Confederate "Tales of the War" in the Trans-Mississippi
Part Five

Price's Raid: From Pocahontas to Boonsboro
(September 19–November 3, 1864)

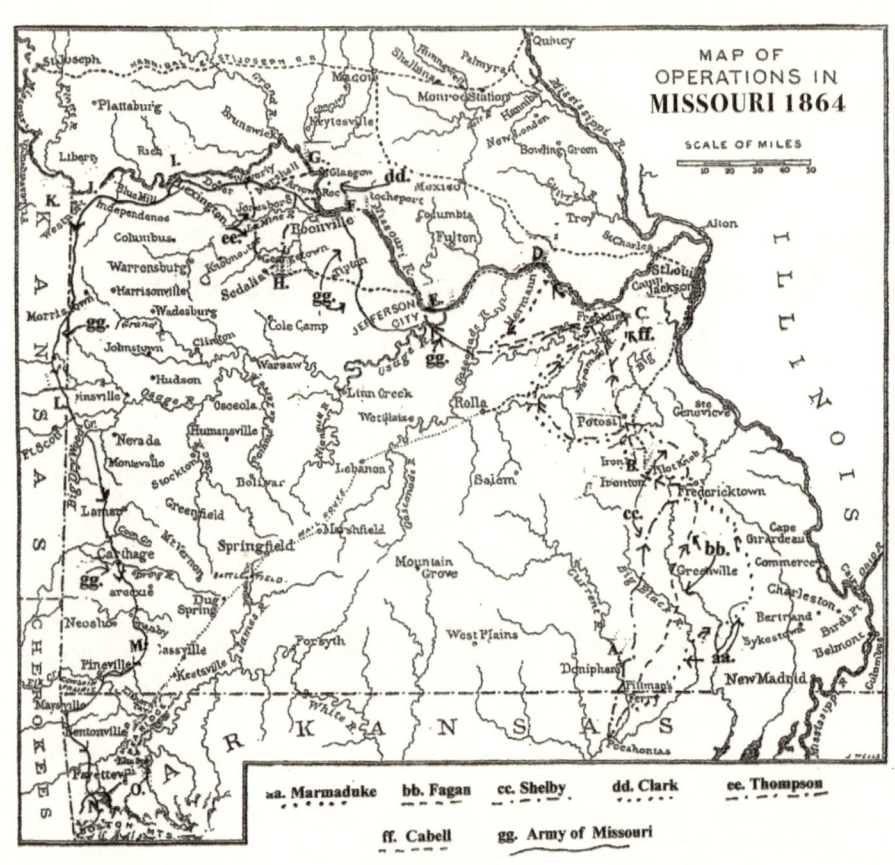

A. Doniphan, Sept. 19
B. Pilot Knob, Sept. 27
C. Franklin, Oct. 1
D. Herman, Oct. 3
E. Jefferson City, Oct. 6–7
F. Boonville, Oct. 9–12
G. Glasgow, Oct. 15
H. Sedalia, Oct. 15
I. Lexington, Oct. 19
J. Independence, Oct. 21–22
K. Westport, Oct. 23
L. Mine Creek, Oct. 25
M. Newtonia, Oct. 28
N. Boonsboro, Nov. 1–3
O. Fayetteville, Nov. 2

UNWRITTEN CHAPTERS OF
THE CIVIL WAR
WEST OF THE RIVER

VOLUME VII

Confederate
"Tales of the War"
In the Trans-Mississippi

Part Five: May 1864–August 1865
End of the Trans-Mississippi Confederacy, with
River Operations, Price's 1864 Missouri Raid,
Irregular Operations (1861–1865), and
The Confederate Exit to Mexico

Authors/Editors Michael E. Banasik
and Brenda F. Banasik

Camp Pope Publishing
2019

Copyright © 2019 by Michael E. Banasik

Library of Congress Control Number: 2019938395

ISBN: 978-1-929919-89-5

Camp Pope Publishing
P.O. Box 2232
Iowa City, Iowa 52244
www.camppope.com

Series Dedication:
Dedicated to the forgotten soldiers of both North and South, who fought in the American Civil War west of the Mississippi River; their deeds of perseverance and valor shall not be lost through the ravages of time, but rather recorded for all to remember.

Volume VII, Part Five Dedication:
To our daughter Marisa Banasik and her husband David Peirce on their recent marriage. May your love last forever.

Acknowledgments:
Two individuals deserve special recognition for their assistance with Chapter 3 of this book, Bryce Suderow, author of *Thunder in Arcadia Valley*, and Terry Justice of Arkansas City, Kansas. Bryce provided useful insight, access to little known sources, and reviewed parts of Chapter 3, all of which proved extremely useful in preparation of this book. Terry provided transcribed copies of several key courts martial associated with Price's Raid as well as the use of a relative's diary on the Expedition. To both individuals, I give my thanks.

CONTENTS

Chapter 1—River Operations in the Trans-Mississippi (May–June 1864)...... 1

Recovering from the Camden Expedition (May 1–23, 1864) and Operations on the Mississippi River (May 24–29, 1864), including engagements between May 24–26, by Henry C. Luttrell, Company G, 10th Missouri Cavalry (C.S.A.). 1

Operations on the Mississippi River (May 29–August 15, 1864), including engagements on June 1–2, 5–7 (Ditch Bayou), and 22 (White River Station, Arkansas), 1864, Henry C. Luttrell, Company G, 10th Missouri Cavalry (C.S.A.). 11

Operations on the White River, Arkansas (June 20–29, 1864), including the capture of the Union Gunboat *Queen City* (June 24, 1864), by R. W. Crabb........ 25

Chapter 2—The Final Infantry Operations, Surrender, and Death of General M. M. Parsons (May 1864–August 1865).. 40

Continuing history of Parsons's Missouri Division, following the Battle of Jenkins' Ferry, Arkansas, until the end of the war, by James H. McNamara. 40

The continuing history of Company A, Tenth Missouri Infantry in 1864-1865, following the Battle of Jenkins' Ferry (April 30, 1864) to the end of the war, by James L. Grubbs, Company A, 10th Missouri Infantry.............................. 54

Introduction to the Confederate Exodus to Mexico and the murder of General Mosby M. Parsons.. 58

The murder of General Mosby M. Parsons on August 16, 1865, by Colonel Richard H. Musser, 9th Missouri Infantry.. 63

Another account of the death of General Mosby M. Parsons on August 16, 1865, by Colonel Sidney D. Jackman. 72

Chapter 3—Price's 1864 Missouri Raid 83

Price's 1864 Missouri Raid, by Henry C. Luttrell, Company G, 10th Missouri Cavalry (C.S.A.). Part One.. 83

The Battle of Pilot Knob, Missouri (September 27, 1864), by Henry C. Luttrell, Company G, 10th Missouri Cavalry (C.S.A.). Part Two. 96

Continuation of Part One of Price's 1864 Missouri Raid, by Henry C. Luttrell, Company G, 10th Missouri Cavalry (C.S.A.).. 107

The continuation of a Missouri trooper's account of Price's 1864 Missouri Raid, from Glasgow to the Kansas state line, by Henry C. Luttrell, Company G, 10th Missouri Cavalry (C.S.A.). Part Three... 129

A Confederate cavalryman continues his tale of Price's 1864 Missouri Raid, copied from a diary, beginning on October 24, 1864, including the Battle of Mine Creek, Kansas, by Henry C. Luttrell, Company G, 10th Missouri Cavalry (C.S.A.). Part Four. 149

The continuation of a Missouri trooper's account of Price's 1864 Missouri Raid, from Carthage, Missouri to the end of the war, by Henry C. Luttrell, Company G, 10th Missouri Cavalry (C.S.A.). Part Five. 165

Chapter 4—Irregular Operations, 1861–1865 178

Biography on Colonel Sidney D. Jackman; Member MSG, Guerrilla and Confederate Officer, by Richard H. Musser, Colonel 9th Missouri Infantry. 179

Recruiting for the Confederacy in the Spring of 1863, by S. D. Jackman.. 205

The Capture and Execution of Lieutenant August T. Doley, Confederate Guerrilla and Scout, April–May 1863, by C. H. Burch, late member Company B, 10th Missouri Infantry (CSA). 208

Colonel Charles Harrison's Failed Expedition to Colorado (May 12–19, 1863), by Colonel Richard H. Musser, 9th Missouri Infantry (C.S.A.). 213

Irregular Operations in the Indian Territory, Northwest Arkansas and in Southwest Missouri, 1863-1865, including numerous skirmishes and attacks on Federal trains, by J. W. Cooper. 223

Appendix A: Orders, Circulars, and Correspondence 246

Appendix B: Selected Biographies 262

Richard P. Crump 262
Archibald S. Dobbin.. 262
John N. Edwards 265
General Mariano Escobedo 267
Thomas R. Freeman 269
Charles Harrison.. 270
Samuel B. Maxey 271
Thomas H. McCray 273
William H. Parsons 274
John F. Rucker... 277
Richard Waterhouse 278

John A. Wharton 279
David A. Williams 282
John I. Worthington 283
Richard F. "Dick" Yeager 285
Index to Previous Biographies 287

Appendix C: Extended Comments on Selected Items 290

Appendix D: Army of Missouri Order of Battle and Additions to the Army 341

Appendix E: Confederate Order of Battle, Pilot Knob (September 27, 1864) 386

Appendix F: Confederate and Union Orders Of Battle, Glasgow, Missouri (October 15, 1864) 400

Appendix G: Confederate Order of Battle, Westport (October 23, 1864) 410

Appendix H: Confederate Losses At Mine Creek, (October 25, 1864) 439

Appendix I: Summary of Price's 1964 Missouri Expedition 450

Bibliography 466

Credits 497

Index 499

Photos and Illustrations

"Tales of the War" nameplate xiv
USS *Tyler* 6
Alfred W. Ellet 7
Joseph A. Mower 17
Andrew J. Smith 21
Joseph O. Shelby 26
Simon B. Buckner 46
John B. Magruder 47
Servando Canales 67
Juan N. Cortina 69
Sir Edward Thornton 71
Pierre Jeanningros 74
William M. Gwin 79

John B. Sanborn 86
Thomas Ewing 95
Egbert B. Brown 140
Sidney D. Jackman 180
Archibald Dobbin 263
John N. Edwards 266
Mariano Escobedo 268
Samuel B. Maxey 272
Thomas H. McCray 273
William H. Pasrons 275
Richard Waterhouse 278
John A. Wharton 280
Richard F. Yeager 285
John B. Clark, Jr. 300
William S. Rosecrans 312
M. Jeff Thompson 315
Alfred Pleasonton 319
James G. Blunt 320
William L. Cabell 324
John P. Bull 335

Maps

Price's 1864 Missouri Raid ii
Operations on the Mississippi River 12
Battle of Ditch Bayou 16
Price's Raid: From Camden to Pocahontas 84
Pilot Knob and Its Approaches 94
Gun Emplacements at Fort Davidson 98
Westport and Big Blue Area 142
Battleground of Westport 145
Battle of Mine Creek 152
Battle of Newtonia 166
Price's Raid: From Maysville to Layneport 170

Series Introduction

The Civil War in the Trans-Mississippi region provides a fascinating study of nineteenth century warfare under the most severe conditions. Soldiers serving in the region faced an almost complete lack of a railroad net, a decrepit road system, and terrain that varied from arid deserts to rugged mountains. Battles were few, but the constant strain of living under less than ideal conditions wore heavily upon the soldiers serving west of the Mississippi River. Often the stories told by the frontier soldiers were not of great engagements, but rather of long marches, poor living conditions, or of simple survival. And for each story told there were always two parts, one told by a man in gray and another by one who wore the blue.

Introduction to Volume VII, Part Five

This latest volume of my series comprises an extensive group of reminiscences published by the St. Louis *Missouri Republican* between 1885 and 1887. These pieces were written by the participants of the Civil War and cover the entire conflict from the firing of the first guns until the surrender of the Confederacy in 1865. The first story was printed on July 4, 1885, and the last one, that I discovered, appeared on July 2, 1887—in all, 95 pieces were published.

Typically, in each Saturday issue, the *Republican* printed assorted reminiscences by the lowliest private to the most exalted general, all veterans of the war, and covering the conflict from every aspect, both North and South, and from every front of the action, including the high-seas. This volume completes the *Confederate "Tales of the War" In the Trans-Mississippi* and will be followed by the "Union Tales" in the coming years.

As to why these articles were published, the *Missouri Republican* wrote the following:

> The publication of the official orders and correspondence of the war of the rebellion made it comparatively easy for military writers to get at the exact facts of many disputed questions, and all the campaigns have been discussed by the record in recent years by competent officers of both the contending armies. Probably it is the publication of these numerous volumes, which, as much as anything else, has aroused a renewed interest in all manner of literature based on the incidents of the civil war. In response to what seems a public desire the *Republican* will hereafter publish in its Saturday edition a series of war papers, either original or selected from the best current sketches in contemporary publications.
>
> It is not desired to make this department especially a medium for criticism of military operations. The incidents of camp life and the experiences of the private soldier will find as ready access to these columns as the history of great campaigns. What ever war reminiscences will interest the thousands of old soldiers and the greater thousands of their

children, will gladly be published in the full ballet that these chronicles of personal experiences from both sides, while reviving the memories, will at the same time aid in obliterating the animosities of the great struggle.[1]

This volume of the "Tales of the War," begins following the Battle of Jenkins' Ferry, on April 30, 1864, and continues through to the Confederate Exodus to Mexico, covering Price's 1864 Missouri Raid, as well as Irregular Warfare. In the first chapter, Operations on the Mississippi and White Rivers are presented, including numerous operations against Union shipping on said rivers. Highlights include the Battle of Ditch Bayou (June 6, 1864) and the Capture and Destruction of the *Queen City* (June 24, 1864) on the White River by General J. O. Shelby. Chapter 1 also notes the beginnings of Price's 1864 Missouri Raid, as the various cavalry commands recruit in preparation for the expedition.

Chapter 2 fully embraces the Confederate planning for Price's Raid as well as the infantry operations that supported the raid. Additionally, the Confederate surrender in the Trans-Mississippi is covered, followed by the exit of some Confederates to Mexico. The highlight of the rebel exodus is the little known, or covered, murder of General Mosby M. Parsons, near China, Mexico, in the early morning hours of August 16, 1865.

Chapter 3 is by far the most ambitious of this volume, embracing one of the most extensive diaries kept by any Confederate trooper on Price's Raid, that has ever been found. Henry Luttrell, of the 10th Missouri Cavalry (CSA), wrote a series of letters, taken form his diary, to the *Republican*, detailing Price's Raid from beginning to end. He covered all the major battles, including a special piece just on the Battle of Pilot Knob. Also in this chapter are extensive accounts of Pilot Knob (September 27), Glasgow (October 15), Westport (October 23) and Mine Creek (October 25), to name but a few.

Where Chapter 3 is the most ambitious of this volume, Chapter 4 is the most unusual. When one thinks of guerrilla operations in the Trans-Mississippi, one immediately thinks of William Quantrill and his men. However, in this chapter you will find the names of Charles or Charlie Harrison, Sidney Jackman, James W. Cooper, and August Dolley—hardly well-known guerrillas, with the possible exception of Jackman. Sidney Jackman's story begins in 1861, and takes the reader though to his death following the war. Of prime interest in the Jackman story is the capture of Union General Thomas Bartholow from his headquarters in Glasgow, Missouri, in April 1863, an episode of the war that has been largely forgotten and untold by Civil War historians.

Where Jackman may be known, few have ever heard of Charles Harrison, much less his ill-fated expedition to Colorado Territory with a party of rebel officers, to recruit for the Confederacy. Harrison's party was attacked by Osage Indians and all were killed save two, one of whom recorded his account of the

---

1. Editorial Comment, *The Missouri Republican* (St. Louis, Missouri), July 4, 1885.

expedition and related the tale to Richard Musser, the author of this fascinating piece of "Irregular Warfare."

Not to be outdone, James W. Cooper presents his wartime experiences as a guerrilla under the command of General Stand Watie, while operating primarily in northwest Arkansas. Cooper covers the period 1863–1865, including numerous accounts of his attacks on Union forage or supply trains operating in the area, and the Siege of Fayetteville during Price's Raid. Of particular note was Cooper's attack, with Dick Yeager, on a Union train in the spring of 1864, where he inflicted a horrific loss on the 2nd Arkansas Cavalry (Union)—the worst that regiment suffered during the war.

Finally, August Dolley brings to light an interesting tale of a typical Confederate recruiter, who was summarily executed upon his capture in 1863.

Also included in this volume are several appendices, with detailed Confederate Orders of Battle for the Battles of Pilot Knob, Glasgow and Westport as well as a detailed Order of Battle for the Army of Missouri as it entered Missouri on September 19, 1864. Other appendices include Extended Comments on a variety of subjects, including the legend surrounding the evacuation of Ft. Davidson, rebel losses at Pilot Knob, Shelby's Operations on the Iron Mountain Railroad, and M. Jeff Thompson's Sedalia Expedition, an analysis of rebel losses at Mine Creek, and a summary of Price's Expedition, detailing the rebel general's accomplishments, his losses, his captures, and the destruction that his army wrought.

As in previous volumes, selected, detailed biographies are presented, with an assortment of correspondence from the principle personalities of the book, plus a detailed index for easy reference.

The publication of Part Five of the "Confederate Tales," brings to completion the assorted stories of Confederate veterans, as they were printed in the *Missouri Republican*. In five volumes, a total of 89 pieces on the Trans-Mississippi Civil War by 52 different authors have been gathered together, which probably constitutes the greatest single collection of primary material ever assembled on the Trans-Mississippi to date.

I hope you find these pieces as fascinating as I did in researching and preparing them for your reading pleasure.

Michael E. Banasik

Nameplate which appeared ahead of most of the "Tales of the War" in the *Republican*.

Confederate "Tales of the War" in the Trans-Mississippi
Part Five

Chapter 1

River Operations in the Trans-Mississippi (May–June 1864)

Item: Recovering from the Camden Expedition (May 1–23, 1864) and Operations on the Mississippi River (May 24–29, 1864), including engagements between May 24–26, by Henry C. Luttrell, Company G, 10th Missouri Cavalry (C.S.A.).[1]
Published: January 29, 1887.

Marmaduke's Brigade and the Tinclads.

Editor *Republican*

With the termination of the battle of Jenkins Ferry, April 30, 1864, closed the campaign against Gen. [Frederick] Steele.[2] As has been stated in a previous sketch

---

1. Henry C. Luttrell, a resident of Pettis County, Missouri, was enlisted by Colonel John C. Tracy in what became Company G, 10th Missouri Cavalry (CSA) on August 10, 1862. He fought at Lone Jack, Missouri, on August 16, 1862, where he was wounded. He also participated in the Little Rock Campaign of 1863, and fought at Pine Bluff (October 25, 1863), in Arkansas, and Price's 1864 Missouri Raid. He survived the war and was paroled at Shreveport, Louisiana, on June 8, 1865. After the war Luttrell, returned home and eventually moved to Baldwin, Chickasaw Nation, Indian Territory, where he wrote a series of articles on his wartime experiences, which appeared periodically in the *Missouri Republican* (These articles have appeared in Parts Two, Three and Four of this series.). Note: Luttrell's previous residence was incorrectly listed as being in Missouri; however, this Baldwin was located in modern-day Oklahoma. Joanne C. Eakin, *Battle of Lone Jack August 16, 1862* (Independence, MO, 2001), 166, hereafter cited as Eakin, *Lone Jack*; National Archives, Record Group M322 (roll no. 57), Confederate Compiled Service Records, 10th Missouri Cavalry; Henry C. Luttrell, "Price's Great Raid," *The Daily Missouri Republican*(St. Louis, MO), March 6, 1886; "War Echoes," *Missouri Republican*, October 31, 1885.
2. On April 30, 1864, the retreating Federal column under General Frederick Steele was attacked at Jenkins' Ferry on the Saline River. The battle saved Steele's Army from destruction as they successfully beat back the rebel assaults and withdrew across the Saline River. The Federals suffered about 700 casualties, while the Confederates lost two artillery pieces and about 1,000 men. United States War Department, *The War of the Rebellion: A Compilation of the Official Records of the Union and Confederate Armies*, 70 vols. in 128 (Washington, D. C. 1880–1901), vol. 34, pt. 1:810, 816, hereafter cited as *O.R.* All citations of *O.R.* refer to Series 1 unless indicated otherwise; Edwin C. Bearss, *Steele's Retreat From Camden and The Battle of Jenkins' Ferry* (Little Rock, AR, 1966), 161, hereafter cited as Bearss, *Steele's Retreat*.

Frederick Steele was born on January 14, 1819, in New York, attended West Point Military Academy, where he graduated in 1843 (number 30 of 39). During Mexican War, Steele received two brevets for gallantry at the Battles of Contreras and Chapultepec. At the beginning of the Civil War he was stationed at Fort Leavenworth, Kansas. Steele rose quickly in rank was appointed col-of those operations, the old Tenth Missouri cavalry found itself in a sad plight.³ On the morning of the 1st of May hardly half of the men are mounted, and not one-fourth the regiment is reported for duty.⁴ The men in dirty tattered uniforms are stretched at full length upon the wet ground sleep, or mope about the camp stiff and sore from their last desperate march to intercept the enemy at the very point where the battle has been fought. Our poor horses stand with drooping heads, and ears drooping down on either side [of] their heads; their flanks are drawn, and they are so stiff they can hardly move. Many of them will never be able to bear a saddle again.⁵ When we break camp to-day we bid farewell to at least a hundred

onel of the 8th Iowa Infantry on September 23, 1861, a brigadier general on January 29, 1862, and a major general on November 29, 1862. Steele was best remembered for capturing Little Rock, Arkansas, in September 1863, and leading the Camden Expedition in 1864. Following the war, he remained in the Regular Army, dying by a freak accident on January 12, 1868, when he fell from a buggy he was driving. Michael E. Banasik, *Missouri Brothers in Gray* (Iowa City, IA, 1998), 152, 154–155, hereafter cited as Banasik, *Missouri Brothers in Gray*.

3. The 10th Missouri Cavalry (CSA) was originally commanded by Emmett MacDonald and consisted of 3 companies with 2 more added forming the "regiment" on December 1, 1862. The unit at that time was known as MacDonald's Regiment, even though it only contained 5 companies. MacDonald's command eventually joined with the 11th Missouri Battalion (CSA), paroled returnees from the First Missouri Brigade captured at Vicksburg, and Lawther's Temporary Cavalry Regiment (dismounted) to form the 10th Missouri Cavalry Regiment (CSA) on December 12, 1863. *O.R.*, vol. 22, pt. 1:156; *O.R.*, vol. 22, pt. 2:781; Joseph H. Crute, *Units of the Confederate States Army* (Midlothian, VA, 1987), 203, hereafter cited as Crute, *Confederate Army*; Janet Hewett, ed. *Supplement to the Official Records of the Union and Confederate Armies*, 100 vols. (Wilmington, NC, 1994–2001), pt. 2, vol. 38:253–259, hereafter cited as *O.R.S.*; National Archives, Record Group 109, Inspector General Report, in Confederate Muster Rolls, 10th Missouri Cavalry; National Archives, Record Group M322 (roll no. 57) Confederate Compiled Service Records, 10th Missouri Cavalry.

4. On December 31, 1863, a few weeks after Lawther's Regiment was organized, its monthly return showed 559 "aggregate Present for Duty." This would suggest that the command numbered no more than 140 officers and men Present for Duty on May 1. *O.R.*, vol. 22, pt. 2:1127.

5. Following the capture of Camden, Arkansas, on April 27, General E. Kirby Smith, ordered Marmaduke's Division (also known as the "Light Horse Division") to cross the Ouachita River below Camden and get in front of the retreating Union Army. Marmaduke's Division, consisting only of Colton Greene's Missouri Brigade, departed the area at 10:00 a.m. on the 27th, crossing the river at White Hall (about 8 miles south of the city). Even while Marmaduke's Division was crossing, Greene was directed to detach Lawther's command (Luttrell's regiment) to continue to the southeast to escort the prisoners (POWs) captured at Marks' Mill. Crossing the river at El Dorado Landing, Lawther moved northward and on April 28, near noon, the regiment linked up with the POW train at Moro Landing. Detaching Companies C and H, to assist in the escort duties, Lawther moved northward toward Princeton, via Warren and Edinburg. Several miles from Princeton, cannon fire was heard, prompting Lawther to quicken the pace. "For an hour," wrote Luttrell in a (previous article),

> we hold to a steady gallop. Now horses are giving out, and the best efforts of those riders cannot keep them in their places in the moving columns. The march is now slowing down to a trot, but the reckless gallop has done its work. The poor beasts drop their heads and fall to the rear.

Toward twilight, following a 60 mile march, the regiment arrived at Jenkins' Ferry, completely exhausted, only to find the battle was over. *O.R.*, vol. 34, pt. 1:826–827, 829, 834; Henry Luttrell, "A Confederate Trooper's Diary," *Missouri Republican*, February 6, 1886; Bearss, *Steele's Retreat*, map on 88, 94; John Ballard Draper, Diary of William Custis Ballard in *William Curtis*

fine horses who at the beginning of the campaign were full of life and vigor, and pawed the ground and chomped the bit with impatience at restraint. On the commons at Tulip, two days after the battle, I bid goodbye to my noble charger. Tears are in my eyes and a lump in my throat as I turned away and leave the faithful fellow to his fate. In those days the loss of a good horse was a sad blow to the Confederate trooper, for he had to

Furnish His Own Horse,

and they generally cost from $300 to $500 in Confederate money. In a word, we are sadly in need of rest; but there is no rest for the Confederates in the days.[6] The unequal contest is being waged with fury and desperation. But we are desperately in love with the cause for which we fight, else we could not stand before our enemies a single hour. This deep devotion and firm conviction in the justice of our cause is the mainspring to our courage and valor. Of this people will read and wonder in years to come. A cavalryman's duty is an everyday affair, and if he is in the face of the enemy it is simply continuous. He must be the eyes and ears and legs of the whole army. Upon him rest a great responsibility. A single vidette [vedette] failing to do his duty has frequently caused great loss of life and destruction of property.

The month of May is filled with marches and counter marches, scouting, picketing and foraging, until on the 23d the Tenth regiment finds itself doing scout and picket duty at Gaines' Landing on the Mississippi River.[7] On the morning of

---

Ballard: His Ancestors and Descendants (n.p., 1979), April 26–30, 1864, hereafter cited as Ballard Diary; "From Arkansas," *The Weekly State Gazette* (Austin, TX), June 23, 1864; Michael J. Forsyth, *The Camden Expedition of 1864 and the Opportunity Lost by the Confederacy to Change the Civil War* (Jefferson, NC, 2003), 143.

6. The loss of a horse by a cavalryman was made even more desperate for those wishing to remain in the cavalry, for failure to procure another would result in their transfer to the infantry or artillery, per paragraph 2, General Orders No. 67 (May 25, 1863) which stated: "Whenever a cavalryman fails and refuses to keep himself provided with a serviceable horse, he may, upon order of the corps commander, be transferred to any company of infantry or artillery of the same army that he may select." In further support of this regulation, with slight amendment, E. K. Smith issued General Orders No. 29 (May 26, 1864), which gave the authority of the transfer to the Department or District commanders. And with the growing shortage of forage, Smith was more than willing to transfer cavalryman to the infantry. Smith further specified in his General Orders, paragraph 2, that "District commanders will have their cavalry commands immediately (and hereafter monthly) inspected for the purpose of enforcing" the order. *O.R.*, vol. 34, pt. 4:631; *O.R.*, Series 4, vol. 2:568.

7. On May 5, 1864, Joseph O. Shelby's Brigade was detached from Marmaduke's Division and ordered to northeast Arkansas to recruit and make demonstrations against the Little Rock-DeVall's Bluff Railroad. About the same time, Price ordered the remainder of Marmaduke's Division (Greene's Brigade, with Pratt's Texas Battery), to operate between the Cypress Bend and Lake Village areas, there "to scout the west bank of the Mississippi, from the mouth of the Arkansas down to Louisiana." On May 17, 1864, General Smith further directed General Price to order Marmaduke's command, "if practicable, to place his batteries, with sufficient support, in position on the Mississippi River for the purpose of attacking the transports of the Sixteenth and Seventeenth Corps," that were en route from Louisiana, via the river. Marmaduke's Division made their initial

the 24th we moved down the river and joined the rest of the brigade with Maj. [Joseph] Pratt's battery. The guns are brass, eighteen-pounder rifles and twelve-pounder smooth bores.[8]

---

headquarters 15 miles from the Mississippi River, on Bayou Bartholomew at the intersection of the Gaines Landing and Monticello roads. At this time William L. Jeffers, of the 8th Missouri Cavalry, commanded Greene's Brigade, which consisted of 3rd, 4th, 7th and 8th Missouri Cavalries, with Pratt's 6-gun Texas Battery. In addition to scouting, the brigade collected deserters and broke up renegade bands. With Greene's return to command shortly after May 13, the brigade moved up to Leatherman's Plantation, on Bayou Macon (at the time the bayou was known as Bayou Mason) where the brigade began its active operations on May 23, 1864. *O.R.*, vol. 34, pt. 3:824, 828; Clement A. Evans, gen. ed. *Confederate Military History*, 13 vols. (Atlanta, 1899; reprint ed., Secaucus, NJ, 1974), vol. 10: *Arkansas* by John M. Harrell, 269, 271, hereafter cited as Harrell, *Arkansas, Confederate Military History*; Chester G. Hearn, *Ellet's Brigade: The Strangest Outfit Of All* (Baton Rouge, LA, 2000), 232, hereafter cited as Hearn; Deryl P. Sellmeyer, *Jo Shelby's Iron Brigade* (Gretna, LA, 2007), 177, hereafter cited as Sellmeyer; Don R. Simons, *In Their Words: A Chronology of the Civil War in Chicot County, Arkansas and Adjacent Waters of the Mississippi River* (Sulphur, LA, 1999), 107, hereafter cited as Simons; War Department, *The War of the Rebellion: Official Record of the Union and Confederate Navies*, 31 volumes (Washington, DC, 1894-1922), Series I, vol. 24: 124, hereafter cited as *O.N.R.* All citations of *O.N. R.* refer to Series 1 unless indicated otherwise.

8. Pratt's Texas Battery was organized by Joseph H. Pratt, an east Texas railroad man, with men from Harrison, Marion and Cass Counties, Texas, in the spring of 1861. However, the battery was not mustered into the Confederate Service until March 1, 1862, at Jefferson, Texas. It was then ordered to Little Rock, Arkansas, in the spring of 1862, where it was assigned to duty with Parsons's Texas Cavalry Brigade. It participated in Marmaduke's Second Missouri Raid in 1863, was at Little Rock during the 1863 Campaign, and participated in the assault on Pine Bluff as part of Carter's Texas Brigade. The battery continued in the service of cavalry commands throughout its existence. Its guns were captured during Price's 1864 Missouri Raid, but the battery was reconstituted and completed its war service in the Trans-Mississippi Reserve Artillery Battalion. Joseph Pratt was promoted to major in the summer of 1865, and the battery was then commanded by H. C. Hynson. During its time in the service Pratt's Battery was considered one of the best batteries serving west of the Mississippi River, prompting an Inspector General of the army to record, the battery "is in very fine order, and a model command. Their discipline is very good. The men are well drilled."

In June 1862, the battery was armed with six 6-lb iron guns, which were replaced with four new guns from Woodruff's Arkansas Battery (two 6-lb James Rifles and two 10-lb Parrots). By May 1864, the battery added two additional guns, probably 12-lb James Rifles from Collins's Missouri Battery, which was refitted for operations in northeast Arkansas with Shelby's Brigade, and replaced the 6-lb rifled guns with 6-lb smoothbores (See note no. 55 for comments on Collins's Battery). In making the various reports on the actions from May 23–June 4, 1864, Colonel Greene reported being nearly out of ammunition, reporting "There are only 12 rifled shells, 6 solid smooth-bore and 30 shells for howitzers." Greene further "ventured the opinion that with 18 and 24 pounder rifles no boat could safely pass a battery," indicating that he didn't have anything heavier than 12-lb guns. As to the existence of 18-lb rifles, one Union commander speculated that he had a portion of "a 12 or 18 pounder." Further, the 18-pound gun was rare, as to usage in the war, with apparently only Confederates in the East using the "out modeled" gun. The 18-pounder was also a siege gun weighing 4,913 pounds and totally unsuitable for cavalry operations. *O.R.*, vol. 22, pt. 2:1051; *O.R.*, vol. 34, pt. 1:950, 952; *O.N.R.*, vol. 26:323, 339, 354, 356; *O.R.S.*, pt. 2, vol. 68:483; Michael E. Banasik, *Embattled Arkansas: The Prairie Grove Campaign of 1862* (Wilmington, NC, 1996), 520 (n. 3), hereafter cited as Banasik, *Embattled Arkansas*; J. Gorgas, *The Ordnance Manual For the Use of the Officers of the Confederate States Army* (Charleston, SC, 1863; reprint ed., Dayton, OH, 1976), 9, 14; Leon, Letter to the Editor (June 25, 1863), *Gal-*

Here the levy is near the river bank, and I see that the guns are unlimbered and ready for action, the troops are

Dismounted and Formed

behind the levy.[9] I also see a gunboat steaming up the river. It is the first one I ever saw, and I mount the levees; along with a hundred others, to get a better view of the black monster moving up under a cloud of coal-smoke. But we are instantly ordered down. Had the order been delayed a few moments longer we would have anticipated it, for before we were all back in our place a huge shell came screeching across the water and shattering the limbs in the treetops above our heads. We could hear the crash of falling timber in its wake as it rushes through the dense forest to the westward then a dull explosion in the distant as it bursts, perhaps in some dismal cypress swamp.

How indignant our little guns appeared in answering the thunder claps of the ironclad steamer. Our shot glanced from her side and dropped about in the water like pebbles. This Maj. Pratt's eagle eye soon detected, and he ordered the guns to retire behind the levy. This is our first experience with an ironclad, and it terminates as many others of a like nature, by our quietly withdrawing from such a one-sided contest.[10] The enemy however, continued to shell the river bank and

---

veston *Tri-Weekly News* (Galveston, TX), July 4, 1863; Warren Ripley, *Artillery and Ammunition of the Civil War* (New York, 1970), 32, hereafter cited as Ripley; Special Orders No. 29 (July 17, 1862), Special Orders Letter Book (June 1–December 18, 1862), Hindman's command, Peter W. Alexander Collection, Columbia University, hereafter cited as Special Orders Book No. 1; Ralph A. Wooster, *Lone Star Regiments in Gray* (Austin, TX, 2002), 304–305, hereafter cited as Wooster, *Lone Star Regiments*.

9. On May 23, Greene departed Leatherman's Plantation, with the 3rd Missouri Cavalry (CSA) and bivouacked near Gaines' Landing. The following morning, at 5:00 a.m., after placing Pratt's Battery on the river, Greene engaged the U.S.S. *Curlew*, a tinclad, for about 30 minutes, striking the *Curlew* several times without any serious damage. Greene, however, reported the *Curlew* was "badly damaged" and was towed up river to Napoleon. After the engagement Greene moved his battery southward, again went into battery at Daniel Simmon's Plantation (Luna Landing) and attacked two transports, which he disabled and were later burned or so Greene was "informed." A short time later, Lawther arrived with his regiment, and Greene detached a section of Pratt's Battery to operate with Lawther. Meanwhile, Greene moved on to Columbia to continue his harassment of Union shipping. *O.R.*, vol. 34, pt. 1:950–951; *O.N.R.*, vol. 26:323–324; "From Cairo and Below," *Chicago Daily Tribune* (Chicago, IL), May 30, 1864; Hearn, 234; Simons, 107, 110.

10. In his official report of operations, Greene does not mention Lawther's engagement with an ironclad, which was probably the U.S.S. *Tyler* as it was the only ironclad in the area at this time. However, Greene did mention Lawther's attack on a gunboat and a transport before leaving his position at Luna to rejoin the main body in the Columbia area. Unfortunately, Luttrell does not address the issue. According to period records, following Greene's attack on the *Curlew*, at Gaines' Landing, the tinclad signaled the *Tyler*, which was two miles upstream, for assistance. By the time that the *Tyler* had arrived, Greene had already departed the area. About the same time, the transport *Nicholas Longworth*, which was heading downstream, arrived under the escort of the tinclad *Romeo* (Gunboat No. 3). Lieutenant Commander James Prichett, commanding the *Tyler*, directed the *Curlew* and the *Romeo* escort the transport pass Gaines' Landing where the battery was located. Once pass Gaines' Landing, the *Curlew* again headed north to Cairo, Illinois, while the *Romeo* remained in the area. Sometime later, the *Longworth* arrived in Greenville, where the

USS *Tyler*

surrounding country for hours after we were miles away. We moved on down the river to Columbia, where we intercepted two gunboats—not ironclads—and one transport.[11] This class of vessel we know as the "mosquito fleet" and "tinclad."[12]

---

ship's captain informed Lieutenant Colonel George E. Currie, the commander of a detachment of General Ellet's Marine Brigade, that he had been fired on 10 or 12 times, without damage (This was probably the tinclad *Romeo* and *Longworth* that Greene reported as being engaged by Lawther). As a result of the intelligence, Currie lashed the *Longworth* to the tinclad *Baltic* and with the *Diane*, brought on the engagement at Columbia/ Leland Landing, as describe by Luttrell in his next paragraphs. [Note: From Greene's and Luttrell's description of events, Greene places Lawther at Leland, while Luttrell has his unit dashing back and forth between Columbia and Leland. However, Greene's basic description of the engagement matches fairly well with what Luttrell recorded.] *O.R.*, vol. 34, pt. 1:951; *O.N.R.*, vol. 26:324; Hearn, 233; "From Cairo and Below," *Chicago Tribune*, May 30 and June 5, 1864.

11. Prior to Lawther engaging the *Longworth*, Greene engaged the cotton laden *Delta*, which was steaming up river past Columbia and riddled her with shot and shell. Badly damaged, the *Delta* limped back to Greenville, Mississippi, and was towed into the port. And a short time after Lawther engaged the *Longworth*, the transport passed by Columbia, where Greene also engaged the vessel. Hoping to re-engage the *Longworth*, Greene moved his command, including Lawther's, to Leland Landing, 1 ½ miles south of Columbia, where he expected to meet the Federal vessel. With new orders, Lawther moved the 2 miles from Luna Landing up to Greene's position, where Lawther placed his two guns above Greene's four pieces and prepared to re-engage the *Longworth*. *O.R.*, vol. 34, pt. 1:951; Warren Daniel Crandall and Denison Newell, *History of the Ram Fleet and the Mississippi Marine Brigade in the War For the Union on the Mississippi and Its Tributaries* (St. Louis, 1907), 397, 399, hereafter cited as Crandall & Newell, 397, 399; Hearn, 233.

One period sailor described Columbia as "a little town of 15 houses, 3 stores [and] 4 groceries– not a living person to be seen." Quoted in Hearn, 233.

12. The "Mosquito Fleet" were a group of "two side-wheel steamers" of shallow draft which were part of the Confederate Navy. The steamers were armed with only one gun, except for The *Seabird* (the flagship of the fleet) which carried two guns. The Mosquito Fleet, under Flag Officer William Lynch, defended Roanoke Island, North Carolina, in February 1862. The fleet consisted of six steamers with a floating battery and was captured or destroyed by February 10. Only the *Appomattox* escaped and was "dismantled and abandoned" later in the month. *O.N.R.*, vol. 6:594–597; *O.N.R.*, Series 2, vol. 1:248; Kevin J. Dougherty, *Encyclopedia of the Confederacy* (San Diego, CA, 2010), 239, hereafter cited as Dougherty; Patricia L. Faust, ed. *Historical Times Illustrated*

They were generally painted black, or left the color of the iron, being covered with sheet or boiler iron, and armed with

Heavy Guns.

They also at times carried a contingent of cavalry. We called them "marine cavalry."[13] Our battery is carefully masked between the levees and the riverbank, in a patch of young willows and cottonwoods, where the channel runs near the bank. Our guns opened on them with solid shot. The tinclad returned the fire, steaming between the transport and us, thus protecting her from our fire until she is well out of range. One of the gunboats remained below with the transport; thinking she is badly damaged by our fire, the other boldly returns, spurting shells at us from the bow guns. At this point the Mississippi makes a monster bend, almost in the shape of a mini shoe, the narrow place being at the heel. This narrow

---

Encyclopedia of the Civil War (New York, 1986), 636, hereafter cited as Faust; Ivan Musicant, *Divided Waters: The Naval History of the Civil War* (New York, 1995), 129–132; "The Opposing Forces At Roanoke Island and New Bern, N.C.," in *Battles and Leaders of the Civil War*, 4 vols. (New York, 1887–1888), vol. 1:670, hereafter cited as *BLCW*.

Tinclads were 4th Class, light draft vessels of the Union fleet, meant for operations on the shallow rivers and bayous that permeated the South. In all, more than 60 vessels were so designated. They were generally armed with either 32-lb smoothbores or a 24-lb boat howitzers, while gunboats carried the heavier guns like the 8" Dahlgren naval gun. Faust, 757.

13. The "marine cavalry," also known as "Ellet's Scouts" or "Ellet's Horse Marines," was part of the Union Mississippi Marine Brigade. The brigade was authorized on November 1, 1862, and began recruiting by Alfred W. Ellet, the brother of Charles Ellet, who commanded the Ram Feet at Memphis until he was killed on June 6, 1862. To enhance recruitment efforts, the brigade was recruited from convalescent camps and consisted of an infantry regiment, a cavalry battalion (4 companies), and a battery of artillery. On February 21, 1863, the brigade numbered 527 infantry, 368 cavalry and 140 artillerymen, with 500 infantry still to be recruited. (By the latter part of 1863 the entire brigade was mounted and added two 12-lb mountain howitzers in December 1863.) In addition to the troops, the brigade contained seven ships; five carried troops, one was the quartermaster ship, while the other was a hospital ship. The *Autocrat* was the flagship of the brigade. As its mission, the brigade plied the various rivers of the Mississippi waterways in search of irregular Confederate forces, which attacked Union shipping. On March 13, 1863, the brigade entered upon active service. During May 1864, the *Adams*, *Baltic*, and *Diana* were all stationed at Greenville and tasked by General Ellet with escorting transports up and down the Mississippi River. The *Adams* carried Companies A and G of the 1st Infantry Mississippi Marine Brigade; the *Baltic* carried Companies B, H, and I; while the *Diana* had Companies C, D, E, and F. The cavalry battalion would join the rest of the brigade in early June for the engagement at Ditch Bayou. *O.R.S.*, pt. 2. vol. 92:681; Norman E. Clarke, Sr., *Warfare Along the Mississippi: The Letters of Lieutenant Colonel George E. Currie* (Ann Arbor, MI, 1961), 61, 72, 74; hereafter cited as Clarke; Crandall & Newell, 252–253, 255, 258-259, 261, 333, 341, 343; Faust, 501; Hearn, 146.

Alfred W. Ellet

strip was then called the neck, about a mile and a half wide. It had also been in cultivation. It was said then that to follow the river around the bend was 25 miles.[14]

The tinclad continued her fire, and steamed steadily ahead, and during her advance to the conflict, our artillerymen are training down our guns to the proper range. Then as she veers around to deliver her broadside, our fire is delivered with a single clash, followed the next instant by the heavy metal of the enemy. For a time our little guns are not heard. The continuous roar of the heavy artillery is filling the river the valleys and the hills. A cloud of white sulphurous smoke shrouds the conflict. But now

There Is a Break

in that heavy roll of thunder, and I can now distinguish the sharp, it's spiteful crack of our rifled guns. A moment later and the enemy's fire ceases, and I see her emerging from the pall of smoke; drifting in the current. A slight breeze drives away the smoke. Another volley from our battery, and her whistles are set going in all the agony of a lost soul. The other gunboat below whistles to her in reply. Another round from our guns, fire rises from her furnaces, and we call to her to come to land. Evidently she is not in a condition to do so, for now her stern is to us and she is drifting below. A few more shots are fired at her, but she finally drifts beyond our reach. Now a dense cloud of black smoke is seen below and across the neck. The Tenth regiment and part of the battery are detailed to intercept them, but we go there too late. They have scented danger from afar. The transports are beyond our reach, and the gunboats are not disposed to come inside our range. So we gallop back across the neck in plain view of the enemy boldly, who content themselves by sending a shower of shells after us. We again take position at the

---

14. From Columbia to Leland was a scant 1 ½ miles, while the river route to the same location was 18 miles. There was no levee in the Leland area, according to Don Simons, but Luttrell has at least part of the battery behind a levee. In Hearn's account, he assumes Pratt's entire battery was in an "exposed" position, "on the beach," as recorded by Colton Greene. However, it's clear from Luttrell's account, that at least some of the guns were concealed, or partially so. When the engagement opened, the *Diana*, under Colonel Currie led the way, opening on Pratt's Battery with a 20-lb Parrot rifle. Greene's men held their fire waiting for the *Baltic* and the *Longworth* to get within range. For the next two hours the two forces slugged it out. In the end, the *Baltic* was "badly riddled from stem to stern," and returned to Greenville with the *Diana*, while the *Longworth* passed on down the river with slight damage. The *Diana*, according to one participant, was unharmed, while the "*Baltic* was hit nine times [14 according to the *Tribune*], and her chimneys completely riddled with canister. One shell burst in the wheel house, another in her cabin" killing a member of the Marine Brigade. The losses on board the *Baltic* totaled one dead and three wounded, while the physical damage to the boat forced it back to St. Louis for repairs on June 2. Confederate casualties were either minimal or none, given that the total losses between May 23–June 2, 1864, were only six slightly wounded. Note: The *Prairie Bird* (*Tinclad No. 11*) was also in the area and not engaged, according to most sources; however, the *Chicago Tribune* recorded that the *Diana*, *Baltic*, and *Tinclad No. 11*, "replied with vigor." The *Adams* remained behind at Greenville and guarded the brigade's coal and horse barges. *O.R.*, vol. 34, pt. 1:951–952; *O.N.R.*, vol. 26:886; *O.R.S.*, pt. 2, vol. 92:693; Crandall & Newell, 397, 399; "From Cairo and Below, *Chicago Tribune*, June 5, 1864; Hearn, 233–234, 237; Simons, 111.

willow patch. Meanwhile, the gunboat, which we have just tried to intercept below the neck, has steamed to an opening, where she can command a view of our position, and has begun a lively cannonade.[15] Now a small squad of our men are crossing the neck. They have been left to sharpshoot the enemy and distract his attention from our position above. But such a shower of grape and canister is rained about them that they are finally obliged to abandon their position. As they cross the open space at the neck heavy shells are bursting and ploughing [plowing] the ground all about them. In the midst of this John H. Bell[16] breaks this stirrup strap. He reins in his steed, dismounts and picks it up, then mounts and

Gallops On.

Now a great shell sinks into the ground before him and explodes; a cloud of dust and smoke for a moment shut horse and rider from view; for a moment I hold my breath, thinking my gallant comrade and messmate is torn to pieces. But no, the next instant the gallant trooper emerges from the screen of dust and smoke, hat in hand, waving it defiantly at his enemies. The two gunboats below us, above the neck, are drifting farther away, blowing their whistles alternately, presumably for assistance. Now the artillery is moving back through the cut in the levee. One of the artillerymen is carried through the cut and laid on the grass. He has been struck by a piece of shell or spent ball in the breast. There is no gash, no blood, but he is unconscious. For a time we think him dead, and we are not wont to jump to hasty conclusions either, for we are used to ghastly wounds and dead men, but this time we are fooled, for the man revives and fought his gun on other fields.[17] We camp three miles above Columbia behind the levee, while the gunboats are expending an immense quantity of ammunition. On the 25th we move up to Gaines' Landing, where we sharpshoot another gunboat.[18] During this affair John H. Bell

---

15. This gunboat was probably *Tinclad No. 11*, the *Prairie Bird*, which stayed out of range of Pratt's guns, while the *Baltic*, with the *Longworth* and the *Diana* did close in work. "From Cairo and Below," *Chicago Tribune*, June 5, 1864.

16. John H. Bell, a resident of Pettis County, Missouri, was a member of Company G, 10th Missouri Cavalry (CSA). Bell joined the Confederate service on August 18, 1862, in Henry County and was wounded at White River Station on June 22, 1863. He survived the war and was paroled at Shreveport, Louisiana, on June 8, 1865. Carolyn M. Bartels, *Missouri Confederate Surrender New Orleans & Shreveport May–June 1865* (Independence, MO, 1991), "Bell, J. H." entry, hereafter cited as Bartels, *Missouri Confederate Surrender*; Henry C. Luttrell, "Battle of Lake River," *Missouri Republican*, February 19, 1887; National Archives, Record Group M322 (roll no. 56), Confederate Compiled Service Records, 10th Missouri Cavalry.

17. After the engagement in the Leland area, Greene pulled his command back to Columbia, where he discovered the tinclad *Romeo*. Going into battery, Pratt's gunners managed to score 15–17 hits on the tinclad. The *Romeo*, according to Greene, was "greatly damaged,…and has not made her appearance before my batteries" between May 24–June 2, 1864. The losses on board the *Romeo* were not known; however, at least one acting ensign was shot in the thigh. *O.R.*, vol. 34, pt. 1:951; *O.N.R.*, vol. 26:326–327; Hearn, 234.

18. Even while Greene's command was busy during May 24, he later learned that one of his scouts, under Captain John W. Jacobs, commanding Company F, 4th Missouri Cavalry (CSA), had captured a Federal transport. Early on the morning of May 24, Jacobs's 40-man party stole a yawl

is stunned by a huge shot passing through the levee under him, though not seriously. On the 26th, late in the evening, we fire into another transport and cripple her very badly, but she drifts to the far side of the river, entirely out of our reach.[19] The 27th and 28th are spent in annoying the enemy, shooting at the pilots and firing at the port-holes. In this manner we kept up a perfect din along the river. The "tinclad" gunboats have been learned in the meantime to keep out of our range. The 29th finds us in a snug camp ten miles below Lake Village, on the Old River Lake. But I will tell you what took place while in this camp in another sketch.[20]

and boarded the *Lebanon*. The steamer was burned with a loss of assorted dry goods (valued at $20,000 dollars), with an additional $20,000 dollars in cash, which was secured by Jacobs, before the vessel was destroyed. Meanwhile, following his engagements at Leland and Columbia, Greene's command camped at Sanders (three miles above Columbia), where they remained until 2:00 a.m., the next morning. Moving up to Gaines' Landing on May 25, Greene's command discovered 3 tinclads—probably the *Marmora, Prairie Bird,* and the *Romeo.* (The *Tribune* reported the *Romeo* as the *Juliet;* however that vessel was undergoing repairs at Mound City, Illinois, at the time.) Of the three Federal boats, the *Prairie Bird* received 30 cannon shots, even while the rebel troopers peppered the fleet with musket fire. Later, Greene's command pulled back, taking a wide birth of the landing, avoiding any further contact with the Federals. By the end of May 25, Greene's Brigade was camped 10 miles above Gaines' Landing, on the river near Adair's Plantation a short distance from Eunice, Arkansas. About 10:00 p.m. on May 25, the same three gunboats, that Greene had engaged earlier made their appearance near Greene's position, but no action took place. A transport was also spotted on the far bank of the Mississippi, but it couldn't be reached before it moved off the next morning. *O.R.*, vol. 34, pt. 1:951; *O.N.R.*, vol. 26:326; "From Cairo and Below," *Chicago Tribune,* June 2, 1864; Naval History Division, Navy Department, *Civil War Naval Chronology* (Washington, DC, 1971), IV:62, hereafter cited, *Naval Chronology.*
19. May 26 was a day of maneuver and feints for Greene's Brigade as he searched for a target, similar in nature to the circumstances surrounding the capture of the steamer *Lebanon* on May 24. First Greene made a "feint at Gaines' Landing and Columbia, which caused the enemy to assemble two fleets" at both of those places. At Columbia, rebel sharpshooters engaged the *Diana,* which bombarded the area for several hours. During the day the ironclad *Tyler* was seen escorting two large transports, the *Leviathan* and the *Empress,* but was not engaged as artillery ammunition was down to just three rounds per gun in Pratt's Battery. In another instance, Greene successfully engaged an enemy transport and "struck her several times," though the damage was not known. By the evening of the 26th Greene was back at Adair's Plantation, where he conferred with General Marmaduke as to future operations. Note: Simons has Greene returning to Leatherman's Plantation on the evening of May 26; however, Luttrell's comment on attacking the transport "late in the evening," seems to support the return to Adair's. Federal reports on the day's operations make no comments on the "crippling" of a ship. *O.R.*, vol. 34, pt. 1:947–948, 951; Crandall & Newell, 400; Simons, 114.
20. During the hiatus of artillery operations between May 26–28, Greene's Brigade was resupplied with the necessary ammunition, allowing it to move to the Mississippi to re-engage the passing Federal ships with more than just dilatory musket fire. On May 27 Greene moved his command to the Parker Plantation on Bayou Mason, which was just west of Lake Village and well south of Gaines' Landing where the river operations began. The next day Greene's Brigade camped on the Old River Lake (also known as Lake Chicot or Lake Village), near Ditch Bayou, which was about 5 miles from the Lakeport and Ford Landing areas on the Mississippi River. Farther to the north, on the 28th, the ironclad U.S.S. *Louisville,* took some pot-shots at some rebel scouts, who were secreted about Gaines' Landing, driving them away from the area. And during this same period Lieutenant Commander E. K. Owen, commanding the Sixth District, Mississippi Squadron, alerted Admiral David D. Porter of the need for a "cooperating land force...to effectively drive away the enemy guns"—assuming they were still in the area, since all had been relatively quiet

H. C. LUTTRELL,
Co. G, Tenth Missouri Cavalry, C.S.A.

* * * * * * *

Item: Operations on the Mississippi River (May 29–August 15, 1864), including engagements on June 1–2, 5–7 (Ditch Bayou)[21], and 22 (White River Station, Arkansas), 1864, Henry C. Luttrell, Company G, 10th Missouri Cavalry (C.S.A.).
Published: February 19, 1887.

Battle of Lake River [Ditch Bayou].

Editor *Republican*

The 29th of May finds Marmaduke's old brigade in a snug, comfortable camp some ten miles below Lake Village, on the Old River Lake. For a few days we occupied this delightful camp, changing shots with the enemy as they pass our picket posts, taking pot-shots at the pilots or port-holes, as the case may be; always having the complement returned with heavy interest added.[22] It was a kind of dare-devil excitement that pleased a great many of the boys to perfection.[23]

---

from May 26–28. In alerting Porter, Owen was admitting that the detachment of the Marine Brigade was not sufficient to handle the rebel force then located on the river. This in turn would bring about an even greater commitment of Federal troops, which would finally have the desired effect at Ditch Bayou on June 6, 1864. *O.R.*, vol. 34, pt. 1:951; *O.N.R.*, vol. 26: 326–326, 331; Ballard Diary, May 28–29, 1864; Crandall & Newell, 400; Hearn, 238 n. 15; Simons, map 109.

21. Ditch Bayou was also known as Fish Bayou, Chicot Lake, Old Lake River, Grand Lake, Grand Village, and Lake River. Henry Luttrell, the author of this piece, called it Lake River. F. H. Dyer, *A Compendium of the War of the Rebellion* (Des Moines, IA, 1908; reprint ed., Dayton, OH, 1978), 684, hereafter cited as Dyer.

22. On the morning of May 29, Greene departed his camp on Old River Lake with Pratt's Battery and the 3rd, 4th and 8th Missouri Cavalries; Lawther's 10th Missouri remained behind, to picket the area and protect Greene's rear. Skirting Old River Lake to the south, Greene's command came to rest 3 ½ miles south of Columbia at Smith's Plantation, where he attacked the *Rocket*, a transport which was carrying the adjutant general of the Army, Lorenzo Thomas and staff. The *Rocket* "was struck many times," according to Greene, "but got off safely." Meanwhile, at Columbia, Lieutenant Colonel Currie, commanding the detachment of the Marine Brigade, heard the cannon fire and moved to assist the troubled transport. The *Adams* and the *Baltic* escorted the *Rocket* back to Greenville, while the *Diana* shelled the shoreline. Greene, for his part had already moved his command to Columbia, in the hopes of catching the *Rocket*, and was not in the area when Currie arrived with his detachment. Assessing the damage to the *Rocket*, Federal sources noted that it was "Badly handled." *O.R.*, vol. 34, pt. 1:950–951; Crandall & Newell, 400; Hearn, 334; Simons, 114.

23. On the morning of May 30, Greene returned to Smith's Plantation, where he engaged the cotton laden *Clara Eames*, putting 17 shots into her and penetrating her boiler. The *Eames* signaled her surrender and moved to the shore. "Everything aboard of her that was needed by us was taken," according to W. R. McGuire of the 8th Missouri Cavalry. A short time later a passing gunboat was lured to the *Eames*, which Greene engaged and drove off. With the gunboat gone, "fire was touched" to the *Eames*, continued McGuire, "and what was left [of the cargo], together with the boat, was burned." In addition to capturing the *Eames*, Greene reported taking 15 POWs and seven Negroes, while noting that his artillery ammunition was again nearly exhausted. "There are

Operations on the Mississippi River

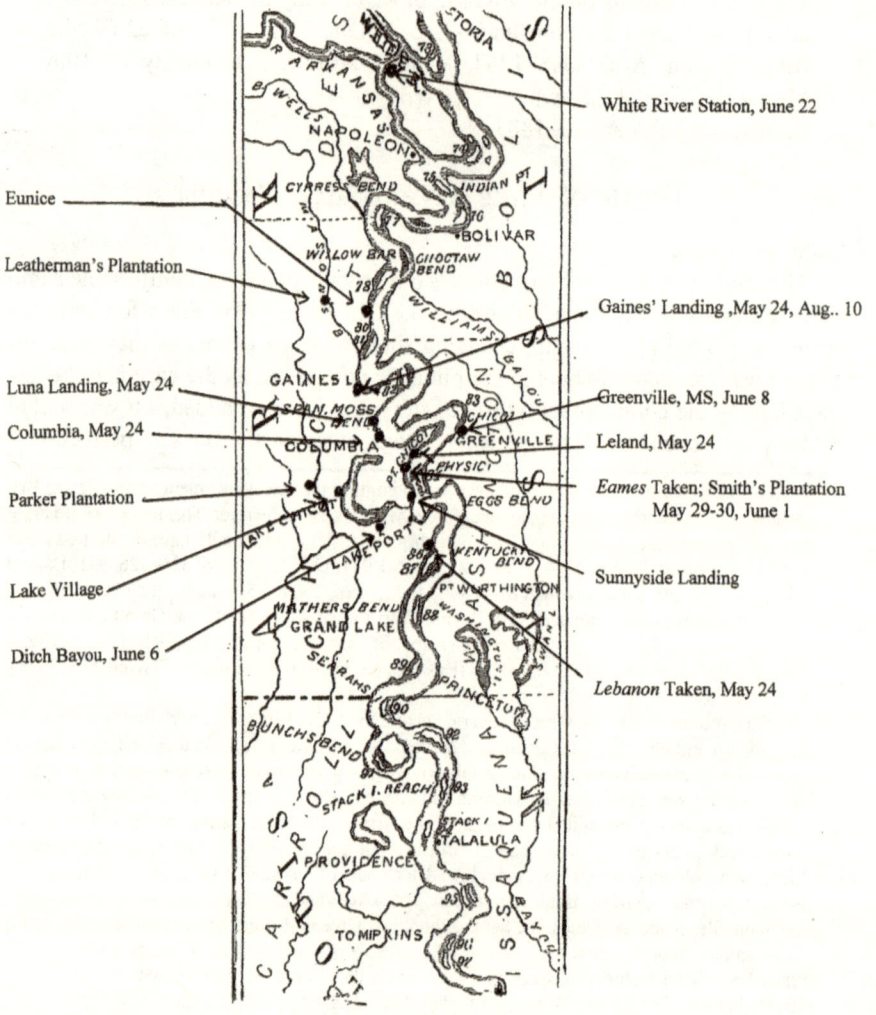

On the 1st day of June a party of sharpshooters is posted on the riverbank just below Sunnyside in charge of a reckless lieutenant from Co. A.[24] Soon a side wheeled tin-clad hove into sight. Two lookouts are in the cross trees between the smokestacks. The ports are up and everything is snug and trim, ready for action at a moments warning. When she is in good easy range we deliver our fire. The two men in the cross trees

Tumbled Out.

Our rash lieutenant springs from cover and hurrahs with delight. In the next instant he goes down with a bullet through his head. Our fire is returned from the decks of the gunboat, the port-holes, and every conceivable hiding place. Then the boom of cannon drowns the rattle of small arms, and the federal commander goes ahead bent on the destruction of the fine cypress trees in the dismal swamp far back in the interior. I've always thought that the two lookouts were dummies, placed there to draw our fire.[25]

---

only 12 rifle shell, and 6 solid smooth-bore and 30 shells for the howitzers," wrote Greene. "It is impossible for me do anything unless I am supplied at once." After burning the *Eames*, Greene moved back to Columbia. May 30 also saw the safe departure of the *Rocket* from Greenville, under the escort of three Marine Brigade ships.

May 31 brought the arrival of a detachment of the Cabell's Cavalry Brigade, under Colonel James C. Monroe, with Hughey's 4-gun battery. Lawther's Regiment was also brought up and posted at Smith's Plantation, where they sniped at passing boats. Greene with Pratt's Battery, the 3rd Missouri, and Monroe's detachment moved to Columbia, while the 4th Missouri guarded the approaches north of Columbia. The 8th, though not mentioned by Greene, probably took over the picket duty, including "fishing and fighting mosquitos," that Lawther had previously performed. *O.R.*, vol. 34, pt. 1:949–950, 952; Crandall & Newell, 401; William Crowley, *Tennessee Cavalier in the Missouri Cavalry: Major Henry Ewing, C.S.A., of the St. Louis Times, A Biographical Sketch* (Columbia, MO, 1978), 133, hereafter cited as Crowley; Harrell, *Arkansas, Confederate Military History*, 272; James E. McGhee, *Campaigning With Marmaduke: Narratives and Roster of the 8th Missouri Cavalry Regiment C.S.A.* (Independence, MO, 2002), 17, hereafter cited as McGhee, *Campaigning With Marmaduke*; Simons, 115–116.

24. Sunnyside Landing was located about 5 miles upstream from Lakeport Landing, and near the tip of the southern "foot" of Old River Lake. *O.R.*, vol. 34, pt. 1: 984; Simons, map on 124.
25. On June 1, while posted at the Smith Plantation, Lawther's Regiment attacked two gunboats (probably the *Autocrat* and the *Monarch*), which had arrived in the area on May 31. Back at Columbia, Greene's command successfully engaged the tinclad *Exchange*, disabling the *Exchange*'s port engine, thus making the vessel difficult to control. It took 45 minutes for the disabled boat to exit the area, at which time its engines stopped. Acting-Master James C. Gibson, commanding the *Exchange*, though severely wounded in three places, managed to drop anchor on the eastern shore of the river; there to make temporary repairs. Eventually the *Exchange* was towed to Greenville, and then to Memphis, to complete her repairs. The *Exchange* lost one dead with two wounded, was struck 35 times, including one shot that "entered the port shell locker," but fortunately did not explode. June 2 marked the end of Greene's initial operations on the Mississippi River as he engaged a series of boats, including the ironclad *Louisville*, which was escorting the transport *W. R. Arthur* by the Columbia area. The *Arthur* carried General John McArthur, his staff, McArthur's wife, and 300 men of the 1st Kansas Infantry. Five men were seriously hurt on board the *Louisville*, while the *Arthur* sustained 17 hits, killing two members of the 1st Kansas. In describing the damage to the *Arthur* a member of the 1st Kansas recorded: "The boat was considerably shattered

The morning of the 6th of June broke with lowering clouds and falling rain, and, through the moaning of the wind in the cypress boughs, and the pattering of raindrops, can be heard the rattle of small arms.[26] We listen for the ever accompanying boom of cannon, but no, the thunder peals are lacking this morning, no echoes breaking the shores. A hasty preparation is going on in camp. Each trooper is putting things to rights, as if in anticipation of a sudden call. Then comes the shrill bugle call, "Boots and Saddles," and then everybody is on his feet. The squadrons assembled promptly and soon we are in battle line on the east [west] bank of Lake River, facing to the west [east].[27] The firing is in the direction of

---

in her upper works and one wheel, but the hull and machinery escaped damage." Greene also engaged the *Adams* and the *Monarch* as they escorted a transport through the area; in all, the *Adams* sustained 28 hits, resulting in three dead and one seriously wounded. In his report of June 8, Greene stated: "On the 3rd and 4th no boats appeared. The river was blockaded." In summing up his operations from May 23–June 4, 1864, Greene reported the loss of six men wounded while engaging "21 boats of all descriptions, of which 5 gun-boats and marine-boats were disabled, 5 transports badly damaged, 1 sunk, 2 burned, and 3 captured." *O.R.*, vol. 34, pt. 1:952; *O.N.R.*, vol. 26: 353–356, 429, 447; W. S. Burke, *Official Military History of Kansas Regiments During the War For the Suppression of the Great Rebellion* (Leavenworth, KS, 1870; reprint ed.. Ottawa, KS, n.d.), 13, hereafter cited as Burke; Crowley, 133; "From Cairo and Below," *Chicago Tribune*, June 7, 1864; Harrell, *Arkansas, Confederate Military History*, 272; Hearn, 235–236; *Naval Chronology*, IV:66; David D. Porter, *Naval History of the Civil War* (New York, 1886; reprint ed, Secaucus, NJ, 1984), 561, hereafter cited as Porter, *Naval History*; Simons, 118–119.
26. On June 3, General A. Ellet departed Greenville, per orders, with his Marine Brigade and headed to Vicksburg, thus providing the reason why the Columbia Bend area was quiet on June 3–4. According to Crandall and Newell, Ellet had "played gunboat" long enough with his Marine Brigade. "Convoying was the special work of the gunboats," not the Marine Brigade. Arriving at Vicksburg at 5:00 p.m. on June 3, Ellet conferred with the newly appointed commander of the Military Division of West Mississippi, Major General Edward R. S. Canby. Canby had already directed General A. J. Smith to use the 16th and 17th Corps "to drive away the rebels" from the river. Ellet informed his superiors that he faced not guerrillas, who typically ran when confronted, but a portion of Marmaduke's Cavalry Division. With Ellet's timely intelligence on the situation, Smith loaded his command on 28 vessels, including four of the Marine Brigade's ships, and headed up river on June 4. In all Smith's force totaled 7,000 effectives, and consisted of the 2nd and 3rd Brigades of Joseph Mower's 1st Division, and the 2nd Brigade, 3rd Division, under Colonel David Moore, all of the 16th Corps, with a portion of the Marine Brigade. The fleet was led by the badly cut-up *Diana*, under Lieutenant Colonel George Currie and per his suggestion, landed the force at Sunnyside Landing, Arkansas, on the evening of June 5. On the morning of June 6, at 6:00 a.m., Smith's Federals headed inland toward Lake Village, amid a rain storm. Two miles after departing camp, the Unionists hit a skirmish line of Greene's 4th Missouri Cavalry, commanded by Colonel John Q. Burbridge. A short time later, the 8th Missouri Cavalry reinforced the 4th's right. Meanwhile, Lawther's 10th Missouri deployed behind Ditch Bayou, supporting the artillery. Greene also used another detachment, with S. S. Harris's Artillery Battery, to cover the command's rear at Lake Village. And still another detachment to cover an escape route over Bayou Mason. *O.R.*, vol. 34, pt. 1:971–974, 984; *O.R.*, vol. 34, pt. 4:185–186; Clarke, 103; Crandall & Newell, 405-407, 413; Hearn, 237–238; Simons, 126, 128; Emmet C. West, *History and Reminiscences of the Second Wisconsin Cavalry Regiment* (Portage, WI, 1904; reprint ed., Rochester, MI, 1982), 11, hereafter cited as West.
27. Luttrell has his directions mixed up. The 10th Missouri was deployed on the west bank of Ditch Bayou or Lake River, facing east. They were supporting four guns of Pratt's Battery. *O.R.*, vol. 34, pt. 1:984.

Sunnyside, below us. Lake River is a deep though narrow stream, which empties into the old lake from the north.[28] On the west [east] of Lake River and in our immediate front is a large plantation, covered with a coat of weeds about waist high. This plantation is about two and one-half miles long by one mile wide.[29] South [North] of us is the Old River Lake. Along its banks is the wagon road leading from Lake Village to Sunnyside.[30] On the north [south] side of the plantation is a cypress swamp, impassable, which reaches around and rest on Lake River. From the cypress swamp, running parallel with Lake River and about fifty yards distant, runs a ditch to the old lake. This ditch is about knee deep fringed by a growth of young cottonwood and willow, eight to fifteen feet high. On the east [west] bank of Lake River, where

We Lie In Battle Line

awaiting the onslaught of the enemy, is a mass of fallen logs and cane. The wagon road mentioned above crosses Lake River on a corduroy bridge submerged underwater two or three feet deep with posts on either side to guide the traveler on the safe road. As I have said, our battle line is along the east [west] bank of Lake River in the edge of the cane and fallen logs. Maj. Pratt's battery is posted at the corduroy road, a position that commands the entire plantation. Our baggage has been sent to the rear, across Bayou Mason four miles away. For when the heavy columns of infantry were seen passing up the lake shore we did not expect to so much as check their advance guard.[31] Our skirmish line is pushed in rapidly. They

---

28. Lake River was actually Ditch Bayou and located about three miles from where the action began. Ibid.
29. The plantation was "an open cotton plantation grown up in weeds." McGhee, *Campaigning With Marmaduke*, 17.
30. Lake Village was a small hamlet of about 100 people and the county seat of Chicot County, Arkansas. Sometimes referred too as Lake City, it was located on the west bank of Old River Lake, about 8 miles from either Luna or Sunnyside Landings. At the time of the Battle of Ditch Bayou, Lake Village was the location of Marmaduke's Headquarters. It was also the home city of Arkansas General D. H. Reynolds, who was serving east of the Mississippi River. *O.N.R.*, vol. 26:364; Clarke, 102; Crandall & Newell, 413; Crowley, 132; "From Arkansas," *State Gazette*, June 23, 1864; Letter to the Editor (June 11, 1864), *The Houston Daily Telegraph* (Houston, TX), June 20, 1864; Mrs. J. W. McMurray, "Sketch of Mrs. D. H. Reynolds, of Lake Village," The United Confederate Veterans of Arkansas, *Confederate Women of Arkansas in the Civil War, Memorial Reminiscences* (Little Rock, 1907; reprint ed., with Intr. by Michael B. Dougan, Fayetteville, AR, 1993), 132–133, hereafter cited as *Confederate Women*; Arthur G. Sharp, "Battle At Lake Chicot," *Civil War Times Illustrated* (October 1982), 18, hereafter cited as Sharp; Simons, 117, 138, 140.
31. On the morning of June 6, the Federal advance was led by the Marine Brigade with Companies E & I of the 2nd Wisconsin Cavalry (Currie incorrectly recalled that it was the 4th Iowa Cavalry), followed by Mower's 2nd Brigade, under Colonel L. F. Hubbard. About 7:00 a.m. the cavalry of the Marine Brigade made contact about two miles from Sunnyside; there, "vainly endeavoring to press back" the rebel skirmishers, according to Hubbard. Between 8:00 and 9:00 a.m., the contending cavalry sniped away at each other, waiting for the Federal infantry to arrive. Amid a falling rain, the infantry began arriving shortly after 9:00, being held up by muddy roads. Deploying five companies of the 47th Illinois to skirmish with the grayclads, Hubbard deployed the rest of his brigade in line of battle to follow behind. My troops "fell back slowly before the increasing

Battle of Ditch Bayou*
(June 6, 1864)

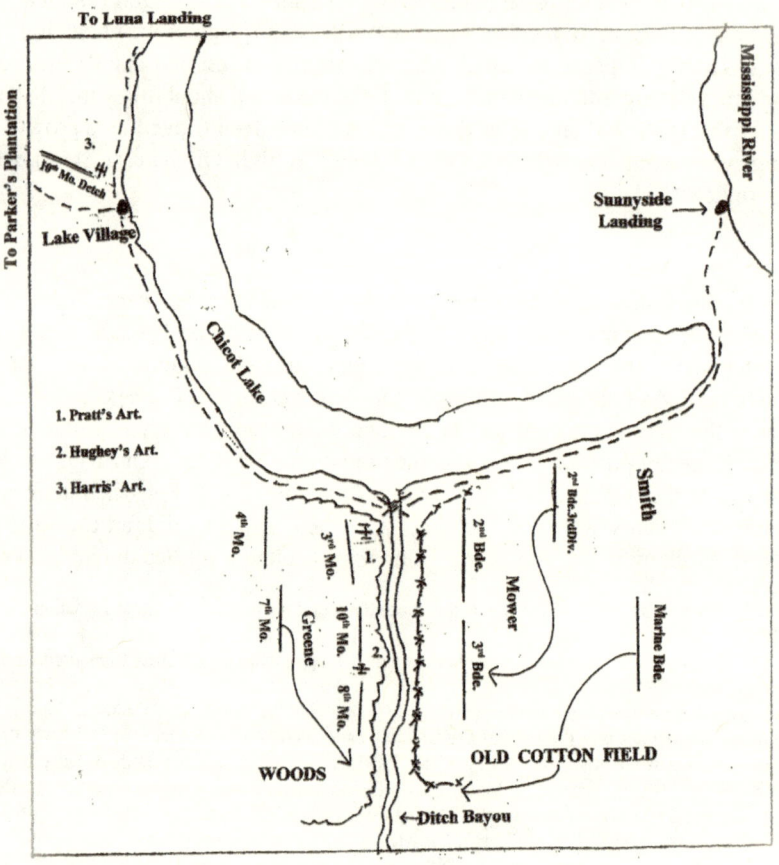

x—x—x—x Fence   Road — — — —

*Also known as Battle of Fish Bayou, Chicot Lake, Old Lake River, Grand Lake, Grand Village, or Lake River.

seem to be in great hurry. Heavy columns of infantry are maneuvering in the rear of their battle line. It seems as though the federal commander is trying to intimidate us by the display of the immense host under his control.[32] If the day had been clear the sight would have been grand. But the rain and the gathering smoke of battle are fast shutting out the panorama. As a federal skirmish line comes up to the willow fringed ditch we greet them with a sharp fire, send them to the shelter in the ditch. Then, as their battle line nears the ditch, our battery opens a terrific fire, every man along the line is tearing cartridges for dear life.[33] They disappear,

---

force," wrote Greene, while Hubbard noted that the gray troopers were "somewhat stubborn at first,... and suddenly retire[d] before my advance." The skirmishing continued all the way back to Ditch Bayou, which was reached near 11:00 a.m. A feeble Federal artillery barrage followed for the next hour, which proved "impotent." *O.R.*, vol. 34, pt. 1:974, 984; *O.R.S.*, pt. 2, vol. 92:670, 675; Clarke, 104, 106; Dyer, 684; "From Cairo and Below," *Chicago Tribune*, June 13, 1864; Hearn, 239–240; Letter to the Editor (June 11, 1864), *Houston Telegraph*, June 20, 1864; Sharp, 22; West, 11.

32. When Greene's line was formed on the west side of Ditch Bayou, it extended about a mile to the south. The position was a strong one, with a lake on his left and a swamp on his far right. One Federal captain called the rebel position "almost impregnable." Additionally, though Ditch Bayou was not that deep, it was about 200 feet wide at its mouth where the bridge crossed. Of the bayou Private W. R. McGuire of the 8th Missouri Cavalry (CSA) recalled: "The bayou had but very little water in it, but the mud and slush had no bottom." Colonel Currie, of the Marine Brigade also noted that the bayou was shallow, but a "thick muck" covered the bottom, making the bayou extremely hazardous to cross. To cover the ditch, Greene had Pratt put four guns opposite the corduroy bridge, which Greene had "torn up" after he had crossed; the 3rd Missouri supported Pratt's Battery. Next came Lawther's 10th Missouri, which supported two guns from Hughey's Arkansas Battery, with the 8th Missouri Cavalry on the far right. Greene held Kitchen's 7th Missouri, commanded by Lieutenant Colonel Jesse Ellison, and Burbridge's 4th Missouri in reserve. Greene's total force numbered about 600 men with six cannon. About noon, General Marmaduke arrived at Ditch Bayou when "the rain began falling in torrents," and on came the Yankees. *O.R.*, vol. 34, pt. 1:984–985; Ballard Diary, June 6, 1864; Clarke, 106–107; "From Cairo and Below," *Chicago Tribune*, June 12, 1864; Hearn, 240–241; McGhee, *Campaigning With Marmaduke*, 17; Simons, 132, 136, 140.

33. Lieutenant Colonel George Currie had recommended that Captain C. G. Fisher of the Marine Brigade serve as an aide to General A. J. Smith, during the battle, as Fisher was familiar with the terrain. Smith "thought he knew best," and despite Fisher's warnings of the "foolhardy" attack, ordered in the infantry. With the rebel skirmishers pushed across the bayou, General Mower aligned his command to assault the rebel line, even as the 3rd Indiana Artillery attempted to soften the rebel position. Dashing up to the front line, "waving his sword as he galloped," Mower exclaimed "'Forward Second Brigade, to the charge!'" The 2nd Brigade advanced *en échelon*, the 47th Illinois on the far right, next to the 5th Minnesota, with the 8th Wisconsin on the far left of the brigade. Greene's command held their fire until the bluecoats had closed to within 100 yards, when they opened a "galling fire" on the charging Unionists. To the left of the 2nd Brigade, Mower deployed his 3rd Brigade, consisting of but two regiments; the 33rd Missouri was on the left of the 8th Wisconsin and the 35th Iowa came next. Unfortunately, the 33rd Missouri and the 35th Iowa were not

Joseph A. Mower

laying down or crawl into the ditch. But other battle lines come up; other lines and columns moved warily through the fogging rain and gathering smoke. The rattle of musketry has increased to a sullen roar. Sulfurous smoke fills the air. Bullets are glancing from the logs and trickling through the cane.[34] A cry for ammunition runs along the line, and, as our ammunition gives out, spiteful hiss of the bullets is more plain. But all things have to end and, this battle is ended as abruptly at as it began, by our quietly moving to the rear, mounting our horses and marching up the lake shore.[35] Across the curb of the lake shore we can see the

Blue Masses of Infantry.

To the north is the pall of battle smoke rising above the treetops. Overhead the gray clouds are scudding before a rising breeze and the rain is ceasing. We swing our hats in defiance at the moving columns of blue coated infantry across the

---

informed of the bayou that was protecting the rebels; though surprised by the bayou, on the 3rd Brigade pressed, with some of the men even trying to ford the mucky river, but they were shot down. The Union line came to a halt, and firing erupted along the whole line; the rebels protected by the "dense forest" and fallen timber, while the Feds lay down in the soft muddy field. Mower, for his part lost two horses during the engagement, while Smith earned the praise of the *Tribune* as he "inspired his command with courage, his position being constantly in advance of his line." *O.R.*, vol. 34, pt. 1:972, 974, 976–978; Clarke, 107; "From Cairo and Below, *Chicago Tribune*, June 12, 1864; Sharp, 22–23; Quoted in Simons, 130, 133, 136.

34. As the Federal line extended to rebel right, Greene ordered Ellison's 7th Missouri Cavalry to extend his line in that quarter. Meanwhile, General Marmaduke, who had arrived at the battlefield at noon, suggested that Greene should withdraw his command, considering the overwhelming odds that he faced. However, according to a civilian, who witnessed the battle, Greene responded that "he would not retreat until all of his ammunition was used, at which Gen'l Marmaduke said 'All right Greene, this is your fight.'" And so the battle continued unabated. In recalling the ferocity of the battle one Confederate veteran wrote: "The enemy would move on us column after column through the field, and when they would get near the bayou, firing was opened on them from our lines, and such slaughter for the short length of time was seldom ever witnessed." *O.R.* vol. 34, pt. 1:985; McGhee, *Campaigning With Marmaduke*, 17; Quoted in Simons, 140.

35. By 3:00 p.m. (Faust and Sharp put the withdrawal time at 2:30), with his ammunition exhausted, Greene finally ordered a measured retreat. However, unknown to Greene or Marmaduke, even as the 7th and 8th Missouri Cavalries with Pratt's Battery began to withdraw, the Unionists were likewise out, or nearly out of ammunition. General Mower requested support to replace his 3rd Brigade, from General A. J. Smith, who sent in the 2nd Brigade, 3rd Division. Next, Greene withdrew the 10th Missouri, with Hughey's section of artillery, followed by the remainder of his command. Meanwhile, as the battle raged, the Marine Brigade was tasked to protect the Union left flank. When it became known that the rebels were retreating, Smith ordered the Marine Brigade, with the 2nd Wisconsin Cavalry, to cross Ditch Bayou on the rebel far right and attack the retreating grayclads. Colonel Currie led off his command and gamely slogged across the mucky bayou. The crossing proved to be quite difficult and exhausting to both man and beast; fortunately for Currie he had no opposition. In the end the Confederates made good their escape, their rear being protected by Lawther's 10th Missouri. *O.R.*, vol. 34, pt. 1:972, 977, 985; Clarke, 107; "From Arkansas," *State Gazette*, June 23, 1864; Faust, 423; Letter to the Editor (June 11, 1864), *Houston Telegraph*, June 20, 1864; Sharp, 23; Simons, 130, 140.

[Note: A year after the battle an engineer from General Smith's staff told a local resident that had the Confederates "held out 15 minutes longer, they (the Union troops) would have retreated." Simons, 140.]

curve of the lake shore and hurrah back at them lustily. We retired to Grigg's ferry on Bayou Mason three or four miles, where we expected the enemy would follow in furious pace. But alas, no! He is not anxious to punish us, for he continues up the lake shore to Lake Village stops for the night.[36] Early in the morning of the 7th we move out to attack the enemy. As we enter Lake Village, that camping-ground of the enemy, we find he has taken an easy leave and left the work of a vandal behind him. About his bivouac fires laid the broken half burned doors, shutters, sash and furniture that only yesterday adorn the villagers' houses. The beautiful lawns and shrubbery that yesterday reminded us of our cozy homes in Missouri are this morning broken, torn and demolished. The palings and fences are gone—only the smoldering ashes lie on the street. Cattle, hogs, chickens lie dead upon every hand. On the naked streets stand the Village people, old and young, the women in tears, the children wailing for bread. More than one generous hearted trooper shares his rough soldier fare with the little ones. How eagerly their little fingers closed over the rough johnny-cake and jerked beef, then nestled back among their mothers skirts and eyed us timidly as they nibble the rough rations.[37] We push on

---

36. With the last of the rebel units departing the area, General Smith ordered his command to advance. However, "We were detained for some time," wrote General Mower, "in repairing the bridge that the enemy had partially destroyed." By 4:30 the bridge was repaired and Hubbard's Brigade crossed over, followed by Gilbert's of the 3rd Division, and finally George Van Beck's Brigade. Even as the Smith's infantry crossed the bridge, the Marine Brigade was out in front, having previously forded the bayou. Traveling another three miles the Federal command entered Lake Village, where they camped for the night near 6:00 p.m. Meanwhile, Greene's command crossed Bayou Mason and camped at Parker's, near Grigg's Ferry. Federal losses at Ditch Bayou were reported as 40 killed and 70 wounded, total 110 (Dyer or West); or 33 killed and 98 wounded, total 131 (Simons or the *O.R.*). Other sources reported the Union losses as 250 casualties. Greene reported the loss of four killed and 33 wounded, total 37, while William Crowley put the number at 44. As to the victor, Colonel George Currie wrote: "The Battle of Lake Village [Ditch Bayou] was no victory. Although the field was won, it was a field dotted with the graves of our soldiers and reddened with the blood of our wounded." *O.R.*, vol. 34, pt. 1: 972, 975–979, 983, 985; James Trooper Alexander Correspondence, Letter (June 15, 1864), Southern Historical Collection, Chapel Hill, NC, hereafter cited as J. T. Alexander, Letter; Crowley, 133; Dyer, 684; Faust, 423; "From Arkansas, *State Gazette*, June 23, 1864; Sharp, 23; Quoted in Simons, 130, 141–143; West, 12.
37. Of their stay at Lake Village, Colonel Currie recalled:
> Every available house and building in the town was converted into sick rooms for the wounded…Fences, chicken-coops, out buildings, and every thing that would burn was used for fires to warm and dry the thoroughly drenched men, and cook their evening meal…The little gem that yesterday lay shining in the morning sun was now torn from its beautiful setting and lay trodden in the mud.

Judge Henry Hayes, of Lake Village, wrote of the Federal incursion–"The Yankees camped here over night, robbing all the roosts, kitchens, pantries, meat houses, and in some instances every thing else womens [sic] and childrens [sic] clothing etc. tearing down much of the fencing, destroying gardens etc." To Judge Hayes, the bluecoats were nothing more than "damned thieving, lousy, cowardly, servile" soldiers. "They find they can't conquer our soldiers, so they vent their spleen and indulge their avarice in pillaging and robbing unarmed citizens women and children, whenever they get the opportunity." The judge put the total loss in the county at "some $300,000.00 worth of property." Arthur G. Sharp wrote that the Unionists "denuded the little village, taking everything they need;" or simply put, Smith's Federals "sacked Lake Village."

and strike the enemy's rear guard near the river levee. The last of the regiments are re-embarking as we dash over the levee and take a few prisoners.[38] Among our captures are a colonel's horse, his orderly, etc. The colonel dismounted and sped on board on foot. I wish I could tell that he fearlessly galloped his horse over the stage-plank. How novel it would sound. But I suppose

He Did Not Have Time

to imitate his great chief, Gen. Grant, by taking a more dignified method of riding over.[39]

Despite the seemingly total destruction of Lake Village, the town survived the war. Clarke, 108; Faust, 423; Sharp, 23; Simons, 142–143.

38. The Federals departed Lake Village at 8:00 a.m., the next morning, led by the Marine Brigade; General Smith's command followed. Colonel Currie took his Marine Brigade back to Columbia, where they burned the remainder of the town and boarded their waiting boats. General Smith's boys went to Luna Landing where they met their fleet and likewise boarded their ships for Memphis, but not before looting Richard Session's house, where the 5th Minnesota burned all his furniture and stole $5,000.00 in monogrammed silverware. Meanwhile, Lawther's 10th Missouri caught up with Smith's command just as they were finishing boarding, capturing eight POWs, according Greene or 10 by General Marmaduke's count. Additionally, back at Columbia, Colonel Currie rode to Luna Landing to confer with General Smith. For his return trip Currie took a tug and sent his horse, "Johnnie," back by land to board the *Diana*. Unfortunately, the animal was taken by Lawther's men and eventfully became the trusted mount of General Marmaduke. Clarke, 108–109; Letter to the Editor (June 11, 1864), *Houston Telegraph*, June 20, 1864; Hearn, 242–243; Sharp, 22; Simons, 143–144; West, 12.

39. Ulysses S. Grant was born on April 22, 1822, in Ohio, graduated from West Point (number 21 of 39) in 1843, and fought in the Mexican War where he was breveted a captain. Resigning on July 31, 1854, Grant tried farming, selling real estate, and clerking in a store. He was appointed colonel of the 21st Illinois Infantry on June 17, 1861, and was sent briefly to Missouri. He commanded in Jefferson City for a week in August 1861, as a newly appointed brigadier general, after which he was transferred to southeast Missouri. On November 7, 1861, he fought and lost the Battle of Belmont, Missouri, his only engagement in the Trans-Mississippi area. Grant completed his Civil War service in the East, rising to the rank of Lieutenant General and Commander of the United States Army. He was elected president of the United States in 1868, and served two terms, after which he traveled and entered into some unfavorable business adventures. Grant died on July 23, 1885, in New York City. Mark Mayo Boatner III, *The Civil War Dictionary* (New York, 1959), 352–352, hereafter cited as Boatner; Francis B. Heitman, *Historical Register and Dictionary of the United States Army from Its Organization, September 29, 1789, to March 2, 1903* (2 vols., Washington, DC, 1903; reprint ed., Gaithersburg, MD, 1988), 1:470, hereafter cited as Heitman; Ezra J. Warner, *Generals in Blue: Lives of the Union Commanders* (Baton Rouge, LA, 1964), 183–186, hereafter cited as Warner, *Generals in Blue*.

The event that Luttrell described happened at the Battle of Belmont, Missouri on November 7, 1861. Recalling the incident Grant wrote:

> The captain of the boat that had just pushed out, but had not started, recognized me and ordered the engineer not to start the engine; he then had a plank run out for me. My horse seemed to take in the situation. There was no path down the bank...My horse put its fore feet over the bank without hesitation or urging, and, with his hind feet well under him, slid down the bank and trotted aboard the boat, twelve or fifteen feet away, over a single gang-plank.

Quoted in Nathaniel Cheairs Hughes, Jr., *The Battle of Belmont: Grant Strikes South* (Chapel Hill, NC, 1991), 171.

The river is dotted over with transports loaded to the guards with infantry. The gunboats steamed between us and the transports and greet us with a round of shell. While we are exchanging shots with the gunboats, the transports passed around a curve. Then the gunboats follow them, tossing back at us by way of adieu a dozen or two heavy shells. There we camped on the river bank, and on the 8th we give a transport a plunging fire as she passes up, closely hugging the farther bank. After this we return to our old [camp], near the battlefield at Lake River.[40] Here we learn that we have been fighting Gen. A. J. Smith's Sixteenth Army Corps.[41] He left quite a

Andrew J. Smith

---

40. After the Federal Army departed the western shores of Arkansas, the area proved to be relatively quiet. Union forces continued their burning ways on June 8 as Greenville, Mississippi, on the east bank of the River, went up in smoke. Arthur Sharp says the Federal "troops were extracting revenge for past guerrilla tactics and for the heavy losses they sustained during the fighting at Ditch Bayou." Meanwhile, Lawther's Regiment returned to their camp at Redleaf Plantation, about two miles from Sunnyside, and near where the skirmish began on June 6; And the rest of Greene's Brigade continued to harass Federal boats with but limited musket fire, causing Lieutenant Commander Owen, the area naval commander to report on June 11:

> With the exception of small squads of sharpshooters on the bank of the river between Cypress Bend and Sunnyside, we have had no firing since my last [June 6]. What the enemy has done with his battery I do not know, nor can I find out, as not a soul is ever seen on the Arkansas shore save guerrillas and sharpshooters.

O.N.R., vol. 26:383; Crandall & Newell, 418; Faust, 423; McGhee, *Campaigning With Marmaduke*, 18; Sharp, 21, 23; Simons, 126, 144.

41. Andrew Jackson Smith was born on April 28, 1815, in Buck City, Pennsylvania. He was educated locally and graduated from West Point in 1838 (number 36 of 45). Prior to the Civil War Smith served primarily in the west and during the Mexican War was in California. At the beginning of the Civil War Smith, a regular army major, was elected colonel of the 2nd California Cavalry. He resigned after six weeks, being posted to the staff of General Halleck as Chief of Cavalry. Promoted to brigadier general on March 17, 1862, he led a division in numerous campaigns east of the Mississippi River. In addition to his operations in the Red River Valley in 1864, Smith also helped repulse Price's 1864 Missouri Raid. He later returned to the east side of the river, fought at Nashville, where he "was commended for his actions." Smith commanded the 16th Corps in February 1865, which he led at Mobile until the close of the war. After the war Smith remained in the army and was breveted a brigadier general for his performance at the Battle of Pleasant Hill. In 1869 he left the army for assorted government jobs. Smith was briefly reinstated in the army by Congressional Act in 1888, and retired from the army the following day. He died in St. Louis on January 30, 1897. Boatner, 768; Faust, 694; David S. Heidler and Jeanne T. Heidler, eds., "Smith, Andrew Jackson," in *Encyclopedia of the American Civil War* (New York, 2000), hereafter cited

graveyard behind him. We had only one man killed, and that one belongs to the artillery.[42]

Early on the morning of the 22nd the Tenth regiment crosses the Arkansas river and attacked a federal post, known to us as the navy yard, located on what is known in this vicinity as the island on the White River side (see map of Arkansas).[43] We, however, find the place newly fortified by a picket wall of split logs, with loop-holes for musketry. We immediately charge the little fort thinking we could scale the walls, but we find the walls are too high. At the first fire of the

---

as *Encyclopedia of the Civil War*; Gary D. Joiner, *Through the Howling Wilderness: The Red River Campaign and the Union Failure in the West* (Knoxville, TN, 2006), 67, hereafter cited as Joiner; William C. Winter, *The Civil War in St. Louis: A Guided Tour* (St. Louis, 1994), 120, hereafter cited as Winter.

The 16th Corps was constituted on December 18, 1862. The first commander of the Corps was Major General Stephen A. Hurlbut. Abolished on November 7, 1864, the corps was reconstituted on February 18, 1865, with A. J. Smith as its commander, and was finally disbanded on July 20, 1865, at the end of the war. During the Red River Campaign, the men of the 16th Corps were labeled Smith's "gorillas" by Admiral D. D. Porter, because of their ragged appearance when they first appeared in Alexandria, Louisiana, in March 1864. Edwin Davis recorded in his book, *Heroic Years*, that the nickname was given to the men because they were "'coarse, uncouth, ill-dressed braggarts and chicken thieves.'" Edwin Adams Davis, *Heroic Years Louisiana in the War for Southern Independence* (Baton Rouge, LA, 1964), 55; Joiner, 67; Frederick Phisterer, *Statistical Record of the Armies of the United States* (New York, 1907), 59.

42. Mrs. Martha P. Sanders, who housed several of the rebel wounded following the battle, described the Confederate losses as "one Confederate killed on the field, 6 mortally wounded, and 34 wounded but recovered"—41 total verses the four killed and 33 wounded that Colonel Greene reported—total 37. J. T. Alexander, who was visiting Marmaduke's headquarters, put the loss at 33 killed and wounded. *O.R.*, vol. 34, pt. 1:985; Quoted in Simons, 140; J. T. Alexander, Letter (June 15, 1864).

43. Following the Battle of Ditch Bayou, operations on the river were exceedingly meager, with little more than some sniping or scouting taking place. Greene's Brigade was again short of artillery ammunition and this time he added the need for Enfield rifled ammunition. On June 18, Marmaduke's demi-division left their base camp at Lake Village and headed north toward the Arkansas River. On June 20, Greene's Brigade was reported four miles west of Eunice, across Cypress Creek, within easy marching distance of Napoleon, on the Mississippi River, and an equal distant from the Arkansas River. It was also clear on June 20th, that the target was White River Station (the Federals name for the "naval yard" as Luttrell noted) at the confluence of the White and Arkansas Rivers. The station was on an island at the mouth of the Arkansas River and contained "three trade stores and an extensive Government wood-yard." Lieutenant Commander James Prichett, commanding the District Mouth of White River, requested that the normally unoccupied station be garrisoned with two companies. General Canby sent six companies of the 12th Iowa Infantry, numbering "200 muskets," recently returned from veteran furlough. The 12th departed Memphis on May 16 and arrived the next day, when they began constructing a stockade. Five days later, Lieutenant Colonel John H. Stubbs wrote his district commander stating: "I can see no need of troops here except a force to act as detectives and pickets." General C. C. Washburn agreed, and upon General Canby's approval, ordered Stubbs to return to Memphis, leaving 55 men from Companies A and F behind to serve as a garrison, in addition to 50 Negro wood choppers. On May 27, Stubbs returned to Memphis, leaving Captain J. R. C. Hunter in command. Lawther's 10th Missouri crossed the Arkansas River at midnight and attacked the station between 4:00–4:30 a.m. on June 22. *O.R.*, vol. 34, pt. 1:1045; *O.R.*, vol. 34, pt. 3:695–696; *O.R.*, vol. 34, pt. 4:122, 455, 664–665; *O.R.S.*, pt. 1, vol. 6:429; *O.R.S.*, pt. 2, vol. 20:132, 139, 152, 157; *O.N.R.*, vol. 26:406–407; *Naval Chronology*, IV:70, IV:76, IV:82.

enemy, Old John M about faces and makes for the rear like a scared wolf, losing his gun at almost the first jump, and exclaiming as he runs "It's all a blame lie! An infernal lie!" His flight ends at the boat. Into one of which he jumps, admonishing the guards to "get aboard before they are all killed, every ——— one of them!" He is the only man in the command whose belligerent propensities are not sufficient to stand the shock of battle. Upon this occasion however, the boys have managed to make him believe there will be no fighting, and hence his presence in the ranks, and his exclamation as recorded above.[44] Breaching the wall, and not being able to scale it we endeavor to drive the garrison out by

Firing through the Loop-Holes

thinking we have got as safe a position as they. In this close fighting John H. Bell catches a ball and his side. As he goes down, his and a federal gun is left crossed in a loop-hole. But we don't get the chance to end the fight as we expected, for about this time a gunboat in the river opened a raking flank fire, which admonishes us to retire.[45] Aiming at some cabins, presumably their quarters, we give them a parting salute. Ben F. Wheatley is slightly wounded while emptying his revolver.[46] He is apparently in no great hurry, notwithstanding the cannon shot ploughing up the ground all about, making the splinters and boards fly in all directions. And their presence is kindly lent us on our return journey. I suppose they put them gratis. Our loss in this little affair is twenty-five killed and wounded, which shows how fatally such petty fighting occasionally terminates.[47]

---

44. The rebels arrived at the Station at 4:00 a.m., according to the garrison commander Captain J. R. C. Hunter, while according to Ensign Henry Booby, commanding the gunboat *Lexington,* the attack began 30 minutes later. After surprising the Federal pickets, Lawther's command stormed the recently completed stockade. Fortunately for the 55-man garrison, 48 of whom were armed, the *Lexington* already had steam up and came to the immediate aid of the Station and "opened on them a rapid fire." However, by the time the *Lexington*, "got clear of the driftwood," the rebels were already retreating, limiting the Lexington's response to "a few parting shots." The *Chicago Tribune* credits the survival of the garrison on the very opportune arrival of the *Lexington*, which allowed the garrison to withstand "several and desperate charges of the enemy" or "might have fared worse." Captain John Bremmer, commanding Company F, 12th Iowa Infantry, credited the victory to the failed attempt to surprise the meager garrison, which resulted in the rebels "needlessly losing many of their men." *O.R.*, vol. 34, pt. 1:1045; *O.R.S.*, pt. 1, vol. 6:428–430; *O.N.R.*, vol. 26:415–416; "From Arkansas," *Chicago Tribune,* June 28, 1864.
45. The timely arrival of the *Lexington* ended the battle for the Confederates, who had no artillery support of their own. After a 30 minute battle, Lawther wisely withdrew his command into the nearby woods, at which time the *Lexington* continued to pepper the rebels, ensuring the rebels did not return to the Station. Instead of pursing the rebels to find their landing point, the *Lexington* remained on picket duty, per orders, which allowed Lawther to successfully withdraw from the island and back to the south side of the Arkansas River. *O.N.R.*, vol. 26: 415–417.
46. Benjamin F. Wheatley, a resident of Johnson County, Missouri, joined the Missouri State Guard (MSG) on December 2, 1861, at Warrensburg. He later became a member of Company G, 10th Missouri Cavalry (CSA)., Wheatly survived the war and was paroled at Shreveport on June 8, 1865. National Archives, Record Group M322 (roll no. 58), Confederate Compiled Service Recorded, 10th Missouri Cavalry.
47. Federal losses were put at one killed and three "severely wounded," who later died, with one

On the 20th of July a scout of 100 is sent to Lake Village under the command of Capt. [Thomas B.] Murray.[48] Two days later he received orders to remain at the village and do scout and picket duty until further orders. On the morning of the 29th, while lounging in the upper story of the courthouse—our quarters—I observed a dense cloud of dust far below town on the lake shore. I at once go in quest of the captain, who, I find is uptown, engaged in a little game of poker. I quietly make known to him the nature of my observation. He throws his cards upon the table and grabbed the money, as he explains, "Beat three queens and take the pool! Fall in, men! Load your guns." The three old planters who sat at the table open wide their eyes in astonishment and drop their jaws in wonder. As I followed the captain from the room I hear one of them ask. "What the deuce has come over the gallant captain? I wonder if that is a little trick to get my money? My hand is

A Little Six – Full!"

Meantime the captain is speeding down the street shouting: "To arms, men! To arms! Fall in! Fall in!" When we reach the courthouse the men are hustling into line. A detail is sent to saddle horses, and a skirmish line is ordered. As they are forming the village people come fleeing from the western suburbs of town, and quite a crowd of frightened women and children have collected in front of us. The dust cloud is moving up the lakes more rapidly. "Load your guns, men!" shouts Murray, and in the next breath he explains; "This way, ladies. Not a hair of your precious heads shall be harmed." Then turning to me he raves forth: "Take charge of the skirmish line, sir! Move to the edge of the suburbs; post your men undercover so as to command the shore road, and hold your fire until you can see the whites of their eyes. Then, sir, shoot the red hot sauerkraut out of every son-of-a-gun of them." Then as the line moved forward I see the gallant captain offering his arm to a woman with a wailing child, and excusing himself thusly: "I

---

additional wounded—all from Company F, 12th Iowa Infantry. Additionally one Negro laborer was also killed. The *Lexington* suffered no losses, while reporting that the rebels had carried off "two families of the refugees." Coincidentally, the *Tribune* reported the rebel losses as 24 killed and wounded, almost identical to what Luttrell recorded. The Federal command reported finding 11 rebel dead on the battlefield following the engagement. *O.R.*, vol. 34, pt. 1:1045; *O.N.R.*, vol. 26:416; *O.R.S.*, pt. 1, vol. 6:429; *O.R.S.*, pt. 2, vol. 20:139; "From Arkansas," *Chicago Tribune*, June 28, 1864.

48. Thomas Benton Murray was born on May 2, 1837, in Johnson County, Missouri. At the beginning of the Civil War he enlisted as a private in Company D, 16th Missouri Infantry. Murray was later promoted and transferred to Company G, 11th Missouri Cavalry Battalion, where he initially served as a 2nd lieutenant (October 15, 1862) and later the unit's 1st lieutenant (May 10, 1863). By war's end he had been promoted to captain, commanding Company G, 10th Missouri Cavalry (CSA). Returning to Missouri, Murray married Clara Davenport, with whom he had two sons. Murray later remarried Lucretia Jane Wood, with whom he had four more children. Thomas Murray died in Empire, Montana, on July 4, 1893. Joanne C. Eakin, *Confederate Records From the United Daughters of the Confederacy Files*, 8 vols. (Independence, MO, 1995-2001), 6:33–34, hereafter cited as Eakin, *Confederate Records*; National Archives, Record Group M322 (roll no. 57), Confederate Compiled Service Records, 10th Missouri Cavalry Regiment.

beg a thousand pardons, madam, ladies!" and he bows profoundly. "A thousand pardons, ladies, madam, for being obliged to use such harsh language in your presence." Meantime the skirmish line takes position as ordered. A few minutes after the last man has been secreted, and the orders again repeated, the dust cloud sweeps up in our front. The day is dry and hot, scarcely a breath of air, and what little there might be is inclined up the lake. The horsemen in the dust cloud look like dark shadows. The flag droops down the staff, completely covered with gray dust. The order "ready" has passed down the line, and "aim" quickly followed it. Then a gust of wind from the lake sweeps the dust from the moving column; the drooping flag lashes forth upon the breeze. It is the red cross banner! and a glad shout of welcome goes up from the little skirmish line, whose fingers a moment ago were feeling for the trigger with deadly intent.[49]

Of such incidents as those related in a soldier's life filled, and as such is war.

H. C. LUTTRELL,
Tenth Missouri Cavalry, C.S.A.

* * * * * * *

Item: Operations on the White River, Arkansas (June 20–29, 1864), including the capture of the Union Gunboat *Queen City* (June 24, 1864), by R. W. Crabb[50]
Published: July 3, 1886.

Cavalry Fight against Gunboats

Uniontown, Ky., June 30.

---

49. Following the engagement at the White River Station, Marmaduke's Brigade (Luttrell's command), under Colton Greene continued to operate near the Mississippi River. Its headquarters was at Lake Village and remained so until mid-August 1864, as the various regiments scouted and harassed Federal boats with musket fire and occasional artillery rounds. On July 27, the brigade attacked the Marine boats, the *Fairchild* and *Adams*, hitting the *Fairchild* 27 times. And on August 10, rebel artillery severely damaged the *Empress* near Gaines Landing, killing six and wounding several others. On August 14, Marmaduke's Brigade was relieved of duty on the Mississippi River, and headed west toward Mt. Elba to refit for Price's 1864 Missouri Raid. General John B. Clark, Jr. assumed command of the brigade on August 18, replacing Greene, who was removed because of "mutinous conduct," which "proved [him]...unfit for command." However, according to Jerry Ponder, Greene was relieved for political reasons and was later reinstated to command his regiment during Price's 1864 Missouri Raid (also known as Price's Missouri Expedition). At the time Greene was relieved, the brigade numbered 888 officers and men present for duty, with 120 present, but sick, and another 443 absent sick. Additionally another 211 men were at a convalescent camp and were expected to be ready in a few days. *O.R.*, vol. 41, pt. 2:1040, 1065, 1071; Ballard Diary, July 21, 1864; McGhee, *Campaigning With Marmaduke*, 18; Jerry Ponder, *Major General John S. Marmaduke C.S.A.* (Mason, TX, 1999), 157, hereafter cited as Ponder, *General Marmaduke*; Simons, 146, 150.
50. The only Crabb found in the *Confederate Roster* was a W. R. Crabb, who was a member of Fristoe's Missouri Regiment. Janet Hewett, ed., *The Roster of Confederate Soldiers 1861–1865* 16 vols. (Wilmington, NC, 1995–1996), 4:198, hereafter cited as Hewett, *Confederate Roster*.

Joseph O. Shelby

Editor *Republican*

I have been reading with a great deal of interest your series of war stories, and will relate the following experience our old brigade had with the gunboats:

In the early part of the summer of 1864 Gen. Joe Shelby was detached;[51] and, [Thomas R.] Freeman's, [Archibold] Dobbin's, [Thomas H.] McCrary's [McCray's] and his own brigade, sent north of the Arkansas River to watch the Federals, who had been depredating in the White River valley, carrying off all the cotton, Negroes, work-horses and everything they could confiscate, to the horror and disgust of the people of that valley.[52]

51. Joseph Orville Shelby was born on December 12, 1840, in Lexington, Kentucky, educated at Transylvania University, moved to Waverly, Missouri, in 1852, where he was a wealthy planter. At the beginning of the Civil War, he joined the MSG and fought in all the early battles in the Trans-Mississippi. Shelby later joined the Confederate Army, organized a cavalry regiment in the Summer of 1862, commanded a Brigade at Prairie Grove, Helena and during Marmaduke's two Missouri raids in 1863. In October 1863, Shelby led his own raid into Missouri and eventually commanded a division during Price's 1864 Missouri Raid. In 1864, Shelby was branded "the greatest horse thief on record," and described as "a dashing young fellow...; he has light hair and eyes and a reddish beard, quiet long; he is nearly six feet high, very well built and as brave as a lion. He wears nothing in the way of a uniform, and no badge to mark his high rank. His dress was a scarlet covered flannel shirt and dark pants tucked in a pair of high cacavlry boots...His hat was a plain gray felt with a large black ostrich feather in it." At war's end he moved briefly to Mexico, returned to Missouri where he died at Adrian on February 13, 1897. Banasik, *Missouri Brothers in Gray*, 150-151; Walter E. Busch, *General Sterling Price's Great Missouri Raid: The Missouri Democrat Articles* (Jefferson City, MO, 2010), 172, hereafter cited as Busch, *Missouri Democrat Articles*; Don Mc. N. Palmer, *Four Weeks In the Rebel Army* (New London, CT, 1865), 16, hereafter cited as Palmer; Ezra J. Warner, *Generals in Gray: Lives of the Confederate Commanders* (Baton Rouge, LA, 1959), 273-274, hereafter cited as Warner, *Generals in Gray*, 273-274.

52. Shelby's Iron Brigade was ordered northward on May 5, 1864, from its camp at Arkadelphia, but delays prevented its departure until May 9. Shelby's mission was simple—"Prevent the use of the railroad east of Little Rock and the navigation of the White River." Additionally, he was to recruit his command and bring order to the region. Reaching the Arkansas River on May 13, Shelby found it impossible to cross near Lewisburg and moved toward Dardanelle. He captured Dardanelle on May 17, along with 74 POWs and "many supplies," and crossed the Arkansas the following day. On May 19 the Iron Brigade headed eastward, crossing the White River on May 26, and capturing an undefended Batesville the same day. Jacksonport was evacuated by the Federals on May 25-26, even as Shelby approached and captured Batesville. When Shelby arrived in northeast Arkansas, he called together all the scattered commands and announced his authority over them. Thomas McCray's, Archibold Dobbin's and Thomas Freeman's Brigades were mere skeletons, basically unorganized bands of men. Of the three, it appears that Freeman's had some type of organization, containing about "seven hundred effective men—a brave brigade truly,"

River Operations in the Trans-Mississippi / 27

Gen. Shelby accordingly took up his headquarters at Jacksonport, a small town on the north bank of the White River, and sent out his scouts over the country to discover the situation of affairs.[53] They soon brought the news that a fleet of gunboats and transports had left Memphis and was then ascending White River.[54]

Leaving Freeman's, McCray's, and Dobbin's brigades to watch enemy near his base, Shelby took his old brigade and four pieces of [Richard A.] Collin's battery, and started out with the determination to intercept and drive them back if possible.[55]

---

according to John N. Edwards, Joe Shelby's Adjutant. In addition to the three named units, Shelby also brought Major R. G. Rutherford's and General C. W. Adams's bands under his control during the same time period. Between May 27 and May 31, the various commands were ordered into camps to perfect their drill and instruction, there to await further operations. See Appendix B for biographies on McCray, Freeman and Dobbin. *O.R.*, vol. 34, pt. 1:924, 926–927; *O.R.*, vol. 34, pt. 4:632, 637; *O.R.S.*, pt. 2, vol. 35:681, 691; *O.R.S.*, pt. 2, vol. 38:736; John Newman Edwards, *Shelby and His Men or the War in the West* (Cincinnati, OH, 1867; reprint ed., Waverly, MO, 1993), 299, 317–318, hereafter cited as Edwards, *Shelby and His Men*; Harrell, *Arkansas, Confederate Military History*, 269–270; Freeman K. Mobley, *Making Sense of the Civil War in Batesville-Jacksonport and Northeast Arkansas 1861–1874* (Batesville, AR, 2005), 166–167, hereafter cited as Mobley; Sellmeyer, 177–181.

53. Jacksonport, the county seat of Jackson County, Arkansas, was located at the confluence of the White and Black Rivers in central Jackson County. Situated on the north bank (or east bank, depending on your perspective) of the White River, the city was first occupied by Federal forces on May 4, 1862, later abandoned, and reoccupied several times during the war. Federal soldiers considered Jacksonport "the meanest secesh place," that had in "peaceful times…been a point of considerable business importance." In 1864, a Nebraska doctor noted Jacksonport as an "unhealthy place, exposed to floods from the White and Black rivers." The town was constructed of largely wooden buildings, made of cypress, with "only a few made out of brick," while "minor fortifications" protected the town. With the arrival of Shelby in northeast Arkansas, Jacksonport was again abandoned by Federal troops on May 25 (mounted troops) and May 26 (infantry left by boats). *O.R.S.*, pt. 2, vol. 38:736; Banasik, *Embattled Arkansas*, 12; Albert O. Marshall, *Army Life; From A Soldier's Journal* (Juliet, IL, 1883), 97; James E. Potter and Edith Robbins, *Marching With the First Nebraska: A Civil War Diary* (Norman, OK, 2007), 274–275, 278–279, hereafter cited as Potter & Robbins; A. W. Sanford, "Letters From Curtis's Army," *Indianapolis Daily Journal*, in H. L. Hanna, ed., *The Press Covers the Invasion of Arkansas, 1862–Vol. 2, July-December* (Widener, AR, 2012), 65.

54. Even as Shelby consolidated his position in northeast Arkansas he issued a proclamation to the "Men of Northeast Arkansas," which called them to arms within two weeks or face conscription (See Appendix A for copy of proclamation). "This proclamation spread like wild-fire," according to John Edwards. During the next two weeks "camps sprang up suddenly in every healthy locality, and drilling, marching, parading went on from day to day with eagerness and enthusiasm." Shelby and staff were in the saddle daily, inspecting camps, mustering the troops, and "infused the exuberance of his confidence" in the new commands. Shelby also used the two weeks to recruit his command and his horses which were "completely wore out, unshod, unfed, and [needed]...rest." In a letter to General Price, Shelby estimated that he would be ready to make "demonstrations against the railroad" between June 10–15, 1864. On June 13, Shelby moved his brigade from Jacksonport to Bell's, just 7 miles south of Augusta, in preparation to raiding the Union supply lines. Finally, on June 15, Shelby started his brigade "for Clarendon, on the White River, determining to see what was going on there." The remaining units were left behind to continue their organizing. *O.R.*, vol. 34, pt. 1:925–926, 929; Edwards, *Shelby and His Men*, 312–313; Mobley, 172; Sellmeyer, 181, 184.

55. Collins's Battery was originally commanded by Captain Joseph Bledsoe, the brother of Hiram

Engaging gunboats with cavalry was something new to this brigade, although they had fought everything from a federal outpost picket to an army corps of infantry. Fighting was their business and they made it a business to fight.[56]

From Jacksonport to Augusta the trip was made in one day (forty-two miles) without incident. Arriving at Cache River about noon the second day, we found that stream bank full from recent rains, also the bottoms and the bayous were flooded. After much delay we ferried over this river,

Swam and Waded

for twenty miles more and arrived on high ground back of Clarendon.[57] Twelve miles above this place and on the west bank of White River was situated DeValls

---

Bledsoe. The battery was organized on September 20, 1862 (*Trans-Mississippi Men* has the date as April). Bledsoe was elected captain and Richard A. Collins was elected the 1st Lieutenant. The battery initially contained 87 officers and men and consisted of two iron 6-lb guns and would add and subtract guns over the next two years. The first, and only known, reorganization of the battery, occurred on November 8, 1862, but unlike its guns, the battery remained cemented in Shelby's Brigade for the war. On December 2, 1863, S. T. Ruffner's Battery turned over its guns, consisting of two 12-pound James Rifles and two 12-pound howitzers, to Joseph Bledsoe. On April 15, 1864, at the First Battle of Poison Springs, the battery lost one of the howitzers, leaving the command with just 3 pieces for the remainder of the Camden Expedition. Following the Camden Expedition, it appears that the battery received a new set of guns, composed of two 10-lb Parrot Rifles and two 12-lb Iron howitzers. The battery was considered Shelby's "pet" and adopted a black bear cub, which they named "Postlewait," as its mascot. See Appendix C for a biography of Richard Collins. *O.R.*, vol. 34, pt. 1: 794; Banasik, *Embattled Arkansas*, 515; Michael E. Banasik, *Reluctant Cannoneer: The Diary of Robert T. McMahan of the Twenty-fifth Independent Ohio Light Artillery*. (Iowa City, IA, 2000), 233, hereafter cited as Banasik, *Reluctant Cannoneer*; Carolyn M. Bartels, *Trans-Mississippi Men at War, Volume I: Missouri C.S.A.* (Independence, MO, 1998), 141, hereafter cited as Bartels, *Trans-Mississippi Men*; Edwards, *Shelby and His Men*, 253–254, 268; "From the White River," *Chicago Tribune*, July 6, 1864; John S. Marmaduke, *Confederate States Trans-Mississippi Order and Letter Book* (Independence, MO, 2000), 16, 43, 73, 77 322, 409, hereafter cited as Marmaduke; Sellmeyer, 41–42, 186; Coleman Smith, "Capture of the Gunboat Queen City," *Confederate Veteran* 22 (March 1914), 120, hereafter cited as Smith, "Queen City."

56. According to Captain S. H. Ford, the Iron Brigade had three separate engagements with ironclads, including the *Queen City*. Their first encounter came at Helena, where the *Tyler* threw shells at them from afar. Next the brigade encountered the *Cricket*, the *Lexington*, and the *Kaskaskia* on August 14, 1863, on the Little Red River, where Colonel Charles Gilkey was killed. The *Queen City* was the third, and final encounter with gunboats or ironclads. Edwards, *Shelby and His Men*, 172; Reminiscences of Capt. S. H. Ford, Missouri Historical Society (St. Louis), 24, hereafter cited as Ford Reminiscences; Sellmeyer, 114-116, 185.

57. Shelby's Brigade camped seven miles below Augusta on June 15, and remained there for several days scouting the area. On the 19th Shelby resumed his march toward Clarendon, which was situated about 12 miles, as the crow flies or 30 miles by river, below DeValls Bluff, on the White River. "The march was terrible," according to Shelby, but he still managed to cross the Cache River by 10:00 a.m. on the 20th. Next Shelby crossed the Cache and Bayou DeView Bottoms, which were three feet deep in water. "All that portion of Arkansas was a swamp," wrote John Edwards. "It was springtime and it was raining incessantly, which will tell the whole story of roads without bottoms, streams without bridges, and swamps without boundaries." "We marched, camped, cooked, and slept in water from two to six inches deep," recalled Coleman Smith of the brigade. Shelby finally camped two miles (Ford says five miles) from Clarendon at 2:00 p.m. on June 23, there to rest and scout the area. It was here that Shelby learned of the presence of the

Bluff, a strongly fortified federal garrison. This place was connected with Little Rock by railroad, and it was by boat up White River to this point, and thence by railroad that the federal army at Little Rock was supplied.[58] Gen. Shelby knew that any interference on this line would be like severing their arteries, so he determined to attack the first boat that passed Clarendon.

Scouts reported that a fleet of boats had passed up that morning, but knowing that he would bag some game before waiting very long, Gen. Shelby put out pickets all around the town and moved cautiously to within sight of the river. Just at dark the reconnoitering party reported a large ironclad having rounded to an anchored near the wharf. Well, sure enough here was some game, rather large to bag, and it looked defiant too. What should we do? Pull up and run or fight? Gen. Shelby resorted to strategy and determined to wait and fight.[59]

---

tinclad *Queen City*, which was anchored in "mid-stream," about 10 rods from the eastern shore, opposite of Clarendon, where it had been ordered to "guard the town." Even as Shelby was advancing down the eastern side of the White River, the Federal command was confused as to his location and strength. Most reports put his command on the western side of the White River, intent on attacking the railroad, and that's where the Unionists concentrated their efforts to find and engage the elusive Missourian. Even when reports arrived placing Shelby on the east side of the White River, they failed to react, even though they were aware that Shelby's mission was to interdict their supply line. On June 23, General Steele notified the navy of the increasing risk of Price moving on Little Rock, but no mention was made of any threat to the White River by General Shelby. And still on the 23rd, Shelby was again reported on the west side of the White and on the 24th he was placed at Cotton Plant on the east side. *O.R.*, vol. 34, pt. 1: 929, 1050–1051; *O.R.*, vol. 34, pt. 4:469, 483–485, 502, 516–517, 532–533; *O.N.R.*, vol. 26:421, 425, 432; Edwards, *Shelby and His Men*, 320–321; Ford Reminiscences, 24; "From Cairo and Below," *Chicago Tribune*, July 4, 1864; "Romance of War, Number One," *Mexican Times* (Mexico City, Mexico), January 27, 1866; Sellmeyer, 184–185; Smith, "Queen City," 120.

58. DeValls Bluff was the terminus of the Little Rock & DeValls Bluff Railroad and the main supply line for the garrison at Little Rock. The town contained but "few buildings," which by June 1864 had been destroyed. However, the wharf and dock, such as they were, provided a landing place for the needed supplies in Little Rock. Clarendon "had never been much of a town…so the little left of the place was not particularly valuable or attractive," according to A. F. Sperry. And by 1864, much of the town had been burned to the ground. A. F. Sperry, *History of the 33rd Iowa Infantry Volunteer Regiment 1863-1866* (Des Moines, IA, 1866), 39–30, 42.

Prior to Shelby's arrival in the Clarendon area, the DeValls Bluff garrison consisted of Livingston's Brigade with two pieces of artillery. The brigade numbered 1,774 present on May 31, and was previously based in Batesville and Jacksonport, having relocated to the Bluff when Shelby arrived in northeast Arkansas on May 26, 1864. Also present at DeValls Bluff on June 23, were the gunboat *Tyler* with the tinclads *Fawn* (also known as the *Grace*) and *Naumkeag*, plus an additional nine transports. *O.R.*, vol. 34, pt. 4:155; *O.N.R.*, vol. 26:423; Carolyn M. Bartels, *Elliott's Scouts 9th Missouri Cavalry Battalion* (Independence, MO, 2005), 59, hereafter cited as Bartels, *Elliott's Scouts*.

59. On June 19, naval Captain George Bache, with the *Tyler*, the *Fawn*, and the *Naumkeag*, left the mouth of the White River heading for Little Rock, having under escort nine transports. Upon approaching Red Fork Landing, on the Arkansas River, Bache turned back from Little Rock, as Marmaduke occupied the bluffs overlooking the river, and escorted his fleet up the White River to DeValls Bluff. On the afternoon of June 23, as the Federal fleet passed by Clarendon they were spotted by scouts from Shelby's command, who also reported the presence of the *Queen City* anchored at Clarendon. Shelby quickly formulated his plan, which called for the capture of the *Queen City* as it lay in anchor at dawn the next day. *O.R.*, vol. 34, pt. 1:1050; *O.N.R.*, vol. 26:422.

Every road leading into town was well guarded, and every person, going or coming, to or from the town, was placed under arrest, every precaution was taken to conceal our presence. The command waited impatiently until 10 o'clock, when the horses were taken from the battery and a detail of twenty men to the gun were made to haul them into position, the night being a little hazy and a slight fog on the river favored us. We move the guns along cautiously. It became necessary to pull our coats off and lay them on the bridge for the cannon wheels to roll on, to prevent noise. All this was done with the greatest care, until we had the four pieces of cannon brought up in line

Within Fifty Yards

of this silent, grim monster. We could hear the steam hissing through her machinery and see the blue smoke from the dying embers in her furnace curl above the mist.[60]

The whole brigade drew up in line above and below the battery, with eager eyes bent on the black object riding at anchor out in the stream.

The clear round moon made its appearance late in the night. The "stars and stripes" hung lazily at her flagstaff, her black ironside with her porthole closed rocked slowly in her cradle of blue waves.[61] No sound save the change of guards, and the time pealing forth the hour of the night, and the sentinel on his beat responding "all is well," but little realizing the true situation on shore. For there was

---

60. After taking assorted security measures, Shelby issued orders at 10:00 p.m. for Collins's Battery to take only shot and shell for the upcoming engagement, but not specifying what the target was. At 11:00 p.m., the gun crews were told they were going after the gunboat at Clarendon. The men "were familiar with gunboats. At Helena the *Tyler's* huge guns had thrown shot and shell at them from a distance so great that they could not even reply." Each man believed it was "his last night on earth." At midnight, "four-hundred picked riflemen" from Shelby's Brigade left camp on foot, passed through Clarendon and left the horses of the artillery about a mile from the sleeping Federal boat. One hundred men then pulled and pushed Collins's 4 guns by hands the last mile, the men muffling the wheels of the cannon, with socks or shirts to prevent detection. By 2:00 a.m. the brigade came to rest on the river bank, in an area "abundant with dog fennel, four feet high" and about 100 yards from the quietly resting *Queen City*. (The distance from the *Queen City* was placed at 50 feet, 60 yards, 100 yards or 200 yards, depending on the source. As the best estimate, Coleman Smith had two guns at 50 yards, with the other two at 100 yards.) To supply the guns, five rounds of ammunition were carried by hand from where the caissons were left. A lone sentry walked the upper deck of the Federal boat, while Shelby's Brigade awaited the coming of dawn. "Heavily and wearily the time sped on" while the brigade waited in silence and eager anticipation. *O.R.*, vol. 34, pt. 1:929, 1050–1051; *O.N.R.*, vol. 26:418; "Capture of the Queen City," Frank Moore, ed., *The Rebellion Record: A Diary of American Events*, 12 vols. (New York, 1861–1868; reprint ed. New York, 1977), 11:Doc-638, hereafter cited as *Rebellion Record*; Edwards, *Shelby and His Men*, 321–322; "From White River," *Chicago Tribune*, July 6, 1864; "Romance of War, Number One," *Mexican Times*, January 27, 1866; Don Roth, *General J. O. Shelby at Clarendon, Arkansas: The Capture and Destruction of the U.S.S. Queen City* (Iowa City, IA, 2017), 27, hereafter cited as Roth; Sellmeyer, 185–186; Smith, "Queen City," 120.
61. Coleman Smith, a member of Collins's Battery, noted that the portholes were open, making a "splendid target for midnight practice." But the brigade waited in silence waiting for the "first dawn of day" before firing on the *Queen City*. Ford Reminiscences, 25; Smith, "Queen City," 120.

a brigade of as determined men as ever look through the sight of a rifle lying flat on the ground, elbows touching, that sixty yards away.

The idea of surprising a gunboat with cavalry is something not recorded in history. A gunboat with an armament capable of sweeping us from the face of the earth laying right under the muzzles of Shelby's guns.[62]

The gray dawn of a bright June morning made its appearance in the East finally. Shelby moved cautiously up and down the column to see that everything was in readiness. The men were waiting eagerly for the word. I was lying flat on the ground between Joe Terry and Mike Roach,[63] and I thought I could hear their hearts beat as the word "ready" was passed along the line. Then came the word "fire." 1,000 muskets and carbines and four cannon heavily loaded like a flash of lightning and a clap of thunder

Broke the Long Stillness,

and sent a shower of iron and lead rattling and crashing upon the decks of this new antagonist—this enemy encased in its iron armor.[64] This is repeated once, twice, thrice and until she was rent with shot and shell fore and aft and lay helpless upon

---

62. Upon its capture, the *Queen City* was found to be carrying two 32-lb smoothbore cannon; two 30-lb Parrot rifles; four 24-lb howitzers and one 12-lb "heavy howitzer" (Shelby listed the captures as four 32-lb guns; four 24-lb howitzers; and one 12-lb howitzer). Shelby for his part had two 10-lb Parrot Rifles with two 12-lb, iron howitzers. *O.R.*, vol. 34, pt. 1:1051; *O.N.R.*, Series 2, vol. 1:187; Sellmeyer, 347 (n. 4); Smith, "Queen City," 120.

63. No Michael Roach, or variation thereof, was found as a member of the Iron Brigade, though it appears he was associated with Quantrill's band. Roach was born in 1847, and carried letters between Quantrill and Kate King. Joe Terry could be J. H. Terry, a resident of Independence, also a member of Quantrill's original band as noted on a July 6, 1862, muster roll. He was later noted as being a member of Elliott's Scouts, company unknown. Bartels, *Elliott's Scouts*, 113; Joanne C. Eakin and Donald R. Hale, *Branded as Rebels: A List of Bushwhackers, Guerrillas, Partisan Rangers, Confederates and Southern Sympathizers from Missouri During the War Years* (Independence, MO, 1993), 372, 425, hereafter cited as Eakin & Hale; Hewett, *Confederate Roster*, 13:196, 15:149–151.

64. At 3:45 a.m. as the "little shreds of daylight" greeted the dawn, Shelby "gave the eager order" to fire. Collins's Battery, which was double-shotted, let loose a devastating volley, which crashed into the *Queen City*, disabling her starboard engine and "burst the steam pipe" in the first few shots. Shot after shot were fired, from Collins's cannons, even as the *Queen City* cut loose its anchor and drifted into mid stream, with only its port engine still functioning. Another set of volleys took out its port engine, as the vessel drifted to the western shore of the White River. The Federal boat returned the "fire briskly," according to a period account, "but the range being too short, was without effect"—the guns were poorly sighted and fuses too long, thus overshooting their targets. After a short engagement of 10–20 minutes, the pilot of the *Queen City* appeared on the deck, waving a white flag of surrender, but not before Acting Master Michael Hickey allowed his men an opportunity to swim to the western shore of the river to avoid surrender. Of the surrender of the *Queen City*, a disgusted Admiral David D. Porter wrote: "Acting-Master M. Hickey...decided to surrender, not having the bravery to fight it out, as many of his contemporaries would have done." On August 8, 1864, a Court of Enquiry met in Mound City, Illinois, to investigate the loss of the *Queen City*. Hickey was found blameless in the loss of his vessel, while his junior officers were judged to have failed to do their duty (See Appendix A for the findings of the Court). *O.R.*, vol. 34, pt. 1:1050–1051; *O.N.R.*, vol. 26:418, 421; Bartels, *Elliott's Scouts*, 59; Edwards, *Shelby and*

the water, her crew was so badly disabled that she could not fire a shot. She struck her colors and whistled defeat. At once the firing ceased, and Gen. Shelby took charge of his prize, the Queen City. She proved to be one of the enemy's finest ironclad war vessels. Her armament consisted thirteen heavy Parrot guns manned by a large crew of "salty tires" that knew their business well.[65]

This was truly one of the most brilliant episodes of the war. A complete surprise. The muffled wheels of the cannon forged up to within fifty yards of one of the enemy's ironclad and the men for five long hours lie on the ground, not permitted to speak above a whisper.[66]

His Men, 322; Ford Reminiscences, 25; "From Cairo and Below," *Chicago Tribune*, July 4, 1864; Porter, *Naval History*, 562; Roth, 28–29; Sellmeyer, 187; Smith, "Queen City," 121.

65. The *Queen City* (*Tinclad No. 26*) was a 4th Class, side-wheeled steamer of 212 tons. She was purchased in Cincinnati on February 13, 1863, for $16,000 and commissioned on April 1. Armed on April 9 with two 30-lb Parrot rifles; two 32-lb smoothbores; and four 24-lb howitzers, the battery remained unchanged until October 7 when a "heavy 12-pdr", a Dahlgren 12-lb boat howitzer, was added to her complement (Bartels has the boat with two 12-lb boat howitzers). The upper deck was wooden, while the lower structure was covered with 1 ¼" iron plating. The draft of the vessel was 3 to 3 ½ feet, ideal for operating on a shallow river. *O.R.*, vol. 34, pt. 1:1050; *O.N.R.*, vol. 26:423; *O.N.R.*, Series 2, vol. 1:187; Bartels, *Elliott's Scouts*, 59; David E. Castro, *Arkansas Late in the Civil War: The 8th Missouri Volunteer Cavalry, April 1864–July 1865* (Charleston, SC, 2013), 51, hereafter cited as Castro; Ripley, 88–89; Roth, 24–25.

66. In addition to capturing the *Queen City* with her nine guns, Shelby also garnered 50 small arms, boxes of ammunition, "a good supply of clothing," and $6,000 dollars (Edwards says it was $10,000 dollars, while Ford said it was $25,000 or $30,000) in cash from the paymaster's cash box. As to losses, Shelby recorded none in his command while the *Queen City* lost of one (Roth has two killed) killed, nine wounded and 25 POWs out of a crew of 65 (Roth has the crew at 60). The assistant surgeon of the *Queen City* put their losses at one killed, nine wounded, with three unwounded officers and "about 20 seamen" made POWs (Sellmeyer has 27 POWs). Of the 65 crew members it appears that between 29 to 33 escaped capture, of which two drowned, according to Surgeon Lewis Westfall. Period newspapers reported that escapees were shot in the water, while captured Negroes were summarily killed. No sailors were shot in the water, though some blacks were shot while swimming, and the surrendering black prisoners, in this case, appear to have been executed, based upon a statement made to Surgeon Westfall, who recorded: "I did not hear General Shelby say what would be made of the contrabands, but one of his officers said he supposed they would be treated as are the rest they had captured, kill them." Of the prisoners, three officers were sent to DeValls Bluff for exchange on June 25. For Captain George Rutherford (captured May 1864), 1st Lieutenant A. C. McCoy (captured February 10, 1864) and 2nd Lieutenant C. R. White (captured Jun 1, 1864) the exchange never took place. McCoy had escaped custody at DeValls Bluff while en route to Alton, Illinois Prison; Rutherford and White were both placed in Little Rock penitentiary where they remained until the close of the war; the three Federal officers were all subsequently paroled, to await exchange. Another group of 20 *Queen City* POWs were sent to Helena for exchange; 17 of the seamen were eventually paroled and sent north; as to the other POWs, no record was found of their fate. *O.R.*, vol. 34, pt. 2:321; *O.R.*, vol. 34, pt. 4:579; *O.R.*, vol. 41, pt. 2:996; *O.R.*, Series 2, vol. 7:414, 960, 1159; *O.N.R.*, Vol. 26:219; Anonymous, Carolyn M. Bartels and James E. McGhee, eds., *The Gallant Breed the 5th Missouri Cavalry: A Roster of the Men Who Rode Under the Flag of Shelby's Iron Brigade* (Independence, MO, 2009), 19, hereafter cited as Anonymous, *5th Missouri Cavalry*; Anonymous, Carolyn M. Bartels and James E. McGhee, *The Gallant Breed the 12th Missouri Cavalry: A Roster of the Men Who Rode Under the Flag of Shelby's Iron Brigade* (Independence, MO, 2009), 54, hereafter cited as Anonymous, *12th Missouri Cavalry*; "Capture of the Queen City," *Rebellion Record*, 11:Doc-638; Edwards, *Shelby and His Men*, 322, 324; Ford Reminiscences, 25; "From Cairo and Below,"

Gen. Shelby knew the enemy at DeVall's Bluff had heard the guns and that they would know what it meant. The gunboats were soon heard on their way down and we knew the day's work had only commenced.[67]

Taking two of the largest Parrot guns from the prize a land battery was improvised. Having disabled the boat so badly that she would be of no further use, and removing everything off that would be of any benefit to the commands she was blown up and sunk.[68]

The Wounded

were taken care of by the brigade surgeons and everything was done to relieve them. Capt. [Michael] Hickey, the commander of the Queen City, and seventy-five soldiers and sailors were sent to the rear as prisoners.[69]

Chicago Tribune, July 4, 1864; "From the White River," *Chicago Tribune*, July 6, 1864; Mobley, 172–173; Porter, *Naval History*, 562; Roth, 30; Sellmeyer, 187; Smith, "Queen City," 121.

67. The Federals at DeValls Bluff had not heard the gunfire at Clarendon, which began at 3:45 a.m. on June 24. In fact, Lieutenant Commander S. L. Phelps recorded that General Steele "was incredulous as to the existence of a rebel force on" the White River until the *Queen City* was reported lost. "At daylight" on June 24 (4:20 a.m.), George Bache departed DeValls Bluff, per orders from General Steele, with his fleet of three war ships and nine transports, to again try the Arkansas River and get to Little Rock. Steele did not believe that Marmaduke was on the Arkansas River in force, despite all the intelligence to that fact. Prior to leaving Bache notified General Steele of his departure, making no mention of the cannon fire from Clarendon, which had ended by the time that Bache left DeValls Bluff. The tinclad *Fawn* took the lead out of DeValls Bluff followed by the rest of the fleet. En route for the Arkansas River, the *Fawn* met the transport *Pike* which informed the war-vessel of the loss of the *Queen City*. The *Pike* also transferred several of the *Queen City* crew, who had escaped by swimming the river. Acting Master John M. Grace of the *Fawn* subsequently halted his forward movement and awaited the arrival of the fleet under Bache. At 9:00 a.m. Bache arrived, heard Grace's report, and promptly ordered the transports (now 10 in number, including the *Pike*) back to DeValls Bluff and organized his command for engaging Shelby's Brigade. The *Tyler* would lead, the *Naumkeag* would come next followed by the *Fawn*. Bache reasoned that "the enemy had not had much time to get anything out of her [*Queen City*], but thought they might attempt to fight her in cooperation with the shore batteries." *O.R.*, vol. 34, pt. 4:532–533; *O.N.R.*, vol. 26:422–423, 425; "Capture of the Queen City," *Rebellion Record*, 11:638; Porter, *Naval History*, 562.

68. Shelby removed two guns from the *Queen City*, one 24-lb howitzer and the 12-lb boat howitzer. Separating "the pieces of his battery to prevent a fire being concentrated upon them," Shelby concealed his guns, all except for the 12-lb boat howitzer, which he placed on some open ground for some unknown reason. A volunteer crew was assigned to the captured guns, even as preparations were made to dispose of the *Queen City*. At about 9:15 a.m., having been informed of the approach of Bache's fleet, Shelby ordered the *Queen City* destroyed. Captain W. J. McArthur, assistant adjutant general on Shelby's staff, "an old and experienced steam boatman, laid the mine and applied the torch," and the *Queen City* exploded, setting the boat on fire. And a short time later, after the fire had burned down to the magazine, there was another explosion," according to Coleman Smith, "that shook the earth for miles around like an earthquake." *O.R.*, vol. 34, pt. 1:1051; *O.N.R.*, vol. 26:423; Edwards, *Shelby and His Men*, 324; Ford Reminiscences, 25; Romance of War, Number Two," *Mexican Times*, February 3, 1866; Sellmeyer, 187; Smith, "Queen City," 121.

69. Michael Hickey joined the U.S. Navy on September 12, 1861, commissioned a mate. He was made an acting master on November 19, 1863, and was assigned to command the *Queen City* in late February 1864, when the previous commander George W. Brown was assigned to command

Hasty works arranging the batteries along the bluff, putting out sharpshooters along the river and securing shelter for the men soon brought everything in readiness, for we knew the final struggle was close at hand.

The long black smoke curled above the river and the popping and blowing an occasional whistle from the foremost boat to the others to keep well closed up told us in an unmistakable terms that, we had aroused the "hornet's nest" and that they were upon us.

A long stretch of a mile in the river above gave us time to size up our enemy, who soon came in full view in the shape of four ironclads, their flags floating out against the fresh morning air.[70]

The *Tyler*, the flagship, was in the lead, and when within 400 or 500 yards of

---

the recently commissioned monitor *Ozark*. Hickey remained in command until he lost his boat on June 24, 1864, at Clarendon, where he was wounded in the leg. Of the loss of the *Queen City*, John Edwards wrote:

> No blame could possibly attach itself to...Captain Hickey. Every naval regulation had been strictly observed. The vessel was anchored in the stream, steam well up, the lookout man at his post and vigilant, the guns all loaded, and the reliefs stationed constantly and in order. Nothing but a cavalry patrol on shore could have warned him of danger—and even with his seamen, just at nightfall, Captain Hickey had ordered a reconnaissance through the streets of Clarendon, which was thoroughly made.

Following the Court of Enquiry, which exonerated Hickey, he was given command of the *Curlew* in late 1864 or early 1865. Hickey operated in the 9th–11th Districts, Mississippi Squadron, doing river surveys, until his reassignment to the tinclad *Silver Lake*, which he commanded until it was decommissioned on August 12, 1865. Despite the misgivings expressed by Admiral Porter over the loss of the *Queen City*, Hickey was highly thought of by his last commander, who wrote: Acting Master Hickey was "a very hard-working, reliable and intelligent officer." On December 27, 1865, Hickey received an honorable discharge from the Navy and reenlisted on July 9, 1866, as a boatswain. He died on April 30, 1876. *O.N.R.*, vol. 25:692, 722, 754, 758; *O.N.R.*, vol. 26:24, 419, 421, 749; *O.N.R.*, vol. 27:14–15, 56, 129, 145, 175, 320, 339–340; Edward W. Callahan, *List of Officer of the Navy of the United States and of the Marine Corps From 1775 to 1900* (New York, 1901), 264; Edwards, *Shelby and His Men*, 323; Porter, *Naval History*, 562.

The number of POWs totaled about 23 and not 75, as the writer recorded or 65 as Shelby implied in his official report. Additionally, the POWs who were "sent to the rear" were stripped of their clothing, according to one period source. The source has Shelby's men appropriating the captives clothing, "as was evident from the amount of rags left on the bank." *O.R.*, vol. 34, pt. 1:1050; "From White River," *Chicago Tribune*, July 6, 1864.

70. With the *Queen City* gone Shelby's troopers waited. "An hour went by—an hour of eager suspense and anxious waiting." At 9:45 the Federal fleet of three boats—not four—passed the confluence with the Cache River, about 300 yards from Shelby's guns. Collins's Battery opened fire first, "putting one of his first shots through the pilot house" of the *Tyler*. Steaming slowly forward, the *Tyler* opened fire with her bow gun, a 30-lb Parrot rifle. She in turn was followed by the *Naumkeag* and the *Fawn*, both of which began the engagement with their bow guns, as the only guns that could bear. Steaming past the rebel position, Commander Bache's fleet sent broadsides of canister and shrapnel into the Confederate position, even as the dismounted cavalry peppered the portholes with rifle fire. Once past, the *Tyler* "rounded to," and came to rest at about 50 yards from the rebel guns, followed by the other two vessels. "Well did" Shelby's Brigade "stand the repeated broadsides of the boats," according to a Federal source. And for the next 45 minutes the two commands slugged it out. *O.N.R.*, vol. 26:423, 425; "Capture of the Queen City," *Rebellion Record*, 11:638; Edwards, *Shelby and His Men*, 324; Ford Reminiscences, 26; Smith, "Queen City," 121.

the battery on Clarendon bluffs fired her bow gun, a 164-pounder, as a challenge to combat, every man on shore stood ready awaiting the word.[71] The *Tyler* came on until she was in short range and opened with a full broadside. Then the word was given to concentrate the fire on her. Capt. Collins, with the two new guns added to his battery (I was detailed as powder boy to one of them), seemed to be in his glory; he gave shot for shot, and handled his guns so skillfully that it seemed to surprised even his iron-based enemy.[72] The men that lined the banks above were firing volley after volley into the boats,

Killing Every Man

that showed himself on their decks or at their portholes.[73]

The *Tyler* and her consorts were pouring in all the time an enfilading fire of grape and canister that ploughed [plowed] the earth and rent the air, making great gaps in our ranks.[74]

---

71. The 180-foot, 575-ton, U.S.S. *Tyler* was built in 1857 of white oak and was purchased by the War Department in June 1861. It was a side-wheel steamer, mounting eight guns by the Battle of Belmont: six 8-inch shell guns and two 32-lb smoothbores. During the war the *Tyler* served on the western waters fighting at Belmont, Missouri, Forts Henry and Donelson, in Tennessee and engaged the rebel ram *Arkansas* on the Yazoo River. The *Tyler* was part of the Western Flotilla and played an important role in defeating the Confederate attack on Helena on July 4, 1863. At Helena, the *Tyler* was armed with 10 guns: one 12-lb heavy (a Dahlgren 12-lb boat howitzer); one 30-lb Parrot rifle on stern; on broadside two 30-pound Parrot rifles; and six 8-inch guns. On March 17, 1864, the *Tyler* mounted 14 guns, adding four 24-lb howitzers to its previous armament. *O.R.*, vol. 22, 1:385–386; *O.N.R.*, Series 2, 1:227, 229; Tony Gibbons, *Warships and Naval Battles of the Civil War* (New York, 1989), 73; Roth, 32.
72. "General Shelby had chosen a position to give...battle, and, with a bravery worthy of a better cause," according to a Federal source, "worked their batteries" fearlessly despite the odds. Collins's Battery deployed "on the naked beach," wrote John Edwards, while Lieutenant Bache recorded that all the guns were "masked" except for the 12-lb boat howitzer, which was visible in the open. As the fight developed, the *Tyler* set its fuses at "one-half and one-quarter second for shrapnel and canister from their smoothbore guns...[The] fire was terrific." For 45 minutes (Shelby put the time at 90 minutes) the Confederates held their own, putting 11 shots into the *Tyler*. In all, Lieutenant Bache reported six men wounded while one period source put the losses at 8–10, including the *Tyler's* pilot, who was wounded in the head, while another reported the pilot killed. *O.R.*, vol. 34, pt. 1:927, 1050–1051; *O.N.R.*, vol. 26:423–424; "Capture of the Queen City," *Rebellion Record*, 11:638; Edwards, *Shelby and His Men*, 324–325; "From Cairo and Below," *Chicago Tribune*, July 4, 1864.
73. With the beginning of the engagement, Shelby's Brigade was on "open ground and not 60 yards from the boats." And, according to Shelby, his "skirmishers charged up to the river bank, keeping up a merciless fusillade," causing serious damage to the *Naumkeag* and the *Fawn*. *O.N.R.*, vol. 26:425–426, 433; Ford Reminiscences, 26.
74. The *Naumkeag* was the next vessel in line, and like the *Tyler*, moved on past the rebel guns, trading broadsides with the Confederates. Moving back upstream the *Naumkeag* came to rest and let loose at close range and, with the *Tyler*, drove Shelby's gunners away from the 12-lb boat howitzer, making "scrap even of the carriages" which were "completely demolished." The *Fawn* was the third vessel in the line and unlike the other two boats immediately ran into trouble. "A 12-pounder shrapnel entered the port shutter of the pilot house, mortally wounding the only pilot on board...and carrying away the bell wires and ringing the bells, thereby causing the engineer to stop the boat directly under" Collins's guns. With no direction from the wheel house, the *Fawn*

But our fire had been so deadly on the *Tyler* that her decks were running with blood—every officer killed and two thirds of her men dead or wounded. She retired up the river. The *Sunbeam, Fawn,* and *Namukeag* closed up and took her place at short range, belching forth forty-two charges of grape and canister per minute.[75] In this trying ordeal I noticed among those of my intimate friends and mess mates, who displayed unusual coolness and daring bravery, were W. F. Burk, and Joe Terry, Cam Bucher [Boucher], Ike Shelby, Mike Roach, John Edwards, James Gray, Capt. Will Moreman [Moorman], Capt. Collins and Gen. Shelby himself, and a number of others whose names I have forgotten.[76] Five

---

"floated listlessly" in place above the rebel battery, firing their bow and broadsides guns. Within minutes the *Tyler* and the *Naumkeag* returned to the battle, engaging Shelby's command at close range. The rebels were now caught in a cross fire, with the crippled *Fawn* firing from the north while Bache's other two boats were hitting Shelby from the west. By battle's end the *Fawn* had been hit 13 times, fired 124 shots, and sustained one killed and 13 wounded, while two gun crews had been "disabled." The *Naumkeag* was "struck several times" with the vessel's cutter being badly damaged. Casualties were not reported, though they did have least one man killed. And for his performance of duty, "Acting Master John Rogers of the *Naumkeag* was...mentioned handsomely," according to David Porter, "for the cool and efficient manner in which he fought his vessel." Overall the Federal fleet lost nine killed with 27 wounded suggesting that the *Naumkeag* lost eight killed and eight wounded. *O.N.R.*, vol. 26:424–426; Castro, 53; Ford Reminiscences, 26; Porter, *Naval History*, 563; Roth, 35; Sellmeyer, 188–189.

75. The comment on losses from the *Tyler* were not true (see note no. 72 above) and seems to be taken from Edwards book. Edwards, *Shelby and His Men*, 325.

Of the 3 vessels mentioned the *Sunbeam* was not present in the White River. It was a British steamer that was caught running the blockade at New Inlet, North Carolina, on September 28, 1863. The vessel was sent to the New York Prize Court, where it adjudicated on November 20, 1863, its cargo being evaluated at $74,966.74. Porter, *Naval History*, 842; *Naval Chronology*, II:99.

Originally known as the *Fanny Barker*, the *Fawn* (Bartels also called the *Fawn* the *Grace*) was commissioned on May 11, 1863, and procured by the Navy on May 13. It was 158 feet long, 174 tons and a 4th rate tinclad. By the Battle of Clarendon it was armed with seven guns: one 12-lb rifle and six 24-lb howitzers. Initially operating on the Tennessee River, the *Fawn* was assigned to the Mississippi Squadron in July 1863. Reassigned to the 7th District, Mississippi Squadron, the *Fawn* operated primarily from Memphis to the Arkansas River. Its sole major combat appears to have been at Clarendon on June 24, 1864. The boat survived the war, being decommissioned June 30, 1865. *O.N.R.*, vol. 25:146, 187, 315, 379, 427; *O.N.R.*, vol. 26:319, 502, 554, 692, 730, 749; *O.N.R.*, vol. 27:55, 77, 100, 128, 144; *O.N.R.*, Series 2, vol. 1:83; Bartels, *Elliott's Scouts*, 59; *Naval Chronology*, IV:83, IV:109.

The *Naumkeag* was commissioned on April 18, 1863, at Mound City, Illinois, and purchased at Cairo on July 23. It was a 4th rate tinclad, 154 feet long, 148 tons and mounted six guns, in June 1864: two 30-lb Parrot rifles and four 24-lb howitzers. After entering the service, the *Naumkeag* operated on the Ohio River against John Hunt Morgan. In August 1863 the *Naumkeag* was moved to Memphis and operated between there, Helena, and the Arkansas River, with convoy duty up the White River, for the remainder of the war—except for repairs undergone in Mound City from October–December, 1864. Its only major engagement occurred on June 24 at Clarendon. The *Naumkeag* survived the war and was sold at public auction on August 17, 1865, at Mound City. *O.N.R.*, vol. 25:336, 379; *O.N.R.*, vol. 26:318, 502, 555, 693, 731, 749; *O.N.R.*, Series 2, vol. 1:156.

76. The only W. F. Burk found, who was associated with the Trans-Mississippi and from Missouri, was a William Francis Burke or Burks. This Burke was from Perry County, joined Company C, 5th Infantry Regiment, 1st Division, MSG on September 1, 1861, and was appointed 1st Sergeant of his company. Serving out his term in the Guard, Burke left the army on February 17, 1862,

bushels of grape and canister shot tearing through per minute is enough to make the heart sick to think of even now, and the wonder is that a man was left to tell the tale.

This fusillade was kept up for two long hours. The *Fawn* drew off and sunk in the bend above half an hour later. The *Sunbeam* and the *Naumkeag* were literally riddled with shot and shell and hardly men enough left steer or steam them up the river. Thus they left Shelby and his cavalry in possession of the field.[77]

The battle was a desperate one, but it showed what flesh and blood could endure against steal.[78]

---

after which his name disappeared from all known records. Carolyn M. Bartels, *The Forgotten Men Missouri State Guard* (Shawnee Mission, KS, 1995), 42, hereafter cited as Bartels, *Forgotten Men*; Wayne H. Schnetzer, *More Forgotten Men: The Missouri State Guard* (Independence, MO, 2003), 36, hereafter cited as Schnetzer, *More Forgotten Men*.

There were 2 James Grays associated with Missouri and the Confederate Army. One was James D. (or J. M.) Gray, who commanded Company B, 4th Infantry Regiment, 8th Division, MSG. Gray, from Osceola, Missouri, was elected captain of his company on June 5, 1861, and later resigned on September 21. The other was from Jackson County and enlisted in the 6th Division, MSG. No further records were found on either man. Bartels, *Forgotten Men*, 133; Eakin & Hale, 172; Richard C. Peterson, et al., *Sterling Price's Lieutenants: A Guide to the Officers and Organization of the Missouri State Guard* (Jefferson City, MO, 1995), 233, hereafter cited as Peterson.

See Appendix B for John N. Edwards's biography. See Appendix C for Extended Comments on Cam Bucher [Boucher], Ike Shelby and Captain Will Moorman. Captain Collins, Mike Roach, General Shelby and Joe Terry have already been covered.

77. After the *Tyler* and the *Naumkeag* came to rest 50 yards from the rebel position, the Federal boats "peppered" Shelby's Brigade for several minutes, before Shelby ordered a withdrawal. "I thought it was several hours," remembered Coleman Smith, though "some of the boys said it was only about fifteen minutes." Even as the gunboats moved into position, the dismounted troopers of the Iron Brigade "charged up to the bank of the river and kept the port-holes closed for a while." In the end, following the 45-minute battle, from the first gunshot until the last, Shelby ordered his brigade to withdraw "from the unequal contest." Moving back to his camp of the previous night, Shelby kept sharpshooters in the area, even as Acting Master John Rogers of the *Naumkeag* put men ashore to recapture the 12-lb boat howitzer that lay shattered and abandoned on the bank of the river. With Shelby gone, the *Tyler* took all the wounded on board and returned to DeValls Bluff, while the other two boats remained in the area to engage the rebel sharpshooters. And contrary to the author's comments, the *Fawn* was not sunk. Though badly damaged, the *Fawn* was able to make herself serviceable before the battle ended. With the coming of darkness, the *Fawn* and the *Naumkeag* anchored above the confluence of the Cache River to await the following day and Shelby's next move. And before nightfall, the Federals, "with their usual spirit of vandalism, took revenge for the loss of their boat by burning all the public and private buildings in Clarendon," including "a gristmill, a sawmill and two timber trucks." On the evening of June 29, according to author David Castro, Carr's command finished the destruction of Clarendon and "illuminated the town by burning every house in it." The Federals justified the destruction because the citizens failed to notify then of the presence of Shelby's command in the area. (John Edwards has the town being burned by E. A. Carr's men on June 26). *O.R.*, vol. 34, pt. 1:929, 1050–1051; *O.N.R.*, vol. 26:424–425, 432; "Capture of the Queen City," *Rebellion Record*, 11:639; Castro, 54, 58; Edwards, *Shelby and His Men*, 325, 328; Ford Reminiscences, 28; Sellmeyer, 189–190; Smith, "Queen City," 121.

78. Of Shelby's operations against the *Queen City*, Admiral Porter wrote: "We have nothing to say against this attack of the Confederates [at Clarendon]—it was all legitimate...General Shelby showed no want of gallantry" in taking the *Queen City*. Lieutenant Commander S. L. Phelps blamed General Steele for the loss of the *Queen City*, having been warned by the Navy that

Shelby, with less than 1,200 men and four pieces of cannon, capturing one, sinking one, and puts to flight three other ironclad gunboats. They were protected behind the iron-cased armor while there was not a tree, bush or weed to protect Shelby's battery. Hereafter I may have something to say about the second day fight at Clarendon.[79]

R. W. Crabb,
Courier to Shelby's Regiment.

[Editor note: A Postscript on Shelby's Operations on the White River.

On June 25, the *Fawn* and the *Naumkeag* returned to Clarendon, where they found that Shelby had returned to the river, building 12 rifle pits and planning to fortify the area for his artillery. However, Shelby's men were again driven from the area.

On morning of June 26, a 3,000-man force under General Eugene A. Carr landed at Clarendon and drove Shelby for the next three days. Shelby finally eluded the Federals, escaping across the swollen Bayou DeView on June 28. During Carr's expedition, he managed to recapture two 24-lb boat howitzers, one of which Shelby had retrieved from the Queen City after it was sunk. Carr reported his losses as one killed and 16 wounded, while capturing two, including Colonel David Shanks; however a period newspaper reported Carr's losses as five killed, 20 wounded, with an unknown number affected by sunstroke or captured.

Shelby reported the loss as 30 killed and wounded for the entire operation, including Colonel David Shanks, who was wounded three times, according to John Edwards, on June 24. Shanks, for his part, had predicted that he would be wounded during the battle "but not bad." Shanks was later captured at Munn's Farm, where he was left with the other Confederate wounded. However, Shanks later returned to his command, to lead Shelby's Brigade during Price's 1864 Missouri Raid. Further, Shanks also predicted that Shelby's command would eventually go to Missouri, where he would "be killed or wounded." During Price's 1864 Missouri Raid, Shanks, who was thought mortally wounded, was captured, but survived the war, dying in Denver, Colorado in 1870.

Of Carr's pursuit Lieutenant Commander S. L. Phelps, of the U.S. Navy, recorded that "Many of Carr's men, after his return to Clarendon from the lame pursuit of Shelby, spoke contemptuously of the whole operation, declaring that they might have captured half the enemy and all his artillery if their pursuit had been vigorous in any sense." Though contemptuous of Carr's pursuit, Phelps admired Shelby for his operations, calling him "a daring and enterprising fellow."

In summing up Shelby's operation on the White River, author David Castro

---

Shelby was heading for the river at Clarendon. Phelps wrote: "I thought the army should watch his [Shelby's] movements. Nothing of the kind was done, and when he [Shelby] captured the *Queen City* there [at Clarendon] it came as a complete surprise to the army." *O.N.R.*, vol. 26:464; Porter, *Naval History*, 563.

79. No additional articles by R. W. Crabb were ever found.

wrote: "Shelby had dealt a stunning blow to the Union forces, but ultimately had been unable to block the river for any length of time. He had wanted to impede the flow of supplies upriver for eight or nine days, but Carr's rapid reaction and the power of the gunboats had made it impossible."[80]]

* * * * * * *

---

80. *O.R.*, vol. 34, pt. 1:1047, 1052; *O.N.R.*, vol. 26:427, 464; Bruce S. Allardice, *Confederate Colonels: A Biographical Register* (Columbia, MO, 2008), 337, hereafter cited as Allardice, *Confederate Colonels*; Bartels, *Elliott's Scouts*, 59; Castro, 58; George R. Cruzen, "Story of My Life," Missouri Historical Society, St. Louis, hereafter cited as Cruzen; Edwards, *Shelby and His Men*, 326, 329; "From White River," *Chicago Tribune*, July 6, 1864; Sellmeyer, 190–192, 309.

Chapter 2

The Final Infantry Operations, Surrender, and Death of General M. M. Parsons (May 1864–August 1865)

Item: Continuing history of Parsons's Missouri Division, following the Battle of Jenkins' Ferry, Arkansas, until the end of the war, by James H. McNamara.[1]
Published: July 16, 1887.

[Continued from Volume 7, Part 4: Spring 1864]

Sketch of Operations of Parsons's Division,

Missouri Confederates
[Garrison Duty—May 1864 to June 1865]
The following sketch of operations of Parsons's division,[2] Missouri Confederates,

---

1. James H. McNamara was born in Ireland in 1837, immigrated to the United States in 1852, and settled in St. Louis. An architect by profession, McNamara was a member of the St. Louis Militia, the Emmett Guards, and was captured at Camp Jackson on May 10, 1861. After his parole, he journeyed to north Missouri where he engaged in farming until October 1861, at which time he joined the 6th Division, MSG. He served initially as an orderly sergeant to A. M. Standish, and then as a volunteer in Gorham's, MSG Battery at the Battle of Pea Ridge, in March 1862. Following a short stint on the east side of the Mississippi River, McNamara returned to the Trans-Mississippi, where General M. M. Parsons appointed him the Division Paymaster, replacing Colonel H. A. Parmales, who had died. McNamara remained on General Parsons's staff until the Battle of Helena, when he volunteered to serve in Tilden's Battery. Severely wounded at Helena, McNamara recovered and returned to duty with Colonel Standish. In January 1865 he joined the engineers and in May 1865, McNamara was appointed a captain. Following the war he returned to St. Louis to practice engineering, including a period where he was a professor at what is now St. Louis University. Clement A. Evans and Robert S. Bridgers, gen. eds., *Confederate Military History Extended Edition* 19 vols. (Atlanta, 1899; reprint ed., Wilmington, NC, 1987), vol. 12: *Missouri* by John C. Moore, 258–259, hereafter cited as Moore, *Missouri, Confederate Military History, Extended*; Peterson, et al., 173.
2. Parsons's Division comprised two brigades. The 1st Brigade was commanded by John B. Clark, Jr. and contained the 8th and 9th Missouri Infantry Regiments, with Ruffner's 4-gun battery. The 2nd Brigade was commanded by S. P. Burns and contained the 10th, 11th, 12th, and 16th Missouri Infantries with the 9th Battalion Missouri Sharpshooters and Lesueur's 4-gun battery. The division was organized on March 25, 1864, at Shreveport, Louisiana. Michael E. Banasik, *Confederate "Tales of the War" In the Trans-Mississippi, Part Four: 1864* (Iowa City, IA, 2015), 40–42, hereafter cited as Banasik, *Tales of the War, Part Four.*

was read before the Southern Historical society last Thursday night by Capt. J. H. McNamara...

On 12th of May [1864] Parsons's division took up the line of march in the direction of Camden, the other infantry divisions having gone in the same direction some days before ahead.³ One regiment of cavalry was left to protect the hospital established at Tulip.⁴

Passing through Camden on the 14th, on the trail of the other divisions, Parsons reached Calhoun on the 16th, where he issued the following address to his troops:⁵

---

3. Following the Battle of Jenkins' Ferry (April 30, 1864), the Confederate Army withdrew to Tulip, Arkansas, where it rested and licked its wounds. On May 3 T. J. Churchill's Arkansas Division and J. G. Walker's Texas Division left their camps at Tulip and headed to Camden, there to await further orders. General E. K. Smith had supposedly ordered his infantry to Louisiana to support General Taylor, who was still engaged with General Nathaniel Banks in the Red River Valley; however, it was clear from various accounts that General Smith did not order his infantry to Louisiana until May 8. Left behind in the Tulip area was M. M. Parsons's Missouri Division, which would wait more than a week for orders to move southward. While waiting for orders an election for the Confederate Congress was held in Parsons's command on May 2, which proved to be the only excitement that the troops had for many days, save "eating & sleeping." *O.R.*, vol. 34, pt. 1:482; *O.R.*, vol. 34, pt. 3:810–811; Michael E. Banasik, *Serving With Honor: The Diary of Captain Eathan Allen Pinnell of the Eighth Missouri Infantry (Confederate)* (Iowa City, IA, 1999), 160–161, hereafter cited as Banasik, *Serving With Honor*; Joseph Palmer Blessington, *The Campaigns of Walker's Texas Division* (New York, 1875), 259, hereafter cited as Blessington; Letter to the Editor (May 7, 1864), *Houston Daily Telegraph*, May 18, 1864; Cythia Dehaven Pitcock and Bill J. Gurley, *I Acted Out of Principle: The Civil War Diary of Dr. William M. McPheeters, Confederate Surgeon in the Trans-Mississippi* (Fayetteville, AR, 2002), 152, hereafter cited as Pitcock & Gurley; William N. Hoskin's Civil War Diary, Western Historical Manuscript Collection, State Historical Society of Missouri, Columbia, Missouri, May 1–11, 1864, hereafter cited as Hoskin Diary; E. Kirby Smith, "The Defense of the Red River," in *Battles and Leaders of the Civil War* 4 vols. (New York, 1887–1888) 4:373, hereafter cited as Smith, "Defense of the Red River."

4. The Confederates established a field hospital a short distance from the battlefield and within a few days "every house between...[Tulip] & the battlefield...[had] been taken for the benefit of the wounded." By May 2 two additional hospitals were established at Tulip and a few days later another medical facility was created at Princeton, primarily for the wounded Federals, who were moved there on May 9. The same day the Federal wounded were moved, Parsons's Division received orders "to be ready to move at a moment's notice." Back in Camden, Walker's Division left camp, moved toward Alexandria, even as Parsons's boys waited, and on May 10, Walker was followed by Churchill's Division. On May 12, Parsons's Division left Tulip and headed "reluctantly" back to Louisiana, for the men had their "heads set North" and toward Missouri. Blessington, 259; Thomas W. Cutrer, ed., "'An Experience in Soldier's Life' The Civil War Letters of Volney Ellis, Adjutant Twelfth Texas Infantry Walker's Texas Division, C.S.A.," *Military History of the Southwest* 22 (Fall 1992), 160–161; Hoskin Diary, May 1, 9, and 12, 1864; Pitcock & Gurley, 152; John P. Quesenberry Manuscript Diary, Western Historical Manuscript Collection, State Historical Society of Missouri, Columbia, Missouri, May 9 and 12, 1864, hereafter cited as Quesenberry Diary; S. C. Turnbo, "History of the Twenty-seventh Arkansas Confederate Infantry With Many Interesting Accounts of the Countries Through Which it Passed During the Civil War and Accurate Accounts of the Battles in which it Engaged," S. C. Turnbo Collection, University of Arkansas (Little Rock), hereafter cited as Turnbo.

5. Breaking camp at 6:00 a.m., Parsons's Division made 15 miles on May 12, passing through Princeton, and 22 miles the next day, camping within 6 miles of Camden. On May 14 the division made 16 more miles, crossing the Ouachita River, at Camden, and camping 8 miles south of town on the

[Circular 14.] – Headquarters Parsons Division, Camp Near Calhoun, May 16, 1864.

SOLDIERS OF MISSOURI – The enemy in Louisiana, by the aid of your gallant prowess so recently defeated have again filled up their depleted ranks and threaten the immediate invasion of the Trans-Mississippi department.[6] The general commanding the department has this day directed me to forward you with all possible speed to meet them the enemy. Remember, Louisiana was the first to aid her sister, Missouri, in clothing and munitions of war, and among the first to show her devoted friendship to our state, by shedding her blood upon our own soil, at the memorable battle of "Oak Hills."[7] She now appeals to you for immediate relief – a high compliment. Let's there be no straggling, no laggards, no noise, complaints upon the march to the rescue, which will be conducted at a greater rate of speed, per day then here to for, but, so far as practicable, to the ease and comfort of the command

M. M. Parsons, Major General.[8]

The address was received by the troops with a cordial enthusiasm. Besides,

---

road to Shreveport. The weather had been pleasant during the march, while the men, according to Captain John Quesenberry, "seem to be nearly worn out." May 15 began with a "heavy rain," but the division still marched, making only 12 miles before camping. Departing at daylight, on May 16, Parsons's Division logged 22 miles, passing through Calhoun and camping 2 miles beyond, at the fork of the Homer Road. Farther south, Churchill's Division was near Mount Lebanon (about 70 miles away), while Walker's, the advanced division, was 36 miles closer to Alexandria, the destination of all three divisions. Banasik, *Serving With Honor*, 161–162; Blessington, 261–262; Hoskin Diary, May 12–16, 1864; Pitcock & Gurley, 161; Quesenberry Diary, May 12–16, 1864; James T. Wallace Diary (1862–1865), Southern Historical Collection, University of North Carolina (Chapel Hill, NC), May 13–16, 1864, hereafter cited as Wallace Diary.

6. Parsons was referring to the Battles of Mansfield (April 8, 1864) and Pleasant Hill (April 9, 1864), after which the Federals retreated back to Grand Ecore and then to Alexandria.

7. At the Battle of Oak Hills or Wilsons' Creek, as it was known by Federal forces, the 3rd Louisiana Infantry played a prominent role in the battle, where it lost 9 killed and 48 wounded. The battle south of Springfield, Missouri, on August 10, 1861, was a Confederate victory and one of the first major battles of the war. The Confederates, commanded by Generals Ben McCulloch and Sterling Price, lost 257 killed, 900 wounded, and 27 missing, while the Unionists under General Nathaniel Lyon posted losses of 223 killed, 721 wounded, and 291 missing. Michael E. Banasik, *Missouri in 1861: The Civil War Letters of Franc B. Wilkie, Newspaper Correspondent*. (Iowa City, IA, 2001), 378, hereafter cited as Banasik, *Missouri in 1861*; Boatner, 932–935.

8. Mosby M. Parsons was born in Virginia in 1822, moved to Missouri at age 13, and was a veteran of the Mexican War. On May 17, 1861, he was appointed a brigadier general, commanding the 6th Division, MSG. Parsons led his command in all the 1861 battles that his division participated in, but was not present at the Battle of Pea Ridge, being absent at the time in Richmond, Virginia. On April 8, 1862, Parsons succeeded Price as commander of the MSG, and on November 5, 1862, he was commissioned a brigadier general in the Confederate Army. At the Battle of Prairie Grove (December 7, 1862), Parsons commanded a brigade and later led a division during the Red River and Camden Campaigns. Parsons spent his Civil War years, save for three months, entirely in the Trans-Mississippi Department. At war's end he went to Mexico, where he was killed on August 16, 1865. Banasik, *Missouri Brothers in Gray*, 146–148; Banasik, *Missouri In 1861*, 380–381; Peterson, et al., 34; Thomas L. Snead, *The Fight For Missouri From the Election of Lincoln to the Death of Lyon* (New York, 1866), 313, hereafter cited as Snead.

it relieved their minds of a thought of where they were marching, and now what purpose.

The Missourians

were much attached to the Louisianans. They were satisfied with their brief campaign against Banks, and desired to again march into that lovely and hospitable state.[9] Louisiana had a Missourian ([Henry W.] Allen) for governor,[10] and her legislature adopted all the Missouri Confederates as her children—to provide for them in the field the same as for her own soldiers.[11]

---

9. Banks's Red River Expedition began on March 10, 1864, and ended on May 22. Prior to May 16, Banks's army was already in retreat, having suffered a disastrous defeat at Mansfield on April 8 and a further rebuke on April 9 at Pleasant Hill. Of the two battles, Parsons's and Churchill's Divisions were only in the battle on April 9, after which they headed back to Arkansas, with Walker's Texans, where they fought the Battle of Jenkins' Ferry on April 30. By May 16, the three divisions were well on their way to Alexandria, Louisiana, to support General Richard Taylor's efforts to further punish Banks's army and attempt to destroy it. However, Banks had evacuated Alexandria on May 12–13, following the successful rescue of the Union fleet, that had been trapped above the falls. Boatner, 685–688; Smith, "Defense of the Red River," 371–373.

10. Though not a Missourian by birth, Henry Watkins Allen did reside in the state from 1833 to 1837. He was born in Virginia in 1820, moved to Missouri in 1833, and in 1837 moved to Mississippi. By the time of the Civil War, Allen had also lived in Texas and finally settled in Louisiana in 1852. At the beginning of the war, Allen enlisted as a private, and was appointed the lieutenant colonel of the 4th Louisiana Infantry on May 1, 1861. At the Battle of Shiloh (April 6–7, 1862), Allen led his regiment as a colonel, was seriously wounded on the first day, but continued to lead the unit through the remainder of the battle. At Baton Rouge (August 5, 1862), while leading a brigade, Allen was again wounded, receiving a canister blast at close range that crippled him for life. He was promoted to brigadier general in August 1863, and ordered to Shreveport for duty. Elected governor of Louisiana in November 1863, Allen took office the following January. After the war, he moved to Mexico City, where he died on April 22, 1866, of Yellow Fever. Ezra J. Warner wrote that, as governor, Allen "was certainly one of the finest administrators produced by the Confederacy." Anthony Arthur, *General Jo Shelby's March* (New York, 2010), 173–174, hereafter cited as Arthur; Banasik, *Tales of the War, Part Four*, 144–146; Arthur W. Bergeron, Jr., "Henry Watkins Allen," in *The Louisiana Governors From Iberville to Edwards* (Joseph G. Dawson III, gen. ed.; Baton Rouge, LA, 1990), 142–145, hereafter cited as Dawson; editorial comment on "Henry W. Allen," *Mexican Times*, April 28, 1866; Warner, *Generals in Gray*, 4.

11. C. B. Lotspeich of the 16th Missouri also remembered the kindness of the Louisiana people, who opened their homes to the "exiles" from Missouri. Concerts and theatrical performances were held, "for the benefit of the 'adopted sons of Louisiana,'" as Governor Allen, "affectionately called the desolate Missourians." Through these efforts "funds enough…to clothe the Missouri troops" were raised, "for they were exiled from their own State, and almost neglected by all," including the Confederate government. One such concert was given by the "Shreveport Glee Club" on September 15, 1864, and was a rousing success, netting $5,000.00 for support of the Missourians. In appreciation of Louisiana's generosity, Governor Thomas C. Reynolds, wrote a letter to the *Caddo Gazette*, with which he closed: "We exiles of Missouri will not forget kindness shown us by our Confederate brethren; and the name of Henry Watkins Allen will be as a household word throughout her limits." Governor Reynolds then attached a copy of a personal letter to Governor Allen, where he again heaped praise upon Louisianans for their uncommon generosity. See Appendix A for a copy of Governor Reynolds's letter to Governor Allen. Sarah A. Dorsey, *Recollection of Henry Watkins Allen, Brigadier General Confederate States Army Ex-Governor of Louisiana* (New York, 1866), 253–254, 385, hereafter cited as Dorsey; C. B. Lotspeich, Unpub-

The division continued on the march till the 19th. Near Haynesville, La. orders were received for the Missouri and Arkansas troops to counter-march, while the Louisiana and Texas troops continued on. Further danger of an invasion by Banks was not looked for.[12] On the 26th the division went into the present "Camp Kirby Smith."[13] The following was the order

[General Order No. 1]
Headquarters Parsons's Division, Missouri Infantry, May 25, 1864. – In

---

lished manuscript, "Personal Experiences of C. B. Lotspeich," 19, Arkansas History Commission; W. H. Tunnard, *A Southern History. The History of the Third Regiment Louisiana Infantry* (Baton Rouge, LA, 1866), 329.

12. The Missouri Division continued its march on May 17, even as orders were winding their way to the division canceling the movement. After 22 miles, "the day hot, sand deep, [and] dust very bad," Parsons's boys came to rest at Haynesville, in Claiborne County, Louisiana. The 18th began with a shower, which cleared off by 9:00 a.m., followed by a march of 15 miles, which ended 10 miles from Minden. Even while the division was making camp orders arrived in Parsons's Division announcing the evacuation of Alexandria by Banks's Federals. New orders directed the division back to Camden, by "easy marches." Previous to Parsons receiving his orders, General Churchill had been turned back to Camden on May 17. General Walker, for his part was not notified of the fall of Alexandria until May 19; however his orders still directed him on to Alexandria where he arrived on May 22—the Red River Expedition was at an end. *O.R.*, vol. 34, pt. 3:826–827; Banasik, *Serving With Honor*, 162–163; Blessington, 263–263; Hoskin Diary, May 17–19, 1864; Richard Lowe, *Walker's Texas Division C.S.A. Greyhounds of the Trans-Mississippi* (Baton Rouge, LA, 2004), 230–231, hereafter cited as Lowe; Pitcock & Gurley, 161; Quesenberry Diary, May 17–19, 1864; Wallace Diary, May 18, 1864.

13. Parsons's Division came to rest in Union County, Arkansas, near Three Creek Store on May 24. The camp was promptly named "Camp Kirby Smith" in honor of the department commander, even though an official order, naming the camp, was not issued until the 26th. Banasik, *Serving With Honor*, 164; Hoskin Diary, May 24, 1864; Quesenberry Diary, May 24, 1864; Wallace Diary, May 24, 1864.

Edmund Kirby Diary Smith was born on May 16, 1824, in St. Augustine, Florida, He attended West Point and graduated in 1845 (number 25 of 41). Assigned to duty in Texas, Smith was cited for "gallant and meritorious conduct" in the Battles of Cero Gordo and Contreras & Churubusco, Mexico, for which he earned a brevet to captain. Following the Mexican War, Smith served as an instructor at West Point, returned to active duty in 1855, and was wounded in a fight with Indians on May 13, 1859. At the beginning of the Civil War, Smith offered his services to the Confederacy. He was promoted to general on June 17, 1861, fought at First Bull Run and was promoted to major general on October 11, 1861. Given command of the Department of East Tennessee, Smith was promoted to lieutenant general for his operations in 1862, and on January 14, 1863, was given command of the Southwestern Army, embracing Louisiana and Texas. On March 18, 1863, Smith was appointed the commander of the Trans-Mississippi Department. Promoted to full general in February 1864, Smith survived the war, still commanding the Trans-Mississippi Department, which he officially surrendered on June 2, 1865. As commander in the Trans-Mississippi, one period newspaper wrote that Smith was "well fitted for his high and distinguished position he occupie[d]; calm, deliberate, far-seeing as a commander-in-chief, dashing and impetuous in action." He died on March 28, 1893, at Sewanee, Tennessee, where he had worked as a mathematics instructor at the University of the South. *O.R.*, vol. 22, pt. 1:7; Banasik, *Missouri Brothers in Gray*, 152–153; Boatner, 769–770; Heitman, 1:896, 2:36; Joseph H. Parks, *General Edmund Kirby Smith C.S.A.* (Baton Rouge, LA, 1954), 119, hereafter cited as Parks; Jeffery S. Prushankin, "Smith, Edmund Kirby," in *Encyclopedia of the Civil War*, 1810–1811; "Trans-Mississippi Generals," *Mobil Daily Advertiser and Register* (Mobil, AL), April 21, 1864.

honor of the distinguished department commander this encampment will be styled "Camp Kirby Smith." By Order of

Maj. Gen. Parsons.
Austin M. Standish, A. A. G.[14]

This camp was beautifully located and the men generally had a pleasant sojourn in their "doghouses."[15] They had abundance of rations, with such other additional luxuries as green corn and other vegetables. The general himself and his staff shared heartily in the pleasures afforded them through the kindness of the neighboring people.

An Evening Pleasure Raid,

in the way of a picnic, fishing excursion and ball was gotten up by the good ladies of El Dorado and Champaignville in which the general and some thirty of his officers participated with the utmost enthusiasm.

The men, too had their picnic. It consisted in detailing them by companies out in all directions to the neighboring plantations to save the crops.

The usual drill and discipline, with inspections and reviews, were resumed in this camp.[16]

---

14. Austin M. Standish was the brother-in-law of General Mosby M. Parsons. A civil engineer by profession, Standish helped "locate the first railroads constructed in Missouri." The "Protestant Irishman" Standish was appointed a colonel and Adjutant General of Parsons's 6th Division, MSG, on June 12, 1861. He later transferred to the Confederate Service, remaining on Parsons's staff as his Adjutant General throughout the rest of the war. Standish was captured at Wilson's Creek, but escaped before the battle ended. He was praised for his actions at the Battle of Prairie Grove and during the Red River Campaign of 1864. Following the war, he left for Mexico with General Parsons and was murdered in the early morning hours of August 16, 1865, with Parsons, near the town of China, Mexico. *O.R.*, vol. 34, pt. 1:603; *O.R.*, vol. 53:434, 461; Michael Flanagan, "The Memoirs of Dr. Robert J. Christie," http://flanaganfamily.net/genealo/memoirs.htm, Chapter XIX, hereafter cited as Christie Memoir; R. H. Musser, "Murder of Gen. Parsons," *Missouri Republican*, January 23, 1886; Peterson, et al., 172.

15. The "doghouse" was one of the many names given to the "shelter tent." "Invented in late 1861 or early 1862" the tent was constructed of cotton, and was first issued to Union troops early in the war, replacing the "Sibley" and "wedge" tents. It was commonly referred to as a "dog" or "pup" tent because its size (about five feet by four feet), which barely accommodated a small dog. Other names included the "dog shanty" or "dog kennel. Used primarily during the campaigning season (April–November), the tent would become unbearably hot during the summer, necessitating raising the bottom of the tent to allow some type of circulation to occur. Though easy to carry and transport, the tent was not-well liked by the troops, as one solider penned: They "'are the worst things that was ever invented for soldiers.'" Francis A. Lord, *Civil War Collectors Encyclopedia Volumes I & II* (Dayton, OH, 1995), vol. 1:279–280, hereafter cited as Lord; Quoted in James I. Robertson, Jr., *Soldiers Blue and Gray* (Columbia, SC, 1988), 45–46.

16. After Parsons's Division settled in to Camp Kirby Smith, in late May 1864, they entered into a period of "rest," where the men spent their time "in drills and cleaning arms." Churchill's command entered the same period of rest at "Camp Grinsted," but a short distance from the Missourians. Inspections were occasionally held and division reviews ordered "to gratify foolish and devilish pride" of the commanding officers for the benefit of the local women. Officers would take rides into the countryside to partake of homemade meals, while many in the division joined the Masons or took part in a religious "revival" that was taking place in the camp. With the wheat crop ready

In General Order 20, the general made two valuable additions to his staff. Maj. John B. Ruthven was made chief commissary of subsistence and Dr. R. J. Bell chief surgeon.[17]

Maj. Ruthven had been his old brigade commissary, and the Trans-Mississippi army could not boast of a better one. Dr.

Simon B. Buckner

to harvest, men were furloughed throughout the army to bring in the crop, which was "light" for the year. In time, the men became bored, as one captain recorded: "We have but little to do and the men are getting quite lazy." However, behind the scenes, General Smith had sent a confidential letter to General Price, on June 3, detailing the requirements needed "to make a campaign into Missouri" (see Appendix A for a copy of the letter). For the infantry of the Trans-Mississippi Army, their active campaigning was done, as the cavalry, under General Price, would soon be making a raid into Missouri, while the doughboys sat about waiting for the end of the war. *O.R.*, vol. 34, pt. 4:642; Banasik, *Serving With Honor*, 167–173; T. J. Gaughan, ed., *Letters of a Confederate Surgeon* (Camden, AR, 1960), 235, 237, hereafter cited as Gaughan; Hoskin Diary, May 28, 31, June 1, 4–5, 9, 19, 24, 26–28, 30, 1864; Pitcock & Gurley, 166–167, 170, 172–174, 178; Quesenberry Diary, May 28, and 30, June 2, 6, 8, 11, 23–24, 26; Wallace Diary, May 31, 1864.

17. John B. Ruthven joined the MSG early in the war and served under General Mosby M. Parsons as his brigade commissary. He was present at the Battles of Prairie Grove and Helena, Arkansas, where General Parsons noted that Ruthven deserved "great praise for the activity [with] which" he "discharged the duties of...his department." In June 1864 Ruthven was appointed the division commissary, being elevated from the same position in S. P. Burns's 2nd Brigade, after which his name disappears from all known records. *O.R.*, vol. 22, pt. 1:423; *O.R.*, 53:459; Joseph H. Crute, *Confederate Staff Officers 1861–1865* (Powhatan, VA, 1982), 145, hereafter cited as Crute, *Confederate Staff Officers*; Letter (October 7, 1862), Mosby M. Parsons Letters, Peter W. Alexander Collection, Columbia University; National Archives, Record Group 109, chapter VIII, vol. 394, Parsons's Division.

Robert "Joe" (or Joseph) Bell, a resident of Hannibal, Missouri, at the beginning of the Civil War, was born in Ralls County, Missouri, on January 2, 1835, and married Virginia R. Hagan on April 16, 1861, even as the war was beginning. He joined the 3rd Battalion, 2nd Division, MSG, being commissioned the battalion commissary on March 22, 1862. He transferred to the Confederate Service at Camp Anderson, Arkansas, as chief surgeon, 10th Missouri Infantry, on October 25, 1862. Bell was made post surgeon of Tulip, Arkansas, following the Battle of Jenkins' Ferry in early May 1864, and chief surgeon of Parsons's Missouri Division on May 12, with an official appointment date of June 7, 1864. Bell returned to Hannibal after the war, where he died on January 25, 1867, just shy of his 32nd birthday. Mrs. R. J. Bell Diary (January–August, 1864), April 16, May 4, 7, & 12 and June 7, 1864, M. M. Parsons Papers, Missouri Historical Society, hereafter cited as Mrs. R. J. Bell Diary; Eakin, *Confederate Records*, 1:79; Harrell, *Arkansas, Confederate Military History*, 382; Peterson, et al., 99; Pitcock & Gurley, 354–355; Wayne H. Schnetzer, *Men of the Tenth: A Roster of the Tenth Missouri Infantry Confederate States of America*. Independence, MO, n.d), 2, hereafter cited as Schnetzer, *Men of the Tenth*.

The Final Infantry Operations, Surrender, and Death of General Parsons / 47

Bell had been long acting as chief surgeon, and his devotion to his profession and great energy in providing hospital accommodations and comforts for the sick earned for him the confidence of the general.

On June 29, the general entertained a distinguished visitor in the person of Maj. Gen. Simon Buckner, who was just from Richmond, to take command in this department.[18] Parsons and his staff were captured by Buckner, who was a keen, dashing-looking officer.[19]

Early in August the troops learned of their new district commander: Maj. Gen. Magruder to the command of Arkansas, Maj. Gen. Walker to that of Texas, and Maj. Gen. Buckner to Louisiana.[20]

---

18. General Simon B. Buckner graduated from West Point in 1844 (no. 11 of 25), served mostly east of the Mississippi River during the Civil War, but was best known for surrendering Fort Donelson to General U. S. Grant on February 16, 1862. Buckner was assigned to duty in the Trans-Mississippi Department on April 28, 1864, replacing General Richard Taylor as commander of the District of West Louisiana on August 4, 1864. Promoted to lieutenant general on September 20, 1864, Buckner was not confirmed until January 17, 1865. In April 1865 Buckner commanded the combined Districts of Arkansas and West Louisiana. Together with Generals Price and Joseph Brent, he negotiated the surrender of the Trans-Mississippi Department, signing the document on May 26, 1865. Following the war Buckner lived briefly in New Orleans, then returned to Kentucky in 1868, where he became the editor of a local newspaper. He was elected governor of Kentucky (1887–92), later ran for vice-president in the "Gold Democratic Party" in 1896, and died near Munfordville, Kentucky, on January 8, 1924. *O.R.*, vol. 34, pt. 4:801; *O.R.*, vol. 41, pt. 2:1039; *O.R.*, vol. 48, pt. 1:7; Mrs. R. J. Bell Diary, June 29, 1864; Boatner, 95–96; Faust, 88.

19. Buckner arrived in camp late on the evening of June 29, en route to visit the daughter of his sister, Mrs. Mary Tooke, who was his only living relative. Of Mrs. Tooke, Mrs. R. J. Bell wrote that she was a "pleasant lady, much more so than most ladies I meet" for she was "a real, warm-hearted, whole-souled woman." Staying with Mrs. Tooke, who lived but a mile from Parsons's camp, Buckner spent the next few days getting acquainted with the army, attending dinners and reviewing the troops, while he awaited official orders as to his next assignment. Speculation was that Buckner was to assume command of the District of Arkansas. Mrs. R. J. Bell Diary, June 29, July 3, and August 3, 1864; Hoskin Diary, June 30 and July 25, 1864; Quesenberry Diary, May 25 and June 30, 1864.

20. Even as the Red River Expedition ended, General E. K. Smith relieved General Richard Taylor from command of the District of Western Louisiana, placing in his stead General Walker. On August 4, 1864, General Smith shuffled his entire command structure, in preparation for Price's 1864 Missouri Raid; General Magruder was given command of the District of Arkansas; Walker the District of Texas, New Mexico and Arizona; and Buckner took over for Walker in western Louisiana. *O.R.*, vol. 34, pt. 4:664; *O.R.*, vol. 41, pt. 2:1039.

Major General John Bankhead Magruder graduated from West Point (no. 15 of 42) in 1830 and served in the Seminole and Mexican wars, receiving two brevets for gallantry. On June 17, 1861, he was appointed a Confederate brigadier general and a major general on October 7. Magruder served east of the Mississippi River until October 10, 1862, when he was assigned to command the District of Texas. He captured Galveston, Texas, on January 1, 1863, and on August 4,

John B. Magruder

The Missourians had a feeling that Gen. Parsons was

Pushed Aside.

The fact that the other major generals outrank him did not remove that feeling.[21]

On the 12th Gen. Parsons was summoned to Camden, where a council of the district commanders was held. He returned to camp on the 16th, and marching orders were immediately issued.[22] The orders found the command unable to move. The mules were away in pasture, fifty miles off, and the streams much swollen

---

1864, was appointed commander of the District of Arkansas, thus allowing Sterling Price to lead his raid into Missouri. With the war winding down, Magruder assumed command of the District of Texas, New Mexico, and Arizona on April 4, 1865. Following the war, he moved to Mexico where he served as a major general under Maximilian and later returned to Houston, Texas, where he died on February 18, 1871. *O.R.*, vol. 41, pt. 2:1039; *O.R.*, vol. 48, pt. 2:1263; Boatner, 501; Warner, *Generals in Gray*, 207, 208.

21. Even though his subordinates felt that Parsons should have been given command of the District of Arkansas, he was never considered for the post. The following are the date of ranks (and order of rank) for major generals considered for command of the District of Arkansas: S. P. Buckner, August 16, 1862 (no. 32); J. B. Magruder, October 7, 1861 (no. 10); J. G. Walker, November 8, 1862 (no. 40). R. A. Brock, ed., *Southern Historical Society Papers*, 52 vols. (Richmond, VA, 1876–1959; reprint ed. Wilmington, NC, 1990–1992), vol. 2:334, 336, 338, hereafter cited as Brock, *SHSP*; Faust, 560.

22. On August 1 1864, General Price departed Camden en route to Shreveport, there to report to General Smith. Price and party arrived at Shreveport on the evening of August 3, met with General Smith, Governor Thomas C. Reynolds, and Senators Johnson and Mitchell of Arkansas that same evening and again on August 4. By 2:00 p.m. on August 4, Price was given his orders for an expedition into to Missouri (see Appendix A for a copy of those orders). Prior to Price's arrival, Governor Reynolds had met with General Smith to discuss who should command the Missouri Expedition. Reynolds supported Price as the commander after querying him in late June 1864, as to whether he would lead the expedition. Price responded on July 22, stating "I would like to command the expedition." Overall Reynolds had two basic reasons for supporting Price; both of which were political. First: none could match Price's "skill as a politician and especially as a military demagogue" or simply put, his men adored him. Second: the "other irregular consideration...was the dread by the Richmond government of political dissension." In supporting Price, Reynolds caveated his recommendation, stating "that the best and most reliable division and brigade commanders should be furnished him." Smith eventually approved Reynolds's suggestion, despite his misgivings of Price, whom he considered "'absolutely good for nothing" and "'was not even a military man...[who was] greatly exaggerated by his partisans.'" Price returned to Camden on August 8 and began meeting with his various commanders and staff the next day, setting the stage for his Missouri raid. Following the initial briefings, General Fagan informed his staff on August 10 of the pending expedition, further directing them that the details of the expedition's destination were confidential. However, that did not prevent J. T. Alexander, his ordnance officer, from telling his wife what was happening. On the evening of August 12 General Parsons arrived in Camden, staying at Dr. Thomas D. Wooten's and, like the others before him, met with Price and others to discuss the upcoming expedition. Four days later Parsons returned to camp with orders to march. *O.R.*, vol. 41, pt. 2:1011–1012, 1020, 1040; J. T. Alexander Letter (August 11, 1864); Mrs. R. J. Bell Diary, August 12, 1864; Albert Castel, *General Sterling Price and the Civil War in the West* (Baton Rouge, LA, 1968), 200–202, hereafter cited as Castel, *Sterling Price*; Pitcock & Gurley, 195, 199–200, 203–206; quoted in Robert G. Schultz, ed., *General Sterling Price and the Confederacy* (St. Louis, 2009), 124–125, 128, 131, hereafter cited as Schultz.

from heavy rains. These hindrances delayed a move till the 19th, on which date the division struck tents, or rather struck "doghouses," and took up the line of march; the first brigade for Washington and the second brigade, with Parsons, for Monticello. Passing through hospitable El Dorado, the division crossed over the Washita, at Moro Landing, on the 21st. The Saline was crossed on the following 24th, halting at Monticello on the 25th.[23] The following order increased the general's importance and responsibility:

[General Order No. 33.]
HEADQUARTERS M. S. DISTRICT ARKANSAS, August 27, 1864.
– In obedience to orders from headquarters, District of Arkansas, the undersigned assumes command of the middle sub-district of Arkansas.
M. M. PARSONS, Maj. Gen..

His first act in taking command was to visit the general hospital and carefully inspect every department of it.

About the end of this month, Gen. Price in command of all the cavalry of the district, moved forward to Missouri[24]

---

23. Shortly after Price returned to Camden, stories began floating in from the various camps predicting a movement to Missouri. General John B. Clark, Jr. was reassigned from Parsons's 1st Brigade, on August 12, to command Marmaduke's Cavalry Brigade, which ignited rumors of an impending move to Missouri. J. A. Cocker, serving in the 8th Missouri Cavalry recalled that "our hearts were glad by the whispers of a projected raid into Missouri, and many were the protestations heard, from the long haired half-clad Missourians, that they would rather die in Missouri than live in Arkansas." By August 13, there was "a good deal of talk" in Parsons's 2nd Brigade, "about Gen'l Price going to Mo. All wanted to go." Rumor had Parsons's Division marching northward on August 15; however, that never happened as the infantry learned on the 15th that Price would be leading the cavalry northward. Still, on the 15th, the infantrymen hoped for a return home as all their wagons were ordered loaded and stock returned in preparation for a movement northward, for an unknown purpose. At the time that the orders were issued, the livestock were located in Claiborne County, Louisiana, some 50 miles away, thus delaying the march. On August 19, following a "steady rain during the night," Parsons's Division "broke up Camp Kirby Smith at sunrise after a stay of eighty-four days" and headed north. The 1st Brigade headed northwest toward Washington, Arkansas, while the 2nd Brigade moved northeast to Monticello. On August 24, the 1st Brigade camped 3 miles northeast of Washington, there to wait further orders. Farther to the east, in Drew County, Arkansas, the 2nd Brigade came to rest a half mile north of Monticello on August 25, and like the 1st Brigade, awaited further orders. In the end, the District of Arkansas' infantry would be used as a feint to hold the Federals in place in Little Rock, while the rebel cavalry crossed the Arkansas River on their way to Missouri. Banasik, *Serving With Honor*, 175–178; Castel, *Sterling Price*, 204; Gaughan, Letter (August 1, 1864 should read September 1, 1864) 243–244; Hoskin Diary, August 13, 15, and 25, 1864; Robert L. Kerby, *Kirby Smith's Confederacy: The Trans-Mississippi South, 1863–1865* (New York, 1972), 333, hereafter cited as Kerby; Robert E. Miller, "General Mosby M. Parsons Missouri Secessionist," *Missouri Historical Review* 80 (October, 1985), 56, hereafter cited as Miller; Quesenberry Diary, August 13 and 25, 1864; Recollections of J. A. Cocker, in Thomas Ewing Papers, The Library of Congress, 8, hereafter cited as Cocker; Wallace diary, August 8, 1864.

24. Price had wanted to start the expedition on August 13, 1864, but various delays in procuring ordnance supplies from Shreveport, proved to be a habitual problem and prevented the start for over two weeks. The blame for the shortage of ordnance material, according to James T. Alexander,

On His Memorable Raid.

On the second of September the enemy's cavalry, some 450 strong, was reported crossing the Saline River at Mt. Elba;[25] Gen. Parsons at once dispatched

---

Fagan's ordnance officer, rested with Major Benjamin Huger, E. Kirby Smith's "Chief of Bureau of Ordnance." Finally on August 28, Dr. William McPheeters, chief surgeon of Price's Cavalry Corps, "arose early," in Camden, "finished packing," and mounted his "horse to join Gen. Price and staff, including Governor Thomas C. Reynolds, and set out on...[the] grand expedition" to Missouri. Reynolds, who wanted to legitimize his position as governor "hoped and even expected to be installed in the governor's office in Jefferson City, if only temporally" (see Appendix A for the eulogy on Thomas C. Reynolds, upon his death by suicide, in St. Louis, on March 30, 1887). The infantry of the District remained behind, being positioned at Washington (1st Brigade, Parsons's Division), Monticello (2nd Brigade Parsons's Division with T. P. Dockery's and A. T. Hawthorn's Arkansas Brigades of Churchill's command) and at Princeton (J. C. Tappan's and L. C. Gause's Brigades of Churchill's Division). Additionally, Marmaduke's and Fagan's Cavalry Divisions were also at Princeton, awaiting the arrival of General Price and the trains of the corps, which arrived on August 29. On August 30, Price's Cavalry Corps departed Princeton, continuing northward toward Missouri. Note: Price's 1864 Missouri Raid will be covered in detail in the next chapter. *O.R.*, vol. 41, pt. 1:754; *O.R.*, vol. 41, pt. 2:1086; *O.R.*, vol. 41, pt. 3:904; J. T. Alexander, Letters (July 10 & 18, 1864); Castel, *Sterling Price*, 203, 206; Crute, *Confederate Staff Officers*, 177; Gaughan, Letter (August 1, 1864, should read September 1, 1864) 243–244; Arthur Roy Kirkpatrick, "Missouri Secessionist Government, 1861–1865," *Missouri Historical Review* 14 (October 1950): 136–137; Henry C. Luttrell, "Price's Great Raid," *Missouri Republican*, February 27, 1887; Parks, 433; Pitcock & Gurley, 212–213; Cocker, 8; Stewart Sifakis, *Who Was Who in the Confederacy: A Comprehensive, Illustrated Biographical Reference to More Than 1,000 of the Principal Confederacy Participants in the Civil War* (New York, 1988), 241–242, hereafter cited as Sifakis, *Who Was Who in the Confederacy*; Wallace Diary, August 8, 1864.

25. Even as Price's Corps headed north, Little Rock, Arkansas, was rife with rumors of an impending attack or a "grand movement" of some type. Refugees, prisoners, and scouts reported that the target was Little Rock, others that it was Pine Bluff and still others stated that it was Missouri. General Frederick Steele, commanding in Arkansas, was "inclined to think that there may be some humbug about the grand movement." Still, Steele took precautions, ordered the strengthening of Little Rock defenses, reinforced his pickets, made plans against an attack on Little Rock, and ordered out scouts to determine what Price was doing. From Pine Bluff, General Powell Clayton ordered out a patrol on August 31 to the Saline River, that came within 13 miles of Churchill's camp at Princeton on September 2, thus precipitating a rebel response. General J. C. Tappan, commanding Churchill's Division, ordered his pickets to "hold themselves prepared for an attack." Parsons in turn, was informed that the picket at Mt. Elba was attacked, causing him to send Craven's "1st Infantry Regiment Consolidated, Trans-Mississippi Department" to protect Warren, while another force was detailed for Cornishe's Ferry which crossed the Saline River near Harrison, Arkansas. Parsons's and Tappan's commands never made any appreciable contact with the Federal force, making the Unionist scout a mere nuisance. By the time the Federal scout had returned to Pine Bluff, General Clayton reported, "All quiet here. No news from the enemy, except that there are none this side of the Saline." However, it appears that Clayton's scout failed to check the Monticello area, where Parsons's 2nd Brigade was located with A. T. Hawthorn's and T. Dockery's Arkansas Brigades. Back at Little Rock, General Steele ordered out his scouts to Benton on September 3, where they discovered the presence of Price's force. As Little Rock was lightly defended, with the bulk of his command chasing after Joe Shelby, Steele ordered the pursuit of Shelby halted, and the troops returned to Little Rock. Additionally, Steele requested reinforcements from General Canby, believing that Little Rock was the target of the rebel movement. The Confederates, for their part, were using their infantry movements as a ruse to hold Steele in place at Little Rock until Price crossed the Arkansas River. *O.R.*, vol. 41, pt. 2:936–937; *O.R.*,

Col. [Jordan E.] Cravens with his regiment of infantry, 223 strong, to occupy Warren, where we stored a large quantity of corn, and also to hold Cornishe's ferry nearby.[26]

On the 7th there was excitement in camp caused by the reported presence of a heavy force of the enemy's cavalry. Gen. Parsons had the infantry at once in line—he had no cavalry—while he with his staff rode in the front. On the 10th the enemy presented himself, received a few volleys from the infantry, and retired.[27]

---

vol. 41, pt. 3:43–44, 905, 907; Castro, 77–78; Gaughan, 244; Hoskin Diary, September 1, 1864; Kerby, 333; Stewart Sifakis, *Compendium of the Confederate Armies. Florida and Arkansas* (New York, 1992), 106–107, hereafter cited as Sifakis, *Arkansas*; Quesenberry Diary, September 2, 1864; William E. Whitsett Letter (July 13, 1900), http://gen.1starnet.com/civilwar/whitsett.htm, hereafter cited as Whitsett Letter.

26. Jordan Edgar Cravens was born on November 7, 1830, in Fredericktown, Missouri. He later moved to Logan Country, Arkansas, and attended the Cane Hill Academy in northwest Arkansas. From Cane Hill Cravens joined the California gold rush (1850–1851), then returned to Arkansas, where he became a lawyer in Clarksville, Johnson County. Cravens subsequently served as an Arkansas State Representative (1860–1861). At the beginning of the war, Cravens was serving as a member of Governor Henry Rector's staff and by November 1861 was the acting adjutant, 3rd Brigade, 1st Division, Arkansas Militia. He was a volunteer at the Battle of Wilson's Creek, where he was wounded. On November 18, 1861, Cravens joined Company C (Harrell has it as Company G), 17th Arkansas Infantry as a private and was elected major of the unit, from the ranks, on April 24, 1862, following the death of Major Cornelius Lawrence. With the consolidation of the 17th and the 9th/14th Arkansas Infantries, on May 15, 1862, Cravens was elected colonel of what became the 21st Arkansas Infantry. The unit served east of the Mississippi River and was captured at Vicksburg on July 4, 1863, while Cravens himself was captured at Big Black River Bridge on May 17. Cravens was sent to Johnson's Island Prison, then was exchanged in March 1864. He later rejoined his newly-created unit, the Arkansas 1st Infantry Regiment Consolidated, Trans-Mississippi, which was organized in January 1864 by the consolidation of four Arkansas regiments, including the 21st. Following the war, Cravens returned to Clarksville, was active in reorganizing the Democratic Party, then became a judge, state senator, and later a U.S. Senator. He died at Ft. Smith on April 8, 1914, and was buried at his hometown cemetery. *O.R.S.*, pt. 2, vol. 2:514, 598–600, 649–654; *O.R.S.*, pt. 3, vol. 1:493–494; Allardice, *Confederate Colonels*, 113; Harrell, *Arkansas, Confederate Military History*, 316–317; Carl H. Moneyhon, *The Impact of the Civil War and Reconstruction on Arkansas: Persistence In the Midst of Ruin* (Baton Rouge, LA, 1994), 246–247; Sifakis, *Arkansas*, 69, 106.

27. From September 6–9, General Steele still believed that Price was intent on taking Little Rock, despite reports that he was headed to Missouri. Steele believed that the rebel prisoners "always report something that they are not going to do," though he did concede that there were "some strong arguments in favor of ...[the] supposition," that Missouri was Price's target. Even while Steele pondered Price's intentions, reinforcements began arriving in Steele's area from Memphis and the Department of the Gulf, thus securing Little Rock. By September 7, Steele had received Clayton's report of no rebel troops on the east side of the Saline River. However, other reports had rebel infantry "moving toward Princeton," which prompted Steele to query Clayton on September 8 as to "any rebel troops at Monticello." On September 9 Clayton ordered a 390-man patrol, under Colonel Albert Erskine to scout the area from Mt. Elba to Monticello. General Parsons was alerted to Erskine's presence on the evening of September 9, with orders issued to the command before "tattoo." At 1:00 a.m., on September 10, Parsons had his troops in line of battle ready to receive the bluecoats. "All was in readiness at the dawn of day," recorded William Hoskin of Lesueur's Battery. "After sunrise the enemy drove our pickets," Hoskin continued, "some firing took place" and "after a fiew [sic] rounds it ceased." Having no cavalry, Parsons's boys remained in line until 11:00 a.m., at which time Texas cavalry arrived and went in pursuit of the Federals, while the in-

That evening some 500 Texas cavalry, under Col. [R. P.] Crump, reached us and pursued the retreating enemy.[28]

Gen. Parsons ordered in the whole of Gen. [John A.] Wharton's cavalry, commanded by Col. [Walter P.] Lane, and sent them forward to occupy Bayou Bartholomew and operate against the enemy as circumstances directed.[29] On the

fantry returned to their camps. *O.R.*, vol. 41, pt. 1:753–755; *O.R.*, vol. 41, pt. 3:78–79, 82, 89–90, 103; April Goff and John Tarbell, eds., *Traveled Through a Fine Country: The Journal of Captain Henry Brockman Company K, 10th Missouri Volunteer Infantry, C.S.A.* (Little Rock, AR, 2011), 52, hereafter cited as Goff & Tarbell; Hoskin Diary, September 9–10, 1864; Quesenberry Diary, September 10, 1864; Dick Titterington, *A Day Late and a Dollar Short: The Fate of A. J. Smith's 16th Army Corps during Price's 1864 Missouri Raid* (Oakland Park, KS, 2014), 27, hereafter cited as Titterington.

28. Having no cavalry present, Parsons's men remained in line until the arrival of R. P. Crump at 11:00 a.m. at the head of two regiments (one regiment according to the *O.R.*) and immediately took up the pursuit of the Union scouts. *O.R.*, vol. 41, pt. 1:756; *O.R.*, vol. 41, pt. 3:926; Hoskin Diary, September 10, 1864.

R. P. Crump was born in January 1824, in Powhatan, Virginia, moved to Texas in 1842, eventually settling in Jefferson. At the beginning of the Civil War he joined the 1st Texas Cavalry Battalion and led his battalion at the Battle of Pea Ridge (Elkhorn Tavern), in March 1862. Crump returned to Texas in May 1862, helped raise the 1st Texas Partisan Cavalry Regiment, with Walter P. Lane being appointed lieutenant colonel. He fought at Prairie Grove and in the Red River Campaign. After the war Crump returned to Jefferson, Texas, where he was arrested for hanging the brother of a Unionist Texas judge during the war. Crump later escaped from prison, joined the "Knights of the Rising Sun," and was again arrested for killing a former Union officer. He was tried, and found not guilty. Freed from prison, an ill Crump never recovered, dying in October 1869. See Appendix B for a complete biography. *O.R.*, vol. 22, pt. 1:155–156; *O.R.*, vol. 22, pt. 2:774–775; *O.R.*, vol. 34, pt. 1:618; Allardice, *Confederate Colonels*, 117; *Confederate Women of Arkansas*, 85–86; "From North-West Arkansas and Missouri," *The Weekly Dallas Herald* (Dallas, TX), February 4, 1863; Walter P. Lane, *Adventures and Recollections of General Walter P. Lane, A San Jacinto Veteran Containing Sketches of the Texan, Mexican and Late Wars with Several Indian Fights Thrown In* (Marshall, TX, 1928), 105, hereafter cited as Lane; Richard B. McCaslin, *Tainted Breeze: The Great Hanging at Gainsville, Texas 1862* (Baton Rouge, 1994), 183, hereafter cited as McCaslin; Wooster, *Lone Star Regiments*, 109, 315.

29. Wharton's Texas Cavalry consisted of three brigades commanded as follows: 1st Brigade, Colonel William H. Parsons (Parsons was replaced by General William Steele in October 1864); 2nd Brigade (Lane's Brigade), Lieutenant Colonel R. P. Crump; 3rd Brigade, Colonel William Hardemen. *O.R.*, vol. 41, pt. 3:969, 998; Anne J. Bailey, *Between the Enemy and Texas: Parsons's Texas Cavalry in the Civil War* (Fort Worth, TX, 1989), 198, hereafter cited as Bailey, *Between the Enemy and Texas*.

John A. Wharton was born near Nashville, Tennessee, on July 3, 1828, was educated in Texas and South Carolina, and became a lawyer. At the beginning of the Civil War, he joined the Confederate Service on September 7, 1861, as a captain commanding Company B, 8th Texas Cavalry. Wharton served principally east of the Mississippi River He was promoted to colonel, effective January 9, 1862, following the death of Thomas S. Lubbock, commanding the 8th Cavalry. On November 18, 1862, Wharton was promoted to brigadier general and to major general on November 10, 1863. He was transferred to the Trans-Mississippi for health reasons on February 4, 1864. Wharton commanded a cavalry unit until he was shot and killed in a duel on April 6, 1865. See Appendix B for a complete biography. *O.R.*, vol. 34, pt. 2:943; *O.R.S.*, pt. 2, vol. 67:785, 790; Allardice, *Confederate Colonels*, 246; Boatner, 909; Faust, 817–818; "Maj. Gen. Jno. A. Wharton," *Houston Daily Telegraph*, June 13, 1864.

Walter Payne Lane was born in Ireland on February 18, 1817, emigrated to the United States in 1821, and came to Texas in March 1836. He fought in the War for Texas Independence, the

11th the enemy turned his course in the direction of Mt. Elba, Col. Crump still to pursue.[30] Gen. Parsons sent forward Col. [Isham R.] Chisum with his regiment of cavalry direct to Mt. Elba, to cooperate with Col. Crump.[31] Col. [W. H.] Parsons of Texas with his regiment he forwarded to Red Fork on the Arkansas River to watch the enemy between South Bend and Cypress Bend on the Mississippi.[32] For

Mexican War, and was living in Marshall at the beginning of the Civil War. He was elected lieutenant colonel of the 3rd Texas Cavalry Regiment and fought at the Battles of Wilson's Creek, Chustenahlah, Indian Territory (December 9, 1861), and Pea Ridge. In mid-1862 Lane organized the 1st Texas Partisan Cavalry Regiment and led the unit in the West Louisiana Campaign of 1863. On April 8, 1864, he was severely wounded at Mansfield, Louisiana. On March 17, 1865, Lane was confirmed as a brigadier general. A supporter wrote of him: "He is impetuous in the charge, and a terror to his enemy, still his undaunted courage is controlled by discretion and penetrating forethought, ...unpretending and modest as he is brave and patriotic." Following the war Lane returned to Texas and spent his remaining years writing his memoirs and pursuing a mercantile business. He died, having never married, on January 28, 1892, and was buried in his hometown of Marshall. *O.R.*, vol. 26, 1:218; *O.R.*, vol. 34, 1:618; Boatner, 471; "Col. W. P. Lane," *The Shreveport Weekly News* (Shreveport, LA), May 31, 1864; Lane, 7, 9, 124, 146; Harold B. Simpson, *Texas in the War 1861–1865* (Hillsboro, TX, 1965), 85–86, hereafter cited as Simpson; Warner, *Generals in Gray*, 173–174.

30. On the evening of September 9 the Federal force camped 14 miles from Monticello. The following morning Colonel Erskine divided his command, sending a small portion to Mt. Elba, while the main body moved on Monticello. After making contact with Parsons's pickets on the 10th, Erskine withdrew, heading back toward Pine Bluff, having captured 3 prisoners. The Confederates under Colonel Crump overtook Erskine's Federals on September 11, attacking them in the rear and flanks. The 13th Illinois Cavalry, with a 12-lb mountain howitzer, initially broke in confusion, but were rallied by Lieutenant Colonel T. W. Scudder of the 5th Kansas Cavalry, who arrived with a detachment of his regiment from the Mt. Elba area and stabilized the situation. A "severe contest" ensued over the howitzer, which had been abandoned by its crew, but for a lone sergeant. Scudder managed to save the artillery piece, following the timely arrival of Company G, 5th Kansas, under Lieutenant Edwin W. Jenkins. For the next 4–5 miles the Federals fought a running battle, finally breaking contact about 6 miles from Pine Bluff. Overall the expedition had cost the Federals 2 killed, 5 wounded, with 13 missing (7 of whom were wounded); one Confederate report put the Federal losses at 6 killed, 12 wounded with 4 prisoners), while Crump lost 3 men wounded. *O.R.*, vol. 41, pt. 1: 754–756; Burke, 118; Hoskin Diary, September 11, 1864.

31. Isham Russel Chisum was born on August 5, 1818, and moved to Texas in 1837, where he settled in Rusk County. A planter who owned eight slaves, Chisum was living in Rockwell, Kaufman County, Texas, when he was appointed a delegate to the Texas Secession Convention. At the beginning of the Civil War, Chisum joined Company F, 3rd Texas Cavalry, and was elected captain on June 13, 1861. On May 20, 1862, he resigned while in Mississippi (*O.R.S.* says he was dropped on May 2, 1862). Returning to Texas, Chisum joined Company K, 2nd Texas Partisan Cavalry Regiment and in November 1862, was elected lieutenant colonel of the command. On December 14, 1863, he was promoted to colonel following the resignation of B. W. Stone. Chisum fought at Chustenahlah, Indian Territory, and led his regiment during the Red River Expedition (April–May 1864). Following the war, Chisum returned home, where in addition to farming he became a tanner and rancher. He died in February 1884, in Bandera County, Texas, where he was living at the time. *O.R.S.*, pt. 2, vol. 67.703, 711; *O.R.S.*, pt. 2, vol. 68:354, 356; Allardice, *Confederate Colonels*, 97; Douglas John Cater, *As It Was: Reminiscences of a Soldier of the Third Texas Cavalry and the Nineteenth Louisiana Infantry* (Austin, TX, 1990), 88; Douglas Hale, *The Third Texas Cavalry in the Civil War* (Norman, OK, 1993), 29; Roberts, *Texas, Confederate Military History*, 36; Simpson, 175; Wooster, *Lone Star Regiments*, 71, 176, 180.

32. William H. Parsons was born on April 23, 1826, near Elizabeth, New Jersey, moved to Montgomery, Alabama, at an early age, and later attended Emory College, near Atlanta, Georgia, while

all these movements the general had reliable information of the presence of part of the enemy's Sixteenth Army Corps on the Mississippi, and other reinforcements for Gen. Steele.[33]

[James H. McNamara]

* * * * * * *

Item: The continuing history of Company A, Tenth Missouri Infantry in 1864-1865, following the Battle of Jenkins' Ferry (April 30, 1864) to the end of the war, by James L. Grubbs, Company A, 10th Missouri Infantry.[34] Published: January 9, 1886.

---

in his teens. With the beginning of the Mexican War, Parsons left school in the 1844 "midterm" and went to Texas to join Zachary Taylor's army. Following the war he settled near Tyler, married in 1851, and by the time of the Civil War was living in Waco, where he edited a newspaper. Appointed a colonel by the governor of Texas on June 10, 1861, Parsons raised what became the 12th Texas Cavalry Regiment, which he led or was part of his brigade throughout the war. As the colonel of the 12th, B. P. Gallaway wrote that "no commander west of the Mississippi could deliver more fiery, colorful and enthusiastic speeches from the saddle," than William H. Parsons. Gallaway further dubbed Parsons "the western Confederacy's answer to Napoleon Bonaparte." The men that Parsons led were duly impressed with their commander, who primarily saw action in Arkansas in 1862, operated along the Mississippi River in 1863, and participated in the Red River Campaign of 1864. Following the war Parsons moved briefly to British Honduras, but later returned to Texas. As a civilian Parsons promoted railroads, edited yet another newspaper, joined the Republican Party, and was elected to the Texas Senate (1870–1871). The 1880s–1890s found Parsons living in either New York or Baltimore. Toward the end of his life Parsons moved to Chicago, Illinois, to live with his son, where he died on October 2, 1907. For a complete biography see Appendix B. Allardice, *Confederate Colonels*, 299; Bruce S. Allardice, *More Generals In Gray* (Baton Rouge, LA, 1995), 177–179, hereafter cited as Allardice, *More Generals In Gray*; Bailey, *Between the Enemy and Texas*, 5–7; B. P. Gallaway, *The Ragged Rebel: A Common Soldier in W. H. Parsons's Texas Cavalry 1861–1865* (Austin, TX, 1988), 20–21, hereafter cited as Gallaway; Ralph A. Wooster, *Lone Star Generals In Gray* (Austin, TX, 2000), 245, hereafter cited as Wooster, *Lone Star Generals*.

33. With Joe Shelby's increased activity in northeast Arkansas and Sterling Price moving northward, Frederick Steele requested reinforcements to prevent the fall of Little Rock. Joseph A. Mower's 1st Division, 16th Corps, departed Memphis and arrived at St. Charles, Arkansas, on September 5 (the portion of the 16th Corps under A. J. Smith, was known as the Right Wing of the corps, of which Mower was part; Smith's other division, the 3rd, was at Cairo, Illinois, and was eventually ordered to St. Louis). From Memphis, General C. C. Washburn crossed Edward Winslow's 1,900-man cavalry division on September 2, to assist General Steele. On September 6, Mower and Winslow were ordered to DeValls Bluff and eventually to Brownsville, where Steele formed a force, under Mower, to stop Price and Shelby from mounting their expedition. By September 12 Mower and Winslow were located at Brownsville awaiting necessary supplies before starting their expedition against Price and Shelby. At the head of the White River another force under General E. S. Dennis awaited orders. On September 18 Mower's command finally started in pursuit of Price; however, Price was also on the move the following day, having a 130-mile head start over Mower's troops. Mower's infantry never caught Price's force and eventually gave up the pursuit, being ordered back East on October 30. *O.R.*, vol. 41, pt. 3: 61–62, 78, 103, 162; Titterington, 8, 27, 37–39, 52, 83–84.

34. James L. S. Grubbs of Lewis County, Missouri, initially joined Company A, 1st. Cavalry Regiment, 2nd Division, MSG at the beginning of the Civil War. He then enlisted in Company A, 10th Missouri Infantry (CSA) on September 1, 1862, at Camp Mitchell, Monroe County, Arkansas.

The Last Company to Surrender...

After the battle [of Jenkins' Ferry we fell back to Princeton, where we

Established Our Hospital.

Co. A was then detailed to take charge of it, to care for the wounded and bury the dead, which we did and stayed there until ordered to join our regiment, when we immediately moved south to Three Creeks, Ark., where we went into camp and remained quite a while.[35] We found the people in this vicinity of Three Creeks more hospitable than many we had ever met. The Joneses and Moores will never be forgotten by many of our soldiers. While in this camp there was a great religious revival among the soldiers. Men who had been very wild and reckless suddenly became very religious. Of evening after dress parade they would repair to some secluded spot and there offer their devotion to Almighty God, and never after that did we have so much recklessness or games among our men.[36]

We then went from Three Creeks to Monticello in Drew County. While at Monticello one of our men conceived the idea of raising some flour that was stowed away in a large store-room. As there was a cellar under the house and a guard in the first story, our men took a two-inch auger and bored through the floor from the cellar, expecting to strike a bag of flour, but instead of flour he happened to bore into the guard's back as he was lying down to take a nap. It is needless to say that he got up. The guard helloed to him to stop, he had struck the wrong sack. Those little incidents are amusing to me when I recall them, therefore, I cannot forbear to mention a few.

(Camp Mitchell was about 22 miles southeast of Clarendon, near the White River and located on the farm of a "General Mitchell."). Grubbs survived the war and was paroled at Camp Allen in Shreveport on June 8, 1865. He returned to Missouri and was living in Canton, Lewis County, in 1906. Wade Ankesheiln, *The Last Guardsmen* (Independence, MO, 2008), 92, hereafter cited as Ankesheiln, *Last Guardsmen*; Banasik, *Missouri Brothers in Gray*, 35; National Archives, Record Group M322 (roll no. 152), Confederate Compiled Service Records, 10th Missouri Infantry; Schnetzer, *Men of the Tenth*, 7; Schnetzer, *More Forgotten Men*, 99.

35. The 10th Missouri Infantry (CSA) went into camp two miles east of Three Creek Store, Union County, Arkansas, on May 24, 1864. They remained in camp until August 19, when they marched northward as part of the Confederate feint to hold Steele in place while General Price crossed the Arkansas River. Banasik, *Serving With Honor*, 164; Gaughan, Letter (August 1, 1864; should read September 1, 1864) 243–244; Goff & Tarbell, 49, 51; Hoskin Diary, May 24, 1864; Miller, 56; Quesenberry Diary, May 24, 1864; Wallace Diary, August 8, 1864.

36. According to William R. Barney, "religion played a central role in forging separate sectional identities in the generation that fought the Civil War," and revivals were an integral part of that role. "Revival" was a popular term in that era. It signified a new and deep interest in religion—"an awaking following a period of indifference to spiritual matters." During the Civil War there were several religious revivals that occurred in the Confederate Army and all occurred during periods of military inactivity. Overall it was estimated by one Confederate chaplain "that 150,000 Confederate soldiers made professions of faith during the war." See Appendix C for extended comments on religious revival in the Trans-Mississippi in 1864. William L. Barney, *The Oxford Encyclopedia of the Civil War* (New York, 2001), 263, hereafter cited as Barney; Dougherty, 234–235; Robertson, 186.

From Monticello we went back to Camden, arriving there about November 1, 1864, and we remained there until about the 1st of April, 1865.[37] Many incidents of note happened while there, of which I will mention the shooting of Capt. [John] Quinn [Guynes] of the Texas Army for encouraging desertion among his men.[38] Also two or three privates were shot while there.[39] During the winter quite a few

---

37. Parsons's Division, less the 1st Brigade, remained in the Monticello area from August 25 to October 5. While at Monticello, Parsons's command and Churchill's Division (McNair's or Dockery's and Hawthorn's Brigades) were joined by Walker's and Polignac's Divisions on September 20. Upon arrival at Monticello, General John H. Forney, commanding Walker's old Texas Division, assumed command of the area from General M. M. Parsons. On September 26, a "Grand Review" of the troops was held by General Magruder. The troops began deploying into three lines at 6:00 a.m. for the review; the Texas Division occupied the first line; Churchill and Parsons occupied the second line; and Polignac's Division constituted the third line. When formed, the review consisted of 8 infantry brigades, numbering 9–10,000 troops, with 36 pieces of artillery. After the division had formed, General Magruder inspected the troops while the band played Dixie. Next the troops passed in review followed by a half hour drill conducted by General Magruder. As to the review, a member of the 10th Missouri recorded: "It was the largest that I ever saw and more artillery than usual on such occasions." After the Grand Review the troops returned to their camp, where they remained until ordered to Camden. By mid-October the four infantry divisions, including Parsons's 1st Brigade lately returned from Washington, Arkansas, were concentrated at Camden (the 1st Brigade arrived on September 18, while Parsons's 2nd Brigade arrived on October 14). Active campaigning was at an end for the infantry of the Trans-Mississippi, and rumors, news, and camp life constituted the daily routine for the foot-soldiers. There would be other marches to winter camp or readjusting their positions to meet the perceived conditions for the war, but for all intents and purposes the infantry war was over for the grayclads west of the Mississippi River. Parsons's 2nd Brigade (Burns's) left winter camp on March 25, 1865, arriving at Shreveport on April 2 after a tedious, muddy march. Burns's Brigade was followed by the 1st Brigade on April 5, 1865, arriving at Shreveport on April 7. There, at Shreveport, Parsons's Division sat until the surrender. *O.R.*, vol. 41, pt. 3:943–944; Banasik, *Serving With Honor*, 182–183, 214; Blessington, 277–278; Goff & Tarbell, 52–53, 58; Hoskin Diary, September 20, 26 and October 14, 1864; Wallace Diary, September 26, 1864.

38. John Guynes was born about 1825. He was a farmer by profession, a Mexican War veteran, and lived in Big Sandy, Polk County, Texas, at the beginning of the Civil War. On March 10, 1862, Guynes enlisted in the Jeff Davis Guards (Company B, 5th Texas Infantry Battalion), for which he received a $100 dollar bounty, and was subsequently elected 2nd lieutenant on March 10, 1862. A popular man within his unit, Guynes was elected captain of his company on June 30, 1862, when the unit became Company F, 22nd Texas Infantry. The unit continued to operate in the Trans-Mississippi as part of Walker's Texas Division. Guynes was "much admired by his men, and well liked by the officers of his brigade." Following impending orders to move to the east side of the Mississippi River, Guynes urged his men to desert if so ordered. He was subsequently court-martialed and executed on October 15, 1864. See Appendix C for an extended comment on Guynes execution. *O.R.S.*, pt. 2, vol. 81:50, 56; Blessington, 279–280; Goff & Tarbell, 54; Jon Harrison, ed., "The Confederate Letters of John Simmons," *The Chronicles of Smith County, Texas* 14 (Summer 1975), 44, 56, hereafter cited as Harrison; Hoskin Diary, October 15, 1864; Kerby, 324–328; L. Davis Norris, ed., *With the 18th Texas Infantry: The Autobiography of Wilburn Hill King* (Hillsboro, TX, 1996), 81, hereafter cited as Norris; Jerry Thompson, ed., *Tejanos In Gray: The Civil War Letters of Captains Joseph Rafael de la Garza & Manuel Yturri* (College Station, TX, 2011), 59–60, 114–115, hereafter cited as Thompson, *Tejanos In Gray*; Turnbo, 378–379.

39. Silas Turnbo of the 27th Arkansas Infantry was stationed at Camden, where his regiment served as the provost guard of the city. In August 1864 Turnbo recorded the execution of three soldiers, all for desertion—an offense Turnbo called "so common among the troops that the privates hardly looked upon it as a crime." All three were shot near the river, two on one day and the third on an-

men were furloughed.⁴⁰ We then went from Camden to near Shreveport, La. It was while at this camp we received the news of the assassination of President Lincoln.⁴¹ From there we moved a short distance south of Shreveport where we remained until the terms of the surrender were agreed upon. While at this camp nearly all the men who had been captured at Helena returned.⁴² As soon as it became known that we were compelled to surrender our men suddenly became demoralized, and all was excitement.⁴³ Gen. Parsons then ordered Co. A to take

---

other, while seated on their coffins. The dead were subsequently "hauled away to where…graves had been prepared for their bodies." Turnbo, 377–378.

40. On November 26, 1864, orders reached Parsons's Division, from General Magruder authorizing the furlough of 12 percent of the men at a time. A policy that James T. Wallace called "a liberal indulgence. One which we are able to appreciate. It being almost the first of the kind." Banasik, *Serving With Honor*, 194; Goff & Tarbell, 56; Wallace Diary, November 25, 1864.

41. President Lincoln was shot by John Wilkes Booth on April 14, 1865, at Ford's Theater. Word of Lincoln's assassination reached the troops in the Trans-Mississippi during the last week of April. Little rejoicing took place at the news of Lincoln's death; in fact, the opposite seemed to be the case, as recalled by Dr. Robert Christie of the 10th Missouri Infantry. Christie wrote: "I well remember it created a feeling of dread for the time. I have never heard any one express any word of approval of the assassination. As the details were given us later, I think nearly all sensible Confederates saw, that so far from helping our cause, it could only be an injury, and as we had time to consider the fate of Lincoln, a sympathy was felt amongst us for him." And Silas Turnbo of the 27th Arkansas supported Christie's comments, recording: "We were sorry to hear of the assassination of President Lincoln and were convinced that none of the Confederate soldiers had anything to do with it. Still we were satisfied the crime would be laid to the people of the South and the true and loyal people would suffer on account of the black deed of some fanatic." In Joe Shelby's Missouri Cavalry Division, "some of the men foolishly cheered." However, Shelby quieted his command, saying: "this is the heaviest blow yet dealt us. Lincoln's slaughter was the act of a mad man. If he had lived he would have been just and generous to the South." Banasik, *Serving With Honor*, 218; Boatner, 484; Christie Memoir, 67; Hoskin Diary, April 23, 1864; Pitcock & Gurley, 295–296; Quesenberry Diary, April 24, 1864; Thomas Reid, *Spartan Band Burnett's 13th Texas Cavalry in the Civil War* (Denton, TX, 2005), 181; Quoted in Sellmeyer, 278; Turnbo, 410.

42. The cartel for the exchange of the Helena, Arkansas, POW's was agreed to by General E. Kirby Smith and General Frederick Steele on July 28, 1864; however, any deal had to be approved by the U.S. War Department. By October 1864, the cartel had still not been approved, as General U.S. Grant had prohibited further exchanges. Following a period negotiations, Federal authorities agreed to honor all cartels entered into prior to General Grant's prohibition. On December 30, 1864, the Office of Commissary-General of Prisoners issued Special Orders No. 49, which directed that the exchange proceed. Colonel Charles C. Dwight, the Federal Agent for Exchange, received notice of the pending operation on January 17, 1865, 18 days after the Special Order was issued. The exchange finally took place the first week of February 1865, after which the various Confederates returned to Parsons's Missouri Division, where they arrived during the second week of February 1865. *O.R.*, Series 2, vol. 7:1055–1056, 1232-1233, 1298; *O.R.*, Series 2, vol. 8:15, 85, 93, 157; Banasik, *Serving With Honor*, 204–205.

43. Negotiations for surrender of the Trans-Mississippi Department began on April 19, when General John Pope, commander of the Military Division of Missouri, sent a letter to E. K. Smith, regarding the surrender of Generals Robert Lee and Joseph Johnston in the East. Lieutenant Colonel John T. Sprague, Pope's Chief of Staff, conveyed the message to General Smith, who received the communication on May 8. Smith then called a conference of the various department governors, whom he met with at Marshall, Texas, the following day to discuss the surrender. On May 13, Smith sent his reply to the surrender terms, attempting to procure better treatment than either Lee or Johnston had received. However, in the end, Smith left the surrender of the department in the hands of his

charge of the mules and wagons and hold then until the proper authorities came to take charge of them, which we did, and performed camp duties until relieved by Federal soldiers. Consequently Co. A was the last company to surrender of the so-called "Lost Cause."[44] During all three years Co. A never had a man in the guardhouse, nor one to desert, and seldom a cross word among them. All seemed to get along like a well regulated family. And since the war many of them have filled honorable positions in life.

Jas. L. Grubbs,
Late of Co. A, Tenth Regiment, Parsons's Brigade.

* * * * * * *

Item: Introduction to the Confederate Exodus to Mexico and the murder of General Mosby M. Parsons.

With the Civil War coming to an end, many Southerners who supported the Confederacy, "felt they no longer had a homeland. The burgeoning lands of the South were burned out, dead, and uninviting. Her cities, desolated by shellfire, did not seem places in which to start a new future." Thousands left the South and headed to countries like Canada, England, Cuba, Brazil, and, the most popular destination, Mexico. By the time the emigration ended in mid-1866, an estimated 10–20,000 had departed the southern states and made their homes abroad. Of those who left, the largest organized group followed General Joseph O. Shelby,

---

Chief of Staff, General Simon Buckner, who with General Sterling Price and General Joseph L. Brent, journeyed to New Orleans on May 20 to negotiate the surrender. On May 26, 1865, Buckner's party reached an agreement, with General Peter J. Osterhaus, representing General E. R. S. Cabby, at New Orleans; all subject to General Smith's approval. The terms were the same as those accepted by the other Confederate commanders (See Appendix A for a copy of the cartel that the Confederate authorities accepted.). Even while negotiations were proceeding, the Trans-Mississippi Department was quickly disintegrating, with whole companies, regiments and even brigades disbanding. On June 1, 1865 (Castel has the date as June 2), Price met with the Missouri troops and announced the surrender of the department. The following day, Smith reviewed and accepted the surrender document, thus ending the Civil War. *O.R.*, vol. 48, pt. 1:186–194; Banasik, *Serving With Honor*, 223; Castel, *Sterling Price*, 271–272; Faust, 760; Kerby, 415–418, 422–424; Sellmeyer, 280; Wallace Diary, May 27, 1865.

44. With the surrender of the Trans-Mississippi Department, the 10th Missouri Infantry cut up their regimental flag "in small pieces, and in that way divided it amongst the soldiers of the 10th." With their flag gone, Company A, 10th Missouri, left Shreveport, bound for transport back to Missouri. En route for the Shreveport wharf, they were met by one of their regimental surgeons, Robert J. Christie, who noted of the "Last Company to Surrender" in the Shreveport area:

> I met Company A marching down the principal street, to take the boat for home; in proper form, with cadence step, through force of habit, I suppose, with the regularity of veterans. How different it was! Before, they marched proudly through the same street, to inspiring music, with arms in their hands; now with empty but willing hands, to take hold of the implements of civil life.

Christie Memoir, 69; Charles W. Logan, "Roster and Battles of Company A, 10th Missouri Confederate States Infantry," Western Historical Collection, State Historical Society of Missouri; Schnetzer, *Men of the Tenth*, 2.

whom Andre Rolle branded "the most spectacular of the Confederate leaders who escaped to Mexico."[45]

On June 1, 1865, even as General Price was addressing his troops for the last time following the surrender, similar scenes were taking place or had taken place throughout the Trans-Mississippi Department. Most of the troops were directed to Shreveport, there to lay down their arms and sign their paroles. At Corsicana, Texas, General Joseph O. Shelby also addressed his troops about the surrender, reminding them of the "hardships and struggles" that they had endured. Unlike most of his contemporaries, Shelby decided to accept exile in lieu of surrender or parole.[46]

Assembling his command on June 1, Shelby divided his division into three lines; those who wished to go to Mexico with him were asked to take three steps forward to the first line, while the other two lines contained men who would accept parole and those who would not, but would remain in the United States. Those who desired parole were placed under Major George P. Gordon's command and departed Corsicana about June 11. Prior to leaving Corsicana, the men of Shelby's escort

> formed a circle around the loved Shelby and a two gallon jug of Brisbane whiskey took the rounds, of the circle, each fellow sitting in his saddle and taking hereby the word of mouth from the brown jug. [W]e all shook hands, lots were in tears, the Genl. and quite a following pulled out for Mexico.

About 150 men of Shelby's Division elected to join their commander and cross the border south. Thus began one of the last chapters of the Civil War, which became known as "Shelby's Expedition to Mexico."[47]

Chronicled by John N. Edwards, Shelby's Adjutant, Shelby's Expedition to Mexico was published in 1872, and formed the basis of most of the books written on the Confederate Exodus following the Civil War. After a week of preparation, Shelby gave the order to depart for Mexico City on June 9 (W. H. Bradley says June 2). Leading about 150 men of his old division, 150 from other commands,

---

45. Robert L. Kerby put the number of exiles at a mere 2,000, well below other estimates. Kerby, 428; M. M. McAllen, *Maximilian and Carlota: Europe's Last Empire in Mexico* (San Antonio, TX, 2014), 185, hereafter cited as McAllen; Andrew F. Rolle, *The Lost Cause: The Confederate Exodus to Mexico* (Norman, OK, 1965), 4–5, 9, 11, hereafter cited as Rolle.
46. See Appendix A for Shelby's Address to His Division upon Surrender of the Trans-Mississippi Department. "Address of General J. O. Shelby to His Division," Western Historical Manuscript Collection, State Historical Society of Missouri.
47. Anonymous, *5th Missouri Cavalry*, 9; Sam Box, "End of the War–Exiles In Mexico," *Confederate Veteran* 11 (March, 1903), 121–122, hereafter cited as Box; Jennie Edwards, *John N. Edwards Biography, Memoirs, Reminiscences and Recollections and Also A Reprint of Shelby's Expedition to Mexico An Unwritten Leaf of the War* (Kansas City, MO, 1889), 239–241, hereafter cited as Edwards, *John N. Edwards Biography*; Goff & Tarbell, 62; Thomas W. Westlake Memoirs, Watson-Westlake Papers (C186), Western Historical Manuscript Collection, State Historical Society of Missouri, Columbia, Missouri, 130-131, hereafter cited as Westlake Memoirs; Whitsett Letter.

6 wagon-loads of women and children with a small arsenal of assorted weapons, including 4 brass James rifles "captured at Mark's Mill," a herd of 35 cattle, and assorted other supplies, Shelby's exiles struck out for their new home on a journey that would take three months.[48]

Arriving at San Antonio on June 16, Shelby found several ex-generals and politicians waiting to join him on his journey to Mexico, including Generals John B. Clark, Sr., Sterling Price, E. Kirby Smith and John Magruder, with Governors Henry W. Allen (Louisiana), Charles S. Morehead (Kentucky) Pendellton Murrah (Texas), Thomas Reynolds (Missouri), as well as "a number of other politicians and low ranking officers," numbering "about fifty or seventy-five." Among this latter group were Colonel William Broadwell, head of the Trans-Mississippi Department Cotton Bureau and Colonel Thomas L. Snead, the author of the *The Fight for Missouri*.[49]

---

48. The estimates of Shelby's strength vary wildly, with John Edwards recording from 500 to 1,000 men depending on the book. Edwin Davis initially puts Shelby at 500, but raises the number to 1,000 by the time he left San Antonio. Other sources, including Arthur Anthony, put the numbers closer to 300, including those he would pick up on the way. Three ex-Confederates who traveled with the party put the numbers at: 132, Sam Box; 130, S. D. Jackman; and 150, Thomas Westlake. Still another, old-time Confederate estimated the number at 200, while Shelby, in his latter years, would put the number at 600. George Cruzen, a bugler in the 5th Missouri Cavalry puts the number at 500, as does Joseph Pollock of the 12th Missouri Cavalry, while W. H. Bradley of Slayback's Regiment says that Shelby took 302 men from his old brigade. In the end "there was no way of telling, for sure," according to Daniel O'Flaherty, how many men were in Shelby's column, for "the size of the expedition would vary, not from day to day but from hour to hour." Anthony Arthur, *General Jo Shelby's March* (New York, 2010), 65–68, hereafter cited as Arthur; Box, 122; W. H. Bradley, "Shelby's Expedition into Mexico," *Confederate Veteran* 22 (December, 1914), 551, hereafter cited as Bradley, "Shelby's Expedition"; Wm. P. Borland, "General Jo. O. Shelby," *Missouri Historical Review* 7 (October, 1912), 17, hereafter cited as Borland; George Creel, *Rebel at Large: Recollections of Fifty Crowded Years* (New York, 1947), 25, 27, hereafter cited as Creel; Cruzen, 36–37; "Deeds of Gallantry," in Shelby Scrapbook (C3558), Western Historical Manuscript Collection, State historical Society of Missouri; Edwin Adam Davis, *Fallen Guidon: The Saga of Confederate General Jo Shelby's March to Mexico* (College Station, TX, 1995, edition), 31, 53, hereafter cited as Davis, *Fallen Guidon*; John Newman Edwards, *Noted Guerrillas or the Warfare of the Border* (St. Louis, 1877; reprint ed., Dayton, OH, 1976) ii, hereafter cited as Edwards, *Noted Guerrillas*; Edwards, *Shelby and His Men*, 543; Sidney D. Jackman, "A Horror of the Chaparral," *Missouri Republican*, January 23, 1866, hereafter cited as Jackman; R. P. Marshall Letter (January 29, 1912), W. L. Skaggs Collection, Arkansas History Commission, hereafter cited as Marshall Letter; Daniel, O'Flaherty, *General Jo Shelby Undefeated Rebel* (Chapel Hill, NC, 1954; reprint ed., Wilmington, NC, 1984), 234–235, hereafter cited as O'Flaherty; Joseph Pollock, "Shelby's Old Iron Brigade," *Confederate Veteran* 32 (January, 1924), 50; Rolle, 18; Sellmeyer, 281, 283–284; Westlake Memoirs, 130–131.

49. John B. Clark was also an ex-Confederate senator and house member from Missouri at the time of the Confederate exodus, and like most Confederate politicians would have been arrested and imprisoned if caught by Federal authorities. Later, when Clark did return to the United States, "he was arrested, brought to New Orleans and imprisoned...in Fort Jackson, near the city." Governor Murrah would not survive the march, dying of tuberculosis in Monterrey, Mexico, on August 4, 1865. And like Murrah, H. W. Allen would never return to the United States, dying in Mexico City on April 22, 1866 (Arthur said April 11) of a "stomach disorder," though yellow fever was probably the actual cause. In addition to the governors mentioned in San Antonio, ex-governors Thomas O. Moore (Louisiana) and Isham Harris (Tennessee) also fled to Mexico, proceeding Shelby to

On June 18, 1865 (Rolle has the date as June 17), Shelby departed San Antonio, leaving behind the women and children, who were expected to rejoin their men after they had settled in Mexico. Shelby headed to Eagle Pass on the Rio Grande River, where he intended on crossing into Mexico. He reached the river on the 29th (Sam Box has the date as June 25, while W. H. Bradley says July 2) and crossed over on July 1, following negotiations (Thomas Westlake has the negotiations taking "perhaps a week") with the local Liberal Mexican governor for the sale of his excess weapons and stores for $16,000–30,000 dollars in silver and a like amount in "Juarez Script." That same day Shelby famously buried his battle flag in the Rio Grande River, thus ending the last active Confederate force still under arms in the United States.[50]

Though never part of Shelby's party, General M. M. Parsons also headed for Mexico at about the same time. On June 3, 1865, Parsons addressed his division near Shreveport on the surrender, then waited for the arrival of General F. J.

Monterrey. Arthur and Edwards both have Shelby meeting T. C. Hindman at San Antonio, when they arrived on June 16; however, that was an error. According to Hindman, who arrived in Monterrey on June 24 after a three week journey, it wouldn't have been possible for Shelby to have met him in mid-June. Thomas Kremm has Hindman departing San Antonio in "early June," probably June 1–5, and could not have been in the Meager Hotel, awaiting Shelby's arrival. Also mentioned as meeting Shelby at San Antonio was Trusten Polk, ex-Governor of Missouri; however, that was not true. Polk was actually a few days behind Shelby; caught him and made it to Eagle Pass on June 28, a day ahead of Shelby. Arthur, 69–72, 173-174; Banasik, *Tales of the War, Part Four*, 145; Box, 122; Davis, *Fallen Guidon*, 47, 99; Dawson, 140; Editorial Comment on "Henry W. Allen," Mexican times, April 28, 1866; Edwards, *John N. Edwards Biography*, 245–247, 255, 300; Edwards, *Shelby and His Men*, 545; Faust, 518; Thomas W. Kremm, *The Lion of the South General Thomas C. Hindman* (Macon, GA, 1993), 204, 206, hereafter cited as Kremm; O'Flaherty, 237, 242; Trusten Polk Diary (January 1–October 24, 1865), Southern Historical Society Collection, Chapel Hill, NC, June 22 & 28 and July 1, 1865, hereafter cited as Polk Diary; Rolle, 79–80; Sellmeyer, 284; W. D. Vandiver, "Reminiscences of General John B. Clark," *Missouri Historical Review* 20 (January, 1926), 231; Ted R. Worley, "A Letter Written By General Thomas C. Hindman In Mexico," *Arkansas Historical Quarterly* 15 (Winter, 1956), 265–266, hereafter cited as Worley.

50. Thomas C. Hindman, who departed San Antonio about two weeks before Shelby, took a route to Laredo, where he crossed the border and eventually made it to Monterrey. Hindman's route was quite rough, causing him to record that the route from Eagle Pass to Monterrey "would be the best to travel." Kremm, 205; Worley, 367.

According to John Edwards, W. H. Bradley and W. L. Webb, Shelby's battle flag was buried on July 4; however, Sam Box clarified what actually happened: "This took place on the 1st day of July. It has been written as the fourth;" by John Edwards, no doubt, to make the burial more dramatic. Shelby would later identify the real date as July 3. Regardless, the Burial of Shelby's flag was subsequently immortalized in a poem by A. W. Slayback and was presented in Michael E. Banasik, *Confederate "Tales of the War" In the Trans-Mississippi, Part Three: 1863*. (Iowa City, IA, 2012), 200–202, hereafter cited as Banasik, *Tales of the War, Part Three*; Arthur, 70–72, 77, 82–83; Box, 122; Bradley, "Shelby's Expedition," 552; Borland, 17; Creel, 28; Cruzen, 39–40; Davis, *Fallen Guidon*, 99; Edwards, *Shelby and His Men*, 547; Polk Diary, June 22 and July 1, 1865; Rolle, 19; Sellmeyer 353 n. 20; Bettie Shelby, "War Experiences," in *Reminiscences of the Women of Missouri During the Sixties* (Jefferson City, MO, 1911; reprint ed., Dayton, OH, 1988), 105; W. L. Webb, *Battles and Biographies of Missourians or the Civil War Period of Our State* (Kansas City, MO, 1900; reprint ed., Springfield, MO, 1999), 309, hereafter cited as Webb; Westlake Memoirs, 134, 136.

Herron, to officially turn over command of the area to the Federal general. In the end, a bitter Parsons reluctantly accepted parole, writing on June 5, 1865—"My self and Division are prisoners of war but not by my consent or judgement....We were and are the last in the field[;] Arkansas, Texas and Louisiana most shamefully abandoned us when we might have prolonged the struggle for years." Parsons departed Shreveport sometime after June 6, and initially tried for Mexico though Brownsville. Finding the route was overrun with lawlessness, Parsons backtracked to San Antonio and then followed the same route as Shelby, but lagged several days behind.[51]

Parsons's party never caught up with General Shelby, and in the end, without support or escort, they were killed, according to John Edwards, for "being Americans." Andrew Rolle implies that decrees issued by Benito Juarez targeted ex-Confederates, which in turn encouraged Liberal Mexican supporters to eliminate the unwelcome guests from the north. The decree, issued by Juarez stated that any foreigner who was captured was subject to "four years' imprisonment to death for...serving in the forces of Maximilian." According to Rolle, "In time this would bring harassment to a number of Confederates," including General Parsons and party, who would be killed by forces loyal to Juarez.[52]

The two letters that follow provide accounts of what happened to General Parsons and his party, even while Shelby eventually made it to Mexico City. Parsons's band, like many others who reached Monterrey, became disillusioned with the prospects of living in Mexico and decided to return to the United States, even if it meant imprisonment. Many of the early returnees, like Parsons, made for Matamoras, on the gulf coast, across from Brownsville, Texas. The story of Parsons's eventual murder, as portrayed in these two accounts, varies from what pervious authors like Anthony Arthur, Edwin Davis, Andrew Rolle and even John Edwards have recounted. Those differences will be noted where possible.[53]

Michael E. Banasik, Editor/ Author

* * * * * * *

---

51. As the various Confederate parties left Texas they proceeded by assorted routes; Hindman crossed at Laredo; A. W. Terrell crossed at Roma, between Brownsville and Laredo; Shelby's party crossed at Eagle Pass; and Parsons crossed downstream from Eagle Pass. Arthur, 105; Goff & Tarbell, 62; M. M. Parsons's Letter to Parents (June 5, 1865), M. M. Parsons's Papers, Missouri Historical Society, St. Louis; Worley, 365-366.
52. Edwards, *John N. Edwards Biography*, 295; Rolle, 23.
53. Arthur, 106–107; Davis, 100–101; Edwards, *John N. Edwards Biography*, 294-297; Polk Diary, July 9, 1865.

Item: The murder of General Mosby M. Parsons on August 16, 1865, by Colonel Richard H. Musser, 9th Missouri Infantry.[54]
Published: January 23, 1886.

Murder of General Parsons.

Very soon after the surrender of Shreveport, Louisiana, to the federal forces under Gen. Frank Herron, Maj. Gen. Mosby Monroe Parsons, formally of Jefferson City, Mo.,[55] Col. Austin M. Standish, his brother-in-law and the chief of staff, and Aaron H. Conrow, then lately a member of the Confederate Congress, whose

---

54. Richard H. Musser was born on February 6, 1829, in Claysville, Kentucky, moved to Missouri in 1848, and settled in Brunswick, Chariton County. He was admitted to the Missouri Bar in 1854 and was elected a court of appeals judge in 1855. Musser started the Brunswick *Gazette* newspaper and later bought the *Brunswicker*, which he combined with his own to form the *Brunswicker and Gazette*. At the beginning of the Civil War, Musser was appointed judge advocate general of the 3rd Division, MSG, on June 23, 1861. He was at the Battles of Wilson's Creek and Lexington, Missouri, where he served as aide to the division commander. At Pea Ridge, Musser had a horse shot out from under him while rallying some troops. Following Price to Mississippi, Musser spent a short time east of the Mississippi River, returned to the Trans-Mississippi Department and raised a battalion of infantry in late November 1862. His new command was known as Musser's Battalion or the 8th Missouri Infantry Battalion. On January 4, 1863, it united with Clark's and Mitchell's Missouri Infantries, and Ruffner's Missouri Battery to form John B. Clark's Missouri Infantry Brigade. On September 30, 1863, Musser's Battalion and Clark's Infantry were consolidated to form the 9th Missouri Regiment and on January 1, 1864, Musser was appointed the colonel of the regiment. Musser participated in the 1863 Campaign for Little Rock, the Red River Campaign and the Camden Expedition. Following the war he relocated to St. Louis, practiced law in the city until 1877, then returned to Brunswick, where he reestablished himself. He died at St. Joseph, Missouri, on November 24, 1898. *O.R.*, vol. 8:320; *O.R.*, vol. 22, pt. 2:851; *O.R.* vol. 34, pt. 1:603, 812; *O.R.*, vol. 53:423, 439, 824; Allardice, *Confederate Colonels*, 287; Banasik, *Serving With Honor*, 44–45, 93; *History of Howard and Chariton Counties, Missouri, Written and Compiled from the Most Authentic Official and Private Sources Including a History of Its Townships, Towns and Villages* (St. Louis, 1883), 761–764, hereafter cited as *History of Howard and Chariton Counties*; National Archives, Record Group 109, Confederate Muster Rolls, 9th Missouri Infantry; Peterson, et al., 108; Schnetzer, *More Forgotten Men*, 171.

55. Francis Jay Herron was born in Pittsburgh, Pennsylvania, in 1837, and moved to Dubuque, Iowa, in 1855, where he entered into the banking business with his brothers. At the beginning of the Civil War he commanded the city militia unit, the Governor's Greys, which later became Company I, 1st Iowa Infantry. Herron went on to become the youngest major general in the Union Army. After negotiating the surrender of the Trans-Mississippi Department, Herron was ordered to Shreveport from Baton Rouge, where he arrived on June 6, 1865. The following day, under Herron's supervision, the Confederate troops stationed about Shreveport began the parole process. June 7 was also the date that Herron resigned from the service. On June 21, Herron was relived of command at Shreveport, departing the area on July 2, upon the arrival of General James C. Veatch, who assumed command of the area. Returning to New Orleans, Herron remained for a time, practicing law and later moved to New York. Falling on bad times, Herron died in a New York tenement on January 8, 1902. *O.R.*, vol. 48, pt. 2:956, 1040; Banasik, *Reluctant Cannoneer*, 28–85; Jacob Bess Journal (R1330), June 6, 1865, Western Historical Manuscript Collection, State Historical Society of Missouri (Rolla, MO), hereafter cited as Bess Journal; Thomas Burnell Colbert, "Herron, Francis Jay," in *Encyclopedia of Civil War*, 967-968; Edwards, *Shelby and His Men*, 543; Goff & Tarbell, 63; Hoskin Diary, June 6, 1865.

residence was at Richmond, Mo., departed for Mexico or some other place of exile.[56] They were accompanied by Standish's orderly and body servant, named William Wenderling, better known as "Dutch Bill."[57] The Federal commander allowed the officers and soldiers to keep such effects as was conducive to their comfort and convenience, so that Gen. Parsons and company retained their wagons, teams and effects and such stores as they had used, before the surrender, to which, it is said, the generous Federal commander added some contributions of his own of luxuries and convenience the Confederate officers had

---

56. Aaron H. Conrow was born on June 19, 1824 (Hale says June 9), in Cincinnati, Ohio, and moved to Missouri at an early age, settling in Ray County. By the age of 20, Conrow was married to Mary Ann Quisenberry, with whom he had three sons and one daughter. In 1860, Conrow was living in Richmond, Missouri, where he served as a lawyer and judge and was elected to the Missouri Legislature. While in the legislature, Conrow became a confidant of Governor Claiborne F. Jackson, and in 1861, at the request of the governor, went to Little Rock, Arkansas, to request military aid from that state. A strong secessionist, Conrow supported the Military Bill and upon its passing, raised and equipped the first MSG company from Ray County. Conrow was later appointed the Adjutant General of the 4th Division, MSG, fought at Wilson's Creek and the Siege of Lexington, in 1861. Appointed a member of the Confederate Congress, Conrow represented the 4th Missouri District, serving in the Provisional Congress (December 2, 1861–February 17, 1862) and both secessions of the regular Confederate Congress, the First Congress (February 18, 1862–February 17, 1864) and the Second Congress (November 7, 1864–March 18, 1865). While in the Congress, Conrow's committee assignments included the Finance Committee, Post Offices and Departments, Public Buildings, and the Quartermaster and Commissary Departments. With the end of the war near, Conrow returned to the Trans-Mississippi, where he remained for a time in Shreveport. On June 8, 1865, believing that amnesty did not cover elected Confederate officials, Conrow headed for Texas and joined up with General Parsons's party on its way to Mexico. For his part, Conrow intended on eventually going to England; however, he never made it. Early on the morning of August 16, 1865, Conrow was murdered, near China, Mexico, along with General Parsons's entire party. Colonel A. M. Standish was previously covered. *O.R.*, vol. 53:437, 440; *O.R.*, Series 4, vol. 3:1185–1186, 1188, 1190–1191; Castel, *Sterling Price*, 22; Eakin, *Confederate Records*, 2:90; Donald R. Hale, *Branded as Rebels Volume 2* (Independence, MO, 2003), 67, hereafter cited as Hale, *Branded As Rebels Volume 2*; "Members of the First and Second Congresses of the Confederate States, *SHSP*, vol. 2:447–448; Peterson, et al., 136; Quesenberry Diary, June 8, 1865; Sifakis, *Who Was Who in the Confederacy*, 62; Marcus J. Wright, *General Officers of the Confederate Army* (New York, 1911), 160, 170, 180, hereafter cited as Wright, *General Officers*.
57. Edwards also has Parsons's accompanied by three "brave and faithful young Irish soldiers, James Mooney, Patrick Langdon and Michael Monarthy," all members of Parsons's Missouri Division. Of the three names, a James Mooney was noted as being a member of Parsons's Division, serving in the 8th Missouri Infantry, while no references were found for the other two men in the *Confederate Roster*. Mooney originally enlisted in William O. Coleman's Missouri Cavalry on August 4, 1862, and became a member of the 8th Missouri Infantry on August 7, when Coleman's command was combined with Charles C. Mitchell's Missouri Infantry. Mooney was left sick at West Plains, Missouri, on October 11, 1862, after which his name disappears from the rolls. Of the other sources, Davis and O'Flaherty put the party at six members, but do not list the names, while Arthur has the party as five members, including Parsons. Nothing was found on William Wenderling, save that he was a "German servant." Arthur, 106; Banasik, *Serving With Honor*, 232, 320; Bartels, *Trans-Mississippi Men*, 188; Davis, *Fallen Guidon*, 100; Edwards, *John N. Edwards Biography*, 294–295; Hewett, *Confederate Roster*, 11: 205, 231; O'Flaherty, 419.

Long Been Unused To.

Gen. Parsons's immediate objective point was Mexico, but there are reasons to suppose he intended, then, ultimately to settle in South America.[58] Those who accompanied him, not knowing what would be the action of the Federal administration toward them, were seeking for some asylum and exile, where they could earn a living and be, if not permitted to return to Missouri, ultimately joined by their families. They were all in the prime of life, Parsons 44 years old and the other gentlemen younger.

In the early days of August they reached the Rio Grande, having disposed of their surplus teams and wagons for a considerable amount of money.[59] They were at Monterrey and remained a few days, being treated politely by the Mexican military authorities.[60] The long journey across Texas and the kindly disposition

---

58. General Parsons was the commander in Shreveport who surrendered the Confederate troops in that quarter to General Francis Herron upon his arrival on June 6, 1865. Parsons accepted parole, but preferred relocating to Brazil, via Mexico, rather than remain in a country that would "tie" his hands and "seal" his "lips against anarchy and tyranny," while being forced to "breath its polluted air." Ultimately, Parsons was seeking a place for the settlement of like-minded Missourians; after which he could "come home" with "free papers" and let his friends know his "opinions and views [and]...what can be done for immigrants" to his new country. Mark Boatner and Patricia Faust both simply contend that Parsons fled to Mexico "to recoup" his fortune. Boatner, 622; Faust, 560–562; Goff & Tarbell, 62; Miller, 56; M. M. Parsons's Letter to Parents (June 5, 1865).

59. Upon arriving at Eagle Pass, Texas, on the Rio Grande River and opposite Piedras Negras, Mexico, Parsons found the area occupied by Mexican Guerrillas, who entered the town after Shelby had departed the area. Parsons's party proceeded down river, sold their excess baggage for about $1,200, successfully crossed the Rio Grande and continued on to Monterrey, about 250 miles from Eagle Pass, where they hoped to join Shelby. Parsons's party missed Shelby's column, which had departed Monterrey in the first week of August. They remained in Monterrey for a time, assessing their situation. In the end, they decided to return to the United States via Matamoras. Arthur, citing Rolle's account of Parsons's death, has Parsons moving toward Matamoras, after crossing into Mexico, where he was ambushed and killed about July 10, 1865—clearly not correct. Davis implies that Parsons crossed at Camargo, Mexico, where he was killed after crossing—again not correct. Edwards' account appears to be the correct version, in this case, which is also supported by Jackman's account of the incident. Arthur, 106, 117; Davis, *Fallen Guidon*, 100; Edwards, *John N. Edwards Biography*, 261, 295; Jackman, "Horror of the Chaparral;" Rolle, 67, 76.

60. Monterrey had been captured by the French on September 21, 1864. It was the provincial capital of the Mexican State of Nueva Leon, and the site of a Mexican War battle (September 20–24), which was won by Zachary Taylor. The city proved to be "much larger" than Trusten Polk expected, numbering 15,000 residents, and was a strategically important place for controlling Nueva Leon. Colonel Pierre Jeanningros was appointed the French governor of the Monterrey District, shortly before Shelby's arrival at the end of July 1865. Since Shelby had only recently departed the area, Jeanningros had made an arrangement with the ex-Confederates to settle and operate on the Pacific coast, near Mazatlan, in support of the French; as such, Parsons and party were welcomed as guests and not treated as potential supporters or allies of Benito Juarez or the Mexican Liberals. Parsons, for his part, waited at Monterrey for several days, hoping for an escort to Matamoras, where the French were drawing their supplies. On August 12 Parsons's party departed Monterrey, as part of a train escorted by a "regiment of Imperial Mexican Cavalry," heading for Matamoras. The French, for their part, finally abandoned Monterrey on August 26, 1866, marking a general retreat of the French in northern Mexico (McAllen has the date as July 26, which actually was the date that Marshal Bazaine, commanding the French forces in Mexico, had ordered

being envisioned by the victorious authorities of the United States had led these gentlemen to momentarily modify their views about continuous exile. This news is received by the papers and through Mexico had determined Gen. Parsons to take the shortest route to Camargo and sail for the United States and home.[61] To this end, he procured passports and was permitted to depart from the military lines about the 12th day of August, 1865. His party was accompanied by

Another Confederate Officer,

from, I think, Tennessee, Col. Williams.[62] They were practically accompanied by another party of Confederate exiles, one of them headed by Gen. John B Clark, Sr., who although not of the same party were in reach.[63] Traveling by themselves they were on the evening of 15th of August near the San Juan River and passed

---

Monterrey evacuated). Arthur, 113–114, 117; Box, 123; Bradley, "Shelby's Expedition," 552; Creel, 29; Davis, *Fallen Guidon*, 98; McAllen, 279; Percy F. Martin, *Maximilian In Mexico: The Story of the French Intervention (1863-1867)* (London, 1914), 207, 219, hereafter cited as Martin; Polk Diary, July 9, 1865; Sellmeyer, 291; Otis A. Singletary, *The Mexican War* (Chicago, 1960), 33, 37–41, 164, hereafter cited as Singletary; Worley, 367.

61. Camargo, Mexico was a "small village on the Rio Grande," across from Rio Grande City, Texas, and located in the State of Tamaulipas. It was founded on March 5, 1749, by 85 Spanish families and was the first settlement on the Lower Rio Grande. During the Mexican War it was occupied by United States troops on July 14, 1846, and served as a base of operations for the invasion of Mexico and the capture of Monterrey. It was about 90 miles from Matamoras, Mexico. The town number over 5,000 residents during the Mexican War and about 10,000 today. George B. Davis and Leslie J, Perry and Joseph W. Kirkley, *Atlas to Accompany the Official Records of the Union and Confederate Armies* (Washington, DC, 1891-1895), plt. no. 44, hereafter cited as Davis, *Civil War Atlas*; Singletary, 34; Wikipedia.

62. A review of the *Official Records* and the *Supplement to the Official Records* shows that there are well over 30 entries for "Williamses" from Tennessee, who served in various units and positions ranging from privates, surgeons, adjutant generals up to general, with less than a handful as a major or above. Only one, Captain William Orton Williams (*O.R.S.*, Index, vol. 5:5655), was associated with a Tennessee Artillery unit, Tobin's Tennessee Battery. Captain Williams later served on various staffs and was promoted to colonel on December 14, 1862. At Shiloh (April 6–7, 1862) he served as "Chief of Artillery" on Braxton Bragg's staff. However, W. O. Williams was executed as a spy in June 1863, in Franklin, Tennessee. *O.R.*, Index, 1057; *O.R.S.*, Index, vol. 5:5639–5656; Allardice, *Confederate Colonels*, 399.

63. As will be seen, Clark's party was just a short distance behind Parsons's party and was assaulted, supposedly by the same band Mexicans that had attacked Parsons shortly after Parsons's band was attacked.

John B. Clark, Sr. commanded the 3rd Division, MSG. He was born on April 17, 1802, in Kentucky, moved to Missouri in 1818, and became a lawyer and a successful politician. At the beginning of the Civil War he was appointed a general in the MSG (May 18, 1861), suffered a wound at Wilson's Creek, and thereafter became a Confederate senator representing Missouri (February 18, 1862–February 17, 1864) and a member of the Confederate House (May 2, 1864–March 18, 1865). After the war Clark fled to Mexico, but later returned to the United States. He was captured and imprisoned at Fort Jackson, Louisiana, on September 28, 1865, but was paroled for health reasons on November 13, 1865. Returning to Missouri, Clark resumed his practice of law. He died in October 1885, in Fayette, Missouri. *O.R.*, Series 2, 59–61; Banasik, *Serving With Honor*, 382–383; Peterson, et al., 107; Wright, *General Officers*, 177, 180.

through the little Mexican town of China.⁶⁴ Williams's horse had fallen lame and he stopped on the road to find a farmer, so that he did not come up with the party in time to camp with them that night. At a water-tank or as near it as was convenient they encamped on the edge of the chaparral. Parsons was a man of peculiar habit in many respects, and always preferred encamping off by himself. He, therefore, remained away a good distance from where Gen. Clark's party was bivouacked to by himself.

That night Gen. Clark's party were attacked by marauders, but not until as he testifies, he heard some sharp firing in the distance of Gen. Parsons's camp. We know nothing of what occurred at Parsons's camp except what we gather from the sworn statements of the witnesses submitted by myself as counsel

For the Widows and Heirs

before the joint commission organized under the joint treaty of July 4, 1868.⁶⁵ The first definitive information derived of their fate was received through the good offices of the German council at Camargo. This was very meager, but gave a clue that enabled us to make the following state of facts: about the time of Gen. Parsons's departure the military secretary of Gen. Canales, who answers and ranked in official duties to ours of inspector and adjutant general, applied for a leave of absence and departed. We judge from Clark's statements and that Parsons was attacked at a late hour—past midnight. That he may have made some resistance was evidenced from the firing which soon ceased. Don [Rafael] Panton [Plato] Sanchez, at the head of a body of Mexican soldiers, claiming to be acting under the orders from Gen. Canales, summoned him and his party to surrender, saying he had orders to arrest them and take them before the Mexican

Servando Canales

---

64. China was about 60 miles northeast of Monterrey, Mexico, and on the east side of the San Juan River. Davis, *Civil War Atlas*, plt. 171.
65. On July 4, 1868, a commission was set up between Mexico and the United States to settle claims "for losses suffered due to acts of one government against nationals of the other." The American-Mexican Claims Commission was established following the departure of the French from Mexico in 1867. Sir Edward Thornton, an English diplomat, was appointed arbitrator. In the case of Parsons's party, the claim was settled in the ex-Confederates' favor, as it was proven that Mexican Liberals were responsible for the death of the Parsons and his men. Wikipedia.

commandant.⁶⁶ Gen. Parsons recognized Sanchez by his uniform. He also recognized those who accompanied Sanchez by their uniforms, among them a captain named Nicholas Alanez, and apprehending only a delay of a few days from this capricious arrest, surrendered.⁶⁷ We have reason to believe, from the testimony, that the very plausible pretext for the arrest was the near proximity of the French lines and that there were in the party

Spies

in the interest of the [Archduke Ferdinand] Maximilian.⁶⁸ The prisoners were immediately bound and taken off some considerable distance into the chaparral and then most brutally murdered.⁶⁹ Col. Don Plato Sanchez took possession of the

---

66. Rafael Plato Sanchez was born in 1831, in the Mexican State of Vera Cruz. He participated in the fight at Puebla on May 5, 1862, and was promoted to lieutenant colonel in the Liberal Army. He served under General Canales and later became an adjutant for General Mariano Escobedo. In addition to being named as the leader of the band that killed Parsons, Sanchez is best remembered as the president of the court that tried and convicted Maximilian of bearing "arms against the Republic." Sanchez was later shot and killed by his own men in 1867, shortly after the execution of Maximilian. The town of Plato Sanchez in Vera Cruz, founded in 1868, was named after him. Martin, 349, 354; Wikipedia.

    Colonel or General Servando Canales, served as a lieutenant under General Escobedo, operating on the Texas-Mexican border. Canales, who styled himself a leader like Juan Cortina, harassed the French under General Thomas Mejia, who held Matamoras for the French. McAllen, 111, 187.

67. No information on Nicholas Alanez could be found.

68. Archduke Ferdinand Maximilian von Hapsburg, was born in Austria on July 6, 1832. Following a debt crisis in 1860, Mexico owed large sums of money to England, France, and Spain, which it could not repay. When he was elected president of Mexico, Benito Juarez put a hold on all debt repayments. In response, the three European nations threatened force to collect the debt, eventually sending troops. England and Spain departed almost as quickly as they arrived, leaving France as the sole European power in Mexico. After securing the country, France sent Maximilian to rule its new acquisition. Maximilian arrived in Mexico City in June 1864 and was installed as "Emperor of Mexico," with guarantees by Napoleon III of France of military support. Following our Civil War, the French withdrew their troops and support for Maximilian, who was captured, tried, and shot on June 19, 1867. Arthur, 79–80; Boatner, 521; Creel, 34; Michael S. Werner, *Encyclopedia of Mexico History, Society & Culture* (2 vols.; Chicago, 1997), vol. 2:785–787.

69. In his account of the murder, Anthony Arthur has the party of five captured, with four of them "shot down in cold blood, not all at once but one by one to prolong the agony and let those who remained anticipate what was coming to them." The final member, General Parsons, according Arthur, escaped, was recaptured, and then executed. Davis has the 6-member party captured and then executed. O'Flaherty has Parsons's party captured by the notorious guerrilla Louis Figueros, just north of Monterrey, and "executed under particularly revolting circumstances."

    John Edwards has two accounts of what happened to Parsons. In *Shelby's Expedition to Mexico*, Edwards elaborates on Parsons's fate after leaving Monterrey with an Imperial escort en route for Matamoras. A few days after leaving Monterrey the party was ambushed and retreated back toward Monterrey. Parsons, not wanting to return to Monterrey, convinced the members of his party to abandon the French column and continue on to Matamoras by themselves. The party was captured the day that they left the train, but escaped the following morning "under a fierce fire of musketry." The next day Parsons's group was recaptured, this time by Figueros, "a robber in chief...among the Mexicans." The party was then executed, one at a time; Standish was first; then came Conrow, and finally the three soldiers who accompanied them. Because of his stature as a major general in the Confederate Army, Parsons was taken prisoner, possibly for ransom,

The Final Infantry Operations, Surrender, and Death of General Parsons / 69

effects of the prisoners and in the presence of their stripped and mutilated bodies the spoils were divided according to the military rank of the robbers. Sanchez appropriated Parsons's gold watch and most of the money of the party, which was in gold. Nicholas Alanez, captain, and Jesus Tigerino, private soldier of the Liberal army of the Republic of Mexico testified to the manner of the division of the spoils. Col. [A. M.] Standish, who was a civil engineer and hoped for the employment and his profession while in exile, had a case of instruments with him. These were given to one of the murderers and by him offered shortly after to an American civil engineer at Camargo for sale. Another of the murderers appeared in China dressed in uniform of a major-general of the Confederacy, of which he had despoiled the body of Gen. Parsons.[70]

The bodies were hidden in the chaparral by Col. Don Plato Sanchez. After

---

and continued with his Mexican captors towards Monterrey. Parsons later escaped on horseback, was recaptured, and immediately executed, his body "literally shot to pieces." In Edwards's other account (in *Shelby and His Men*), Parsons's entire party escapes, is then recaptured, and executed en masse. Arthur, 106–107; Davis, 100–101; Edwards, *John N. Edwards Biography*, 294–297; Edwards, *Shelby and His Men*, 550–551; O'Flaherty, 419 (n. 23).

70. The leader of the group that killed General Parsons was himself later killed, according to most accounts. However the capture and killing of Parsons's murderer was quite different than what was described by Richard Musser, who subsequently won a monetary settlement for the murder of the ex-Confederates. Musser states that the leader of the band was Don Panton Sanchez (actually Rafael Plato Sanchez), a lieutenant colonel of the Liberal Army. Edwards and O'Flaherty both write that the leader was Louis Figueros, a notorious outlaw. O'Flaherty makes few remarks on the matter and simply defers to Edwards's account of the murder. In Edwards's account, Figueros is later tracked down and killed in Camargo, on the Mexican side of the Rio Grande River, by Frank Moore, an ex-Confederate officer at the head of a squadron of cavalry, riding under the French flag. Davis has Moore killing Parsons's murderer in the village of "Las Flores," though he never mentions the murderer's name. Arthur disputes Edwards's account, stating that Figueros was killed in July 1866, following a raid on the ex-Confederate town of Carlota, near Vera Cruz, and could not have been Parsons's killer. Arthur, citing Rolle as his source, has Parsons being killed by General Juan N. Cortina around July 10, 1865, also clearly wrong. L. A. Pindall, provides the best explanation of Parsons's murder and murderer, following the receipt of two letters (not found) of individuals, who knew the details of the attack on Parsons. In his own letter on the matter, Pindall acknowledges that Escobedo's forces, which included Cortina, attacked the French train that Parsons was trying to catch. Escobedo then sent a group under his adjutant, Lieutenant Colonel Sanchez, on a reconnaissance around the French forces. Discovering Parsons's party, they killed the ex-Confederates. Arthur, 106–107, 175–176; Davis, *Fallen Guidon*, 99–101; Edwards, *John N. Edwards Biography*, 294, 297–299; Martin, 307; O'Flaherty, 301; L. A. Pindall Letter (February 3 1869), M. M. Parsons Papers, Missouri Historical Society, St. Louis, hereafter cited as Pindall Letter; Rolle, 76, 83.

Juan N. Cortina

having been absent from duty with his commander for eleven days, returned to duty,

Wearing Gen. Parsons's Watch

and carrying his purse. Efforts were made by Gen. Clark, [and] by Col. Williams, whose life had been saved by the lameness of his horse, and by other American and ex-officers of the Confederacy, to ascertain their fate. It was feared for some time they were incarcerated in some remote dungeon in Mexico and enduring all indignities and privations of Spanish imprisonment. General Canales seemed anxious to facilitate a search for the missing gentlemen, and all this time that chief murderer was at the head of the military family. There was then serving in the Legion of Honor of the Liberal army, an American who was taken service after the disbandment of the volunteer armies called into being by our Civil War. He was a captain, and his name was Siler.[71] A true soldier, and a true Yankee, full of adventurous spirit, but full of truth and honor. One day Sanchez filled himself up with mescal and the brandy of Paras, with pulque and other abominable Mexican drink. This inspired him with boastful

Courage and Braggadocio,

and while thus in his drunken war-paint he was incited to tell his deeds of the chivalry. He supposed Siler would, having been in the Federal army, have a brutal pleasure hearing the details of the death of the Confederate general. He, in a fit of drunken confidence, gave him a full account of his brutal crime, which occurred during his eleven days' absence. To confirm his story, which Siler hesitated to believe, he produced the watch which he swore he had taken from the body of the "Confederate general." This and other evidences of the crime convinced Siler of the fact, whereupon with honest indignation he denounced his poltroon and murderer. Capt. Siler, on making investigations, found there stood on the place indicated by Sanchez's statement, four rude crosses the Mexican peasants always erect over the unknown dead who are found murdered, and these crosses mark the burial places of Parsons, Standish, Conrow and Dutch Bill.

Under the joint treaty heretofore named I filed claims against the Republic of Mexico for the

---

71. The only Siler discovered in the *Official Records* or the *Supplement* was a Calvin Siler of the 8th Kentucky (Union), who was reported missing following the skirmish at Dobbin's Ferry, Tennessee, on September 9, 1862. All other known Silers were Confederate. However, L. A. Pindall, who wrote a letter concerning Parsons's death, gives the name as either "Stiles" or "Silus;" neither of which appear in the *Official Records* or the *Supplement*. *O.R.*, Index, 877; *O.R.S.*, pt. 1, vol. 3:623; *O.R.S.*, Index, vol. 5:4780–4781; Pindall Letter.

Murder and Robbery

of the three gentlemen.[72] I filed none for William Wenderling, for he had no heirs that I could hear about. After delays aggregating 10 years, I secured an allowance by the umpire Sir Edward Thornton, of $51,000 for Gen. Parsons, $42,400 for Col. Standish and $50,000 for Col. Conrow.[73]

The Mexican government in defense first denied the gentleman were murdered by soldiers, and then denied the responsibility for lawlessness and unauthorized acts of officers and soldiers.

But Sir Edward, like a true Briton, declared that when a government kept in its service and pay, wearing the uniform and in its commission, such men, it assumes a responsibility for their conduct and action toward the citizens of other and friendly countries.

Sir Edward Thornton

Sanchez, shortly after his confession to Capt. Siler, was assassinated at a fandango.[74] For much of the evidence on which these statements are based, I sent

---

72. Following the death of Maximilian, Bonito Juarez resumed the leadership of Mexico as president in the autumn of 1867. However, Mexico's problems were far from over, as it entered a period of reform and revolution that would not end for decades. Juarez died unexpectedly on July 18, 1872, shortly after being elected to his fourth term. With Juarez's death "the last hope for at least half a century of combining peace with freedom" had ended, as the republic descended into a series of dictatorships. Porfirio Diaz was the first, followed by a succession of presidents/dictators that would not end until the middle of the twentieth century. Henry Bamford Parkes, *A History of Mexico* (Boston, 1960), 278–282, 285, 411, 416–417, 421, hereafter cited as Parkes.
73. Sir Edward Thornton, a career diplomat from England, was born on July 13, 1817, in London, was educated at King's College London and Pembroke College Cambridge. He began his diplomatic career at the age of 25, serving in South and Central America, until his assignment as Minister to the United States in 1867. With the end of the French intervention in Mexico, Thornton served as the arbitrator for the Commission on Mexico and United States Claims, to resolve any monetary compensation due to either side, as a result of the French occupation of Mexico. In 1881, Thornton departed the United States for Russia and served there until 1884, when he was sent to Constantinople as the ambassador to the Ottoman Empire. Thornton later returned to London, where he died on January 26, 1906. Wikipedia.
74. Edwards and Davis have Parsons's murderer, Louis Perez Figuero, being tracked to the village of Las Flores, where he was killed. Arthur names the killer as Juan Cortina, but has no further comments on his status. In his notes Arthur acknowledges Edwards's support of Figueros as the killer of Parsons, but favors Andrew Rolle's contention that it was Cortina. The disposition of Figueros has been previously covered (see note 70). Following the American Civil War, Cortina was arrested by Mexican authorities in about 1878 and died in a Mexican prison at Atzapozalco on October 30, 1894. Arthur, 106–107, 236 (n. 106); Roy R. Barkley and Mark F. Odintz, *Porta-*

in to Mexico to the scene of the murder and they were taken for me by Michael Duffy, an honest Irishman of Roma, Tex. I found Capt. Siler living in Jacksonport, Ark.; he had resigned from the Mexican service and I took his statement myself. The late Gen. John B Clark gave a most edifying statement of facts, and the whole case was made by such irrefragable statements, both American and Mexican, that before an English ambassador for umpire, the United States taught her sister republic the lesson that the lives of all her citizens are precious in the sight of the government.

R. H. Musser

* * * * * * *

Item: Another account of the death of General Mosby M. Parsons on August 16, 1865, by Colonel Sidney D. Jackman.[75]
Published: January 23, 1886.

A Horror of the Chaparral

Col. Jackman's account of the murder of Gen. Parsons's party is as follows:
SAN MARCOS, Tex., Jan. 15. – While recently at Brownsville,[76] Tex., 400 or

---

ble *Handbook of Texas* (Austin, 2000), 248, hereafter cited as Barkley & Odintz; Davis, *Fallen Guidon*, 101, 136; Edwards, *John N. Edwards Biography*, 298.

A fandango "resembles a French *ducasse*," or parish feast, "with the additional excitement of gambling. It commences at 9:30, and continues till daylight." Arthur J. L. Fremantle, *Three Months in the Southern States April-June 1863* (New York, 1864; reprint ed., Lincoln, NE, 1991), 19.

75. Sidney D. Jackman was born in Kentucky, moved to Howard County, Missouri, in 1830, and settled in Bates County in 1855. At the beginning of the Civil War, he raised a company in Bates County and was elected captain of the unit, which became part of the 9th Cavalry Regiment, 8th Division, MSG. Operating behind enemy lines, Jackman raised two regiments during the war; the first was organized in the fall of 1862, and the second was raised in late spring of 1864. During the war, Jackman was basically a guerrilla leader, participating in only two major engagements: Lone Jack (August 16, 1862) and Westport (October 22–23, 1864). He moved to Texas following the war, where he died on June 2, 1886. Allardice, *More Generals in Gray*, 133–135; Banasik, *Confederate "Tales of the War" In the Trans-Mississippi, Part Two: 1862.* (Iowa City, IA, 2011), 174–175, hereafter cited as Banasik, *Tales of the War, Part Two*; Crute, *Confederate Army*, 201, 208; Mrs. Mary Jackman Mullins, "Sketch of Col. Sidney D. Jackman," in *Reminiscences of the Women of Missouri During the Sixties* (Jefferson City, MO, 1911), 93–96, cited hereafter as Mary Jackman; Richard L. Norton, *Behind Enemy Lines: The Memoirs and Writings of Brigadier General Sidney Drake Jackman* (Springfield, MO, 1997), v, 3-9, 19, hereafter cited as Norton.

76. Brownsville, Texas, was located on the Rio Grande River, a short distance from the Gulf of Mexico and across the border from Matamoras, Mexico. In 1781, Jose Salvador de la Garza was given a Spanish land grant that covered the area that encompassed what would become Brownsville. Squatters came and a small settlement formed in 1836. In the late 1840s Charles Stillman bought a portion of the land, where Brownsville sits, from an heir to the land grant, and with Samuel Belden, plotted the city. In December 1848, Juan Cortina filed a lawsuit against Stillman, stating that Stillman did not own the land as it was illegally sold to him. On January 13, 1849, Brownsville was established as the county seat of Cameron County, Texas, even while Cortina's lawsuit worked its way through the Texas courts. The matter would not be settled until 1879, when the courts ruled that Stillman did own the land and had the right to form the city. During the

more miles south of this, in attendance on one of the courts of this district, and finding the murder of Gen. Parsons's party still fresh in the minds of the people and much talked of, I determined to learn all the facts possible concerning the same for the benefit of the *Republican* and the friends of the murdered men. The following extract from the Old Ranchero, published at that time in Matamoras, and kindly furnished by Col. Maltby, one of its then editors, now running a job office in Brownsville, is the sole result of my investigation, and this, as the writer knows, contains several mistakes.[77] Following is

The Brownsville Account.

By this arrival we have the particulars of the murder of Gen. M. M. Parsons late of the Confederate States Army. He did not have his family with him, as previously reported, nor was he traveling in an ambulance. He was on horseback, accompanied by three gentlemen, who had been members of his staff. One was Capt. A. M. Standish, late assistant-adjutant general. We have not been able to learn certainly the name of the other two. This shocking occurrence took place on the 5th [16th] ult., between Toro and Coma, on the road from Monterrey to this place. The unfortunate exiles were met by the robbers, who pretended to be friendly until they had surrounded and disarm the party. They were then stripped and taken one side in the chaparral where they were barbarously murdered.

Col. Wilson [Williams], also late of the C. S. A., had been one of the party, but his horse became lame and had caused him a few hours detention; he passed over the same road and saw nothing of the robbers nor any sign of the affray. From this it is rendered certain that their destruction was accomplished by treachery. The other men, both young Missourians, being unmarried, were murdered in cold blood at the village of China a few days afterwards.[78] Their names were Kelly

---

Civil War Brownsville served as a major point of entry of goods coming into the Confederacy. The goods were sent to Matamoras to avoid the Union blockade and then trans-shipped across the river to Brownsville. The city was captured on November 6, 1863, abandoned on July 28, 1864, and recaptured by Confederate troops two days later. Michael E. Banasik, *Duty, Honor and Country: The Civil War Experiences of Captain William P. Black, Thirty-seventh Illinois Infantry. Unwritten Chapters of the Civil War West of the River Volume VI* (Iowa City, IA, 2006), 262 n. 39, 306 n. 65, hereafter cited as Banasik, *Duty, Honor and Country*; Barkley & Odintz, 189–191; Davis, *Civil War Atlas*, plt. no. 54.

77. The more common name for the *Old Ranchero* was the *Weekly Ranchero* or *Daily Ranchero*. According to *Newspapers on Microform*, the paper was published in Matamoras from 1862–1865, with the 1863 issues apparently being printed in Santa Margarita, Texas. After the war, the *Ranchero* returned to Brownsville, where it continued to be printed as a weekly, tri-weekly, or a daily until 1879, when it merged with the *Rio Grande Democrat* to form the *Democrat and Ranchero*. The newspaper survived but another year, when it disappears from the records. In 1865, there were two Maltbys that were listed as editors of the newspaper: H. A. Maltby and W. H. Maltby. It's not known as to which individual Jackman was referring. Matamoras will be covered in a later note. Library of Congress, *Newspapers in Microfilm, United States, 1848-1983*, Volume 2, P-Z (Washington, DC, 1984), 129, 168; Library of Congress online, Internet site chroniclingamerica. loc.gov/lccn/ SN83025706.

78. As seen in other accounts, the party was either murdered one at a time or all at once. This is but

and Wheary. These occurrences were previous to the fight which Col. Tiberind, commanding escort of the baggage train, had with [General Mariano] Escobedo's band.[79]

Some Errors Corrected.

The Ranchero having to rely almost entirely on Mexicans for the truth of the matter, it was but natural that some mistakes would be made. The writer having been with Gen. Parsons a few days before, and within a few miles of him when murdered, perhaps knows as many of the facts of that lamentable affair as any other one man. And as the particulars have never been published so far as he knows, and as they are of deepest interest to many, he will now give them. The writer was one of Gen. Shelby's party of 130 men, who went to Mexico after the war, reaching Monterrey some weeks in advance of Gen. Parsons; Col. Standish; his brother-in-law, A.A.G., Col. Conrow of Platte County, Missouri, and of the Confederate Congress; Lieut. Col. Williams of Tennessee, and battery commander, as he informed me; and Dutch Bill, teamster for Parsons. Five in all and no more.

Pierre Jeanningros

another account of what happened to the lesser members of Parsons's party. Colonel Musser's account, as shown above, has all the members killed at once, shortly after they were captured.

79. General Mariano Escobedo was born on January 16, 1826, in San Pablo de los Labradores (modern-day Galena), and rose to the rank of general under Juarez, being one of his most trusted and competent officers. Escobedo was captured when Puebla fell to the French on May 17, 1863, but escaped with the help of French General Mejia, who took a "liking for the young Escobedo." Considered the "most talented military man" in the Mexican Army, Escobedo commanded Liberal Mexican forces in northeast Mexico, which operated along the Texas-Mexico border. He captured Matamoras on March 23, 1866, and received the surrender of Emperor Ferdinand Maximilian on May 15, 1867, at Queretaro, Mexico. On June 19, 1867, Escobedo became the "executioner" of the emperor. Percy Martin labeled Escobedo a "ferocious leader," further noting that Escobedo was a "confirmed liar and trickster," who "was also a great physical coward..., having a horror of flying bullets, and invariably keeping under any available cover which presented itself during an engagement." After the death of Juarez, Escobedo led a rebellion against Porfirio Diaz in the 1870s, was captured and imprisoned in 1878, and died on May 22, 1902. See Appendix B for a complete biography. *O.R.*, vol. 41, pt. 2: 1244, 1257, 1259; Martin, 108–109, 219, 307–308; McAllen 88–90, 184; Robert Hammond Murray, ed., *Maximilian, Emperor of Mexico: Memoirs of his Private Secretary Jose Luis Blasio* (New Haven, CT, 1934), 164, 232; O'Flaherty, 303; Parkes, 268, 273; Wikipedia..

During Shelby's march to Mexico City, the ex-Confederate engaged Escobedo's forces at Matehuala, where he "scattered and demoralized" the Mexican force, saving the French garrison of the city. Davis, *Fallen Guidon*, 129, 134; Edwards, *John N. Edwards Biography*, 321.

The Final Infantry Operations, Surrender, and Death of General Parsons / 75

We were all disarmed by the French Gen. Jeanegros [Jeanningros], who receipted for the same, and promised to return them when we wished to leave.[80] Parsons and party were on their way to Brazil. Shelby and party were in search of homes, for its permanent location.[81] But after remaining here some weeks, that seemed impracticable during the murderous war then existing in that country. And thus our party became sadly and terribly demoralized, every man acting for himself, but evidently without any definite object in view. We therefore scattered in every direction, some for the Pacific coast, some for the City of Mexico, some for Texas, and really, it seemed, the "devil for us all." Feeling now that I had no country, my first duty was to my family, composed of a wife and six children who had been robbed and burned out, then banished in destitution to a strange country. [82] But I

---

80. Pierre Jeanningros arrived in Vera Cruz, Mexico, on March 26, 1862, at the head of the 1st and 2nd Battalions, French Foreign Legion. A 30-year veteran of the French Army, Jeanningros began his "military career as a common soldier, rising from corporal to captain of a Zouave regiment in Algeria" and held the rank of colonel when he captured in Monterrey in July 1864. Jeanningros was wounded 13 times during his military career and also served in Italy, China, Algeria, and the Crimea. Appointed French Governor and commander of the Monterrey District, the "grayhaired," "bushy-faced" Jeanningros was promoted to brigadier general following his victory over the Juaristas at Buneva Vista, shortly after the departure of General Shelby's party in early August 1865. Jeanningros returned to France after the French left Mexico and continued in service to the Empire, becoming a lieutenant general and commanding a French Corps during the Franco-Prussian War. Arthur, 97–98, 109; Davis, *Fallen Guidon*, 104, 106; Edwards, *John N. Edwards Biography*, 262, 273, 288; Edwards, *Shelby and His Men*, 550; Kremm, 209; O'Flaherty, 265, 267–268, 276, 429; Rolle, 67.

81. Shelby's band, with no more than 150 men remaining (John Edwards has it as 50 men), reached Mexico City on September 3, 1865. On September 5 Shelby offered the service of his command to Maximilian, who turned down his offer, fearing reaction from the United States (Rolle has Shelby meeting the emperor on August 16, 1865). In the end, Maximilian offered land to the ex-Confederates in a decree he issued on September 5 and published "in full" on November 3, 1865. The ex-Confederates promptly established the colony of "Carlota," named in honor of Maximilian's wife. The colony was located in the Cordoba Valley, about 150 miles southeast of Mexico City and 70 miles from Vera Cruz (Rolle has it 70 miles from Vera Cruz) in the Mexican state of the same name. The colony flourished for a time, but in the end was abandoned, following attacks by Mexican guerrillas in the spring of 1866, and the French withdrawal from Mexico in March 1867. Arthur, 135, 141–142, 144, 150, 187; Edwards, *John N. Edwards Biography*, 363, 368–369, 379; Edwards, *Shelby and His Men*, 551; O'Flaherty, 285–288, 291–292, 295; Rolle, 74, 89 n. 8, 91; Sellmeyer, 292.

82. Within days of leaving San Antonio, Shelby's band began to lose some of its members. General E. Kirby Smith departed the group as it neared Piedras Negras, taking with him an escort of 10 men under Captain Maurice Langhorne, and crossed into Mexico shortly before Shelby. Upon arriving at Eagle Pass, Shelby negotiated for several days with the local authorities at Piedras Negras, crossed over the border, and then rested a few days, during which time a reorganization took place. Colonel Ben Elliott and 65 men (Westlake says it was 36 men; George Cruzen has it as two companies—one with 44 men, the other with 20, total 64; and W. H. Bradley estimates 52 members) of the expedition would stay with the column until it reached Monterrey and then they would turn toward the Pacific Ocean and Mazatlan. (Of the 65 men only 52 would be left at Monterrey for the trip to the Pacific.) After Monterrey, Shelby's band pressed on to Mexico City, where the final breakup occurred. On September 5, following his meeting with Maximilian, Shelby disbanded his command. Some became colonists in the Cordova Valley, some 50 joined the 3rd French Zouaves, while others "took shipping for California, for China, for Japan, and for

am indebted to [John M.] Schofield and Col. [James O.] Broadhead for sending them among my friends of the South.[83] Those of

Our Party

who determined to return with me to Texas, were Col. D. A. Williams of Dallas, Tex.,[84] Col. Warner Lewis, Rainey McKinney, and Camp Bucher [Cam Boucher],

---

the Sandwich Islands." Still others went in search of Captain Kidd's pirate treasure. Box, 122–123; W. H. Bradley, "Through Mexico In 1865," *Confederate Veteran* 23 (July, 1918), 311; Creel, 32; Cruzen, 40; Davis, *Fallen Guidon*, 168–169; Edwards, *John N. Edwards Biography*, 369; Edwards, *Shelby and His Men*, 545, 551; O'Flaherty, 290; Rolle, 53; Sellmeyer, 285, 288–289, 292; Westlake Memoir, 134, 137.

83. John M. Schofield was born in New York in 1831, attended West Point and graduated toward the top of his class in 1853. At the beginning of the Civil War, he was on a leave of absence, teaching school in St. Louis. Schofield became General Nathaniel Lyon's chief of staff in mid-1861, was promoted to brigadier general on November 21, 1861, and to major general on November 29, 1862 (and again on May 12, 1863, after his original appointment had expired). In May 1863, he departed the Trans-Mississippi and completed his military service east of the Mississippi River. By the time of his death on March 4, 1906, Schofield, had risen to the rank of lieutenant general and was Commander in Chief of the U.S. Army. Banasik, *Missouri In 1861*, 360–362; Heitman, 1:865; Warner, *Generals in Blue*, 425–426.

James O. Broadhead was born in Virginia in 1829 and spent a brief time at the University of Virginia before coming to Missouri in 1837. He settled in St. Charles County and studied law, becoming a lawyer in Bowling Green. Broadhead moved to St. Louis in 1859, where he entered Missouri politics, first as a Whig, and then as an Unconditional Unionist and Republican, and aligned himself with Frank Blair. A founding member and secretary of the St. Louis Committee of Safety, Broadhead was also a member of the Missouri Senate and an active participant in the convention called to decide if Missouri should secede from the Union. Even though Broadhead was a slave owner, he argued persuasively that economics dictated that Missouri remain in the Union, remarking that "I am not willing to sacrifice to the slave interest the commercial, mining of other interests of the State." Following the convention Broadhead joined the Missouri Reserve Corps as a major and quartermaster. He later became the lieutenant colonel of the 3rd MSM Cavalry, was appointed the Provost Martial for the Department of Missouri on June 6, 1863, and, on July 10, joined the staff of John M. Schofield. Broadhead returned to his regiment, on January 8, 1864. Following the war, Broadhead became a Democrat and a law partner with Alonzo Slayback. Other post-war activities included "special counsel in the prosecution of the Whiskey Ring cases" (1876), first president of the American Bar association (1878), member of U.S. Congress (1882), and Minister to Switzerland (1895). Broadhead returned home from Switzerland in 1897, and died in St. Louis in 1898. *O.R.*, vol. 22, pt. 2:315, 364; *O.R.*, vol. 34, pt. 2:48; Arthur, 211; Louis S. Gerteis, *Civil War St. Louis* (Lawrence, KS, 2001), 59, 80-81, 336, cited hereafter as Gerteis; Steven Rowan, ed., *Memoirs of a Nobody: The Missouri Years of an Austrian Radical, 1849-1866* (St. Louis, 1997), 279 n. 16; Walter Harrington Ryle, *Missouri: Union or Secession* (Nashville, 1931), 66, 131, 190, 194, 196, 206, 213, 228.

84. David A. Williams was born in Prince Edward County, Virginia, in 1832, and moved to Missouri at an early age, eventually settling in Mercer County. Educated in Grand River College in Grundy County, Williams was a farmer, merchant, a lawyer, and a veteran border ruffian by the beginning of the war. On July 4, 1861, he joined the 8th Division, MSG, and was elected 1st lieutenant of his command, then was promoted to captain and adjutant on September 20, 1861. Transferring to the Confederate service on June 22, 1862, Williams was subsequently promoted to captain of Company D, 6th Missouri Cavalry Regiment (CSA) on January 27, 1863. During Price's 1864 Missouri Raid, Williams raised a cavalry regiment. He fled to Mexico at the end of the war, later returned to Arkansas, where he farmed in Chicot, Jefferson, and Desha Counties, eventually set-

Missouri Gen. John B Clark, Sr., Senator Wayne, who we found in Monterrey, and a man and a woman from the City of Mexico and bound for St. Louis, were also returning to the United States, and traveling in an old-time four-horse United States mail coach.[85] Gen. Dick Waterhouse of Texas and a few soldiers, and also two captives from Arkansas, who names are forgotten, constituted the entire number of Americans returning to Texas and all were under the protection of an imperial or Maximilian force of Mexicans, numbering 800 strong, going to Matamoras.[86] Before leaving we called for our arms; the pistols were returned but the

---

tling in Dallas, Texas, in 1876. He died on March 29, 1898, in Terrell, Texas. See Appendix B for a complete biography. Allardice, *Confederate Colonels*, 397; Anonymous, *The Gallant Breed the 6th Missouri Cavalry: A Roster of the Men Who Rode Under the Flag of Shelby's Iron Brigade* (Independence, MO, 2009), 69, hereafter cited as Anonymous, *6th Missouri Cavalry*; Arthur, 66; Bartels, *Forgotten Men*, 392; Eakin, *Confederate Records*, 8:65; Peterson, 243, 252–253, 283.

85. Colonel Warner Lewis, a nephew of famed explorer Meriwether Lewis, was born on January 5, 1834, in St. Louis County. He graduated from the University of Missouri in 1854, married the following year, and settled in Mt. Olive, Cass County, where he worked as a stockman and merchant. At the beginning of the war Lewis was appointed lieutenant colonel and paymaster of the 8th Division, MSG. He was captured while on recruiting service in Johnson County in the latter part of 1861. Exchanged or paroled, Lewis resigned from the Guard on January 1, 1862, and journeyed to Richmond, where Jefferson Davis commissioned him a colonel "in Ranger service." Lewis returned to the Trans-Mississippi and fought at the Battle of Lone Jack, after which he worked to raise recruits. In November 1862 he left Missouri for Arkansas and served as a volunteer aid under General Daniel M. Frost at the Battle of Prairie Grove (December 7, 1862), where Frost noted that he made "himself particularly useful." Lewis then joined an ill-fated expedition to the Colorado Territory with Colonel Charles Harrison in May 1863. Lewis was wounded and was only one of two men who survived the expedition. Upon recovering from his wound, it appears that Lewis was assigned to Cabell's Brigade in 1864. At the end of the war Lewis went to Mexico with General Shelby, stayed a short time, then returned to the United States, settling in Danville, Montgomery County, Missouri. Post-war, Lewis worked as a politician and lawyer, passing away on October 22, 1915, at the age of 81. *O.R.*, vol. 22, pt. 2:849; *O.R.S.*, pt. 1, vol. 4:79; Bartels, *Forgotten Men*, 217; Eakin, *Battle of Lone Jack*, 166; Eakin, *Confederate Records*, 5:61; William H. Gregg, "A Little Dab of History Without Embellishment," Western Historical Manuscript Collection, State Historical Society of Missouri, 41, cited hereafter as Gregg; Hale, *Branded as Rebels Volume 2*, 189–190; Warner Lewis, "Civil War Reminiscences," *Missouri Historical Review* 2 (April, 1908), 221, 228, cited hereafter as Lewis; Richard Musser, "Doomed Expedition," *Missouri Republican*, January 15, 1887; Bruce Nichols, *Johnson County Missouri in the Civil War* (Independence, MO, 1974), 31.

Rainey McKinney carried a letter of introduction from General Shelby to Colonel Jeanningros, when the Confederate column arrived at Monterrey. This could possibly be Rane James McKinney, who was born on June 20, 1820, in Wayne County, Kentucky, moved to Missouri, and died in Andrew County on January 26, 1908. No other information found on the name McKinney or any variation thereof. Arthur, 97–98; Edwards, *John N. Edwards Biography*, 289; Internet site www.tribalpages.com /tribe/familytree?uid= styxmark&surname=McKinney.

Cam Boucher and General John B. Clark, Sr. have already been covered. Senator Wayne not found.

86. Richard Waterhouse was born in Rhea County, Tennessee, on January 12, 1832, and fought in the Mexican War as a youth, after which he returned to Tennessee. He moved to Texas in 1849, settling near St. Augustine. By the time of the Civil War he was a rich merchant and helped raise the 19th Texas Infantry. He fought at Milliken's Bend, Louisiana (June 7, 1863), and participated in the Red River and Camden Campaigns. Promoted to brigadier general, Waterhouse led a brigade in Walker's Texas Division until the end of the war. He lived briefly in Mexico, then returned

guns kept. Jeanningros would neither give them up nor pay for them. And thus we were treacherously robbed, and in a measure left to the mercy of the murderous banditti, then investing that whole country. Gen. Parsons and party having an ambulance and wagon and eight mules, which they hope to sell to the French, were not ready to move when our army of protection was ready, and hence, determined to remain, sell out, then follow us.

I visited him in person, and urged that he go on; that he could sell his property in Matamoras, and pointed out the danger of remaining and following up our rear.[87] He expressed no fear. Having a passport that he had purchased from an alcalde (Justice of the peace) at a cost of 50 cents, he felt safe. I assured him that ours had cost us $2.50 each, and were granted by the governor of the state, and yet two of our party had been killed and two badly stabbed. I asked: "If ours will not protect us, how will yours protect you?" He nevertheless felt safe, and remained. Our army of 700 infantry and 100 cavalry moved out, marching at the rate of 30 miles a day in the most excessively hot weather imaginable. On the second day we reached the San Juan River, but this day's march was terrible on our infantry,

Fifty Were Stricken Down

by heat (sunstroke, I suppose), nine of whom died and were buried on the bank of the river.[88] The balance were barely saved.[89] Dr. [William M.] Gwin did all in

---

to Texas and spent his remaining days in either St. Augustine or Jefferson. He died on March 20, 1876, as a result of a freak accident in Waco on March 18. For a complete biography see Appendix B. Anne Bailey, "Richard Waterhouse," in The *Confederate General* (William C. Davis, gen. ed.; 6 vols. Harrisburg, PA, 1991), 6:108–109, hereafter cited as *Confederate General*; Simpson, 94.

87. Matamoras was the capital of the Mexican state of Tamaulipas. The town was founded in 1765, and was originally known as San Juan de Los Esteron. Colonel John Black of the 37th Illinois Infantry described the city as follows:
> It is a town of about fifteen thousand people but covers scarcely more ground than the sum of four thousand would with us. The biggest house is but two stories or two & one half high. The roofs are all flat & have a wall from two to three feet high around them as a kind of breastwork to be used in case of insurrection, I suppose. The windows are iron banded like those of our goats—the doors, thickly battered—the walls very strong. The outsides are very plain & have no front of arbor. They are arranged after the style of oriental houses with courts in the center in which are the gardens, flower patches, stables &c.

During the course of the Civil War, "as many as eighty ships at one time awaited discharge of their cargoes," bound for Matamoras and eventually the Confederacy. John C. Black Letters (November 21, 1863 and January 12, 1864), Black Family Collection, Abraham Lincoln Presidential Library, Springfield, IL; Barkley & Odintz, 189; Rolle, 26.

88. This account of Parsons leaving Monterrey is different than John Edwards put forth in his book on Shelby's expedition (see note no. 69 for details). In his earlier account, Edwards has Parsons leaving with the escort, and when the escort returned to Monterrey, Parsons decided to go it alone to Matamoras. Parsons and party were later captured and executed. Edwards, *John N. Edwards Biography*, 294–297.

89. The route taken by the French command, and ultimately also General Parsons, was known to be devoid of "dependable water sources," especially in the summertime. The San Juan River

his power to save those poor creatures.[90] Many of those soldiers had their wives with them, who would go clipping along with their bare feet, carrying their shoes and a big neck gourd filled with water in their arms for the convenience of their husbands, who were not allowed to leave the line. and a chicken or parrot in one hand, and baby, ranging from an infant to 3 years old, slung in a pouch on the back. They seem never to tire, or even know that the weather was hot.

After this burial, our command crossed the river, encamped at the village of China. The next day our usual march was made, and after going into camp, the colonel commanding notified the Americans to report to his quarters. The summons was obeyed, when we were informed that the enemy was quite strong in his front, and feared that he would not be able to go much further, felt it his duty to inform us

William M. Gwin

---

represented the only water available to the column that marched from Monterrey to Matamoras. McAllen, 246.

90. William McKendree Gwin was born in Tennessee in 1805, and graduated from Transylvania University in 1828 with a degree in medicine and the "Classics." He moved to Mississippi, served a term in the U.S. Congress in the1840s, and joined the California gold rush in 1849. Gwin struck it rich and stayed in California, becoming one of its first U.S. Senators in 1850. As a senator, Gwin "helped to orchestrate the Gadsden Purchase of lands" from Mexico in 1853. An ardent supporter of the South, Gwin had thoughts of making California either a separate county or another Confederate state. Andrew Rolle described Gwin as "an enigmatic pro-slavery advocate with a shady past, a real intriguer." With the beginning of the Civil War, Gwin, fearing arrest by local officials, left California on October 22, 1861. En route for New York, Gwin was arrested at sea on November 12, by General Edwin V. Summer, who was also traveling to the city. In New York, Gwin was detained and eventually directed to Washington, where he was interviewed by both Secretary William Seward and President Lincoln. In the end, Gwin was released and all charges dropped, on the condition that he would return to his Mississippi plantation (Edwin Davis says Gwin was imprisoned for two years). Later Gwin, who "was an experienced statesman and knew the Mexican diplomatic situation," traveled to Paris, where he convinced Napoleon III, to allow him to recruit Americans to work the precious metal mines of Senora, Mexico. Named the "Duke of Senora," by Napoleon, Gwin went to Mexico to convey his plan to Maximilian, who eventually turned the scheme down. Gwin left Mexico and returned to San Antonio, Texas, where he was arrested and sent to New Orleans on September 27, 1865. Imprisoned at Fort Jackson, Gwin was offered parole on April 13, 1866, but refused, not willing to accept the conditions that required him to leave the country. On May 16, 1866, Gwin was released "upon the parole usually required in such cases." Final disposition unknown. *O.R.*, Series 2, vol. 2:1009, 1011–1013, 1017, 1020; *O.R.*, Series 2, vol. 8:755, 760, 897, 902, 909; Arthur, 114–116; Davis, *Fallen Guidon*, 107; Edwards, *John N. Edwards Biography*, 300; McAllen, 193; Rolle, 62.

of the situation. The night, however, was spent at the place without interruption, the Americans camping together. About 10 o'clock of this night Col. Williams (not Wilson, as above) rode into camp and inquired for Gen. Parsons and party. Of course we could not give him any information. He stated that at the San Juan River, where the soldiers died and were buried, his horse had given out, and he was forced to remain all night to exchange for another, Parsons and the others going on a few miles. That day he passed through Ranchero, or Woman's ranch, following up his friends, and was told by a Louisiana creole French woman that they were only a hour or two ahead of him, and that she so described them that he knew it was them. Parsons was mounted on a black war horse. The others were also mounted, and one leading a pack horse. He therefore expected

To Find Them With Us.

All felt more or less concerned about them, and many expressed the hope that, knowing they were near us, they had encamped night and would be up in the morning. Feeling differently, I so expressed myself, and the result proves that my fears were well-founded. No enemy having appeared that night, our command went forward and made a march of some twenty-five miles. Here we were again notified to appear before the colonel, when we were informed that Col. Canales lay in our front with a force so strong that we would have to retreat, and we would do so in a few minutes, and that we could return with the command or go on, as we saw proper. We at once began the retreat, and, as we had no time for consultation, we were forced to return with our party. Quite a rapid march was kept up all night, with an occasional shot from the brush by an enemy into our ranks. Rancho was reached about 8 o'clock in the morning, where a halt was made for breakfast. Some of our party called on the old French woman referred to above for something to eat, when she informed them of the murder of Gen. Parsons and party. I was informed of the fact, when Lieut. Col. Williams and I called to see her and learn the facts. She talked good English and cheerfully gave us all the particulars as she had gotten them from a Mexican who lived in the town and was not at home and was a witness to the transaction, but denied participation. We went immediately to see the Mexican, but he refused to see us, and had his doors barred against us. But when he found we would see him or break open the doors, he met us. And when confronted with the facts here given he admitted their truth, but when closely questioned by Williams, who could talk some Spanish, he became sullen and refused to answer a question. Williams went to see our colonel and ask his aid in the matter, while I remained and questioned the Mexican. The colonel

Refused To Take Action,

stating the military was subordinate to civilian authority, and referred him to the alcalde. We then went to see the alcalde, who claimed that the country was under martial law, and that therefore he had no authority. Just at this particular junction the enemy came upon us, when our party rapidly retreated. We, too, were forced to go, and thus our interrogation of that terrible tragedy was suddenly terminated. The particulars, however, as gathered from the old woman are these: That the Mexican referred to saw four Mexican soldiers meet the four Americans with the pack-horse and demand their surrender, which was complied with, when they were pushed off a short distance in the timber and murdered. And while this proceeding was going on, the lone man, who was Col. Williams, passed to the front and reached our camp in safety. This capture, robbery and murder took place within three or four miles of our command. They had $1,200 in money, four pistols, five horses and rigs, clothing, etc. This was a grand hall for greasers, and whether they were soldiers or simply robbers, they were one in the same, and the results would doubtless have been the same, no matter as to the captors. It will doubtless be thought strange that four Americans, three of whom were distinguished men, armed with revolvers, would under any circumstances surrender to four Mexican greasers. And I admit it is strange. But the facts are these: They had fought for a cause they loved and had lost. They were now in exile and felt that they were without hope and country, and away from kindred and friends. They were in a foreign country and unable to speak the language of the country, and without suspicion of treachery on the part of the people. They had but little means and were going still further [farther] off. They were greatly humbled and discouraged, and in the hands of a murderous foe – on his own soil – they were but little better than so many children.

Had Williams been with them, the results, I have no doubt, would have been different. On the Lower Rio Grande there are various reports as to the

Disposition of the Bodies.

One is that they were buried where they were murdered, and that sometime after the authorities of the country had them removed. Another report says that a Capt. Miller,[91] wife and child were killed at the same time, and all were left where they

---

91. This was probably Captain A. B. Miller of the Commissary Department. Miller was a resident of Denver, Colorado, at the beginning of the Civil War, where he operated a freight company. In September 1861, Miller openly led rallies in Denver, urging men to join the Confederacy. He organized an expedition to Texas with supplies for Sibley's New Mexico campaign. Miller's train was captured, but he escaped with his family. Later Miller probably joined Sterling Price's Missouri Army, commanding a company in the 8th Division, MSG. As the war progressed, Miller was made a captain in the Confederate Commissary Department, working in eastern Texas, where he procured supplies for the Confederacy via the trade of cotton for military goods through Brownsville-Matamoras, Mexico. Edwin Davis called Miller "one of the most remarkable men in the Confederacy" for his administration of the trade with Mexico. Of Miller, John Edwards wrote:

> He was a magnificent *athlete* in the supply department and a giant in manufacturing and developing. His trains upon the roads from Matamoras to Shreveport were thick as vessels in a harbor, and the hats and shoes given out from his steam houses at Tyler and Gilmer were enough for the army. In the field he would have been overpowering; in the bureau he was the most valuable man west of the Mississippi.

Davis, *Fallen Guidon*, 43; Edwards, *Shelby and His Men*, 544; Ovando J. Holister, *Colorado*

fell, and a few days later the robber's returned, put them in a pile and burned them. But all these reports need confirmation. I now desire to ask of my friends and comrades of those unforgettable men if they do not think it's time we were looking after their bones. If they were the most humble of men of our cause we would act readily, willingly and long since. But three of them were men of distinction, men of mark, and all were honest, faithful and true men. They were with us at the first and with this at the last. Shall we act? Anything asked of me within my power will be cheerfully done.

The retreat was continued and rapid pursuit made by the enemy for some fifteen miles, and a few incidents occurred that are worthy of mention. At the St. John River our road followed the bed of the river some 300 yards before we could ascend the hill on the other side. While in the river the enemy dashed up and formed on the bank of the river immediately over us and about 30 feet above us, when they poured it into us as rapidly as possible. But our party displayed considerable courage. They fought well,

But Shot Badly,

firing from the hip and of course without aim. They kept moving and firing until the level land on the west, when our four little mountain howitzers, mounted on the backs of as many little poor mules, were swung into position and turned loose. This was too much for the enemy, who then broke and ran. To the Americans the artillery practice was funny. When a gun was fired away went the little mule, falling and catching sometimes on his knees and sometimes almost standing on its head. All four guns were going through this same sort of procedure at the same time. When the mules would recover and get on their feet they were again brought into position and the same amusing scene gone through with. The fight now ended, the retreat was resumed, and our damage all told, if I remember correctly, was that the lieutenant colonel was shot in the jaw. The enemy, I feel very certain lost not a man. After a march of some fifteen miles a halt was made for the night. And here a sad scene presented itself. A poor woman, whose husband had died on the march from the sunstroke, was seen coming in with him thrown across a horse. To appreciate this it would have to be seen. The coach, with all its mail, was abandoned during the fight. What became of the man and woman I do not remember. But Gen. Clark and Dr. Gwin got back together to Monterrey in safety. Ten days later word reached our colonel that this stage and mail were still where they were left. They were sent for and brought up, and had not been molested.

Respectfully,
S. D. Jackman

* * * * * * *

Volunteers In New Mexico 1862 (Denver, 1863; reprint ed., Chicago, 1962), 41; "Our Kansas Letter," *Chicago Tribune*, December 19, 1861; Duane A. Smith, *The Birth of Colorado: A Civil War Perspective* (Norman, OK, 1989), 20–21, hereafter cited as Smith, *Birth of Colorado*.

Chapter 3

Price's 1864 Missouri Raid

Item: Price's 1864 Missouri Raid, by Henry C. Luttrell, Company G, 10th Missouri Cavalry (C.S.A.). Part One.
Published: February 27, 1887.

Price's Great Raid.

[Incidents related by a Confederate trooper, from a diary kept on the march.]
Editor *Republican*

As I have never seen an account of Gen. [Sterling] Price's raid through Missouri in 1864, I have concluded to send you an article covering that period.[1] Most of the incidents here set down, are gleaned from an old diary, written while the events were fresh on my mind and many times as we were bivouacked on the field in the presence of the enemy. I shall confine myself to the career of the "old Tenth Missouri," as we pride ourselves if it's title—and especially in the career of "G Company." This diary is, properly speaking, an account of my own personal career—just such an affair as any 18-year-old boy would be guilty of under similar circumstances. But I shall endeavor to keep the big "I" as much behind the scene as possible.

So that the reader may be able to comprehend the magnitude of this expedition—that is, the magnitude of the undertaking—not of its numbers, for in numbers we did not exceed 6000 of all arms, I will state that our brigade ([John S.] Marmaduke's), then commanded by Col. [Colton] Greene of the Third Regiment, was in camp in the northern part of Lincoln County, Arkansas.[2] On the 7th of Au-

---

1. Sterling Price was born in September 1809 in Virginia, and moved to Missouri in 1831. He served in the U.S. Congress (1844–1846), was governor of Missouri (1853–57), and became a brigadier general during the Mexican War. At the beginning of the Civil War he cast his lot with Missouri and subsequently the Confederacy. Price was one of the principle Confederate commanders at the Battle of Pea Ridge and earned the reputation by early 1864 as of "one of the very greatest... citizen Generals" of the Confederacy, according to the *Mobile Advertiser*. In 1864, Price was described as "a large and rather good looking man....His height is about six feet and his general appearance much like Gen. [Winfield] Scott. He has however rather a hard face and impressed us very favorably. He is very corpulent, so much so that he cannot ride very pleasantly on horseback, as he generally rode in a comfortable coach, drawn by four mules." Price also sported "white hair and whiskers," according to Don Palmer, a rebel conscript. Following the war Price moved briefly to Mexico, settling in Cordova, about 70 miles from Vera Cruz, but returned to St. Louis, where he died in 1867. Banasik, *Missouri Brothers in Gray*, 148–150; Boatner, 669; Palmer, 20–21; "From Mexico," *Mexican Times*, January 6, 1866; "The Trans-Mississippi Generals," *Mobile Advertiser and Register*, April 21, 1864.
2. John S. Marmaduke was born in 1833, graduated from West Point (number 30 of 38) in 1857, and served on the frontier until the beginning of the Civil War. He resigned from the U.S. Army on April 17, 1861, and was appointed a colonel in the MSG. He commanded the MSG troops at

Price's Raid: From Camden to Pocahontas
(August 28–September 18, 1864)

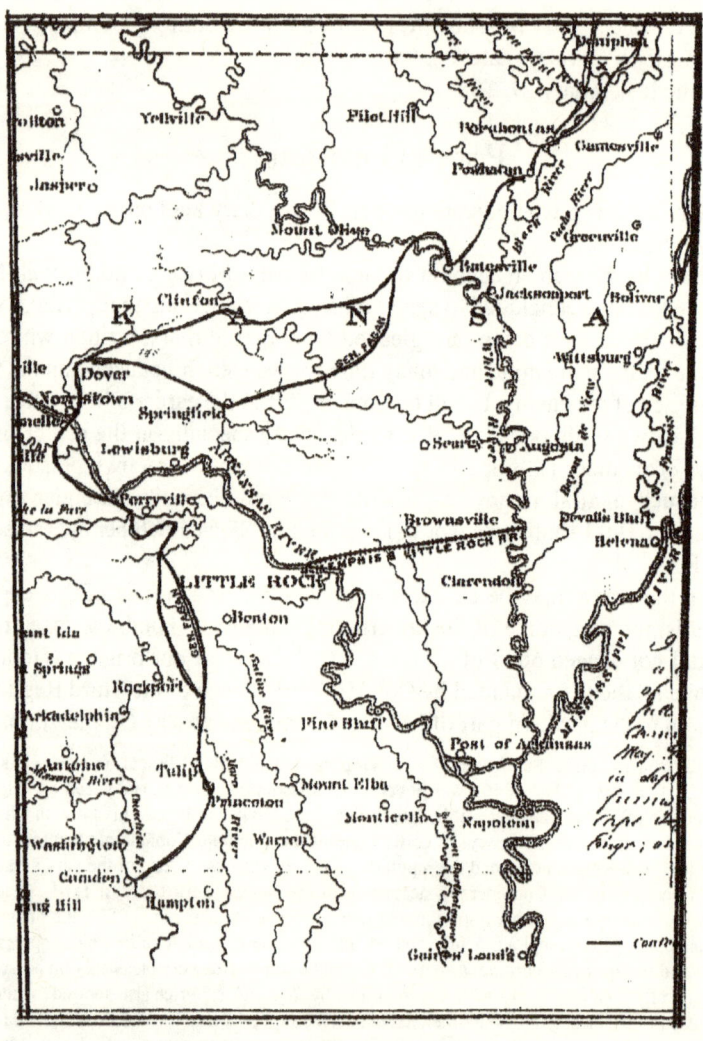

gust, 1864, all the sick of the brigade were sent to the convalescent camp at Tyro.³ As I have been chilling for nearly a month, I was sent off with the contingent. August, the 18th, Gen. Clark took command of the brigade.⁴ Since my sojourn in the convalescent camp, the regimental forces have been run night and day, and

---

Boonville and later entered the Confederate service. On November 15, 1862, Marmaduke was promoted to brigadier general and major general on March 15, 1865. He was described in 1864, as "tall and thin, with light hair and eyes, and the most partial judge would not be guilty of calling him handsome, or even fine looking;...he is generally regarded as [a good general], and is also held in high esteem by his men." Following the war Marmaduke was elected governor of Missouri in 1884, and died while in office in 1887. Banasik, *Missouri Brothers in Gray*, 143, 146; Palmer, 21.

Colton George Greene was born on July 7, 1833, in South Carolina and moved to St. Louis in the 1850s. A wealthy merchant in pre-war St. Louis, Greene, described as a "man of delicate physique and cultivated mind," helped organize the St. Louis Volunteer Militia. Following the capture of Camp Jackson (May 10, 1861), Greene served as an aide to Governor C. F. Jackson, joining the MSG on August 8, 1861. In the early part of 1862, Greene joined the Confederate Army, led a brigade at Pea Ridge, and on November 4, 1862, was appointed colonel of the 3rd Missouri Cavalry Regiment and frequently commanded a brigade thereafter. "No braver man nor better officer ever drew a sword," wrote John Edwards of Shelby's Brigade. Greene moved to Memphis, TN, following the war, where he became a successful businessman and "civic leader." He died, unmarried, on September 23, 1900. Allardice, *Confederate Colonels*, 173–174; Banasik, *Confederate Tales, 1862*, 173–174; Edwards, *Shelby and His Men*, 251; John McElroy, *The Struggle For Missouri* (Washington, DC, 1909), 38.

Marmaduke's Brigade, commanded by John B. Clark, Jr., during Price's Raid, consisted of the 3rd, 4th, 7th, 8th and 10th Missouri Cavalry Regiments, the 14th Missouri Battalion with Hynson's Texas Battery and Harris's Missouri Artillery. Also attached was Hogane's Engineer Company. See Appendix D, for composition and strength of Price's Army of Missouri.

3. Tyro, "a little town," was located about six miles from Bayou Bartholomew, in Drew County, on the road leading to Mt. Elba, Arkansas. *O.R.*, vol. 41, pt. 2: 1074; McGhee, *Campaigning With Marmaduke*, 18–19.

4. John B. Clark, Jr. was born in Fayette, Missouri, on January 14, 1831, educated at the University of Missouri, and received a law degree from Harvard in 1854. At the beginning of the Civil War, Clark was elected captain of Company C, 1st Infantry Regiment, 3rd Division, MSG in May 1861. He was wounded at Wilson's Creek while leading Burbridge's Regiment. He subsequently rose in rank, commanding his regiment and then the 3rd Division, MSG. While in the Guard, Clark also fought at Lexington and Pea Ridge. Clark was appointed a Confederate colonel on June 28, 1862, and in November 1862 assigned by Thomas C. Hindman to command what became the 9th Missouri Infantry (CSA), which he led at Prairie Grove. He was promoted to brigadier general on March 8, 1864, and led a brigade of troops at the Battles of Pleasant Hill (April 9, 1864) and at Jenkins' Ferry (April 30, 1864). With the advent of Price's 1864 Missouri Raid, Clark was transferred to the cavalry, commanding Marmaduke's Cavalry Brigade and later Marmaduke's Division. After the war, Clark returned to Missouri and was elected to the U.S. Congress (1873–1883). He died on September 7, 1903. Banasik, *Serving With Honor*, 380–381; Moore, *Confederate Military History, Missouri*, 206–208; National Archives, Record Group M861 (roll no. 36), Records of Confederate Movements and Activities, 9th Missouri Infantry; Special Order No. 38 (November 10, 1862), Special Orders Book No. 1, 111–112; Peterson, et al., 107, 113, 115; Warner, *General in Gray*, 52.

Horseshoeing Has Gone On

continually.⁵ Everyone is on the qui vive, an expedition is afoot, and we suspect that Missouri is the objective point.⁶

---

5. By the time General Clark took command of Marmaduke's Brigade on August 18, the brigade reported "120 sick present and 443 absent sick," while the convalescents at Tyro numbered 211. The report for Clark's command came just after it had withdrawn from the Arkansas and Mississippi Rivers where they had been actively engaged since mid-May, disrupting Union river traffic. After taking command of Marmaduke's Brigade, Clark moved his command to Mt. Elba, where he prepared for the expedition. The horses of the command were reported as in "fair condition," but would be ready "in a very short time"; however, the condition of the horses was contingent on the shoeing, which if not completed prior to the expedition, would leave the horses unfit for service. Overall the health of the brigade was declared as "bad" by General Clark, though the procurement of quinine would solve "nine-tenths of the cases." Additionally, among the many problems the brigade faced in getting ready for the expedition, was a lack of shoes, as "a great many of the men" were barefooted and also in need of clothing. Fagan's Division, composed of William L. Cabell's and W. F. Slemons's Brigades, was likewise preparing for the Missouri Expedition, making their headquarters at Princeton. Cabell "made every preparation" to put his brigade "in good order," recording that he had his "horses and mules shod, wagons repaired, commissary stores gathered, issued all the shoes and clothing...[he] could get, replenished...[his] stock of ammunition of every kind, both artillery and musketry." Slemons's Brigade experienced the same preparations, after which a member of the unit declared that as "the men and horses are refreshed and recuperated, it was now in fine condition for any service." *O.R.*, vol. 41, pt. 2: 1065, 1071, 1075–1076; *O.R.S.*, pt. 1, vol. 7:390. John Crowell Wright Papers, "Memoirs of Colonel John C. Wright C.S.A," Typescript copy in possession of author, unnumbered pages 64–65, Arkansas History Commission, hereafter cited as Wright Memoirs; Crowley, 136.
6. Prior to launching the Missouri Expedition, Price envisioned three objectives, according to Michael Forsyth. First, capture St. Louis and Jefferson City, and install Thomas C. Reynolds as governor of the state. Second, replenish his command with new men, supplies and horses. And third, influence the national election in favor of the Democrat peace candidate, George B. McClellan. Union General John B. Sanborn, a witness to Price's Raid, put forth the same rebel objectives, adding that Price intended to occupy the state as well as draw Union troops from other quarters. In reaching his conclusions, Sanborn cites "ex-Confederate generals" as his source. General W. L. Cabell, who was probably one of Sanborn's sources, also added that the expedition sought "to restore confidence in the ability of the Confederate government," in Missouri, by "relieving the State...of Federal rule." Other authors and expedition participants, generally support the objects that Forsyth listed, while some, like J. W. Gibson or Paul Jenkins simply have the invasion as a means to divert Union troops from other theaters of the war or to re-occupy the state. And the *Chicago Tribune*, in an early assessment of the raid, wrote that "one of the main objects of the invasion is to conscript its inhabitants to replenish the Southern armies, and to obtain supplies." Overall the raid would eventually yield thousands of recruits and numerous supplies, and divert Union troops, but would not accomplish the main objectives of taking St. Louis or Jefferson City, much less reoccupy the state. D. Alexander Brown, "The Battle of Westport," *Civil War Times Illustrated* 5 (July, 1966), 6, hereafter cited as D. Brown; Busch, *Missouri Democrat Articles, 41*; Castel, *Sterling Price*, 202–203; Michael J. Forsyth, *The Great Missouri Raid: Sterling Price and the Last Major Confederate Campaign in Northern Territory* (Jefferson, NC, 2015), 7–8,

John B. Sanborn

August 20 the brigade arrived at Tyro. Ben F. Wheatley pays us a flying visit. "We are getting to Missouri as sure as fate," he says, and he puts his hands on the ground and kicks his feet up in the air and makes his spurs rattle. That he mounts his horse and gallops off giving a ringing cheer for the "Old Tenth." Going back to my quarters I gather up my saddle and blankets, strap them on my horse and avoiding the guards, I make my way to the brigade. I find a dozen other convalescents have beat me into camp. What a rejoicing there is about the mess-fires tonight.[7]

On the 21st we march to Mount Ellby [Elba] and camp on the Saline River.[8] I chill severely while on the march. August 22d forage duty and chill again. On the 23rd and 24th the convalescents are sent back to Tyro. Again some of us few evade the guards and return to the brigade. On the 25th, to keep them from being sent back to the convalescents, at Tyro, I take one of the boy's places on the picket duty. I remain on this duty until the 27th, when the brigade moves to within five miles of Warren, Bradley County. On the 28th we camp at Bucksnort and on the

---

hereafter cited as Forsyth, *Great Missouri Raid*; "From St. Louis," *Chicago Tribune*, September 22, 1864; Louis Fusz Diary, Missouri Historical Society, 2:64, hereafter cited as Fusz Diary; J. W. (Watt) Gibson, *Recollections of a Pioneer* (St. Joseph, MO, 1912; reprint ed., Independence, MO, 1999), 158, hereafter cited as Gibson; Douglas L. Gifford, *Where Valor and Devotion Met: The Battle of Pilot Knob* (Winfield, MO, 2014), 20–21, hereafter cited as Gifford; Harrell, *Arkansas, Confederate Military History, Extended*, 439; Paul B. Jenkins, *The Battle of Westport* (Kansas City, MO, 1906; reprint ed. Digital Copy, n.c, n.d.), 27–28, hereafter cited as Jenkins; John B. Sanborn, "The Campaign in Missouri in September and October, 1864," *Glimpses of the Nation's Struggle. Third Series. Papers Read before the Minnesota Commandery of the Military Order of the Loyal Legion of the United States*, 70 vols. (St. Paul, MN, 1893; reprint ed., Wilmington NC, 1992). vol. 28:137–140, hereafter cited as Sanborn, "Campaign in Missouri;" Sellmeyer, 208; Robert E. Shalhope, *Sterling Price Portrait of a Southerner* (Columbia, MO, 1971), 262, hereafter cited as Shalhope; Joseph Conan Thompson, "The Great Little Battle of Pilot Knob," *Missouri Historical Review* 83 (January, 1989), 140–141, hereafter cited as Thompson, "Great Little Battle of Pilot Knob."

7. Luttrell was right as to the rapid recovery of the sick men in Marmaduke's Brigade once the rumored destination of the expedition became general knowledge. One of those who recovered quickly was F. M. Hope of the 4th Missouri Cavalry (CSA). Hope refused to be left behind in Arkansas, recording in his later years: "I foolishly went with him [Price] before my broken leg had healed properly, but the idea of going back to old Missouri was too great to withstand." Neither Luttrell nor Hope were alone in the excitement of going back to Missouri; for on August 22, General Clark reported: "I send up a field return this morning showing large increase in the command in the last few days." And still more could be added to the rolls, according to Clark, if the quinine could be provided, as requested. Fortunately for Marmaduke's Brigade, and Price's Army, "a large shipment of newly arrived medical supplies, including one hundred boxes of quinine and smaller quantities of morphine and opium, were sent to the Price's command on August 23, 1864. This in turn probably produced a further increase in the command's strength *O.R.*, vol. 41, pt. 2:1076; F. M. Hope Statement, *Confederate Veteran* 33 (February, 1925), 73; Kyle S. Sinisi, *The Last Hurrah: Sterling Price's Missouri Expedition of 1864* (New York, 2015), 35, hereafter cited as Sinisi.

8. On August 21, Clark made camp on the north side of the Saline River, about 3/4 of a mile above a pontoon bridge that was laid at Mt. Elba. The position was not an ideal one, being devoid of forage, though there was a "two or three day's supply within four or five miles on the south side" of the Saline River. Further, Clark notified headquarters that "it was of the first importance that the command be well foraged" before the expedition began. *O.R.*, vol. 41, pt. 2:1075–1076.

29th we camp one mile south of Princeton on the Camden road. Our next march brought us to within four miles of Rockport, on the Little Rock road.[9] September 1 we march twenty miles. On the 2d we camp on the middle fork of the Saline River. Our next camp was on the Little Push or Lafay [La Fourche] River. On the 4th we camp within six miles of the Big Push. On the 5th we camp within four miles of the Petit Jean River. The 6th we crossed the Petit Jean on a bridge, the first one since our march began. We passed through Dardanelle and cross the Arkansas River.[10] I go down on the river and watch the train cross. Our advanced-guard

9. Price and staff, with his ordnance and headquarters train, departed Camden on August 28, experienced a "violent storm of rain, hail and wind" in the afternoon, and finally made camp after traveling 16 miles. The next day, Price's entourage, consisting of "the General, the attachés, hangers-on, and body guard," which numbered about 300, arose before dawn and were off to Princeton by sunrise. After traveling another 16 miles, Price's party arrived at Princeton by 11:00 a.m., joining his train with Fagan's and Marmaduke's commands, giving him roughly 250 wagons (Webb says 300, as does Monnett). Later that day Price met with his principal officers, setting the stage to begin the "grand expedition" into Missouri. On August 30, Price headed north 8 miles to Tulip, as rain pelted the column during the march. Before noon, Price halted the command for the remainder of the day "to allow all trains to get up and get everything in order" before moving onward. Additionally, Price was hoping that I. F. Harrison's 1,500-man Louisiana Brigade would catch up with the column before he pushed on to northeast Arkansas, but Harrison never did. The following day started off "cloudy and pleasant," but later "became very warm." Prior to starting, two 6-lb iron guns of Hughey's Battery were sent back to Camden, "not having suitable horses." When the column moved, it set a pattern that was followed until it reached northeast Arkansas—"Start every morning at daylight and travel all day." J. B. Clark's Brigade of Marmaduke's Division led off Price's army on September 1, followed by the train, with Price and staff, and then Fagan's Division. The column made 27 miles before day's end. September 1 also saw a flurry of orders governing Price's Army, one which stated that the various commands, from regiments to divisions, were to alternate their position in the march every day. *O.R.*, vol. 41, pt. 1:626, 642, 679; J. T. Alexander, Letters (September 6, 1864); Carolyn M. Bartels, *Battle of Pilot Knob As Told by Dr. Seymour Carpenter and Eye-witness Account by a Participant* (Independence, MO, 1995), 6, hereafter cited as Bartels, *Battle of Pilot Knob*; Howard N. Monnett, *Action Before Westport 1864, Revised Edition* (Niwot, CO, 1995), 26, hereafter cited as Monnett; Pitcock & Gurley, 212–214; Sinisi, 33–34, 41; Webb, 209.

10. From September 1–6 the weather was generally warm, with the column starting at or before sunrise and stopping by early afternoon. On September 1, Price divided his army into two columns (Forsyth has the separation taking place on August 31); Fagan's Division, constituted the right portion of the command, departing from the remainder when within 7 miles of Benton, Arkansas. Crossing the Saline River, Fagan's mission was to deceive the Federals in Little Rock into believing that Price was marching on the city, a mission which he successfully executed. Union General Frederick Steele for his part was totally confused as to Price's intentions, believing that Little Rock was the target of the rebel advance and any rumored advance into Missouri was "humbug." In the end Steele did nothing to impede Price's advance, leading one staff officer to remark that Steele "must be weak and timid," while remaining "in a virtually catatonic condition," according to author Kyle Sinisi. On September 5, Fagan rejoined Price, just as the army was nearing the Arkansas River. The rest of the column, led by Clark's Brigade, with Price's trains moved off to the northwest on September 1, over a rough, hilly and mountainous road, toward Dardanelle where they intended to cross the Arkansas River, which was about 65 miles from Little Rock. In all, the column made about 100 miles from September 1–6, reaching the Arkansas River on September 6. *O.R.*, vol. 41, pt. 1:626, 642–43; *O.R.*, vol. 41, pt. 2:936; *O.R.*, vol. 41, pt. 3:25–26, 44, 53–54, 78, 906; J. T. Alexander, Letters (September 6 & 13, 1864); Lumir Buresh, *October 25th and the Battle of Mine Creek* (Kansas City, MO, 1977), 33, hereafter cited as Buresh; Crowley, 135;

has a slight skirmish with the Yankees near Norristown. Our brigade takes the advance. The Tenth regiment in the lead with Cos. A and K as advanced-guard. We camp near Norristown. On the 7th we passed through Russellville and camp on Illinois Bayou.[11] On the 8th we passed through Dover, take the right-hand road and camp on a creek eighteen miles from Dover in the direction of Clinton.[12]

Forsyth, *Great Missouri Raid*, 109; Wright Memoirs, unnumbered page 70; Pitcock & Gurley, 214–216; Sinisi, 37–39.

11. Clark's Brigade arrived at Dardanelle on the morning of September 6, and was greeted by flag-waving Confederate women who lined the streets. Lawther's 10th Missouri Cavalry immediately crossed the Arkansas River, even as the rest of Clark's Brigade filtered into the city. Shortly after crossing the river, Companies A and K, 10th Missouri Cavalry, engaged Company A, 3rd Arkansas Cavalry (Union) near Norristown, which was just across the river from Dardanelle. The Federals reported no losses in the affair; however, rebel sources noted that "four or five" Federals were killed or wounded, with "eight or ten good horses" captured. Additionally, Price's advance also managed to capture the Federal correspondence of the garrison commander at Dardanelle, including a cipher code for all his correspondence. Pushing aside the Federal scouts, Clark's Brigade secured the northern bank of the river. Meanwhile, Captain Thomas J. Mackey, the corps chief engineer, arrived shortly thereafter and evaluated the area to determine if a pontoon needed to be laid to cross the corps train. Upon inquiry, and then inspection, Mackey found a ford "a half mile southeast of Dardanelle—a ford three or three and half feet in depth, the river 290 or 300 yards in width. Ammunition was removed from caissons; ordnance stores necessarily raised in the wagons" and the wagons prepared for fording the river. Meanwhile, General Price ordered General William Cabell to take charge of the crossing. After crossing Clark's Brigade, Cabell started the ordnance train across the Arkansas "late in the evening." Immediately behind the train came Cabell's then Slemons's Brigades, which had to delay crossing until the following day. On September 7, the remainder of the army crossed the Arkansas and proceeded on to Dover 14 miles away. Of the river crossing General Cabell recalled: "Never did anyone see a grander or more imposing sight." Dr. McPheeters agreed, noting that "It was a really grand and picturesque... [crossing] and is well worthy of being sketched and perpetuated. I cannot now pretend to describe it but I shall never forget it." *O.R.*, vol. 41, pt. 1:679, 703; *O.R.S.*, pt. 1, vol. 7:391–392; *O.R.S.*, pt. 2, vol. 2:84; J. T. Alexander, Letter (September 6, 1864); Crute, *Confederate Staff Officers*, 158; John C. Darr, "Price's Raid in Missouri," *Confederate Veteran* 11 (August, 1903), 359, hereafter cited as Darr; Davis, *Civil War Atlas*, plt. no. 154; Dyer, 686; "Journal of Sterling Price's Missouri Expedition by an unnamed officer, August 31–November 10, 1864," *Washington Telegraph* (Washington, AR), November 30, 1864, hereafter cited as *O.R.S.*, pt. 1, vol. 7; National Archives, Record Group 109, Confederate Correspondence (MSS 03-26, Box 1, file 2), Letter (September 7, 1864), hereafter cited as Confederate Correspondence; Pitcock & Gurley, 216–217; Sinisi, 39; Wright Memoirs, unnumbered page 70.

12. On September 7 the remainder of the train began crossing the Arkansas River "at an early hour," and by 9:00 a.m. the army was on the road to Dover. After the crossing was completed, Captain Mackey ordered 18 of the 25 wagons in the pontoon train burned as they were no longer needed. Meanwhile, Clark's Brigade expanded the army's bridgehead, moving four miles to the vicinity of Russellville on the road to Dover, where they remained as the army moved northward, thus assuming the role of the rear guard. Led by Cabell's Brigade, Fagan's Division reached Dover at 1:30 p.m. At Dover, due to the scarcity of forage on the route to northeast Arkansas, Price divided his command; Fagan's Division moved to the front and was sent on a longer southern route via Springfield to Batesville, while Marmaduke, with the train, took a northern road to Clinton and on to Batesville. The delay in moving Fagan to the front prevented the trains and Marmaduke's command from moving until 9:00 a.m. on September 8, "the latest start" that they had made since the beginning of the expedition. *O.R.*, vol. 41, pt. 1:626; *O.R.S.*, pt. 1, vol. 7:391–392; Pitcock & Gurley, 216–217; Sinisi, 39.

On the 9th we leave the camp early and make Moon Pint Creek. On the 10th our advance has a brush with the mountain boomers. One of our men is wounded. We camp within eight miles of Clinton on the south fork of Little Red River.

On the 11th we take the Batesville road and camp on the middle fork of Little Red River.

[Editor Note: From this point on Luttrell has mis-dated his diary entries; all of which should read one day earlier. The correct dates are listed in brackets]

13th [12th]—Pass over Greenbrier Mountain and camp on White River.

14th [13th]—Lay in camp and repair the train, many wagons having been broken while crossing the mountain. I have a desperate chill. They come regularly every third day.[13]

On the 15th [14th] we camp within 10 miles of Hookrum.

16th [15th]—Leave Hookrum one mile to the left when we cross Piney Creek and camp on Strawberry River.[14]

---

13. Of the two routes, Marmaduke's proved to be the worst. From September 8–12, Marmaduke's column logged about 97 miles, with the 12th being "the roughest and worst day's march." The terrain was "rocky, steep, rough and...the whole way without water for stock or men," according to Dr. McPheeters. The medical wagon capsized and some medicine was lost, wagons broke down, causing the train to delay the march to Batesville, as repairs needed to made to the various conveyances on the 13th. While Marmaduke guarded the train, Price hurried on to Batesville with his staff, en route to Powhatan, Arkansas, where he met General Shelby on the evening of September 13. On September 14, Marmaduke finally arrived at Batesville and headed to Powhatan, while the remainder of the army was already on the road to Powhatan, with the ultimate destination being Pocahontas in northeast Arkansas. *O.R.*, vol. 41, pt. 1:627, 643; Pitcock & Gurley, 217–219; Sinisi, 41, 43.

14. While Marmaduke struggled on the northern route to Batesville, Fagan's Division moved on toward Springfield with Cabell's Brigade in front. After making 17 miles, on September 8, the division camped at Point Remove or Glass Village, about 23 miles from the Union garrison at Lewisburg. After the pickets were placed, a scout from Cabell's Brigade came running into camp followed by a 300-man detachment of the 3rd Arkansas Cavalry (Union), from Lewisburg. A volley from J. C. Monroe's Arkansas Regiment (Cabell says it was Gordon's Regiment), assisted by Hughey's Battery sent the bluecoats running. Anderson Gordon's Arkansas Regiment was then sent in pursuit, capturing "several good horses and a number of carbines." The Confederates reported killing one, wounding five and capturing seven, while losing none of their own; there was no Union report on this skirmish. Fagan's Division made 52 miles from September 9–11, while noting "my horses and mules tired, very, and need shoeing badly." By the 11th Fagan was also out of "breadstuff." On the evening of the 12th Fagan reached Batesville, the same day that Price and staff pulled into town. September 13 saw Fagan's ordnance officer make a bold and prophetic prediction on the pending invasion of Missouri—"I have always thought this move a very uncertain and precarious one," wrote Captain James T. Alexander, "but if successful will result in great benefit to the cause. If disastrous will greatly demoralize the army and will be attended by the loss of our train." With Fagan in Batesville, Marmaduke's command was still 18 miles farther back, repairing its wagons, planning to rejoin the army in "a few days." Both commands reached the Strawberry River, 13 miles from Powhatan, on September 15, where they halted early in the day to allow their wagons to catch the main column and to forage their horses, which were in a "wearied condition." *O.R.*, vol. 41, pt. 3:116, 919, 924–925, 934; *O.R.S.*, pt. 1, vol. 7:302, 405; J. T. Alexander, Letter (September 13, 1864); Darr, 359; Dyer, 686; Pitcock & Gurley, 219; Sinisi, 43; Wright Memoirs, unnumbered page 70.

17th [16th]—Lay up and rest our jaded horses; miss my chill.[15]

On 18th [17th] we camp on Spring River, marching on the Smithville and Pocahontas road.

19th [18th]—Move out at sundown, cross the Seven Points and reach Pocahontas about midnight. We cross the wagons on a raft and swim our horses.[16]

20th [19th]—This morning we finished crossing Black River and getting through the swamp; we build fires, dry ourselves, feed our horses and cook rations: laying up about two hours. We then move on Poplar Bluff road, and camp fifteen miles from Pocahontas on Current River.[17]

21st [20th]—To-day we crossed the state line, and camp on a bayou two miles inside the state of Missouri, name of bayou not known.

22d [21st]—Camp on Big Black River, one mile north of Poplar Bluff.

---

15. Colonel William L. Jeffers's 8th Missouri Cavalry departed Powhatan on September 16 or 17 on a "scout" into southeast Missouri and were not part of Price's army when he crossed into Missouri three days later. The rest of Marmaduke's command remained another day, resting and making repairs, before heading to Pocahontas, where it arrived on the evening of September 18. *O.R.*, vol. 41, pt. 1:703; Cocker, 9; McGhee, *Campaigning with Marmaduke*, 21; Bryce A. Suderow, *Thunder in Arcadia Valley: Price's Defeat, September 27, 1864* (Cape Girardeau, MO, 1986), 31, hereafter cited as Suderow, *Arcadia Valley*.

16. On September 16 Fagan's command arose before sunrise and was off to Pocahontas, where Price concentrated his army, including J. O. Shelby's command. By 1:00 p.m. Price's command were all in camp, with the exception of Marmaduke's Brigade, which did not arrive until late on September 18. In all, Price's column had made about "324 miles in eighteen days and averaged 18 miles per day, a slow pace for cavalry." Final preparations took place between September 16–18 before the army moved to Missouri; horses were shod, wagons repaired, ammunition issued, Medical Department organized and on September 18, per General Orders No. 8, the "Army of Missouri" was organized. As organized, the Army consisted of the three divisions, commanded by Generals Fagan, Marmaduke, and Shelby, with several attached regiments and battalions. Note: The organization presented in the *Official Records* (vol. 41, pt. 1:641–642) is a composite that was developed based upon the entire expedition and was not reflective of what it looked like when the expedition began. See Appendix D for the Army of Missouri Organization, when the expedition entered Missouri, including known additions as the expedition progressed. *O.R.*, vol. 41, pt. 3:943; *O.R.S.*, pt. 1, vol. 7:392; Wiley Britton, *The Civil War on the Border A Narrative of Military Operations in Missouri, Kansas, Arkansas, and the Indian Territory, During the Years 1863–65, Based Upon Official Reports and Observations of the Author, Volume 2* (New York, 1899), 390, hereafter cited as Britton, *Civil War on the Border, 1863–65*; Buresh, 30, 32–33; Edwards, *Shelby and His Men*, 382–383; Forsyth, *Great Missouri Raid*, 111; Pitcock & Gurley, 220–221.

17. On September 19 the Army of Missouri moved out of its camps around Pocahontas, and set off on three different paths to Fredericktown, Missouri, which was about 120 miles from the starting point and 20 miles southeast of Pilot Knob. Fagan's Division, with Price's headquarters and trains, took the direct route "by way of Martinsburg, Reeve's Station and Greenville"; Marmaduke's Division (Luttrell's command) was to Fagan's right, taking the longest and poorest route, that skirted swamps, taking the division across the Current River at Pitman's Ferry, to Poplar Bluff, then to Dallas, Bloomfield, and finally into Fredericktown. To the west of Fagan, Shelby's Division headed to Patterson, via Doniphan and then to Fredericktown. *O.R.*, vol. 41, pt. 1:627; Britton, *Civil War on the Border, 1863–65*, 390; Crowley, 136; Harrell, *Arkansas, Confederate Military History, Extended*, 440–441; "The Invasion of Missouri—Sept. 19, 1864," in *The Civil War In Ripley County, Missouri* (Doniphan, MO, 1992), 20–21, hereafter cited as *Ripley County*; Rob't L. Lindsay, "Pilot Knob, Mo.—The Battle Fought There, September 26 and 27th, 1864," *The Forge* (Ironton, MO), October 19, 1865, hereafter cited as Lindsay; Schultz, 168–169; Sinisi, 46.

23d [22nd]—March on the Cape Girardeau road, and camp five miles north of the St. Francois River.
24th [23rd]—March on the Fredericktown road and camp on the Castor River.[18]
25th [24th]—Passed through Dallas, and camp eight miles beyond.[19]

---

18. Of the three rebel columns marching into Missouri, Shelby's moved rapidly forward lead by M. Rector Johnson's Company, lately arrived from southwest Missouri. About daylight on the 19th, Johnson's advance was attacked, by an 86-man patrol from the 3rd Missouri State Militia (MSM) Cavalry (Union), under Lieutenant Erich Pape, and driven out of Doniphan. Pape later burned the town and moved on to Ponder's Mill to camp for the night, not believing that the invasion had begun. Shelby's Division arrived at the still-smoldering Doniphan at 3:30 p.m., on the 19th, and went into camp. Lieutenant Colonel B. A. Johnson, commanding a portion of the 15th Missouri Cavalry, from Fagan's Division, who was familiar with the area, was sent in pursuit of Pape soon after Shelby made camp, taking with him 150 men from the division. At daylight, the next morning, Johnson attacked the Federals, assisted by the guerrilla Sam Hildebrand, and scattered Pape's command. Federal losses varied depending on source, ranging from 11–45 killed and 43–45 wounded. Confederate sources reported losing two killed and five wounded (See Appendix A for Extended Comments on Doniphan. Also see Appendix D, Additions to the expedition, Matthew Rector Johnson's Battalion, for details on Johnson at Doniphan.). On September 20 Shelby slowed the pace of his advance, camping at Reeve's Mill, and fearing that he "would be too much in advance of the main line." On the 21st Shelby was 12 miles from Patterson, and the following morning Elliott's Battalion, with Hildebrand, took Patterson at 10:00 a.m. According to John Edwards, 29 were killed, 40 captured and several wounded. Federals for their part admit abandoning Patterson and 35 wounded men, probably from Pape's command, at the fort following its capture, while another seven were noted as either killed, wounded or captured. On September 23, following a 33 mile forced march, through a rain and lightening storm, Shelby took the abandoned Fredericktown after dark the same day. There he waited for the remainder of the army. *O.R.*, vol. 41, pt. 1:455–455, 644,672–673; *O.R.*, vol. 41, pt. 3:945–946, 948, 951, 954; 131–132; Carl W. Breihan, *Sam Hildebrand Guerrilla* (Wauwatosa, WI, 1984), 131–132, hereafter cited as Breihan; Gifford, 56–60; Busch, *Missouri Democrat Articles*, 43; Edwards, *Shelby and His Men*, 383; "From St. Louis," *Chicago Tribune*, September 23, 1864; Moore, *Missouri, Confederate Military History*, 181; Pitcock & Gurley, 221; Confederate Correspondence (MSS 03-26, Box 1, file 2), Shelby to MaClean (September 20, 1864); Bruce Nichols, *Guerrilla Warfare in the Civil War, Volume IV, September 1864–June 1865* (Jefferson, NC, 214), 47, hereafter cited as Nichols, *Guerrilla Warfare, Volume IV*; Jerry Ponder, *A History of the 15th Missouri Cavalry Regiment, C.S.A.* (Doniphan, MO, 1994), 88, 90, 93, hereafter cited as Ponder, *15th Missouri Cavalry*; Sellmeyer, 209–210; Suderow, *Arcadia Valley*, 38; Henry Wilkinson (Letter Nos. 15, 16 & 18), in Peterson Pilot Knob Collection, Missouri Historical Society, hereafter cited as Wilkinson.
19. From September 19–24, the Army of Missouri advanced steadily northward. Of the three columns, Fagan's experienced few if any problems, having only limited contact with Union guerrillas during its initial entry into Missouri. However, Union raiders left their mark as they vacated the area, burning both Doniphan and Martinsburg as Confederate troops crossed into Missouri. Major Isaac Brinker, Price's quartermaster, opened a bottle of "native wine" to celebrate his return to his home state. During the march the "weather [was] pleasant but roads dusty" and generally remained so during the march to Fredericktown, except for a heavy rain which fell on the evening of the 23rd. Fagan's column camped at Ponder's Mill at the end of the second day, the site of an engagement that very morning, where the Doniphan raiders were dealt a serious blow. The command made 24 miles the next two days, passing through Poplar Bluff on the 21st, arriving at Greenville, the county seat of Wayne County, Missouri, on September 22, where they found only two families living. Overall Fagan's column traveled at a leisurely pace, "starting just after daylight" and camping by early afternoon, finally arriving at Fredericktown at 1:00 p.m. on September 24. *O.R.*, vol. 41, pt. 1:643–644; *O.R.S.*, pt. 1, vol. 7:392–393; "An Overview," in *Ripley County*, 11; Diary of the Raid (September 19–October 15, 1864), Civil War Collection, "Army of Missouri" file,

26th [25th]—Pass through Patten, and camp five miles from Fredericktown.[20]

27th [26th]—Today we passed through Fredericktown. Heavy skirmishing in the direction of Ironton. We camp ten miles west of Fredericktown.[21]

Missouri Historical Society (St. Louis), hereafter cited as Diary of the Raid; Pitcock & Gurley, 221-223; Ponder, *15th Missouri Cavalry*, 90; Sinisi, 59.

20. On the "late evening" of September 24, Captain Thomas J. Shaw of Coffee's Battalion reported to General Shelby at Fredericktown, after a scout up the Little Black River. Shelby ordered Shaw to take Captain M. Rector Johnson's company and capture Farmington, the county seat of St. Francis County. Shaw's 54-man command left Fredericktown that same night, marched through the darkness, and waited two miles outside of the town until "it was light enough to shoot." At 9:00 a.m. Shaw's command, led by M. Rector Johnson, charged into Farmington and surrounded the courthouse, where the Federal garrison had taken cover. Unable to compel a surrender, Shaw called for volunteers, who fired the courthouse, causing the Federal commander immediately to capitulate. Federal accounts have one man wounded, with five or six captured. However, Captain Johnson reported to Shelby that he had taken 14 prisoners and captured "25 stand of new arms" with large "quantities of goods," while losing one mortally wounded and one slightly wounded (Bartels has 30 captured). All the prisoners were taken back to Shelby at Fredericktown, except for one civilian, who was executed "for carrying information to the enemy of the approach of" Shaw's command. September 25 also saw Price meeting with his division commanders to discuss their next move. In the end, despite a protest by General Shelby, Price decided to bypass St. Louis and march on Jefferson City. But first Pilot Knob had to be dealt with. Shelby argued against an assault, while both Marmaduke and Fagan supported an attack. Price agreed with his two senior commanders, ordering them to march the next day for Pilot Knob, while Shelby circled the city to the east to cut the Iron Mountain Railroad leading to the city. *O.R.*, vol. 41, pt. 1:652; *O.R.*, vol. pt. 3:359, 956-957; Bartels, *Battle of Pilot Knob*, 13; Busch, *Missouri Democrat Articles*, 23-24; Edwards, *Shelby and His Men*, 385; Gifford, 63; Danny Odom Letter (June 10, 2013), "Coffee's Regiment," Internet site, The Arkansas in the Civil War Message Board, hereafter cited as Odom Letter; Sinisi, 64-65; R. M. Winns, "Scouting In Arkansas and Missouri," *Confederate Veteran* 21 (November, 1913), 538-539, hereafter cited as Winns.

21. To the east of Fagan, Marmaduke's Division, which had a farther route to travel, finally arrived at Fredericktown on September 26, having "had a few skirmishes with the Federal militia, killing and wounding four and capturing 11." Marmaduke, like Fagan moved at a rather slow pace, arriving at Bollinger's Mill on September 23, about 30 miles from Fredericktown. "Unsure about what to do next," Marmaduke slowly marched on to Fredericktown, while awaiting further orders from General Price. He camped five miles from the city on the 25th and finally passed through and camped north of the city on September 26. Additionally, prior to departing Arkansas, William Jeffers' 8th Missouri Cavalry, of Clark's Brigade, was detached from the brigade, with instructions to take Bloomfield, the county seat of Stoddard County. Jeffers was about 18 miles from Bloomfield when he was detected by a 10-man Federal scout, under a Captain Smith, on September 21. Smith immediately informed Captain Lewis Sells, the garrison commander, "that a large body of rebels was moving upon Bloomfield, estimated at from eight to fifteen thousand." Sells, commanding the 200-man garrison of Bloomfield, evacuated the city late into the night, with the final troops leaving at about 2:30 a.m. on the 22nd. At 10:30 a.m. Jeffers' command caught the retreating Union garrison at the Castor River and put them to flight. The next five miles was a running fight with the road "literally strewn with sugar, coffee, flour, crackers, boots and shoes and in fact all kinds of goods." In all, Jeffers captured "75 small arms and 6 wagons loaded with army and sutler stores," while the remaining wagons were burned by the Unionists, before their capture. The Federal command reported losing "3 killed, 7 wounded and some 10 missing," in the running fight, while claiming to have caused a 20-man loss in Jeffers' command. Jeffers entered the undefended Bloomfield later in the day and promptly burned all the military facilities, as well as sacking the town. On the 23rd, Jeffers rejoined his brigade at Bollinger's Mill, was detached the next day for an expedition to Old Jackson. Jeffers "charged into Jackson about sunset, captured 18 prisoners

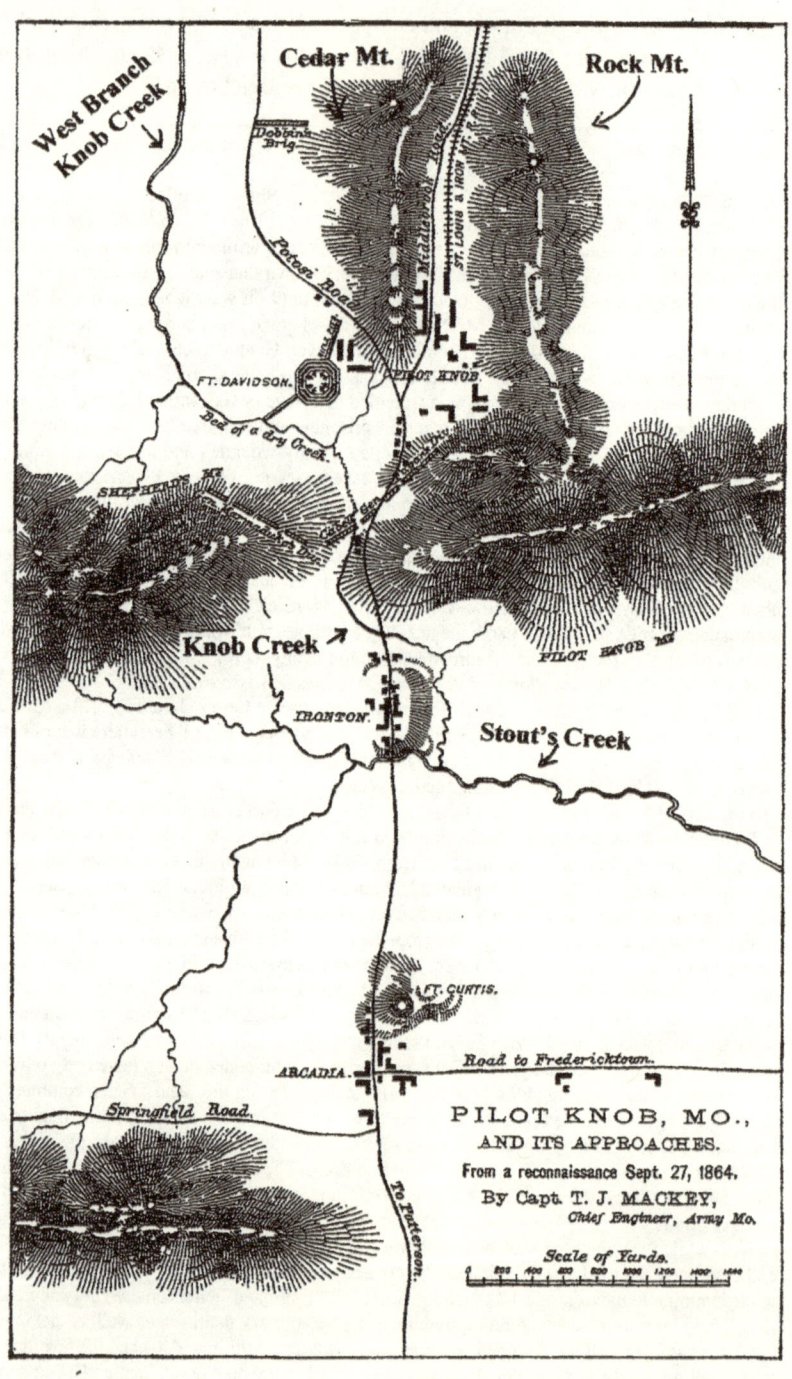

28th [27th]—We find this morning that Shelby's brigade had fought the enemy at Ironton day before.[22] We could see plenty of signs of the fight around some unfinished works which they had abandoned.[23] We find enemy occupying their strongly fortified position at Pilot Knob. Our brigade, Clark's, occupying Cedar [Shepherd] Mountain; Fagan's brigade Shepherd's [Pilot Knob] Mountain; while Shelby's brigade is swinging around to Caledonia.[24]

---

and 40 horses," while losing one man wounded. Two days later, Jeffers rejoined his division on the 26th, which was already at Fredericktown. *O.R.*, vol. 41, pt. 1:453, 628, 679; *O.R.*, vol. 41, pt. 3:361, 951, 953–954; *O.R.S.*, pt. 2, vol. 34:669; Britton, *Civil War on the Border, 1863–65*, 393; Busch, *Missouri Democrat Articles*, 19–20; Cocker, 12–13; Gifford, 60–61; McGhee, *Campaigning With Marmaduke*, 21–22; Nichols, *Guerrilla Warfare, Volume 4*, 47; Suderow, *Arcadia Valley*, 40.

22. Not true. Early on the morning of September 26, Shelby's Division, departed Fredericktown and headed northwest. According to Price's plan, Shelby was tasked with cutting the Iron Mountain Railroad, thus preventing reinforcements from reaching Pilot Knob. By the evening of the 26th, Shelby was located about 26 miles north of Pilot Knob on the road between Potosi and Farmington and within five miles of the Iron Mountain Railroad, having bypassed Pilot Knob to the east. For Extended Comments on Shelby's operations on the Iron mountain Railroad see Appendix C. *O.R.*, vol. 41, pt. 1:628, 652; Castel, *Sterling Price*, 210; Cocker, 13; Richard L. Norton and Troy Massey, eds., *Hard Trials and Tribulations of An Old Confederate Soldier* (Van Buren, AR, 1897; reprint ed., Springfield, MO, 1997), 63, hereafter cited as Norton & Massey.

23. On September 26 Fagan's Division led off Price's Army, departing Fredericktown, "early in the morning," with William F. Slemons's Brigade in the lead, commanded by Colonel William C. Wright. Next came Thomas McCray's and Archibald Dobbin's Brigades, while Cabell's Brigade brought up the rear. Stopping eight miles from Pilot Knob, Fagan sent Slemons's Brigade forward to secure Shut In Gap, the entrance to Arcadia Valley, and take Ironton if possible. Ironton was about two miles from Pilot Knob and just outside of the Ironton Gap, which barred the way to Pilot Knob. Wright became engaged near 1:00 p.m., briefly occupied Ironton, was driven out by Federal troops at 3:00 p.m., and settled in by nightfall just outside the town of Arcadia, following a day of "light attacks" and counterattacks. Few casualties were reported on either side (Albert Castel says that Wright's command suffered "heavy casualties"), while the Confederates had secured the entrance to Arcadia Valley. Further, the Union command was still unsure as to what troops they actually faced and what action General Thomas Ewing, the commander of Pilot Knob, should take: stay and fight or evacuate? "The advantages of delaying the enemy two or three days," wrote Ewing, "in his march northward and of making a stubborn fight before retreating were so great,... that I resolved to stand fast" *O.R.*, vol. 41, pt. 1:628; *O.R.S.*, pt. 1, vol. 7:393, 406; Busch, *Missouri Democrat Articles*, 21; Castel, *Sterling Price*, 210; Gifford, 90–92, 99, 112–113; Pitcock & Gurley, 224; Lindsay, *Forge*, October 19, 1865; Schultz, 160; Sinisi, 69–70; Suderow, *Arcadia Valley*, 47, 61–70; Wilkinson (Letter No. 17); Wright Memoirs, unnumbered page 74.

24. Caledonia was located about eight miles west from the Iron Mountain Railroad and 12 miles north of Ironton. It was the place that Shelby moved to after destroying the Iron Mountain Railroad. Davis, *Civil War Atlas*, plt. no. 152; Schultz, 170.

Thomas Ewing

Reminiscence of Pilot Knob.

In a former article I gave an account of the battle of Pilot Knob, which is not materially different from that in my diary, only I gave the date of the battle as occurring on the 25th of September. My diary says it was on the 28th [27th]. I wrote it entirely from memory.

Henry Luttrell,
Gen. Hindman's Escort, Co. G, and
Tenth Missouri Cavalry, C.S.A.

[Editor Note: Luttrell's piece on the Battle of Pilot Knob is inserted here, where it properly belongs. The remaining portion of Luttrell's February 27, 1887, article on Price's 1864 Missouri Raid will immediately follow this piece.]

* * * * * * *

Item: The Battle of Pilot Knob, Missouri (September 27, 1864), by Henry C. Luttrell, Company G, 10th Missouri Cavalry (C.S.A.). Part Two. **Published:** October 24, 1885.

Baldwin, Mo., Oct.21

As well as I remember, it was on the evening of the 24th of September, 1864, that Gen. Joe Shelby, with his brigade, struck the enemy a short distance east of Ironton and south of Pilot Knob.[25]

After a spirited and somewhat prolonged engagement he drove them from some unfinished works into their strongly fortified position at Pilot Knob.[26]

The fort, as I remember it, was an eight square work, with two sally ports, a

---

25. Not true. There was no record of Shelby striking anywhere near Ironton on September 24. Luttrell was probably referring to Shelby's attacks on the Iron Mountain Railroad, between Irondale and Mineral Point, which occurred on September 27. See Appendix C, for Extended Comments on Shelby's Operations on the Iron Mountain Railroad.
26. There were two major forts built in the vicinity of Arcadia Valley. Fort Davidson was located on the plain just southwest of Pilot Knob, while Fort Curtis was located between Ironton and Arcadia and guarded the south entrance to the valley. Curtis was the unfinished works that Luttrell was referring too and played no role in the upcoming battle, having been built in early 1862. Originally called Fort Hovey, after the commander of the 33rd Illinois Infantry, the name was changed to Fort Curtis, following General Samuel R. Curtis's victory at the Battle of Pea Ridge. Neither Fort Curtis nor Davidson were ever intended to withstand a well-organized opposing force, but rather to discourage guerrilla attacks and small cavalry raids. Curtis, which mounted six guns, was recommended for abandonment in early 1863, because the fort "did not protect what was truly important to the military," the Iron Mountain Railroad terminus and the iron deposits. By the Battle of Pilot Knob, Fort Curtis housed no troops, and its artillery had been removed to Fort Davidson. Still, Fort Curtis was used periodically by Federal troops, who "camped around...but less used" fort. On September 26, according to Price's corps engineer, Fort Curtis contained an "outpost" or picket force that was intended to warn Pilot Knob of any pending rebel attack. For details of operations on September 26, at Pilot Knob see note 21 above. Walter E. Busch, *Fort Davidson and the Battle of Pilot Knob: Missouri's Alamo* (Charleston, SC, 2010), 15, 17, 19, 21, 26, hereafter cited as Busch, *Fort Davidson*; Busch, *Missouri Democrat Articles*, 41; Forsyth, *Great Missouri Raid*, 120; Schultz, 177; Wilkinson (Letter No. 15).

parapet 12 feet high and 12 inches in depth, with a ditch surrounding the whole work 12 foot deep and 12 feet wide, making a distance of 24 feet from the bottom of the ditch to the top of the parapet. The armament of the work was about as follows: Seven 64-pound guns, three 100-pounders and four heavy howitzers, besides a number of smaller field guns; but 14 heavy guns were mounted on the works.[27] The fort sits in an open valley, once a farm, surrounded on all sides by mountains and high hills. Cedar Mountain is on the south and about 300 yards to its foot, around which winds a small branch.[28]

Shepherd Mountain is on the east, and in the gorge between Shepherd and Cedar Mountains nestles the little village of Ironton.[29] Through this gorge ran the road and approaches to the fort. Farther to the north and east is Iron Mountain. Then a range of little high hills complete the circle to the north and west.[30]

27. Fort Davidson was named after General John W. Davidson, "a man for whom the people of South-East Missouri have very little respect." Davidson was born in Virginia and falsely suspected of rebel sympathies early in the war. Luttrell was incorrect as to the armament of Fort Davidson. At the time of the battle, Fort Davidson mounted four 32-lb smoothbore siege guns, three 24-lb howitzers, two 24-lb Coehorn mortars, with two 2-lb Woodruff guns. Additionally, Battery H, 2nd Missouri Artillery, commanded by Captain William C. F. Montgomery was added to the garrison on September 22, bringing six 3-in rifled cannon to the post. Montgomery's command later joined the Pilot Knob retreat and continued to serve in other capacities throughout the expedition. See Figure No. 1 for Sergeant Henry Wilkinson's drawing and gun placements of Fort Davidson. See also Appendix C for Extended Comments on Fort Davidson. *O.R.*, vol. 41, pt. 1:458; Banasik, *Reluctant Cannoneer*, 282; Busch, *Fort Davidson*, 23; Lindsay, *Forge*, October 19, 1865; Sinisi, 61; Suderow, *Arcadia Valley*, 48; Wilkinson (Letter Nos. 16 & 17).

28. Cedar Mountain was north of Fort Davidson, not south, and northwest of the town of Pilot Knob. It was located in what was known as the upper or northern part of Arcadia Valley. The Iron Mountain Railroad was to the east of Cedar Mountain, while to the west of the railroad, Rock or Depot or Iron Mountain was the prominent feature. The Middlebrook road ran next to the railroad, while the road to Farmington passed between Rock and Pilot Knob Mountains. West of Cedar Mountain one finds the Potosi Road. The East Branch Knob Creek ran between Rock and Cedar Mountains, while the two mountains marked the boundary between the upper and lower Arcadia Valley. Before passing onto the lower valley the East Branch Knob Creek links up with the West Branch and then heads south between Shepherd and Pilot Knob Mountains, emptying into Stouts Creek. Stouts Creek lay to the east and between Arcadia and Ironton, running to the west of Shepherd Mountain and southeast to Shut In Gap, which barred the entry to the southern part of Arcadia Valley. And the southern-most road into the valley was the Fredericktown Road. *O.R.*, vol. 41, pt. 1: map on 708; Busch, *Fort Davidson*, 19; Birdie Haile Cole, "The Battle of Pilot Knob," *Confederate Veteran* 22 (September 1914), 417, hereafter cited as Cole; Sinisi, 78; Suderow, *Arcadia Valley*, 47, 87; Thompson, "Great Little Battle of Pilot Knob," 150–151.

29. Shepherd Mountain was to the south and southwest of Fort Davidson, while Pilot Knob Mountain was to the east of the fort. Between the two mountains lay a gap of 300 yards, that marked the division between the Upper and Lower Arcadia Valley. Pilot Knob Mountain was about 500–600 yards from Fort Davidson. Ironton was the county seat of Iron County and was located in what was known as the lower or southern part of the Arcadia Valley. It was described by one Union soldier as "one of the prettiest little towns that I have seen." Banasik, *Duty, Honor and Country*, 241; Castel, *Sterling Price*, 213; Cole, 417; Sinisi, 82; Suderow, *Arcadia Valley*, 47, 83; Thompson, "Great Little Battle of Pilot Knob," 151.

30. Fort Davidson "was located three hundred yards northwest of the base of Pilot Knob [Mountain], about the same distance north of the base of Shepherd Mountain, and one thousand yards nearly north of the gap between the mountains," according to Wiley Britton (Captain T. J. Mackey, Con-

Gun Emplacements at Fort Davidson

11. Ewing's HQ
12. 32 lb Siege Gun
12A. Dismounted 32 lb Siege Gun
13. 24 lb Howitzer
14. 3" Rifle Cannon
15. Mortars (unmanned)
18. Abandoned 3" Rifle Cannon
19. Woodruff Guns (unmanned)

Shepherd's Mt.

Pilot Knob Mt.

The morning of the 25th [27th] finds us in position on the crest of Edan [Shepherd] Mountain.³¹ Maj. [Joseph] Pratt's battery opened the engagement by shelling the enemy

At Long Range.³²

The enemy respond with thunderous effect.

---

federate engineer, has the distance at 600 yards from the base of each of the mountains, while General Ewing puts it at 300 yards from Shepherd and 600 yards from Pilot Knob Mountain). Pilot Knob was to the northeast of the fort, about 400 yards. Much of the land around the fort had been stripped of its timber, laying the ground bare, while the southern slope of Shepherd Mountain, according to General John B. Clark "was as rugged as one could imagine," being covered with "huge boulders, fallen timbers, and deep and almost impassable ravines." Another soldier, in the 8th Missouri Cavalry, noted that the mountains were "so rough with brush and rocks that a man can hardly climb them afoot." Pilot Knob mountain, according to author Joseph Thompson was "the rockiest of the four...[and] proved the most difficult to climb." Overall, the condition of both Shepherd and Pilot Knob Mountains lent themselves to breaking up any order to the Confederate assault as they descended from these two peaks. This in turn would cause time to be taken to reorder the commands as they emerged on the plain below the two mountains before any final assault could be made. *O.R.*, vol. 41, pt. 1:679, map on 708; Britton, *Civil War on the Border, 1863–65*, 395–396; Cole, 417; Thomas Ewing, "Battle of Pilot Knob and Leesburg, Missouri," Rebellion Record, vol. 11:136; Benjamin J. Farmer Memoir, 11, William L, Skaggs Collection, Arkansas History Commission, hereafter cited as Farmer Memoir; Thompson, "Great Little Battle of Pilot Knob," 150.

31. The evening of September 26, found Marmaduke's Division camped 10 miles west of Fredericktown, near the St. Francis River, and about two miles from Price's headquarters. Fagan's command moved up to the Arcadia Valley, camping just inside the valley, near the town of Arcadia. Going into the evening hours, Marmaduke ordered Colonel Thomas R. Freeman to issue 25 rounds of ammunition to every man and "be ready at early daylight to move out" to Ironton. Further, Freeman was to "carry into the fight, if there be any, all your armed men." The unarmed men were to serve as horse holders or to form an "infirmary corps," while all excess men were to remain with the train. For the upcoming battle, Freeman would combine with Alonozo Slayback's Battalion, providing just 500 armed men. By sunrise, Price expected Marmaduke to join him at his headquarters, ready for action. On the Federal side, Ewing continued to picket the area near Ironton, setting his lines north of Stouts Creek for a distance of about a mile. The night also found Ewing determining to fight and not evacuate Fort Davidson. That decision was based in part upon on a false belief that Ewing did not face Price's entire army. Ewing confidently telegraphed to General William S. Rosecrans, commander of the Department: "I can hold out against 4,000 or 5,000 cavalry and four pieces of artillery." To that end, Ewing dispatched several trains out of the area, carrying excess supplies; however, the railroad train was delayed until daylight, for fear the road had been cut, which proved to be incorrect. The wagon train, with some 64 wagons (Gifford says 70 wagons), 40 of which were empty, under Lieutenant M. P. Tate, departed the area sometime between midnight and 1:00 a.m., during a light "mist" which continued most of the night. The wagon train never made it to DeSoto, its destination, having been attacked and captured by Shelby's command near Potosi the following afternoon. *O.R.*, vol. 41, pt. 3:959; "Arrival of Captain Hills," *Missouri Republican*, September 30, 1864; Bartels, *Pilot Knob*, 26–27; Busch, *Missouri Democrat Articles*, 55; Quoted in Forsyth, *Great Missouri Raid*, 126; "The Rebel Invasion," *Missouri Republican*, September 28, 1864; Letter (September 26, 1864), Ewing to Freeman, Civil War Collection, "Army of Missouri" file, Missouri Historical Society; Gifford, 110–111; Pitcock & Gurley, 223; Sinisi, 71–72, 74–75; Suderow, *Arcadia Valley*, 72, 74, 76–77; Wilkinson (Letter No. 18).

32. At the beginning of the expedition Joseph Pratt was appointed J. S. Marmaduke's assistant ord-

Dark, heavy clouds swing near the ground; heavy fog and rifts of rain completed the picture of a dark and lowering day. Under foot the ground is wet and oozy from heavy rain of last night.[33]

The fort nestling below us in the valley does not appear much larger than a good size barn. With the naked eye you can scarcely tell anything of its construction. We seemed to be doing literally nothing. The heavy guns of the enemy seem to completely drown us out, but we keep pounding away. And now the enemy's

---

nance officer, and was responsible for the artillery of the division, which consisted of two batteries. Pratt, according to General John B. Clark, commanded a battalion in the brigade, which contained the two 3-gun batteries; Captain Henry C. Hynson's Texas Battery (Pratt's old command or the 10th Texas Light Artillery) and Captain Samuel S. Harris's Missouri Battery. Pratt's Battery consisted of one 12-pound James Rifle; one 6-pound smoothbore; and one 12-pound mountain howitzer, while Harris' Battery contained the same three guns (See Confederate Artillery in Appendix D for details). Pratt's command was about nine miles away from Pilot Knob when the battle began on September 27, and would not arrive until sometime after 10:00 a.m., but well before noon. By about 11:00, according to Bryce Suderow and Douglas Gifford, Confederate artillery posted near Ironton fired some rounds in support of the Confederate attackers. Gifford has the battery from Clark's Brigade, while Suderow says that it was one of Fagan's; however, it appears, according to Luttrell, that it was Pratt's or Hynson's Texas Artillery, which had just arrived in the area. *O.R.*, vol. 41, pt. 1:679; *O.R.*, vol. 41, pt. 3:959; Crute, *Confederate Staff Officers*, 132; Gifford, 128; Suderow, *Arcadia Valley*, 97; Wooster *Lone Star Regiments*, 305–306.

33. The sun rose at 6:01 a.m. on September 27, with a light mist still falling and fog blanketing the area. Marmaduke's Division was on the road before daylight and headed for Pilot Knob, 10 miles away. Back at Ironton, Fagan's Division was up well before dawn, with Cabell's Brigade aligned along the south side of Stouts Creek, while the rest of the division was held in reserve. All was quiet until it was "light enough to discern the outlines of a man's body." A lone rifle shot started the battle, followed by the "continuous roll" of assorted gunfire, which was heard, according to one witness, 39 miles away, near where Piedmont, Missouri, now stands. Cabell's Brigade charged at about 7:00 a.m., sending the Union pickets scurrying for their support. A short time later Hughey's Arkansas Battery opened fire in response to two Federal guns that were peppering Cabell's Brigade. After firing a few rounds, Morgan Simonton's section of Montgomery's Battery withdrew to Fort Davidson, eventually being positioned outside the fort on the north side. Meanwhile, withdrawing Union troops occupied the northeastern and northwestern slopes of Pilot Knob and Shepherd Mountain, respectively, leaving an avenue for the Fort Davidson guns to rake the area. The time was about 9:15 a.m., when the artillery in Fort Davidson sent a volley of shells into the Ironton Gap, which did little damage, according to Union Dr. Seymour Carpenter, though they did disperse the rebels who had gathered there. By 10:00 a.m. J. C. Monroe's Confederate regiment had pushed back the Union troops holding Shepherd Mountain. Other troops from Cabell's command took the summit of Pilot Knob at 10:15 a.m., driving off Joseph A. Hughes and Colonel James Lindsay, volunteer civilians, who were sending information on the rebels, via the "'wiggles'" of a signal flag. Bartels, *Pilot Knob*, 28; Britton, *Civil War on the Border, 1863–65*, 398; Farmer Memoir, 11; Thomas C. Fletcher, "The Battle of Pilot Knob, and the Retreat to Leasburg," in *War Papers and Personal Reminiscences. 1861–1865. Read Before the Commandery of the state of Missouri, etc.* (St. Louis, 1892; reprint ed., Wilmington, NC, 1992), vol. 14: 37, hereafter cited as Fletcher; Gifford, 117–118, 121, 131; Mark A. Lause, *Price's Lost Campaign: The 1864 Invasion of Missouri* (Columbia, MO, 2011), 45, 47–48, hereafter cited as Lause; Sinisi, 75; Suderow, *Arcadia Valley*, 79, 81–82, 84–89; Joseph Conan Thompson, "The Great Little Battle of Pilot Knob [Part II]," Missouri Historical Review 83 (April, 1989), 227, hereafter cited as Thompson, "Great Little Battle of Pilot Knob;" Wilkinson, (Letter No. 18).

position is hid from view. A cloud of white sulphurous smoke hangs over the fortress.[34]

Suddenly the order comes, "Attention! Right dress! Guide Center! March!"

Then over the crest of the mountain we step and begin to descend its rugged side. The line widens, and the men slip and slide and jump from rock to rock, or shrub to shrub, or scoot down feet first with a bushel of dirt and small rocks pouring down over their heads.[35]

At the foot of the mountain the line reforms and we step upon the level plain in a trim straight line.[36] As we near the works the battery on the crest of the

---

34. While Fagan was securing Shepherd and Pilot Knob Mountains, General Price arrived at 10:00 a.m., making his headquarters at Fort Curtis. Price sent Captain T. J. Mackey, his corps engineer, to make a reconnaissance of Fort Davidson. Ascending Shepherd Mountain, Mackey observed that the fort was partially obscured by smoke, noting that there "appeared to be but a slight ditch around" it. This proved to be a critical error, as the ditch, from bottom to the top of the parapet, was about 12–14 feet deep. Mackey returned to Price and recommended that six or eight guns be placed on Shepherd Mountain, after which a short bombardment would cause the place to surrender. Following a consultation with Fagan, who wanted an immediate assault (Marmaduke was absent, but also desired an immediate assault), Price decided on a frontal attack of the fort. It was about 11:30 a.m. when the meeting broke up, followed by preparations for the attack. Marmaduke's Division was to assault the fort from the south, using Clark's Brigade, while all the armed men of Freeman's Brigade, with Slayback's Battalion, would block the western approaches to the area and then attack the fort from the north. Additionally, two pieces of artillery from Hughey's Battery were placed on Shepherd Mountain to support the attack. Fagan's Division was slated to attack through Ironton Gap, and from the east, while Dobbin's Brigade was sent around the fort to cut off Ewing's retreat to the north by occupying the Potosi Road. Finally, S. G. Kitchen's Regiment, from Clark's Brigade, would guard the army trains (See Appendix E for Confederate Order of Battle). To further ensure that Ewing could not escape, Price sent riders to Shelby ordering his command southward to block the enemy's retreat down the Potosi Road. By 1:30 p.m. Fagan's Division was in position and awaiting orders to assault Fort Davidson. By 2:00 p.m. all was ready. *O.R.*, vol. 41, pt. 1:695, 707, 709; Britton, *Civil War on the Border, 1863–65*, 401; Farmer Memoir, 11; Forsyth, *Great Missouri Raid*, 128; Freeman Memoir, September 27, 1864, The Arkansas in the Civil War Message Board, key word "Thomas Freeman Memoir," hereafter cited as Freeman Memoir; Gifford, 127, 129–131; Lindsay, "Pilot Knob," *Forge*, October 19, 1865; Pitcock & Gurley, 224; Sinisi, 76–78; Suderow, *Arcadia Valley*, 92–94; Wilkinson (Letter No. 18); Wright Memoirs, unnumbered page 74.

35. Between 1:00–2:00 p.m., Marmaduke's command moved into position. Clark's Brigade moved up the wet, southern slopes of Shepherd Mountain, "with skirmishers deployed," taking their position just behind the crest. Clark then deployed the 4th and 8th Missouri Cavalries on his left, while the 10th Missouri and Wood's Battalion were on the right, with Greene's 3rd Missouri taking a position as the reserve. Meanwhile, Freeman's command moved around the southern side of Shepherd Mountain, to its assigned position, guarding the western approaches to Fort Davidson. At 2:00 p.m. the artillery was fired from Shepherd Mountain, signaling the start of the attack. *O.R.*, vol. 41, pt. 1:679, 687–688; Busch, *Missouri Democrat Articles*, 57; James W. Campbell Memoir, Internet site www.history-sites.com, "The Missouri in the Civil War Message Board," hereafter cited as Campbell Memoir; Lause, *Price's Lost Campaign*, 51; Shalhope, 266; Sinisi, 80; Suderow, *Arcadia Valley*, 104, 107–108.

36. With "unfaltering courage" and a "high, screaming cheer," Clark's Brigade "pressed forward, each one seeming eager to reach the enemy's entrenchments first." And not to be outdone, General "Marmaduke and his staff, out in front and continually exposed to the vicious fire from the fort" urged his command forward. Not a gun was fired as Clark's command advanced the 1200 yards to Fort Davidson. The slope of Shepherd Mountain was wet causing men to slip, slide and stumble

mountain stops firing. Now the enemy's guns boom out louder that ever. Minnie balls hiss spitefully near our ears. Cannon shot of all sizes and description whir and shriek through the air. A storm of iron hail—a panorama, ghastly, horrible, yet sublime.

Breasting this terrible blast from the Federal batteries we gain the edge of the ditch. Here we gain our breath and exchange shots with the enemy as he shows himself above the parapet. Finding the ditch impassable the order is given

To Retreat.[37]

Fifteen steps from the edge of the ditch, we pass the silent form of Fredric Munm, then William Farnsworth, G Co., both shot through the neck (messmates).[38]

At last we reach cover in the run of the small branch mentioned above. At this moment Gen. Fagan's [Cabell's] Brigade deploys on the plain from the foot of

---

their way to the plain below, which was about 600 yards from Fort Davidson. It took Clark's Brigade about an hour to reach the bottom of Shepherd Mountain, "owing to the irregular decent. Upon emerging into the open space around the fort the brigade was found divided." The left and right wings of the brigade were separated by about 150 yards (Lause incorrectly says it was 150 feet.). "It being impossible to bring...[the brigade] together without great loss of time as well as life," Clark ordered his command forward. Greene's Regiment moved from the reserve, partially filling the gap between the two wings of the brigade, further encouraging the right wing of Clark's Brigade to move on the fort. "Like wheat before the reaper" the men began to fall. By the time the brigade hit the West Branch of Knob Creek they were greeted by a volley from Fort Davidson, which shocked the right wing of Marmaduke's assault. Encouraged by Colonel Greene, the right wing made one last effort to close on the fort. Joined by Cabell's Brigade on their right, for their final assault, Clark's Missourians approached Fort Davidson. *O.R.*, vol. 41, pt. 1:679–680, 687–688, map on 708; Bartels, *Battle of Pilot Knob*, 29; Campbell Memoir; Crowley, 137; Lause, *Price's Lost Campaign*, 51; Shalhope, 266; Sinisi, 80; Suderow, *Arcadia Valley*, 104, 107–109.

37. The right wing of Clark's Brigade, including the 4th Missouri, continued to move forward, encouraged by Cabell's Brigade to their right, which arrived "with banners flying and marching gallantly forward." Advancing "with a desperate courage," the Missourians moved "to the very muzzles of the enemy's guns"; and then they hit the dry moat surrounding the fort. Finding the moat impassable and coupled with too few men reaching it, the right wing buckled, and back went the 4th, 10th and Woods's Missouri units. The retreating right wing found a refuge in a dry creek bed, or the West Branch Knob Creek that was located about 200 yards from the fort and 400 yards from the base of Shepherd Mountain. There the right wing waited until darkness before completing their withdrawal. Meanwhile, on Clark's left, Jeffers's and Burbridge's regiments, seeming to have a more difficult time advancing, halted when they saw the remainder of the brigade repulsed. Taking refuge in the same creek bed, the 4th and 8th Missouri hunkered down and began sniping at the fort with the rest of Clark's Brigade, while Freeman's command attempted to draw fire away from the beleaguered members of the division, allowing them to reach the safety of the dry creek bed. *O.R.*, vol. 41, pt. 1:679–680, 687–688, map on 708; Campbell Memoir; Crowley, 137; Freeman Memoir, September 27, 1864; Suderow, *Arcadia Valley*, 104.

38. William Farnsworth joined the Confederate Army on August 15, 1862, in Johnson County, Missouri. With the formation of the 11th Missouri Cavalry Battalion, Farnsworth became a member of Company G and on December 12, 1863, when the 10th Missouri Cavalry was organized, became a member of the same company. He was killed at Pilot Knob on September 27, 1864. Nothing found on Frederick Munm or any variation thereof. National Archives, Record Group M322 (roll no. 56), Compiled Service Records, 10th Missouri Cavalry.

Shepherd Mountain.³⁹ They step over the ground as if they were on parade battalion drill. How our hearts bled for those brave fellows, as we see them pass under the withering fire from the fort.⁴⁰ With the retirement of Fagan's Brigade our battery on the crest of Cedar [Shepherd] Mountain again opens fire.⁴¹ From every

---

39. With the firing of the signal guns on Shepherd Mountain, Fagan's two right-most brigades, Slemons's's and McCray's, charged down Pilot Knob Mountain "in a scattered order," while Cabell remained in place, awaiting the word to attack. "The Rebs swarmed from the brush on the mountain sides like bees from a hive," wrote Dr. Seymour Carpenter of the Union command. They came "yelling like incarnate fiends," continued Carpenter, as "our skirmish line was driven before them like chaff." McCray's command easily overwhelmed and captured a small Union detachment under Major James Wilson near the base of the mountain, while the remaining Unionists made good their escape. With their skirmishers mostly out of harm's way, the Federal gunners in Fort Davidson then concentrated their all their fire on Fagan's two right-most brigades, causing them to falter and take refuge in East Branch Knob Creek, which was about 500 yards from Fort Davidson. There they remained for the rest of the battle, with the exception of John C. Wright's Arkansas Regiment, which would later join Cabell's Brigade in their assault on Fort Davidson. *O.R.*, vol. 41, pt. 1:709; Bartels, *Pilot Knob*, 29; Gifford, 140–141; Memoirs of John Wilson, Wilson Family Papers (C348), Western Historical Manuscript Collection, State Historical Society of Missouri (Columbia, MO), 13, hereafter cited as Wilson Memoirs; Wright Memoirs, unnumbered pages 76–77.

40. With McCray and Slemons no longer a threat, Marmaduke's troops became the next target of concern. And like Slemons and McCray, Marmaduke's command were also brought to a halt, even as Cabell finally broke out of the underbrush, about 600 yards from the fort. Cabell's Brigade had never received word to begin the attack and delayed moving, believing that Price first intended to soften up the target. About 2:30 p.m., a staff officer finally arrived from Fagan, directing Cabell to attack. Moving out at a "double quick" on Fort Davidson, Cabell advanced "in a most gallant style," being joined by Colonel John C. Wright's Arkansas Regiment, and then the right wing of John B. Clark's Brigade. At 200 yards Cabell's extended command delivered their first volley at the fort, causing but little damage. On Cabell rushed, "without a bobble or a break," all the time "under a terrific fire of grape and canister." At 50 yards from the fort Colonel Wright had his horse shot out from under him, while General Cabell lost his at the edge of the moat. After rushing through a "seething hell," Cabell's extended command reached the moat, delivered another volley, which also proved ineffective. Finally, "without any support and on reaching the Fort, [Cabell] found the ditches deep and so wide that they could not scale it without ladders," and so he ordered a retreat. Or, as Dr. Seymour Carpenter recalled, "The rebels went back as fast as they had come forward and when the smoke cleared away, an awful sight presented itself...more than 300 lay dead and severely wounded" about the fort. Within two hours of its start, the Battle of Pilot Knob was over, except for some occasional sniping. *O.R.*, vol. 41, pt. 1:448, 629, 709; *O.R.S.*, pt. 1, vol. 7:393–394, 406; Bartels, *Pilot Knob*, 30; Campbell Memoir; Castel, *Sterling Price*, 215; Cocker, 16; Gifford, 140, 152, 154–155, 158; Sinisi, 80–81, 83; Quoted in Suderow, *Arcadia Valley*,112; Wright Memoirs, unnumbered page 75.

41. Hughey's Battery continued to fire for a time, from Shepherd Mountain, until the 32-lb siege gun, in the southeast corner of Fort Davidson, got the proper range and shattered one of the wheels of Hughey's guns (Gifford has the gun being silenced even as the attack began). Then Hughey went silent, and at 5:58 the sun set ending the battle. Even though every Union account of the Battle of Pilot Knob has Union gunners being able to bear on the rebel guns on Shepherd Mountain, there was one account published in the St. Louis *Democrat* that stated otherwise. The Union telegraph operator from Pilot Knob, a Mr. Burns, reported the gunners in Fort Davidson "were unable" to fire on the rebel guns on Shepherd Mountain, "owing to the elevated positions held by the rebels. This seems to give pause to other accounts on the silencing of Confederate artillery. Busch, *Missouri Democrat Articles*, 42; Gifford, 139, 159; Suderow, *Arcadia Valley*, 116; Wilkinson (Letter No. 18).

available place our sharpshooters reply to the discharges from the fort. During this sharp practice Maj. [George W. C.] Bennet, Ben F. Wheatly and a few others from G Company are sharp-shooting from a small house some thirty steps in advance of our line. Maj. Bennet is standing at the corner looking through his field glasses. A large cannon shot tears through the house and cuts the brave Bennet in two at the knees.[42] How we missed our gallant major! Stubbornly the fight went on until dark; which put a stop to the showers of iron hail, which had filled the air all day. Scaling ladders were ordered for the morrow, and we slept on our arms that night. About 4 o'clock the next morning a terrific explosion shook the very earth where we lay. "There," exclaims Ben F. Wheatly, jumping up. "There, they have busted Long Tom as sure as hell!" Long tom was a

Monster Big, Black Gun

that had heaped dust upon us the evening before, seemingly trying to bury us alive.[43] Turning our eyes, we see the flame and cloud of debris as they fly heaven-

---

42. George W. C. Bennett was born about 1837 in Monroe County, Indiana. He later moved to Missouri, eventually settling in Platte County. At the beginning of the Civil War, Bennett became a member of the 5th Division, MSG, commanding a cavalry company in the 1st Battalion. In November 1862 he joined what became the 11th Missouri Cavalry Battalion, as major and inspector general of the command on November 16, 1862. Bennett was cited for bravery at the Battle of Prairie Grove (December 7, 1862), and rose to command of his regiment in January 1863, after Colonel Emmett MacDonald was killed at Hartville, Missouri, on January 11. During the remainder of 1863, Bennett was also at the fall of Little Rock in September and Pine Bluff in October. On December 12, 1863, upon the organization of the 10th Missouri Cavalry, Bennett was elected major of the command, a position he held until his wounding at Pilot Knob. Bennett also participated in the Camden Expedition of 1864 and Price's Missouri Expedition, where he was wounded on September 27, 1864. However, contrary to what Luttrell recorded, Bennett lost only one leg. Of Bennett's wounding John Edwards wrote: "His name has been associated ever in his brigade with deeds of knightly daring, and the purity of his stainless life had endeared him to all." Final disposition unknown, through he probably died at Pilot Knob sometime after the battle due to the wounds he received. *O.R.*, vol. 41, pt. 1:698; *O.R.S.*, pt. 2, vol. 38:256–257; Busch, *Missouri Democrat Articles*, 142; Edwards, *Shelby and His Men*, 388; Marmaduke, 57, 82–83, 188, 403; John S. Marmaduke Letter (December 4, 1862), Peter W. Alexander Collection, Columbia University; National Archives, Inspector General's Report (December 1, 1862), Record Group 109, in Confederate Muster Rolls, 10th Missouri Cavalry; National Archives, Record Group M322 (roll no. 56), Compiled Service Records, 10th Missouri Cavalry; Peterson, et al., 166, 344.
43. At 1:00 a.m., even as Fort Davidson was being evacuated, Captain Henry Milks, of the 3rd MSM Cavalry, was assigned the responsibility of destroying the fort's magazine. General Ewing further directed Milks to wait two hours after the fort had been evacuated before executing his mission. By 3:00 a.m., the full evacuation of Fort Davidson had taken place, or so everyone believed, and thirty minutes later the magazine was rigged for detonation. At 4:00 a.m. (some sources say 2:00 a.m. and others 3:00 a.m.), a nervous Milks had the fuse lit an hour earlier than ordered. Sergeant William Moore (Gifford says he was a private) lit the fuse, and, with the magazine party, quickly evacuated the fort. Minutes later Fort Davidson exploded. Unfortunately, several sleeping men were still in the fort, when the explosion occurred, burying them with dirt, while outside of the fort some of the wounded, were thrown into the air by the concussion. It was two hours before daylight and no one on the Confederate side had any idea that the fort had been evacuated. Busch, *Fort Davidson*, 34, 37–38; Walter E. Busch, *General, You Have Made the Mistake Of Your Life* (Independence, MO, 2004), 116, hereafter cited as Busch, *General*; Busch, *Missouri Democrat*

ward, in a moment, a buzz runs along the line. "The enemy has flown! The works are blown up!" Men who look somber and stern a moment ago are smiling now.[44] Detachments are sent out in hot haste. The enemy have gone in the direction of Caledonia, but Shelby is supposed to be there by this time, and no extra haste is made to overtake him.[45]

Burial squads are now passing over the field, gathering up the dead for

---

Articles, 86; Crowley, 138; Forsyth, *Great Missouri Raid*, 133–134; Farmer Memoir; Gifford, 168, 170, 173–175; Suderow, *Arcadia Valley*, 126–130; Wilkinson (Letter No. 19).

44. When darkness fell, General Ewing called a conference of his officers and principle citizens to discuss his options. Some present suggested surrender, to which General Ewing "curtly replied, that he would never surrender." His command was down by 25 percent, his artillery ammunition was almost exhausted and his men had each expended 300 rounds of ammunition. When the battle began Ewing had 280 fixed rounds for his "large cannons" and "320 for the smaller ones"; and what he had remaining would have run out early the next day. Ewing wanted to stay and fight, but nevertheless conducted a secret ballot on what action to take. By a majority of one the group urged Ewing to evacuate. Not convinced one way of the other, Ewing then consulted Dr. Seymour Carpenter, his longtime friend, at 11:00 p.m., before making a final decision. According to Carpenter the discussion "did not allow of much debate. With his jaded troops he must make a run for it." At midnight, Ewing issued orders to evacuate Fort Davidson. Prior to evacuating Ewing discovered that Freeman's command was covering the Mineral Point Road, while he was uncertain as to the Potosi Road, which was actually being watched by Dobbin's Brigade. To prepare a route for retreat, according to Captain Charles Hill, who was supported by David Murphy, Ewing selected a "small gorge" to the north of the fort, "shelled all the bark off the trees to clear" out any rebels. Between 1:00–2:00 a.m., with cannon wheels muffled, the Federals "marched out of the fort." With his command assembled outside the fort at 3:00 a.m., Ewing silently marched through the area they had shelled, passing within 600 yards (some say 60 yards, others 300 yards) of a rebel brigade. According to one participant the column was challenged by one lone sentry, who let the column proceed after the lead replied "Confederate troops changing position." At 4:00 a.m. the fort's magazine exploded. For the Confederates' part, they did not realize that the Unionists had evacuated the fort, believing only that a gun had exploded, and continued throughout the night preparing "300 scaling ladders" and placing artillery on Shepherd Mountain. (See Appendix C for the legend surrounding the Federal evacuation of Fort Davidson.). *O.R.*, vol. 41, pt. 1:448–449; Bartels, *Pilot Knob*, 30, 32, 36; Britton, *Civil War on the Border, 1863–65*, 408; Busch, *Fort Davidson*, 31–32, 74; Busch, *Missouri Democrat Articles*, 58–59, 84, 96; Castel, *Sterling Price*, 216; Crowly, 138; Forsyth, *Great Missouri Raid*, 132; Gifford, 166; Lause, *Price's Lost Campaign*, 54–55; Lindsay, "Pilot Knob," *Forge*, October 19, 1865; Mobley, 192; Suderow, *Arcadia Valley*, 124–126; Thompson, "Great Little Battle of Pilot Knob," 289; Wilkinson (Letter No. 19).

45. At Potosi, many of Shelby's Division were drunk, following the capture of the town. This in turn possibly slowed Shelby's reaction in coming to Price's aid, given that a messenger appears to have arrived at Shelby's headquarters in sufficient time to beat Ewing's Federals to Caledonia. According to the *Missouri Democrat*, a "Mr. Holland" was present at Potosi, when Shelby received the order from General Price requiring him "to send reinforcements as soon as possible" to Pilot Knob. Meanwhile, Shelby, who said he never received Price's message, sent a courier back to Price, informing him that he would be at Pilot Knob by 10:00 a.m. The courier was captured by Ewing's advance, according to H. C. Wilkinson, "sometime about, or near sun up" as "the rebels ran out of the saloon" in Caledonia. The dispatch that was captured "was Shelby's reply to Price's orders, which read about as follows: 'I will be at Pilot Knob by ten o'clock to-day.'" *O.R.*, vol. 41, pt. 1:653; "The Battle of Pilot Knob by One Who Was There," Western Historical Manuscript Collection (C3425), State Historical Society of Missouri, hereafter cited as "The Battle of Pilot Knob by One Who Was There;" Busch, *Missouri Democrat Articles*, 96–97, 142; Cruzen, 24; Norton & Massey, 62; O'Flaherty, 218; Wilkinson (Letter No. 19).

internment. When I reach the fort most of our dead have been gathered up. I ask an officer "How many of the Tenth do you find?" "Twenty-five," was his reply.[46] As to our entire loss, I don't know, for I have never heard anyone who had a chance to know, say what it was.[47] We were participated in so many fights and battles afterwards that all interest in the Battle of Pilot Knob died out or was swallowed up by other more exciting events.

The next day we drove the enemy into another fortified position at Leesbourgh [Leasburg], or Steelville, on the railroad, where we left him in peace, and continued out journey down the railroad to Union.[48]

According to my notion at the time, the Battle of Pilot Knob, was a drawback to the expedition. It is true we demolished a strong post of the enemy, but the time and material it took to reduce it, ripped our force and delayed the expedition. I certainly saw nothing to compensate us for the brave men that were sacrificed. But perhaps the officers of the army could show it up in a different light. Would be glad if they could do so.[49]

Henry Luttrell,
Gen. Hindman's Escort, Co. G, and
Tenth Missouri Cavalry, C.S.A.

* * * * * * *

---

46. For the Battle of Pilot Knob, including the actions that preceded the final assault, Colonel Robert R. Lawther reported losing 4 killed and 26 wounded. *O.R.*, vol. 41, pt. 1:698.
47. The most extensive analysis of the Confederate losses at Pilot Knob was made by author Bryce Suderow, who puts the number at about 510. Other authors, participants, and assorted newspaper accounts vary depending on whose side reported the loss. Douglas Gifford believes there was some type of "group-think infecting Union reports of Confederate casualties," which "universally accepted the 1,500-man loss that was prevalent in 1864; and the various personal accounts that followed the battle and war." With few exceptions, Confederate accounts put the loss in the 500-man loss range. "We will never know for certain exactly how many of Price's men fell at Pilot Knob," wrote Gifford; however see Appendix C, for Extended Comments on the Confederate losses at Pilot Knob, and, Appendix E for my breakdown of the Confederate losses at Pilot Knob, by division, brigade and in many cases individual units. Gifford, 195–196; Mobley, 195–196; Suderow, *Arcadia Valley*, 121, 138–139.
48. Steelville was about 8 miles south of Leasburg, which was located a few miles from the South Pacific Railroad. Leasburg would prove to be the destination for the retreating Union forces, where they hoped to find some relief from Rolla, which was 30 miles to the southwest. Union, on the other hand, was about 30 miles to the northeast of Leasburg and would fall to Price's army before the expedition had ended. *O.R.*, vol. 41, pt. 1:449; Davis, *Civil War Atlas*, plt. no. 152.
49. See Appendix C for Extended Comments on the effect of the Battle of Pilot Knob on the Confederate Army and its overall impact on the remainder of the campaign.

Item: Continuation of Part One of Price's 1864 Missouri Raid, by Henry C. Luttrell, Company G, 10th Missouri Cavalry (C.S.A.).
Published: February 27, 1886.

Price's Great Raid.

[Incidents related by a Confederate trooper, from a diary kept on the march.] Passing over the battle and referring to my diary I see the following, which may be interesting to many readers of the *Republican*.

Sept. 28—After the explosion we emerge from our cold and shivering bivouac in the run of the branch. Details are sent for horses. Everything is hurry and bustle. Squadrons are sent out in hot haste.[50] Everyone is expecting to hear Shelby's guns open on the enemy in the foothills to the north, for he has been ordered to intercept the enemy if he retreats by way of Caledonia.[51]

---

50. As the sun rose a little after 6:00 a.m. on September 28, Dr. Seymour Carpenter rode out of Pilot Knob, with a white flag and met the rebel pickets. The surprised pickets discovered that Fort Davidson had been abandoned and relayed the information to General Price (according to Thomas Fletcher, Price did not receive the information until 8:00 a.m.). The Confederate pursuit began "very early in the morning," according to Colonel James R., Shaler, "with some of the troops moving at daylight." However, Governor Thomas C. Reynolds, who accompanied the expedition, recorded that "Price refused to order an immediate pursuit." I suspect that Shaler's comments, supported by Luttrell, suggest that a scouting party was sent after the fleeing Federals, to ascertain their location, numbers, etc., while the remainder of the army prepared to follow. Regardless, a few squadrons of John B. Clark's Brigade were sent in a "rapid pursuit" after Ewing's command, while Fagan's Division remained behind to clean up the battlefield and secure whatever spoils they could find. Meanwhile, Confederate troops entered and looted Pilot Knob at 6:30 a.m. By 8:00 a.m., after feeding their horses and themselves, the remainder of the 10th Missouri Cavalry led out the remainder of Clark's Brigade, on the road to Potosi. General Price followed at 10:00 a.m., while Fagan's Division departed Pilot Knob at 2:00 p.m. Bringing up the rear was John C. Wright's Arkansas Regiment, while Freeman's Brigade guarded the Army trains. And after a leisurely march of 12 miles the lead element of the army camped near Caledonia, at 3:00 p.m., where they made contact with Shelby's Division and waited for further orders. *O.R.*, vol. 41, pt. 1:653, 698, 710; *O.R.*, vol. 41, pt. 3:962; Carolyn Bartels, *Iowa Boy Makes Good etc.* (Shawnee Mission, KS, 1966), 156, hereafter cited as Bartels, *Iowa Boy*; Ballard Diary, September 28, 1864; Campbell Memoir; Fletcher, 45–46; "Generals Price, Marmaduke, and Cabell in the Missouri Campaign," *Marshall Republican* (Marshall, TX), December 23, 1864, hereafter cited as "General Price in the Missouri Campaign;" Richard J. Hinton, *Rebel Invasion of Missouri and Kansas* (Chicago, 1865; reprint ed., n.c., n.d.),23, hereafter cited as Hinton; Pitcock & Gurley, 225; Sellmeyer, 2134; Sinisi, 85; Suderow, *Arcadia Valley*, 79; Wright Memoirs, unnumbered page 78.

51. Meanwhile, father to the north at Potosi, Shelby had departed the area early on September 28, intent on joining with Price's main body. Moving southward, Shelby's advance unexpectedly made contact in Caledonia, with Ewing's command shortly after daylight. Scattering the rebel troopers as they emerged from a saloon, Ewing's men managed to capture a Shelby messenger, who, upon being threatened with hanging, relayed Shelby's location and strength, which was a few miles to his rear. General Ewing also learned that Shelby was headed for Pilot Knob, where he intended to arrive at 10:00 a.m. Facing a superior force, and without the protection of entrenchments or superior artillery, Ewing altered his path from the Potosi Road, to the Webster Road, reaching the targeted town at sundown. Shelby for his part stopped his movement toward Pilot Knob at 10:30 a.m., mistakenly believing that he faced General A. J. Smith's troops, who had gotten around him from Mineral Point. Digging in, Shelby waited four hours for Ewing to attack, thus giving Ewing

Getting permission from Capt. [Thomas B.] Murray I go to the field to seek my mess mates, Frederick Munm and Wm. Farnsworth, killed in yesterday's action. I find the burial parties have carried them from where they fell on the field. They are covered with dust and powder stains from the explosion. They have met their death like gallant soldiers that they were, and they will sleep under the walls of the fortress before which they sacrificed their lives to conquer. With a sad heart I say farewell to my dead comrades and turn to the dismantled fortification, wondering how soon I may meet same sad fate. Now I am on the walls of the fortress. The Federal dead lie all about—inside the works, on the parapets, in the ditch even out on the plain 50 yards away. They are torn and mangled by cannon shot and many of them almost covered up by dirt and debris of the wreck. A great hole is torn in the center of the enclosure, where the magazine had been deposited. Great beams and squared timbers have been hurried to the top of the parapet and even clear beyond the outer ditch. The great guns that had guarded the works the day before are wrenched and tumbled from their carriages. By one of the monster guns, pitched from its carriage, is a

Well Thumbed Testament.

I picked it up. Bloody finger marks are on it, and the first leaves are torn out. There is no name or inscription on it, but many marked verses, showing that the former owner had read it well. I put the book in my pocket for luck, and read many pleasant lessons from its pages.[52] The "mount" call rings out sharp and shrill from the brazen throat of our brigade bugle, and I hasten back to my place in the ranks. Five miles out on the Caledonia road, in the rough foot-hills we go into camp. We draw rations and cook a square meal of flour bread and bacon, cooked on sticks over the fire. Ere we swallow this last bite, "boots and saddles" is sounded and an all-night march follows.[53]

time to distance himself from the pursuing Confederates. In the late morning Shelby finally made contact with Marmaduke's Division, and, per orders, his command was attached to Marmaduke's command for the upcoming pursuit. *O.R.*, vol. 41, pt. 1:449; "Battle of Pilot Knob by One Who Was There;" Britton, *Civil War on the Border, 1863–65*, 409; Busch, *Missouri Democrat Articles*, 96, 142; Hinton, 23; Lause, *Price's Lost Campaign*, 66; Sellmeyer, 213; Sinisi, 87; Wilkinson (Letter No. 19).

52. A female reader of the *Republican* would later write to the newspaper stating that she believed that her father, the Reverend George T. Gray, was the owner of the Bible. According to Mrs. Phoebe Roberts, of Higbee, Randolph County, Missouri, Reverend Gray, a resident from Chariton County, disappeared during Price's Raid. Gray was later reported wounded and tore a page out of the Bible to send a dying message to his wife. "War Echoes," *Missouri Republican*, March 13, 1886.

53. On the morning of September 28, General Price issued orders to General Marmaduke, directing him to lead an expedition to "overtake and capture" General Ewing's command. General Shelby, with the armed men of his division, was likewise made part of Marmaduke's force. General Clark's Brigade, led by Lawther's 10th Missouri Cavalry and supported by the 4th Missouri, led the rebel advance. Upon reaching the Caledonia area, near 3:00 p.m., Marmaduke halted his command, linked up with Shelby, foraged and fed his troops before proceeding. The pursuit finally began in earnest at 8:00 p.m. and continued throughout the night, as they headed for Webster

September 30 [29]—Daylight find us yet in the saddle, going at a "trot march." A little after sunrise we pick up half a dozen prisoners, at the fork of a small branch—we are near the enemy's rear. Small squads of prisoners are frequently sent to the rear. At noon crackling rifle shots tell us that our advance has fallen in with the enemy's rear. The enemy has well-chosen his line of retreat. It is long a narrow backbone ridge with deep gulches and steep, rocky declivities on either side, where it is almost impossible for the cavalry to maneuver. Heavy skirmishing is the order of the evening. Heavy crashes of artillery, followed by the sharp rattling of musketry, are constantly echoing along the old hills. Finally we drive them into their works at Leasburg [Leasburg].[54]

October 1 [September 30]—After some desultory firing we resumed our march down the railroad, leaving the enemy in his fortified position to nurse his wrath as he may deem proper after his discomfort at Pilot Knob. Along our line of march

(modern-day Palmer) even as rain began to fall. *O.R.*, vol. 41, pt. 1:629, 644, 673; *O.R.*, vol. 41, pt. 3:963; Britton, *Civil War on the Border, 1863–65*, 410; Busch, *General*, 117; Busch, *Missouri Democrat Articles*, 146; Cruzen, 24; Sellmeyer, 213; Wilkinson (Letter No. 19).

54. Ewing departed Webster sometime between 11:00 p.m. and midnight, following a needed three hour rest, and hurried on to Leasburg and the Southwest Branch of the Pacific Railroad, where he hoped to find a Union militia regiment that was stationed there. Guiding Ewing was a "Mr. Wingo," a man who was familiar with the area. However, a heavy rain and almost total darkness caused them to halt after only a few miles and wait until dawn before moving forward. Meanwhile, Marmaduke's boys passed through Webster, leaving in their wake 12 dead Union Home Guard, who were found in the area. At 8:00 a.m. the advance of Lawther's Regiment made contact with the surprised Federals, sending one panicked man screaming "The rebels are on us! The rebels are on us!" This in turn caused panic in the rear element of Ewing's command, but they soon rallied around the 14th Iowa Infantry, who calmly stood their ground. When the rebels appeared it was but a few men, probably scouts of the advance party; after which the Federal retreat continued to Leasburg, 22 miles away. For the remainder of the day, the Federal column was sniped at constantly as they trudged along the narrow winding road. Owing to "the topography of the country it was impossible [for the rebels] to deploy rapidly, and in consequence failed to bring [Ewing] to a general engagement." At 11:30 a.m. Clark made his first "major attack" on the Federals' rear, which easily beat off the attack with the assistance of Montgomery's Artillery. Closing in on Leasburg as the sun was setting, Shelby's command took over the lead from Marmaduke's boys at 6:00 p.m. and made one last effort to take Ewing's command. Making a "heavy charge" upon the Federals, Shelby lost 3 killed "and a number wounded," according to Colonel Thomas Fletcher. Shelby, like Clark, before him was repulsed, recording "with night alone" saving "Ewing from capture." In the end, following "several slight skirmishes" and the one last-minute attack by Shelby, Clark's Brigade reported losing one killed and six wounded, while Shelby's losses were unknown. Ewing's losses, including those suffered at Pilot Knob, totaled about 150 killed and wounded with another 50 captured, after all missing detachments had been accounted for. At Pilot Knob Ewing lost 22 killed or mortally wounded, with 47 wounded; total 69. Another 131 were killed, wounded or captured during Ewing's retreat to Leasburg. *O.R.*, vol. 41, pt. 1:450–451, 453, 680, 688, 692, 698; *O.R.*, vol. 41, pt. 3:961–962; Britton, *Civil War on the Border, 1863–65*, 410; Busch, *Missouri Democrat Articles*, 97; Fletcher, 47–48; Hinton, 23–24; Sellmeyer, 214; Wilkinson (Letter No. 19).

[Note: In a contrasting, though incorrect view, Douglas Gifford has Marmaduke stopping at Webster sometime after midnight, having missed Ewing's command. Not wanting to risk a night engagement, according to Gifford, Marmaduke halted the pursuit and waited until dawn to chase down his Federal foes. Period reports clearly have the Confederates riding throughout the night to catch Ewing, though I would suspect that they halted at intervals for short rests. Gifford, 184.]

today the telegraph wires have been cut, the railroad track is torn up, and bridges burned. We camp this night at B station, fifteen miles below Leasburg [Leasburg].[55]

October 2 [1]—We break camp early this morning, and resume our march.[56] We pass through St. Clair. As we approach Union, county seat of Franklin county, a small detachment of Home Guards

---

55. Having failed to capture Ewing's force on September 29, Marmaduke waited until dawn on the 30th, to renew the effort; but, discovering that the Federals had fortified their position during the night, "deemed it" unadvisable to attack them. Leaving Colton Greene's 3rd Missouri to demonstrate at Leasburg, Marmaduke moved off to Sullivan on the S.W. Branch of the Pacific RR at about 10:30 a.m. Meanwhile, on the previous day, Marmaduke had detached Wood's Battalion and the 4th Missouri Cavalry, under Colonel John Q. Burbridge to destroy the railroad between Leasburg and Rolla at Cuba. Burbridge reached Cuba at 5:00 p.m., burned the depot, destroyed a mile of track and a "large amount of cord wood," as well as torching the town of Cuba. Completing their work, Burbridge's command rejoined his brigade at Sullivan on September 30, while Greene's Regiment broke contact with Ewing at 2:00 p.m. and headed for Sullivan Station. Shelby's advance was the first to reach Sullivan, in the "middle of the afternoon." Surrounding the town, they gathered up all the men for questioning as to their loyalty, then "burned the railroad depot, ties, cord wood, water tank, and a lot of bridge timber," as well as tore up the track and destroyed the telegraph line. Their work completed, Shelby's Division camped a mile northeast of Sullivan on the Springfield Road. After Marmaduke's Division arrived they camped southwest of the town, in what is now known as the "Lake View Addition." *O.R.*, vol. 41, pt. 1:680, 688, 694; *O.R.*, vol. 41, pt. 3:964–965; Busch, *Missouri Democrat Articles*, 97, 99; Campbell Memoir; Ralph Gregory, *Price's Raid In Franklin County, Missouri* (Washington, MO, 1990), 2, hereafter cited as Gregory; Hinton, 26; "War In Missouri," *Chicago Tribune*, October 1, 1864.
56. While Marmaduke's and Shelby's commands finished up with Ewing, the remainder of the army under Price had not been idle. Price moved his troops down the road to Potosi, on September 29, passing through Caledonia and then Potosi. After making 22 miles, Price camped at 4:00 p.m., near Shibboleth, after which he was joined by General M. Jeff Thompson, lately exchanged and returned to the army. The next day Price made a hapless 10 miles, camping at the "small settlement" of Richwoods, where a Lieutenant Christian arrived with 150,000 rifle and pistol caps. The same day Price dispatched Cabell's Brigade to cut the railroad above Franklin (also known as Pacific City, which was part of Franklin) and then take the city. Also on the 30th, General Fagan sent another 300 men, under a Colonel Davis to DeSoto to destroy the railroad facilities in that area (Sinisi believes it was Lieutenant Colonel J. E. Davies; however Davies's command was with the 7th Missouri at Sullivan on the 30th). Both parties were successful. Cabell reached the railroad late on September 30, burned the Moselle Bridge, rested and entered Franklin at 6:30 a.m. on October 1. Later that day, Cabell fought Edward H. Wolfe's Brigade of Federal infantry for nearly two hours before leaving Franklin during the noon hour, losing two killed, six wounded with "eight or ten captured while too much under the influence of liquor." Federals reported killing "5 or 6" and wounding "between thirty and fifty" rebels while losing only four wounded. However, according to another newspaper, Wolfe supposedly lost 37 killed and 43 wounded, while three of Wolfe's regiment reported losing seven wounded. However, a subsequent newspaper account places Wolfe's losses at just 11 wounded. In a like manner, DeSoto was entered at 6:00 p.m. on September 30, after which the rebels burned the local railroad facilities, along with the "Mooney's bridge." *O.R.*, vol. 41, pt. 1:322–325, 630, 644; *O.R.*, vol. 41, pt. 3:538, 964; *O.R.S..* pt. 1 vol. 7:394, 407; Ballard Diary, September 28–20, 1864; Busch, *Missouri Democrat Articles*, 70–72, 78, 80, 325; Gregory, 3; "Operations On the Pacific Railroad," *Missouri Republican*, October 2, 1864; Palmer, 19; Pitcock & Gurley, 225; Sinisi, 94.

Open Fire

on our advance.[57] A skirmish line of two companies, I and K, is deployed. A section of Pratt's Battery is whirled into position and opens fire. The Tenth regiment swerves from its line of march to the right at a "trot march," passes to the rear and south of our skirmish line, and under cover of a skirt of timber forms in platoons, and in solid column charges into the town from the south. As we approach the courthouse, the Home Guards have come out and surrendered. During the little excitement attending the security of the prisoner's arms I raise my eyes to our skirmish line—whose position is to the westward, it's left resting on the point of timber to the southwest, the same behind which the regiment formed—and this is what I see: A white puff of smoke spurts out from a skirmisher's Enfield rifle, a dull report, that hiss and thud of a rifle ball, and Col. Lawther's black charger sinks lifeless under him.[58] We gather about him with the query, "Are you hurt,

---

57. Marmaduke and Shelby took St. Clair before noon, meeting the remainder of the army under Price near the same time, and as before destroyed the depot, water tank and tore up the track. Pushing on to Union, General John B. Clark's Brigade led the way. When within a mile of town, Clark dismounted his brigade, save for the 8th and 10th Missouri Cavalries. Lawther's 10th was sent to the eastern approach to the city, while Jeffers's command covered the west. Federal militia in Union built a makeshift fort to guard the local bridge and initially it seemed that they would make a stand. However, as Lawther's men approached, Captain Henry Detmer's Federals fired but two volleys. Meanwhile south of town, General Clark opened with his artillery which unnerved the Union defenders under Detmer, even though they weren't under artillery fire. Detmer panicked and ordered "everybody for himself." Then the chase began as Lawther charged into Union pursuing the hapless Federal militia, killing 10 and capturing 65 (General Price recorded Federal losses as 32 killed and 70 wounded, while Clark has the 70 as captured and Joel Bolton of the 10th Missouri says 60 were taken at Union). By 4:00 p.m. Union was in Confederate hands, with the loss of three killed and one wounded. That night Clark, Marmaduke and Shelby took dinner at the Jeffies place, just south of Union and planned their next move. Learning that there was a militia force at Washington, en route for St. Louis, Marmaduke directed General Clark to send the 10th Missouri out as the advance of the division to secure Washington. *O.R.*, vol. 41, pt. 1:630, 680, 698; *O.R.*, vol. 41, pt. 3:674–675; Joel M. Bolton Memoir, Western Historical Manuscript Collection, State Historical Society of Missouri (Columbia); Gregory, 5–6, 9.
58. Robert R. Lawther was born in Kittanning, Pennsylvania, on January 21, 1836. Prior to the war he lived for a time in Muscatine, Iowa, and moved to Jefferson City, Missouri, where he was a grocer. He joined the MSG and was elected major of the 1st Missouri Cavalry Regiment (CSA) on December 30, 1861. Lawther departed his regiment on June 12, 1862, with the permission of President Jefferson Davis, to organize the 1st Regiment, Missouri Partisan Rangers during the summer of 1862. Captured in September 1862, he was exchanged in the early part of 1863, and was given command of a "Temporary Regiment of Dismounted Cavalry," during the Little Rock Campaign. Later, his command was incorporated into the 10th Missouri Cavalry, of which he was elected colonel on April 20, 1864. Lawther led his command until he resigned on February 27, 1865 (Service Record has the date as January 10), with a surgeon's Certificate of Disability. During the war, he participated in the Arkansas engagements at Pea Ridge, Pine Bluff, the Camden Expedition and Price's 1864 Missouri Raid. He was paroled at Galveston, Texas, on June 20, 1865. Following the war Lawther settled in Dallas, where he died on October 1, 1911. *O.R.*, vol. 22, pt. 1:731–732; *O.R.*, vol. 34, pt. 1:781; *O.R.*, vol. 41, pt. 1:698; *O.R.S.*, pt. 2, vol. 38:253; Banasik, *Confederate Tales, 1863*, 162–163; R. S. Bevier, *History of the First and Second Missouri Confederate Brigades 1861–1865. And From Wakarusa to Appomattox, A Military Anagraph* (St. Louis, 1879), 77, hereafter cited as Bevier; Crute, *Confederate Army*, 203; Eakin & Hale, 261; "The 'Invader,'"

colonel?" to which he replies, "Not much." But I see his trousers are cut near the knee, and further examination reveals the fact that he has received a considerable flesh wound.

Finally the prisoners are ordered into line. One of them, a German, refuses to take his place in line with his comrades. One of the guards thinking perhaps he did not understand the order, puts his hand on the shoulder and attempts to show him what is to be done. Quick as wink, the German strikes the guard a left-hander in the jaw which staggers him across the sidewalk. Recovering from the blow the guard charges down upon the German, knocking him on the head with the butt of a Sharp's rifle and felling him like an ox.[59] Two of the guards picked the fallen men and carry him between them to the fairgrounds, where we camp for the night. As we lay in the soft grass under the young trees in the fairgrounds, Ben Wheatley rolls over on his elbow and, shutting one eye, says "Luttrell, wasn't that a——fine shot, though?"

"Did you notice it?" I asked.

"You're blamed right I did. That's the outcome of that

Cotton Burning Affair

at Monticello last winter; Col. Lawther had no right to arrest the man for setting cotton on fire, for we all thought the colonel was smuggling the cotton through to the Yankees. You know how we took him from the guard the night after he was arrested and sent him to Shelby's brigade to save him from court-martial. But the darned fool won't stay away from the regiment. He had a racket with the colonel during our brush with the Yankees on Prairie de Ann in Arkansas.[60] I thought they

---

Muscatine Daily Journal (Muscatine, IA), May 28, 1863; James E. McGhee, *Letter and Order Book Missouri State Guard 1861–1862* (Independence, MO, 2001), unnumbered page 29 (entry pages 56–57), hereafter cited as McGhee, *MSG Order Book*; National Archives, Record Group M322 (roll no. 57), Confederate Compiled Service Records, 10th Missouri Cavalry Regiment.

59. The Sharps was made by the Sharps Rifle Manufacturing Company of Hartford, Connecticut. There were two basic models that Luttrell could be referring to—a cavalry carbine and an infantry rifle (Model 1859). The rifle measured 47 inches long, while the carbine was 39 inches. Both used percussions caps and employed interchangeable parts. A total of 80,512 carbines were produced during the war, while 9,141 rifles were manufactured. The carbine was considered "among the best" in the world. In all likelihood the man who fired the shot was armed with a carbine. The Sharps Carbine was patented in 1848 by Christian Sharps, and was "one of the first successful breech-loading systems." A total of five models were produced for the Federal service, while the Confederates developed their own model using the Sharps as their guide. The carbine was intended for cavalry use, with .52 caliber bore as normal. To load the weapon the user cocked it, opening the breech, into which was inserted a paper cartridge. When closed the paper cartridge was cut allowing ignition of the powder and the firing of the weapon. A competent soldier could fire off 10 rounds a minute using this weapon, with accuracy up to 600 yards. Boatner, 735–736; Edwards, *Civil War Guns*, 293–294.

60. April 10, 1864, marked the beginning of the three day engagement at Prairie D'Ane, which took place during the Camden Expedition of 1864. The heaviest fighting took place on April 10, when the Confederates made a determined attack on the Union line but were repulsed. The next two days would see mostly heavy skirmishing and maneuvering, as Frederick Steele seemed reluctant

had things settled, but it seems as though they hain't. If he wants to kill the colonel why don't he take the time at close range? I call this half mile practice foolishness. But it was a splendid shot. There is no h——l [hell] if it wasn't!" and Wheatley walks off to attend to his horse.[61]

Sunday, October 3 [2]—This day we reached a point within thirty-five miles of St. Louis, so the country people say. Here quite a damper is thrown over the boy's enthusiasm in addition to the cold rainy and muddy roads. We change our course farther to the north, and we see that St. Louis is not our objective point.[62] Late in the evening we reach Washington.[63] Here many stores are gutted of their con-

---

to launch an all-out assault on the rebel lines. On April 11, Steele managed to flank the rebel lines, causing Price to withdraw. Federal losses were placed at 20 killed with 42 wounded. Confederate losses were not known. Banasik, *Reluctant Cannoneer*, 230–232; Dyer, 683.

61. October 1, 1864 also saw the arrival of Major General Alfred Pleasonton, in St. Louis, where he assumed command of the St. Louis District. *O.R.*, vol. 41, pt. 3:539.

62. It appears that the troops of Price's army were in the dark as to where they were going or what the ultimate objectives were. Following his repulse at Pilot Knob, Price had already decided to make Jefferson City the next objective of the expedition, though it appears that he may not have let his staff know of his decision. On September 30, Dr. McPheeters, of Price's staff recorded, "We are now 80 miles from St. Louis and must expect fierce opposition." On October 2, Price changed the direction of his march, issuing orders for the capture of Jefferson City, such that by the end of the day "officers freely told the men that 'we are going to march on Jefferson City,' formally inaugurate Reynolds, and 'hold him in by force of arms.'" And on October 3, Dr. McPheeters recorded that they were on the road to Jefferson City. *O.R.*, vol. 41, pt. 1:630; Forsyth, *Great Missouri Raid*, 145; Quoted in Lause, *Price's Lost Campaign*, 138; Pitcock & Gurley, 225, 227.

63. Lawther's 10th Missouri arrived at South Point, two miles from Washington in the late evening of October 1, after first burning the railroad facilities at Gray's Summit. The remainder of Clark's Brigade followed later on in the early morning of October 2. At dawn Lawther burned the South Point railroad depot, bridge, and two "freight cars," but failed to capture two ferryboats; however, the 10th managed to "perforate" the steamboat *Wide Awake* with more than one hundred musket balls. Prior to Lawther's arrival the *Wide Awake* and the *Bright Star* had managed to evacuate a militia regiment and save the military stores that were housed in the city. At 8:00 a.m., the remainder of Clark's Brigade arrived, after which they took the town without opposition. Shelby's Division with the rest of Marmaduke's Division stayed at Union, awaiting the remainder of the army. Meanwhile, Fagan's Division, with Price's headquarters, had spent the night of October 1 at St. Clair. Price left St. Clair early on October 2, moving to Union where he found Shelby and Marmaduke awaiting orders. Also present was Cabell's command, lately returned from their raid on Franklin where they "had destroyed a large amount of stores and buildings of the enemy, also a splendid & costly bridge. He destroyed near a million dollars worth of property." Following a meeting with his principle commanders, Price directed Shelby and Fagan to move toward Jefferson City, while Marmaduke's Division was to continue down the Missouri River road, from Washington to Herman. By nightfall, of October 2, Shelby and Fagan were camped 8–10 miles southwest of Union, while Marmaduke camped near New Port on the road to Herman. During the day, Marmaduke sent Freeman's Brigade back to the main column, fearing that he could not "take care of it." *O.R.*, vol. 41, pt. 1:645, 680; *O.R.*, vol. 41, pt. 3:975, 977; *O.R.S.*, pt. 1, vol. 7:407; J. T. Alexander, Letter (undated, but probably October 2, 1864); Busch, *Missouri Democrat Articles*, 82–83; "From St. Louis," *Chicago Tribune*, October 4, 1864; Gregory, 9, 12, 15; Anita M. Mallinckrodt, *A History of Augusta, MO. And Its Area(I) 1850s–1860s As Reported in the St. Charles Democrat* (Washington, MO, 1998), 120-121, hereafter cited as Mallinckrodt; Pitcock & Gurley, 226; "The War In Missouri," *Chicago Tribune*, October 6, 1864.

tents; who began the pillage I do not know.[64] Store doors have been smashed in and the goods of all kinds are strewn on the street as we entered town. Soon the men begin to break and appropriate such wearing apparel as they stood in need of. I see men riding at a gallop with a bolt of calico trailing in their air after them. They think it is great fun. "Why don't you draw yourself a new rig?" asked a trooper as he passed me dressed up in a new suit of gray cashmere.

"Because I don't approve of that kind of drawing. I will wait until we make a new draw on Uncle Sam's fat quartermaster depots and then I'll draw a rig of Yankee blue. It will be preferable to your style of drawing clothing."

As we move out of town I pick up a new militia hat by the roadside. It is

A Gaudy Affair

as compared to our plain, gray sombreros.[65] It has yellow cord and tassels, feather and half pound brass "E pluribus unum." I find it to be a good fit, and cast my old ragged gray to the road side. I'm laughed at some for my ungainly appearance, a new militia man's hat over a dirty, ragged gray uniform. We camp, this night near town. While on foraging duty tonight, some mile and a half from camp, some of the boys begin a rapid firing. They said it was at Yankees, but I am inclined to think it was an imaginary enemy, for I can neither see or hear anything indicative of an enemy. Such another stampede and scattering of forage sacks I never saw in a forage detail. We remain in camp but about three hours. Then remove on and camp near Newport.

Monday, 4th [3rd].—This day we reach Hermann and have more skirmishing, capturing one piece of artillery. The side-tracks along the railroad on the river are literally jammed with freight cars. Rain begins to fall in the night and sleep is impossible. I have been chilling every third day since the middle of July. But tonight—the second day—I chilled desperately. Perhaps it is a cold rain and the exposure that has brought it on ahead of time.[66]

---

64. Author Ralph Gregory puts the Franklin County losses of destroyed property at $500,000. See Appendix I, "Property Destroyed, Captured or Stolen" During Price's Expedition for a listing of known losses suffered by the Union command and the Missouri citizens. Gregory, 19.

65. Federal Militia reoccupied Washington on October 5, and on the 11th General E. C. Pike's Militia Brigade arrived in the city from St. Louis. And even at that late date one militiaman recorded: "The streets are littered with boxes of every kind, paper, rags and lots of things of no value." Ibid., 14.

66. October 3 proved uneventful for the main column under General Price, except for the parole of several hundred prisoners. Prior to paroling the prisoners, Colonel James R. Shaler, Price's inspector general, queried the men as to their units. If they answered the 3rd MSM Cavalry, they were removed from the group and marched off to another location. Eventually they were turned over to Colonel Timothy Reeves for summary execution (For Extended Comments on the execution of Major J. Wilson and his men, see Appendix C). Meanwhile, John B. Clark's Brigade succeeded in taking Miller Landing toward noon, and entered Herman between 4:00 and 5:00 p.m. At Miller Landing (current location of New Haven), Clark captured a freight train, three locomotives, and 30 cars (another source says 40–50 cars), including eight stock cars, 14 box cars and eight others, with one of the box cars containing 1,200 weapons, according to Lieutenant John A. Bennet of the

Tuesday, 5th [4th]—Day has dawned at last, but the cold rain continues. I'm sick with a high fever and drenched to the skin by the pouring rain. The battalions are marshaling for the march; at last we filed down into the streets of Hermann. One of the exasperating halts so common to moving columns of a cavalry command is at hand. Such a pour of rain; the streets are almost knee deep in mud and water. By permission of the captain I take shelter from the downpour under an awning. Presently Gen. Marmaduke rides up and seeks shelter from the storm. "Hello! Good morning, general; it's a ——— nasty day; take something to drink?"

The speaker is John Medlock [or Matlock] of Company G, who has just turned the corner with an

Armful of Wine Bottles.[67]

Now he is opposite the general and is holding up one of the long-necked bottles as he talks on to in his maudlin, drunken, thick tongued voice. "Jus' put a bottle under your belt, general, and it'll help you wonderful—darned if [it] don't, general. It's good stuff; 'cause I've ———."

8th Missouri Cavalry. General Clark noted that 400 of the guns were Sharps rifles (the *Missouri Democrat* and *Chicago Tribune* say there were 800 and Marmaduke stated there were only 250 Sharps, actually Sharps carbines), while Kyle Sinisi pegs the other weapons as Austrian rifles. Proceeding on to Herman, Clark's Brigade, led by Colton Greene's 3rd Missouri Cavalry, approached the town in the late afternoon. Per orders, Greene dismounted his command and charged into Herman easily dispersing the Union defenders. And in the process Greene captured one 6-lb iron smoothbore (Clark says it was an iron 12-lb smoothbore and Mark A. Lause says the defenders threw the gun in the river.). Herman secured, Marmaduke camped for the night just outside of town. Price, for his part, made but 12 miles, following a late start, and camped near the border of Franklin and Gasconade Counties, on the road to Jefferson City. *O.R.*, vol. 41, pt. 1:680, 688, 696; *O.R.*, vol. 43, pt. 3:544; Busch, *Missouri Democrat Articles*, 99–101; Campbell Memoir; Gregory, 18; Lause, *Price's Lost Campaign*, 139, 148–149; Mallinckrodt, 121; McGhee, *Campaigning With Marmaduke*, 22; Sinisi, 97–98; "The War In Missouri," *Chicago Tribune*, October 6, 1864.

67. John [w/wo B.] Medlock [or Matlock], a resident of Reynolds County, Missouri, was born about 1840. He joined the MSG on June 16, 1861, at Holden, in Johnson County. He fought at Wilson's Creek and Lexington as a member of Company A or G, 3rd Infantry Regiment, 8th Division MSG. He mustered out of the MSG on December 14, then joined the MSG units that were organizing at Milford, Missouri. Captured at Milford on December 19, 1861, Matlock was sent to the Alton Illinois Prison, where he was later exchanged. Matlock then joined what became Company G, 11th Missouri Cavalry Battalion (CSA) on August 16, 1862, in Johnson County. On August 11, 1863, he went AWOL, until September 3, 1863, probably in search of a new horse, when he returned to his command In December 1863, the company became Company G, 10th Missouri Cavalry. Matlock survived the war and was living in Crane, Stone County, Missouri, in 1913, at the age of 73. Ankesheiln, *Last Guardsmen*, 136; Bartels, *Trans-Mississippi Men*, 213, 249; Joanne C. Eakin, *Battle of Blackwater River Milford, Johnson County, Missouri on December 19, 1861, Including a List of 736 Captured* (Independence, MO, 1995), "Medlock, John" entry, hereafter cited as Eakin, *Battle of Blackwater*; Joanne C. Eakin, *Missouri Prisoners of War From Gratiot Prison & Myrtle Street Prison, St. Louis, Mo. and Alton Prison, Alton Illinois Including Citizens, Confederates, Bushwhackers and Guerrillas* (Independence, MO, 1995), "Medlock, John" entry, hereafter cited as Eakin, *Missouri Prisoners of War*; National Archive, Record Group M322 (roll no. 57), Confederate Compiled Service Records, 10th Missouri Cavalry; Peterson, et al., 231 (n. 304); Schnetzer, *Men of the Tenth*, passim.

Gen'l Marmaduke takes the proffered bottle and throws it down on the pavement.

"Oh; devilish slippery weather, general. Take another. Accidents will happen in the best of regulated ———"

Crash went another bottle. "What command do you belong to?" asked Gen. Marmaduke.

"Co. G, Tenth Missouri, ———, sir. Take another bottle general; I've got lots of 'em, and a cellar full right over there. Just help yourself, general."

"Captain of Co. G, arrest this man, and keep him in durance until he is sober," orders the general.

"Well now, if that don't beat ———! That's what I call politeness with a vengeance: me a offering to treat the general on wine and he orders me under arrest; it's a pretty way to show a man raisin'," says John, as he is marched out in the pouring rain between two guards.[68]

Wednesday, 6th [5th]—This day we have a brush with the enemy at the Gasconade Bridge. We capture and burn blockhouse and bridge.[69]

---

68. On October 4, Marmaduke's command made about 25 miles on the road to Linn, encountering no resistance except for "copious showers of rain" that fell, making for an uneventful, though muddy day. Prior to leaving Herman, Marmaduke had loaded one of the captured trains with a portion of Wood's Battalion, plus a piece of artillery, and directed them to destroy the Gasconade bridge near its mouth at the Missouri River. Accompanying the train was another part of Wood's command, which led the horses of the men on the train. Wood's unit easily captured the Gasconade bridge, which was guarded by two companies of the 34th Enrolled Missouri Militia (EMM). The militia companies tore up some track and then fled to Jefferson City. Repairing the torn up track by bringing up rails from the rear, Wood ran his train onto the trestle and burned the bridge. Wood secured some oxen from a local farm, hooked ropes to them to pull the artillery. Later, on October 5, Wood secured "a pair of big, fat, gray German horses and succeeded to carrying...[the] artillery and equipment back to the command" without further incident, where he arrived late on October 5. Meanwhile, the main column under Price made 17 miles, crossed the Gasconade River at Mt. Sterling, and camped a mile beyond Shelby's command. Shelby led the army past Mt. Sterling and captured Linn on October 4, taking in the process 100 prisoners with as many arms (John Edwards greatly exaggerated the captures as 372). *O.R.*, vol. 41, pt. 1:630, 653, 680–681, 696; Ballard Diary, October 4, 1864; Campbell Memoir; Edwards, *Shelby and His Men*, 392; McGhee, *Campaigning With Marmaduke*, 22–23; Pitcock & Gurley, 227; Sinisi, 98.

69. With the "morning clear and beautiful; air pleasant and bracing," on October 5, Marmaduke resumed his march to rejoin the main army as it approached Jefferson City. Detaching Lawther's command, Marmaduke ordered Lawther to burn the Gasconade River bridge, near Fredericktown, and yet another bridge across Bailey's Creek. When Lawther reached the Gasconade River bridge he discovered that Wood's Battalion had already destroyed it. After destroying the Bailey bridge, Lawther rejoined his brigade and camped 25 miles from Herman with the remainder of Marmaduke's Division. Meanwhile, the main army, led by Shelby's Division, made 14 miles, camping near Linn, while Shelby's Division pushed on to Westphalia. As Shelby pressed forward, he detached Colonel David Shanks at Linn on the evening of October 4, with three (Cruzen says only two) regiments to capture and "completely destroy" the Osage River bridge. Capturing Westphalia on the afternoon of October 5, Shelby awaited the arrival of Shank's detachment, which arrived during the early morning of October 6. Shanks for his part had marched through the night of October 4–5, briefly camping at the village of "Loose Creek" to feed and forage before moving forward. Shanks easily captured and destroyed the Osage River bridge at sunrise on October 5, where the militia fled without firing a shot. In addition to capturing "80 old men," Shanks de-

Thursday, 8th [6th]—Shelby's brigade leads the advance today. He encounters the enemy at the Osage bridge.[70] It is Ewing with the Pilot Knob contingent.[71] Heavy firing is heard the front.[72] As we near the bridge we begin to see dead horses—a little further on dead men—Federal—along the roadside. We move at a "trot march," yet I see plenty of signs of the fierce fighting along the road, brush cut and twisted down, trees shattered by cannonballs, the ground torn by hoofs of the charging squadron and dead men and horses strewn along. This night we lie on our arms in battle line around Jefferson City, expecting to attack the place at daybreak.[73]

---

stroyed the local deport, railroad property, Mr. McKermsan's warehouse, and a mill. As a bonus, the militia had just been preparing their breakfast when they fled, which Shanks' men appropriated for themselves, including thirty gallons of coffee, cooked bacon, bread, and some sugar. *O.R.*, vol. 41, pt. 1:3369–370, 680–681, 696, 698; *O.R.*, vol. 41, pt. 3:642, 982, 985; Cruzen, 25–26; Edwards, *Shelby and His Men*, 392; Lause, *Price's Lost Campaign*, 145; McGhee, *Campaigning With Marmaduke*, 23; Pitcock & Gurley, 227; Sellmeyer, 216–217; Sinisi, 105.

70. On October 6, Shelby was tasked with crossing the Osage River, which offered several possible fords. Previous scouts had determined that all the fords were guarded, but unknown as to the enemy's strength. Dividing his command, Shelby sent Gordon's Regiment to cross at Castle Rock Ford, thus creating a diversion, while the remainder of Shanks's Brigade crossed at Prince's Ford. Jackman's Brigade served as a reserve and brought up the rear at Prince's Ford. It was about noon when Gordon's command moved out, followed shortly thereafter by the remainder of the division. *O.R.*, vol. 41, pt. 1:654; *O.R.*, vol. 41, pt. 3:985–986; Cruzen, 26–27.

71. Not true. Ewing eventually made it to Rolla, and from there his men moved to St. Louis where they received a hero's welcome for their successful stand at Pilot Knob. Busch, *Missouri Democrat Articles*, 96, 98.

72. Reaching Prince's Ford during the noon hour, Shelby dismounted Shanks's Brigade, with the exception of Elliott's Battalion and D. A. Williams's Company. Jackman's Brigade was in reserve. With the artillery in place and firing, Elliott and Williams charged across the ford, while the dismounted men splashed across at the same time. Caught by surprise, the Federals under Major A. W. Mullins, were initially driven from the ford, rallied a short time later, but were eventually driven from the area and pursued by Shanks's Cavalry. Federal losses totaled two killed, three wounded, with four mortally wounded. (The *Missouri Democrat* puts the Federal loss at 13 killed, three wounded. The additional seven killed or mortally wounded were probably men who were caught on the wrong side of the Osage River when the assault began, tried to swim the river, but drowned. Four of the drowned came from the 7th MSM.) Federal sources put Shelby's losses at two killed, with seven wounded. However, Dr. McPheeters, the army's medical director, puts the Confederate losses at but one severely wounded—Colonel David Shanks, whose wound was thought mortal. Later Shanks was captured, survived his wound and the war, eventually passing away in Denver, Colorado, in 1870. Meanwhile, Gordon's detachment had no difficulty crossing the river at Castle Rock, meeting only light resistance three miles north of the ford. It seems that once Shelby began his assault at Prince's Ford, the Unionists at Castle Rock moved to assist in repelling the rebels, but failed. At dark Gordon made camp near the Dixon Plantation and sent a scout in search of Shelby, whose division was camped near Taos, about three miles from Prince's Ford and seven from Jefferson City. *O.R.*, vol. 41, pt. 1:362, 654, 673; *O.R.*, vol. 41. pt. 3:667; *O.R.S.*, pt. 2, vol. 35:463; Allardice, *Confederate Colonels*, 337; Busch, *Missouri Democrat Articles*, 125; Lause, *Price's Lost Campaign*, 167; Pitcock & Gurley, 227; Sellmeyer, 217–218; Sinisi, 106; *The Union Army A History of Military Affairs in the Loyal United States 1861–1865—Records of the Regiments in the Union Army—Cyclopedia of Battles—Memoirs of Commanders and Soldiers* (8 vols., New York, 1908; reprint ed., Wilmington, NC, 1998), 6:717, cited hereafter as *Union Army*.

73. While Shelby forced the river crossing of the Osage River, the remainder of the rebel army

Friday, 9th [7th]—This morning we

Hear the Long Roll

in the Federal camps, and we are greatly surprised when we receive marching orders to move out on the Russellville road. About noon we hear heavy firing close by our right (north).[74] We suppose it is Shelby's or Fagan's brigade at the Morol [Moreau] bridge.[75] This night we camp at the Russellville.

was still 18 miles behind, at Linn. During the day Fagan's Division, led by Cabell's Brigade, headed for the Osage, and by nightfall they were encamped near the river, waiting for the dawn. Farther back at Linn, John B. Clark's Brigade of Marmaduke's Division finally arrived from its operations on the Pacific Railroad and joined the rear of the column, reuniting with the division. Meanwhile, in Jefferson City, commanded by General Clinton Fisk, the Federals made final defensive preparations. A network of five forts, with "three miles of entrenchments, palisades, rifle pits, chevaux-de-fise" encircled the city. Occupying the city were 3,000 EMM, MSM, and citizens under E. B. Brown; 1,000 cavalry under John McNeil; and another 1,400 cavalry under J. B. Sanborn. Also present were 1,800 MSM and EMM that Fisk had gathered from his district for the defense of Jefferson City. In all the Unionists numbered 7,200 effectives, "with no more than 6,000 reliable," and 10 pieces of artillery. (Forsyth has only eight pieces of artillery, failing to add in the two mountain howitzers from E. B. Brown, while the *Missouri Republican* said there were 18 pieces of artillery, including six mountain howitzers.) The whole command was divided into four brigades. General McNeil held the far right of the entrenchments; the one-armed Brown was given the left; Sanborn held the center; and the reserve was under Colonel Franklin Hickox. *O.R.*, vol. 41, pt. 1:375-376, 418-419, 631, 696; Ballard Diary, October 6, 1864; Busch, *Missouri Democrat Articles*, 176; Forsyth, *Great Missouri Raid*, 149; Lause, *Price's Lost Campaign*, 165; Jay Monaghan, *Civil War On the Western Border 1865–1865* (New York, 1955), 331, hereafter cited as Monaghan; Occasional, "From Jefferson City," *Missouri Republican*, October 19, 1864; A. Pleasonton, "General Pleasonton's Narrative," in *Rebellion Record*, vol. 11:394; Pitcock & Gurley, 227–228.

74. October 7, began with the "morning pleasant," according to John A. Bennett of the 8th Missouri Cavalry (CSA). The day was filled with "beautiful sunshine," continued Bennett, and "light fleecy clouds....Delightful autumnal winds giving everything a magnificent appearance." All was ready for the final Confederate push on the Missouri capital, with Fagan's Division given the responsibility of leading the Army of Missouri. Shelby's Division would be supporting operations, as it moved from the far right of the rebel line to the left, where it was tasked to cut the Pacific Railroad coming into Jefferson City from the west. Meanwhile, Marmaduke's Division remained in the rear of Price's Army. For Marmaduke's boys, October 7 proved to be a lazy day as they leisurely moved forward, crossing the Osage at the Bolton Ford during the noontime. By the end of October 7, Marmaduke's command was camped two to three miles, southwest of Jefferson City on the Russellville Road, having not been engaged during the day. *O.R.*, vol. 41, pt. 1:655; Ballard Diary, October 7, 1864; McGhee, *Campaigning With Marmaduke*, 23; Order of March (October 7, 1864), Civil War Collection, "Army of Missouri" file, Missouri Historical Society (St. Louis), hereafter cited as Order of March, Army of Missouri.

75. About 6:00 a.m. on the morning of October 7, Fagan's Division, led by W. F. Slemons's Brigade (not Cabell's Brigade as stated by John Edwards and Mark Lause), moved to the front of the army, making contact an hour later. John C. Wright, whose Arkansas Regiment spearheaded the advance, was assured by General Fagan, that he would be supported by the whole division, once contact was made; however that support came too late to do any good. Wright crossed the Osage River at the Bolton Ford, pressing toward Jefferson City. Five miles from the city Wright encountered the 6th and 8th MSM Cavalry, commanded by Colonel Joseph J. Gravely, and fought a series of short skirmishes as they pushed the Federals steadily back toward the main defenses of the city. At the Moreau Bridge, resistance stiffened, with "the firing very intense at times,"

Saturday[Sunday], 10th [8th–9th][76]—About noon today my horse cast a shoe, and in a short time he is so lame I am obliged to stop and drive on another.[77] Before I get through our rearguard comes up. "Fall in!" called the officer in command.

according to Peter Brooks of the 6th MSM Cavalry. And then Federal artillery came into play, as two companies of the 45th EMM Infantry (one newspaper said it was the 48th EMM) advanced to relieve the cavalry; however, the infantry panicked, then scattered, as Gravely's command withdrew, causing Wright's Arkansans to charge. Federal artillery came to the aid of the retreating Companies C & I, 45th EMM, halting the rebel advance after a few rounds of artillery. By 1:00 p.m. the front quieted for a period, as Cabell's Brigade came from the rear of Fagan's column to bolster Wright's attack. Placing Hughey's Battery in support, Cabell deployed, but never attacked, making only a demonstration on the Federal troops, who withdrew into their entrenchments. By 3:00 p.m. the engagement, described as "hardly a battle but a continuous skirmish," had ended. Federal losses in the 6th and 8th MSM numbered three killed, with 19 wounded, while the EMM losses were not unknown; however a period newspaper put the overall losses at the Moreau at seven killed, with 49 wounded, suggesting that the EMM lost four killed and 30 wounded. (Later the *Missouri Democrat* stated that the EMM lost 17 killed, wounded or missing, while Major L. H. Boutell recorded "Loss as far as known was 3 killed, 9 wounded, and 4 missing in action.") Overall Confederate losses were "very slight" according to one participant; however, even though the exact number of rebel killed was not known, "a number" of men from Wright's Arkansas Regiment, including Major James W. Bowie, were mortally wounded or killed, according to Colonel John C. Wright, while Dr. McPheeters recorded that the Confederates had lost "10 to 12 of our own men wounded." This would suggest that rebel losses were about 15. *O.R.*, vol. 41, pt. 1:370, 395, 412, 419; *O.R.*, vol. 41, pt. 3:689; *O.R.S.*, pt. 1, vol. 7:370, 395, 407–408; Britton, *Civil War on the Border, 1863–65*, 420–421; Peter Brooks Diary (September 26–November 11, 1864), October 8, 1864, Terry Justice Private Collection, hereafter cited as Brooks Dairy; Busch, *Missouri Democrat Articles*, 120, 126; Edwards, *Shelby and His Men*, 395; Forsyth, *Great Missouri Raid*, 151; Lause, *Price's Lost Campaign*,170; Mallinckrodt, 121; Pitcock & Gurley 228; Sinisi, 108; Wright Memoirs, unnumbered pages 82–83.

76. It appears that Luttrell actually skipped October 8 altogether. Saturday was October 8, but the events that he describes are from October 9. From here on Luttrell's dates and days don't match and have been corrected as needed.

77. During the night of October 7–8, General Price reevaluated his chances of taking the Missouri capital. Central to that decision was a report that placed the Federal defenders at 12,000 men, with 3,000 more just north of the Missouri River and getting ready to cross. Upon consulting with "his chief of engineers, General Shelby and others," at his headquarters in the Wallendorf house in the Frog Hollow area, Price was uncertain as to whether he should attack Jefferson City. The next morning, October 8, Dr. William McPheeters, who was at Fagan's headquarters, accompanied the Arkansas general as they searched for Price, whom they found four miles away with General Marmaduke. "It was determined," according to McPheeters, after meeting Price and Marmaduke, "not to attack the Yankee fortifications at Jefferson, so we resolved to move on." With the debacle at Pilot Knob still fresh in his mind, Price decided to bypass Jefferson City and continue the march westward toward Kansas. As an additional take as to why Price gave up Jefferson City, author Dino Brugioni wrote that Price possibly had a "fatal weakness of Southern temperament—that capacity for romantic sentimentality—that he could not bring himself to destroy a city he helped build, to kill helpless friends, or destroy the edifices where he had labored as a representative, speaker and governor." With Price's decision, any hope of reestablishing Confederate control over Missouri had ended, as the expedition was now oriented to securing men and supplies for future operations. To Michael Forsyth, Price's failure at Jefferson City marked "the real turning point" in the expedition, as the general gave up his last major strategic objective. *O.R.*, vol. 41, pt. 1:376, 631, 645; Britton, *Civil War on the Border, 1863–65*, 421–422; Busch, *Missouri Democrat Articles*, 177; Dino A. Brugioni, *The Civil War In Missouri As Seen From the Capital City* (Jefferson City, MO, 1987), 121, 127, hereafter cited as Brugioni; Castel, *Sterling Price*, 224–225; Crowley,

"All right, as soon as I fasten this shoe," I replied, hacking away with all my might. "Don't tarry, more than five minutes," said the officer, "the enemy is not more than a mile behind."[78]

I drove two nails and clench down the shoe, put up my tools, set my foot in the stirrup to mount just as a voice sang out "Halt!"

As I swung into the saddle and look back I see the road is full of blue-coats and a dozen shots are fired at me before I could say Jack. A good 150 yards is between us, and lying low on my horse's back, I hold the spurs into his flank and urge him to do his best. The enemy do not chase me, as I expected they would, but a few of

---

139–140; Forsyth, *Great Missouri Raid*, 152, 158; Lause, *Price's Lost Campaign*, 174; Pitcock & Gurley, 228–229; Sellmeyer, 220; Shalhope, 267; Sinisi, 108–109.

Note: Most writers, with the exception of Albert Castel, have Price making the decision to withdraw on the night of October 7; however, a close reading of Price's comments on the matter leave it open as to when the final decision was made. Governor Thomas C. Reynolds agrees with Dr. McPheeters. In a letter to the *Marshal Republican*, Reynolds wrote: The "next morning [October 8], whether wisely or correct information that large reinforcements had reached the enemy in the night, or unwisely from hesitating generalship or mistaken policy, General Price suddenly ordered a retreat, on the road to Springfield." Castel, Sterling Price, 224–225; Thomas C. Reynolds, Letter (December 14, 1864), *Marshall Republican*, December 23, 1864.

78. "Daylight came and the sun rose broad and clear" on October 8, "yet no forward movement came," according to John Edwards. "And finally," continued Edwards, "about ten o'clock, instructions were received to march westward." To protect Shelby's withdrawal, John Schnable's Missouri Battalion, better known as the "Straw Hat Regiment," was given the mission to picket the front. With no attack materializing on the morning of the 8th, General Sanborn ordered the 2nd Arkansas Cavalry (Union) to advance "and try the enemy's position." For the next several hours, Colonel John E. Phelps's boys fought Schnable's command, in a series of attacks and counterattacks, during which Schnable lost three horses. After driving Schnable four miles, the Federals broke contact, returned to Jefferson City, where they reported the withdrawal of Price's army. Even while the bluecoats were probing his line, Price's army moved out on the Russellville Road. Marmaduke's Division had the advance followed by the army trains, then Shelby's command, with Fagan's Division bringing up the rear. (Most writers, except James Thoma, have Shelby's Division leading the way, which is incorrect.) Meanwhile, General Alfred Pleasonton arrived in Jefferson City at 10:30 a.m. and assumed command of the Union forces. Pleasonton organized a provisional cavalry division under John Sanborn, whom he directed to pursue the retreating rebels. Sanborn's 1st Brigade, under Colonel Philips took up the pursuit down the Russellville Road, while Sanborn's other two brigades headed toward California via the Pacific Railroad. After Philips made contact in the late afternoon with the rebel rear, commanded by General Cabell, Sanborn diverted his 3rd Brigade under Colonel Gravely to support Philips. After driving back Cabell's Brigade from the Moreau Creek area, Sanborn's command camped, with his 2nd Brigade still located on the California Road. Cabell for his part camped 14 miles from Jefferson City, while Marmaduke's Division, with the army's trains made Russellville. Shelby's Division was sandwiched between Fagan's and Marmaduke's Divisions. For the day, Schnable reported the loss of four killed with 14 wounded; Cabell recorded "my loss quite heavy in wounded, but few killed." *O.R.*, vol. 41, pt.1:305, 386, 395, 401–402, 420, 655; *O.R.S.*, pt. 1, vol. 7:397; Crute, *Confederate Units*, 210; Edwards, *Shelby and His Men*, 395; Norton & Massey, 64; Order of March, Army of Missouri, October 8, 1864; Pitcock & Gurley, 229; Sanborn, "Campaign in Missouri," 159–160; Sellmeyer, 220–221; Stewart Sifakis, *Compendium of the Confederate Armies. Kentucky, Maryland, Missouri, The Confederate Units and the Indian Units* (New York, 1995), 108, hereafter cited as Sifakis, *Missouri*; James F. Thoma, *This Cruel Unnatural War: The American Civil War in Cooper County, Missouri. Second Edition* (Kingsport, TN, 2006), 82, 96, hereafter cited as Thoma.

them content themselves with sharp rifle practice until I clear the crest of the next ridge, where I fall in with the rearguard.[79] A little before sundown, as our baggage train is passing through California, a column of the enemy makes a dash at it and opens fire with a six-gun battery. As it happens one section of Pratt's battery is with the train. It wheels into position and replies with great spirit.[80] The Tenth regiment gallops to its support in hot haste. Following up at a dead run comes another section of artillery; it is unlimbered and opens up in fine style; shot and shell hiss and shriek through the air at a fearful rate—six guns against four. The enemy shows up a solid battle line, stretching out to the railroad on the north, and into the timber on the south. And now

---

79. During the night of October 8, General Shelby directed General M. Jeff Thompson to send a regiment in advance of the army to take California. Colonel Moses Smith's 11th Missouri (CSA) was selected, reaching its target by early morning on October 9, where they began the destruction of the local railroad facilities. Meanwhile, Shelby's Division moved to the front on the morning of October 9, followed by the trains, Fagan's Division, with Marmaduke's Division bringing up the rear. At Highpoint the rebel army headed north toward California, on the road to Boonville. Meanwhile the Union pursuit, led by J. J. Gravely's 3rd Brigade, and supported by Sanborn's 2nd Brigade, which had marched cross-country to join the division, made contact with Colton Greene's 3rd Missouri Cavalry (CSA), of Clark's Brigade, at about 9:00 a.m. near the village of Stringtown. Easily repulsing Sanborn's troopers, Clark's Brigade continued its retreat while its Federal adversary maneuvered on its flank. Toward noon, John Philips's 1st Brigade moved to Sanborn's front and led the Federal division north, on the rebel eastern flank, via back roads, in an attempt to reach California before the rebels did. At the head of the Confederate column, Shelby's Iron Brigade, now under M. Jeff Thompson, entered California well before noon. Looting the town, Thompson was soon joined by Shelby and then Price just before noon. Shelby then obtained permission from Price to hurry on to Boonville, where he arrived before sunset, on the 9th, and took the town, with 300 prisoners, without firing a shot. *O.R.*, vol. 41, pt. 1:354, 414, 681, 688; Diary of the Raid, Army of Missouri, October 9, 1864; Charles H. Lothrop, *A History of the First Regiment Iowa Cavalry Veteran Volunteers, etc.* (Lyons, Iowa, 1899; reprint ed, Salem, MA, 1998), 196, hereafter cited as Lothrop; Order of March, Army of Missouri, October 9, 1864; Sanborn, "Campaign in Missouri," 161–162; Sellmeyer, 221–222; Donal J. Stanton, Goodwin F. Berquist, and Paul C. Bowers, eds., *The Civil War Reminiscences of General M. Jeff Thompson* (Dayton, OH, 1988), 240–241, hereafter cited as Stanton, et al.; Thoma, 133–134.

80. Between 4:00–5:00 p.m., Philips's Brigade approached California from the southeast, breaking out of the timber to an open prairie. Discovered by Clark's Brigade, the rear guard of the army, Clark deployed two guns of Hynson's Battery in the town, supported by Kitchen's 7th Missouri to hold the Federals at bay, while the brigade passed through the town. Meanwhile, Philips dismounted his command and deployed for action, while Captain Charles H. Thurber placed Lieutenant Albert Wachsman's section of his battery to respond to Hynson's rebel artillery. Note: There's no indication that Thurber deployed his entire battery, as noted by Lause or Luttrell, though I suspect that they were there. Further, Lause has Wachsman's section as a separate unit when it was actually part of Thurber's Battery. *O.R.*, vol. 41, pt. 1:354–355, 387, 681, 696; *O.R.S.*, pt. 2, vol. 36:131; Britton, *Civil War on the Border, 1863–65*, 419–420; Campbell Memoir; Mark A. Lause, *The Collapse of Price's Raid: The Beginning of the End in Civil War Missouri* (Columbia, MO, 2016), 19, hereafter cited as Lause, *Collapse of Price's Raid*; Sanborn, "Missouri Campaign," 162.

Another Section of Artillery

wheels into position and the thunder of battle swells—it's six guns to six.[81] The cavalry supports on either side stand still and watch the panorama in silent admiration. An artillery man, No. 1, on the section next to "G" Co., falls like a log. Sergt. Pratt a mere youth, son of Maj. Pratt jumps to the gun and rams shot after shot. Presently the wounded man rises to a sitting position feels about with his hands like one in the dark. The young sergeant without a handkerchief, wiped the blood from the man's face, ties a handkerchief around the wound, ramming a shot and swabbing the gun at intervals. Now No. 1 gets on his feet; takes the swap, rams a shot and stands to his post to the end of the action. Soon after the sergeant gives the rammer back to No. 1, some of the artillery horses are wounded. They reared and plunged, and fairly lifted drivers off their feet.

Sergt. Pratt sees that commotion, runs to the drivers, whips out his sword and brandishing over their heads, swears he will "cut the first man down that turns a horse loose." For half an hour the artillery duel lasts.[82] Then the enemy limber up their guns and put for the timber in their rear; we march on into town. The boom of cannon breaks loose again. We form in the street. Some of the men break ranks to hunt whiskey. A saloon is in our rear; into it they swarm. But someone has knocked in the head of the barrels. Shells are falling about at a lively rate. One passes over our heads, comes down inside the saloon door and crashes through the floor into the cellar and bursts. That clears the saloon of stragglers. Another shell

---

81. Union accounts have only Wachsman's Section of Thurber's Battery being engaged at California, while Confederate accounts are sketchy as to their numbers. General Clark says that he used Pratt's Battalion, which was composed of six pieces of artillery. J. F. Davies, of the 7th Missouri Cavalry says that only Hynson's three guns were engaged. Other rebel participants say Pratt's Battery was engaged, but don't specify the number of guns, while yet another account just simply says "our artillery was thrown into" the engagement. And Luttrell has all six guns of Pratt's Battalion engaged. The additional guns could have been added after Clark repositioned his command a mile north of California as the fight was ending. *O.R.*, vol. 41 pt. 1:354–355, 387, 681,696; Campbell Memoir; McGhee, *Campaigning With Marmaduke*, 23.

82. Passing through California, Clark redeployed his brigade about a mile north of town. Greene's and Kitchen's commands supported Hynson's Battery, while Lawther's 10th Missouri brought up the rear. With no further attacks, Clark broke contact and moved his command up the road, passing Fagan's Division. Clark made another three miles past Cabell's command, and bivouacked for the night with the rest of Marmaduke's Division on Montineau Creek. For the day the army made 27 miles, being scattered from north of California (Cabell), to Montineau Creek (Marmaduke), with the remainder of Fagan's command and Jackman's Brigade two miles farther down the road on Wonder Creek, while Thompson's Brigade of Shelby's Division was in Boonville. The Federals under Sanborn, with night upon them, camped at California. The engagement at California lasted about an hour resulting in but few casualties on either side. Lawther reported losing two men wounded, Hynson another, while Greene reported four men wounded during the earlier fights of the day near Russellville. No other rebel losses were reported; however, Union troops reported finding five dead rebels in California when the town was finally taken. Union losses were three wounded at California, and one killed and three wounded earlier in the day at Russellville. *O.R.*, vol. 41, pt 1:355, 631, 414, 645, 673, 688–689, 696, 698; Ballard Diary, October 9, 1864; Forsyth, *Great Missouri Raid*, 158–159; Hinton, 109; Lause, *Collapse of Price's Raid*. 19; McGhee, *Campaigning With Marmaduke*, 23; Pitcock & Gurley, 229; Sinisi, 115–116; *Union Army*, 5:205.

knocks the top off the chimney, falls in the street at our feet, spins around in the dust like a top, then bursts. Fortunately no one is hurt. We camped this night eight miles from California on the Boonville road.

Sunday [Monday], 11th [10th]—Nothing worthy of note transpired today, only we have done one more weary march. We camp

Just above Boonville,

on the riverbank, at about 3 in the evening.[83] How thankful we will be, if we can have a half-day and night rest. It has been about fifty days since we started on this expedition. Let me see. I left the convalescent camp on the 20th of August, at Tyro, Lincoln County, Ark. Yes; ran away from the convalescent camp and go on this expedition. I expected then to get to see my mamma and my little sweetheart. Blamed if I wouldn't go through a part of torment to see them. But my hopes are flown. We won't strike Pettis County at all.[84] How I wish I had got permission to join Shelby's brigade. It will strike Sedalia, and I might get to see the folks. But I'm always out of luck. It's unlucky for me to have these beastly chills. Everyone gets harder. Ha! ha! ha!

Ben Wheatley is trying to cook some rice. He put it on in a camp kettle, and filled it over half-full. It has not raised the "bile" yet, and it is run out over the top of the kettle, putting out the fire. He is a having a time of it. If he ever gets married, there is one thing in the culinary department that he will understand thoroughly, and that thing is cooking rice. He has gotten enough piled out now about the fire for the whole company. Now he's put out about five pounds of brown sugar in with it. "Going to have a candy pulling, Ben?" I asked, from my place under an oak tree?

---

83. The "morning was clear and pleasant" on October 10, though the roads were "dusty and dry" when Fagan's and Marmaduke's command began their march to Boonville. Price arrived in Boonville at 11:00 a.m., and was greeted like a conquering hero. His "reception was enthusiastic in the extreme." "The citizens flocked to see him and for the rest of the day the scene baffled description," according to Dr. McPheeters. Jackman and Marmaduke arrived next at 3:00 p.m., followed an hour later by Fagan's Division. Some of Marmaduke's men camped near the Missouri River on the north side of town, while others were to the south, connecting with Cabell's Brigade. The remainder of Fagan's troops bivouacked in a "beautiful blue grass pasture" to the east or southeast of Boonville, and Shelby's Division camped west of town. The troops were welcomed guests of the Southern population of Boonville and were given "an abundance of good and substantial things." For the next two days the Army of Missouri remained basically inactive, recruiting replacements, and taking its first meaningful rest since entering Missouri 22 days previously. *O.R.*, vol. 41, pt. 1:631, 711; *O.R.S.*, pt. 1 vol. 7:396; McGhee, *Campaigning With Marmaduke*, 23; Pitcock & Gurley, 229–230; Sinisi, 116; Stanton, et al., 242; Thoma, 135.

84. Boonville was located in Cooper County, while Pettis County was to the southeast. Though Marmaduke's Division never made it to Pettis County, a portion of Shelby's Division under James C. Wood did, making a scout of the Sedalia area on October 13. Additionally, Thompson's Brigade, following Wood's scout, took Sedalia, in the center of the county on October 15. See Appendix C for Extended Comments on General M. Jeff Thompson's Sedalia Expedition. *History of Pettis County, Missouri, Including an Authentic History of Sedalia, Other Towns and Townships, etc.* (Reprint ed., Clinton, MO, n.d.), 443, 449, hereafter cited as *History of Pettis County.*

"No, I'm going to have rice for supper, by ———. What put candy into your head, you darn galoot? Come and help me fix the blasted stuff; it don't fit the pot," he says as he casts a forlorn look at the rice pot, and wipes the perspiration from his brow.

You're doing quite well, Bennie; we will have lots of candy, spiked with rice, as soon as it has time to cook a little," I reply.

"You go to ———. You don't know as much about cooking as you did a year ago," he snaps back.

At Supper I Call for Rice.

"We don't have rice for supper; besides hot rice is not fit to eat. I have got the rice away to cool—we'll have it for breakfast," says Ben.
Monday [Tuesday], 12th [11th]—Wheatley brings out the rice for breakfast. He lifts the cover and peeps in the pot. Then he drops the cover steps to the other side of the fire with the injunction to "help ourselves." Sam Calvert makes a dive with a wooden spoon, but he don't get any rice.[85]

"What the blazes is the matter wid yous?" says Sam, and he turns the kettle so he can see inside. A hard crust of burnt sugar is frozen over the top, and it is half cooked rice and dry sugar in the middle.

"Zounds, boys!" Says [John D.] Taylor, "when we want rice cooked again let's put Ben at it; he understands it so well."[86]

"I'm highly in favor of it, provided he ever gets his pot clean again," says old Sam with a chuckle.

---

85. Sam Calvert was a resident of Davis Township, Henry County, Missouri. He joined what became company G, 10th Missouri Cavalry, on August 13, 1862, being enlisted by Colonel Jeremiah Vardeman Cockrell. At Lone Jack, on August 16, 1862, Calvert was wounded in the thigh, but recovered. Calvert served throughout the war and was paroled at Shreveport on June 8, 1865. Eakin, *Lone Jack*, 151; Hale, *Branded As Rebels, Volume 2*, 48; Kathleen White Miles, *Bitter Ground: The Civil War in Missouri's Golden Valley Benton, Henry, and St. Clair Counties* (Warsaw, MO, 1971), 300, hereafter cited as Miles; National Archives, Record Group M322 (roll no. 56), Confederate Compiled Service Records, 10th Missouri Cavalry.

86. There was only one Taylor in Company G, 10th Missouri Cavalry, John D. He was enlisted in Lafayette County, Missouri, by Colonel Cockrell, on September 8, 1862, into what became Company G, 10th Missouri Cavalry. Taylor appears to have been captured during Price's Raid, sent to Myrtle Street Prison in St. Louis, but was later transferred to Gratiot Street Prison for court-martial on November 7, 1864. While at Gratiot, Taylor was held "for examination for trial," having to wear a ball and chain for a period of time. I suspect that Taylor, like many of Price's men, was captured wearing a blue uniform, which marked him as a guerrilla and subject to court-martial and execution, or he could have been held for violating an oath he had previously taken. Additionally, John D. Taylor, according to another source, was also a member of George Todd's guerrilla band, who was captured on October 25, 1862, in Webster County, Missouri, shortly after he had enlisted, and sent to Alton Illinois Prison. This Taylor took the Oath of Allegiance and paid a bond for his release in March 1863. This could be the same Taylor, who violated his oath and returned to the army, rejoining his regiment. If the two Taylors are one and the same individual, there is no indication that either Taylor was ever executed or even tried for that matter. Eakin, *Missouri Prisoners of War*, "Taylor, John D." entry; Hale, *Branded as Rebels, Volume 2*, 318; National Archives, Record Group M322 (roll no. 58), Confederate Compiled Service Record, 10th Missouri Cavalry.

"Oh, I'll agree to clean the pot," says Ben, as he kicks the kettle down the bank into the river, "I'll just leave it in [and] soak until we come back by here, it'll be easy to clean. You fellers don't understand the culinary department a bit."

I go on picket duty about a mile and a half south of town. Heavy skirmishing goes on all day to our left (east); sometimes cannon shot fly high sky above our heads.[87]

I take another chill about noon; my teeth chatter in spite of every effort to the contrary. At dark we are relieved from duty. With the assistance of a comrade I get back to camp, but I am crazy all night with fever.[88]

---

87. The day of October 11 began quietly for the Army of Missouri, as it rested about Boonville. At City Hotel, where Price had his headquarters, the Missouri general greeted numerous visitors, including over 100 ladies that came to see "Old Pap." "The ladies were brought forward and introduced by Gen. Marmaduke. Some were so enthusiastic that plain shaking of the hands would not due for them, so they put their arms around his neck and kissed him." As the morning moved along Bill Anderson arrived with his men and was received by Price, who gave him a mission to return to north Missouri to disrupt the railroad traffic in that area. By 10:00 a.m., even as Price met with his senior officers, bugles were sounding in Marmaduke's Division, as the absent Federals had reappeared, making contact on the Tipton/ Pisgah Road (also known as the Upper Tipton road), to the southeast of Boonville. Following the engagement at California on the 9th, General Sanborn headed west on the 10th, toward Tipton, breaking contact with the rebels, before turning north to Boonville. Sanborn was guarding against Price's movement farther west, before following him northward. After contact was made on the 11th, both Marmaduke's and Fagan's commands responded. Cabell's Brigade, supported by Slemons's Brigade, vigorously attacked the Federals, just inside the outer limits of Boonville, driving them out of the city. After the Federal line broke, following a brazen attack by Captain Galveston Reed of Wright's Arkansas Regiment, other units of Fagan's command followed up the attack, pushing Sanborn's troops for about five miles across the Petite Saline River. Meanwhile, Marmaduke's Division, to the right of Fagan's Division, was only lightly engaged, losing three killed, five wounded, with one man missing (Private James H. Grant, Company I, 10th Missouri). Cabell's Brigade suffered nine killed and 15 wounded, for a total of 12 killed, 20 wounded and one missing on the 11th. Federal reports of losses, which were incomplete (2nd Brigade losses unknown), show three killed, 10 wounded and two men missing on October 11. Jackman's Brigade, of Shelby's Division, also advanced on the 11th, initially marching down the Georgetown or "West Tipton Road" before turning toward the southeast and taking a position just north of the Petite Saline River, near the Wilkin's Bridge and a short distance from Sanborn's 2nd Brigade. Darkness brought an end to the day's skirmishes and the various commands camped where they had ended the day. *O.R.*, vol. 41., pt. 1:356, 407, 409, 645, 692; *O.R.*, vol. 41, pt. 3:1002; *O.R.S.*, pt. 1, vol. 7:397, 408; *O.R.S.*, pt. 2, vol. 2:248; Britton, *Civil War on the Border, 1863–65*, 427–428; *History of Howard and Cooper Counties, Missouri, etc.* (St. Louis, 1883), 768, cited hereafter as *History of Howard and Cooper*; Lothrop, 196; McGhee, *Campaigning With Marmaduke*, 24; Palmer, 24; Pitcock & Gurley, 230–231; Sinisi, 117–119; Thoma, 135, 137, 139; Wright Memoirs, unnumbered pages 85–86.

88. On the morning of October 12, Sanborn's command withdrew to California, having been unsupplied for over 36 hours. Philips's 1st Brigade and Beveridge's 2nd Brigade withdrew before dawn at 4:30 a.m., while Gravely's 3rd Brigade left shortly thereafter. To the west, even while Beveridge's 2nd Brigade left camp, Joseph Eppstein's 5th MSM Cavalry, per orders, advanced toward Boonville, via the Belair Road (also known as the main Tipton-Boonville Road) to reconnoiter the city. Eppstein made contact at 5:00 a.m., with Jackman's Brigade near the Wilkin's Bridge (Thoma and Charles Lothrop correctly identify the bridge, while Eppstein incorrectly labels it the Gravely Bridge). For the next three hours the two sides skirmished about the bridge, while Jackman waited for assistance to arrive. At 10:10 Colonel W. F. Selmons arrived with his brigade followed by General Shelby with the remainder of his command. Finding himself flanked and

Wednesday [and Thursday], 14th [12th–13th]– We stop at [Chouteau] Sulfur Springs and feed our jaded horses, cook rations and move in the direction of Arrow Rock and camp on the Blackwater River.[89] I am on picket duty again tonight, but don't chill, thank fortune.

Tuesday [Friday], 15th [14th]—We cross the Missouri River at Arrow Rock, and camp just opposite town.[90]

greatly outnumbered, Colonel Eppstein wisely chose to withdraw at 1:00 p.m., and joined the remainder of his brigade then retreating toward California. By noon Sanborn's command was well on its way to California, where it arrived at 5:00 p.m. and received four days' rations. The Confederates did not pursue but returned to camp at 4:00 p.m., where they cooked their meal and prepared for a night march. The losses for the day amounted to four killed and 20 wounded in Jackman's Brigade, while Eppstein's Regiment lost two killed and four wounded. *O.R.*, vol. 41, pt. 1:356, 382–383, 383, 388, 632, 645, 664, 674, 696; *O.R.* vol. 41, pt. 3:816, 837, 1001–1002, 1006; *O.R.S.*, pt. 2, vol. 35:157; Ballard Diary, October 12, 1864; Britton, *Civil War on the Border, 1863–65*, 429–430; Lothrop, 196; Sinisi, 119–120; Thoma, 139–140 (n. 347).

89. Meanwhile, back at Boonville, General Price broke camp at 10:00 p.m. on October 12 and headed west toward Lexington. Fagan's Division led the army followed by the trains, Marmaduke command, with Shelby's Division bringing up the rear. After marching 11 miles, Fagan's division, with the trains, camped at Chouteau Sulphur Springs at 1:00 a.m. the next morning, while Marmaduke camped in the vicinity of the LaMine River, and Shelby's Division lingered in the Boonville area until about 10:00 a.m. on the 13th. Having received information that ultimately proved to be a rumor, of a large stock of weapons at Glasgow, that same night Price ordered General John B. Clark with his own brigade and 800 men (most sources say it was only 500, while Shelby says 800) of Jackman's command to take the city and its cache of weapons. Moving up to the head of the column on the 13th, Clark's Brigade camped on Blackwater River, about 16 miles from Arrow Rock, and seven miles from Jonesborough; Shelby came next, then the trains, and Freeman's Brigade, while Fagan's Division was now protecting the rear. "Starting at daylight" on October 14, Clark headed for Arrow Rock, with Jackman's Brigade following. *O.R.*, vol. 41, pt. 1:645, 674, 681, 704; *O.R.*, vol. 41, pt. 3:1012; Ballard Diary, October 14, 1864; Busch, *Missouri Democrat Articles*, 187; James M. Denny, *The Battle of Glasgow, Missouri* (Independence, MO, 2001), 1, hereafter cited as Denny; Diary of the Raid, Army of Missouri, October 12–13, 1864; "From Missouri and Arkansas," *Chicago Tribune*, October 16, 1864; McGhee, *Campaigning With Marmaduke*, 24; Order of March, Army of Missouri, October 12, 1864; Pitcock & Gurley, 230–231; Sanborn, "Campaign in Missouri," 116.

90. On October 14, Clark's command made it to Arrow Rock at 10:00 a.m., followed by Jackman's troops later in the day. With the use of a "steam ferry boat" that Shelby had captured at Boonville, Clark began his crossing of the Missouri River which proved "difficult on account of the landing." Jeffers's 8th Missouri was the last of Clark's men to cross, followed by Jackman's command, which began its crossing about 5:00 p.m. As the various units crossed they grabbed a few hours sleep, while waiting for the remainder of the force to cross. By midnight the two commands were across and had moved to Glasgow, 16 miles away. As his brigade crossed the Missouri River, Clark sent a request to General Price, asking for support of the Glasgow attack from the west side of the river with a section of artillery. Price agreed, sending General Shelby that same night with his two 10-lb Parrot rifles, with 125 men from Schnable's Battalion and his escort company as support. The attack was scheduled for dawn. Meanwhile, the main army marched to Jonesborough, where Price ordered Shelby to send a second expedition to Sedalia to capture that town and drive a herd of livestock back to the army. M. Jeff Thompson was given command of the force that numbered about 1,200 men, with 2 pieces of artillery. Before sundown, Thompson started on his expedition. See Appendix C for Extended Comments on Thompson's Sedalia Expedition. *O.R.*, vol. 41, pt. 1:532, 664, 682, 689, 696; *O.R.*, vol. 41, pt. 3:1010–1011; Ballard Diary, October 14, 1864; Confederate Correspondence (MSS 03-26, Box 1, File 3), Jackman to Price (October 13

Friday [Saturday] 16th [15th]—We reach Glasgow about sunrise and

Attack the Enemy,

who are 800 strong.[91] After a stubborn fight of four or five hours, they surrender. About an hour before the close of the battle, the detachment of about 200 Federal cavalry attempts to escape up the river. The Tenth regiment is thrown around to the right (north), in front of them; they take possession of a brick house and make a desperate fight for escape, but we hold them and press the fight. The Federal skirmish line now reaches from town to the brick house along the road. Our original skirmish line east of town and our new one, which covers the last movement of the Tenth regiment, lap across each other at a bridge which spans a creek about half way between town and the brick house.[92]

    A general advance is ordered, and our skirmishers break through the Federal line at the bridge, driving the Federals south and north into town and up the hill to the brick house. In this affair at the bridge, reckless Ben Wheatley runs down the bank, wades the Creek under the bridge, and crawls up under the abutment with cocked gun. He looks about him and sees a Federal skirmisher crouched behind a shivered stump. Wheatly slips down the bank and crawls up behind the old log.

---

    [14], 1864); Denny, 3; Edwards, *Shelby and His Men*, 404–405; Gibson, 158; *History of Howard and Cooper Counties*, 288; McGhee, *Campaigning With Marmaduke*, 24; Moore, *Missouri, Confederate Military History*, 184; Sinisi, 128.

91. Clark and Jackman marched through the night toward Glasgow, and were still three miles away when Shelby let loose with Collins's guns. Shelby had arrived an hour before daylight and began his attack promptly at 5:00 a.m., as the sun was rising. After seventeen rounds, the *West Wind*, the supposed tinclad, was disabled, and Shelby then began to bombard the city, concentrating on military targets, until his ammunition was "entirely" expended. Finally, Clark arrived at 7:30 a.m., moving at a "trot." The Federals in Glasgow numbered between 600–900 officers and men, according to several sources. Colonel Chester Harding, commanding the Federals, recorded that he had 481 officers and men from assorted units, with 150 citizens and militia, for a total of 631. However an accounting of the Federal forces has the militia from Saline and Chariton Counties and Glasgow numbering 310, while Harding added another 481, and assorted detachments of the 9th and 13th MSM, Cavalry numbered another 150 for a total of 941. See Appendix F for the Confederate and Union Order of Battles at Glasgow. *O.R.*, vol. 41, pt. 1:436, 656, 675, 681–682, 694, 696; "The Attack Upon Glasgow," *Missouri Republican*, October 21, 1864; Busch, *Missouri Democrat Articles*, 187, 190, 200–201, 226; Confederate Correspondence (MSS 03-26, box 1 file no. 3), Shelby to McLean (October 15, 1864); Denny, 17; Edwards, *Shelby and His Men*, 405; Lause, *Collapse of Price's Raid*, 50.

92. Greene's rebel brigade led Clark's command at a run as they approached Glasgow. Heading cross-country Greene established his line about half a mile from the city and south of Greggs Creek, with five of his units. The 3rd Missouri was on the far right and occupied the eastern approaches to the town. On the south side, the 8th held the far left. Davies's Battalion was in the center, while to its right, the 4th Missouri under Burbridge deployed, and to the left of Davies, Solomon Kitchen's 7th Missouri took its post. The 10th moved to the right of the 3rd Missouri, dismounted briefly, before remounting, per orders, and worked its way to the north side of the town where it was in position by 8:00 a.m., blocking any possible Federal retreat. Williams's artillery was placed upon the hills to the south of Glasgow, while Jackman's Brigade took the main road into town, from the south, extending Clark's line toward the river. *O.R.*, vol. 41, pt. 1:437–438, 681,689; Busch, *Missouri Democrat Articles*, 307; Denny, 17, 19; Sinisi, 132.

"Hist! Come down here, pardner. They have crossed the bridge, and will be down on us in a minute. Come down, and let's take the bed of the creek for it." "So?" says the Federal, lowering his gun slipping down the hill feet foremost.[93]

"Come over the log; you're my fry," commands Ben, as he covers the Federal with his rifle and takes possession of his gun and marches him to the rear. We escort the Federal cavalry back to town.[94] The infantry have stacked arms in the street, while the guards are forming to escort them back to camp.[95] A Federal trooper eyeing my equipment closely for a moment or two finally says: "Well, Johnny, you have got a pretty good rig with the exception of your spurs. Allow me to

---

93. Slowly the Confederates pushed the Unionists back, eventually taking "every available shelter" that covered the main Federal positions—a fort and a few rifle pits. Williams's artillery advanced to within a few hundred yards of the Federal fort, which a Federal participant described as "miserable." The situation was grim. By noon, it was apparent to Colonel Harding that the end was near. His men had been crowded into a poor fort and rifle pits designed to hold but 250 men. Further, his troops were exhausted and ammunition was nearly gone. Dr. J. P. Vaughn, a Glasgow resident, left the town, met with General Clark, and agreed to carry a message to Colonel Harding, asking for his surrender. Following a meeting between Harding and Clark, Glasgow surrendered, at 1:30 p.m., with Harding being granted the Honors of War. The Federal command marched out of the city at 2:00 p.m., with their arms and with flags flying, stacked arms and were later paroled. Officers were allowed to keep their horses and sidearms, while the entire Union garrison was escorted to Federal lines near Boonville, to prevent their being attacked by rebel guerrillas which were in the area. Overall, Federal losses were reported as 11 killed with 32 wounded and 81 missing, with "between five and six hundred soldiers and two or three hundred civilians surrendered." However, Dyer's *Compendium* lists the losses as 11 killed, 52 wounded, with 469 missing. Confederate losses were incomplete with only Greene's Brigade reporting losses as seven killed and 45 wounded. Estimated losses in Jackman's and Shelby's commands places the Confederate losses at 11 killed, 69 wounded with none missing. See Appendix E for the Confederate and Union Order of Battles and Losses at Glasgow. *O.R.*, vol. 41, pt. 1:438–439; Busch, *Missouri Democrat Articles*, 190–191, 202, 228, 307; Denny, 21; Dyer, 813; *History of Howard and Cooper Counties*, 288–289; McGhee, *Campaigning With Marmaduke*, 24–25 (n. 57); Moore, *Missouri, Confederate Military History*, 184.
94. Lawther's command captured 157 Union cavalrymen from the 9th MSM, the 13th Missouri, and the 17th Illinois Cavalries, with their horses. As to the 10th's actions at Glasgow, writer James Denny wrote that they "turned in the most lackluster performance" of all the Confederate commands at Glasgow, because they were stopped upon entering the town and failed to press forward. However, for but a few casualties of one dead and four wounded, Lawther did prevent the escape of any Federal cavalry, netting in the process 157 prisoners. *O.R.*, vol. 41, pt. 1:699; Denny, 19.
95. The Battle of Glasgow produced a windfall of goods and weapons for the Confederates. By most accounts they captured 1,200 arms, 150 horses, the *steamboat West Wind*, which they briefly put back in service before burning it, 1,000 new cavalry uniforms, 1,200 overcoats, with assorted commissary and quartermaster supplies. Unfortunately, prior to the surrender Colonel Harding ordered his quartermaster, Major John B. Moore, to destroy 50,000 rations that were housed in City Hall. Burning the municipal building was accomplished, but because of a strong west wind, 13 other buildings, including a local church, were destroyed, resulting in thousands of dollars worth of damage. As James Denny noted, "$100,000 in personal property was destroyed in an effort to keep $30,000 of government property from falling into rebel hands." (See Appendix I, List of Property Destroyed for an accounting of losses at Glasgow.) *O.R.*, vol. 41, pt. 1:438; Denny, 23; Busch, *Missouri Democrat Articles*, 230; Sellmeyer, 228.

Make You a Present

of a good pair, for you will need them before you get back to ARKANSAW," and he hands me up a new pair of brass militia spurs.

"Many thanks for your kind consideration," is my reply, as I buckle them on and ride back to camp. I am wore out with the exertions of the day, and I lie down under a tree. The boys are eating their supper, laughing and joking and discussing the events of the day. Stuttering Bill Grover, a brave kind-hearted man, seeing my forlorn condition, comes over to where I lie and blurts out in his stuttering way: "We—we—we—well, Lu- lu- trell, a—a—are y—y- you d—d—d—done for?"

"Nearly so," I reply.

"D–don't y—y—you want some supper?"

"Not much; I am feeling very badly; I think I will chill again soon."

He turns away but soon returns with a can of cove oysters and some soda crackers and insists on my eating a few bites at least. I try to eat, but my stomach rebels at food. What a terrible chill I have this night, the cramps and aches and vomiting!

Henry C. Luttrell,
Tenth Missouri Cavalry.

* * * * * * *

Item: The continuation of a Missouri trooper's account of Price's 1864 Missouri Raid, from Glasgow to the Kansas state line, by Henry C. Luttrell, Company G, 10th Missouri Cavalry (C.S.A.). Part Three.
Published: March 6, 1886.

Price's Great Raid

[Incidents related by a Confederate trooper from a diary kept on the march: second paper, from Glasgow to the Kansas line.]

Camp near Glasgow, Saturday [Sunday], October 17 [16], 1864.—This is one morning in many that "boots and saddles" is not sounded at peep of day. The boys are lolling about, which shows that they appreciate a rest. United States blankets and Federal uniforms were appropriated by the men generally. The nights have grown cool and our thin, gray, ragged uniforms are not sufficient for the inclemency of the weather. I don a blue uniform with repugnance. But it is that or worse.[96]

---

96. On the day following the capture of Glasgow, Clark's command paroled its Federal prisoners, sending them across the Missouri River, via the captured ferry boat. The men of Clark's command, "after a distribution of as much of the property, ordnance, etc., captured as the troops could conveniently carry," began leaving Glasgow, with Jackman's Brigade departing first in the latter part of the morning. Greene's Brigade came next, departing Glasgow shortly after darkness set in on the 16th. On the morning of the 17th, the 4th Missouri Cavalry (CSA) was the last unit to leave Glasgow and cross the Missouri River, reaching the far shore about 1:00 p.m., when Clark's

Sunday [Monday], the 18th [17th].—This morning we crossed back to the south side of the Missouri River. The brigade looks like a column of Yankees. When off at a distance the only way we can distinguish friends from foes is by our red cross battle flags. We camp tonight within eight miles of Waverley.[97]

Monday [Tuesday], the 19th [18th].—Nothing worthy of note transpires. We camp three miles west of Waverley.[98]

Tuesday [Wednesday], 20th [19th]—Ben Wheatley comes into camp early this morning. He says he stayed Sunday night [17th] in Glasgow, and that the enemy

command resumed its march to rejoin the main army. Meanwhile, back at the main army, Fagan's Division, with the army's trains, made 17 miles on October 15, and camped on the Salt Fork of the Blackwater River, near the Keiser Bridge, which was about 10 miles northwest of Marshall, the county seat of Saline County. There the army rested for two days, awaiting the return of Clark's expedition to Glasgow, and Thompson's raid on Sedalia. While inactive until October 17, recruits "by the hundreds" were coming in to the Army of Missouri, with 700 arriving on the evening of the 15th and more each day thereafter. *O.R.*, vol. 41, pt. 1:675, 682, 690, 694, 696, 699; Ballard Diary, October 16, 1864; R. L. Brown Journal, R. L. Brown collection, Missouri Historical Society (St. Louis), October 16, 1864, hereafter cited as Brown Journal; Confederate Correspondence (MSS 03-26, box no. 1, file no. 3), Fagan to McLean (October 16, 1864); Davis, *Civil War Atlas*, plt. No. 152; Edwards, *Shelby and His Men*, 403; McGhee, *Campaigning With Marmaduke*, 25; Moore, *Missouri, Confederate Military History*, 184; Pitcock & Gurley, 231–233; Sellmeyer, 229.

97. Clark's Glasgow Expedition rejoined the main rebel army near midnight on October 17, camping on the banks of the Salt Fork River. Meanwhile, M. Jeff Thompson's command rejoined the main army in the latter part of the day, camping at Grand Pass and about seven miles east of Waverly. As October 17th closed, Thompson's Brigade stood at the head of the Army of Missouri, followed by Fagan's Division with the army's trains and Freeman's Brigade of Marmaduke's Division, then Jackman's Brigade and finally Clark's Brigade. Meanwhile, the Federals were slowly closing in on the rebel command. To the west the Army of the Border, under Samuel R. Curtis, was assembling and moving to pin Price's Confederates, hopefully at Lexington, while Generals Alfred Pleasonton and A. J. Smith closed in from the east. See Appendix C for Extended Comments on the Concentration of the Federal Command in October 1864. *O.R.*, vol. 41, pt. 1:675, 704; *O.R.*, vol. 41, pt. 4:16–17; Ballard Diary, October 17, 1864; Busch, *Missouri Democrat Articles*, 213; Cruzen, 28; McGhee, *Campaigning With Marmaduke*, 24; Sinisi, 143, 166.

98. On October 18, the Army of Missouri moved westward toward Lexington, led by Cabell's Brigade, with the remainder of Fagan's command following. Next came Marmaduke's Division, the trains, Jackman's Brigade, while Thompson's Brigade fell in at the rear of the column as it moved on to Waverly. Protecting the rear of the army on the 18th was Archibald Dobbin's Brigade, of Fagan's Division. John C. Wright's Arkansas Regiment led the army, departing at 4:00 a.m., with instructions to take Waverly and two "Steam Boats" that were based in the city. Following a forced march, Wright's command took Waverly at 10:00 a.m., but found no boats; instead, the regiment promptly looted the local stores, picketed the area, then sat and waited for the remainder of the army to arrive. Fagan's Division, which led the army, made 22 miles during the day, following a late start, while Thompson's Brigade made only seven miles. In the center, Marmaduke's Division marched 18 miles before it camped about one to three miles west of Waverly in the latter part of the day. Dobbin's Brigade lagged behind, camping five miles east of Waverly, near Grand Pass. Overall, as one soldier noted, "Nothing of importance occurred today." However, Michael Forsyth notes in his book on Price's raid, that the "picnic period" of the raid was over and the initiative of the raid was shifting from the Confederates to the Union command *O.R.*, vol. 41, pt. 1:642, 704; *O.R.*, vol. 41, pt. 4:1004; *O.R.S.*, pt. 1, vol. 7:397; Ballard Diary, October 18, 1864; Brown Journal, October 18, 1864; Confederate Correspondence (MS 03-026, box no. 1, file no. 3), Marmaduke to MacLean; Forsyth, *Great Missouri Raid*, 171; Pitcock & Gurley, 233; McGhee, *Campaigning With Marmaduke*, 25; Wright Memoirs, unnumbered page 87.

is crossing at that point in force; that he crossed the river with a boatload of Federal cavalry just before daylight, his blue uniform protecting him.[99] Co. G is furloughed to-day, and about noon starts to Johnson County (south). They are under command of Lieut. [George P.] Roberts.[100] Capt. Tom Murray remains with the regiment in command of the recruits. I start with the furloughed men when, a few miles south of our moving column, I am taken with another one of those break-bone chills, and am left by the side of the road near a farm house, where the men got dinner. The distant

Boom of Cannon

comes to me across the country, and I know that some part of the army is engaged with the enemy.[101] When I reach the road on which the army is moving, I see that the fencing has been thrown right and left. Further on are dead horses torn and mangled by cannon shot. Near Gen. [Tom] Shield's residence dead horses are lying thick, and a few dead Federals here and there.[102] The shrubbery about the

---

99. Luttrell is mistaken. By Sunday the 17th, no Federal troops had reentered Glasgow. However, William C. Quantrill's guerrillas entered Glasgow on the 17th and proceeded to extort $21,000 from a local banker, who had previously hidden his stash of cash. And on October 21, Bill Anderson arrived at Glasgow and ransomed Benjamin Lewis, a Union millionaire and tobacco factory owner, for $5,000 in cash and $1,000 in gold and jewelry. If Wheatly crossed over with some other men in blue uniforms, they were probably the 4th Missouri Cavalry, the tail end of Greene's Brigade, who also wore blue as their coverings. *O.R.*, vol. 41, pt. 1:694; Busch, *Missouri Democrat Articles*, 216–218; Denny, 24; "From Kansas City," *Chicago Tribune*, October 25, 1864.

100. George P. Roberts was born in Coffee County, Tennessee, in about 1840, and was a resident of Johnson County, when the Civil War began. Joining the Confederate service as a private, Roberts was elected a lieutenant on October 15, 1862, of Company G, 11th Missouri Cavalry Battalion (CSA), which became Company G, 10th Missouri Cavalry in December 1863. Roberts survived the war and was paroled on June 7, 1865, at Shreveport. National Archives, Record Group M322 (roll no. 58), Confederate Compiled Service Records, 10th Missouri Cavalry.

101. Price's army resumed its march westward at "daybreak" on October 19, heading to Lexington. Led by Shelby's Division, the Confederates made contact with the enemy at about 11:00 a.m. The Unionists, under the command of General James G. Blunt, offered "spirited resistance" throughout the day, but in the end gave up Lexington. Overall the casualties were light for the day, with Union accounts placing their losses at about 40–50, while Confederate losses were "very slight." On its surface, the "Action" at Lexington seemed to be of little importance, but it did mark a significant turning point in the expedition. For the first time Price's rebels were confronted by Federal troops from the west— Samuel R. Curtis's Army of the Border had arrived, Blunt's command representing but a small portion of that force. The next week would prove to mark the crescendo of Price's Expedition, as major engagements would occur almost every day and would eventually end in the disastrous Confederate defeat at Mine Creek on October 25, 1864. See Appendix C for Extended Comments on the "Action" at Lexington on October 19, 1864. *O.R.*, vol. 41, pt. 1:573, 582, 646, 666; Busch, *Missouri Democrat Articles*, 213–214; Dyer, 813; "From Kansas," *Chicago Tribune*, October 24, 1864; Palmer, 27.

102. Pitcock & Gurley misidentify the owner of the Shield house, recording that it was James Shield, a Union general. And in a similar manner, Charles Jennison says it belonged to Tom Shields, while John Edwards says it was William Shield's house. And Margaret Frazier, in the Mendenhall diary has the house belonging to Tom. Further, it appears from the Mendenhall account, that Tom was as wealthy as his father and in all probability both lived in Lexington, with William's house being the one that was occupied by Price. Tom Shields was born in 1822, in Salem, Virginia, the son of

house and grounds is cut and broken and bent and twisted. Marks of the deadly missiles are on the fencing, and cannonballs can be seen lying about on the ground. The army is in camped three miles east of Lexington. Shelby's brigade has had the advance and a lively time he has had.

Wednesday [Thursday], 21st [20th]—Shelby's brigade leads out this morning, driving the enemy before him. Clark's brigade covers the rear which is threatened by a column of the enemy who has been following steadily since we left Glasgow[103]. Small-pox has broken out in the army, several cases have been reported.[104] About noon I am taken with another jerky cramping chill, but I keep my

General William Shields, who was the paymaster of the Trans-Mississippi Department. Both father and son joined the MSG in May 1861, and served throughout the war. Tom eventually became a colonel in the MSG, before joining the Confederate Army and Joe Shelby's staff. William, on the other hand, was a general officer in the Guard, serving as the commissary of subsistence, under the Missouri governor before joining he Confederate Army. Both survived the war, with Tom being paroled while his father never took the oath or accepted parole. Both settled in St. Louis following the war. William became involved in Democratic politics after the war, dying in St. Louis in 1878. Tom appears to have eventually moved to or was visiting Cairo, Illinois, when he died on March 12, 1900. Bartel, *Missouri Confederate Surrender*, "Shields/Theild, T. W." entry; Burke, 389; Crute, *Confederate Staff Officers*, 173; Eakin, *Confederate Records*, 7:23–24; Edwards, *Shelby and His Men*, 44, 449,627; Margaret Mendenhall Frazier, *Missouri Ordeal 1862–1864: Diaries of Willard Hall Mendenhall* (New Hall, CA 1985), 22, 25, 139; McGhee, *MSG Order Book*, unnumbered pg. 78; Peterson, et al., 32; Pitcock & Gurley, 233, 371.

103. October 20 began as a cold, raw day, with the temperature hovering in the 30s, followed by a "cold and misty" rain and then a dusting of snow. Overall the day was "very wet and disagreeable." The Army of Missouri "moved at daylight rapidly towards Independence," with Fagan's Division in the lead. Marmaduke's command brought up the rear, while Shelby's Division was sandwiched in between the other two commands. In all the army made 22 miles, camping at noon above Wellington in Jackson County, at Fire Creek Prairie, and six miles from the Little Blue River, where the Federals were posted. While Fagan's Division led the way, Thompson's men lingered for a time in the Lexington area, where "several hours were spent thus pleasantly," with friends and families, after which they resumed their "place in the column" on the road to Independence. Even though there was no fighting on October 20, the day did not go without incident. Fifteen miles to the east of Price's army several rebels, who were visiting family members, were joined by others who had been on recruiting service, having just crossed the Missouri River at Dover. At sunrise on the 20th, they were attacked by the 2nd Arkansas Cavalry (Union). Three or four rebels were killed and 13 captured, including four officers, among whom were 1st Lieutenants J. S. Plattenberg and William Redd from the 5th Missouri Cavalry, Captain E. S. Stanford, the assistant adjutant from Williams's Missouri Regiment, and 1st Lieutenant W. B. Walker from Elliott's Battalion. And in the late evening of the 20th, the 5th MSM Cavalry entered Lexington, capturing seven rebels, following a brief engagement. O.R. vol. 41, pt. 1:402–403, 646, 666, 704; *O.R.S.*, pt. 1 vol. 7:397, 409; J. H. P. Baker Diary (October 1, 1864–May 31, 1865), J. H. P. Baker Collection, Western Historical Manuscript Collection, State Historical Society of Missouri (Columbia), October 20, 1864, hereafter cited as Baker Diary; Brown Journal, October 20, 1864; Britton, *Civil War on the Border, 1863–65*, 445, 463; Brooks Diary, October 20, 1864; Davis, *Civil War Atlas*, plt. no. 161; Edwards, *Shelby and His Men*, 423; Lause, *Collapse of Price's Raid*, 175; Pitcock & Gurley, 233–234; 313; Report of Prisoners of War, List no. 75 (November 15–20, 1864), Bryce Suderow Collection, Western Historical Manuscript Collection, State Historical Society of Missouri, hereafter cited as Report of POW's; Sellmeyer, 232; Sinisi, 180; Stanton, et al., 248.

104. Overall smallpox did not prove to be a debilitating impediment to the expedition. The medical director of the army, William McPheeters, made only one reference to the disease in his diary, noting on November 14 that "6 or 8 cases of smallpox recently developed in the command." Other

place in the ranks until the fever begins to rise. I turned blind and dizzy and pile off by the side of the road. When the rear guard comes up they passed on declaring that I have got the small-pox. Whether they are really afraid of me on account of the dread disease which is reported in the army, or whether they do not want to be bothered with me, I do not know. However, they leave me to my fate. The next I remember is a woman's voice, saying, "Are you sick or wounded?"

"Sick with a chill," I replied.

"The enemy is coming up the road. You'll be captured if you remain here. Let me bring your horse and help you to mount, then you can ride out into the brush until they pass by. You can then come up the road to the house and we will give you some medicine."

She has led my horse to where I lie and with a little assistance,

Get into The Saddle.

My horse has become restive and strikes the road at a brisk trot. Whether the woman is old or young I do not know for I never saw her face. But certain it is it was a woman's kindness that saved me from capture this day. About 100 yards from where I lay a road from the southeast intersects the one on which the army is moving. As I pass the road half a dozen voices pitched in different keys call out "halt!"

As far down the road as I can see it is full of Federal cavalry. I spur my horse to a gallop as the blue-coated troopers open fire and lunge forward in hot pursuit. Holding my spurs in my horse's flanks and lying down on the horse's back, I try his speed down a long stretch of straight road with the Federals shooting and yelling uncomfortably close in the rear. Halfway down the slope a comrade, mounted on a mule, dashes into the road from the north, the mule braying like Old Nick was after it, but making good time. Suddenly the brazen voice stopped, and I see mule and rider struggling on the roadside. As I reached the level ground I use my militia spurs again and urge the "Flying Dutchman" to his best speed. As I ride over the crest of the next ridge, I see my pursuers are falling rapidly behind. The spiteful hiss of the bullets has subsided, and I pulled my horse down to a gallop. Two miles farther on I overtake our rear-guard—soon afterwards I hear musketry—and know that our rear-guard is engaged. This night the army camps twenty miles west of Lexington.[105]

---

than Luttrell's account, only W. L. Webb wrote in the waning days of the expedition that "small-pox—an ally of winter—carried off hundreds." No other references to smallpox were found, in any other sources, including the other doctors of the army. Baker Diary, passim; Pitcock & Gurley, 244; Webb, 243.

105. Following the Battle of Lexington, on October 19, Blunt's command made good its retreat, camping about a mile east of the Little Blue at 2:00 a.m.; "the men of the division were so exhausted they simply fell down to sleep." On the 20th Blunt was up early, moving his command to the west side of the Little Blue, where he arrived at 9:00 a.m. Surveying the area, Blunt found it well suited for defense and deployed his forces. He then sent a staff officer to General Curtis, who was eight miles away at Independence, requesting rations and additional support to hold the line.

Thursday [Friday], 22d [21st]—Gen. Clark's brigade takes the lead with Tenth regiment as advanced guard. I am assigned today on the left flank. About two miles from the Little Blue timber

We Give Chase

to a squad of Federal cavalry.[106] As we near the timber we hear the rattle of small arms. On we rush, hip and thigh, pass a line of white tents just at the edge of the

---

Curtis refused and ordered Blunt "to leave two or three squadrons of troops at the Little Blue," while the remainder were directed back to the Big Blue, where Curtis intended to make his stand. Blunt reluctantly complied, but instead of a few companies, Blunt, upon Thomas Moonlight's "remonstrance," left the entire 11th Kansas Cavalry and four pieces of artillery to hold the area. Moonlight then picketed the area; two companies were placed at the bridge-crossing of the Little Blue, and two additional companies were sent to cover fords a mile north and four miles south of the bridge (Hinton says the southern ford was two miles from the ford, while the other ford was four miles away.). The remainder of the 11th Kansas was placed behind a stone wall on a hill to the west of the bridge. During the 20th, while the 11th waited at the Little Blue, Moonlight's men felled trees and fortified their position as best they could. A mile to the east, an advanced picket was stationed to provide early warning of the Confederates' approach. All was set for October 21, and the Action at the Little Blue. *O.R.*, vol. 41, pt. 1:583, 592; *O.R.*, vol. 41, pt. 4:144–145; James G. Blunt, "General Blunt's Account of His Civil War Experiences," *The Kansas Historical Quarterly* 1 (1931–1932), 255, hereafter cited as Blunt, "Civil War Experiences"; Forsyth, *Great Missouri Raid*, 175; Britton, *Civil War on the Border, 1863–65*, 444-445; Hinton, 93; Kip Lindberg, transcriber, *Wartime Reminiscences of Colonel Thomas Moonlight*, Topeka, KS, Kansas State Historical Society, Thomas Moonlight Collection, hereafter cited as *Moonlight Reminiscences*; Monnett, 53; Sinisi, 178, 181.

106. On October 21, the Army of Missouri "started at an early hour for Independence," led by Marmaduke's Division, then Shelby's command, the army trains, and finally Fagan's Division (Edwards and W. L. Webb have Shelby's Division in the rear at the beginning of the march, while M. Jeff Thompson, says they were in the middle.). Guiding Marmaduke's command was a Captain West, from Charles Tyler's Brigade of recruits. D. R. Stallard's Escort, which had recently been increased to a battalion, followed behind West and made contact with the Federal pickets about a mile from the Little Blue River Bridge between 7:00–8:00 a.m. With the rebel advance engaged, the Union picket rushed a rider back to Little Blue Bridge to inform Major Martin Anderson that Price's army was approaching the river. Following an hour of "stout resistance," Major Anderson ordered the bridge burned, using a previously loaded hay wagon. Anderson then withdrew his command back to Thomas Moonlight's main defensive line, about two miles from the burning bridge. Meanwhile, General J. B. Clark arrived at the Little Blue River, with Robert Lawther's 10th Missouri leading his advance. Clark quickly ordered Lawther's command to find a crossing downstream, while Stallard's command was tasked to secure the burning bridge. About a half mile downstream, near the Blue Mill, Lawther found an unprotected ford which he crossed and deployed for action. Lawther was followed by the 4th Missouri, under Lieutenant Colonel William Preston, whom Clark sent upstream to secure a ford south of the bridge. From this point on the battle developed rather quickly, though initially not as the Confederates expected. Brown Journal, October 21, 1864; Britton, *Civil War on the Border, 1863–65*, 445–446; Campbell Memoir; Collins, 196; Confederate Correspondence, Maclean to Marmaduke (October 20, 1864); Edwards, *Shelby and His Men*, 420–421; Hinton, 93; Paul Kirkman, *The Battle of Westport: Missouri's Great Confederate Raid* (Charleston SC, 2011), 87, hereafter cited as Kirkman; Pitcock & Gurley, 234; Sellmeyer, 232; Sinisi, 181-183; Webb, 221; Ellen Williams, *Three Years and a Half in the Army; or History of the Second Colorados* (New York, 1885; reprint ed., Albany, MO, 1999), 95, hereafter cited as Williams, *Second Colorados*.

prairie. Now the fugitive Federals take to the brush. We dash on down the road, cross the stream at the mill and find the regiment dismounting. They had been repulsed from the ridge in front. The horses are left on the riverbank. We form and move up the timber slope.[107] The enemy greets us with a heavy fusillade of small arms. We can just see their heads. A little further on the road, running parallel with the enemy's position, is reached. It is considerably washed. Using this old road as rifle pits, we open a galling fire upon the enemy, which causes him to fall off a few points in his aim. But now the enemy opens up the right and left oblique fire from each flank. Our position is getting uncomfortably warm.

Again now the scene changes.[108] The rest of the brigade has crossed the river,

107. Crossing the Blue Mill Ford, Lawther's troopers dismounted, leaving their horses near the western river bank. Seeing James Greer's Company I, 11th Kansas fleeing just to the north of him, Lawther prematurely launched an attack. (Monnett has Greer's command south of the bridge, while Joel Huntoon's Company H was to the north, and Paul Kirkman has Greer guarding the Blue Mills Ford, while Luttrell has his command crossing there unopposed.) Taking a portion of his command, Lawther raced "indiscreetly" up a wooded hill after the retreating Kansans, straight into the bulk of the 11th Kansas behind the stone wall. A hail of bullets and howitzer canister greeted the 10th Missouri, halting them in their tracks and back they went, even as Luttrell's Company G was dismounting and heading to the front. Company G, halted in a washed out portion of the hill, with the rest of the regiment, and exchanged fire with the 11th, which was armed with repeating rifles. Behind the stone wall, Colonel Moonlight noticed the lack of support for his opponent and ordered two of his companies to flank the 10th, eventually routing it back toward the river. Back at the smoldering bridge, which had not been destroyed, General Marmaduke ordered Stallard's command across the river in support of Lawther, while his engineers reinforced the heavily damaged bridge so that artillery could cross. Clark, for his part, sent the rest of his brigade across at the Mill Ford, dismounting them after crossing the river. The 3rd Missouri, under Colonel Greene, sloshed across the Little Blue first, then Robert Wood's Battalion, and finally Solomon Kitchen's 7th Missouri. *O.R.*, vol. 41, pt. 1:682–683; Ballard Diary, October 21, 1864; Britton, *Civil War on the Border, 1863–65*, 446; Samuel J. Crawford, *Kansas In the Sixties* (Chicago, 1911), 146, hereafter cited as Crawford, *Kansas In the Sixties*; Hinton, 95; Jenkins, 57; Kirkman, 86; Lause, *Collapse of Price's Raid*, 76; Monnett, 54, 58; O'Flaherty, 221; Sinisi, 183–184; Webb, 220.

108. With the rebels across the Little Blue and the bridge burning, Colonel Moonlight sent a dispatch to General Blunt, then located at Independence with General Curtis, detailing the situation (Note: In his memoirs Blunt stated that he received a telegram, while in the *Official Records* he stated that it was a dispatch.). Blunt had convinced Curtis to send him back to the Little Blue with the rest of his division, minus the Kansas State Militia (KSM). At 10:00 a.m., just as Blunt prepared to head for the Little Blue, he received Moonlight's message. Blunt spurred his command on to the Little Blue, accompanied by General Curtis, who wanted to see the situation for himself. Back at the Little Blue, J. B. Clark managed to stabilize his front, thanks to the extraordinary efforts by Colton Greene's 3rd Missouri, and T. J. Williams' Battery, which had crossed on the hastily repaired bridge. Assailed from the front and both flanks, Greene held his own, while he waited for the rest of Clark's Brigade to arrive. Wood's Battalion arrived first and took a position on the right of Clark's Brigade, even as Blunt's reinforcements began arriving from Independence at 11:00 a.m. Blunt placed Jennison's 1st Brigade on the far right of the Federal line, while James Ford's 4th Brigade was split, with part placed on Moonlight's left while the remainder occupied the center between Moonlight and Jennison. Blunt then pushed forward on Clark's disjointed command, which sent the Confederates reeling. Greene's 3rd Missouri and Williams' Artillery were nearly out of ammunition and forced to withdraw; the situation was grim and the "day seemed lost," according to Clark. However, at noon, Kitchen's Regiment, with Davies's Battalion, arrived just in time, positioning themselves to Wood's left and resting on the Independence Road, covering the

and our guns open up on the left flank of the enemy. In two minutes more the Battle of the Little Blue Mills is ended, the Federals retreating by way of Independence.[109] Our horses coming up we mount and press on after the retreating enemy. As we gain the top of the timbered ridge on which the battle has been fought we discover that the enemy was protected by a stone fence. Among this fence, and scattered through the field which it surrounded, we passed dead Federals—victims of our sharpshooters and Pratt's artillery.[110] Pressing the enemy closely in his rapid

3rd Missouri's retreat. The timely arrival of Kitchen and Davies stabilized Clark's line for the final time. The Unionists were repulsed along the rebel line and "lay in piles of two and three across each other" in front of Wood's Battalion. Behind Clark's command, Freeman's Brigade finally made it to the Little Blue, where it waited for its turn to cross the river, which it finally did late in the engagement, barely in time to participate in the final pursuit of the day. In the meantime, Shelby's Division entered the field of battle and deployed to the left of Marmaduke's Division, setting the stage for the final Confederate push at the Little Blue. *O.R.*, vol. 41, pt. 1:574–575, 583 607, 633–634, 682–683, 690; Ballard's Diary, October 21, 1864; Blunt, "Civil War Experiences," 236; Britton, *Civil War on the Border, 1863–65*, 446; Campbell Memoirs; Forsyth, *Great Missouri Raid*, 176; Lause, *Collapse of Price's Raid*, 76; *Moonlight Reminiscences*, 31; O'Flaherty, 221; Sinisi, 184–187, 190; Williams, *Second Colorados*, 95-96.

109. Shelby arrived "with his characteristic dash and gallantry" at the "old Camp Holloway Ford" about noon, dismounted his division and sent it across the Little Blue. Gordon's 5th Missouri led Thompson's Brigade across as they double-quicked into position adjacent to Kitchen's 7th Missouri and immediately engaged the enemy. They were about 1/4 of a mile from the Union line, positioned behind a fence and were soon joined by the rest of the brigade, extending the line to the left. Jackman's Brigade, with the exception of C. H. Nichol's Regiment, was dismounted behind Thompson's command, which they supported during the subsequent advance. Nichol's command was sent to the far right of the Confederate line, where it operated for the remainder of the engagement. By 1:00 p.m. Shelby was fully engaged as "the fight opened fast and furious." For almost an hour Blunt's command continued to hold, but the arrival of Collins's Artillery again turned the tide, as it had done at Lexington. Collins's Parrot rifles began hitting the stone wall and "every shot knocked a big gap in that rock fence and the Feds lit out." And the chase was on, with the Iron Brigade leading, joined by Jackman's, Freeman's, and Cabell's Brigades. On the far right, Nichol's Regiment "made a brilliant and desperate charge," driving the enemy before them. Clark's Brigade, being almost out of ammunition, did not take part in the pursuit; instead they resupplied before moving on to Independence. *O.R.*, vol. 41, pt. 1:657,675; O.R.S., pt. 1, vol. 7:397–398; Cruzen, 28–29; Edwards, *Shelby and His Men*, 421; Ponder, *General Marmaduke*, 197; Sinisi, 189; Wright Memoirs, unnumbered page 89.

110. On the Federal side, overall losses were reported by several sources as about 200, with one reporting 400 casualties. It appears that Moonlight lost 100, Ford another 60, while Jennison lost the remaining 40, out of the 200 reported casualties. Adding to those losses, Mark A. Lause wrote that Federal losses could have been as high as 300, "with some losses in the other brigades and the presence of militia units" not included. However, in Dyer's *Compendium* the Union losses were listed as 18 killed, 83 wounded, with 14 missing; total 115. This might further suggest that slightly wounded were not counted in the total Federal losses. Also, many of the units listed by Dyer were not at the Little Blue, and others, like the Warrensburg Militia, were not included, making the overall Federal losses as recorded by Dyer suspect. In Marmaduke's Division only Clark's command filed any reports, posting 7 killed, 53 wounded, with six missing or captured. The 4th and 8th Missouri Cavalries appear not to have been engaged, while Stallard's Escort lost five wounded. Thompson failed to report any losses, while Jackman was never engaged. Similarly, neither Thomas Freeman nor William Cabell reported any losses in the pursuit that followed the battle. Overall, one Confederate source reported their total loss as 100 killed, wounded and missing, suggesting that Shelby lost about 29 (100 - 66 - 5 = 29). Additionally, Captain George Todd,

retreat, he occasionally turns and gives us a spiteful, spasmodic shower of rifle balls.

Passing through Independence we camp three miles out on the Kansas City road.[111] Though worn out with the fatigue of the day I get permission from Capt. Murray to visit my cousin, Mrs. Dick Nelson.[112] On presenting myself at the Nelson residence I am informed that,

---

infamous Missouri guerrilla, was killed "shortly after" Thompson's Brigade crossed the Little Blue, giving rise to the question as to how many Missouri guerrillas were casualties at the battle. (Others, including General Cabell and John Edwards recorded that Todd was killed in the last charge of the day.) The losses for both sides are not as clearly stated as could be expected. *O.R.*, vol. 41, pt. 1:525, 692, 697. 699; *O.R.S.*, pt. 1, vol. 7:398, 409; Brown Journal, October 21, 1864; Busch, *Missouri Democrat Articles*, 239; Edwards, *Noted Guerrillas*, 321; "From the Army of the Border," *Leavenworth Daily Conservative* (Leavenworth, KS), October 25, 1864; Hinton, 103; Jenkins, 61; Lause, *Collapse of Price's Raid*, 83; Stanton, et al., 249; Whitsett Letter; Williams, *Second Colorados*, 97–99.

111. With both of his flanks collapsing, and Moonlight's boys out of ammunition, General Curtis ordered a general retreat, beginning about 2:00 p.m. Blunt's 4th Brigade, under Colonel James Ford, was given the task to cover the Federal retreat. "Falling back slowly," the 2nd Colorado, of Ford's brigade, parried every attempt of the rebels to cut off the retreat. Using multiple lines of defense, and, assisted by four mountain howitzers from General Curtis's Escort, the 2nd Colorado had no difficulty covering the Unionists' withdrawal, in part, because Thompson's rebel brigade was dismounted and simply had difficulty keeping up with the retreating foe, which was mounted. By sundown, Curtis formed his final line just outside of Independence, after which he pulled his command back to the Big Blue, which was five miles west of Independence, where he intended to make his stand with his combined command of volunteers and the KSM. Though not wanting to fight at the Little Blue, General Curtis saw the positive results of the engagement: "I had thus delayed and seriously embarrassed the enemy without demoralizing any of my forces... and at a small loss in killed and wounded." The Confederates for their part had crossed the Little Blue, allowing them to continue on westward, without being trapped between Curtis's army and that of General Pleasonton, which was close upon his rear. Still, Price had to cross the Big Blue, where Curtis waited with 15,000 men in a fortified position. And no matter how one chooses to understand the events of the day, Price's army was in trouble. Up to October 21 Price's Expedition "was a perfect success," according to William Hazen; however, Price should have "commenced the southward move...five days before." On the evening of October 21, the Army of Missouri "had to either fight or flee south," according to Deryl Sellmeyer. For the present they were camped about Independence and "slept an untroubled sleep for the brave." However, disaster was fast approaching and Price seemed oblivious to the actual situation. *O.R.*, vol. 41, pt. 1:476, 478; Britton, *Civil War on the Border, 1863–65*, 448–450; William Hazen Letter (December 21, 1864), Western Historical Manuscript Collection, State Historical society of Missouri, hereafter cited as Hazen Letter; Hinton, 99, 101; Jenkins, 62; A.B. Scholes, "Army of the Frontier," *National Tribune* (Washington, DC), March 13, 1890; Sellmeyer, 236; Wm., A. Timbooker, "Skirmish In Advance," *National Tribune*, November 21, 1898; Webb, 223; Williams, *Second Colorados*, 100; Wright Memoirs, unnumbered page 89.

112. Nothing found on the Nelson family in Independence or in Jackson County. However, an R. H. Nelson and family had been expelled from western Missouri in September 1863, as a result of General Ewing's infamous Order No. 11. This Nelson lived in one of the counties immediately north of Independence. Regardless, it appears that the Nelson family had fled or was banished from the area prior to October 1864. "Disloyalists Banished From Western Missouri," *Wyandotte Commercial Gazette* (Wyandotte, KS), September 19, 1863; W. Z. Hickman, *History of Jackson County Missouri* (Topeka, KS, 1920), passim, hereafter cited as Hickman.

The Family Is Not at Home.

The hall and corridors were brightly lighted and gay animated voices came to me from the rooms within. My object in this visit was to thank the lady for the kindness she had extended to me while I was lying under the hospitable roof of those good Samaritans, Mr. And Mrs. James Wilson, (near Pleasant Hill), recovering from a wound received at Lone Jack in 1862.[113] Also to hear from home or, if possible, send a letter to my mother. But I am again disappointed. Disappointments are daily occurrences with me now. This, my last chance to hear from home, has failed, and I go back to camp with sad heart, miserable and dejected.[114] Saturday, [October] 23 [22nd]—Early this morning the enemy makes a dash on Fagan's [Cabell's] brigade and, report says, captured two guns and 300 prisoners.[115] Companies G, H, I and K of the Tenth regiment are sent to the scene of

---

113. Confederate forces under Jeremiah V. Cockrell assembled at Lone Jack following the Confederate victory at Independence, on August 11, 1862. Responding to the rebels, General James Totten ordered Major Emory Foster to attack the Confederate concentration in conjunction with a force under General Fitz Warren coming north from Clinton. Foster arrived at Lone Jack on August 15, as planned, but found no support. On the morning of the 16th the rebels attacked and following a four hour battle the Union forces gave way. The Federals lost 43 killed, 154 wounded, and 74 missing, while the Confederates lost 34 killed and 70 wounded. Additionally, the Federals lost two 12-pound James rifled cannons. Banasik, *Embattled Arkansas*, 163–164, 173–174.

    A review of the Cass and Jackson County histories shows but one possibility for James Wilson. Born in 1819, in Cooper County, Wilson moved to Jackson County, with his family in 1825, being one of the oldest settlers of the county. He later married Elizabeth, settling somewhere between Pleasant Hill and Lone Jack. Nothing further found. Hickman, 288, 614.

114. The night of October 21 found the Army of Missouri camped near Independence. Marmaduke was two miles west of the city on Rock Creek, while his escort and headquarters were "camped in the Court House yard." To secure the area, Colton Greene's 3rd Missouri was tasked to picket the roads west and south of Independence. Shelby's command camped just to the west of Independence, with Jackman's Brigade in the town. East of town Fagan made his camp, while the army's trains were located between Fagan and Shelby's Divisions. To picket their eastern flank, Fagan assigned John C. Wright's Arkansas Regiment, which galloped back to the crossing of the Little Blue where they made camp, without food or forage. Wright placed his command near the burnt out remains of the bridge, which had been destroyed after the army's trains had passed over. Farther to the east, at Fire Creek Prairie, Pleasonton's advance, under Brigadier General John McNeil, made camp about 10 miles from the Little Blue and Wright's pickets. *O.R.*, vol. 41, pt. 1:371, 683, 690; Britton, *Civil War on the Border, 1863–65,* 465; Baker Diary, October 21, 1864; Brown Journal, October 21, 1864; Campbell Memoir; Freeman Memoir, October 23, 1864; Stanton, et al., 249; Webb, 220; Wright Memoirs, unnumbered page 91.

115. The morning of the 22nd dawned "clear and cool," with Shelby's Division leading the advance; Jackman's Brigade took the Kansas City Road at 9:00 a.m., while Thompson's Brigade moved down the Westport Road. The army's trains escorted by C. H. Tyler's Brigade, and Fagan's Division, less Cabell's Brigade, followed behind Shelby at "mid-morning." Marmaduke constituted the rear division, with Cabell guarding the army's rear. Back at the Little Blue, John McNeil's Federals moved at 5:00 a.m., making initial contact with Wright's rebels, just "before sunrise," while the bulk of McNeil's Brigade arrived at the Little Blue at 10:00 a.m.. With the temporary rebel bridge still smoldering, part of McNeil's Brigade crossed at the Blue Mill Ford, and within 30 minutes had forced Wright's command back toward Independence. Informed of Wright's contact with the Federal advance, General Cabell deployed his brigade to the east of Independence. Meanwhile, General Pleasonton had arrived at the Little Blue and personally supervised the con-

the disaster. We find the enemy active and aggressive, driving everything before him.[116] Companies I and K deployed into line. Enemy dashes upon the flank of Company I and runs them over a rail fence that in the hurry uncertain light of the new day has been overlooked and left standing. But company K changing front gives the enemy a volley from their Enfields that checks their wild career.[117] Companies G and H deployed to the right and left to protect the flanks, and I and K dismount, send their horses to the rear, and lying upon their faces, send a well aimed volley into the ranks of the approaching enemy which causes them to stagger and break ranks. H and G firing and charging at the gallop, send them down the road in confusion.[118] After this the enemy are more careful how they dash in

---

struction of a temporary bridge, using fence rails, which allowed the artillery to cross. By 11:00 a.m. the rest of Pleasonton's Division was crossing the Blue and headed toward Independence. Toward the front, Wright's rebels continued to resist the Federal advance, using successive lines, that would fire several volleys and then pull back. By noon, Wright had broken contact with McNeil's Federals, passed through Cabell's lines, the town of Independence, and finally came to rest several miles away, where he rested and fed his command. The time was about 2:00 p.m., when Cabell's Brigade made contact with McNeil's Federals. And within an hour Cabell had been routed, losing Hughey's Battery and several prisoners. See Appendix C for Extended Comments on Cabell's Rear Guard Action. *O.R.*, vol. 41, pt. 1:340, 371; "The Battle of Westport," Shelby Scrapbook; Britton, *Civil War on the Border, 1863–65*, 463; Crawford, *Kansas In the Sixties*, 147; J. W. Halliburton, "That Charge." *Confederate Veteran* 28 (July 1920): 264, hereafter cited as Halliburton; Jenkins, 67, 74; McGhee, *Campaigning With Marmaduke*, 25; Monnett, 77; National Archives, Record Group 153 (File no. LL 2942), James McFerran , General Court-Martial, Thomas Doyle Testimony, 46, hereafter cited as McFerran Court-Martial; S. R. Nelson, "Chasing Price," National Tribune, November 26, 1903; Sanborn, "Campaign in Missouri," 176–177; Sinisi, 209–211, 249-250; Wright Memoirs, unnumbered pages 91–92.

116. With Cabell's Brigade in a disorderly retreat, a battalion of the 10th Missouri was ordered to the front to stabilized the situation, allowing Cabell's command time to reform, check the enemy and move to the left and rear of Marmaduke's Division which waited at Rock Creek to receive the pursuing Federals. Thomas Freeman's Brigade, of about 900 men, was posted a half mile west of the creek, at the edge of a wood, and about a mile and a half from town. J. B. Clark's Brigade, less the 3rd Missouri, formed a second line, immediately behind Freeman and about a half mile father back. Hynson's Artillery Battery was with Clark, while the 3rd Missouri remained on picket duty on the west and south, until ordered otherwise. And here they awaited the Federal attack and the return of Lawther's Regiment. *O.R.*, vol. 41, pt. 1:683, 690; *O.R.S.*, pt. 1, vol. 7:398; Freeman Memoir, October 23, 1864.

117. The Enfield Rifle was the standard issue for the British Army in 1855, and widely used by both sides during our Civil War. The official Enfield was manufactured at the Royal Small Arms Factory in Enfield, England, while the exported models were produced by private contractors throughout England The weapon weighed 9 pounds, 3 ounces and was chambered in .577 caliber. It was very accurate to 800 yards and effective to 1,100 yards. About 400,000–500,000 were imported during the war, and it was considered the most popular weapon in the Confederate Army, while the Springfield Rifle was the preferred weapon in the Union Army. Boatner, 266; Faust, 243–244.

118. Following the successful charge of McNeil's and Sanborn's commands, the Federal troops were exhausted, unorganized and not capable of further pursuit. To keep the momentum of the attack going General Pleasonton ordered E. B. Brown's 1st Brigade to the front to continue the pressure. Pushing "rapidly forward," Brown's Brigade passed though Independence, with the 1st MSM Cavalry leading the way. About 200–300 yards west of town, Brown encountered the forward elements of W. F. Freeman's Brigade and the 10th Missouri on the eastern side of Rock Creek.

upon us. In a couple of hours we are relieved by other troops and take our place in the moving column.¹¹⁹ On the high prairie divide just east of Brush Creek, the command comes to a halt. The enemy is

Egbert B. Brown

The 1st MSM quickly dismounted and began to actively skirmish with Freeman's and Lawther's rebels, who were about 500 yards to a half mile away. The battle quickly developed into a "fierce fight," even as the remainder of Brown's Brigade was nowhere to be found, causing Brown to send repeated orders for his command to press forward. Finally after almost an hour absence the brigade began to arrive. As it turned out Colonel Nelson Cole, Pleasonton's chief of artillery, and acting chief of staff, had halted Brown's column in Independence, while he detailed one company of the 4th MSM to remove the captured artillery, and another was assigned as Provost Guard. After a 30 minute delay the absent portion of Brown's Brigade moved to the front, arriving as the 1st MSM was on the verge of breaking. Deploying by 4:00 p.m., the 4th MSM occupied the far left of Brown's line, while one battalion of 7th MSM was placed between the 1st and 4th MSM, and the other battalion under Colonel John Philips, was briefly placed in reserve before joining the rest of regiment. Opposite the center of the Federal line Lawther's 10th gamely held on, having deployed by a brick house and "hedge fence." For about two hours Brown and Freeman were engaged, when Colonel Thomas Crittenden, ordered his men forward. Back went the rebel line, though not without cost, for the 10th Missouri (CSA), had lost Lieutenant Colonel Merit Young, who was mortally wounded, captured, then died on October 23, in Kansas City. *O.R.*, vol.41, pt. 1:346–347, 699; "Diary of Colonel John Philips," in *Battle of Westport* (Fred Lee, gen. ed.; Kansas City, MO, 1976), 39, hereafter cited as Philips Diary; National Archives, Record Group 153 (File no. LL 2941), Egbert B. Brown General Court-Martial, George W. Kelly Testimony, 266, hereafter cited as Brown Court-Martial; McFerran Court-Martial, E. B. Brown Testimony, 230–231; McFerran Court-Martial, Nelson Cole Testimony; McFerran Court-Martial, T. T. Crittenden Testimony, 196–197, 199, 205; McFerran Court-Martial, Thomas Doyle Testimony, 43; McFerran Court-Martial, John Phillps Testimony, 207, 209; "Price's Invasion," *Daily Journal of Commerce* (Kansas City, MO), October 24, 1864; Sinisi, 213–214.

119. Meanwhile, E. F. Winslow's 4th Brigade, also known as the "Yelling Brigade," arrived at Independence, and Pleasonton hurried them to the front, telling them to report to Brown for orders. Arriving at the front, about 5:00 p.m., as "it was growing dark," Winslow's Brigade found Brown's command deployed about a half mile from the rebel line, "doing nothing." From about 4:00–5:30 p.m., Brown's Brigade had skirmished with Freeman's Brigade, inflicting but few casualties because of the long distance skirmishing. About 30 minutes before sunset, Freeman successfully withdrew his brigade, using Ford's Battalion to cover his retreat. The Federals, led by T. T. Crittenden, finally attacked, even as Brown ordered Winslow to cross Rock Creek to pursue the retreating rebels. Farther back, Brown's 1st Brigade came to a halt; his command was out or nearly out of ammunition, and the men, who had had little to eat over the previous two days, were spent. Winslow's Brigade, which was basically still fresh moved to the front with "the rush of an express train" to carry on the attack, even as the sun set. *O.R.*, vol. 41, pt. 1:346–347. 349, 635, 683; Freeman Memoir, October 23, 1864; Wilson B. George, "The Drive After Price," *National Tribune*, March 13, 1924, hereafter cited as George; Sanborn, "Campaign in Missouri," 178; Wm. Forse Scott, *The Story of a Cavalry Regiment: The Career of the Fourth Iowa Veteran Volunteers From Kansas to Georgia 1861–1865* (New York, 1893; reprint ed., Iowa City, IA, 1992), 319–320, hereafter cited as Scott, *Fourth Iowa*; Sinisi, 213–214; A. A. Stuart, *Iowa Colonels and Regiments Being a History of Iowa Regiments in the War of the Rebellion; And Containing a Description of the Battles in Which They Have Fought* (Des Moines, IA, 1865), 600, hereafter cited as Stuart.

Hovering in Our Rear

and spiteful volleys of musketry occasionally greet our ears as small detachments come into collision.[120]

From the west the boom of artillery is incessant, and one can see with the naked eye the charging squadrons of Shelby's fierce fighters, as they drive Gen. Blunt's cavalry before them across the prairie. In one of these fierce encounters Shelby captures a 24-pound field gun.[121] This night there is no camping or resting for the old Tenth. She guards one of the approaches to our camp, which is only a few miles from Kansas City. She stands between the vigilant foe and the sleeping army. This is truly a night of horror. The country about us is covered thickly with a young growth of blackjacks. It is almost impossible for cavalry to maneuver. We are obliged to dismount and act as infantry. The enemy, not content with the day's fighting, is feeling our line to find a weak point through which he can make a dash. The swish of a brush or the snapping of a stick is the signal for a fusillade or volley of musketry. Through the darkness the flash of the enemy's guns is like lightning bugs. The bullets hit spitefully by—or spat the sapling, or cut the brush—reminding one of how near he came to being the victim.[122]

---

120. When Freeman's Brigade withdrew from Independence, General Marmaduke ordered Freeman to Byram's Ford, while Clark's Brigade covered the army's retreat. Clark staggered his units to block the Federal advance, as each command in turn fended off Winslow's Brigade. Led by the dismounted 3rd Iowa Cavalry, Winslow continued to press the Confederates back well into the night. "First Wood's battalion was driven back, then Burbridge's regiment, then Kitchen, then Lawther's, and the last Jeffers's who contended longest and last with this fierce advance." "The confusion in the night was terrible," according to Lieutenant William Ballard, of the 7th Missouri Cavalry (CSA). "The enemy," Ballard continued, "sometimes within 20 paces of us, and we could see nothing but the blaze of their guns." The pursuit, according to General Clark, was made "with a reckless fierceness that I have never seen equaled." Finally, about 10:00 p.m., Winslow broke off the attack, just west of Byram's Ford. Meanwhile, Greene's 3rd Missouri Cavalry (CSA), which was cut off from Clark's Brigade on picket duty, finally returned to the brigade, camping west of the Big Blue, with the rest of Marmaduke's Division near Byram's Ford, which had been captured earlier in the day by Shelby's command. To the east of the Big Blue, at Byram's Ford, Clark posted Jeffers's 8th Missouri and Wood's command as pickets for the division. During the day Pleasonton's command had lost 14 killed, 58 wounded, with 11 missing for a total of 83. Confederate losses were generally unknown, though estimated at 31 Killed, 61 wounded with 41 missing; total 133 (See Appendix I, Confederate Prisoners Lost, Casualties Suffered for details.). *O.R.*, vol. 41, pt. 1:683, 690, 692, 694, 696–697, 699; *O.R.*, vol. 41, pt. 4:184; Ballard Diary, October 22, 1864; Campbell Memoir; Dyer, 813; Freeman Memoir, October 23, 1864; Moore, *Missouri, Confederate Military History*, 190; Scott, *Fourth Iowa*, 320; Sinisi, 214–216; Stuart, 600.

121. October 22, 1864, was one of those rare days in the Civil War where an army found itself attacking on one front while defending on the other. To the rear of the Army of Missouri, General Pleasonton attacked Price from the east, precipitating an all-day struggle, where Marmaduke's Division and Cabell's Brigade fended off aggressive Union attacks. Meanwhile, to the front and west of Price's Army, General Shelby attacked General Curtis's Army of the Border at the Big Blue. Shelby's objective was simple—secure a crossing of the Big Blue to allow passage of the rebel army southward back to Arkansas and safety. See Appendix C for Extended Comments on Shelby's Operations on the Big Blue for October 22, 1864.

122. The night of October 22nd found the rebel army bivouacked west of the Big Blue River. The train had successfully crossed at Byram's Ford late in the afternoon, camping on Harrisonville

Westport and Big Blue Area
(October 22, 1864)

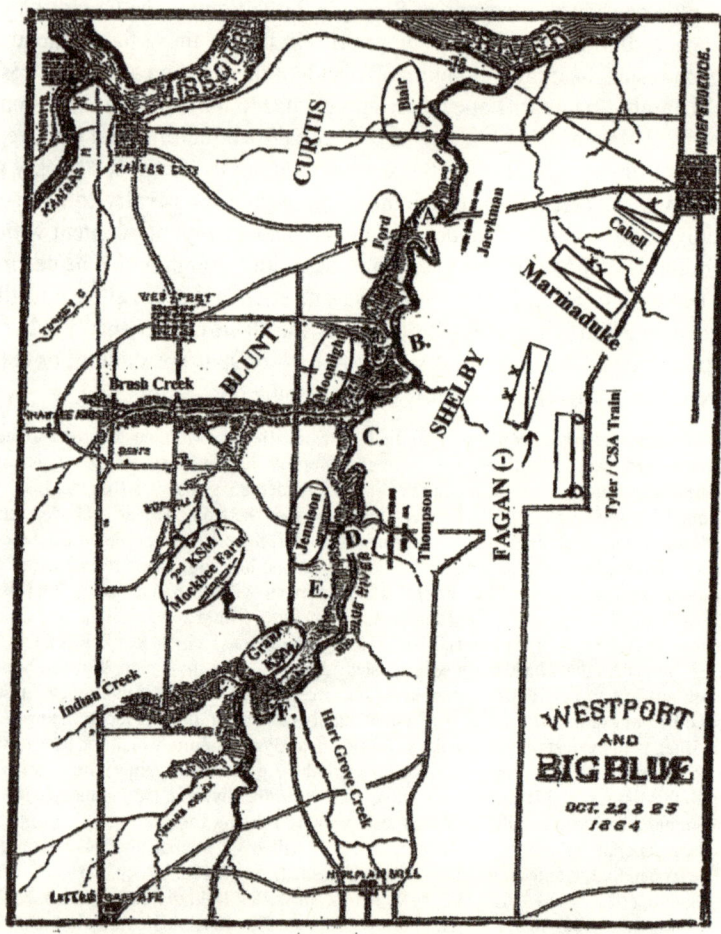

A. Main Ford B. Simmon's Ford C. Hinkle's Ford D. Byram's Ford
E. Cattle Ford F. Russell's Ford

[Sunday,]October 24 [23]—The enemy presents a solid front and seems bent on mischief. With the coming of daylight rifle practice begins along the picket line.[123] Before sunrise the pickets are pushed in and the firing becomes heavier. Soon the

---

Road just south of Shelby's Division, which was camped on the "open prairie" in the vicinity of the Mockbee Farm. For the night, many of Shelby's men "camped without food or water," except for Gordon's 5th Missouri. George Cruzen, of the 5th, scoured the captured wagons of the 2nd KSM, finding "bacon, flour, sugar and hardtack," enough for "supper and breakfast" for the entire regiment. To the east, Marmaduke's Division guarded the army's rear, opposite of General Pleasonton, with Freeman's Brigade, augmented by the 3rd and 4th Missouri holding Byram's Ford The remainder of Clark's Brigade was positioned 500 yards behind, on what was "Potato or Bloody Hill," except for Jeffers's 8th Missouri and Wood's command, which picketed the Big Blue east of Byram's Ford. And unlike Shelby's boys, Marmaduke's Division, which had fought late into the night, managed to get but a "few hours to cook and rest...[their] weary frames." The bulk of Fagan's Division was with the trains and no doubt had no trouble obtaining rations for the night, while Cabell's Brigade may not have had an opportunity, given their precipitous retreat from Independence. *O.R.*, vol. 41, pt. 1:658,667, 676, 684; *O.R.S.*, pt. 1, vol. 7:398; Bonebrake, 35; Campbell Memoir; Cruzen, 31; Edwards, *Shelby and His Men*, 427–428; Freeman Memoir, October 23, 1864; Lause, *Collapse of Price's Raid*, 119; McGhee, *Campaigning With Marmaduke*, 26; Sellmeyer, 242; Sinisi, 249; Stanton, et al., 249; Webb, 230; Wright Memoirs, unnumbered page 91.

123. The 23rd began long before daylight as both sides prepared for the upcoming battle. Price sent his train and cattle herd off well before daylight, escorted by Cabell's and McCray's Brigades from Fagan's Division, along with C. H. Tyler's Brigade of recruits. Shelby was directed to attack the Federals in his front at dawn, being assisted by Fagan's other two brigades. And Marmaduke was responsible for holding Pleasonton on the eastern front. Overall Price's plan was intended "to get the train out," according to author W. L. Webb, while Valerie Williams believes Price was still intent on capturing Fort Leavenworth's supplies and munitions. To George Maddox of Jackman's Brigade, their mission was simple: "We had to hold them on that side until our trains passed south." On the Union side, General Curtis was undecided as to his next move, thus beginning a "night of anxiety and doubt." His KSM infantry were crowded into the entrenchments guarding Kansas City, while the cavalry and volunteers were positioned to the north of Brush Creek and south of Westport. Initially, Curtis intended to retreat across the Kansas River, but a courier arrived at his headquarters near Wyandotte at 6:00 p.m. on the 22nd, announcing that General Pleasonton was at Independence and driving the enemy. His spirits revived, Curtis returned to Kansas City, where he rested until midnight. He then called a "council of war" to discuss the actions for the 23rd. During the late night meeting that proved "quite lively," Curtis wanted to retreat toward Leavenworth and leave the rebel army to Pleasonton. Following a heated discussion, Curtis was still undecided as to what to do. A frustrated Blunt asked Curtis for a decision, to which Curtis responded. "General Blunt, I will leave the whole matter to you. If you say fight, then fight it is." Blunt said fight, and by 3:00 a.m. the Council broke up to prepare for the morn. To the east, in Independence, General Pleasonton directed that his command attack at dawn, via Byram's Ford, with E.B. Brown's 1st Brigade leading the attack. Further, John McNeil's 2nd Brigade was directed to Little Santa Fe via Hickman Mills, to attack Price from that quarter. McNeil moved out at midnight on the 22nd. For both sides, the die was cast as the morning October 23rd approached. *O.R.*, vol. 41, pt. 1:341, 484–485; *O.R.S.*, pt. 1, vol. 7:398; "The Battle of Westport," *Freedom's Champion* (Atchison, KS), December 1, 1864; William Connelley, *Life of Preston B. Plumb* (Chicago, 1913), 189–190, hereafter cited as Connelley; Crawford, *Kansas In the Sixties*, 148–149; Edwards, *Shelby and His Men*, 430; Forsyth, *Great Missouri Raid*, 189–190; Hinton, 144, 168; Lause, *Collapse of Price's Raid*, 99–102; Monaghan, 331; Monnett, 93–95; Moore, *Missouri, Confederate Military History*, 190; Norton & Massey, 66–67; Sanborn, "Campaign in Missouri," 180–181; Sellmeyer, 242; Sinisi, 218–219, 250; Valerie Williams, "Battle of Westport, Jackson County Historical Society (Collection no. 720), 2, hereafter cited as Williams, "Westport."

booming of cannon, mingled with the roar of musketry. It seems that the whole of Clark's brigade is engaged; how much more I do not know, perhaps a part of Fagan's. The Tenth regiment has been dismounted and is fighting on foot. During a lull in the battle we are ordered to the rear.[124] As we mounted our horses we hear the roar of cannon in the direction of Westport, and know that Shelby is hard at work.[125]

---

124. Following a sleepless night and an early morning temper tantrum, General Pleasonton arrested General E. B. Brown and Colonel James McFerran, for failing to attack at dawn, calling them "ambulance soldiers," who "belonged in the rear," and subsequently charged them with a variety of offenses for court-martial. Replacing Brown with Colonel John Philips, Pleasonton began the attack about 8:00 a.m. Before that, at daybreak, elements of Winslow's 4th Brigade skirmished with Jeffers's 8th Missouri and Wood's Battalion, from J. B. Clark's rebel brigade, driving them across the river to Clark's main line. Overall Colonel Winslow was in command of the Federal attack, which continued unabated until about noon. As the attack unfolded, Confederate Colonel Thomas Freeman, deployed the 3rd and 4th Missouri Cavalries close to the ford, "to force the enemy to deploy and mount a heavy attack." Philip's 7th MSM initially tried crossing at the ford but was repulsed. Winslow then led them across, assisted by the 4th Iowa, which waded the "chest-deep" Big Blue downstream, undetected, and with the 7th MSM, pushed the rebels back at the ford. To Clark's front, Freeman's command still held firm, though finally giving way near 10:00 a.m. Passing through Clark's Brigade, except for the 3rd and 4th Missouri, which rejoined Clark's Brigade, Freeman's command was done for the day. Supported by Hynson's and Harris's Batteries, Clark's Brigade was protected behind make-shift entrenchments, fashioned from rail fences and felled trees. For two more hours Clark held on, repulsing several Union attempts with a "frightful fire." Finally, near the noon hour, Winslow had gotten both Philips's and his own brigades across the Big Blue, having to cross the river in single file. Supported by artillery from the eastern side of the Blue, Winslow made a grand assault. Across an open field 200 yards in width raced the dismounted Unionists, even as Clark's command was withdrawing, having exhausted all or nearly all their ammunition. Between noon and 1:00 p.m. Winslow's exhausted troops cleared the rebel held woods to their front, as John Sanborn's 3rd Brigade took over the pursuit of the retreating rebels. For all intents and purposes the 2nd Battle of the Big Blue was over; however, the Battle of Westport was far from complete. See Appendix C for Extended Comments on Losses at the Big Blue on October 23, 1864 for the Union command *O.R.*, vol. 41, pt. 1:330, 684, 692, 697, 699; *O.R.S.*, pt. 2, vol. 35:73, 424; Brown Court-Martial, J. F. Philips Testimony, 237, 245; Campbell Memoir; Forsyth, *Great Missouri Raid*, 190; Freeman Memoir, October 23, 1864; Hinton, 169–170; Jenkins, 87, 89; Monaghan, 332–333; Monnett, 111–116; Occasional, "The Pursuit of Price," *Missouri Republican*, November 4, 1864; Philips Diary, 39–40; Scott, *Fourth Iowa*, 321–324, 562; Sinisi, 234–235,237–242; Williams, "Westport," 5.

125. Westport, Missouri, was a "muddy little city," sporting a population of about 800 in 1864. It was a mile from the Kansas line and four miles south of Kansas City. Two miles south of Westport lay Brush Creek, the focal point of Shelby's and Curtis's confrontation on October 23rd. The morning "opened cold and clear" on Shelby's front, as his division headed north to confront Curtis at 8:00 a.m. Deploying his division south of Brush Creek, Shelby positioned Thompson's Brigade in the center, on both sides of the Wornall Road, while Jackman's command was to the left of Thompson. Slemons's Brigade of Fagan's Division held the far left of the rebel line, next to Jackman, and Archibold Dobbin's Brigade, also of Fagan's Division, served as the rebel reserve on the Westport front. The Federals, under Blunt were to Shelby's immediate front, having advanced at daylight and crossing to the south side of Brush Creek. Ford's Brigade was on the left, Jennison's was in the center, while Moonlight's Brigade occupied the right. Blair's 3rd Brigade was in reserve and just north of Brush Creek. About 8:30 a.m., Union artillery opened on Shelby's deploying troops. One of the "first shells knocked off the head of a man in Slayback's Battalion, as smooth as a guillotine could have done it." By 9:00 the battle was in full swing, as Moonlight pushed back

Battleground of Westport
(11:00 a.m. to 1:00 p.m., October 23, 1864)

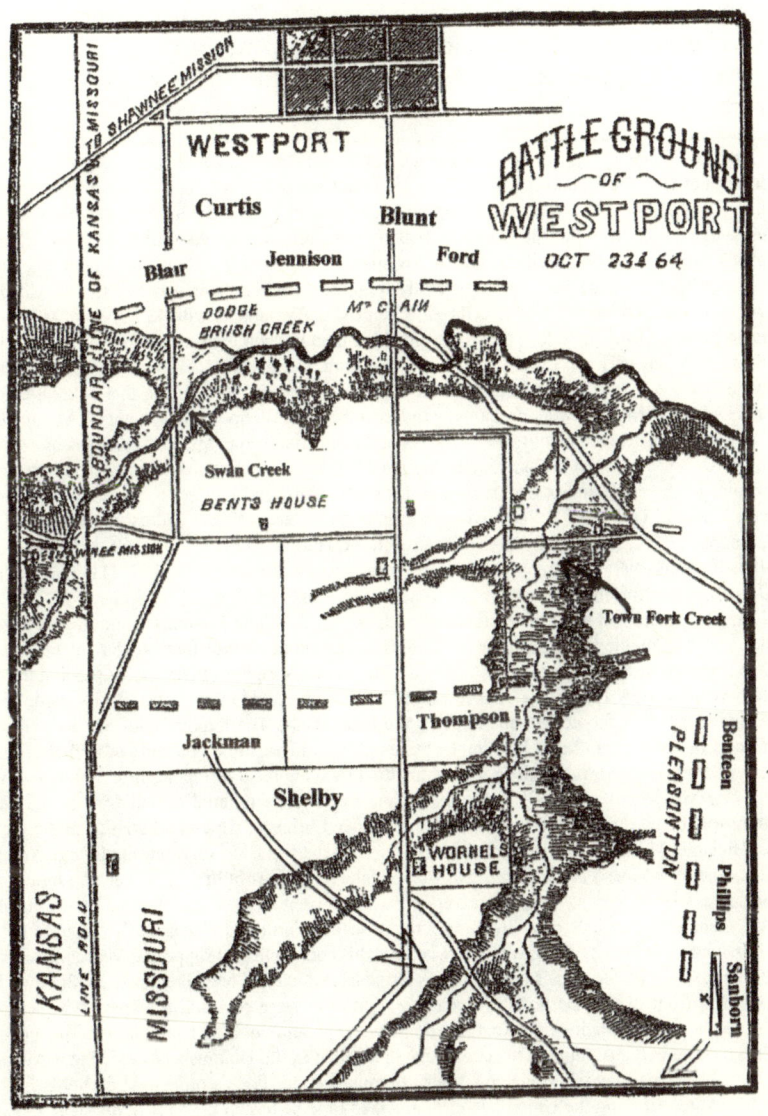

Crossing a Creek,

someone says it is Brush Creek. We strike the road at a gallop and soon gain the high prairie. Now the rattle of small arms accompanies the rapid firing of Shelby's guns. As we gain the crest of a high prairie ridge, we see Shelby's battle line half enveloped in smoke, and beyond it is the enemy's line in a similar condition. Still farther to the northwest is the town of Westport, the streets are swarming with marshaling squadrons of the enemy. For a while I think we are going to the support of Shelby's left.[126]

Slemons's Brigade, only to be pushed back in turn. In the rebel center Collins's Battery dueled for a time with the Federal guns, losing a 10-pound parrot by day's end, when it shattered upon firing. About 10:00 a.m. General Fagan ordered Colonel James McGhee, of Dobbin's Brigade, to charge a section of the 1st Colorado Artillery positioned on the Wornall Road. Supporting the attack was Thompson's Brigade which advanced dismounted. McGhee's mounted charge was counterchanged by the Federals, who easily repulsed McGhee "with a heavy loss in killed and wounded and prisoners." In all McGhee lost 25 dead and wounded, with 33 captured. Meanwhile, racing ahead of his brigade, Thompson urged his men to "come ahead my brave boys," driving Blunt back across Brush Creek. Fortunately for Blunt, the rebels were almost out of ammunition, which caused a delay of an hour while they were resupplied. And during this delay Slemons's and Dobbin's Brigades were probably withdrawn from the Westport line to support Marmaduke's Division. This delay also allowed Blunt to stabilize his line and prepare to attack, as more troops from the KSM came to his assistance. Around 11:00 a.m. the Unionists struck, changing the dynamics of the engagement. Note: Hinton, Monnett, Sinisi and Lause have McGhee making his attack around 11:00 a.m. or later, which was not correct, according to official reports and M. Jeff Thompson. *O.R.*, vol. 41, pt. 1:608, 658; Cruzen, 31; Hinton, 152–153, 155, 160–161; Jenkins, 85, 105–106, 108–109; Kirkman, 109; Lause, *Collapse of Price's Raid*, 105–107, 111–112; Monnett, 98–101, 103; Norton & Massey, 66; Sellmeyer, 242–244; Shalhope, 272; Sinisi, 219–220, 222–225, 227; Stanton, et al., 250; Williams, "Westport," 1, 7; Wright Memoirs, unnumbered page 93.

126. By 11:00 a.m. the Federals on the Westport front had gone on the offensive, having been shown a gully made by Swan Creek, which placed them on the far right of their line, enfilading the rebel left. With artillery hitting the exposed rebel left the bluecoats moved steadily forward, despite Confederate sharpshooters, who peppered the Union right. The remainder of Shelby's line held firm as Jackman encouraged his men to "remember...you are fighting a band of robbers, murderers, and thieves." However, the Kansans finally turned the rebel left flank, forcing Shelby to pull his line back even farther. By noon Shelby and Fagan were ordered to withdraw as the army's train was being threatened by John McNeil's Federal brigade, which had arrived in the vicinity of Hickman Mills Road where the train was crossing the Big Blue, en route southward. Additionally, Shelby was also made aware that Marmaduke's line was falling back, causing him to send Jackman's Brigade to stem the Union advance on his right flank. While moving to Marmaduke's aid, General Fagan halted Jackman near the Mockbee Farm and Harrisonville Road to counter Pleasonton's Division, which was overwhelming his command as it supported Marmaduke's withdrawing division. Slemons's and Dobbin's Brigades, which had been previously withdrawn from Shelby's front, with a portion of McCray's command, were covering the space between Shelby's right and Marmaduke's retreating command and could not hold back Pleasonton's Federals. Jackman quickly dismounted his command and waited as the Unionists advanced at a "swinging trot" toward his line, while Fagan's troops disengaged, per Price's orders. At 80 yards Jackman opened fire, breaking the Union advance, at which time he turned his guns to his right, defeating yet another move from that quarter. Jackman then mounted and rode off after the army and the trains, stopping periodically to fire and prevent further Union pursuit in that quarter. Jackman had saved Fagan's and Marmaduke's Divisions, but now it was Thompson's Iron Brigade that was in trouble, being surrounded and pressed on three sides. *O.R.*, vol. 41, pt. 1:341, 635–636, 658, 676;

Shot and shell from the enemy's guns are flying about us thick and fast. Our baggage wagons and the recruits have left the road, which runs along the crest of the ridge, to escape the fire of the enemy. When nearly opposite or south of Shelby's left the head of the regiment turned square to the south. Cheers from Shelby's brigade, or from the enemy, come to us above the shock of the battle: Looking back ere we leave the crest of the ridge I see Shelby's line is advancing, and the enemy is in confusion.[127]

Dashing on at a headlong gallop, passing baggage wagons and recruits, who hastily make room for us to pass, we cross the Blue River and, as we come to the top of the first high ridge on the south side, we see to the eastward beyond a small creek that empties into the river a long column of Federal cavalry at a six-gun battery deployed into line.[128] Halfway down the east side of the ridge are the

---

Forsyth, *Great Missouri Raid,* 190–191; Britton, *Civil War on the Border, 1863–65,* 496; Edwards, *Shelby and His Men,* 433; Hinton, 160–161; Jenkins, 104–107; Kirkman, 115; Lause, *Collapse of Price's Raid,* 110–112, 128; Monaghan, 335; Monnett, 103–104, 106–107; Sanborn, "Campaign in Missouri," 182; Sellmeyer, 245–246; Shalhope, 272; Sinisi, 227–228, 242–243; Williams, *Second Colorados,* 107; Wright Memoirs, unnumbered pages 93–94.

127. With the collapse of the rebel right and the retreat of Fagan's and Marmaduke's Divisions, Shelby was left with only Thompson's Iron Brigade to hold off the advancing Federals. The time was about 1:00 p.m., as Curtis closed in on Thompson from the north and Pleasonton's boys approached from the east. In a desperate attempt to extricate his command from the impending disaster, Shelby "with much difficulty" pulled Thompson back from Curtis and ordered him to charge John Sanborn, who headed Pleasonton's lead brigade. Shelby hoped to break Pleasonton's line and then turn on Curtis, who was rapidly approaching Thompson's rear. In the attack that followed Thompson broke through the enemy's first lines, but it was already too late. Dismounted Union cavalry of Philips's Brigade was advancing from the east along with Benteen's Brigade, which was mounted to meet the charge. Compounding Thompson's problems, artillery was firing into his front and flanks, and Curtis's men were charging from the north; there was little else that Thompson could do, "and then for the first time in this campaign Shelby's brigade turned its back to the foe." It was every man for himself, as the Iron Brigade fled the battlefield "in wild disorder…with scarcely the semblance of an organization, dropping guns, cartridges and blankets in their reckless flight" southward. With the rout of Thompson's Brigade at 2:00 p.m. the principle part of the battle was over. The Federals under Colonel Frederick Benteen, with the 2nd Arkansas Cavalry from Sanborn's Brigade and Jennison's Brigade from Blunt's command, continued the pursuit of Thompson's Brigade to Little Santa Fe, where some semblance of order was reestablished. Positioned behind a stone wall, Thompson easily defeated the last Union attack, allowing his unit to break contact with the pursuit and rejoin the army about sunset before camping on the Middle Fork of the South Grand River. *O.R.,* vol. 41, pt. 1:341, 390, 658–659, 667–668; Brooks Diary, October 23, 1864; Edwards, *Shelby and His Men,* 435; Geo. S. Grover, "The Price Campaign of 1864," *Missouri Historical Review* 6 (July 1912), 171, 174, hereafter cited as Grover; Hinton, 174–175; Monnett, 108–110; "Price's Invasion," *Chicago Tribune,* November 3, 1864; Sanborn, "Campaign in Missouri," 182–184; Scott, *Fourth Iowa,* 325–327; Sellmeyer, 247–250; Sinisi, 244–246; Webb, 234–235.

128. While the engagements were taking place at Byram's Ford and opposite of Westport, the Confederate train headed south crossing the Big Blue at Russell Ford. To the front of the train C. H. Tyler's Brigade led the way while Cabell's Brigade was tasked to protect the left or eastern flank of the train at Russell Ford, as it crossed the Big Blue. Bringing up the rear of the column was McCray's Brigade. By 10:00 a.m. the train and the extensive livestock herd was well on its way across the river as the Federal troops under John McNeil approached the area. General Cabell, being in charge of the trains deployed his command to successfully hold off Union attempts to in-

Windsor Guards, Gen. Prices escort, deployed as skirmishers. They open fire at a distance of 600 or 800 yards just as we come into line.[129] Cos. I and K go to the front with their Enfields as skirmishers. The Federals come into line in fine style, the sun glistening on their arms and accouterments, making a splendid spectacle. Enfield and Sharp's rifles are crackling along our line.

White Jets of Smoke

leap from the enemy's guns and the crash of artillery and the whizzing of solid shot and the bursting of shells adds at least force and weight to the enemy's argument. After a while a section of artillery comes into action at a dead run.[130] The artillerymen are black—almost as negroes—from powder-stain and smoke, but how they do make these two guns pop. Other troops come to our relief and we shake the enemy from our flank. The army is now moving south, and at a quick pace, too; for the enemy has become bold and aggressive because of his superiority in numbers. Heavy fighting has been done to-day because of a burdensome baggage train. Why we are hampered with this is past my comprehension. Our recruits are worth more to us than the train, for we have got not less than 7000 or 8000—perhaps more.[131] The old Tenth is twice as large as now as it was when we left Arkansas. We camp close to the Kansas line.[132]

Henry C. Luttrell,
Tenth Missouri Cavalry

* * * * * * *

tercept the army's wagons. As the morning progressed, Freeman's Brigade arrived from Byram's Ford about 11:00 a.m. to help protect the train, followed by the remainder of Marmaduke's command sometime after the noon hour. The remainder of the army followed, in a disordered condition. Shelby's command which guarded the rear of the army was the last to break contact with the pursuing Unionists. To save his division from destruction, the command split, with part of Thompson's Brigade heading toward Little Santa Fe, while the rest of the division followed behind the rear of the army, thus ending the Battle of Westport. See Appendix C for Extended Comments on the Trains. See Appendix G for the Confederate Order of Battle and losses at Westport. *O.R.*, vol. 41, pt. 1:636, 668, 676; *O.R.S.*, pt. 1, vol. 7:398; Freeman Memoir, October 23, 1864; Monnett, 118–119; National Archives, Record Group 153 (File no. NN 3336), John McNeil, General Court-Martial, Charge no. 3, 10, hereafter cited as McNeil Court-Martial; Sinisi, 250.

129. The Windsor's Guards was actually Company K, 2nd Missouri Cavalry, which served with Price throughout the war. It began the war as a MSG unit and later became Company K. During the Missouri Expedition, it was commanded by Captain Robert Collins. Confederate Correspondence, Nelson to Maclean (December 15, 1864); Peterson, et al., 37.

130. The artillery probably belonged to Captain S. S. Harris, who had withdrawn from Byram's Ford shortly after the 10th Missouri departed the fight with Pleasonton's command.

131. See Appendix I, Summary of Price's 1864 Raid, Recruits Gained, for details on numbers received.

132. This last statement of Luttrell's provides an interesting indication as to the size of the Army of Missouri following the Battle of Westport, particularly in the Missouri units. See Appendix G for the Confederate Oder of Battle and Losses at Westport.

Item: A Confederate cavalryman continues his tale of Price's 1864 Missouri Raid, copied from a diary, beginning on October 24, 1864, including the Battle of Mine Creek, Kansas, by Henry C. Luttrell, Company G, 10th Missouri Cavalry (C.S.A.). Part Four.
Published: March 13, 1886.

Price's Great Raid.

[Incidents from a trooper's diary kept on the march: third paper; from the Kansas line to Carthage, Mo.]

October 25 [24], 1864.—The army moves south this morning.[133] We crossed the state line near the southeast corner of Johnson County, Kansas. We passed over the site in the village to-day that has been burned to the ground. Not a house is to be seen. Nothing but the foundations of the houses is left. Weeds are waist high in the streets—or what was once the streets. I have failed to learn the name of this desolate place. The enemy has kept at a respectable distance to-day. We camp this night of what I suppose is the Osage River, though some of the boys say it is the Miami River, near a village name not known.[134] We have mutton for supper, which is highly

---

133. Following the Battle of Westport, the commanders of the two Federal armies met by Indian Creek, near the state line, west of Byram's Ford and 10 miles south of Westport. The time was between 2:30–3:00 p.m. on October 23. Following the oftentimes contentious meeting, Curtis, with the consent of his major commanders, relieved the KSM from north Kansas and sent them home to tend their farms and vote in the upcoming elections. The remainder of the reorganized Army of the Border, under General Curtis, continued its less than "vigorous" pursuit, according to Howard Monnett, with "the Union forces... as thoroughly disorganized in victory as the Confederates had become in defeat." By the time the pursuit of Price's army had ended on October 23, Curtis's army, led by Blunt's 1st Division, was camped near Little Santa Fe, with Pleasonton's 2nd Division to its rear, while John McNeil's Brigade was encamped in the vicinity of Russell's Ford, just north of Hart Grove Creek. Following the battle on the 23rd, Price's army continued its headlong retreat southward, which Wiley Britton described as "almost...a reckless flight." After making 24 miles the army trains camped about 1:00 a.m. on October 24, "without unsaddling," near the Middle Fork of the Grand River, with the remainder of the army camped about four miles farther back, while the rear guard was four miles distant from Curtis's advance and eight from Little Santa Fe. On morning of October 24, Marmaduke's Division "started before daylight" and headed south, followed by the army's trains, Fagan's and then Shelby's Division (Forsyth has Marmaduke's and Shelby's commands reversed). *O.R.*, vol. 41, pt.1:486, 684; D. Brown, 41; Brown Journal, October 23, 1864; Britton, *Civil War on the Border, 1863–65*, 438–439; Buresh, 53; Campbell Memoir; Robert Collins, *General James G. Blunt: Tarnished Glory* (Gretna, LA, 2005), 200, hereafter cited as Collins; Forsyth, *Great Missouri Raid*, 196–198, 201; Gene Geer, "'Up and In Line at Day Break; Considerable Skirmish.' The Taylor Bray Diary (September 27, 1864–July 5, 1865)," *White River Historical Quarterly* 1 (Summer 1964), 12, hereafter cited as Bray Diary; Hinton, 175–176, 183; Lause, *Collapse of Price's Raid*, 131–132, 146–147; McNeil Court-Martial, John F. Beveridge Testimony, 17; Monnett, 127–129; Sinisi, 254–256.

134. From the Grand River the rebel army moved southward, crossing the Kansas line near the noon hour after passing through West Point, Luttrell's unnamed, burned out town. The burned out houses, barns, etc. and deserted landscape that the Army of Missouri passed through on its way south were indicative of "Jennison Tombstones" or "Jennison's Monuments," reminding Confed-

Appreciated by the Boys.

October, the 26th [25th].—Some of Co. G's furloughed boys came into camp last night, or rather early this morning. They report that the enemy is moving upon us rapidly, and in force.[135] "Boots and saddles" is sounded at the brigade headquarters at 2 a.m. Rain is falling and thick darkness prevails. Notwithstanding the inclemency of the weather and the annoying darkness, the squadrons formed

---

erate Missourians how much they detested the Kansans. And despite the best efforts of some of the officers, like M. Jeff Thompson, the rebel troops repaid the Kansans in kind as they marched along the Kansas border. Houses were sacked, livestock stolen or butchered, crops burned, wells fouled with dead animals, and seven or eight civilians, in the vicinity of Trading Post who failed to evacuate the area in time, were executed for past wrongs inflicted upon Missourians. The path south was also littered with discarded "debris of a retreating foe," including "hundreds of broken-down and abandoned animals," wagons, forges, and even a spinning wheel. Also mixed in with the debris were "large droves of cattle...as well as many sick men lying beside the road." But despite the looting and devastation wrought upon the area as noted by many participants, a Kansas doctor recorded that overall the Confederates "failed to do any damage to speak of in Kansas." And by the end of the day, Price's army had reached Trading Post, on the Marais de Cygnes or Osage River (Missouri's name for the river), following a 35 mile march. Shelby's command was posted on the west side of the river with Marmaduke and the train, while Fagan's Division protected the rear on the opposite side of the river. To the rear of the rebel army the Union army started at sunrise, with a battalion of the 2nd Colorado leading. Father back, the bulk of the army did not get in motion until almost 10:00 a.m., giving the Confederates a good 15 to 20 mile head start. The Yankees made it to West Pont by 8:00 p.m., rested briefly, and moved on with Pleasonton's Division, now commanded by General Sanborn, taking the lead. Marching into a dark, wet night, Sanborn continued on in the hope of contacting Price's army, while Blunt's Division rested back at West Point, thus setting the stage for October 25. D. Brown, 41; Buresh, 61–63; Crawford, *Kansas In the Sixties*, 153; Forsyth, *Great Missouri Raid*, 201–202; "The Latest From Price," *Freedom's Champion*, November 10, 1864; Monnett, 129; Pitcock & Gurley, 236; Sanborn, "Campaign in Missouri," 185; Scott, *Fourth Iowa*, 328; Sinisi, 259–265; Jerry D. Stalnaker, *The Battle of Mine Creek: The Crushing End of the Missouri Campaign* (Charleston SC, 2011), 56, 62, hereafter cited as Stalnaker; Stanton, et al., 253.

135. Having caught the rebel army, the 2nd Colorado settled into the vicinity of Trading Post on the night of October 24. General Sanborn arrived about midnight and was informed by Captain Ezra Kingsbury, commanding a battalion of the 2nd, that the enemy pickets were near. To further develop the situation, Sanborn directed a nighttime assault of the two mounds that guarded the entrance to Trading Post and a crossing of the river. Using the 6th and 8th MSM, with the 2nd Colorado in reserve, Sanborn ordered the attack, during a "heavy mist," which was quickly responded to by Fagan's Division, holding the mounds and easily repelling the Unionists. "The darkness was so great that the topography of the country and position of the enemy could not be determined," according to Sanborn, who "concluded to defer the general attack until the dawn of day." Also during the night of October 24, Price had received information that led him to believe that there was no enemy to his rear, but there would be Federals to his front and right flank as he moved forward. He set the order to march for 2:00 a.m. on October 25. Shelby's Division would lead the army, with orders to take Fort Scott, followed by the train, Fagan, with Marmaduke's command bringing up the rear. Thus began the day that "ten years to the day after the...charge of the Light Brigade at the Battle of Balaclava, another charge against greater odds" would be made. *O.R.*, vol. 41, pt. 1:413, 636; *O.R.S.*, pt.1, vol. 7:399; Castel, *Sterling Price*, 238–239; Forsyth, *Great Missouri Raid*, 203; Hinton, 188; Kip Lindberg, "Chaos Itself: The Battle of Mine Creek," *North & South* 1 (No. 6), 74, 79, hereafter cited as Lindberg, "Mine Creek;" Sanborn, "Campaign in Missouri," 187; Sinisi, 264–265; Williams, *Second Colorados*, 110–112.

promptly, but we stand for an hour in the rain, waiting for the slow motion train to creep out of camp. Then our march is fitful and sporadic. At daylight a heavy, thick fog prevails, with drizzling rain, and the rattle of distant musketry tells us that the enemy is at hand.[136] Clark's brigade is marching in the rear this morning. The Tenth regiment is thrown to the rear to support the rear-guard. The rattle of small arms grows louder. The regiment wheels into line, skirmishers are sent out and flank guards placed. Now the wind rises and the fog and drizzling rain disappear, and the sun casts a sickly smile through the breaking clouds. Our rear-guard is not more than a half mile distant, stubbornly resisting the advance of the enemy, who was supported by a heavy column close up in the rear.

Soon our skirmish line is busy. For a short time they check the advances of the enemy.[137] But now whole companies wheel into line and our skirmishers are

---

136. At 4:00 a.m., General Sanborn renewed his assault on the mounds, encountering Slemons's Brigade on the western mound, Dobbin's Brigade in the gap between the mounds, supported by two 2-pound Woodruff guns, while Cabell held the eastern hill. Driving up the slippery slopes, with some men crawling on their hands and knees, the Unionists finally gained the top of the acclivities, in a large part because the rebels were withdrawing, having allowed time for the trains to depart the area in apparent safety. About a mile south of the river, Marmaduke formed his line, using Clark's Brigade, supported by Harris's Artillery, while Freeman's small brigade constituted a skirmish line about 400 yards from the main ford. Pushing forward, Sanborn's troops captured an abandoned 2-pound Woodruff gun and 12 wagons (other sources say 20–40 wagons). They then chased away a party of rebels who were attempting to block the river ford with fallen trees after taking down "but two trees of moderate size." Sanborn then crossed the river, pushed Freeman's command back and deployed about half a mile from Marmaduke's main line, manned by Clark's troopers. Clark had divided his command into two parts; one mile from the Osage he had deployed the 7th, 8th, 10th and Wood's Missouri Regiments, while a mile farther back the 3rd and 4th Missouri constituted yet another line. It was between 6:00–7:00 a.m., when Sanborn's command had all crossed the river and deployed for action. "The sun lit the scene with splendor, and all the landscape glowed and twinkled," chasing away the rain, but the fog had arrived. *O.R.*, vol. 41, pt. 1:390–391, 413; Buresh, 72, 78; Busch, *Missouri Democrat Articles*, 454; Forsyth, *Great Missouri Raid*, 203; Hinton, 198–201; Lause, *Collapse of Price's Raid*, 157–158; Lindberg, "Mine Creek," 79; McNeil Court-Martial, George Yates Testimony, 61; "Price's Invasion of Missouri," *Missouri Republican*, November 11, 1864; "Retreat of the Invaders," *Missouri Republican*, October 29, 1864; Sanborn, "Campaign in Missouri," 187–189, 192–193; Scott, *Fourth Iowa*, 329–330; Sinisi, 266–268, 274.

137. After crossing the Osage, Sanborn's men launched an unsupported attack against J. B. Clark's line, which was supported by three pieces of artillery. The 8th MSM, Kingsbury's 2nd Colorado Battalion and the 2nd Arkansas Cavalry (Union), all dismounted and attacked the rebel line. The time was 9:00 a.m. when the Federals, under Colonel John Phelps moved forward; however, both the 2nd Arkansas (Union) and the 8th MSM buckled under the rebel artillery fire and fell back to the safety of the woods near the river, halting the initial Federal thrust. There they waited until more troops arrived with artillery support. Meanwhile, at 10:00 a.m., J. B. Clark withdrew his line, without firing any small arms, back through the 3rd and 4th Missouri Cavalries. Clark's new line was formed a mile to the south of the 3rd and 4th Missouri where they awaited the Federal advance. Colonel Phelps moved forward, as rebels retreated. Back at the Marais des Cygnes Ford, General Pleasonton arrived on the scene, assumed command, and ordered General Sanborn to press the attack, giving him John Philips's and Frederick Benteen's Brigades to bolster the Union drive. *O.R.*, vol. 41, pt. 1: 676, 685, 696; Britton, *Civil War on the Border, 1863–65*, 491–492; Buresh, 83; Hinton, 203, 205; Lindberg, "Mine Creek," 79; Sinisi, 275; Williams, *Second Colorados*, 114–115.

Battle of Mine Creek
(October 25, 1864)

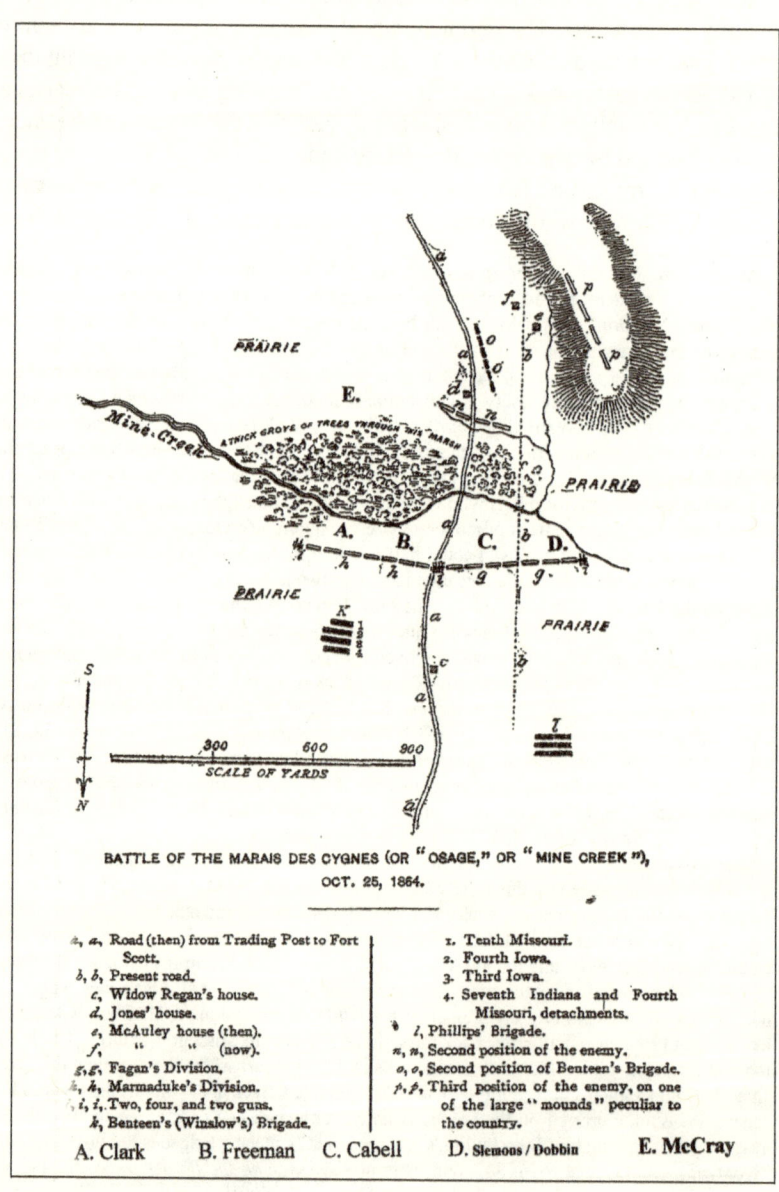

BATTLE OF THE MARAIS DES CYGNES (OR "OSAGE," OR "MINE CREEK"),
OCT. 25, 1864.

a, a, Road (then) from Trading Post to Fort Scott.
b, b, Present road.
c, Widow Regan's house.
d, Jones' house.
e, McAuley house (then).
f, " " (now).
g, g, Fagan's Division.
h, h, Marmaduke's Division.
i, i, Two, four, and two guns.
k, Benteen's (Winslow's) Brigade.

1. Tenth Missouri.
2. Fourth Iowa.
3. Third Iowa.
4. Seventh Indiana and Fourth Missouri, detachments.
l, Phillips' Brigade.
n, n, Second position of the enemy.
o, o, Second position of Benteen's Brigade.
p, p, Third position of the enemy, on one of the large "mounds" peculiar to the country.

A. Clark   B. Freeman   C. Cabell   D. Slemons / Dobbin   E. McCray

pushed back by force of numbers. Heavy flanking columns of the enemy are reaching out around our flanks; steadily we give ground, for we are contending against overwhelming odds.[138]

Now we are on higher ground and I see Clark's brigade in line a little to the rear. To the northward the whole prairie is alive with the hostile squadrons of the enemy. A solid battle line is in our front, reaching to a fringe of timber on a small stream to the eastward. This stream, stretching around to the west runs parallel with and half a mile south of our battle line (name of stream not known)[Mine Creek].[139]

---

138. Between 10:00 and 11:00 a.m., Philips's and Benteen's Brigades crossed the Marais des Cygnes River and deployed. Philips's command took the right of the Federal line, Benteen was in the center, while Sanborn's re–mounted troops were on the left. Pushing forward, the Federals continued to advance, capturing another abandoned piece of artillery (probably the other Woodruff gun), even while Marmaduke's Division withdrew further. With the Confederates retreating, General Pleasonton allowed Sanborn's Brigade to rest and feed as they had been up since before dawn and were exhausted. To the front of the Union advance, Colton Greene, commanding the rebel rear guard with the 3rd and 4th Missouri, held about 30 minutes, when he fell back, joining the rest of the brigade. Both sides were now moving at "a trot," just out of effective gunfire and about 800 yards apart. Back at the crossing of Mine Creek the Confederate train was still struggling to cross, and by 11:00 a.m. several wagons were still north of the creek, along with Marmaduke's Division and Fagan's command, less McCray's Brigade, which had already crossed to the south side. *O.R.*, vol. 41, pt. 1:684, 691; Britton, *Civil War on the Border, 1863–65*, 493; Buresh, 84; Sanborn, "Campaign in Missouri," 192; Sinisi, 275–277; Stalnaker, 73.

139. By the time Clark's Brigade was reunited following the steady retreat from the Marais des Cygnes River, General Marmaduke had already requested the assistance of Fagan's command. Taking up a position about 300 yards north of Mine Creek, Marmaduke's Division held the right of the line, while Fagan's Division positioned itself on the left. Clark's Brigade was on the far right, while to their left was Freeman's command. The far left of the rebel line was occupied by Slemons's Brigade, while Cabell's command took its post next to Freeman. Dobbin's Brigade appears to have been to the rear of Cabell's and Slemons's Brigades, serving as Fagan's reserve. (The placement of Dobbin is sketchy at best, according to Sinisi, who has it to the left of Slemons's Brigade, while John C. Wright has Slemons's Brigade on the "extreme left" of the division. John C. Moore, in the *Confederate Military History* has only Cabell and Slemons's Brigades on the main line, implying that the rest were behind.) Supporting the rebel line were eight pieces of artillery scattered on both flanks and in the center of the line. It was near 11:00 a.m., when the 10th Missouri came into line, and faced about, at which time Luttrell observed the chaos at the Mine Creek Ford. The creek was a winding, "deep, lightly wooded stream with abrupt caving banks," which "was blocked by broken-down wagons." The vast majority of the train had already passed and was headed south to the Little Osage River. Unfortunately, the bulk of the army was pinned against the creek, and Marmaduke, who was in command of the rear guard, had to "either pass and abandon the train or else fight." Marmaduke chose to fight. Normally the grayclads would have dismounted to fight on foot; however, across the prairie, the Unionists were fast closing the gap. Having had but little time to react to the advancing Federals, Fagan and Marmaduke kept their commands mounted, while they deployed, knowing full well that most of their men were armed with long-range rifles that they were incapable of loading while mounted. Compounding Marmaduke's problems was his selection of position, which was at the bottom of a gentle slope, which would ultimately give impetus to the Federal charge that followed. *O.R.*, vol. 41, pt. 1:684, 691; *O.R.S.*, pt. 1, vol. 7:399, 410; Britton, *Civil War on the Border, 1863–65*, 493–494; Brown Journal, October 25, 1864; Buresh, 92; Edwards, *Shelby and His Men*, 440–441; Forsyth, *Great Missouri Raid*, 204; Lindberg, "Mine Creek," 80–81; J. Marmaduke Letter (May 26, 1865), Ken-

Maj. Pratt's Battery

is on the hill at the road. I think it is Fagan's brigade forming on the right of it. Shells are flying thick and fast as we take position on the left. So rapid have been the movements of the enemy, our whole line is instantly engaged.

Turning myself so as to see the south, in the rear of our battle line, I see a mob of our baggage wagons jammed up at the fords of the creek. The enemy's line comes to a halt when in about 200 yards of us, and contents itself with a steady ringing fire. It is a full-grown cavalry fight out on the high rolling Kansas prairie.[140] Now the sun shines out brightly, showing up every feature of the battlefield. Capt. Murray rides along the line exhorting the men to do their duty, for the ranks of the company are mainly composed of new recruits. I don't think a dozen of the old veteran boys are in line. "Keep cool, boys, and aim low—remember that the eyes of the veteran regiment are upon you." Most of the old veteran boys are

---

nerly Papers, Missouri Historical Society; Moore, *Missouri, Confederate Military History*, 193; Sinisi, 277–279; Stalnaker, 87; Stuart, 602; Wright Memoirs, unnumbered page 97.

140. John Philips's 1st Brigade moved forward to the open prairie at 11:00 a.m., faced the rebel line on Mine Creek, and deployed, dismounting skirmishers to his front. Philips's line was anchored on the Fort Scott Road, extending about half a mile to the west. For the next twenty minutes Philips confronted the rebel line, which contained between 6,000–8,000 men, while his 1,400-man brigade was totally unsupported. "It was a grand spectacle. An awful moment," according to Philips, while Lieutenant Colonel Bazel Lazear, of the 1st MSM, recorded: "We were drawn up in line in front of each other more like a picture than reality." But that quickly changed. Just before 11:30 a section of artillery arrived, and then Frederick Benteen's 4th Brigade appeared on Philips's left. But unlike Philips, Benteen had no intention of dismounting, instead sending word to Philips to charge the enemy when he did. Deploying his brigade in a column of regiments in line, Benteen prepared to charge the enemy in what William Crowley declared was "one of the most spectacular cavalry charges in the war." To Benteen the situation was perfect. According to General Pleasonton's orders, Benteen was "to charge the enemy whenever the opportunity offered" and Benteen was determined to attack regardless of odds. About 11:30 a.m. the "chief bugler" of Benteen's Brigade sounded the charge, followed by fifty more taking up the tune, and away the 1,100-man brigade went. Over a hill that "masked" their advance, "down the slope at a full run," went Benteen's troopers. Seeing Benteen's command charging, Philips's Brigade quickly mounted and moved forward to join the charge; however, to Philips's left Benteen's lead regiment, the 10th Missouri (Union), came to an abrupt halt at 200 yards, being hit by artillery fire that "literally mowed the grass just in front" of the regiment. This in turn caused Philips's boys to halt, dismount and fire on the rebel line. After but a few minutes, the 4th Iowa, the second regiment in Benteen's attack column, veered to the 10th's left and continued its headlong charge at Clark's Confederate Brigade. The remainder of Benteen's Brigade followed the 4th's example and continued onward. The 10th Missouri quickly regained its composure and moved forward, mixing in with elements of the 4th Iowa as they passed through their line. To Benteen's right, Philips' Brigade, seeing the charge continue on its left, remounted, and moved forward at the charge. *O.R.*, vol. 41, pt. 1:332, 352, 361; Buresh, 87, 92–93, 105, 113–116; Busch, *Missouri Democrat Articles*, 374; Crowley, 143; Forsyth, *Great Missouri Raid*, 205, 207–208; Wilson B. George, "The Drive After Price," *National Tribune*, March 13, 1924; Hinton, 207–208; Lindberg, "Mine Creek," 81–82; Vivian Kirpatrick McLarty, "The Civil War Letters of Colonel Bazel F. Lazear," *Missouri Historical Review* 45 (October 1950), 58, hereafter cited as McLarty; Philips Diary, October 25, 1864; Scott, *Fourth Iowa*, 332–335; Sinisi, 279–281; Stalnaker, 73, 84; Stuart, 602; J.F. Young, "The Battle of the Osage," *Missouri Republican*, November 14, 1864.

grouped near the head of the company: stuttering Bill Graves is on my right, Long John McKinney and Charlie Howard are on the left.[141]

Now the battle is growing lively. Cavalry horses are breaking from the enemy's line and running riderless across the prairie. Twice the enemy's colors have gone down in our immediate front. Many of our men have dismounted and are firing with a rest upon their knees. John McKinney is jubilant over what he considers his good marksmanship—for he is tallying what he considers his most telling shots—and declares that he has dropped two of the enemies color-bearers. About this time Charlie Howard catches a bullet in the fleshy part of his leg. He slings his gun, takes out his handkerchief and binds up the wound, then goes on firing again as he remarks that "It is better to catch 'em in the leg than in the head." A heavy column of the enemy is moving

Upon Our Left Flank.

I think it is Wood's battalions dashing out, and for a few moments checks them, but they are finally pressed slowly back.[142]

My ammunition is now out. Looking to the right (east), I see that it is in confusion and falling back rapidly.[143] Our line has dwindled down now to a mere

---

141. John McKinney joined the Confederate Service on September 7, 1863, and was a sergeant in Company G, 10th Missouri Cavalry (CSA). National Archives, Record Group M322 (roll no. 57), Confederate Compiled Service Record, 10th Missouri Cavalry.

   Stuttering Bill Graves was W. D. Graves, a member of Company G, 10th Missouri Cavalry. Graves joined the Confederate Army on April 9, 1862, in Lafayette County, being enlisted by J. V. Cockrell. On October 10, 1863, Graves was detailed to the Quartermaster Department, but later returned to the command He survived the war and was paroled at Shreveport in June 1865. Final disposition unknown. Bartels, *Missouri Confederate Surrender*, "Graves, D. W." entry; National Archives, Record Group M322 (roll no. 56), Confederate compiled Service Records, 10th Missouri Cavalry.

   Nothing found on Charles or "Charlie" Howard National Archives, Record Group M322 (roll no. 57), Confederate Compiled Service Record, 10th Missouri Cavalry.

142. Wood's Battalion was organized on August 31, 1863, with six companies, but added four more during Price's 1864 Missouri Raid, making it a regiment. The unit was commanded by Robert C. Wood, who was born on February 20, 1828, in Charlotte County, Virginia. He moved to Marshall, Missouri, in 1842, and married just before the war. Prior to the war Wood was a merchant, livestock rancher, and "noted Indian fighter." Wood joined the MSG, serving in Sterling Price's escort as a major. He was appointed a major in the Confederate Army, on September 25, 1863, commanding what became the 14th Missouri Cavalry Battalion (CSA). Wood survived the war and was paroled on July 27, 1865, settling initially in Texas, where he was a rancher. In his later years, Wood moved to Arizona, where he died on October 12, 1902, in Tucson. *O.R.S.*, pt. 2, vol. 38:285, 288–289; Allardice, *Confederate Colonels*, 405–406; Crute, *Confederate Army*, 204; Peterson, et al., 36; Sifakis, *Missouri*, 102.

   At Mine Creek, Wood's unit occupied the far left of Clark's line, next to Pratt's Artillery Battalion, and his repulse seemingly unhinged the Confederate center, causing Freeman's Brigade to his left to break, even before the Federals hit his line. Sinisi, 278; Stalnaker, 87.

143. Benteen's Brigade made contact first with Burbridge's 4th Missouri, which was positioned on the far right of the rebel line. Firing but one ineffective volley, the 4th "broke and fled in the wildest of confusion." This in turn allowed Companies A and K, of the 4th Iowa Cavalry, to flank Clark's line and get into his rear. To the left of the 4th Missouri, the 7th Missouri, with Davies's

nothing and the men are calling for ammunition. "Stand your ground, men; a reserve is marching to our relief!" is the order. I have but one shot left in my pistol and I return it to the belt. Having nothing to do but look about, I turn my eyes to the south. The train is across the creek and out of sight. Wood's battalion is hotly engaged, but, beyond them, farther to the left, is a column of the enemy moving at a "trot march" to our rear, heading southeast.[144]

Now a regiment forms close up to our rear—I think it is the Eighth.[145] Then

> Battalion, initially held Benteen's troopers, checking their assault "in fine style." Unfortunately, in the center of the Marmaduke's line, Freeman's Brigade behaved badly, having endured heavy fire from the 1st MSM, just before the 3rd Iowa slammed into their line. Firing at most one round at the charging bluecoats Freeman's troopers beat a hasty retreat for the south, opening up Clark's left and Cabell's right flank. *O.R.*, vol. 41, pt. 1:691, 694; Ballard Diary, October 25, 1864; Buresh, 120, 122; Campbell Memoir; Lindberg, "Mine Creek," 82–83; McGhee, *Campaigning with Marmaduke*, 26; Monnett, 131; Sinisi, 282–284.

144. Following a delay of about 10 minutes, and seeing rebel flags retreating in the center of their line, Philips's Brigade remounted and charged. Bazel Lazear, who had seen the rebel flag falling back, started the charge followed by the remainder of Philips's Brigade. Freeman's Brigade had opened a gap in the center of the rebel line allowing Philips's command, led by the 1st and 7th MSM, to pour into the breech and spread out, hitting Cabell's Brigade in the flank. Within moments Cabell's Brigade was caught up in the rebel rout as Fagan's entire command raced for safety. Zimmerman's Battery of Slemons's Brigade got stuck in the muddy bottom of Mine Creek and was captured along with Colonel William F. Slemons, who had come back to help save the battery. General Cabell was likewise captured soon after his line collapsed, managed to escape, not once but twice, but was finally recaptured by Sergeant Calvary D. Young of the 3rd Iowa Cavalry, when his horse fell while attempting to cross Mine Creek. Young was later awarded the Medal of Honor for capturing Cabell. Others in Fagan's command were not so lucky, as any caught wearing a blue uniform were summarily executed by Philips's men, per standing orders from General Pleasonton. General Cabell, who witnessed this atrocity called Colonel William Cloud's attention to the executions. Cloud "tried to excuse their conduct saying they only killed our men who had on Federal uniforms." Cabell then called Cloud's attention to the fact that "he was dressed in civilian's clothes and not a Federal uniform." To end the discussion Cabell also reminded the Federal colonel that four-fifths of his men wore no uniform of any kind. Cloud then said he would stop the indiscriminate killing of wounded and prisoners. *O.R.*, vol. 41, pt. 1:361; *O.R.S.*, pt. 1, vol. 7:399–400, 402, 410; Buresh, 123–124; Lindberg, "Mine Creek," 83–84; Sinisi, 286; Wright Memoirs, unnumbered page 98.

145. To the rear of Clark's line Colton Greene's 3rd Missouri and Jeffers's 8th Missouri served as the brigade's reserve. The 8th was located behind Pratt's Artillery, to the left of Clark's Brigade, while the 4th was to its right. The regiment coming to the 10th's support was likely the 3rd Missouri, while the 8th was busy protecting Pratt's Artillery Battalion in the center of the line. However, before the 3rd even got a chance to move up, it was caught in the masses that were retreating. With but one company still under his control Greene attacked the Unionists to his right, but to no avail, as he ordered his remaining men to "withdraw as best they could." In the center of Clark's line, the 10th Missouri (CSA) charged the advancing Federals, while the 8th Missouri traded blows with the Unionists attempting to capture Pratt's Battery. In the end, finding himself surrounded, Colonel Jeffers surrendered himself, with the remaining men of Pratt's Artillery Battalion, to Colonel William Cloud, commanding a detachment of the 2nd Kansas Cavalry. To make matters worse, within minutes of Clark's line being hit in the front, the two Iowa companies attacked the line from the rear, sealing the fate of the battle. General Marmaduke, who was trying to rally the troops was subsequently captured by Private James Dunlavy of the 3rd Iowa Cavalry. For his capture of Marmaduke, Dunlavy was also awarded the Medal of Honor. *O.R.*, vol. 41, pt. 1: 558–559; 691; Lindberg, "Mine Creek," 82–83; McGhee, *Campaigning With Marmaduke*, 26; Sinisi, 285–286.

comes the order, "Foreward!" I am of the opinion that this order comes from the regiment in the rear, that is now moving up. In the next breath "about-face," and the regiment, with the exception of Company K, moves back in very good order, considering that the reserve regiment has been allowed to get right on our heels before order was given to retire. Co. K, however, with Capt. [Asbury] Vandever at its head, charges at a gallop in the face of the enemy.[146] Evidently Co. K has misunderstood the order or else the rest of the regiment has. Who will ever solve this enigma? We are scarcely separated from the reserve regiment ere we become conscious that the curtain has risen upon another scene that we were not expecting, at least not from that quarter. About halfway, or hardly so far, from us to the creek is a column of cavalry moving rapidly to its southwest. At first we think or at least I do, that they are the Third regiment (Green's), but a second look convinces me

They Are Federals,

where they are wearing their pea-jackets; while Clark's brigade is enveloped in the blue cavalry overcoat. A moment more, and the Federal column wheels into line, and advances at a brisk walk. All this time—which is really but a few moments—Pratt's battery, on the hill in the east, is pounding away furiously, and the fight along the crest of the ridge west to the extreme left, which is wrapped around considerably to the southwest, is hotly engaged.

"Forward! Gallop! Charge!" is the order. With a wild cheer we dash forward. To our surprise, not a shot is fired from the Federal line; but when we are within twenty steps of them, their sabers flash from their scabbards with a clatter. A second more, and we strike them like an avalanche, and a clash of steel rings out as we receive their straight cuts on our guns at a guard. What a God's pity we are out of ammunition, and just at this critical moment, too—not enough for a corporal's guard would have been left of that line. For one moment the two lines hang together, then they break into a whirling eddies, in groups of twos, fours and sixes, the Federals cutting and slashing with their sabers, the Confederates banishing their revolvers and make believe they were going to shoot or using their guns to ward off the saber blows. Everything is in confusion. The Federals and Confederates are mixed up. From a general fight it has turned out to be a personal affair. Now I see a Federal cutting and slashing at a Confederate and calling upon him to surrender; on my right is a Confederate riding knee to knee with a Federal, with

---

146. Asbury Vandiver or Vandever was born in Casey County, Kentucky, in about 1837, moved to Missouri, settling in Missouri City, Ray County. He entered the Confederate Army, being elected a 2nd lieutenant, in Company D, 1st Missouri Cavalry (CSA) and was later promoted to 1st lieutenant. Following his capture at Vicksburg in July 1863, he was exchanged, returned to the Trans-Mississippi, where he organized Company K, 10th Missouri Cavalry on September 1, 1863. Vandiver was subsequently elected captain of the company on November 5, 1863. He was captured at Mine Creek, sent to St. Louis, and then forwarded to Johnson's Island November 12, 1864, where he took the Oath of Allegiance on June 16, 1865, and was released. *O.R.S.*, pt. 2, vol. 38:112, 257; Eakin, *Confederate Records*, 7:163; National Archives Record Group M322 (roll no. 58), Confederate Compiled Service Records, 10th Missouri Cavalry.

his empty pistol at his head admonishing him to throw up his hands; by his side a Federal who has captured his man, on the other side I see a Confederate who is equally triumphant. While doing escort duty for Gen. [Thomas C.] Hindman, Co. G was prepared for just such an emergency—a saber charge.[147] A year ago and more I threw away

My Trusty Old Saber,

calling it "a glittering nuisance." However, I caught the first "cut" at a "guard" close up to the "hilt," and with a slight twist rent the saber from the trooper's hand. Quick as a flash he drew his revolver and aims a shot at my left breast. With my bridle hand I knocked up the pistol as it exploded, cutting through the collar of my coat. Before he can aim another shot I made a "left cut," with my gun, which catches him just at the base of the skull. He sinks down on the horse's neck as the two lines break into confusion. Riding a few steps further through the confused thong I come upon a Federal trooper who had reined up his horse and is deliberately firing his revolver at a Confederate who is lying on the ground resting upon one elbow and holding up his other hand. Remembering that I had one shot left in my old navy I quickly drew it and fired at the cold-blooded wrench as I passed. He dropped his revolver, humped himself in the saddle and lay down on the horse's neck as the animal moved on.

Following a trail to the creek I pass a company of Federals guarding the crossing. Lieut. Harris of Co. E is handing his sword to the officer in command. He looks up at me with a sickly smile as I present arms to the officer.[148]

"Where to?" He asked in a brusk tone. I see that he is fooled in my uniform and rig for it is Federal all through, except a gray blouse, which my big blue overcoat completely covers. So I replied promptly, "To the front, to join my regiment."

Without a second look he replies: "Pass around this way," motioning with his hand to the right. I walked my horse around the end of the company and halfway down the creek bank. Half a dozen comrades come dashing down the bed of the stream hunting for a place to climb the bank. "Open fire upon these men in the

---

147. Thomas C. Hindman was born in Tennessee in 1828, fought in the Mexican War, and moved to Helena, Arkansas, in 1856. At the beginning of the Civil War, he commanded an Arkansas infantry regiment and was promoted to general officer in November 1861. After the Battle of Shiloh, Hindman was again promoted and returned to Arkansas to command the Trans-Mississippi District. He went on to the command the army at Fort Smith, fought and lost the Battle of Prairie Grove, after which he departed the Trans-Mississippi for the east side of the river. Following the war, Hindman emigrated to Mexico, remained a short time, but later returned to Helena, where he was assassinated on September 28, 1868. *O.R.*, vol. 22, pt. 2:781; Banasik, *Missouri Brothers in Gray*, 139–141.

148. No Lieutenant Harris is found in the records of the 10th Missouri Cavalry (CSA), or in the list of prisoners delivered to St. Louis. Harris could have been one of the many Confederates who were subsequently executed for wearing a partial or full blue uniform at Mine Creek. See Appendix H, Executed Prisoners for more details on the execution of captured Confederate prisoners at Mine Creek. Busch, *Missouri Democrat Articles*, 342; National Archives, Record Group M322 (roll no. 57), Confederate Compiled Service Records, 10th Missouri Cavalry, passim.

creek!" ordered the Federal. When I heard the order I picked my horse up on my spurs,

Gave Him a Shake,

and with a bound he strikes the mud and water in the bed of the creek in the midst of my friends just as the rifles ring out on top of the bank. One horse and rider go down under volley, the rest of us scramble up the bank and scatter in the narrow timber bottom. Coming to the edge of the timber, I see a level prairie valley, perhaps half or three-quarters of a mile wide. Deep foothills, or rather prairie edges, rise abruptly along the southern edge of this valley. On this valley to the east Confederates on foot and mounted are fleeing to the southward, and coming out from the timber are companies, platoons and squads of Federals flushed and belated with victory, galloping and picking up prisoners. To the west and south stragglers are more leisurely.

On the north side of the creek the rattle of small arms is yet going on, but the boom of cannon has ceased. Galloping across this valley I come upon a squad of Federals who are calling in and running down the fugitives. For a while they are undecided as to my identity, but when near them the wind caught my bluecoat, two buttons being loosed crossing the creek, and whirled the tail around so my gray blouse could be seen. They took a shot a piece at me, but did no harm other than to cut another hole in my blue coat. When near the foot of the ridge mentioned above I overtake a man with an Enfield rifle. He gives me some cartridges. Dismounting I opened fire on the squad who took such a delight in shooting at me. The man with the Enfield comes up—he is panting and exhausted from his long race—squatting in the grass he levels his gun, resting his arm on his knee. Finally he lowers the gun as he says "It's not a ——— bit of use to shoot, for I could not hit the side of the barn at thirty steps." And he laid down in the grass with his hands pressed tight against his sides, but in a minute he is on his feet. "Here, Jim; this way, old pard," he calls up to a man galloping by. In a minute more and he is mounted behind his pard, and is moving fast

Out of Danger.

Now, I see a battle flag hoisted on the side of the ridge just west of me. Perhaps it is Gen. Price's escort flag, who knows? However, it is a rallying point, and every trooper who is yet willing to fight turns his face to the enemy under its fluttering folds. Someone yells for the Third (Greene's) Regiment.[149] Than another

---

149. The last company of the 3rd Missouri Cavalry (CSA) was organized on November 4, 1862, and Colton Greene was appointed colonel of the unit on the same day. The 3rd served exclusively in the Trans-Mississippi, participating in both of Marmaduke's Missouri Raids in 1863, the Battle of Helena (July 4, 1863), Pine Bluff (October 25, 1863), to name but a few, as well as the Camden Expedition and Price's 1864 Missouri Raid. Colton Greene has been previously covered (See note no. 2 this chapter). *O.R.S.*, pt. 2, vol. 50:171–178; Allardice, *Confederate Colonels*, 175; Moore, *Confederate Military History*, Extended, 303.

whoops for the Eighth (Burbridge's [Jeffers']) Regiment.[150] Thinking that the old Tenth (Lawther's) ought to be represented, I open up in her behalf.[151] When my

---

150. Burbridge's Regiment was the 4th Missouri Cavalry (CSA), not the 8th. It was organized on November 14, 1862, at Yellville, Arkansas, though it didn't add its last company until January 1863. The regiment fought at Clark's Mill (November 7, 1862) and Beaver Creek (November 24, 1862), both in Missouri, as their first two engagements. They were also in both of Marmaduke's Missouri Raids in 1863, the 1863 Campaign for Little Rock and the Battle of Pine Bluff. In 1864, the regiment was in the Camden Expedition and participated in Price's 1864 Missouri Raid. *O.R.*, vol. 22, pt. 1:199, 288, 527, 731; *O.R.*, vol. 34, pt. 1:785; *O.R.*, vol. 41, pt. 1:678; *O.R.S.*, pt. 1, vol. 4:24; *O.R.S.*, pt. 2, vol. 38:200; Carolyn Bartels, "Yankee In Rebeldom," in *Civil War Stories of Missouri* (Shawnee Mission, KS, 1995), 244, hereafter cited as Bartels, *Civil War Stories of Missouri*; John Q. Burbridge Letters (November 10, 1862), Peter W. Alexander Collection, Columbia University.

John Q. Burbridge was born on May 21, 1830, in Pike County, Missouri. At the beginning of the Civil War, he lived in Louisiana, Missouri, as a banker, and was elected a captain in 1st Infantry Regiment, 3rd Division, MSG, and then colonel of his regiment on July 3, 1861. During the course of the war, he led troops in the MSG and commanded regular Confederate troops, serving mostly in the Trans-Mississippi. He was captured at Brownsville, Arkansas, during the Little Rock Campaign of 1863 and was later exchanged. After the war he ended up in Jacksonville, Florida, where he was elected mayor in 1887. He died on November 14, 1892, in Tucson, Arizona. Allardice, *Confederate Colonels*, 82; Banasik, *Serving With Honor*, 378–380; Eakin, *Confederate Records*, 2:186; Peterson, et al., 113, 115.

151. With the collapse of the Confederate line on Mine Creek, it was every man for himself. All were desperate to cross the creek to the safety on the south side and every effort to organize a defense proved futile. North of Mine Creek, elements of Benteen's and Philips's commands, with brigade staffs, rounded up prisoners and secured the area, while John Sanborn's 4th Brigade and John McNeil's 2nd Brigade were sent across Mine Creek to join the reforming commands of Philips and Benteen in their pursuit of the fleeing rebels. The time was about noon. A half mile south of Mine Creek, the Confederates began to form, first in squads, then in larger commands. They held briefly against continued Federal assaults and then fell back yet again, pursued relentlessly by the Yankees. Still farther back, Colonel John C. Wright managed to establish yet another line, by reining in a flag bearer. The new line was well to the rear of Mine Creek, perhaps but a few miles from the Little Osage and several hundred yards long. Wright initially stunned the following bluecoats, then fell back in good order until he was met by Shelby, who had galloped in from the front of the train. Previously, Shelby had crossed the Little Osage about noon, when word reached General Price of the desperate condition of affairs to his rear. Price left the convenience of his ambulance for his "white horse," named "Bucephalus," and ordered Shelby to send the Iron Brigade back to Mine Creek to support the other two divisions. Shelby galloped to the rear with his veteran brigade following and linked up with the remnants of the rout, about a mile north of the Little Osage at about 2:00 p.m. To support his shaky line, Shelby deployed Collins's Battery. Then "meeting the men who were running…[he] rallied them to go back and fight and he seemed to infuse new life into every man he met." Farther to Shelby's left Thompson arrived with his brigade, deployed and waited for the enemy, who were visible to the northwest, but were hesitant to come forward. Farther to Thompson's right, and unseen by Thompson, General Sanborn's Brigade had taken the lead of the Union advance, moving at a walk toward Shelby's shaky, but reformed line. If the army was to be saved, then Shelby would have to hold the Federals at bay until dark; a tall order given the state of the fleeing army. *O.R.*, vol. 41, pt. 1:391–392, 637,659–660, 668, 691; Ballard Diary, October 25, 1864; Buresh, 131, 138,140, 142, 148, 162–163; Castel, *Sterling Price*, 239–240; Crawford, *Kansas In the Sixties*, 180; Edwards, *Shelby and His Men*, 442, 450; Lause, *Collapse of Price's Raid*, 164–165; Norton & Massey, 68; Sanborn "Campaign in Missouri," 185–196; Scott, *Fourth Iowa*, 336–337; Sinisi, 294, 296; Stanton, et al., 253–254; Wright Memoirs, unnumbered page 98.

cartridges are all gone and I am about to mount my horse, someone says: "Young man, what command do you belong too?"

Looking over my shoulder I see Gen. Price. He is on horseback and unattended. He has, apparently, just come from beyond the ridge south. I saluted him and told him my command.

"And where is it now?" he asked.

"Back there, with the exception of what you see on the valley and with the colors," I answered, with my gun so as to indicate the battlefield, the valley, and the rallying point.

"And where is Gen. Marmaduke?" he again asked.

"I saw him last near Maj. Pratt's battery, which now is in the hands of the enemy; he is probably a prisoner."

He mused a moment, and then said, as if he was speaking to himself: "A bad state of affairs, a very bad, a very annoying mishap. But," he said in a louder key, after he had swept the whole scene with his glass, "but we will soon set things to right again." Then he closed his glass and returned it to its case, turned his horse and galloped over to the colors.

Soon after this the enemy becomes aggressive, and the little band of braves who have rallied to the colors and are yet willing to fight, is forced back inch by inch. The enemy is reaching out to crush the last obstacle that stands between him and his prey. Now it seems that resistance is all in vain. That we are about to be swallowed up in a whirlwind of fire and strife. Stout hearts are growing weak, brave men who were never known to flinch, are

Beginning to Waiver.

Has the God of War set his seal upon us and are we to be sacrificed to appease his wrath? No; I look, oh, what! Ye gallant troopers! See what the genius of Sterling Price has done. There is a cheering sight burst upon our vision. Solid battle lines loom up in our rear. At first we think it is Shelby's Brigade come to our relief, who previously had marched in the direction of Fort Scott. But no; it is not Shelby, for when we approach them they melt away and again show up on the crest of the next ridge, like the mirage on the brain. It is our unarmed recruits that Price and has formed on the prairie ridges.[152] But they have the desired effect,

---

152. From roughly 2:00 p.m. to 3:00 p.m., Shelby continued to resist the Federals, led by John Sanborn's Brigade. Back to the Little Osage, then across the river Shelby went, forcing the Unionists to deploy each time he confronted them. As Shelby pulled back from north of the Little Osage, he sent word to Thompson to redeploy south of the river. Shelby's third line, included Dobbin's reformed brigade, which deployed on Thompson's right. For another hour Shelby held on by feigning attacks, then falling back, while Sanborn's men pushed four miles beyond the Osage, where "they were unable to proceed any farther," the men and horses totally exhausted. John McNeil's 2nd Brigade then took over the pursuit, about five miles from the Marmiton River, continuing to press the attack. Time and time again, Shelby reformed his line, only to fall back ever closer to the rear of the Army of Missouri, which was crossing the Marmiton at the Douglas Ford. The Marmiton was about 11 miles from the Little Osage, and though a shallow river, the

for the enemy becomes cautious. Supposing them to be reinforcements he loses much time in preparing for another onslaught, thereby giving us time to place distance between us and them.[153] On Crooked River half of the train is corralled and burned. The march, however, is kept up and we lose a great many recruits during the night, who being unused to such overexertion stray from the ranks and are left behind.[154]

steep banks slowed the train crossing. It was about 3:00 p.m. when Shelby established his final line two miles in front of the Marmiton and "for the first time," according to Kyle Sinisi, "most of the retreating mob had been stopped and formed into line," setting the stage for the Battle of Charlot Farm. *O.R.*, vol. 41, pt. 1: 372–373,392, 637, 660, 668, 691, 697; Ballard Diary, October 25, 1864; Pitcock & Gurley, 237; Charles W. Porter, *In the Devil's Dominion: A Union Soldier's Adventures in "Bushwhacker Country,"* (Nevada, MO, 1998), 173, hereafter cited as Porter, *In the Devil's Dominion*; Sanborn, "Campaign in Missouri," 106–197; Sellmeyer, 255; Sinisi, 295–297, 299–300; Stanton, et al., 254–256.

153. The line that Shelby established at the Marmiton had the Iron Brigade on the left, with the remnants of Fagan's Division to Thompson's right, and then 500 men of Clark's Division, with 400 men from Clark's Brigade commanded by Colton Greene. To Shelby's rear Jackman supported Thompson, while Charles Tyler's Brigade was to Jackman's right. Following on Shelby's heals, John McNeil halted his command about 800 yards from the rebel line; the time was about 3:30 p.m. McNeil dismounted his troopers and began long range fire that lasted about 20 minutes. To buy time for his army to reform, General Price ordered Charles Tyler's Brigade to support the final line "by an ostentatious display." Moving to the right of the line Tyler dashed forward, his command "yelling like devils," threatening McNeil's left flank. Of this charge a veteran of Tyler's Brigade recorded: "The command was placed in motion, and after a short march all the men who did not have anything to shoot with were separated and sent forward, while those with variegated arms were drawn up in line with their backs to the Federals, counted off, and given the command 'Fours right about, charge!' and away we went...the boys shooting the best they could with the arms they had....We were engaged probably five or ten minutes, certainly not more than fifteen....The effect of the charge...was to hold the Federal command until the trained men could reorganize in the rear." And according to John Wilson, of Thomas McCray's Brigade, "it had its effect." To the rear of Tyler's charge, Price placed the unorganized, unarmed recruits, giving the impression of an even larger force. Shortly after Tyler's charge, Colonel Benteen arrived with his 4th Brigade, deployed to McNeil's right, and made a charge; however the charge began half a mile from the rebel line, and the horses could barely move at a walk, much less a gallop. The attack faltered, though it did unnerve the far left of Shelby's line. With the sun getting low in the sky, Jackman's Brigade raced through Thompson's line, "shattering" Benteen's front line with the force of a "thunderbolt," thus ending any further Union threat for October 25. *O.R.*, vol. 41, pt. 1:332–333, 373, 660, 668, 676–677, 685 691,700–701; Buresh, 175–178; Campbell Memoir; Edwards, *Shelby and His Men*, 452–454; Halliburton, 264; Hinton, 234–235; Scott, *Fourth Iowa*, 339–341; Sellmeyer, 255–256; Sinisi, 300–302; Stanton, et al., 256–257; Stalnaker, 102; Wilson Memoirs, 15.

154. Following the Battle of the Marmiton or Charlot Farm, the Confederate Army continued its march, on October 25. Thompson's Brigade was the last command to cross the Marmiton at midnight, after which they stopped briefly to feed and rest with the rest of the army, before continuing southward. "So ended October 25—the Union troops near collapse, the Confederates also completely worn out and thoroughly demoralized." During the night of October 25, Price issued orders for the destruction of all excess wagons, including civilian vehicles. About one third of the train was destroyed which still left 300 wagons (Sinisi has only 50 wagons remaining), by the time the army had moved at 2:00 a.m. A "light sprinkle of rain" greeted the Army of Missouri, according to R. L. Brown of Marmaduke's escort, "and in the distance behind us we could see a magazine explode with a loud noise, like distant thunder. Slowly and silently we wended our way

October 27 [26] dawns on our half famished army moving in a "trot march." Four columns of cavalry, four men deep, are moving southward, with guards between each column to keep the men from straggling. Now the Tenth Regiment, which yesterday with over a thousand strong, is today less than 300. Only a handful of G Company is in the ranks.[155] About noon a slight halt is caused by a jam in the column. I dismount and find I can hardly stand upon my feet, so numb have my legs become from my long continuance in the saddle. But I am not alone in my fatigued and benumbed condition, for I see many others catching hold of their saddles to keep from falling. Poor horses! They are in as sad a plight as the riders, for they are so tired and jaded they drew their head in the grass without attempting to graze. We pass to the left of Lamar (east), in sight of the town, and camp on the Spring River,

Near Carthage.

As we strip the saddles from our horses the hair in many instances sticks to the blankets.[156] How the poor things droop their heads, sniff with their noses to

---

over hills and vales in the direction of Arkansas." And for the first time "desertions commenced" in Shelby's Division, the command that had saved Price's army. *O.R.*, vol. 41, pt. 4:1023–1014; Baker Diary, October 25, 1864; Ballard Diary, October 25, 1864; Brown Journal, October 25, 1864; Buresh, 179, 182; Campbell Memoir; Confederate Correspondence (MS 03–026, box no. 1, file no. 4), Board of Survey at Clarksville, TX (November 29, 1864), General J. O. Shelby Testimony; Monnett, 133; Pitcock & Gurley, 237; Porter, *In the Devil's Dominion, 172*; Sinisi, 306–305; Shalhope, 273.

155. The Battle of Mine Creek lasted a mere 30 minutes by most accounts and produced the greatest losses suffered by the Army of Missouri for the entire expedition. In all, by the end of October 25, Price's army had lost an estimated 124 killed, 237 wounded, with 554 soldiers taken prisoner, not including those POWs executed by the Federals for wearing a blue or partial blue uniform. In contrast the Federals lost about 150 officers and men. See Appendix H for details on the Confederate losses, including executed POW's. Crawford, *Kansas in the Sixties*, 161; Hinton, 213; McNeil Court-Martial, Nelson Cole Testimony, 50.

156. Even as the Confederates broke contact with the Federals on October 25, the latter for the most part had given up the chase. The only commands remaining in close proximity to Price's army on the evening of the 25th were Benteen's and McNeil's Brigades. The remainder of the Northern army, including Blunt's 1st Division, rode off to Fort Scott, there to feed, rest, and proclaim the glory they had richly won at Mine Creek. Though tired and near collapse, the Union Army gave up its last chance to bag Price's entire command, and instead Generals Curtis and Pleasonton spent their time at Fort Scott "disputing who had the right to the prisoner Marmaduke." In the end Pleasonton was given the honor and departed the fort on the morning of the 28th (Porter says it was the 26th), with his prisoner, using the 1st MSM Cavalry as an escort. The remainder of the Army of the Border lingered about Fort Scott until noon, removing all unserviceable men and horses, before heading after Price. Blunt's 1st Division led the way. The Confederates for their part made good their retreat, despite still having 300 wagons in tow. Departing camp at 2:00 a.m., Fagan's Division led, followed by Marmaduke's command, now led by John B. Clark, with Shelby's Division guarding the rear. To Shelby's immediate rear, S. D. Jackman held the rear guard for the day, burning the selected wagons before his brigade followed in the rear of the rebel column. The train followed behind Fagan's Division, crossing Drywood Creek at the Adamson's Ford, which was six miles south of the Marmiton River. During the dark night, the army got briefly disoriented, which cost them a few hours as they sorted the situation out before resuming their march toward

the dust, lie down too tired to roll and only stretch their tired legs and groan. And there is no forage for the poor things. How I pity them. In forty-eight hours we have marched from near Paola, Kan. to Carthage, Mo., a distance of 100 miles as the crow flies, and, as I reckon, the distance covered by our march 125 miles. Then take the battle, together with the maneuvering and countermarching pertaining thereto and one can easily see that the score will be hard to beat. Neither will it be hard for one to believe me when I tell them that, when we received less and a fourth ration, we were too tired to cook and eat it, but tumbled down on our blankets and went to sleep, notwithstanding we had been forty-eight hours almost without food.[157] Here young [J. M.] Bolton of Co. H is buried.[158] He died from a wound received in the battle of the 26th [25th]. What an example of courage and fortitude he has shown to his comrades! The ball ranging through his bowls and passing out of his back, caused him the most excruciating pain; but he sat his horse and kept in the ranks until only a few minutes before his death; and, as for me, my teeth are chattering. I am booked for another of those beastly chills. The camp fire has burned out. What a night I shall have of it!

Henry C. Luttrell,
Tenth Missouri Cavalry

* * * * * * *

Carthage. Marching through the night, with but one short halt for an hour's rest, the Army of Missouri pulled into the outskirts of Carthage at 9:00 a.m. and collapsed after a 62 mile march from their previous battlefield at the Charlot Prairie. The march had been exhausting, "A fatal day to horse flesh," recorded J. H. P. Baker, who also added, "I don't know that a longer march graces modern history." The arrival at Carthage also brought about the parole and release of about 300 Federal prisoners, who still remained with the rebel army. *O.R.*, vol. 41, pt. 1:661, 677; *O.R.*, vol. 41, pt. 4:1013; Baker Diary, October 26, 1864; Blunt, "Civil War Experiences," 261–262; Buresh, 184, 187; Edwards, *Shelby and His Men*, 455; Hinton, 236–238; Lause, *Collapse of Price's Raid*, 172; H. J. McBrayer, "Hurried Price Most Briskly," *National Tribune*, August 25, 1904; Pitcock & Gurley, 238; Porter, *In the Devil's Dominion*, 173; Sanborn, "Campaign in Missouri," 198; Sinisi, 305, 307–308; Williams, *Second Colorados*, 119; Wright Memoirs, unnumbered page 99.

157. When the Army of Missouri arrived at Carthage, "or where it once was, for it had been destroyed by the Yankees," Shelby's Division received a meager ration of some flour and beef, with corn for their horses. In Fagan's command they received a ration of "poor beef without salt or bread," while their horses had nothing, except some occasional dry grass that they found on the march. In Clark's Division, it appears that they received about the same as the other commands when they arrived at Carthage. Brown Journal, October 27, 1864; Cruzen, 34; Pitcock & Gurley, 238; Wright Memoirs, unnumbered page 99.

158. According to Confederate records, there were seven Boltons, who served in Company H, 10th Missouri Cavalry (CSA)—Dixon, F. B., James, Joel, John, Merewether and Thomas. Of the seven F. B., John, and Thomas were captured during the expedition, while Dixon, James, and Joel survived the expedition, eventually surrendering at Shreveport on June 7, 1865. That left only Merewether L. Bolton as the one who died as Luttrell described. Merewether originally joined the Confederate Service on June 25, 1862, in Abbeyville, Mississippi; and later became a member of the 11th Missouri Cavalry Battalion (CSA), which subsequently became Company G, 10th Missouri Cavalry. National Archives, Record Group M322 (roll no. 56), Confederate Compiled Service records, 10th Missouri Cavalry.

Item: The continuation of a Missouri trooper's account of Price's 1864 Missouri Raid, from Carthage, Missouri to the end of the war, by Henry C. Luttrell, Company G, 10th Missouri Cavalry (C.S.A.). Part Five.
Published: March 20, 1886.

Price's Great Raid.

Incidents from a Confederate trooper from a diary written on the march: Fourth paper; From Carthage to the surrender.

October 28 [27], 1864.—A burning fire is consuming me as I take my place in the column. But I manage to get through the day's journey somehow. We camp this night on the Granby lead mines. Here during the night, poor Simp Oliphant of Co. G dies from fatigue and exposure. He was a brave, good man, and served his country well.[159]

October 29 [28], just south of Newtonia, a few minutes' halt is made in a cornfield. I dismount, shell an ear of corn in my frying pan, set a shock of corn on the fire and cook it by parching, shaking the pan in the flames; think it is the best parched corn I ever ate. We go into camp some eight miles south of town, on a small creek; we draw quarter rations. The sun is fast sinking in the West. The mess fires are hung with scant rations. The men's mouths are watering with anticipation of the few morsels they are about to receive.[160] Suddenly the boom of cannon and

---

159. The Confederate Army broke camp and staggered into line between 9:00 and 11:00 a.m., on October 27, and marched at a "leisurely pace," making between 16 to 22 miles, depending on the command, before camping just north of Granby near the lead mines, and on the south side of Shoal Creek. On the 27th, like the previous day, Shelby's Division brought up the rear. And with no contact from the Federal Army, the morale of the troops began to improve; however, there were also "many desertions among the Arkansas troops." Back at Fort Scott, Sam Curtis's command, led by Blunt's Division, departed the area about noon on October 26, (Sinisi says it was before daylight, which is not correct), making 23 miles before linking up with John McNeil's Brigade, near Shanghai, in Barton County, Missouri, at 11:00 p.m. (Sinisi says it was 9:00 p.m., while McNeil states that it was 11:00 p.m.) McNeil had spent the previous night on the Marmiton battlefield, departing at 10:00 a.m. in pursuit of the rebel army. Back at Fort Scott, John Sanborn's Brigade rested during the 26th, before taking up the march on the 27th, at 5:00 a.m., followed by Benteen's command. By the end of the 27th Sanborn and Benteen had made about 62 miles, camping on the Spring River near Carthage at 11:00 p.m. Meanwhile, Curtis's command, including McNeil, moved on to Carthage, where they arrived at 3:00 a.m. on October 28, and camped about five miles south of town. As the 28th dawned Curtis was about 10 miles from Sanborn's two brigades, and about an equal distance from the rebel army (Sinisi has them 28 miles from Price, while Burke says it was 12 miles). *O.R.*, vol. 41, pt. 1:373–374, 392, 405, 408, 587, 637, 647, 669; Blunt, "Civil War Experiences," 262; Bray Diary, October 27, 1864, 13; Brown Journal, October 27, 1864; Burke, 397; McGhee, *Campaigning With Marmaduke*, 27; Pitcock & Gurley, 238; Porter, *In the Devil's Dominion*, 174; Sanborn, "Campaigning In Missouri," 199; Sinisi, 309–311; Larry Wood, *The Two Civil War Battles of Newtonia* (Charleston, SC, 2010), 115–116, hereafter cited as Wood, *Newtonia*; Wright Memoirs, unnumbered page 99.

James S. or "Simp" Oliphant joined what became Company G, 10th Missouri Cavalry (CSA) on November 10, 1862, in Jackson County Missouri. National Archives, Record Group M322 (roll no. 57), Confederate Compiled Service Records, 10th Missouri Cavalry.

160. The Army of Missouri was slated to march at sunrise, with Shelby's Division leading; however,

Battle of Newtonia
(October 28, 1864)

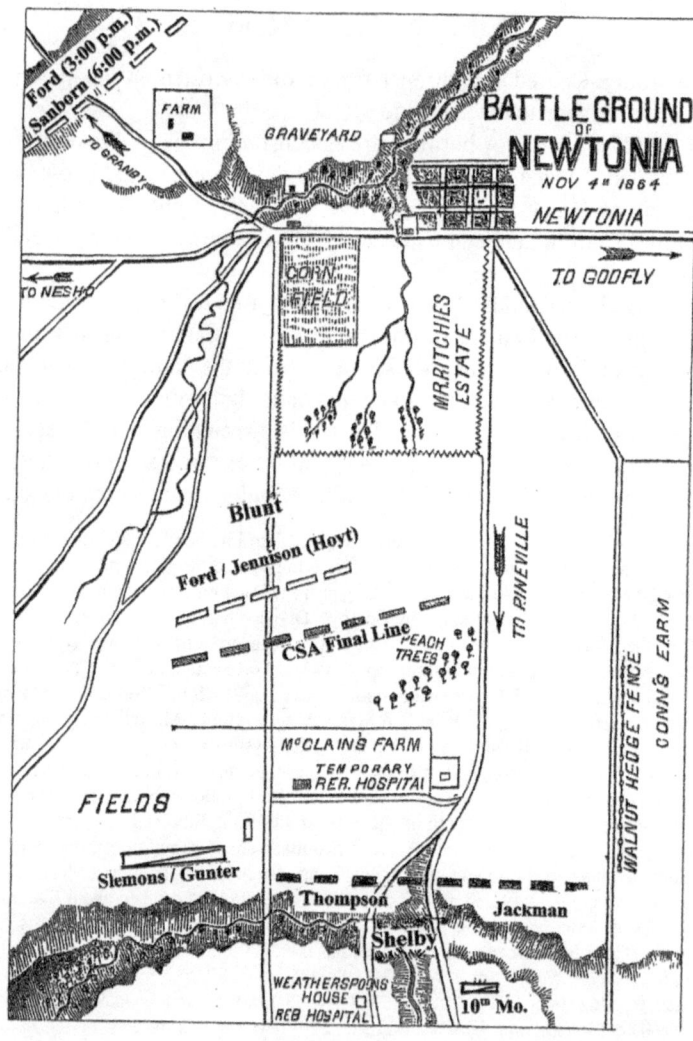

the rattle of musketry bring every man to his feet. Shells are dropping about the campfire. "Boots and saddles," ring out from the bugles' brazen throats.[161] In five minutes we are galloping to the scene of action.

Reaching the prairie we find Shelby's brigade hotly engaged.[162] We deploy by companies to the left in line at a trot march. Reaching the crest of a prairie ridge we find the enemy behind a stone fence to the north.[163] Shelby's battery is playing

---

the troops "were so scattered from getting in after dark," the men "were much longer in forming than usual." Behind Shelby came the train, then Clark's Division, with Fagan bringing up the rear. Marching at a "leisurely" pace, for the second day, and believing they were free of Union pursuit, Shelby's Division reined in three miles south of Newtonia, camping in the timber, while Clark's command, with the train, moved on by. The bulk of his division camped about three miles past Shelby. Fagan's Division also passed by Shelby, except for the rear guard, Cabell's Brigade, under Thomas Gunter. In the town of Newtonia, John C. Wright halted his regiment, per orders, to operate the local grist mill and feed his horses in a nearby cornfield. Wright was also informed at the same time, by Fagan, that Gunter's command was being "threatened" by the enemy. The time was about 1:00 p.m. and all would be quiet for yet another hour. The area was picketed and the troops took their time to make fires, and cook their "scanty rations of meat...and felt that for the first time [that they] were rid of the enemy." *O.R.*, vol. 41, pt. 1:669; *O.R.S.*, pt. 1, vol. 1:410; Ballard diary, October 28, 1864; Brown Journal, October 28; Campbell Memoir; McGhee, *Campaigning With Marmaduke*, 27; Pitcock & Gurley, 238; Stanton, et al., 259; Hemp B. Watts, "Shelby at Newtonia," Shelby Scrapbook, hereafter cited as Watts, "Shelby At Newtonia;" Wright Memoirs, unnumbered pages 99–100.

161. It was about 3:00 p.m. when the quiet of the rebel camp was shattered by artillery shells, prompting an immediate retreat of the army's trains, escorted by the bulk of Clark's and Fagan's Divisions. Previously, Blunt's Division had departed its camp, south of Carthage at daylight, with the advance making contact with Gunter's rebels about 10:00 a.m. at Diamond Prairie near Shoal Creek and 5 miles from Granby. Alerted to the close proximity of the rebel army, as he approached Granby at noon, Blunt pushed on, with Ford's 4th Brigade leading, followed by Jennison's 1st Brigade, commanded by Lieutenant Colonel George Hoyt. To the rear of Blunt's advanced units the other brigades were resting, which left Blunt with a meager force of about 1,000 men to confront the entire Confederate Army. Ford's Brigade arrived first between 2:00–3:00 p.m. Quickly deploying his artillery, Ford opened fire about 3:00 p.m., making his presence known to the startled rebels. *O.R.*, vol. 41, pt. 1:577, 587, 609; Blunt, "Civil War Experiences," 262; Campbell Memoir; Hinton, 263–264; Lause, *Collapse of Price's Raid*, 175; Porter, *In the Devil's Dominion*, 175; Sinisi, 313–314; Volunteer, "Interesting Particulars of the Late Campaign Against Price," *Daily Conservative*, November 5, 1864; Wood, *Newtonia*, 116, 120.

162. Of all the units in Clark's Division, only the 10th Missouri Cavalry was deployed and took part in the engagement, suffering one man wounded. The remainder of the division mounted up and headed farther south with the train, which hurriedly broke camp and marched five or six miles, when they again camped, "for the remainder of the night." *O.R.*, vol. 41, pt. 1:647, 692, 694, 697, 699; Ballard Diary, October 28, 1864; Campbell Memoir; McGhee, *Campaigning With Marmaduke*, 27.

163. When word of the approaching Federals reached General Shelby, he ordered his division to assemble, which was largely ignored as the troops could not believe that the Federals were close at hand, However, within a short time, the booming of the cannon announced the arrival of the enemy. Bugles called assembly, and one soldier recalled "Should I live a century never can I forget the blanched face of the poor, tired, ragged men around me; they were pictures of despair." To these seemingly despondent men General Shelby rode up, delivered a stirring speech, and moved on to the next unit. The men's spirits revived, and they moved into line, leaving their horses to the rear. Collins's Battery, including the captured 24-lb howitzer, took the center, supported by Jackman's Brigade. Thompson's Brigade was to its left. To the front of the army Slemons's and

with the same unerring precision as of yore, causing confusion and spoiling enemy's aim. A general advance is ordered. The enemy retires as we advance and we push them back near to Newtonia; they sending back a few scattered shots at us through the gathering darkness.[164] After the enemy has become reconciled to their retrograde movement we fall back and pass through our old camp. But our suppers which we left about the camp have disappeared and we sleep on empty stomachs this night.[165]

>   Cabell's Brigades were deployed closer to Newtonia, with Wright's Arkansas Regiment located to the southwest of town in a cornfield. With the appearance of the Unionists, the rebel rear guard beat a hasty retreat, save for Wright's Regiment, which charged the oncoming Federals, halting their initial advance. Wright then withdrew back toward Shelby's Division, which was fast forming on the prairie, just in front of its timbered camp site. *O.R.*, vol. 41, pt. 1:669, 677; Cruzen, 34; Edwards, *Shelby and His Men*, 454; Sinisi, 314–318; Watts, "Shelby at Newtonia;" Wright Memoirs, unnumbered page 100.
> 164. Blunt's 4th Brigade, under Colonel James Ford was the first command on the field, his advanced company of the 16th Kansas Cavalry moving rapidly toward Newtonia. Upon encountering Wright's pickets, Ford's advance pulled back to await the arrival of the rest of the brigade, as Wright also moved back to the still-forming rebel line. With all in readiness, Shelby's Division rushed forward to a fence that lay a half mile in front of their timbered camp, coming up on Wright's right flank. Meanwhile, Ford's Brigade deployed in two lines to the northwest of Newtonia, about three miles from Shelby's position; they then moved forward at the gallop, led by General Blunt. Both commands came to rest opposite each other, about 500 yards apart—Shelby's boys occupying a southern fence line of the Thomas McClain Farm, while Ford's troopers held the northern fence. Both sides were supported by artillery. Jennison's 1st Brigade arrived to buttress the Union front, but Shelby was able to extend his line beyond the Federal flanks. Within a short time, his flanks in peril of being turned, Blunt ordered a retreat, which encouraged the rebels to charge. "Soon we were ordered forward," recalled George Cruzen. "I blew the charge," and with a "rebel yell" Shelby's Division and its supports, assaulted the Federal line. Back went Blunt troopers, slowly at first and then more rapidly as their ammunition ran out. The Union artillery was also threatened and barely escaped capture, as the 10th Missouri (CSA) entered the fray. But by 6:00 p.m. General Sanborn's brigade arrived, following a 36-hour, 104-mile march. Sanborn deployed to Blunt's left, saving the Federal army, and, in the words of Colonel John Phelps "turned a defeat into a victory." Shelby's troops fired three volleys at Sanborn's troops and then pulled back, having given sufficient time for the remainder of the Confederates to withdraw from the area. For the men in Shelby's Division, Newtonia marked "the scene of its last glorious victory." *O.R.*, vol. 41, pt. 1:405, 638; Bray Diary, October 28, 1864, 13; Cruzen, 34; Edwards, *Shelby and His Men*, 458; Sinisi, 317–321; Wood, *Newtonia*, 124, 129–130; Wright Memoirs, unnumbered page 100.
> 165. Having successfully blunted the Union pursuit on October 28, the Confederate Army gained a much needed victory, despite the spin later placed on the battle by various Union soldiers and generals. The three hour clash at Newtonia cost the Federal command 18 killed, 95 wounded, and one missing, total 114. Confederate losses appear to have been about the same, with Price's medical director reporting just "24 or 25 wounded men and officers." The dead and slightly wounded would have boosted the total to about 100 or more. Kyle Sinisi speculates that the Confederates losses were possibly "lower than the Union numbers." Richard Hinton put the rebel loss at 275 wounded, 35 seriously, while Charles Porter, of the 3rd Wisconsin, in his diary, claimed the rebels lost 175 wounded, with 35 seriously wounded. Blunt for his part initially recorded the rebel "loss at over 200," citing a captured rebel surgeon; however, in his reminiscences he raised that number to over 800. Author Michael Forsyth puts the rebel losses at between 100–125, while Deryl Sellmeyer definitively places the Confederate losses at 20 killed and 50 wounded, citing the Kansas City *Daily Journal of Commerce*. The *Leavenworth Daily Conservative*, as late as November 5, also put the rebel losses at 20 dead with 50 wounded, supporting what the *Daily Journal of*

October 30 [29]—The army camps on the Cowskin River tonight. The old Tenth Regiment does picket duty. Nothing to eat. Night's very cold. I shake with a chill while on vidette picket.[166]

November 3 [1]—We reach Cane Hill by easy marches. Company at Maysville, and Illinois bayou fifteen miles west of Fayetteville on the state line road. Snow is falling to-day. Our stock is in a deplorable condition, poor and emaciated from overwork and starvation. We draw forage for the first time since leaving Cowskin River. We also draw about

Four Ounces of Meal

to the man, not sifted and no salt. We have an abundance of fruit, apples.[167] The boom of the cannons creates some stir. Rumor says Joe Shelby is having a brush

---

Commerce reported. *O.R.S.*, pt. 2, vol. 3:424; Blunt, "Civil War Experiences," 263; Busch, *Missouri Democrat Articles*, 352; Crawford, *Kansas In the Sixties*, 176; Crowley, 144; Forsyth, *Great Missouri Raid*, 220; "From Arkansas," *Daily Conservative*, November 20, 1864; Hinton, 272; O'Flaherty, 125; Pitcock & Gurley, 239; Porter, *In the Devil's Dominion*, 175; Sellmeyer, 260, 351 n. 9; Sinisi, 322; Volunteer, "Interesting Particulars of the Late Campaign against Price," *Daily Conservative*, November 5, 1864; Wood, *Newtonia*, 130–131.

166. From October 29–31, the Confederate Army continued its retreat, beginning the march at first light of each day. On the 29th they made 26 miles, camping five miles south of Pineville, Missouri, on Sugar Creek. The 12th Missouri (CSA) was left back at Newtonia to guard the rebel rear. They departed the area at 8:00 a.m. when the Federals failed to advance. As it happened, during the night of October 28, General Curtis had received orders from General Rosecrans, directing Pleasonton's remaining brigades back to their respective Missouri Districts. With only about 1,000 effectives remaining, Curtis abandoned the pursuit and moved his command back to Neosho, where it rested pending new orders. October 30 found the Army of Missouri camped about Maysville, Arkansas. That day marked the beginning of the disbanding of the army, as Freeman's Brigade, with several regiments from Shelby's Division, was detached from the army. Freeman was directed to northeast Arkansas, on furlough until December 15, while Coleman's, Hunter's, Nichol's, Schnable's and Slayback's commands were furloughed to visit friends and family, as well as recruit their commands in northern Arkansas. The following day, the march continued down the line road that bordered Arkansas and the Indian Territory. One Confederate from Jackson County, Missouri, noted that "the houses were mostly burned and farms destroyed. The whole country was deserted or nearly so...and everything going to decay." By the end of October 31, the remaining part of Price's Army made it to the Illinois River, in Benton County, Arkansas, 26 miles from their previous camp. Forage was either "scarce" or unavailable, although some of the animals were allowed limited grazing on prairie grass. Rations were scanty at best. The troops were lucky to receive a piece of bread or an ear of parched corn, though beef, without salt for flavoring, seemed to be plentiful. "The men in some instances hungered for food but never approached starvation," according to General Price. But for Hemp Watts of Williams's Regiment, "the retreat southward from Newtonia was a famine." Note: Though furloughed on October 30, Freeman's command did not depart the army until November 2. *O.R.*, vol. 41, pt. 1:638, 647, 661, 677, 705; *O.R.*, vol. 41, pt. 4:318, 330–331, 1020; *O.R.S.*, pt. 1, vol. 7:410–411; Baker Diary, October 28–29, 1864; Blunt, "Civil War Experiences," 263; Britton, *Civil War on the Border, 1863–65*, 511; Brown Journal, October 30–31, 1864; Crawford, *Kansas In the Sixties*, 176–177; Lause, *Collapse of Price's Raid*, 183; McGhee, *Campaigning With Marmaduke*, 28; Pitcock & Gurley, 239; Sanborn, "Campaign in Missouri," 200; Sellmeyer, 263; Sinisi, 323–324; Watts, "Shelby At Newtonia;" Wood, *Newtonia*, 133–134; Wright Memoirs, unnumbered page 102.

167. The weather changed on November 1, as the clouds thickened and the rain began well before

Price's Raid: From Maysville to Layneport
(October 30–December 2, 1864)

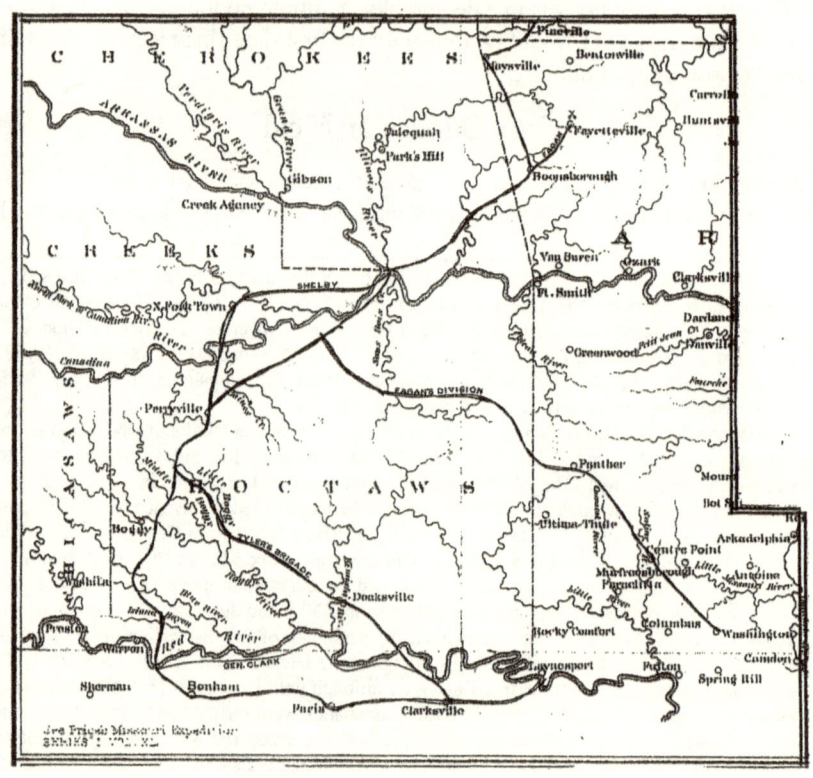

with the Yankees at Fayetteville.¹⁶⁸ We have been expecting to be ordered to his assistance for the last five hours, but things are getting quiet since the cannonading has ceased. Dark, and the snow is yet falling. The camp-fires burn brightly and the men clustering about them in very loving attitude, showing that they appreciate their warmth. The melting snow and the tramping feet about the camp fires has caused quite a stop. We are wet to the skin by the falling snow. The wind is coming from the north with a whoop. No tents and but few blankets, and worst of all, another horrible chill is coming on. So good-bye, old diary, for I don't know when I will need you again.¹⁶⁹

daylight and continued throughout the day, before turning to snow. The rough roads and mountainous terrain further troubled the march, which was all part of "the beauty of army life," according to a sarcastic Dr. William McPheeters. Following a movement of about 16–20 miles, the army camped near Boonsboro, in the Cane Hill Valley. There they rested for several days, enjoying the abundance of the apple crop, gathering supplies, and giving the horses time to recover their strength, as they received, for the first time in days, a supply of forage. Back at Neosho, General Curtis had received orders through General Henry Halleck, from U.S. Grant, to continue the pursuit of Price until he had crossed the Arkansas River. Curtis ordered his command to assemble at Cassville, there to resume the hunt. By November 1, while Price camped at Boonsboro, Curtis departed Keetsville, Missouri. Curtis's command consisted of Blunt's Division, with Benteen's Brigade—in all about 3,000 troops. Of Pleasonton's other two brigades, McNeil never caught up with Curtis and eventually diverted to Ft. Smith; Sanborn, also late in moving, made it to Cassville, where he broke off his pursuit, being well behind General Curtis. Back at Boonsboro, General Price received a request for support, from Colonel William H. Brooks, who was besieging Fayetteville, Arkansas, some 20 miles northeast of Boonsboro. Price agreed to the aid, ordering Fagan's Division to Fayetteville, supported by a detachment from Shelby's Division. Price was hopeful that a significant demonstration would cause the 1,000-man Federal garrison to surrender. *O.R.*, vol. 41, pt. 1:638, 647, 661, 697, 705; *O.R.S.*, pt. 1, vol. 7:411; Britton, *Civil War on the Border, 1863–65*, 514; Campbell Memoir; Hinton, 279–280; E.P. Kirkman, "Driving Price Out of Missouri," National tribune, October 10, 1912, hereafter cited as Kirkman, "Driving Price;" Lause, *Collapse of Price's Raid*, 191; McGhee, *Campaigning With Marmaduke*, 28; Pitcock & Gurley, 240; Sinisi, 325, 327–328; Wood, *Newtonia*, 134–135.

168. Fagan's Division marched to Fayetteville on November 2 in a snow storm and invested the town on the 3rd, while Dobbin's, McCray's, and Freeman's Brigades slipped away to northcentral and northeast Arkansas to recruit their commands. Fagan's remaining troops consisted of a 420-man detachment from Cabell's Brigade, commanded by Colonel Thomas Gunter, and an 80-man detachment from Shelby's Division, with two pieces of artillery from Collins's Battery. The remaining men of the 500-man detachment came from Cabell's Brigade, commanded by Thomas Gunter. In the end, the Federal garrison had no difficulty holding off Fagan's lackluster assault. Late on the 3rd, having given time for Dobbin, McCray, and Freeman to exit the area, Fagan broke contact with Fayetteville and rejoined the army at Boonsboro, leaving a small contingent to bring up the rear on November 4. For details on the Fayetteville operation See Chapter 4, note no. 144. *O.R.*, vol. 41, pt. 1:638, 631, 705; *O.R.S.*, pt.1, vol. 7:411; Edwards, *Shelby and his Men*, 461; Forsyth, *Great Missouri Raid*, 221; Hinton, 286–287; Kirkman, "Driving Price;" Sinisi, 330; Wright Memoirs, unnumbered pages 102–103.

169. The Army of Missouri, or what was left of it, departed the Cane Hill Valley at about 10:00 a.m. on November 4, heading southwest into the Cherokee Nation of the Indian Territory. Left behind were about 100 sick and wounded, along with the remaining cattle and sheep that had accompanied the expedition. The army that marched on the 4th was no longer a cohesive body of men but "a loose undisciplined herd of cavalry." The horrible weather that had plagued the army for the past three days finally gave way to clearing skies, though the prospects of better rations and forage for their animals remained bleak, prompting Kyle Sinisi to label the retreat southward as

November 10—We camp this night on the side of a mountain some thirty miles south of Hick Falls, on the Arkansas River, on the Perryville road. No rations; no forage; Gen. Clark kills his Indian pony for subsistence. The men are eating mule-beef. That would do if there were mules enough to go around, even if the mules are so poor they can hardly walk. I guard my horse to-night to keep him from being slaughtered for food.[170]

November 11—This morning we leave camp with no order of march. The troops struggle along as they please. The brigade does not number 400 men. Small squads are breaking off to the south in quest of food. Mules and horses that give out are skinned, a fire built and a wrangle goes on over the carcass. We camp this night fifteen miles northeast of Perryville. Not a bite to eat for the last three days, and

No Prospect of Any

in the near future. About 9 o'clock this evening I join a small party from Cos. G, D and H, who had determined to take the chances of starvation into their own

"a march of misery." By November 6, following a movement of about 50 miles, the army camped within two miles of the Arkansas River. On November 7, the morning was spent in cutting a road to Pleasant Ford, which was completed about noon. The bulk of the command crossed the river at 1:00 p.m., followed by the 32 remaining wagons of the train, according to a local missionary, and camped three miles beyond in the Choctaw Nation. The 8th saw the army continue southward, in a cold rain, which turned to snow before day's end. The command took three different roads to find food and forage: Fagan's brigades headed southeast toward Washington, Arkansas; Shelby headed southwest toward the North Fork of the Canadian River; and Marmaduke's command headed to Boggy Depot, accompanied by the army's headquarters unit, and Fagan with his escort. Also on the 8th General Curtis arrived at the Arkansas River, where he chased a few scattered rebels. Firing 34 rounds of artillery, as a parting declaration of victory, in honor of the United States, Curtis thus ended his pursuit of Price's army and headed back to Kansas. But for Price the retreat was far from done. From November 4–9, the march was a slow process, with "horses and mules dying by the hundreds." The men fared little better. "The recruits," according to Hemp Watts, suffering "more in spirit than in flesh, and fell out by the wayside to die." Those who died on the retreat remained unburied as there was "no means to bury them," leaving them "to be devoured by cayotas [coyotes]" or wolves. The rest of the retreat would prove little better, until the army reached the vicinity of Boggy Depot, where their fare would finally begin to improve. *O.R.*, vol. 41, pt. 1:647, 705; *O.R.S.*, pt. 1 vol. 7:411; Baker Diary, November 1–9, 1864; Brown Journal, November 4–9, 1864; Edwards, *Shelby and His Men*, 463–464; Forsyth, *Great Missouri Raid*, 223; Hinton, 289–290; Lause, *Collapse of Price's Raid*, 188, 190–191; McGhee, *Campaigning With Marmaduke*, 28; Moore, *Missouri, Confederate Military History*, 195; Pitcock & Gurley, 240–242; Sinisi, 323; T.D.C., "Letter from Fort Gibson," *Freedom's Champion*, November 21, 1864; Watts, "Shelby At Newtonia."

170. The army made 14 miles on November 10, camping on the Canadian River. With nothing to eat for three days, General Clark killed "a fat pony," allowing his escort company to "relish" both a dinner and breakfast. Other commands were not so lucky—the remaining men of Jackman's Brigade had nothing but a few hickory nuts, though most appeared to have had at least some beef. On November 10, General Price continued his policy of furloughing his men, allowing Cabell's and Slemons's Brigades to break from the army, to return on December 10; Cabell's troopers were to report to Spring Hill, while Slemons's Brigade was ordered to Miller's Bluff. *O.R.*, vol. 41, pt. 1:647; J. T. Alexander, Letter (November 13, 1864); Baker Diary, November 10, 1864; Brown Journal, November 10, 1864; Campbell Memoir; McGhee, *Campaigning With Marmaduke*, 29; Pitcock & Gurley, 241; Wright Memoirs, unnumbered page 104.

hands. There are twenty-one of us when noses are counted. We strike south for the mouth of Boggy River, and camp some three miles from the army. I trade twenty cartridges for one quarter of a pound of pork. When I display it at the campfire twenty men ask for just a taste—and just a taste it is when divided up. Wolves are howling all around. I take my gun and watch for quite a while, trying to get a shot, but they are too shy.

November 12—We leave camp in pairs for the purpose of hunting. I am paired with Stubbs of Co. D.[171] About noon we came up with four men. They had killed a skunk, and were quarreling about the title to it. They were then skinning it. How they settle the dispute I do not know, for we left them and went on. This evening as we are crossing a creek a wolf jumps from its lair. I fire a shot and wound it. Stubbs insists on my following it, saying that "wolf meat would best no meat at all."

Following it up the creek half a mile, I come on an old camp, some two or three days old. By the pile of ashes was a backbone, with the loin meat attached, of a beef. It had been roasted whole, the topside was picked bare, but the underside was intact, clean and cooked nice. I cut off a sample and found it was sweet and good. So I sat down and ate what I thought would be good for me. Then cut off a piece for Stubbs. He ate the meat ravenously ad begged me to take him to the old camp, while I begged him to continue the hunt. While parlaying, a volley of musketry rang out to the southwards, then another. "That's the signal to come to camp, for game has been killed," says Stubbs, and he moved out briskly, forgetting all about the old camp. When we reach camp to-night the fires are lined with juicy steak. We spend the night feasting

And the Next Day Vomiting

and purging. It's a wonder we did not kill ourselves. On the 14th we camp on the Gaine's Creek. On the 15th we came to an Indian settlement, where we trade for some corn and grind it in a steel mill. That is the first square meal of bread we have had since the morning we broke camp near Paola, in Miami County, Kan.[172]

---

171. Stubbs: not found in the National Archives, Record Group M322 (roll no. 58), Confederate Compiled Service Records, 10th Missouri Cavalry.

172. It was a day-to-day struggle for the Army of Missouri from November 11–18, where at times "every person seemed to be his own commander." The army averaged about 20 miles a day between November 11–12. On November 13, Clark's Division, with the army headquarters arrived at Perryville, where they rested until the 15th. Four miles from Perryville, a train of six wagons greeted the arriving troops with salt and flour—"only a half pint of flour to the man and about a thimble of salt." Farther to the front of the army, Tyler's Brigade moved on to the Middle Boggy, finally resting on November 16, before heading to Boggy Depot, where it arrived on the 17th, followed by the rest of the army. On November 16, Clark's troops continued their retreat, camping at 1:00 p.m. to graze their horses, following a 16-mile march. Another 22 miles brought the column to General Stand Watie's camp on Muddy Boggy Creek on November 17. And finally, on November 18, following a 10-mile march in "raw drizzling weather," Clark's column pulled into Boggy Depot, the headquarters of General Douglas Cooper. Later that day, Shelby's Division arrived, after a three-day rest on the North Fork of the Canadian, where the men participated in a "wild cat-

On the 20th we cross Red River at the mouth of the Kymisha River, and on 3d December we reach the brigade camp, twenty miles below Lainsport, on Red River.[173] The army has been reorganized and discipline restored and the old Tenth is looking like herself again.[174]

Kind reader, just take a glance at the map of Missouri, Kansas, and Arkansas, and you will see that the road traversed by Gen. Price's raiding column in 1864 covered a distance of at least 1,200 miles. Starting from Tyro, Lincoln County, Ark., and ending at Cane Hill, Ark. But go on down to Lainsport [Laynesport], Texas, and it will reach 1,500 miles. Add to this the many pitched battles participated in by the raiders, to say nothing of the personal encounters as one might say

---

tle hunt" amid a cornucopia of wild game, with lush grass and cane for their exhausted livestock. Of the march from Jackson County, Missouri, to Boggy Depot, Colonel Colton Greene recorded:
> For twenty-five days our animals were without forage. For twenty-three days we subsisted on beef without salt, frequently issued in insufficient quantities, and for three days were without food at all. The loss in animals was heavy, and many wagons were abandoned in consequence.

Though there was never an exact accounting for the loss of horses and mules, during the march through the Indian Territory, one trooper, in Marmaduke's escort, recorded in his diary that he "supposed 10,000" had been left in the Territory. General Price simply put the loss "at not one half," while those still mounted "would be entirely unfit for service," for some time following the completion of the expedition. *O.R.*, vol. 41, pt. 1:647–648, 661, 692, 705; *O.R.*, vol. 41, pt. 4:1076–1077; J. T. Alexander, Letter (November 13, 1864); Baker Diary, November 8–18, 1864; Ballard Diary, November 11–18, 1864; Brown Journal, November 11–18, 1864; Edwards, *Shelby and His Men*, 463–463; McGhee, *Campaigning With Marmaduke*, 29; Mobley, 200; Pitcock & Gurley, 243–246; Sellmeyer, 266–269; Sinisi, 337; Stanton, et al., 266–267.

173. Of the three brigades remaining with the army, Charles Tyler's departed Boggy Depot on the 18th, heading for Doaksville. Fagan, with his escort, accompanied Tyler's Brigade to Doaksville, though its ultimate destination was Washington, Arkansas, where Fagan was to meet Cabell's and Slemons's Brigades. Tyler's Brigade was then directed to Clarksville, Texas, eventually ending up near Laynesport, where the expedition officially ended. Shelby's Division, consisting solely of Thompson's Brigade, with Colton Greene's Brigade, of Clark's Division, left Boggy Depot on November 19, heading to Bonham, Texas. Clark's Division crossed the Red River at Kent's Ferry (Sellmeyer calls it Kemp's Ferry), into Texas on November 21, followed by Shelby's command on the 22nd. Price's army made it to Bonham on November 23. They made Paris on the 26th and Clarksville on the 28th, where they rested until November 30, washing their clothes and themselves following the grueling campaign. The army left Clarksville on December 1 and reached Laynesport on December 2, where it officially terminated the expedition. According to John Edwards, Price's Raid had "begun in joy and high expectation [but] terminated in this little Texas village, in doubt, misery and despair." Writes Kyle Sinisi: "Price's Army of Missouri ceased to exist, and its odyssey had come to a close." *O.R.*, vol. 41, pt. 1:624–625; 648; *O.R.*, vol. 41, pt. 4:1067–1068; Baker Diary, November 18, 22, 1864; Brown Journal, November 21, 1864; Edwards, *Shelby and His Men*, 465; Sellmeyer, 267, 269; Sinisi, 339–340.

174. On December 20, 1864, General John B. Magruder submitted two plans to General Smith, commanding the Department, recommending a reorganization of the cavalry of the District of Arkansas. Essentially, Magruder proposed retaining Shelby's Iron Brigade, Clark's Missouri Brigade, and Cabell's Arkansas Brigade, while the rest of the mounted troops would be dismounted to serve as infantry. Following a review of Magruder's plans, Smith made several suggestions to coordinate with current regulations from Richmond, but overall he approved Magruder's planned reorganization, which took effect in early January 1865. *O.R.*, vol, 41, pt. 4:1117–1119, 1134–1135; *O.R.*, vol. 48, pt. 1:1317, 1330.

of the picket fighting and scout fighting, and desultory skirmishing that is never mentioned in the pages of history, or even in the accompanying article. Then consider the time occupied in this expedition. That is from the 20th day of August to the 3d day of November, about seventy-five days, or about two and a half months, all this, too, in the face of overwhelming odds, and then you will be able to understand how determined was the struggle for the "lost cause."[175]

June 2, 1865.—Gen. Price arrived from Baton Rouge to-day and the terms of surrender are made known by general order. Some of the men jump for joy, while others curse and swear and gnash their teeth in frantic rage, and yet again others are cast down, silent and dejected, sighing as if their hearts were broken.[176] The camp

Presents A Sorry Spectacle.

June 5.—Some of the Missouri infantry of Parsons's brigade is shipped on board the steamer Capitol, and bound for home. The steamer Old Kentucky follows in her wake. As they pass our camp, three miles below Shreveport, their flags are flying and bands playing.[177]

June 6.—Early this morning the old Tenth marches by companies and deposits their arms on board a steamer. It in turn delivers them to a detachment of Confed-

---

175. In his report following the expedition, General Price submitted the following summary of what he had accomplished:

> I marched 1,434 miles; fought forty-three battles and skirmishes; captured and paroled 3,000 Federal officers and men; captured 18 pieces of artillery, 3,000 stands of small arms, 16 stand of colors that were brought out by me..., at least 3,000 overcoats, large quantities of blankets, shoes, and ready made clothing for soldiers, a great many wagons and teams, large number of horses, great quantities of subsistence and ordnance stores. I destroyed miles upon miles of railroad, burning the depots and bridges... [and] destroyed...property to the amount of $10,000,000 in value. On the other hand I lost 10 pieces of artillery, 2 stand of colors, 1,000 small arms, why I do not think I lost 1,000 prisoners, including wounded left in their hands and others than recruits on their way to join me...I brought with me at least 5,000 new recruits and they are still arriving in large numbers daily within our lines.

See Appendix I, Summary of Price's 1964 Missouri Expedition. *O.R.*, vol. 41, pt. 1:640.

176. See note no. 43, Chapter 2, for information concerning the surrender of the Trans-Mississippi Department.

177. The *Old Kentucky* was probably the side-wheel steamer *Kentucky*, also known as *Kentucky No. 2*. It was a 500-ton side-wheel steamer, identified as the *Kentucky* in the official reports surrounding the Battle of Belmont, Missouri (November 7, 1861). According to popular belief, the *Kentucky* participated in the engagement at Island No. 10, was captured at Memphis on June 6, 1862, sold in a prize court, after which an attempt to refit her at St Louis failed, as the vessel was "very much out of repair." The ship was then put up for sale, was purchased by its previous owners, and appears to have reentered the war as a Federal river transport. With the end of the war, the *Kentucky* was used to transport parolees back to Missouri; however, it sank in the Red River in June of 1865, killing 30 parolees. The only thing found on the *Capitol* was that it was sunk in the Yazoo River in 1862, with its machinery subsequently removed and used in the defense of Mobile, Alabama. *O.R.*, 3:409; Naval History Division, *Civil War Naval Chronology*, VI: 207, 258–259.

erate infantry which is guarding the arsenal at Shreveport. Late this evening the Yankee fleet steams up Red River to the wharf.[178]

June 8.—Another contingent of the Yankee fleet arrives—mostly transports loaded with infantry.

June 9.—The steamer *Old Kentucky*, by some mischance, floundered and sank in the "cut off." Some fifty or sixty Confederates were drowned. The Ohio Belle brings back a part of the unfortunate victims.[179] The brigade takes the parole all today. We are marched to the city to receive the oath and parole papers. We marched into a room at the provost marshal's office by companies. While we are standing in line Ben Wheatley nudges me and says, "Let's have some fun out of that ———— Dutch major."

"How?" I asked.

"Why, let's take the ———— parole oath left-handed. He'll cuss like a sea-horse."

"All right," I replied.

"When they say, 'hands up and hats off,' let's take our hats in our right hands and hold up our left."

Before I can reply the order is given. "Hats off and hands up." An officer reads the parole oath and the responses are made. W. T. Steele is passing before the company handing each man a printed parole.[180] The major came out from behind his desk, and, pointing to Wheatley and me, said we had not taken the oath and we must be sworn over. Then Wheatley wanted to know if a left-handed man didn't have the right to take an oath left-handed. But the major ranted around a little more than we expected. Capt. Murray tried to appease the major's wrath and the boys protested for the major

Threatened to Have Us Arrested

and locked up. In the midst of the little commotion the captain gave the order "Right face, forward march." As we marched to the door—where a guard stood on either side—Wheatley whispered: "Let's play drunk." Taking a cue, canteen in hand, I swaggered up to the guard and say, "Have a dram, old pard," and I hold my canteen up. Wheatley has followed me with a drunken lurch, and all three of

---

178. Company A, 10th Missouri Infantry (CSA) was guarding the arsenal, and according to James Grubbs, one of its member, was the last company to surrender at Shreveport. On June 6, 1865, General Francis Herron arrived at Shreveport to begin the parole process. See note no. 55, Chapter 2, for details on Herron's arrival at Shreveport. James L. Grubbs, "The Last Company to Surrender," *Missouri Republican*, January 9, 1886.

179. The *Ohio Belle* was a second class side-wheel steamer, of 406 tons. It was built in Cincinnati in 1855, and used as an "Army watch boat" on the Mississippi River until its capture by the Federals at Island No. 10 on April 7, 1862. Naval History Division, *Civil War Naval Chronology*, VI: 277.

180. William T. Steele was enlisted in the Confederate Service on September 15, 1862, by Colonel J. Vard Cockrell in Jackson County, Missouri. He survived the war and was paroled at Shreveport on June 7, 1865. National Archives, Record Group M322 (roll no. 58), Confederate Compiled Service Records, 10th Missouri Cavalry.

us tumble out on the pavement, Wheatley and I both trying to get the guard to drink. In the midst of the tumble I hear the major exclaim: "By Got, da ish drunk." The guard scrambled up and went back to his post, while Wheatley and I scuffled and tried to make each other drink. Some Yankee soldiers standing on the street clapped their hands and yelled with delight. At the boat landing little Bob Prewitt said to me: "You and Ben Wheatley have got more impudence that all the rest of the company.[181] You two boys always hold a flush or a pat hand, or else play all trumps."

June 10—Leave Shreveport en route for home on board the steamer Adonis; 15th, arrived at Baton Rouge; 16th, re-shipped on board the Lady Gay.[182] Am too sick to write; goodbye old diary.

That is the last entry of in the old diary, for I was sick all the way up the river. At Cairo we changed to the steamer *Belle Memphis*. When I arrived at St. Louis I managed to stagger from the wharf up to the transportation office. It was the last march of the old Tenth and the straw that broke the camel's back, for I was carried from there to the charity hospital at the instigation of a Mr. Hanna by John H. Bell and Ben F. Wheatley.[183] But for the kind ministration of those good Sisters of Charity, I would in all probability never have reached home or gladden the heart of a waiting mother.

HENRY C. LUTTRELL,
Hindman's Escort, Co. G,
Tenth Missouri Cavalry,
Clark's Brigade

* * * * * * *

---

181. Robert H. Prewitt or Prewett was born in Montgomery County, Kentucky, in about 1838, and was living near Holden, Missouri, in Johnson County, when he joined the MSG. He was elected 2nd lieutenant of Company A, 3rd Regiment, 8th Division, MSG, on June 14, 1861. While serving in the Guard, Prewitt was wounded at Wilson's Creek on August 10, 1861. He recovered and resigned his commission on December 12, 1862. On August 1, 1862, Prewitt joined the Confederate Army, in Johnson County, Missouri. As a member of Company D, Cockrell's Regiment, Prewitt fought at Lone Jack on August 15, 1862, and later became a member of the 10th Missouri Cavalry, where he served for the remainder of the war. He was paroled on June 7, 1865, at Shreveport. Bartels, *Forgotten Men*, 295; Eakin, *Lone Jack*, 188; National Archives, Record Group M322 (roll no. 58), Confederate Compiled Service Records, 10th Missouri Cavalry.

182. Nothing found on the *Adonis* or the *Lady Gay*.

183. John H. Bell and Ben Wheatly have been previously covered. Nothing found on a "Mr. Hanna." National Archives, Record Group M322 (roll nos. 56–58), Confederate Compiled Service Records, 10th Missouri Cavalry.

Chapter 4

Irregular Operations, 1861–1865

Introduction

When one thinks of guerrilla warfare in the Trans-Mississippi, the war-torn states of Missouri and Arkansas come to mind. Names like William Quantrill, George Todd, and Bill Anderson are well-known and are covered extensively in the Civil War literature. This chapter deals with some of the less famous men who operated as guerrillas in the Trans-Mississippi and are largely unknown to the Civil War community.

Sidney Jackman is probably the best example of the group and is well-represented in a sketch of his life as a guerrilla in Missouri, from the beginning of the war until he joined Price's 1864 Raid. Included in this account is his capture of Union General Thomas Bartholow from his home in Glasgow, Missouri, in April 1863. Jackman may not have been as flamboyant a guerrilla raider as John S. Mosby, but his capture of Bartholow is worthy of note.

Even more obscure than the exploits of Jackman is the story of August T. Doley. Like many Confederate Missourians, Doley served in a dual role, as both a guerrilla fighter and a regular army officer, who recruited or undertook irregular actions, as need be, for the Confederacy. The story of Doley's capture and execution are typical of what happened to many a man who returned to Union-held territory to recruit for the Confederacy, whether in Missouri or Arkansas. They were all branded as guerrillas and in many cases executed immediately upon capture.

Probably the most unusual account of irregular operations concerns an expedition which left Missouri, bound for Colorado Territory in May 1863. Commanded by Colonel Charles "Charlie" Harrison, the exploit had the goal of recruiting Confederate supporters in Colorado. In the end only two men survived; the rest were killed by Osage Indians in a fight that covered a running battle of 10 or more miles. The story of this expedition has rarely been told and was penned by the only man who survived the war—the other member of the group having being killed shortly after he returned to Missouri.

The names of William "Buck" Brown or James W. Cooper are little known, except by the most informed of Civil War enthusiasts. Both of these men organized Confederate units in northern Arkansas to prevent Federal troops from gaining control of the area, beyond the few towns they occupied. In this chapter you'll find Cooper's extensive account of his operations in Arkansas, none of which ever made it into the *Official Records*. Cooper served initially in the regular army and then as a guerrilla operating under General Stand Watie.

Overall these few articles are a reminder that there was a lot more to the Trans-Mississippi Civil War than Wilson's Creek, Pea Ridge, Prairie Grove, the Red River/Camden Campaigns, or Price's 1864 Missouri Raid. The untold stories of the small engagements, skirmishes, and the civilians who lived through the guerrilla warfare on the border are the real "Confederate Tales of the War."

* * * * * * *

Item: Biography on Colonel Sidney D. Jackman; Member MSG, Guerrilla and Confederate Officer, by Richard H. Musser, Colonel 9th Missouri Infantry.
Published: August 28, 1886.

Sketch of Col. S. D. Jackman.[1]

Sidney D. Jackman was born in the state of Kentucky March 7, 1826. When very young he was brought by his parents to Missouri, where his father, Porter Jackman, first settled in Lewis County, following the occupation of farmer.[2] The elder Jackman in a year or so left northeastern Missouri and settled in Boone County, where he resided for a year or two, and finally established himself in Howard County, where he raised his family, being in very moderate circumstances, amid the simple and modest surroundings of pioneer farm life. The opportunities for education in this new country, along in the 30s, may be readily imagined. The log schoolhouse in the neighborhood with its slab benches and plain rough furniture, afforded all the learning and tuition of those days. These country schools from which statesmen and soldiers, scholars and men eminent in every walk in life have emerged, were not constant and perennial. They could only be afforded in the winter, when the pupils were to be spared from the labors of the crop. Nor were they capable of imparting any great scope of recondite and curious learning. Their teachers only pretended to impart the crudest elements of the rudiments, reading, writing and arithmetic, the latter by no means thorough or exhaustive. A few months each winter at such schools, when the studies were combined with necessary labor, was all that was afforded Col. Jackman in the

---

1. Short biographies of Jackman were presented in Chapter 2 (note 75), of this book and in Banasik, *Confederate Tales, 1862*, 174–175.
2. Porter Jackman was Sidney's uncle, while Thomas Jackman was his father. Porter Jackman was a man who espoused the principle of "hospitality knows no bounds," which meant an open-door policy for Confederate guerrillas, despite the disapprobation of Union officials. This policy eventually led to his arrest, at the age of 74, by Union troops on June 19, 1863. Incarcerated in Gratiot and Myrtle Street Prisons in St. Louis, Porter Jackman was held but a short time, contrary to what Sidney Jackman recorded in his memoirs, where he has his uncle remaining in prison until the end of the war. According to Federal records, Porter posted a $2,000 dollar bond and took the Oath of Allegiance, after which he was released on July 14, 1863. Porter did survive the war but died a short time after. Eakin, *Missouri Prisoners of War*, "Jackman, Porter," entry; Norton, 3, 158; James A. White and Carolyn M. Bartels, *The Men Who Rode With Capt. Wm. C. Quantrill & Capt. Wm. T. Anderson: Their lives, Their Loves, Their Stories* (Independence, MO, 2015), 86–87.

Sidney D. Jackman

way of education. But upon this he built by diligence and study. The facilities for study were not then as now, for books were few and not by any means cheap or choice. There were

Few School-Books.

The arithmetic computed pounds, shillings and pence, and the readers were such chance stories, history or biographies as were in possession of the family or might be borrowed for the occasion. There were no school boards then to select and establish a series of texts, nor enterprising publishers to furnish them to the public. The paucity of books perhaps conduced to a higher scholarship: for one thoroughly studied was worth a whole course or series of those which make learning easy. The aid of such elementary education as could be gained in this manner, combined with habits of diligence, industry and honesty, was sufficient to develop an intelligent, sturdy, truth-telling and self-reliant young farmer of Jackman, and he grew up among his brothers and sisters an American citizen, with firm and fixed convictions, fit to take his place among his fellows in any sphere of duties into which he might be called.[3]

At the age of 24, in 1849 (February 15) he married the daughter of a neighbor in Boone County, Miss Martha R. Slavin, who survives him, and has been a faithful and devoted wife and mother of his children.[4] In 1855, when that part of the country was comparatively new, he moved with his young family to Bates

---

3. Sidney was the eldest of the Jackman children, which included three sisters and two brothers: Margaret (born November 18, 1824), William (born May 11, 1828), Sarah (born May 1, 1830) and the twins Nathaniel and Mary (born March 18, 1836). Norton, 3.
4. The wife that Richard Musser was referring too as "surviving" was Jackman's second wife, Cass. Jackman's first wife Martha Rachael Slavin was born on January 17, 1834, and married Sidney just shy of her fifteenth birthday. Martha had eight children by Sidney Jackman: William (born April 19, 1851), Cora (born September 11, 1853), Mary (born October 1, 1855), Henry (born October 29, 1857), Nathaniel (born December 2, 1859), Sidney Johnston (born September 5, 1863), Nora (born November 18, 1867), and Thomas (born September 15, 1869). At the end of the Civil War, Martha and the children journeyed part of the way to Mexico with Sidney, but were left behind in San Marco, Texas, there to wait until he was settled in Mexico. Sidney became disillusioned with Mexico, however, and returned to Texas, reuniting with his family near Kyle. Unfortunately Martha died in 1870, at the age of 36. Sidney remarried in 1875, to the widow Cass Gaines. Sidney and Cass subsequently had four children, Edward (born November 2, 1876), Nellie (born May 19, 1878), Helen (born February 2, 1880 and Mark (born January 8, 1881). Musser's

County and began to make a home for them. About that time the Kansas excitement began; the settlement of the new territory under the Kansas-Nebraska Bill, involving, as it did, efforts to control the future institutions of Kansas by election, and the violent agitation of the question of slavery, led to many acts of hostility and words or recrimination.[5] The invasion of the border of Missouri by jayhawkers and emissaries of the

Free State Party

kept that part of the state in a condition of constant anxiety and excitement.[6] The question of the right of squatters or first settlers in a territory to the exercise of

---

article on Jackman was published in the *Republican*, 87 days after Jackman died in Hays County, Texas, on June 2, 1886. Norton, 3, 8–9.

5. Passed on May 30, 1854, following five "months of bitter debate over its provisions," the Kansas-Nebraska Act "completely undermined the chances of compromise between North and South," over the slavery issue. Known by some Missourians as the "Squatter Sovereignty Act," the bill was proposed by Illinois Senator Stephen A. Douglas as a means of compromise over the expansion of slavery into the territories. When adopted, the Act nullified the Missouri Compromise of 1820, allowing Kansas to determine if it wanted to enter the Union as a slave or free state through the exercise of "popular sovereignty." Ultimately the Act "altered the politics of the United States...[and] triggered the formation of a new sectionalized Republican Party." Kansas subsequently exploded as the conflicting forces vied for control of the state. Men were killed on both sides of the issue; pro-slavery Missourians sacked Lawrence on May 21, 1856, while abolitionists, under John Brown, murdered five pro-slavery men three days later at Pottawatomie. Small battles took place throughout Kansas, at places like Black Jack (June 2, 1856), Franklin (August 12, 1856), Fort Sanders (August 14, 1856), Bull Creek (August 31, 1856), and Hickory Point (September 13, 1856), to name but a few. These skirmishes continued on and off from 1854 to 1861, as Kansas bled. One of the more famous actions occurred on May 19, 1858, at Marais des Cygnes, where five men were executed and six others were seriously wounded, this time by pro-slavery men. In the end, "Bleeding Kansas," as it became known, eventually entered the Union in 1861 as a free state, after the Southern states had begun to secede. Barney, 35–36, 182–183; Boatner, 69, 448; Nicole Etcheson, *Bleeding Kansas: Contested Liberty in the Civil War Era* (Lawrence, KS, 2004), 109, 114, 119, 134, 192–193, hereafter cited as Etcheson; Faust, 66, 408; Lewis, 224; Loren K. Litter, *"Bleeding Kansas" The Border War in Douglas and Adjacent Counties* (Baldwin City, KS, 1987), 59, 64.

6. Jayhawkers was a common term used on the Kansas-Missouri border to describe anyone who stole property, regardless of whom they stole it from. The term originated, according to Leo Huff, back in 1849, during the California gold rush, when some Illinoisans remarked "that they would jayhawk, their way across the plains." To one Missourian the moniker applied only to Kansans, who had "the propensity...to appropriate their neighbor's property, on the Missouri side" of border; this was particularly true in the years 1854–1860. In the early part of the Civil War the term was generally associated with Kansans, while Missourians were denigrated by their enemies as "border ruffians," "pukes," "guerrillas," or "bushwhackers." Albert Castel, *A Frontier State at War: Kansas, 1861–1865* (Ithaca, NY, 1958), 43, 62–63, hereafter cited as Castel, *Frontier State*; Michael Fellmen, *Inside War: The Guerrilla Conflict in Missouri During the American Civil War* (New York, 1989), 13–14; Leo E. Huff, "Guerrillas, Jayhawkers and Bushwhackers in Northern Arkansas During the Civil War," *Arkansas Historical Quarterly* 24 (Summer 1965), 129, hereafter cited as Huff, "Guerrillas"; Lewis, 227.

The "Free State Party" was better known as the "Free Soil Party." A short-lived group, the Free Soil Party was organized in the late 1840s, participated in the 1848 and 1852 presidential elections, and was the forerunner to the Republican Party. It was concerned with the extension

autonomy in the excluding of immigration of citizens from the Southern States with their property, by a nonrecognition of a portion of their effects as such, was one upon which the Missourians were always sensitive. Jackman had the pronounced views of his class and party and held that the territories being the common property of the states, were open to settlement from all without restraint or disparagement to any, and that no act or sovereignty could be binding until under the Constitution and laws of the Federal Union the territory became competent for admission as a sovereign state and was so admitted.[7] He was soon called upon to leave his farm and family and repel the incursions of jayhawkers. To protect the border, then frequently threatened by predatory bands of desperadoes, was the first occasion of Jackman's military service. The duty at the time was neither arduous nor dangerous, but it served to give him some idea of military training, and led to firm and honest conviction on all of the questions involved in the issues which produced these troubles.

In the fall of 1860 and winter of 1861 the celebrated [James] Montgomery invasion necessitated calling out the organized militia under Gen. Frost and the Southwest Expedition.[8] Jackman's then residence was, if not in the midst of the

---

of slavery into the newly acquired territory obtained after the Mexican War, but was not against slavery, per se. The Free Soilers were concerned about the economic impact that slave labor would have on jobs in any potential state, by lowering wages. Martin Van Buren was the party's presidential candidate in 1848, running on a platform "founded on the values of economic development, social mobility, and political democracy...[that] glorified the working class while denouncing the degradation of the work ethic in Southern society." The year 1848 also marked the high point of the Free Soil Party, which gave way to the Republican Party in 1854, having existed a bare eight years. Boatner, 314; Faust, 290–291.

7. A total of four constitutions were submitted by the territory of Kansas to the U.S. Congress. The Topeka Constitution, a Free Soiler document (Warner Lewis mistakenly identifies this as a pro-slavery document), was adopted on December 15, 1855, but was never finalized due to limited number of voters who participated. The pro-slavery Lecompton Constitution (November 7, 1857) was racked with voter fraud in its first vote in December 1857, but was still sent to the U.S. Congress for approval. A subsequent territorial vote easily defeated the Lecompton Constitution on August 2, 1858. Next came a second free-state proposal, the Leavenworth Constitution, which was completed on May 18, 1858, to counter the Lecompton submission to Congress; however the Leavenworth Constitution "lacked solid legal credentials," so the appointed Kansas territorial governor, James W. Denver, refused to endorse the bill. The Wyandotte Constitution was approved by the voters of Kansas by a 2-1 vote on October 4, 1859, and submitted to the U.S. Congress for approval, but it stalled in the Senate. Kansas was finally admitted as a state on January 29, 1861. Etcheson, 146, 177–179, 206, 220, 224; Faust, 66–67; Lewis, 225; Wendell Holmes Stephenson, *Publications of the Kansas State Historical Society Embracing The Political Career of General James H. Lane* (Topeka, 1930), 57–58, 90, 95, 101, hereafter cited as Stephenson.

8. James Montgomery, a compatriot of John Brown, was from Ohio, having moved to Kansas in 1854 and settled near Mound City. A Free Soiler and staunch opponent of slavery, Montgomery terrorized the Missouri side of the border from Linn County, Kansas, before and during the war, stealing slaves, plundering, and murdering at will. He "saw himself to be the hand of the Lord in striking down slavery and all who supported it." He commanded the 3rd Kansas Infantry during the Civil War. Donald R. Hale, *Jackson County and The Civil War* (Independence, MO, n.d.), 4, cited hereafter as Hale, *Jackson County*; Stephenson, 107, 111; Stephen Z. Starr, *Jennison's Jayhawkers: A Civil War Cavalry Regiment and Its Commander* (Baton Rouge, LA, 1973), 30–31, cited hereafter as Starr.

invaded territory, sufficiently near to give occasion for vigilance and anxiety on the part of himself and neighbors. Those experiences

Prepared His Mind

for what was soon to follow. As soon as the Camp Jackson outrage had precipitated war upon the state of Missouri in May 1861, the governor called out 50,000 militia volunteers.[9] Jackman was among the earliest to respond and went with a

---

Daniel M. Frost was born in 1823, in New York, graduated from West Point (number 4 of 25) in 1844, and served in the Mexican War. On May 31, 1853, Frost resigned from the army and moved to St. Louis. At the beginning of the Civil War, he ran a "planing mill," in St. Louis, and was a general in the Missouri State Militia. Captured at Camp Jackson on May 10, 1861, Frost was exchanged in November 1861, and journeyed to Columbus, Kentucky, where he joined the Confederate war effort. He was at the Battle of Pea Ridge in March 1862, and was promoted to brigadier general in October 1862. At the Battle of Prairie Grove, Frost commanded a Confederate division. Frost was at Little Rock in September 1863, after which he submitted his resignation and escorted his wife to Canada via Mexico. Unfortunately, Frost's resignation was never accepted and he was listed as a deserter, the only Confederate general officer so listed at the end of the war. Frost later returned to St. Louis and became a farmer. He died on October 29, 1900. Banasik, *Missouri Brothers in Gray*, 138; Boatner, 318; Heitman, 1:438. Warner, *Generals in Gray*, 94–95.

The "Southwest Expedition" or the "Ball's Mill Expedition," as it was sometimes known, occurred in late 1860. On November 20, 1860, James Montgomery entered Missouri, rounded up several pro-slavery men near Ball's Mill in northwest Vernon County, and killed them. In response, Missouri Governor Robert M. Stewart called out Daniel M. Frost's St. Louis Militia Brigade, supported by the Jefferson City Militia. Frost's mission was simple; to "protect the lives and property of the people of the border." Arriving at the Kansas-Missouri border in late November 1860, Frost's small brigade positioned itself about 12 miles from Montgomery's headquarters in Kansas, awaiting Montgomery's next move. Within days Montgomery disbanded his command, followed by Frost disbanding the militia, save a 200-man force of three cavalry companies and a battery of artillery, who were left near Ball's Mill to patrol the border. During the expedition, Sidney Jackman served as a scout for the command. Moore, *Missouri, Confederate Military History*, 10; Etcheson, 221; Donald L. Gilmore, *Civil War on the Missouri-Kansas Border* (Gretna, LA, 2006), 100–104, hereafter cited as Gilmore; Norton, 4; Jonas Viles, "Documents Illustrating The Troubles on the Border, 1860. The Southwest Expedition," *Missouri Historical Review* 2 (October 1907), 61, 70–72, 76.

9. On May 6, 1861, Governor Claiborne F. Jackson called for the Missouri Militia to assemble from throughout the state in St. Louis for "instruction in military tactics." Camp Jackson was established on the outskirts of the city in Lindell Grove. Fearing that the pro-secession governor was using the lawfully assembled Missouri Militia as a ploy to take the St. Louis Arsenal, Union General Nathaniel Lyon captured the camp on May 10, without firing a shot, and marched the militiamen off to the St. Louis Arsenal. En route, a mob attacked the Federal troops, who returned fire, killing 25 civilian men, women, and children, along with three of the unarmed Camp Jackson prisoners. This then became known as the "St. Louis or Camp Jackson Massacre," which outraged Southern sympathizers in the city. This was followed by a peace conference on May 21, meant to cool things down in Missouri. It ultimately failed. On June 12, 1861, Governor Jackson issued a proclamation calling for 50,000 men "for the purpose of repelling invasion, and for the protection of lives, liberty and property of the citizens of this State." See Appendix A for a copy of the proclamation. *O.R.*, vol. 53:697; Hans Christian Adamson, *Rebellion in Missouri: 1861 Nathaniel Lyon and His Army of the West* (Rahway, NJ, 1961), 62–64; Banasik, *Missouri Brothers in Gray*, 9–10, 12; Bevier, 24–25; "Governor's Proclamation–General Orders No. 7," *The Missouri Republican*, May 2, 1861; Winter, 34–35, 46.

company to the rendezvous at Jefferson City. The early disbanding of the troops at Jefferson [City] before they were fairly organized, by reason of the Price-Harney Treaty, sent him home to his farm in Bates but only to be called on the 16th of June to another rendezvous at Boonville, in consequence of the breach and repudiation of that treaty by Gen. Harney's government.[10] He barely reached Boonville before the troops were dispersed by Lyon's forces and again ordered to assemble in the Southwest.[11]

Gen. Rains, who commanded the division from that part of the state where Jackman resided, fell back behind the Osage, where he received orders to retreat still farther south and be supported by Confederate forces, then taking position just south of the Arkansas line.[12] Jackman was then a captain and participated in the Battle of Carthage on the 5th of July, 1861, the first success that had fallen

---

10. William S. Harney was born in Tennessee, joined the Regular Army in 1818, fought Seminoles in Florida, served in the Mexican War, and fought Indians on the frontier. On June 14, 1858, he was promoted to brigadier general in the regular army, one of only four at the beginning of the Civil War, and given command of the Department of the West (November 17, 1860), in St. Louis. Unionists in St. Louis did not trust Harney because he was a Tennessean and successfully had him removed from command following the Camp Jackson Affair. Harney never commanded again, retired from the army on August 1, 1863, was breveted a major general for "long and faithful service," before war's end. Harney died in Orlando, Florida, on May 9, 1889. Michael E. Banasik, *Confederate "Tales of the War" In the Trans-Mississippi Part One: 1861* (Iowa City, IA, 2010), 185–186, hereafter cited as Banasik, *Confederate Tales, 1861*; Boatner, 376; Dyer, 254; Heitman, 1:502; McElroy, 30–31; Warner, *Generals in Blue*, 208–209.

The Price-Harney Agreement was signed on May 21, 1861, and temporarily staved off civil war in Missouri. Under the agreement, the Missouri government would maintain order in the state while the Federal government, represented by Harney, would not militarily interfere in Missouri. The agreement lasted three weeks, until General Lyon effectively repudiated the agreement on June 11, at the Planter's House hotel in St. Louis, when he declared that Missouri and the Federal government were now at war. See *Confederate Tales, 1861* for a copy of the agreement; *O.R.*, 3:374–375; Banasik, *Confederate Tales, 1861*, 181–182; Shalhope, 160–162; Snead, 198–200.

11. Boonville was located in Cooper County, on the south side of the Missouri River. It was the point to which Governor Claiborne F. Jackson fled from Jefferson City to avoid the advancing Federal troops under Lyon. On June 17, 1861, Lyon engaged the MSG, under John S. Marmaduke, at Boonville and easily dispersed them after only a few minutes. During the engagement, Lyon lost two killed, nine wounded (two mortally) and one missing out of 1,700 men engaged. Lyon reported capturing 60 rebels, 500 arms, and two brass cannon. *O.R.*, vol. 3:11–14, 809; Christopher Philips, *Damned Yankee: The Life of General Nathaniel Lyon* (Columbia, MO, 1990), 217–220, hereafter cited as Philips.

12. Following the loss at Boonville, Rains's 8th Division, MSG (Jackman's division), was located at Lexington. General Price, commanding at Lexington, ordered Rains back to Lamar, well below the Osage River, there to await further orders, while the MSG concentrated at that site. On July 4, Rains's Division moved southward again, as part of the general retreat of the MSG, to escape the advancing Federals; this time to Cowskin Prairie, in the extreme southwest corner of Missouri, there to drill and prepare for future operations. McGhee, *MSG Order Book*, unnumbered page 8; Philips, 222–223, 226–227.

James Spencer Rains was born on October 2, 1817, in Tennessee, later moved to southwest Missouri, settling near Sarcoxie. He served in the militia in pre-Civil War days, and was a state senator (1854–1861) when the war began. Appointed a brigadier general in the MSG, Rains served throughout the war. After the war he settled in Texas, where he died on May 19, 1880. Allardice, *More Generals in Gray*, 190–192; Banasik, *Confederate Tales, 1861*, 190–191.

to the lot of the Missouri forces.[13] To Cowskin Prairie, in McDonald County, all soon repaired, where the business of organization was hastened. Gen. Price took command of all the Missouri forces and forming a junction with Ben McCulloch at Cassville, moved upon Springfield.[14] Jackman participated in the skirmish at Dug Spring and the Battle of Oak Hills.[15] The army was at the time in a transition

13. On the morning of July 5, 1861, Rains's Division led out the MSG force, commanded by Governor C. F. Jackson, southward toward the town of Carthage. About 7:30 a.m. the two forces collided six miles from Carthage, near the Double Tree Creek (Sigel says it was two miles farther south at Dry Creek). Labeled the "Battle of Carthage," the engagement was actually a running fight of about 10 miles that began at the Spring River and proceeded southward into and through the town. Nightfall terminated the action. The rebel force numbered about 4,000 effectives, while the Federals, under Sigel, fielded about 1,100 men. The Unionists lost 18 killed, 53 wounded, and five missing; Confederates lost 12 killed, 64 wounded and one missing. *O.R.*, vol. 3:17, 20, 25; David C. Hinze and Karon Farnham, *The Battle of Carthage: Border War in Southwest Missouri, July 5, 1861* (Campbell, CA, 1997), frontis map, 202, 205, 278; Ward L. Schrantz, *Jasper County, Missouri In the Civil War* (Carthage, MO, 1923), 23, 31–33, hereafter cited as Schrantz.

14. The MSG, under General Price, departed Cowskin Prairie on July 25, 1861, marching toward Cassville, located in Barry County, Missouri, where a junction of forces was to occur. Price reached Cassville on July 28 and Generals McCulloch (commanding Confederate troops) and N. B. Pearce (commanding the Arkansas State troops), reached the town on July 29. The joint command moved forward toward Springfield on August 1, camping at Crane Creek on August 2, where the army again concentrated. On August 4, General Price agreed to allow McCulloch to command the entire force, after which the army moved out at midnight toward Springfield and the Federals, who were reported advancing on the joint Confederate, MSG, and Arkansas Militia force. *O.R.*, vol. 3:98–99; McGhee, *MSG Order Book*, unnumbered page 22.

Ben McCulloch was born in Tennessee in 1811. He fought at the Battle of San Jacinto, searched for gold in California in 1849, and was a U.S. Marshall in Texas. He received the surrender of the Federal forces in San Antonio in February 1861, and was commissioned a brigadier general on May 11, 1861. McCulloch commanded the District of the Indian Territory, which embraced the territory south of Kansas and west of Arkansas, in the early part of the war. He was the Confederate commander of record at the Battle of Oak Hills or Wilson's Creek (the Federal name for the battle) on August 10, 1861, and was killed at the Battle of Pea Ridge on March 7, 1862. *O.R.*, 3:575; Banasik, *Missouri in 1861*, 356–357; Warner, *Generals in Gray* 200–202.

15. Dug Springs was located about a mile southwest of present day Clever, Missouri. It consisted of a fresh spring of water and "two or three houses in the ravine." The skirmish at Dug Springs began at 9:00 a.m. on August 2, 1861, as the rebel advance, led by Rains's command of about 520 men, including an advance party of 120 men, fired at the Federal Army. In the ensuing skirmish, Rains initially drove back the Federals, but was in turn driven when a portion of his command "became panic-stricken and retired in the utmost confusion." Rains then "fell back, in accordance with instruction," even as Lyon's forces also fell back, thus abruptly ending the engagement. Losses on both sides were minor; the Federals reported losing four killed and seven wounded; Rains lost six wounded. However, in Dyer's *Compendium*, Federal losses are reported as four killed and 37 wounded. News reports at the time put the Confederate losses at "twenty-five killed and sixty to one hundred wounded." Additionally, General Frémont, the department commander, reported the Federal losses as eight killed and 30 wounded, while placing the rebel killed at 40 and wounded at 44. Since the Federals gave up the field immediately after the battle, this last comment seems a bit far-fetched, considering General Rains's report of the affair. *O.R.*, vol. 3:47, 50–51; *O.R.S.*, pt. 1, vol. 1:226–227; Banasik, *Missouri in 1861*, 132, 134; Dyer, 798; Elmo Ingenthron, *Borderland Rebellion A History of the Civil War on the Missouri-Arkansas Border* (Branson, MO, 1980), 78, hereafter cited as Ingenthron.

The Battle of Wilson's Creek was fought on August 10, 1861. The Confederates were commanded by Ben McCulloch and the Unionists were under Nathaniel Lyon. Advancing during

and half-organized condition, so that it was not at any time certain what was an officer's command. He was with Rains's troops, whose disorder in encampment in front of our line on the left center, prevented by its

Blundering Innocence

of military rules and tactics, the surprise of the whole force, and it was the coolness and intrepidity of Jackman and Missouri officers like him that saved us from disaster and annihilation.[16]

Shortly after the victory of Wilson's Creek the unsettled state of the country on the border above and within the vicinity of his home in Bates County rendered it necessary for Capt. Jackman to apply for a leave of absence and recruiting orders to enable him to look after his family and find them a place of safety. [James H.] Lane and [Charles R.] Jennison and [James] Montgomery had made incursions into Jackson and Cass Counties, in June, shortly after the beginning of hostilities.[17] They had sacked and burned Morristown on the edge of Kansas, in Cass,

---

the night of August 9–10, Lyon divided his command into two parts; he commanded one while General Franz Sigel led the other. The Federal attack began a little after 5:00 a.m., taking the rebel forces completely by surprise. In the end the Confederates rallied, driving the bluecoats from the field. The battle was a Confederate victory and one of the first major battles of the war. The rebels lost 257 killed, 900 wounded, and 27 missing, while the Federals posted losses of 223 killed, 721 wounded, and 291 missing. Among the dead was General Lyon. Banasik, *Missouri in 1861*, 143; Boatner, 932–935; Philips, 244, 249-250.

16. On the morning of August 10, the Confederates had no pickets out as they were preparing to march on Springfield. Colonel James Cawthorn, commanding Rains's Cavalry Brigade, ordered out a patrol at daylight to "allay his concerns" of what lay ahead of his advance brigade. A mile from camp the patrol ran into Lyon's scouts. Cawthorn sent a courier to Rains, informing his superior of the presence of Federal troops, but Rains did not believe that Lyon's entire force was present. Colonel John Snyder, of Rains's staff, investigated the scouting report, found it to be true, and per Rains's orders, hurried off to Price's headquarters. At Price's headquarters, Snyder found Price, McCulloch, and James McIntosh, and informed the trio of the presence of the Federal Army. The generals did not believe Snyder, calling it one of "Rains's scares," even as another rider brought in the same message. Seconds later the calm was broken by a cannon blast from Lyon's artillery. The lack of proper pickets and the arrogance of McCulloch, Price, and McIntosh almost cost the rebels the battle, even as the three commanders went forth to rally their commands, eventually to win. William Riley Brooksher, *Bloody Hill: The Civil War Battle of Wilson's Creek* (Washington, 1995), 179-180, 182-183.

17. James or "Jim" H. Lane was born in 1814 in Indiana, led a regiment in the Mexican War, and served a term in Congress and another as the lieutenant governor of Indiana. Moving to Kansas in 1855, Lane was the leading proponent of a slave-free state. He participated in the 1854–1860 Missouri-Kansas border wars and was elected the first senator from Kansas in April 1861. Best remembered for his raids into Missouri at the beginning of the Civil War, Lane burned and looted the town of Osceola on September 23, 1861. Of Lane's actions in Missouri, General Halleck wrote: "The conduct of the forces under Lane...has done more for the enemy in this State that could have been accomplished by 20,000 of his own army." Lane remained a factor of radicalism on the border throughout the war. He died on July 11, 1866, of a self inflicted gun shot, that some believe was a result of brain damage caused by an advanced case of syphilis. *O.R.*, vol. 3:196; *O.R.*, vol. 8:449; Banasik, *Reluctant Cannoneer*, 286–287; Alice L. Fry, *Following the Fifth Kansas Cavalry: The Letters* (Independence, MO, 1998), 24; Miles, 125.

Charles R. Jennison was born on June 6, 1834, in Antwerp, New York. In 1846, his family

and were demonstrating on the border counties below.[18] Jackman was permitted, therefore, with a part of his command to return home. He reached sufficiently near his own farm to view from one of the beautiful mounds with which Bates County abounds, only to witness the burning and destruction of his own house while powerless with the force at hand to save or protect his property. He made therefore the best disposition he could of his effects and took his wife and children to his former home in the hills in Howard County and placed them with his mother and near the residence of Mrs. Jackman's own people in Boone County.

In the Fall of 1861 he was at Lexington, but stayed back on the Missouri River after Price's retreat, being charged still with the delicate and perilous duties of the recruiting service, and only rejoining Gen. Price about the time shortly before the Battle of Pea Ridge.[19] He remained in Missouri after the unfortunate issue of that

---

moved to Wisconsin, where Charles studied medicine. Jennison married at age 20 and moved to Kansas from Minnesota in 1858, eventually settling near Mound City in Linn County, Kansas. Prior to the war "Doc" Jennison led frequent raids into Missouri to plunder slave holders, and he became one of the most hated men of the border region. According to Albert Castel, Jennison's traits were "brutality, unscrupulousness, and opportunism." Jennison raised the 7th Kansas Cavalry, which was mustered in U.S. service on October 28, 1861. When the 7th was ordered to Lawrence, Kansas in March 1862, Jennison resigned from the regiment. He survived the war, dying on June 21, 1884, just fifteen days after his fiftieth birthday. Castel, *Frontier State*, 43; Starr, 28–31, 385; *Union Army*, 4:208.

James Montgomery has previously been covered.

18. On September 10, 1861, James Lane led a brigade of 2,000 men into western Missouri, intent on "clearing out the valley of the Osage" and then the valley of Marais des Cygnes; his target towns were Butler (burned and looted December 14, 1861), Harrisville, Osceola (burned and sacked September 22, 1861) and Clinton. Two days later he reduced his command to protect various points in Kansas from possible attack. After Lane's Brigade entered Missouri, James Montgomery was dispatched with 600 men to attack Morristown on September 17. In the ensuing engagement, the Federals lost two killed, including Lieutenant Colonel H. P. Johnson, with six wounded, while killing seven rebels, according to Lane. However, eyewitnesses put the rebel losses at nine killed—all executed after Morristown was taken. Montgomery then sacked and burned the town. Lane sacked and burned Osceola on September 22 "on the grounds of military necessity and merited retaliation" for a Confederate attack on Humbolt, Kansas. *O.R.*, vol. 3:196, 485; Michael E. Banasik, *Cavaliers of the Brush: Quantrill and His Men* (Iowa City, IA), 2003), 8 (n. 4), hereafter cited as Banasik, *Cavaliers of the Brush*; Castel, *Frontier State*, 53–54; Gilmore, 136; Thomas Goodrich, *Black Flag: Guerrilla Warfare on the Western Border, 1861–1865* (Bloomington, IN, 1995), 19–20.

19. After Lexington, according to Jackman, he remained on the Missouri River, during the winter of 1861–1862, "giving such protection as I could to the people and making battle as occasion offered." He attacked and routed a Jayhawking force near Butler on November 20, 1861. And again at Butler, on December 8, he pursued the Federals, who had burned the town, and "stampeded them at a terrible rate." Contrary to Musser's comments, Jackman never joined Price prior to Pea Ridge (Jackman was north of the Missouri River at the time), but remained in Missouri or Arkansas for months to come. *O.R.*, vol. 8:1; Norton, 35, 37, 40, 43.

Lexington was the county seat of Lafayette County, Missouri, and the site of a siege from September 13–20, 1861. It was located about 300 miles from St. Louis by river with near 5,000 inhabitants, who worked primarily in the hemp industry. The city consisted of some manufacturing (hemp) with two colleges. The Masonic College, which embraced fifteen acres of land, served as the Federal defensive point during the siege. Colonel James Mulligan commanded the Federals, while Sterling Price led the Missourians. In the end, the Federals surrendered some 3,500 men, ac-

affair and reported in the spring of 1862 to Maj.-Gen. [Thomas C.] Hindman, and was by him commissioned to bring out recruits to the Confederate Army from the State of Missouri.

Duly Commissioned

on this service, Jackman spent the summer raising a battalion and recruiting in his old county, Bates, Vernon and the contiguous country, while these recruits kept watch along and protected the border of Kansas from the marauding jayhawkers. In the early days of August Gen. Vard Cockrell of Johnson County ordered a rendezvous of all the recruiting parties in the neighborhood of Johnson and Jackson Counties to meet corresponding dispositions of the Federals and jayhawkers.[20] Independence was then in position of the enemy in strong force, under Col. Buell, and on the 11th of August an attempt was made by the Confederates under Col. Up. Hays, reinforced by Col. John T. Hughes, aided by Capt. Quantrell [Quantrill], to capture the town.[21] The attack was successful, but resulted in the death

---

cording to Price, with five pieces of artillery, two mortars, 3,000 stands of small arms, 750 horses, $100,000 worth of commissary supplies, and the Great Seal of Missouri. Price put the rebel losses at 25 killed and 72 wounded, while Dyer's *Compendium* put Mulligan's losses at 42 killed, 108 wounded and 1,624 "captured and missing." *O.R.*, vol. 3:188; Banasik, *Missouri in 1861*, 182 (n. 79); Dyer, 798; McElroy, 206-207.

The Battle of Pea Ridge or Elkhorn Tavern, as it was known by the Confederates, took place in northwest Arkansas on March 6–8, 1862. General Earl Van Dorn commanded the Confederate forces while General Samuel R. Curtis led the Federals. After a three-day battle, a disorganized Confederate Army fled the area, having suffered as few as 1,000 casualties or as many as 2,000, depending on the source. Curtis reported 203 killed, 980 wounded and 201 captured or missing. *O.R.*, vol. 8:206, 282; Banasik, *Missouri Brothers in Gray*, 148–150; Boatner, 669; William L. Shea and Earl J. Hess, *Pea Ridge Civil War Campaign in the West* (Chapel Hill, NC, 1992), 271, hereafter cited as Shea & Hess.

20. Jeremiah Vard Cockrell was born on May 7, 1832, in Johnson County, Missouri, attended Chapel Hill College, near Lexington, and prospected for gold in California (1849–1853). A farmer and Methodist preacher by profession, Cockrell lived in Warren County prior to the war. On June 13, 1861, he was elected a lieutenant in Company E, 2nd Cavalry Regiment, 8th Division, MSG. During the summer of 1862 Cockrell recruited a regiment of cavalry, which was subsequently dismounted, causing Cockrell to lose command of the unit to S. D. Jackman. Cockrell was wounded in 1863 while recruiting. He recovered in time to participate in Price's 1864 Missouri Raid. Following the war he resided in Sherman, Texas, as a farmer, lawyer, and U.S. congressman (1893–1897). He died in Abilene, Texas, on March 18, 1915. Allardice, *Confederate Colonels*, 104; Norton, 63–64, 70, 123–125; Peterson, et al., 250, 284.

21. Lieutenant Colonel James T. Buell, of the 7th Missouri Cavalry, arrived at Independence on May 24, 1862, and assumed command of the local area. On August 11, 1862, Buell was attacked by the combined forces of John T. Hughes's Confederates and Quantrill's guerrillas. Defeated after a five hour battle, Buell surrendered his command. Federal losses were 26 killed, 74 wounded, with the loss of 300 muskets, 170 naval pistols, 200,000 rounds of ammunition, 300 horses, six wagons, one ambulance, and all the tents and garrison equipment—in all "fifteen to twenty" wagon loads of supplies. Gideon W. Thompson, second in command after the death of Hughes, reported the capture of about 350 Union prisoners, whom he paroled, while losing 11 killed with 27 wounded of his own force. The paroled Federals were sent to Benton Barracks in St. Louis, to await exchange. After details of the fight came out, Federal authorities decided to muster Buell and his entire command out of the service on August 25, 1862. Buell, for his part, was vilified in the press

of John T. Hughes, while leading the assault on Buell's stronghold, and many other valuable lives.[22] Buell surrender at discretion to [Upton] Hays, who shortly afterwards moved southward.[23] But in the meantime it was determined to surprise and capture Lone Jack, some twenty miles south of Independence, in which was a Federal garrison commanded by Maj. Emery Foster.[24] The dispositions were

---

for his actions at Independence. Atchison's *Freedom's Champion* stated that Buell "should be shot" for the debacle, while the *Daily Conservative* of Leavenworth labeled him "an unmitigated traitor." *O.R.*, vol. 13:228; *O.R.S.*, pt. 2, vol. 35:334–335; Banasik, *Embattled Arkansas*, 161–162, 503; Wiley Britton, *The Civil War on the Border: A Narrative of Military Operations in Missouri, Kansas, Arkansas, and the Indian Territory, During the Years 1861–62, Based Upon Official Reports of the Federal Commanders, Volume 1.* (New York, 1899), 323; "From Independence," *Freedom's Champion* (Atchison, KS), August 16, 1862; Joanne C. Eakin, *Battle of Independence August 11, 1862* (Independence, MO, 2000), 35, hereafter cited as Eakin, *Battle of Independence*; "Independence Taken," *Daily Conservative* (Leavenworth, KS), August 12, 1862; G. W. Thompson's Report, September 1, 1862, Miscellaneous Correspondence, Peter W. Alexander Collection, Columbia University, New York, hereafter cited as Miscellaneous Correspondence. See following notes for comments on John T. Hughes and Upton Hays. Quantrill will be covered at a later time.

22. John T. Hughes was born on July 25, 1817, in Woodford County, Kentucky, and moved to Howard County, Missouri, in 1820, where he graduated from Bonne Femme College (1844). He became a teacher, then served in the Mexican War under Alexander Doniphan. He wrote a popular book on the war titled *Doniphan's Expedition*, edited a newspaper, became a plantation owner, militia colonel, and was elected to the Missouri Legislature in 1854. At the beginning of the Civil War, Hughes was living in Plattsburg, Clinton County. He didn't believe in secession, but the capture of Camp Jackson changed his mind. He was elected captain of Company K, 1st Infantry Regiment, 4th Division, MSG on May 25, 1861, 15 days after Camp Jackson, and colonel of his regiment on June 21. He was at the Battles of Wilson's Creek and Lexington, Missouri, having been wounded at the latter place. Hughes was also at Pea Ridge, commanding the 2nd Confederate Brigade, following the wounding of William Slack. In mid-1862, Hughes was on recruiting service in Missouri and led the rebel troops, including Quantrill's guerrillas, to victory at Independence on August 11, 1862. Unfortunately, Hughes was killed while leading a charge at Independence, with a single shot to the forehead. *O.R.*, vol. 53:429, 441; Allardice, *Confederate Colonels*, 204; Allardice, *More Generals in Gray*, 132–133; Eakin & Hale, 220; Eakin, *Battle of Independence*, 38, 45; Peterson, et al., 136, 143, 147.

23. Upton Hays was born on March 29, 1832, in Callaway County, Missouri. He moved to Westport as a child and grew up to become a wealthy planter. Prior to the war he operated a freight line to Utah and Santa Fe. At the beginning of the Civil War he was elected captain of Company E, 1st Cavalry Regiment, 8th Division, MSG, and in December 1861, he was elected lieutenant colonel of the regiment. Hays commanded a regiment of Confederate cavalry in the summer of 1862, and was killed on September 13, 1862, near Newtonia, at Page Crossing, while leading a charge upon some Federal pickets. Earlier he had also been wounded at Independence and Lone Jack. *O.R.S.*, pt. 2, vol. 34:742; *O.R.S.*, pt. 2, vol. 38:260; Banasik, *Cavaliers of the Brush*, 64, 178–179; Eakin, *Battle of Independence*, 35; Eakin, see "Col. David Shanks" entry, *Confederate Records*, 7:14; John S. Krister, "Captured Guns At Lone Jack, Mo.," *Confederate Veteran* 24 (April 1916), 184; National Archives, Record Group 109, Confederate Muster Rolls, 12th Missouri Cavalry Regiment; Peterson, et al., 244; Webb, 322–325.

24. Major Emory S. Foster was born on November 5, 1839, in Greene County, Missouri, near Springfield. Educated locally, he was a printer by trade and co-owner of the *Missourian* newspaper. At the beginning of the Civil War, he organized a Union Home Guard Company, and after the unit was incorporated into the 27th Missouri Infantry, was elected major. Later he formed the "Frémont Scouts," and was mustered out of the service, with his unit, in January 1862. Returning home, Foster recruited a new battalion, was wounded fighting guerrillas in March 1862, and subsequently was appointed major of the 7th MSM Cavalry. Foster was severely wounded at the Bat-

adroitly made and the troops duly concentrated in the neighborhood of Lone Jack without seriously alarming the garrison, which had, as the commander supposed, been sufficiently reinforced on the evening of the 15th. Col. Jackman's regiment, Col. [DeWitt C.] Hunter's and Col. [John C.] Tracy's were in position, while Col. [John T.] Coffey [Coffee] was some four miles south of the Federals.[25] The plan of attack was duly laid, and the battle was to begin at daybreak, Col. Hays

To Give the Signal

by commencing the battle. Unfortunately Hays did not receive his orders promptly and the unsuspicious enemy were allowed to sound reveille, call the roll and be wide awake when the desultory attack was made. Coffee had moved, but had been misguided on the wrong road, only finding out his mistake after the battle began.[26] Tracy fell at the first fire and pretended to be wounded, but was really only scared, which created some confusion and consequent loss of life, but notwithstanding all

---

tle of Lone Jack, left the army, but returned in 1864, raised yet another battalion and participated in the battles of Price's 1864 Raid. After the war, Foster lived for a time in Jefferson City, then St. Louis, where he was the managing editor of the *St. Louis Journal*. In the fall of 1902 Foster moved to California to recover his health. He died on December 23, 1902, and was buried in Oakland. Banasik, *Confederate Tales, 1862*, 171–172.

25. DeWitt Clinton Hunter was born on August 2, 1830, in Manchester, Morgan County, Illinois. He lived for a time in California and Nevada, where he mined for gold. A lawyer by profession, Hunter surveyed and built the first house of Nevada, Missouri. At the beginning of the Civil War, he was the circuit and country clerk for Vernon County. He was elected colonel of the 7th Cavalry, 8th Division, MSG on July 10, 1861, and fought at Wilson's Creek, but resigned on December 10. He reentered the service as a Confederate major and was sent into Missouri on July 11, 1862, to recruit a regiment of infantry. He fought and was wounded at Lone Jack, then organized a cavalry battalion on August 31, 1862. After retreating to Arkansas, Hunter's command was dismounted and formed into an infantry regiment. Hunter led his command at Prairie Grove, Arkansas, on December 7, 1862, after which he again resigned on February 4, 1863. Hunter raised a new cavalry regiment in the spring of 1864, and led that regiment at Marks' Mill, Arkansas (April 25, 1864), where he was again wounded. His regiment was a part of Price's 1864 Raid. Following the war Hunter returned to Nevada, where he resumed the practice of law, then relocated to Oklahoma, where he died at Checotah on October 3, 1904. *O.R.S.*, pt. 2, vol. 38:273–274, 609; Allardice, *Confederate Colonels*, 207; Bartels, *Forgotten Men*, 178; Crute, *Confederate Army*, 208; Hale, *Branded As Rebels Volume Two*, 152–153; National Archives, Record Group 109, Confederate Muster Rolls, 11th Missouri Infantry; Snead, 269; Special Orders No. 28 (July 11, 1862), Special Order Book No. 1.
26. John Trousdale Coffee was born on December 14, 1816, in Smith County, Tennessee. He moved to Missouri in 1842, settling in Springfield and working as a lawyer. After service in the Mexican War, Coffee lived in Greenfield, Missouri, where he owned a local newspaper. He was elected to the Missouri Senate in 1854, and became speaker of the Missouri House (1859–1860). At the beginning of the Civil War, Coffee raised a regiment of MSG cavalry, of which he was elected colonel. Later he organized a regular Confederate unit in the summer of 1862, and another one in 1864. He was at Lone Jack, on Shelby's 1863 Missouri Raid, and Price's 1864 Raid. Following the war he moved to Brownsville, Texas, where he died on May 23, 1890. Allardice, *Confederate Colonels*, 104–105; Banasik, *Confederate Tales, 1862*, 170–171; John K. Hulston and James W. Goodrich, "John Trousdale Coffee: Lawyer, Politician, Confederate," *Missouri Historical Review* 85 (October 1990), 272–273, 275–277, 283, 290, 292, 294, hereafter cited as Hulston & Goodrich; Peterson, et al. 263.

the blunders and mistakes, Jackman, Hunter and Hays succeeded in carrying the enemy's position and capturing the place with many prisoners, among them the gallant Federal commander seriously wounded.[27] Jackman had many criticisms to make of this affair; the commander-in-chief seems to have been satisfied with having it planned, and trusted to it being spontaneously executed without providing sufficiently for the supervision or anticipating any unforeseen contingency. Tracy, who recovered his health and strength as soon as danger was over, having lost the confidence of the troops, made his way to Richmond where he presented to the War Department an elaborate report of the battle, the victory, and his own conduct as the hero.[28] He narrowly escaped being promoted to brigadier-general on his report, and was commissioned colonel, with authority to raise a regiment in Missouri as a reward for his boasted gallantry. But while he could get a commission at Richmond for his charlatanry he could never raise a command of Missourians, and

Disappeared From the State.

Blunders like the promotion of Tracy disgusted and exasperated Jackman. He was an honest man and detested the pretenders who always abound in military and civil life, but his patriotism and loyalty to the South and Missouri never wavered

---

27. John C. Tracy was born in Kentucky in about 1826, and was living in Columbus, Johnson County, Missouri, at the beginning of the Civil War. He was elected lieutenant colonel of the 3rd Infantry Regiment, 8th Division, MSG on June 19, 1861. Wounded at Wilson's Creek, Tracy recovered and spent the winter of 1861–1862 in the Lexington area recruiting for the rebel cause. In late spring 1862 Tracy was in Arkansas, having remained behind when the MSG moved to the east side of the Mississippi River. On June 4 General T. C. Hindman authorized Tracy to return to Missouri to recruit for the Confederacy. On July 31 Tracy began recruiting his regiment, then joined up with Cockrell, Hunter, Jackman, and Hays to fight and win the Battle of Lone Jack. Tracy was wounded at Lone Jack, but there is no further mention of him found in the *Official Record*s or the *Supplement to the Official Records*. However, according to a later comment, D. C. Hunter wrote, Tracy "long ago sleeps under the sod." Banasik, *Cavaliers of the Brush*, 223; Banasik, *Embattled Arkansas*, 170; Banasik, *Confederate Tales, 1862*, 105; Bartels, *Forgotten Men*, 364; Hale, *Branded As Rebels Volume Two*, 324; Letter (June 4, 1862), Hindman to Tracy, Copy Letter Book (June 1–December 18, 1862), Hindman's Command, Peter W. Alexander Collection, hereafter cited as Copy Letter Book No. 1.
28. In the years following the Battle of Lone Jack, Sidney Jackman wrote of the cowardice of Tracy, Hunter, and Hays at the battle, while, he, Jackman, was the real hero of the engagement. It appears that Richard Musser also supported Jackman's comments on Tracy, who feigned being wounded while the battle progressed. Meeting a wounded Tracy en route to the rear, Jackman recalled that Tracy told him that he was "shot all to pieces," but upon examination by Jackman, the latter returned to the battlefield "with a feeling of supreme contempt" for Tracy. Jackman "was thoroughly convinced" that Tracy was "mistaken, as to what it was running down his legs"; it wasn't blood. However, Tracy's men thought differently of their commander. Henry Luttrell wrote that "Jackman's imagination was hard at work when he accused Col. Tracy of cowardice." Tracy "faced the music" and helped capture the Federal artillery during the battle, according to Luttrell, while Jackman's command was struggling to get at the Union artillery. Granville C. Bowen, also of Tracy command, likewise supported Luttrell's comments, adding that "Col. Jackman did Col. Tracy a great injustice when he made his remarks." Banasik, *Confederate Tales, 1862*, 99, 103, 111, 113; S. D. Jackman, "Battle of Lone Jack," *Missouri Republican*, August 29, 1885; Norton, 97.

nor wearied in the midst of many such trials as befell him and many other soldiers. With his regiment he moved southward and rendered good service to Shelby at Newtonia, after which affair he was ordered by Gen. Hindman to turn over his command to his junior officer and once more to undertake the perils and hardships of the recruiting service.[29] This in a measure deprived him of the brilliant chances for promotion and reputation in the field which a distinct and definite command would have given him, but it was a compliment to that cool and vigilant courage, that plain, practical sense and woodcraft that benefitted him for the peculiar duties of recruiting, in the exercise of which he was of more value to the cause than in the field.[30]

The winter of 1862 and 1863 was one of great moments to the Missouri soldier, for the hope that's never altogether died out in him of returning and occupying his own land was strong in him that winter. Hindman, who was a man of genius, had been superseded by Gen. Theophilus Holmes, a soldier honest and brave, but without genius, was still in command of the District of Arkansas, and held practically the Boston Mountains in the earlier months of the winter.[31] He fell back under Holmes's order to Fort Smith, and Gen. Blount [Blunt] came into the state with his forces.[32]

---

29. Jackman makes no mention in his memoirs of rendering any type of service to Shelby at the Battle of Newtonia; indeed, Jackman was down in Arkansas at the time, organizing his infantry regiment. The First Battle of Newtonia took place in southwest Missouri in Newton County and was fought on September 30, 1862. The Federals were commanded by General Frederick Salomon, while the Confederates were led by Colonel Douglas H. Cooper. The battle began shortly after dawn and continued throughout the day. The Unionists eventually withdrew, having suffered 50 killed, 80 wounded, and 113 captured, while the Confederates lost 12 killed, 63 wounded, and three missing. Joe Shelby and Thomas C. Hindman have already been covered. *O.R.*, vol. vol. 13, 286–307; Dyer, 804; Norton, 121–122.

30. Jackman resigned from the service on October 23, 1862, and was subsequently assigned two days later to recruit a cavalry regiment to operate in the state of Missouri. In his letter to General Hindman, Jackman stated that he preferred cavalry service to that of infantry. Overall, Jackman preferred the life of a partisan ranger or a guerrilla to that of regular service. Lieutenant Colonel Josiah Caldwell, from Brook's Arkansas Regiment, was placed in command of Jackman's Regiment. Special Orders No. 22 (October 25, 1862), Special Order Book No. 1; Miscellaneous Correspondence, Jackman to Hindman (October 23, 1862).

31. Major General Theophilus H. Holmes was born in 1804, graduated from West Point (number 44 of 46) in 1829, and served in the Seminole War and Mexican War. He was appointed a Confederate brigadier general on June 5, 1861, and served in the East until named the commander of the Trans-Mississippi Department on July 16, 1862. He was promoted to lieutenant general to rank from October 10, 1862, relieved as department commander on March 7, 1863, and fought and lost the Battle of Helena (July 4, 1863). Following the debacle at Helena, Holmes was relegated to a minor role in the Trans-Mississippi and finally resigned in 1864. Banasik, *Missouri Brothers in Gray*, 141–143; Boatner, 406; Sifakis, *Who Was Who in the Confederacy*, 133, 261.

32. James G. Blunt was born on July 21, 1826, in Trenton, Maine. He obtained a medical degree in Ohio and moved to Greely, Kansas, in 1856. An abolitionist and supporter of John Brown, Blunt led a militia company during the Kansas-Missouri border wars. At the beginning of the Civil War Blunt enlisted as a private, was appointed the lieutenant colonel of the 3rd Kansas Infantry, and on April 8, 1862, was catapulted to the rank of brigadier general. Blunt lead the Kansas Division in the fall of 1862, and later the Army of the Frontier, which fought and won the Battles of Old Fort

The Battle of Prairie Grove

resulted disastrously to the Confederate armies and gave southwest Missouri and northwest Arkansas to the Federals.[33] Hindman could have commanded a department or made a first-class minister of war but he frankly confessed on all occasions he could not command an army in the field or plan and execute a battle.[34] Holmes could do neither. He contented himself with undoing all the good that Hindman could have done and as far as he could thwarting all his plans. Jackman with some chosen and trusted officers, among them Maj. [John F.] Rucker and Capt. [James F.] Wilhite, left Arkansas in the spring of 1863—2d of April—making their way to his old neighborhood in Bates County.[35] Col. Caleb Perkins

---

Wayne, Indian Territory (October 22), Cane Hill (November 28), Prairie Grove (December 7) and Van Buren, Arkansas (December 28). Blunt spent his entire Civil War career in the Trans-Mississippi, participating in his last engagements during Price's 1864 Raid. A popular general with the soldiers, Blunt was promoted to major general on March 3, 1863, a grade he held until the end of the war. After the war Blunt returned to medicine in Leavenworth, Kansas, then moved to Washington, DC, where he died in a government hospital for the insane on July 27, 1881. Banasik, *Reluctant Cannoneer*, 273–277.

33. The Battle of Prairie Grove was fought in northwest Arkansas on Sunday, December 7, 1862. The battle began just before dawn and lasted the entire day. Initially successful, the Confederates failed to hold the initiative, allowing the out-maneuvered Federal forces time to concentrate. By 3:15 p.m. the two wings of the Federal Army, commanded by James G. Blunt and Francis Herron, were united on the battlefield and managed to survive the day. During the night, General Hindman, believing he faced insurmountable odds, and being short of ammunition, ordered his command to retreat, giving the field and the victory to the Unionists. Confederate official losses were reported as 164 killed, 817 wounded, and 336 missing; total 1,317. However this does not correspond with the losses listed by the various brigade or regimental commanders, who reported 204 killed, 872 wounded, and 407 missing; total 1,487. The Union command lost 175 killed, 813 wounded, and 263 missing; total 1,251. *O.R.*, vol. 22, pt. 1:86, 142; Banasik, *Embattled Arkansas*, 338–339, 428–429, 431, 458–459, 513, 515–517.

34. Musser was right. Following the Battle of Prairie Grove, General Hindman lamented his failure to press the enemy, feeling that had cost him the battle. Hindman further spoke of the matter to General Holmes, via a telegraphic conversation:

> I am so completely dissatisfied about my failure to destroy the enemy's force that I think immediately of quitting the service. I believe I am only useful in organizing and providing. Don't know enough to handle an army in the field.

Telegram Collection, Telegraphic Conversation between Hindman and Holmes (December 12, 1862), Peter W. Alexander Collection.

35. Musser was mistaken as to when Jackman returned to Missouri. After giving up his regiment to recruit a cavalry command, Jackman left Arkansas "about the middle of November," 1862, not in April 1863. Norton, 141.

According to Larry Wood there were two John F. Ruckers—one a famous "noted guerrilla," a Missourian Guardsman, and Confederate officer, and another with a similar background. Both men came from Boone County, joined the MSG, and eventually became Confederate majors. The one whom Jackman knew and Musser refers to, John F. Rucker, was born in Virginia, "around 1830," lived in Rocheport, while the other Rucker was ten years younger and lived in Sturgeon. The Daughters of the Confederacy have the two men as one and the same. See Appendix B for a biography. Eakin, *Confederate Records*, 6:197–198; Larry Wood, *Other Noted Guerrillas of the Civil War in Missouri* (Joplin, MO, 2007), 195, 278 (n. 1), hereafter cited as Wood, *Noted Guerrillas*.

departed at the same time in his company for the scene of his dangerous service north of the Missouri River, in Randolph and contiguous counties.[36] After spending some time organizing the service in Bates and southwestern counties, Jackman, with Rucker and Wilhite, proceeded to the Perchi Hills, where their families resided, and there Jackman having opened communications with Perkins and other officers in that region under similar orders, took command of the recruiting parties not yet ordered to the rendezvous for the purpose of going south. The Federal garrisons were composed mostly of militia organizations, the regular volunteers at that season being in the field in front. He made his headquarters in the neighborhood of Boonsbough, nearly the first settlement in North Missouri by the hardy pioneers who

Followed Daniel Boone,

the thickets and paths of which he had known since his boyhood. Here he began to enlist soldiers for the Confederacy, who rallied enthusiastically to his standard. More than ordinary prudence was required to succeed without detection and arrest. His duty frequently led him into the lines of the Federal outposts and to be in the camps of the militia, among whom he secured some valuable recruits who were serving there much against their will.[37] By the 1st or middle of August he had succeeded in partially organizing a good battalion, nearly ready at the

---

James F. Wilhite (or Wilhut or Wilheit) was a resident of Cooper County at the beginning of the Civil War. He was captured at Blackwater or Milford, Missouri, on December 19, 1861, and sent to Alton, Illinois Prison. Exchanged in September 1862, Wilhite returned to the Trans-Mississippi and joined Jackman in the fall of 1862, when the latter returned to Missouri on recruiting duty. Wilhite was captured in Howard County at the house of Jackman's mother, on January 30, 1863, and sent to Gratiot and Myrtle Street Prison in St. Louis. Wilhite attempted an escape on July 22, 1863, by jumping out of a prison window, injuring his leg. He was recaptured and returned to prison. Final disposition unknown. Bartels, *Forgotten Men*, 390; Eakin, *Missouri Prisoners of War*, "Wilheit, Jas. F." entry, "Wilhut, James F.—?" entry; Norton, 145–146, 151.

36. Caleb Perkins was born on December 13, 1829, in Clark County, Kentucky, and was living in Rennick, Missouri, at the beginning of the Civil War. He joined H. T. Fort's Randolph County Company, MSG and later became captain of the unit. On September 24, 1861, upon organization of the 5th Infantry Regiment, 3rd Division, MSG, Perkins was elected major of the unit. Perkins fought with distinction at the Battle of Pea Ridge and later left the unit to operate for a time as a guerrilla, serving with Bill Anderson, while recruiting for the Confederacy. During Price's 1864 Raid, Perkins joined the Confederate Army and was wounded at Glasgow, Missouri, on September 23. Returning to Arkansas with his recruits, Perkins was elected colonel of an infantry regiment in the fall of 1864, but never saw action again. He was paroled at Alexandria on June 7, 1865, and returned home, where he farmed until he died on February 27, 1901, at Prairie Hill, Missouri. *O.R.*, vol. 40, pt. 1:415–418; Allardice, *Confederate Colonels*, 303; Banasik, *Serving With Honor*, 202 (n. 4); Banasik, *Cavaliers of the Brush*, 81 (n. 240); Bartels, *Trans-Mississippi Men*, 33; William Niel Block, *Shades of Gray Confederate Soldiers and Veterans of Randolph County, Missouri* (Shawnee Mission, KS, 1996), 56; Crute, *Confederate Army*, 209; Eakin & Hale, 344; National Archives, Record Group M322 (roll no. 175), Confederate Compiled Service Records, Perkin's Infantry Battalion; Peterson, et al., 126, 128.

37. On one occasion Jackman, with John Rucker's assistance, managed to enlist an entire company of militia. Of the incident Jackman wrote:

appointed signal to concentrate on the Missouri River and march southward. He had accurate information of all that transpired in the militia camps through his men who were in the Federal service and was quietly making his arrangements to cross the river, when on the 27th of August he fell in with a small body of home guards at Morgan Taylor's blacksmith shop, a few miles north of Fayette. The militia were commanded by Maj. Reeves Leonard,[38] and after a sharp fight were repulsed, Jackman having received a severe wound in the affray, from which he was for some time laid up.[39]

After this affray the country was filled with thieves and murders, who pillaged promiscuously the Southern and Union people, claiming to be Jackman's men. It was, therefore, convenient for the Union authorities to assume they were such, and was the occasion of

---

> On reaching the drill ground, I found Capt. James McDonald drilling his company...On our approach, the whole company cheered heartily, throwing up their hats and shouting for Jeff Davis and the Confederacy. I now enlisted the Captain and 40 of his men in an hour.
>
> This incident probably occurred near Rocheport on May 22, 1863. Norton, 161; "Our St. Louis Letter," *Chicago Tribune,* May 27, 1863.

38. Reeves Leonard was a major in the 9th MSM Cavalry and cousin to Charles and Ben Leonard, who were captured by Sidney Jackman on March 31, 1863. Born in Missouri in about 1839, Leonard was educated at Dartmouth University, then spent two more years of study in Berlin, Germany. At the beginning of the Civil War, Leonard returned to the United States and on February 12, 1862, was mustered in as the captain of Company A, 9th MSM Cavalry. He was promoted to major on June 4, 1863, and served his entire military service in Missouri. In January 1865, Leonard took a leave of absence from his command to participate in the Missouri State Convention. On May 9, 1865, Leonard resigned from the army citing "previous private affairs." National Archives, Record Group M405 (roll no. 218), Union Compiled Service Records, 9th MSM Cavalry; Thoma, 82, 96.

39. Musser is mixing up two separate engagements that Jackman had with Federal troops. On June 1, 1863, Jackman made contact with a Federal scouting party under Captain S. W. Steinmetz, scattering the party. Returning to Fayette for assistance, Steinmetz found Captain Reeves Leonard, commanding 75 men of Companies A and G, 9th EMM. Leonard then re-engaged Jackman three miles northeast of Rocheport. In this second fight, the bulk of Jackman's men, being new recruits, buckled, leaving Jackman barely a dozen men to sustain the engagement. After twenty minutes, Jackman retreated, losing two men killed according to Leonard, while the Federals lost, in both engagements, one killed, seven wounded (one mortally), with one missing (1st Sergeant Vance was captured by Jackman and paroled). Jackman stated that he lost one man killed and one man wounded. A Federal participant in the engagement reported "four killed, left on the field, and perhaps twice that number wounded."

The other incident, where Jackman was wounded, occurred at 9:00 a.m. on the morning of June 18. Federal troops, numbering 40 men (25 from Company A and 15 from Company B) pretending to be recruits for Jackman's band, approached the rebel camp, but Jackman was not fooled and opened fire on them. In the ensuing battle Jackman was the only man wounded on the Confederate side, while the Federals reported "several lost, killed and wounded on both sides." O.R., vol. 22, pt. 1:343–344, 373–374; O.R.S., pt. 2, vol. 35, 601; Dyer, 807; Norton, 167, 171; Participants, "Fight Near Rocheport," *Rebellion Record*, vol. 7: Doc 273–274.

A Proclamation

issued by Gen. T. J. Bartholow, who was in command of the militia at Glasgow, against the "notorious" Jackman, treating him as an outlaw and his men and followers as bushwhackers and guerrillas.[40] This proclamation denounced punishments of the most summary nature against Jackman and his troops, placing them beyond the pale of the courtesies of civilized warfare. It also threatened summary vengeance against all persons who might be found or suspected of aiding and abetting by subsistence or otherwise any of them. Jackman knew the loyal part of the militia, many of them Germans and persons of foreign birth, would not be slow to avail themselves of it as a license to pillage his friends, to burn their houses and from wantonness or spite proceed to extreme of murder, if the proclamation was not withdrawn or by some bold stroke counteracted.

He, therefore, being nearly recovered from his wound, communicated with one of his men whom he trusted implicitly, serving in Bartholow's camp, and made preparations for Bartholow's capture. On the night of the 18th of September, Jackman with twenty-seven men, accompanied by Maj. Rucker, repaired to Will's old saw-mill, which they reached about 12 o'clock at night, and were there met by a guide from Glasgow.[41] The old saw-mill was situated on Hurricane Creek, about one and a half miles south of Congreve Jackson's mansion, and perhaps four miles from town.[42] Consulting with Rucker, they arranged their plans

---

40. Thomas J. Bartholow was born in Maryland, on January 31, 1821, a grocer, banker, and tobacco manufacturer among his various trades. He was married with two children. Bartholow was a Mexican War veteran and was living in Glasgow at the beginning of the Civil War. He commanded the 8th District of the Enrolled Missouri Militia, based in Glasgow, and is best remembered for being captured in his house, by Sidney Jackman on April 23, 1863. Bartholow was later released after he agreed not to press "charges against farmer Jazaleel Maxwell...[for] 'providing aid and comfort'" to some of Jackman's men. Returning to duty, Bartholow remained but a short time, when he was pressured to resign on August 31, 1863, in a large part for the deal he had made with Jackman. Living out his remaining years in Glasgow, Bartholow died on May 19, 1879. Karen Carmichael Boggs and Louise Muir Coutts, *Howard County Cemetery Records* (n.c., n.d.), 602; *History of Howard and Chariton Counties*, 265, 451; John B. Gray, *Annual Report of the Adjutant General of Missouri for 1864* (Jefferson City, MO, 1864), 391, hereafter cited as Gray, *Missouri Adjutant General Report*; Heitman, 2:78; Rose Mary Lankford, *The Encyclopedia of Quantrill's Guerrillas* (Evening Shade, AR, 1999), 10, hereafter cited as Lankford; Bruce Nichols, *Guerrilla Warfare in Civil War Missouri, Volume II, 1863* (Jefferson, NC, 2012), 66–67, hereafter cited as Nichols, *Guerrilla Warfare, Volume II*; Norton, 153.
41. According to period newspapers the capture of General Bartholow occurred on April 23, 1863, at 2:00 a.m. The guide was Logan Shipp, whose name is mentioned later in Musser's account of Bartholow's capture. Nichols, *Guerrilla Warfare, Volume II*, 66; "Our St. Louis Letter," *Chicago Tribune*, April 27, 1863; Wood, *Noted Guerrillas*, 200.
42. Congreve Jackson was born in Howard County, Missouri, near Glasgow, in about 1803. He received little schooling during his life, but was called a "man of wisdom...and his judgement without error." A Democrat and a slave owner, Jackson served as a militia general in 1838 during the "Mormon difficulties," then in the Second Seminole War (1835–1842) as a captain, commanding Company D, 1st Missouri Volunteers under Colonel Richard Gentry. During the Mexican War, Jackson commanded a battalion and served as the executive officer (lieutenant colonel) in the 1st Missouri Mounted Volunteers. Jackson was elected colonel of the 2nd Infantry Regiment, 3rd

and proceeded to march the whole force to Bear Creek, about three-quarters of a mile from Glasgow, and to the northeast of town. There they dismounted, leaving twelve men to guard the horses, which hey concealed on the creek in the woodland pasture belonging to L. H. Turner,[43] while Jackman and Rucker, with the balance of the force following their guide, proceeded to

Steal Through the Pickets.

They proceeded to Bartholow's residence on the hill, where they arrived about 3 o'clock in the morning, having silently approached through a vineyard to within about thirty yards of the house to a back picket fence which Rucker proceeded to pull down. They next without noise surrounded the house. Jackman, Maj. Rucker and the guide went to the front door and gave several raps before anyone answered. Bartholow then spoke and asked who was there. Rucker replied, telling him to get up as he had a verbal message for him. The general lighted a lamp and opened the door, upon which Rucker stepped in, and as he did so Jackman covered Bartholow with his shotgun, being still standing out on the steps. Noticing

---

Division, MSG, on August 11, 1861. He led his command at Lexington and Pea Ridge, where he was cited for "great bravery during the hottest part of the engagement." Jackson served briefly as the 3rd Division commander, until Edwin Price was elected commanding general on December 2, 1861. Jackson led his regiment at Pea Ridge, after which he left the Guard, due to age and "infirmities." Indications are that he organized an irregular force in the spring of 1863, and led it into southwest Missouri, in conjunction with Tom Livingston. No further Civil War record was recorded on Jackson. He later crossed the Mississippi River, where he completed his military service, and was paroled at Columbus, Mississippi, on June 15, 1865. Following the war, Jackson returned to his home in Howard County, where he died, a bachelor, on May 19 1869. *O.R.*, vol. 3:191; *O.R.*, vol. 8:319; *O.R.*, vol. 22, pt. 2:109, 225; *O.R.*, vol. 53:438–439; Ephraim McD. Anderson, *Memoirs: Historical and Personal; Including the Campaigns of the First Missouri Confederate Brigade* (St. Louis, 1868; reprint ed., Dayton, OH, 2005), 103, 108, cited hereafter as Anderson; Banasik, *Confederate Tales, 1862*, 162; Eakin, *Confederate Records*, 4:120; Eakin & Hale, 230; Heitman, 2:56, 281; *History of Audrain County, Missouri, Written and Compiled from the Most Authentic Official and Private Sources: Including a History of Its Townships, Towns and Villages* (St. Louis, 1884), 55–56; Peterson, et al., 15; Richard H. Musser, "Two Missouri War Characters," *Missouri Republican*, November 14, 1885.

43. L. H. Turner was probably Lynch Turner, who was born in Howard County on December 19, 1828, and had the same surname as his father. Lynch's father owned the farm while Lynch was living in Huntsville, Missouri, about 20 miles away. The farm passed on to the elder Turner's wife, Nancy, who died in Howard County in 1869. The younger Turner joined the MSG in June 1861, later joined the regular Confederate Service in December 1861, as a member of the 3rd Missouri Infantry (CSA). Turner fought in all the early battles in the Trans-Mississippi, then transferred with his command to the east side of the Mississippi River, where he completed his military service as a captain and commissary officer. After the war Turner returned to Missouri, working as a farmer, a common laborer, a teacher, and in 1897 the superintendent of the Confederate Home in Higginsville, Missouri. In 1903, Turner became a resident of the Home, due to poor health. He died at the age of 88 on March 31, 1917. Wade Ankesheiln, *Eight-Hundred Voices: Each With A Story To Tell. A Guide to the Confederate Memorial Cemetery Missouri Historical Site Higginsville, Missouri* 2 vols. (Independence, MO, 2009), 1:260–261, hereafter cited as Ankesheiln, *Eight-Hundred Voices*; Ankesheiln, *Last Guardsmen*, 208; Eakin, *Confederate Records*, 7:154; Nichols, *Guerrilla Warfare, Volume IV*, 101–102.

Jackman out there he turned to grasp his pistol which was laying on the stand, being suspicious of his visitors. But the general presuming that Jackman had the drop on him, surrendered and asked to know whose hands he had been so unlucky as to fall into.[44] Jackman replied in a loud tone, "this is the *notorious Jackman*." He then ordered Bartholow to dress in a hurry, assuring him he had no time to delay, which somewhat excited Bartholow, but he proceeded to obey, and asked permission to ride his own horse. The horse was brought out in a few minutes by Bartholow's servants, then under guard, and the whole party with the Federal commander, his horse being led walked to where Jackman's party had left their horses in Turner's pasture. Here

They All Mounted,

Jackman riding by Bartholow's side. The march was some ten or twelve miles, and as the day broke about the sixth or seventh mile the general was blindfolded as a precaution that he should not know the locality he was going to. The party arrived in the morning at a thicket not far from the road from Boonsborough to Arrow Rocks, which was Jackman's headquarters. Very little conversation enlivened the trip across the hills through the paths and dense timber in which they traveled. Bartholow being left to his own meditations.[45]

After the long and tiresome ride Gen. Bartholow was given some breakfast and permitted to indulge in such reflections as his situation would naturally suggest to him. Jackman then proceeded to business. He produced the proclamation signed by Bartholow as commander of the state militia under the authority of the United States, he called the general's attention to the fact that he had not issued a counter proclamation but was now in a position to take the initiative by acting on it and not waiting till provoked to retaliation: That it had become possible for him (Bartholow) to be the first victim by the application in his own person of the inhuman doctrine and the practices inculcated by his own teaching; and he wanted to know if such violent and lawless extremities were to be resorted by the Federal authorities and by Gen. Bartholow in particular. He proceeded: "I and my command are not bushwhackers, guerrillas and robbers. I am a regular commissioned officer of the Confederate States, a belligerent power, and so recognized as at war

---

44. A period piece has Jackman, with a party of 12 men arriving at 2:00 a.m. at Bartholow's house. Of Jackman's party only Major Rucker approached Bartholow's residence, while the rest of the band remained hidden. A cautious Bartholow was distrustful of the stranger at his door and kept a pistol on him even after Rucker was allowed to enter the house. Following a ten-minute conversation with Major Rucker, who said he had a message from General Odon Guitar, in Columbia, Bartholow was captured. Despite being armed, Bartholow surrendered when confronted by the rest of Jackman's band. *History of Howard and Cooper Counties*, 286–287; "Our St. Louis Letter," *Chicago Tribune*, April 27 and 29, 1863.

45. Jackman and party traveled through the night, in a southeasterly direction, making about 12 miles by daylight. A little after sunrise Major Rucker departed, taking the rest of the men with him, save one. Jackman and Bartholow, with the one guard, then began a serious discussion centering on Jackman's status and the status of his men. *History of Howard and Cooper Counties*, 287.

with your government. I have orders from the commander of the Trans-Mississippi Department to perform my duties here, and am here because the Federal Army has not heretofore been able to

Dislodge Me.

"I am not lurking in your camp as a spy, and am only using the measure against you recognized as proper in honorable warfare. We do not rob or subsist on the country, but we subsist at the expense of the Confederate government. To satisfy you, general," continued Jackman. "I will show you my orders and authority from the Confederate commander.[46] You can thus determine whether your proclamation ought to apply to my command, whether we are to make war like regular enlisted soldiers or like guerrillas and outlaws."

Bartholow examined carefully the contents of the orders shown him by Col. Jackman. His situation was most perplexing. He was at Jackman's mercy on either hand of the dilemma. If Jackman was to be treated as an outlaw, he was himself to be the first victim on anticipatory retaliation of his own proclamation. If Jackman was a belligerent and recognized as a soldier of the Confederacy, he was at least a prisoner of war and liable to be taken South. Jackman, who comprehended his situation and divined his thoughts, only asked him for his parole of honor for three days, which was given, and the guards dismissed to other duties.[47] Without constraint of threats of influence, the Federal officer was allowed to reflect at his leisure for some time, when, toward noon, Jackman resumed the colloquy, saying: "General, you have seen my papers, and you comprehend the situation entirely. Will you treat my people as bushwhackers, and robbers, and force me into a kind of warfare that you and all other soldiers like myself detest? You can make up your mind without constraint. You and I have been friends many years, and that your judgement may be entirely

Free From the Duress

and constraint you are in, I assure you your captivity will bring you no worse consequences than your three day's parole. I will not begin my retaliations for such acts as your proclamation may induce to be committed on my friends—possibly

---

46. See Appendix A for copies of Jackman's resignation and subsequent assignment to recruit a regiment in Missouri.
47. According to period correspondence by Bartholow and local newspapers, Bartholow gave no type of parole, but rather writing briefly to General John B. Gray, Missouri Adjutant General:
GLASGOW, April 24.
General John B. Gray, A.G.; I was released by Jackman yesterday evening; have just arrived at headquarters. I positively refused to take any oath or accept any parole, or compromise my honor. Particulars by mail.
T. J. BARTHOLOW, Brig. Gen.
History of Howard and Cooper Counties, 286; "Our St. Louis Letter," *Chicago Tribune*, April 29, 1863.

my family—by any act of cruelty to you, whom I have known and respected for long years before this war."

Bartholow answered: "Thus assured that I am paroled for three days, which parole I have given, I will say, Col. Jackman, I was constrained to issue the proclamation upon what I supposed trustworthy information, that the term guerrilla did properly apply to the troops under your command. I issued it in accordance with the orders I received from my superiors, and thought that its application to freebooters and guerrillas made it apply to your troops.[48] I have seen your papers, am satisfied that you are a regularly commissioned Confederate officer, that you are performing here a daring an honorable service, and one full of peril. I appreciate, especially under my current circumstance, but would, were I otherwise situated, that you are entitled to all the courtesies and amenities of civilized war. I am your paroled prisoner for three days. During that time my mouth is sealed as to anything that may transpire in your camp, or between you and me. When it pleases you you can fix limits to my imprisonment on parole, and I will keep to the bonds. I can only tell you what I can do. I will not enforce, nay, I will revoke my orders containing that proclamation, but I can make no promises for the actions of my superiors or the United States Government. I may not be in command on Glasgow long after the news of my being captured in my own quarters at night, amid my own troops, and guarded by my own sentinels, shall have reached the authorities. I suggest to you, therefore, colonel, make your best dispositions pending my parole, for I can only promise for myself and not for the action of my superiors."[49]

Bartholow was soon afterward escorted with due precaution to the high road and

Permitted to Return

to his company, where he had been anxiously looked for, having suffered no other indignity that the necessary restraints of his captivity and parole.[50] Jackman had

---

48. Bartholow was operating under instructions, dated March 30, 1863, from Samuel R. Curtis, commanding the Department of Missouri, which reads in part: "Death to bushwhackers is the order. Have commission always ready to try, determine, and execute immediately, if they are unfortunately taken alive." *O.R.*, vol. 22, pt. 2:184.
49. Bartholow remained in command at Glasgow until at least June 30, 1863, his reputation seemingly unaffected by the experience with Jackman as noted in one piece:
    > General Bartholow is now at his post in attendance upon his ordinary duties, his standing as an officer of the militia unimpeached, and his honor in no wise jeopardized by the unfortunate occurrence. His course under the trying circumstances in which he acted, cannot but be approved by all judicious and just persons.

    However, according to another source, once the details of Bartholow's capture and his promises to exchange captured Jackman guerrillas for Unionists, Bartholow was forced to resign on August 31, 1863. *O.R.*, vol. 22, pt. 2:351; Gray, *Missouri Adjutant General Report*, 392; *Howard and Cooper Counties*, 287; Norton, 153–154; "Our St. Louis Letter," *Chicago Tribune*, April 29, 1863.
50. Bartholow was released on the evening of April 23, and returned to his command the next morning. In addition to Bartholow's agreement on the treatment of captured guerrillas, he also agreed

in the meantime issued orders and made his dispositions to march southward. Perkins was notified and the scattered detachments of recruits were called to rendezvous at the river, when preparations were actively and quickly made. Skiffs and boats were soon prepared so that on the 17 of October, or within about thirty days subsequent to the capture and release of Gen. Bartholow, his command were all safely over and moving southward. He was soon beyond the Osage, and once behind that stream they were in force to make their way through the sparsely settled hills and prairies to the Confederate Armies in Arkansas.

The foregoing statement I can make upon the authority of both parties most interested. Bartholow and Jackman have both related the substantial facts to me, besides which I am indebted to the wonderfully accurate memory of Col. Caleb Perkins for dates, as well as incidents otherwise out of my reach, and to the guide who showed Jackman the way to Glasgow, Mr. Logan Shipp of Chariton County, and who was eyewitness to the capture.

It is hardly necessary to relate that Bartholow kept his parole like an honorable gentleman and soldier, and for keeping his further word not to enforce the proclamation was soon after

Relieved of His Command.

It was only a little time after this incident that the Federal authorities sent a detachment down into the Perchi Hills and arrested the elder Mrs. Jackman, the mother and two sisters, together with Col. Jackman's wife with an infant scarcely a week old, and carried them off to St. Louis as prisoners of war.[51] They were taken before Col. James O. Broadhead, then Provost Marshal.[52] Broadhead released the elder lady and her two daughters, but paroled Mrs. Jackman for a short time that she might return for her other children whom she left standing in the yard, so precipitate had been the arrest, and report to him for banishment South. This affair occasioned Col. Jackman great and honest indignation. In all other matters he was a most forgiving man, but on this subject he was "a good hater." The last time I ever saw him was in this city when we both called on Gen. Frost. In our free conversation about the war the name of the Federal officer was mentioned

---

to pardon Jazaleel Maxwell, a man accused of harboring Jackman's guerrillas. Additionally, Bartholow was supposed to have agreed to reimburse Maxwell $200 dollars in gold for two horses that members of the EMM had taken from him. *History of Howard and Cooper Counties*, 287; Norton, 153; "Our St. Louis Letter," *Chicago Tribune*, April 29, 1863; Wood, *Noted Guerrillas*, 201.

51. The capture and subsequent exile of Martha Jackman, and her six children to St. Louis, occurred in September 1863, following the birth of her son, Sidney Johnston, on September 5. On September 23, 1863, 20 rebel sympathizers were expelled from St. Louis, among whom might have been Mrs. Jackman and family. After their expulsion, the Jackman family settled in Shreveport, Louisiana, where they remained until the end of the war. "From St. Louis," *Chicago Tribune*, September 23, 1863; Norton, 3; Mrs. Mary Jackman Mullins, "Sketch of Col. Sidney D. Jackman," *Reminiscences of the Women of Missouri During the Sixties* (Jefferson City, MO: Missouri Division, United Daughters of the Confederacy, 1911), 95.

52. See Chapter 2, note 83 for a biographical sketch of Broadhead.

who caused this unnecessary arrest, and Jackman spoke of him with execration, as a soldier who warred on women, aged and in child-bed, expressed the hope that he should never meet him, saying he was in love and charity with all who had fought us except this man who had treated with wanton indignity his aged mother and helpless wife and infant.

Of Jackman's subsequent career in the army I must be brief. He reported to the army in Arkansas with his battalion and was placed, I believe in command of a regiment becoming his rank and service.[53] He served for a while under Gen. Marmaduke

In the Cavalry,

but becoming dissatisfied with the prospect of being brigaded with the troops of another state, and hearing of the banishment of his family, asked to be relieved and for a leave of absence to provide for Mrs. Jackman and the children. He went east of the Mississippi and to Richmond, where he applied for leave to organize a regiment out of the lately exchanged prisoners, who were from Missouri. Disappointed in this by reason of an application of Col. Harvey McKinney for the same command, he returned after an absence of some four months and went into service again with Gen. Marmaduke.[54] In 1864 he accompanied Gen. Price on the raid

---

53. Jackman departed for Arkansas in early October 1863, wintered there, and returned to Missouri in April 1864. Dispatching recruiters into southern Missouri, Jackman assembled what men he could and then moved back into northern Arkansas, near Dover, where he rounded up conscripts and former parolees from Vicksburg and Port Hudson. Jackman continued operating along and north of the Arkansas River, gradually raising his reported strength from 200 to between 600 and 1000 men, when he was ordered to report to General J. O. Shelby's camp at Jacksonport, Arkansas, on June 17, 1864. After arriving at Shelby's headquarters, Jackman organized a brigade, composed of his own unit and Hunter's Regiment (assigned July 8), with John Schnable's Battalion (assigned July 17). And prior to the departure of the Missouri Expedition, Jackman's Brigade was completed with the addition of two cannon from Collin's Missouri Battery, commanded by Lieutenant Jacob D. Conner. William O. Coleman's Missouri Regiment (actually battalion), which was already in Missouri when Jackman's Brigade was formed, was added to Jackman's command shortly after the expedition entered Missouri. When completed the brigade was part of J. O. Shelby's Division. *O.R.*, vol. 34, pt. 3:328, 526, 576–577, 829; *O.R.*, vol. 34, pt. 4:121, 231, 293–294, 517, 547, 680; William O. Coleman Letters (October 27, 1909 and November 20, 1914), W. L. Skaggs Collection, Arkansas History Commission, hereafter cited as Coleman Letters; Schrantz, 167; Sellmeyer, 179, 194.

54. Musser is mistaken about Jackman vying for the same command as McKinney. McKinney was in Virginia in early 1863, when he was given command of a company, composed of Trans-Mississippi men, while Jackman was in his home county, seeking recruits for the Confederacy. Additionally, by the time that Jackman went to Virginia, according to Musser, in the latter part of 1863, McKinney was long dead, having been mortally wounded on May 16, 1863, at the beginning of the Vicksburg Campaign. *O.R.S.*, pt. 2, vol. 38:523; Peterson, et al., 128.

Colonel Harvey G. McKinney, a resident of Rocheport (Bartels has it as Columbia), Boone County, joined the MSG in Everetta, in June 1861, and was elected captain of a cavalry company in the 3rd Division, MSG. He fought at Dry Wood (September 2, 1861) and Lexington, after which he was elected colonel of the 6th Regiment, 3rd Division, MSG on September 26, 1861. McKinney left his command prior to the Battle of Pea Ridge and went north of the Missouri River on recruiting duty, where he was captured. After he was exchanged, McKinney went to Richmond

into Missouri, where he as always performed gallant service.[55] He was ordered while on this expedition, to North Missouri, and reported to Gen. John B. Clark, Jr., whom he reached on the eve of the capture of Glasgow, October 16, 1864. He passed the bridge at the east end of the latter town, taking his position in line as the battle begun and, holding his troops steadily in hand under the enemy's fire, contributed largely to the surrender of the enemy with all the stores, munitions and arms in the place, as also by an unfortunate accident the burning of a considerable portion of the town. The Confederate troops were not permitted to rest long at Glasgow, nor indeed anywhere while on this raid, for the enemy concentrated rapidly in overwhelming force, driving Price out of Missouri and with an army of unarmed recruits, through Kansas and into the Indian Territory. On the retreat Jackman commanded first a regiment and then a brigade. He was everywhere distinguished for bravery, vigilance and energy, and on reaching the Red River was

Promoted to Brigadier,

in General orders.[56] The Confederacy was near its end so that no commission came to him from Richmond. Appomattox was at hand.[57]

After the war Gen. Jackman settled with his family in Texas, in San Marcos County, where he applied himself to his former business of farming, laboring with all his energy for the support and education of his family. He represented his county in the Texas Legislature for two secessions and was in the beginning of the present Democratic administration appointed United States marshal for the Western District, in which office he died.[58]

---

and then to Petersburg, Virginia, where he was made a Confederate captain and given command, on March 26, 1863, of Company H, 5th Missouri Infantry (CSA). McKinney joined his regiment at Bovina, Mississippi, on May 7, 1863, but was wounded at Edwards Station, Mississippi, on May 16, 1863, and died the following day. *O.R.S.*, pt. 2, vol. 38:523; Anderson, 77, 111–112, 306; Banasik, *Confederate Tales, 1862*, 162; Bartels, *Trans-Mississippi Men*, 35, 45; Eakin, *Confederate Records*, 5:121; Peterson, et al., 112, 128; Schnetzer, *More Forgotten Men*, 158.

55. Price's 1864 Missouri Raid began on August 28, 1864, when Price and staff left Camden for Princeton, Arkansas, where he assumed command of the expedition. After reaching northeast Arkansas, Price organized his command and invaded Missouri on September 19, 1864. The expedition ended at Laynesport, Texas, on December 2, 1864. See Chapter 3 for details on the expedition, including the role that Jackman played. *O.R.*, vol. 41, pt. 1:303–304, 622.

56. Per General Orders No. 46, Trans-Mississippi Department, dated May 16, 1865, Jackman was promoted to brigadier general. Nine days later, on May 25, General E. K. Smith surrendered the Trans-Mississippi Department. *O.R.*, vol. 48, pt. 1:9; *O.R.*, vol. 48, pt. 2:1307.

57. Robert E. Lee surrendered the Army of Northern Virginia, 26,765 men, at Appomattox Courthouse, to U. S. Grant, on April 9, 1865, effectively ending the Civil War. The fighting would continue for about two more months, until June 2, when E. K. Smith officially signed the surrender documents for the Trans-Mississippi Department, in Galveston, Texas. *O.R.*, vol. 48, pt. 1:9; Boatner, 22, 770.

58. Following the war, Jackman emigrated to Mexico for a short time, while his family waited for him near San Marco, Texas. After arriving at Monterrey, Mexico, Jackman had a change of heart, and returned to Texas in the fall of 1865. Arrested in San Antonio, Jackman was sent to New Orleans, where he was imprisoned until he signed an Oath of Allegiance. Upon returning to Texas, Jackman settled his family near Kyle, where he built a church for his ministry. Jackman's post

Jackman was a perfect specimen of a self reliant, self-assertive, self-educated Missourian of the South. The main strength of his character consisted in his stubborn honesty and practical common-sense, combined as it was with the highest aggressive courage and prudence. Plain spoken and frank, there was never any doubt or hesitation as to his view or opinions, though he was never obtrusive or meddlesome. As he was convinced he always acted, never wavering from his sense of duty and right. Devoted to his friends, he was constant in all attachments, and like all men of pronounced convictions equally tenacious of his personal or political antipathies. His method of thought and action were direct, positive and or a character beyond the suspicion of fallacy or prevarication. In the service he was

Prone to Criticize,

and was quick to discover the errors, blunders and inefficiency of plans, and where the execution of them was weak or ineffectual, because he, like all old soldiers, realized that in the military as in civil life the great occasions for success and the best opportunities for reputation more often fall to the lucky and intriguing than to the meritorious and capable. Often as he perceived occasion for his censure and criticism in an army that was still inchoate in its organization, he never faltered in his obedience or hesitated in the line of duty and discipline. He was a determined foe to all charlatanage [imposters] and pretense, and being a man of that excited courage that intensifies the faculties and inspires courage in others in time of battle, he had little charity for those who sought military rank and glory without the qualities that only can earn it.

In person Jackman was about five feet ten inches high. In earlier life he had red hair and a fair complexion, but we knew him approaching middle age, when his beard began to be tinged with gray. His face indicated the firmness, determination and amiableness of his character, marked with lines of thought and caution rather than speculation. His features indicated the careful and vigilant soldier alive to the responsibilities of his position, blended with marks of industry and constant action, the result of his early avocation as a farmer. Almighty God created him a brave and honest man among his "noblest works," and in his whole life he did nothing to impair or mar the highest art of his Creator.

R. H. Musser.

* * * * * * *

Civil War years included a stint in the Texas Legislature (1874–1876), remarriage in 1878, following the death of his first wife, and service as a U.S. Marshal (1885–1886). He died while still in office in Hays County on June 2, 1886, the 31st anniversary of the surrender of the Trans-Mississippi Department. Norton, 8–9.

Item: Recruiting for the Confederacy in the Spring of 1863, by S. D. Jackman.
Published: November 14, 1885.

Note: This is a portion of an article Jackman wrote for the *Republican* which was not included in Norton's book *Behind Enemy Lines*. The original article was entitled "Retreat From Lone Jack."

[Recruiting In Missouri: A Response to D C. Hunter]

I was on Horse Creek, Barton County, [Missouri]...[59] Finding recruits plentiful here, several officers were left to work up this county, Vernon and St. Clair. Others were dropped in Bates and Henry. Still others were sent to Cass, Johnson, Jackson, Lafayette and across the river into Clay, Buchanan and other counties. After crossing the Missouri River, others were sent into Chariton, Linn, Randolph, and Pike.[60] But Callaway, Boone and Howard were our rallying ground. With few exceptions, the people of those counties were all Southern, but nearly all, who were within the military age had been formed in the ranks of our enemies, and required to meet and drill twice a week, but were too disloyal to be trusted with arms. While drilling I rode into one of these camps, and if Gov. [Hamilton R.] Gamble could have witnessed my reception he would have had

---

59. After Jackman returned to the main Confederate Army in the fall of 1862, he was asked by General Thomas C. Hindman to give up his regiment and return to Missouri on recruiting duty. Recalling the meeting with Hindman, Jackman recorded Hindman's remarks to him:

    And since you were in Missouri, the enemy is persecuting our people greatly by putting our friends into their army and otherwise badly treating them. I fear they will so discourage them that the Southern spirit will be so crushed that when I get into Missouri, I will not be able to accomplish any good. I want to send somebody into the enemy's lines who can in a measure counteract this influence and keep the Southern feeling alive until such time as I can go...I want you to go and I will give you a detail of forty or fifty men. You must give up your regiment.

    Despite Jackman's assertion that Hindman asked him to resign and return to Missouri on recruiting service, Jackman's letter of October 23, 1862, suggests otherwise (See Appendix A for a copy of the letter). Be that as it may, General Hindman accepted Jackman's resignation, on October 25, and assigned Jackman to duty in Missouri, to raise a regiment of cavalry. In mid-November 1862, Jackman headed north to recruit and further harass the Union commands whenever possible. See also note 30 for additional comments on Jackman's resignation). Letter (October 23, 1862), Jackman to Hindman, Miscellaneous Correspondence; Norton, 141, 143–144; Special Orders No. 22 (October 25, 1862), Special Order Book No. 1.

60. On his journey into Missouri Jackman was accompanied by several officers including Captains Robert L. Maupin, John D. Pulliam, James F. Wilhite, George Watkins, and William Marchbanks, in addition to many other unnamed individuals. Maupin was assigned to recruit in the Columbia area; Watkins got the Clinton area; Wilhite went to Cooper County; Pulliam was assigned to Pike County; and Marchbanks, after he was exchanged and joined Jackman, recruited in Bates County. Others of Jackman's party were assigned to other counties as needed. By the summer of 1863, Jackman's command had grown to a reported strength of 400–500 men. *O.R.*, vol. 22, pt. 1:318; *O.R.*, vol. 53:582; Norton, 39–40, 145–147, 153.

no further use for Southern men in his army.[61] I recruited the captain and forty men in one hour. I also, at other times, recruited two other captains and their companies.[62] And yet these men have gone into history as soldiers of the Federal Army. What a fraud upon truth. I also had a number of little battles, in which a number were killed and wounded on both sides—myself among the dangerously wounded.[63] I also made a number of captures, some of whom were quite important.[64] Among them Gen. Thos. J. Bartholow, Capt. R. G. Lyell, Capt. C.

---

61. Hamilton R. Gamble was born in Winchester, Virginia, on November 29, 1798, moved to Tennessee, and then to Missouri. He was a lawyer by profession and opened a law office in St. Louis. While living in Missouri, Gamble served in the legislature, was the secretary of state (1824–1825) and a Missouri supreme court justice (1851–1854). Gamble is also remembered as giving the only dissenting vote on the Missouri court's Dred Scott decision, after which he left Missouri (1858) for Pennsylvania, citing poor health. Gamble returned to Missouri during the secession crisis of 1861 and was appointed provisional governor on July 31, 1861, by the Missouri Constitutional Convention. He did not survive the war, dying on January 31, 1864. Faust, 297; *Rebellion Record*, vol. 2:Diary-50; Stewart Sifakis, *Who Was Who in the Union: A Comprehensive, Illustrated Biographical Reference to More Than 1,500 of the Principal Union Participants in the Civil War* (New York, 1988), 147.

62. During the summer of 1863, Jackman made three separate visits to Union camps of instruction in heavily supported Southern areas. Captain James McDonald joined Jackman with 40 men, followed by Captains William Monroe and Clincy Calloway with their units. These camps were overseen by Federal spies, according to Jackman, who were to "report anything disloyal, that may occur." No Federal records of these events can be found; however, the period press did report on at least one of the events. About May 22, Jackman entered one of the camps, near Rocheport, probably McDonald's, where he "rode along the line" of the assembled troops "and was recognized by all present. Someone asked him to exhibit the pistol stolen from Gen. Bartholow, and instantly the demand became general among the militia. The [militia] officers alone had arms, but stood speechless, without making an attempt to capture Jackman." Shortly thereafter the militia joined Jackman's command. Norton, 161–162; "Our St. Louis Letter," *Chicago Daily Tribune*, May 27, 1863.

63. When Jackman led his command back to Missouri in late 1862, he first engaged some Federals near Huntsville, Arkansas, on November 9, and at Carthage, Missouri, on November 27. After he successfully returned to his home county, Jackman spent the next several months recruiting a new command, though occasionally he did partake in several captures and some additional combats. Jackman engaged a small band of Federals on June 1, 1863, near Rocheport, Missouri, near sunrise, killing two, wounding one, and capturing 1st Sergeant John Vance. Later in the day Jackman was engaged by Captains Reeves Leonard and Henry Cook, in which skirmish two of Jackman's men were killed and six wounded, according to Federal sources; the rest then scattered (Jackman recorded that only one was killed and one wounded. See note 39 for further details). On June 18, Jackman again engaged the Federals near Rocheport, resulting in his wounding, which took him out of action for several months. *O.R.*, vol. 13:7; *O.R.*, vol. 22, pt. 1:1, 343–344; Norton, 144–145, 165–167, 171–172; Wood, *Noted Guerrillas*, 204.

64. Jackman captured Captain Robert G. Lyell on March 14, 1863, Captain Charles E. Leonard and his bother Ben on March 31, 1863, and General Thomas J. Bartholow on April 23. All four were captured at night; Lyell and Bartholow were captured in their homes, while the Leonards were captured returning from the funeral of their uncle Abiel Leonard. Of the four men, according to Jackman, the Leonards honored their paroles, Lyell did not; and Bartholow, according to other accounts was paroled for only three days and subsequently released after he agreed to recognize Jackman's troops as legitimate soldiers and not guerrillas. Further, Bartholow agreed to pardon Jazaleel Maxwell and pay him $200.00 for two horses that Federal troops had appropriated from

E. Leonard and one of the most prominent stock dealers in Missouri, and his brother, Sergt. Ben Leonard.[65] These were incidents quite amusing,

Full of Interest,

and worthy of a place among the "Tales of the War." The *Republican*, which was "hitting me with many hard licks" at the time, will doubtless remember the exciting times of the early winter and spring of 1863, in Western and Central Missouri, and hence can form some idea as to whether the wishes of my commanding officer had been committed to safe hands. Having now answered Col. [DeWitt C.] Hunter,[66] as to why I left the army, and given him some of the results of that leaving, it becomes him to tell what he meant by the question or stand convicted as a slanderer. I know nothing to be ashamed of, but am proud that I complied with the demand of my general, and the honorable part I played towards my subordinates in giving them a chance at promotion. And the coolest and most imprudent thing about this whole matter is that he would make such inquiry, when, in the spring or summer following he abandoned his regiment. Can he give as good a reason why he left? If so it is time he was talking. Being a

---

him. Richard H. Musser, "Sketch of S. D. Jackman," *Missouri Republican*, August 28, 1886; Norton, 153–154, 162–164, 166; Thoma, 82; Wood, *Noted Guerrillas*, 199–201.

65. Robert Gilbert Lyell was born in New York in 1817, educated in "common schools," and "reared to agricultural pursuits," became a teacher at age 19, and was a carpenter, per his "father's vocation." Lyell moved to Missouri in 1840, settled in Boone County, and married Emilia Bishop (1842), with whom he had five children. In 1849 Lyell went to California, in search of gold, but later returned to Missouri, settling in Rocheport. At the beginning of the Civil War he enlisted in the 61st EMM in May 1862, and was later commissioned a captain and quartermaster on December 15, 1862. With the demise of the 61st EMM in 1864, Lyell continued on in the service as a brigade quartermaster, with the grade of major, serving until the end of the war. Following the war he moved to Harrisonburg (1871) and was remarried in 1876 to Mary Rawlings, following the death of his first wife. He served as the Boone County notary, township magistrate, and deputy postmaster of Rocheport in 1881. Final disposition unknown. Norton, 154; William F. Switzler, *History of Boone County, Missouri, Written and Compiled From the Most Authentic Official and Private Sources; Including A History of Its Townships, Towns and Villages. etc.* (St. Louis, 1882), 65–66.

Charles E. Leonard was born on March 27, 1839, on his family's estate in Cooper County, Missouri, educated in Kemper's School in Boonville, then Boonville University. Upon graduation, Leonard entered the family business, managing the stock farm known as Raven Wood, a 1900 acre estate in Cooper County. During the Civil War, Leonard enlisted in the 52nd EMM on September 10, 1862, where he was a captain, commanding Company H. Leonard served for a year and a half and was discharged on July 28, 1864. Following the war he returned to the management of his estate. Final disposition unknown. *History of Howard and Cooper Counties*, 1062–1065; Norton, 162; Thoma, 212.

Benjamin Leonard lived on the Warfield farm, which was 17 miles south of Boonville. No other information was found on him. Thoma, 117.

66. DeWitt C. Hunter wrote an account of the Battle of Lone Jack, Missouri, which was published in the *Republican* on September 12, 1885. The article was critical of Jackman's account of the battle (See Banasik, *Confederate "Tales of the War" In the Trans-Mississippi, Part Two: 1862* for Hunter's and Jackman's accounts). See note no. 25 for a biography of Hunter. D. C. Hunter, "Rightwing Heard From," *Missouri Republican*, September 12, 1885.

very prudent man he, doubtless, thought that with [Simon P.] Burns at the head of his regiment it would be greatly improved by his absence.[67]

S. D. Jackman

* * * * * * *

Item: The Capture and Execution of Lieutenant August T. Doley, Confederate Guerrilla and Scout, April–May 1863, by C. H. Burch, late member Company B, 10th Missouri Infantry (CSA).[68]
Published: March 27, 1886.

Lieut. August Doley's Fate

St. Louis, March 1
Editor *Republican*

I noticed in your "Tales of the War" an article by F. W. Fry, in which he gave what he had heard to be the story of the capture and butchery of Lieut. August Doley.[69] After reading the article I felt constrained to give to the public a correct

---

67. Simon P. Burns was born in Ohio, moved to western Missouri, and settled in Carthage. He was a member of the MSG, a captain of Company D, 5th Cavalry Regiment, 8th Division. Burns resigned from the Guard on December 5, 1861, and later enlisted in DeWitt C. Hunter's cavalry battalion as a private on July 21, 1862. He was elected major of Hunter's command on September 1, 1862, and lieutenant colonel on September 15. When Hunter resigned on March 24, 1863, Burns was made colonel of the regiment. The Confederate Congress officially appointed Burns a colonel on January 8, 1864, to rank from March 24, 1863. In the spring of 1864, Burns was elevated to brigade command, heading Mosby M. Parsons's Brigade, while Parsons commanded the Missouri Division. After the war Burns moved to Texas, became a farmer, and later a member of the Texas Legislature. He died on April 8, 1898, at his Texas home. Banasik, *Confederate Tales, 1863*, 175–176.

68. Charles H. Burch (or Birch) of St. Louis enlisted in the Confederate Service on August 12, 1862, in St. Louis County, eventually becoming a member of Company B, 10th Missouri Infantry. In March 1863 he was on recruiting duty in St. Louis and upon returning to Arkansas was captured on April 20, 1863, by a scout of Company C, 5th MSM Cavalry, commanded by Lieutenant Augustus Benz. Sent probably to Alton, Illinois Prison (no record found of him in St. Louis prisons), Burch took the Oath of Allegiance on April 8, 1864, after which he was released. No other information found. *O.R.*, vol. 22, pt. 1:313; Eakin, *Missouri Prisoners of War*, passim; Schnetzer, *Men of the Tenth*, 18–19.

69. See *Confederate Tales, 1861*, "The Battle of Salem, Missouri (December 3, 1861)" by F. W. Fry. No information found on Fry.
    Augustus or August Doley or Dole (the local Richmond, Missouri, newspaper probably inadvertently dropped the "y" from Dole's name) or Dow (name he used upon capture in Dent County) or Dolle, was originally from Franklin County and lived in St. Louis. Doley killed two men, who had been discharged from Captain Amos Maupin's Company I, 34th EMM "earlier in the war." He was caught in Dent County near the border with Shannon County, on the Current River on April 19, 1863. Sent to Rolla, Doley was taken by train to Franklin County for trial, but never got there. On May 2, 1863, he was hanged in St. Clair. Doley was "'a desperate individual' who had murdered, robbed and threatened Franklin County citizens," according to the *Northwest Conservator* of Richmond, Missouri. *O.R.*, vol. 22 pt. 1:313; Eakin & Hale, 115; *History of Franklin, Jefferson, Washington, Crawford & Gasconade Counties of Missouri* (Chicago, 1888), 246, hereafter cited

account of the last few weeks of Lieut. Doley's life, as I was with him almost hourly during that time. I shall not attempt to give dates as I have forgotten them. To begin with, Doley, at the outset of the war, was a Unionist, and one of the quietest and most peaceable of men, but like many others, was opposed to coercion. He wanted to remain at home and take no sides in the conflict. His neighbors, however, tried to make him join the Union cause. He refused. They burned his house and drove his family away. Then he did go in and proved himself a terrible enemy to those who had aroused the slumbering passions of hate and revenge.

I belonged to Co. B. Stein's [Steen's] Regiment, Parsons's Brigade, C.S.A.[70] We were in camp in Little Rock in the latter part of the Winter of 1862–63, recruiting the army and gathering supplies.[71] About the 1st of March Lieut. Doley came into the brigade and remained several days. He was at that time regarded as

The Best Scout

and most crafty woodsman then engaged in recruiting and piloting men from Missouri to Arkansas. I was detailed about this time to come to St. Louis County for recruits and it was agreed that I should meet Lieut. Doley at Batesville, which I

---

as *History of Franklin County*; Nichols, *Guerrilla Warfare, Volume II*, 79; Schnetzer, *Men of the Tenth*, 18 (See "Burch, Charles" entry), 108.

70. Colonel Alexander Early Steen was born 1828 in St. Louis. His father, Enoch Steen, was a colonel in the U.S. Army and remained loyal to the Union at the outbreak of the Civil War. The younger Steen served during the Mexican War, receiving a brevet for "gallant and meritorious conduct in the battles of Contreras and Churubusco." Steen was mustered out of the army in 1848, but reentered the service in 1852 and was wounded fighting Indians in 1857. At the beginning of the Civil War, Steen was in St. Louis serving both in the U.S. Army and as a lieutenant colonel, 2nd Regiment, St. Louis Militia. Steen remained loyal to the Union until May 10, 1861, when he resigned from the Army upon the capture of Camp Jackson. He joined the MSG, serving first as an aide to Governor Claiborne Jackson, and was then promoted to brigadier general, commanding the 5th Division, MSG, on June 18, 1861. As the "drillmaster" of General Price's army, Steen fought at Wilson's Creek and was present at the Siege of Lexington, though ill at the time. At Pea Ridge, Steen was absent from his command, being in Richmond, Virginia, attempting to secure a generalship in the Confederate Army. On November 10, 1862, Steen was appointed a Confederate colonel and given command of the 10th Missouri Infantry. He was shot in the head and killed at Prairie Grove on December 7. *O.R.*, vol. 8:321; *O.R.*, vol. 53:444; Allardice, *Confederate Colonels*, 355–356; Allardice, *More Generals in Gray*, 215–216; Banasik, *Missouri Brothers in Gray*, 155; Heitman, 1:919; "Military Encampment," *Missouri Republican*, May 7, 1861.

71. Parsons's Brigade, which contained the 10th Missouri Infantry (CSA), reached the Little Rock area on January 14, 1863, where it camped near Crystal Hill. Two days later, during a snow storm, the brigade crossed over the Arkansas River and came to a permanent camp about a mile and a half south of Little Rock on January 21. The brigade remained there until April 27, 1863, when it moved camp to the north side of the Arkansas River, in preparation for a movement against Helena. Banasik, *Serving With Honor*, 47–48; C. B. Lotspeich, Typescript Diary (January 17–September 26, 1863), Arkansas History Commission, Little Rock, AR, January 18–24 and April 27 1863; Quesenberry Diary, January 14–19 and April 26–27, 1863.

did.[72] He was accompanied by James Whitsett.[73] We three traveled together as far as Franklin County at which point Whitsett left us to go to his home. We traveled by night and hid in the chaparral by day and in this way Doley and I arrived just before daylight at the house of one of the Norths, then living in Franklin County.[74] Doley seemed to know all about the premises and in ten minutes our horses were hidden away and we were housed in the barn for a sleep. We slept like logs till noon when the owner found us in the hay and aroused us. He gave us a good meal and after dark we stared for St. Louis. Our horses were nearly worn out and we had to watch all the houses and cross roads for militia guards, but about 4 a.m. we reached the house of a friend within seven miles of the city. Remaining there until dark, Doley went into the city to visit his wife and two daughters,

---

72. Batesville, Arkansas, was the county seat of Independence County, located about 50 miles from the Missouri border. The city was occupied by General Samuel R. Curtis's troops on May 3, 1862, and abandoned on June 24, following severe supply shortages. Confederates reoccupied the city shortly after Curtis left and used it as a base of operations for northeastern Arkansas and Missouri. Union forces under Colonel R. R. Livingston retook Batesville on December 25, 1863. A Union soldier described Batesville as follows:

> The place is about the size of Omaha, yet it is built more compactly. It is located half a mile from the White River...The city is old in comparison with cities of the Northwest. An impressive church, courthouse and various important buildings are here. A large stone building, occupied by stores below and a large hall above, belonging to the Freemasons, is now being used as a warehouse for our commissary department. A large hotel is closed, as are the rest of the stores..., while the doors and windows are shut and empty shelves and chests and crates belie the pompous advertisements.

With the advance of General Shelby into northeast Arkansas, Livingston abandoned Batesville between May 14 and May 20, thus allowing Shelby to capture the town on May 26. No further permanent occupation of Batesville would occur for the rest of the war. Banasik, *Embattled Arkansas*, 12, 39; Mobley, 147, 167–168, 201; Potter & Robbins, 242–243, 277–278.

73. James Whitsett was born on June 10, 1818, in North Carolina, moved to St. Louis County in 1836, married in 1840, and fathered six children. Beginning in 1841, Whitsett moved about the local area, buying land, starting businesses, and establishing himself as a wealthy farmer and businessman. By the beginning of the Civil War, Whitsett owned 320 acres of land in St. Louis County, with another 600 acres in Franklin County near Catawissa, which was on the railroad and about 34 miles from St. Louis. It appears, based upon C. H. Burch's statement, that Whitsett was living on his farm in Franklin County in 1863. There was no military record found for James Whitsett, though several James Whitsetts were found in assorted sources. None appear to be associated with Franklin County or any of the surrounding counties. James A. was a lieutenant and member of Elliott's Scouts from Holden, Johnson County, in western Missouri. James H. was a private in the 5th Missouri Cavalry, and probably from western Missouri. James S., a member of the 12th Missouri Cavalry (CSA), was from near Hickman Mills, located in Jackson County, also in western Missouri. Anonymous, *5th Missouri Cavalry*, "Whitsell, James H." entry, 126; Bartels, *Elliott's Scouts*, 118; Davis, *Civil War Atlas*, plt. 66 no. 3; Eakin, *Confederate Records*, 8:55–56; Eakin, *Missouri Prisoners of War*, "Whitsett, Jas. H." entry; Eakin & Hale, 465; Hale, *Jackson County*, map on back page; *History of Franklin County*, 340, 843–844.

74. There were a total of five "North" families living in Boles Township, Franklin County, in 1860. All were slave owners, with F. J. North owing 23 slaves, while the other Norths owned from 1–11 slaves. Boles Township was located in northeast Franklin County, between the Missouri River and the railroad. Herman Gottlieb Kiel, *The Centennial Biographical Dictionary of Franklin County, Missouri* (Washington, DC, 1925), 35.

then staying at my house which was close by Fort No. 6.[75] Doley was safer in the city than almost anywhere else, for he was known to nearly everyone in Franklin County and the western part of St. Louis County, including all the militia officers. At that time he was probably

More Feared and Hated

than any other man in Franklin County, and I have heard that there was a large reward offered for him, dead or alive.

The exposure of the trip had given me a bad cold that almost destroyed my eyesight, and it was three weeks before I was able to do anything. Then, having lost so much time, it was not safe to try to raise a company. About the 15th or 16th of April Doley met a former neighbor who was his bitter enemy, and it being no longer safe for him to stay in the city, he came to where I was waiting for him and anxious to start. Doley, however, refused to go that night because of a dream of his wife, that if he started on that day he would be captured. Finally we got off and our trip was made in safety until about twenty miles southwest of Steelville we ran into a squad of Federal soldiers, who were watching for paroled rebel prisoners. Of course we did the best we could to avoid capture. The Feds chased us all that night and part of the next day, but Doley's woodcraft and knowledge of the country enabled us to keep away until, their horses were worn out, they gave up the chase. We here learned that the militia stationed at Salem were scouting the county and hanging Southern sympathizers;[76] and our movements became cautious and slow. Halting on a mountain spur, we continued to strike for Texas County, and then for Huntsville, hoping to get beyond the Union lines. But first we had to have food for ourselves and our horses, so we started for a house of a friend who lived at one of the fords of the White River. When within a few hundred yards of the ford we unexpectedly rode right into a company of state militia. We were descending a steep hill when the feds rose on three sides of us, having been concealed in a ravine.

We Wheeled Our Horses

and urged them back up the ridge with the enemy in hot pursuit, turning in the saddle and holding our pursuers off with our revolvers till Doley's stirrup strap broke

---

75. During the summer of 1861, through the fall, a series of ten forts were built, in a semi-circle, to protect St. Louis. Fort No. 6 was located near the intersection of Clark Avenue, Market Street, and Laclede Avenue. The fort was constructed under the supervision of Major Justice McKinstry, a quartermaster officer, and cost nearly as much as the first five forts combined. It contained four heavy guns. Winter, 75–76.

76. Companies C and D, 5th MSM Cavalry were stationed at Salem, Missouri, during the period April 1–July 31, 1863. Captain Peter Ostermayer commanded the post which numbered about 200 officers and men, until June 27, when he went AWOL, at which time Captain Samuel B. Richardson then took command, through July 31. *O.R.*, vol. 22, pt. 2:344, 418; *O.R.S.*, pt. 2, vol. 35:136; Joanne C. Eakin, *The Little Gods: Union Provost Marshals in Missouri, 1861–1865* (Shawnee Mission, KS, 1996), 63.

and he pitched headlong to the ground. He rose instantly, but we were brought to a halt and after a conference, in which it was agreed we should be treated as prisoners of war, we surrendered. None of the Federals knew Doley or his history.[77] We were taken towards Salem, and when we halted for the night were searched and in Doley's saddle blanket was found the pass, giving him across at all times to the Confederate lines. On this it was all the officers could do to keep the men from shooting us on the spot without trial.[78]

I may here relate that while trying to wait for us the Federals left one prisoner, whom they had captured, in the custody of a single guard—a Dutchman. During the excitement the reb made a break for the hill. The guard pursued and the reb, picking up a stone, unhorsed his man, who dropped his hat and gun. The reb secured the horse, gun and hat and made good his escape. The unlucky guard was most unmercifully guyed by his comrades all day.[79]

Arriving at Salem we were kept in jail over night and next morning were taken to the Provost Marshal's Office with three other prisoners, whose necks bore purple marks, showing that they had been struck up to extract information from them. Here we were thoroughly searched, and $400 in gold, which I was taking to a friend, was confiscated, the officer refusing to give a receipt for it. After my release I tried to recover the money, but

Uncle Sam Still Owes It

to one of the "truly loyal." I was taken to a black-smith's shop and had a chain and 32-pound ball riveted to my leg. Then we were put in a wagon and sent to Rolla. As we passed the draw a mammoth Dutchman, seated in front of us, suddenly rose to his feet exclaiming, "Mein Gott in Himmel!! There's Doley."

That was the first intimation they had as to the identity of their capture. Doley was instantly placed in irons and witnesses were summoned from Franklin County for evidence against him. Next train brought up a squad of Home Guards. Doley was taken to the Provost Marshal's Office, and on seeing the man they most feared and hated, these valiant witnesses tried to kill him in irons. I never

---

77. Doley apparently gave his captors a fictitious name—Augustus Dow—after his capture, with Charles Burch. Both men were transferred to a Salem, Missouri jail, there to await a Military Commission and disposition. *O.R.*, vol. 22, p1 1:313.

78. When Burch and Doley were captured, Lieutenant Benz reported finding "a recruiting commission issued by General M. M. Parsons," to Charles Burch, while Doley carried a "splendid secesh flag and a lot of letters." In capturing Doley, Lieutenant Benz also stated that Doley had resigned from the 10th Missouri Infantry and was now a "carrier of secesh mails." It should be noted that there was no record found of Doley ever being an officer in the 10th Missouri Infantry (CSA), even though Burch implied that Doley was a lieutenant in that unit. Ibid.; Schnetzer, *Men of the Tenth*, passim.

79. Lieutenant Benz departed Salem on his scout on April 18, proceeding "as far as about 10 miles on the other side of Eminence." During the scout, Benz found five abandoned "general camping places" of rebels and managed to chase and kill one guerrilla while capturing two. On returning to Salem, Benz captured Burch and Doley on April 20, not the 19th as recorded in *Men of the Tenth*. *O.R.*, vol. 22, pt. 1:313; Schnetzer, *Men of the Tenth*, 18.

saw any man suffer as he did that night thinking of his helpless wife and children, who would be left without home or protection. He knew what awaited him at St. Clair, Franklin County. He was taken there and a crowd of Home Guards was in waiting for the train. As soon as it arrived Doley was taken to the only tree nearby and hanged with the ball and chain still fast to his leg. While hanging, fifty-two bullets were fired into his body. After he was cut down they cut off his leg to save the ball and chain. They stamped mud into his mouth and otherwise mutilated his body. This account of his death I received from one who was present and who never dared speak of it till after the war.

I was taken to St. Louis, kept in irons, tried and convicted for being a spy and military insurgent, and sentenced to go on that tramp from whence no traveler returns. Fortunately for me the sentence was not executed. Mr. Editor, I close this sketch with the statement that I do not believe there was a truer, braver, kinder-hearted man or more faithful friend ever lived than Lieut. August Doley.

C. H. Burch

* * * * * * *

Item: Colonel Charles Harrison's Failed Expedition to Colorado (May 12–19, 1863), by Colonel Richard H. Musser, 9th Missouri Infantry (C.S.A.).

Published: January 15, 1887.

Introduction.

In one of the most unusual accounts published in the "Tales of the War," Richard H. Musser retells the story of an ill-fated Confederate recruiting expedition to Colorado Territory. Led by Colonel Charles (or Charlie) Harrison, the expedition took place in May 1863, and ended disastrously for the Confederates, with the members killed in a most brutal manner by Osage Indians, save for two who managed to escape. The account that follows, with attached notes, is based on several conflicting primary and secondary sources including those from the Sons of Confederate Veteran (Patrick Gerity), Annie Abel (two first hand Indian accounts), Warner Lewis (sole Confederate survivor of the Expedition), George E. Tinker (historian for the Osage Indians), Wiley Britton (covers aftermath of the engagement), Steve Cottrell (general account of the expedition) and Carolyn Bartels and Janice Toms, in Duncan Hansen's work on Quantrill's guerrillas (general and researched account of the expedition) as well as several period newspaper and *Official Records* pieces on the expedition.

What follows is the best blending of the various accounts, including start dates, who was involved, how many participants there were, where the action occurred, and the outcome of the running fight.

Primary Sources:
1. Annie Heloise Abel, *The American Indian in the Civil War, 1862-1865* (Cleveland, OH, 1919; reprint ed., Lincoln, NB, 1992), 237–238, cited hereafter as Abel.
2. Britton, *Civil War on the Border, 1863–1865*, 228.
3. Steve Cottrell, *Civil War in the Indian Territory* (Gretna, LA, 1995), 67, 69–70, cited hereafter as Cottrell.
4. Patrick Gerity, "Charles Harrison," Internet site www.coloradoscv.org, cited hereafter as Gerity, "Charles Harrison."
5. Duncan E. Hansen, *A Reunion in Death: Grave Sites of the Men Who Rode With William Clarke Quantrill* (3 vols.; vol. 1, Independence, MO, 2002; vols. 2, 3, Harrisonville, MO, 2013), 3:91–98, cited hereafter as Hansen.
6. Warner Lewis, "Civil War Reminiscences," *Missouri Historical Review* 2 (April 1908), 228–232, cited hereafter as Lewis.
7. George E. Tinker, "The Osage: A Historical Sketch," Internet site www.ualr.edu, cited hereafter as Tinker, "The Osage."

A Doomed Expedition

In the spring of 1863 Lieut.-Gen. Theophilus Holmes was in command of the Trans-Mississippi Department with headquarters at Little Rock.[80] The Confederate forces occupied the line of Arkansas with outposts of cavalry on the borders with Missouri, while the southwestern counties were full of detached officers and soldiers fresh from various parts of the state, intent on recruiting bodies of troops for the Confederate Service to be commanded by themselves and insure their promotion. There were considerable detachments having their rendezvous in Jasper and the contiguous counties in southwestern Missouri. They were from various parts of Missouri and their purpose was to penetrate, as soon as they could with safety, into north Missouri and other parts of the state in the performance of their perilous duty.[81]

Before they were ready to make a forward movement there appeared among them one Col. Charles Harrison bearing a commission from Gen. Holmes, with authority to recruit a brigade or more of cavalry for service in the territories of

---

80. Holmes was assigned to command the Trans-Mississippi Department on July 16, 1862, but did not arrive in Little Rock until August 12, when he assumed command. Banasik, *Embattled Arkansas*, 179.
81. Confederate recruiters returned to Missouri beginning in March 1862, following the Battle of Pea Ridge. Colonel Joseph Porter was the first of many, proceeding to Lewis County to raise a regiment. Porter was followed by John A. Poindexter, who also operated in northeast Missouri, while Colonels J. Vard Cockrell, Upton Hayes, John T. Coffee, and Gideon W. Thompson conducted their operations in western Missouri. Also operating in western Missouri were Captains J. O. Shelby and William C. Quantrill, as well as Colonels John C. Tracy, John T. Hughes, S. D. Jackman, and D. C. Hunter; all intent on raising regiments for the Confederacy. In the case of Quantrill, his operations were meant to keep the Unionists off balance in Western Missouri while the other men went about recruiting. Ibid., 116–118, 147, 149, 169–170.

New Mexico and Colorado for the purpose of harassing the enemy and interrupting communications with the Pacific coast. The railroads across the continent were not then constructed, and it was thought the enemy's

Trains and Supplies

in transit could be interrupted, captured or destroyed.[82]

Very little was known of Harrison or his antecedents. He was 6 feet in height, of swarthy complexion, with long, jet black hair, as erect as an Indian, athletic and graceful. He was about 30 years old, and looked the bold and fearless mountaineer, and was said to have been reared on the western Plains as the protégé and pupil of Kit Carson.[83] You would have selected him, from his appearance, among

---

82. There were actually several accounts, most of which were speculative, as to the purpose of the Harrison Colorado Expedition. The *Chicago Tribune* reported that Harrison's band was going to Colorado "to rob miners and stage coaches leaving Denver." Duane Smith has the Confederates on recruiting service in Colorado and to "seize gold for the South's waning fortunes." Alvin Josephy has Harrison's party going to Colorado "to induce the plains Indians to assist the Confederacy by attacking Federal forts and supply trains in Kansas and Colorado." Annie Abel, in her book on the *American Indian in the Civil War*, uses two period reports that have the rebels authorized to recruit both rebels and Indians for the Confederacy—nothing more. Bartels and Toms have Harrison slated "to bring back the many Southern men in sympathy with the Confederacy, who for one reason or another could not get out of Denver." Steve Cottrell has the rebels inciting the "Plains Indian tribes to wage war on settlers in Kansas and Nebraska." Wiley Britton supports Abel's comments, but adds that the troops were needed "for the purpose of interrupting or destroying the Federal wagon trains hauling supplies" for the troops in the area. And John Edwards has Harrison's party destroying trains and interrupting routes to California; ultimately Harrison wanted to "eliminate from the military economy of western occupation the frontier post system... [breaking] the only link that bound California and the Union together." Against all the speculation on the purpose of the expedition, Warner Lewis, the only surviving member of the Harrison's party, recorded that it was a recruiting mission to organize Southern supporters "into companies, regiments and brigades, and as soon as this was done to drop down into Western Texas and then unite with the main army." Abel, 237–238; Britton, *Civil War on the Border, 1863–65*, 228; Bartels & Toms, 3:92; Edwards, *Noted Guerrillas*, 126; Cottrell, 70; "From St. Louis," *Chicago Tribune*, May 27, 1863; Alvin. M. Josephy, *The Civil War In the American West* (New York, 1991), 291, hereafter cited as Josephy; Lewis, 228; Smith, *Birth of Colorado*, 146.

83. Charles Harrison was born in New York (Eakin & Hale say he was born in Arkansas), in the later 1820s or early 1830s, and moved to Denver, Colorado, in 1859. Forced to leave Denver on September 19, 1861, for "assaulting a Union sentry," Harrison joined William Quantrill in March 1862, serving on and off with him until early November 1862. Harrison then headed south with Quantrill and joined Emmett MacDonald's Cavalry Regiment, as commander of what became Company A, 10th Missouri Cavalry. Harrison was praised for his performance at the Battle of Prairie Grove, after which he resigned on January 15, 1863, though some writers have Harrison being promoted to lieutenant colonel and taking part in Marmaduke's First Raid. Harrison was commissioned a colonel with authority to organize a brigade of troops, and led an expedition to Colorado Territory, where he was killed on May 15, 1862. Despite Musser's remarks on Harrison's "black hair," he was actually bald, though he did have a full black beard. See Appendix B for a complete biography and Appendix C for details on his death and the men who rode with him to Colorado. *O.R.*, vol. 22, pt. 1:59; *O.R.S.*, pt. 2, vol. 38:254; Abel, 237–238; Banasik, *Cavaliers of the Brush*, 144; Bartels & Toms, 3:91; Eakin & Hales, 193; Patrick Gerity, "Charles Harrison (And the Confederate Cause in the Colorado Territory)" http://nebula.wsimg.com/80bce-074b2a0a280b403e086b4cf422f?AccessKeyId=F7559C48D68C23EC2E5B&disposition=0&al-

a thousand as a fit man to lead a daring and desperate enterprise. The fall before he had served with Quantrill and assisted at the sacking of Lawrence, Kas., and had seen service as a guerrilla with [Bill] Anderson, John Brinker and other desperate chiefs.[84]

Harrison exhibited his orders and commission, and laid before various detachments his plans, and purpose, endeavoring to enlist them in his enterprise. Among other things he represented that he had left Colorado the previous spring to cast his fortunes with the Confederacy, and that there were in that territory a large number of sympathizers in the Confederate cause who had left the states to avoid being drafted into the Federal Army; that they could easily be recruited into

---

loworigin=1, herafter cited as Gerity, "Charles Harrison"; Hale, *Branded As Rebels, Volume Two*, 134–135; Lewis, 228–229, 231–232; Lankford, 92–93; Bruce Nichols, *Guerrilla Warfare in Civil War Missouri, 1862* (Jefferson, NC, 2004), 207–208, hereafter cited as Nichols, *Guerrilla Warfare in Missouri, 1862*; Smith, *Birth of Colorado*, 21.

84. William C. Quantrill was born on July 31, 1837, in Ohio, attended a local school, and later became a teacher. In 1857 Quantrill left Ohio for Kansas, where he was a gambler, wanderer, thief, teacher, and a supposed abolitionist. With the beginning of the Civil War, Quantrill fought at Wilson's Creek as a common soldier, later left the army and formed a gang of Southern partisans in December 1861. A household name by the summer of 1862, Quantrill was feared by most on the Kansas-Missouri border. He played an important role in the capture of Independence on August 11, 1862. Later, Quantrill went to Richmond, Virginia, seeking a colonel's commission. Upon rejoining his command in the summer of 1863, he led them in the infamous Lawrence Raid in August, and in November he attacked General James G. Blunt's escort and band at Baxter Springs, killing most of the members, though Blunt himself managed to escape. Quantrill supported Price's 1864 Missouri Raid, spent the winter of 1864–65 in Texas, after which he headed East, planning to assassinate President Lincoln. En route for the nation's capital, Quantrill was fatally wounded in Kentucky, where he died on May 30, 1865, after converting to the Catholic religion. Banasik, *Serving With Honor*, 391–392.

William Anderson was born in the late 1830s in either Missouri or Kentucky, depending on the source. He was educated in Huntsville, Missouri, and migrated to Kansas in 1857. He joined the MSG at the beginning of the Civil War and fought in all the early battles in Missouri, through Pea Ridge, after which he left the Guard. He subsequently joined Quantrill in August 1862, following his escape from Leavenworth Military Prison. As a guerrilla, Anderson fought in many engagements, the most famous being Lawrence (August 20–23, 1863) and Centralia, Missouri (September 27, 1864), where his command killed 147 men in two separate engagements. Known as "Bloody Bill," for the manner in which he engaged his enemy, Anderson had killed 53 men prior to his own death at Orick, Missouri (October 26, 1864). Banasik, *Cavaliers of the Brush*, 173–174.

John D. Brinker was born in Johnson County, Missouri, in about 1841, and was a merchant in Warrensburg at the beginning of the Civil War. Initially, Brinker joined Quantrill's band in February 1862, and was wounded near Fred Farmer's farm on July 11, 1862. After recovering from his wound, Brinker joined the Confederate Service in the summer of 1862, serving as a 2nd lieutenant in Charles Harrison's Company A, 10th Missouri Cavalry (CSA). One source has Brinker leaving the army, rejoining Quantrill, and fighting at Baxter Springs Kansas, in October 1863. As to Brinker's final disposition, one source has Brinker being killed in August 1863, while another has him resigning from the service in 1865. No other information found. *O.R.*, vol. 13:154–155; *O.R.S.*, pt. 2, vol. 38:254; *O.R.S.*, pt. 3, vol. 2:751; Banasik, *Cavaliers of the Brush*, 58; Eakin, *Confederate Records*, 1:150; Edwards, *Noted Guerrillas*, 89; Lankford, 23.

Harrison was killed in May 1863 and was never at the Lawrence Raid, which occurred in August 1863; however he was at the sack of Shawnee Town, Kansas, on October 17, 1862. Banasik, *Cavaliers of the Brush*, 72–76; Bartels & Toms, 3:92; Gilmore, 205; Lankford, 92–93.

the Southern Service if opportunity was offered them;[85] that he wished to take out with him as many experienced and skillful soldiers as possible to assist him in the work of recruiting and instructing the men, as well as to furnish suitable officers to command and discipline them.[86] His undertaking, though hazardous, seemed feasible and commended itself to the daring fellows gathered on the borders of Missouri, and before the time set for departure a large number expressed a willingness

To Enlist With Him.[87]

It was on the 20th of May, 1863, a beautiful morning, when he ordered his mules packed in readiness for the march. It was at the village of Centrevale on the western border of Jasper County that he ordered his men into line. Only nineteen men were ready at the time to respond.[88] Col. B. H. Woodson of Springfield, Mo., Capt. Parkinson McClure [McLure] of St. Louis (whose venerable mother resides in this city and was then in exile under banishment in Alabama), Capt. Bowen of Howard County, Douglas Huffman [or Hoffman], Frank Roberts, Reuben Pickwell [or Pickerel], John B. Rafferty and Col. Warner Lewis of Callaway County

---

85. The population of Colorado Territory officially numbered 25,329 in 1861, although William Byers, editor of the *Rocky Mountain News*, estimated the number at closer to 30,000. Of Colorado's population Southern sympathizers were estimated at between 6,000–7,500, more than enough to organize a significant military force for the Confederate cause. Smith, *Birth of Colorado*, 11, 14, 18.

86. When Harrison originally formulated his Colorado plan in February 1863, he enlisted the support of Captain John P. Bull, an aide to Colonel Emmett MacDonald. Soon after Harrison resigned from MacDonald's Regiment, Bull was appointed a major to serve with Harrison on the expedition. Bull, for some unknown reason, never went. (After hearing the actual plan, Bull possibly felt it was too hazardous, and like many others who were initially recruited, backed out.) Harrison procured the necessary supplies, men and authority to proceed to Colorado from General T. H. Holmes, the department commander. In all, the expedition contained 19 men, including Colonel Harrison. Several secondary sources correctly identify the expedition as a recruiting venture and not one "to plunder upon the road to Pike's Peak" or other nefarious objectives. *O.R.*, vol. 22, pt. 1:338–339; *O.R.*, vol. 22 pt. 2:286; Abel, 237–238; Banasik, *Brothers in Gray*, 101, 105; Britton, *Civil War on the Border, 1863–65*,, 228; Witt Edwards, *The Prairie was on Fire: Eyewitness Accounts of the Civil War in the Indian Territory* (Oklahoma City, OK, 2001), 46, hereafter cited as Edwards, *Prairie was on Fire*; Lewis, 228.

87. According to John Edwards, General J. O. Shelby did not see the plan as feasible, but finally agreed to recommend it to his superior, General T. C. Hindman. After Hindman approved the plan, it's assumed that Harrison then proceeded to General Holmes's headquarters, where he received final approval to the expedition. Warner Lewis stated in his account of the expedition that the plan was feasible, "though very hazardous; so much so, that many of those who had first volunteered, finally refused to go." Edwards, *Noted Guerrillas*, 126–127; Lewis, 228; University of Arkansas at Little Rock, American Native Press Archives and Sequoyah Research Center, Tinker, George E. "The Osage: A Historical Sketch," https://ualrexhibits.org/tribalwriters/artifacts/Tinker_Osage-Historical-Sketch.html, hereafter cited as Tinker "The Osage."

88. The expedition departed Jasper County, Missouri, on May 12 (not May 20 or 22 as Musser and Lewis say), passing into Kansas at the point where Center Creek crosses the border. The route took the Confederates in a due westerly direction about 10 miles north of the Kansas-Indian Territory border. *O.R.*, vol. 22, pt. 2:286; "Fort Scott Correspondence," *Chicago Tribune*, May 25, 1863; Lewis, 229; Schrantz, frontis map of Jasper County.

were of the party, and these are all the names that can now be learned of these daring adventurers.[89] They were bold, fearless and brave men, expert and cool in action, prudent and untiring in the performance of duty, well mounted on the best Missouri horses, which were trained to hard service, like their riders, and inured to hardships.

This dauntless and high-spirited cavalcade, the nucleus of Harrison's Brigade, armed with revolves and sabers, their supplies placed on mules and equipment in perfect trim, moved out on that beautiful May day to win laurels and victory on the boundless plains.[90] They were full of hope and courage, and burning with the fervor of Southern patriotism. For two days they pursued their line of march on a due westerly direction. Their route lay through the trackless prairies of the Indian country with no sign of habitation or of animal life save the rustling of the startled prairie hen, or the flight of birds with the occasional scampering of the wild deer in the distance, of the nightly

Howling of the Coyote.

At noon on the third day the party had halted on an eminence, unpacked their mules, and unsaddled their horses, which were picketed to browse on the luxurious prairie grass, when the ever alert vigilance of the soldiers discovered a body of mounted men pursuing on their trail.[91] They were pressing their horses at full speed and intent on the surprise and capture of Harrison's little party. The order to saddle horses and pack the mules was instantly given and obeyed, the little troop mounted and formed for battle, by which time about 250 mounted Indian warriors were within hailing distance, but they approached no nearer. Neither party, it seems, knew whether the other were friends or foes till after a short parley, and when the Indians ascertained that Harrison's men were Confederates they opened

---

89. Also included in the party were John J. (or Y.) Yeater, Edward West, John Henderson, J. B. Kimbaugh and Clark Hockensmith. See Appendix C for extended comments on the participants in Harrison's Expedition and what became of them. Bartels & Toms, 3:96; Lankford, 93.

90. After the Osages had killed all of Harrison's command, they reported taking "about 50 revolvers...a carbine and saber." This lack of long guns, like the carbine, was the primary reason that the Osages overcame Harrison's party—the Indians simply sat out of pistol range and rained musket balls down on the hapless Confederates, forcing them into a running fight. The booty captured by the Indians, contained 17 horses (4 of which were killed) and a number of mules; the mules were used by some of the Confederates as mounts, while others were used to carry supplies. Abel, 237; Lewis, 229.

91. According to one period account, on the first night that Harrison's party camped they were visited by "a small, smart Indian boy (who understood English)." The Indian boy in turn "wormed out of them who they were, etc. and reported to the Chiefs." White Hair (Lankford and Britton call him White Wing), Head Chief of the Osages and Little Bear, Chief of the Little Osages, then "hastily" assembled their warriors, about 150 in number, and took after Harrison's party. However, in Gerity's and Cottrell's accounts they have the Indians led by the Osage Chief Long Rope (or Hard Rope), making no mention of the other chiefs that were involved. Tinker also makes no mention of the Osage chiefs who were involved in the combat against Harrison's command. Abel, 237–238; Britton, *Civil War on the Border, 1863–65*, 228; Cottrell, 69; "Fort Scott Correspondence," *Chicago Tribune*, May 25, 1863; Gerity, "Charles Harrison;" Lankford, 93; Tinker, "The Osage."

fire with their long range rifles. The Confederates having only their side arms could not reach them with their fire, and sought safety in flight.[92] Occasionally when closely pressed Harrison would turn and charge them with revolvers and saber, and, notwithstanding the Confederates killed and wounded many of them, the odds were too great. There were 250 Indians against nineteen Missourians. Huffman was killed in the first skirmish, Lewis was wounded in the right shoulder, and his horse was killed, but he mounted Huffman's, and when the little party again retreated after the charge

The Indians Pursued

them with savage fury.[93] It was a running fight on the open prairie for about fifteen miles, in which the safety of the party pursued depended mostly on the superiority of the Missouri horse over the Indian steeds.[94] Harrison often turned

---

92. Harrison's command had just finished mounting when the Osages, numbering 150 (not 250) confronted the invading rebels, about 15 miles southeast from present day Independence, Kansas (Cottrell, Gerity and Tinker have a 10-man or "small" Indian party making first contact). Not wanting to engage, Harrison moved his command away at a "brisk walk," from the Indians, who followed. Finally the Indians questioned who they were, what they were doing in Osage county, and "ordered them off their land." Since the Confederates were clad in blue uniforms, Harrison told the Indians that they were a patrol out of Humbolt, Kansas (another source has the Confederates wearing civilian clothes, with Confederate uniforms found in their packs). Harrison had hoped that the pro-Union Osages would let them pass though their territory. Based upon their previously obtained intelligence of the invaders, the Osages, as instructed by Union officials, ordered Harrison's party to surrender their weapons and accompany them to Humbolt, where their authenticity could be determined. Harrison refused, after which the Indians sent a volley from their long guns, killing Douglas Huffman. The Confederates, in turn, charged the Indians drove them back, killing one of their number (Abel and Britton say two Osages were killed; Tinker has one man killed in the first exchange, with Harrison firing first). Harrison, seeing the disparity in numbers, ordered a retreat, thus beginning a running fight that would last for 10–15 miles, depending on the source and ending where the Elk River enters the Verdigris River near present day Independence (Warner, supported by Bartels & Toms, have the final engagement taking place just south of Coffeyville on the Kansas-Indian Territory boundary.). *O.R.*, vol. 22, pt. 2:286; Abel, 237; Bartels & Toms, 3:95,98; Britton, *Civil War on the Border, 1863–65*, 228; Cottrell, 67, 69; Gerity, "Charles Harrison;" Lankford, 93; Lewis, 229, 232; Nichols, *Guerrilla Warfare, Volume II*, 101–102; T. F. Robley, *History of Bourbon County, Kansas To the Close of 1865* (Fort Scott, KS, 1894; reprint ed., 2nd printing, Fort Scott, KS, 1976), 194; Smith, *Birth of Colorado*, 146; Tinker, "The Osage."
93. During the initial engagement with the Osage, Harrison's party unfortunately lost their guide, according to the Osage, which possibly proved fatal for the expedition. With his guide gone, Harrison may not have known where the crossings of the Verdigris River were, causing him to rapidly flee the area, heading northwest, but not really knowing where to go for safety. Abel, 237; Cottrell, 67.
94. As the battle progressed against the invading rebels, the Little Osages sent a runner to the Great Osage camp at Big Hills, asking for assistance. Chiefs Clarimore and Beaver then assembled another 400 braves of the Great Osages and charged on down Lightening Creek to confront Harrison's party. (In Cottrell's, Tinker's, and Gerity's accounts no mention is made of a second party of Osages confronting Harrison's party.) Surrounded, Harrison's party hunkered down in the Lightening Creek bed, allowing their horses and mules to rest before making another dash for freedom. "The Indians here," according to Warner, "got all around us at gunshot range, and kept up an incessant fire. We had only our side arms and pistols and were out of range." And here, in the creek

on them and drove back their advance upon the main body. Then, as they recoiled, he would make good his retreat, until finally they reached Verdigris Creek.[95] But by this time one-half of his party had been killed, or being wounded, fallen into the hands of the enemy, and of the remainder who reached the Verdigris nearly all were wounded more or less. Besides, they were greatly scattered. The banks of the creek were very steep and high and impassable for horseman at the point where they reached it. Lewis dismounted and abandoned his horse, calling of Rafferty, the only one in hailing distance, to do the same. The two then took to the middle of the stream to hide their trail and kept themselves under cover of the high bank. They eluded the Indians, but could hear their savage and brutal yells of triumph and firing of guns when they came up on and murdered others of the party.[96] They, in moving down in the stream, making no trail for about a mile, when they

---

bed, Frank Roberts was shot in the head and killed. Abel, 237–238; Cottrell, 69; Gerity, "Charles Harrison;" Lewis, 229; Tinker, "The Osages."

95. After their livestock had rested, Harrison ordered his men to mount and make a dash for freedom. "On ascending the bank of the stream the saddle of Captain [William] Park McLure, of St. Louis, slipped back and turned and he fell into the hands of the Indians. Harrison was shot in the face and was captured. Rule Pinkeral had his arm broken." The remaining members of Harrison's party made their escape breaking through the Indian encirclement and raced on to the Verdigris River, which was two miles away. However, by the time the Confederates had reached the river, Colonel Woodson had been caught and clubbed off his mule by the Osage Medicine Man Gra-tah-moie. It was here, at the Verdigris, that the command fell apart. Warner Lewis and John Rafferty gave up their horses and descended the steep banks of the river and hid under its overhang, as the Indians passed them by. The Verdigris also proved to be the end for Harrison's party as the Great Osages had arrived. Pinned down on a sandbar at the confluence of the Elk and Verdigris Rivers, the remaining rebels attempted to surrender, but the Osages ignored their white flag. They surrounded the remaining Confederates and waited until their ammunition was exhausted. Charging the rebel held sandbar, the Osages killed the remaining men in hand to hand combat, then "peeled the scalps from their skulls," and beheaded Harrison's men. Following the battle the Osages celebrated their victory with a war dance about the heads of their victims, even as Lewis and Rafferty made their escape. The Osages, according to their chiefs lost but two men killed, and those died at the beginning of the engagement, when the two sides were in a close battle. *O.R.*, vol. 22, pt. 2:286; Abel, 237–238; Cottrell, 69; Gerity, "Charles Harrison;" Lewis, 230; Tinker, "The Osage."

96. Following the engagement with Harrison's group, the Indians reported the incident to Federal authorities at Humbolt. (One period newspaper has the report coming to Fort Scott, carried by a priest). Captain Willoughby Doudna, commanding at Humbolt, sent Lieutenant W. A. Johnson, with a detachment of the still organizing 15th Kansas Cavalry to investigate the scene of the action (Cottrell has the 9th Kansas Cavalry investigating the battle, while Tinker's account has Doudna leading the burial party, not Johnson). Johnson found the mutilated bodies of the rebel command, including their heads and buried them in a mass grave. Johnson also located two other members of Harrison's party who had been killed in the running fight and buried them where they were found on the prairie. After burying the Confederates, Johnson secured all the documents and papers that the Osages had taken from the dead rebels and carried them back to Humbolt; the papers unfortunately were later lost. The Indians for their part were praised by the Federal authorities for their victory. As their reward the Osages were allowed to keep all the weapons, horses, and other supplies that they had taken. Additionally, Indian Agent William G. Coffin "distributed between two and three hundred dollars worth of goods," to the "elated Indians" and further recommended the four Indian chiefs, White Hair the VI, Little Bear, Clarimore, and Beaver, for government medals "for an important service rendered...in the destruction of those Confederate emissaries." Abel, 237–238; Bartels & Toms, 3:95; Britton, *Civil War on the Border, 1863–65*, 228; Cottrell,

came upon fresh tracks made by bare-footed children on the edge of the water. They also heard the barking of a dog and concluded that the children and the dog belonged to Indians. They secreted themselves in the brush.[97]

Rafferty and Lewis had escaped a horrible death at the hands of the Indians, but they were now threatened with a more horrible one. They were lost on the plains and

Threatened With Starvation.

Besides Lewis having pulled off his cavalry boots to facilitate his movements in the water had the misfortune to lose them and he was bare-footed and foot sore. They were 100 miles from any friendly settlement and they were without food. They must make their way through an open plain, exposed to the vigilance and savage and relentless enemy. Under the cover of the night they began their journey eastward, Lewis bare-footed, both hungry. During the day they had to hide themselves in the fringe of timber and brush on some friendly prairie stream which might cross their way. They took their course by the stars and found their way to the borders of Missouri, which they succeeded in reaching on the fourth day; emaciated, foot sore and wounded, they arrived at the same place from which they had marched so buoyantly a week before.[98] Here they were in danger of being captured by Federal scouting parties who had come in since they left. They very soon found hospitable and sympathetic friends, who relieved their wants and nursed them again to health and strength.

Before reaching the Neosho River in their starved and foot-sore condition, for Rafferty had allowed Lewis to wear his shoes half the time to enable him to travel at all, they startled a wild turkey off his nest. Rafferty secured the eggs, but upon breaking the first one he found instead of a delicious yolk only a young turkey with demonstrations for feathers and a most callow and unappetizing morsel.

69–70; "Fort Scott Correspondence," *Chicago Tribune*, May 27, 1863; Lankford, 93; Tinker, "The Osages."

97. In recalling the events, Warner Lewis mentioned that when the tracks were discovered they also found some fishing poles nearby. Departing the stream, Warner and Rafferty hid out during the remainder of the day and did not continue their journey until nightfall. The two men were "eighty miles from a place where relief could be obtained." Also, Warner was the one who lost his boots first, not Rafferty, causing the two men to rotate the use of Rafferty's shoes. And when not wearing footwear the two men used pieces of clothing tied to their feet to protect them from the terrain as they walked back to Missouri. Lewis, 230.

98. As Warner and Rafferty proceeded eastward, they crossed the Neosho River, where they lost Rafferty's shoes in the river. Now without footwear of any type, save the cloth wrappings, the two men continued their trek. During the journey the only food the two men secured was from a turkey nest that contained "nine unhatched eggs in an advanced state of incubation." Warner "ate one with relish," while Rafferty's "dainty appetite refused them." The two men finally reached the area of their starting place at 11:00 p.m. of May 27. Ibid.

The Delicate Stomach

of the starving soldier revolted at it, and he turned it over to Lewis, who gulped it down with great relish and laid away the remaining eggs for future use. But on reaching the Neosho, the river was not fordable, and Rafferty could not swim. They constructed a rude raft and Lewis undertook to ferry him over the deep stream. Having put Rafferty on the logs, he placed his commissariat in the shoes he was wearing at the time, so as to save his provisions, and placed them on the raft with Rafferty. But, unfortunately, the latter, though a brave soldier, like Peter the Great was afraid of water, and becoming frightened, capsized the raft, and the shoes and the commissariat were lost. Bare-footed and hungry as they were, they found in the amusement the accident afforded some compensation for their irreplaceable loss, and both laughed heartily.

The report soon reached them that news had been carried to Fort Scott of the fight, and defeat of Harrison's Brigade on the Verdigris, and the casualties were accurately reported as seventeen killed, thus giving a sad account for everyone of the gallant and daring spirits who started out to make war for the Confederacy on the plains.[99]

Rafferty was shortly afterwards killed at Cowskin Prairie, and Col. Lewis joined Gen. J. Shelby's Brigade, which about that time entered Missouri and fought its way to the Missouri River.

Of the seventeen killed, our captain, Parkinson McLure, was particularly well known and admired by the Missouri soldiers, and all hearts went out in yearning sympathy for his bereaved and widowed mother, then in her exile Cis-Mississippi. She for years nursed in her motherly breast the hope that would die for his escape and return to her maternal arms that he might be the comfort and stay of her declining years.[100] He was an officer of great prominence. Educated and ac-

---

99. The Fort Scott report that Warner refers to, puts the date of the engagement with the Indians at May 15, 1863, and not May 23, as Warner implies throughout his recollections of the expedition. The correspondence in the *Chicago Tribune* seems to support the Fort Scott report, recording via letter to the *Tribune*, dated May 18, 1863, that the incident occurred on May 15. *O.R.*, vol. 22, pt. 2:286; "Fort Scott Correspondence," *Chicago Tribune*, May 25, 1863.

100. Even as William P. McLure was meeting his fate in the Indian Territory, his mother Margaret, was being banished from St. Louis for allowing her house to become the Confederate "headquarters for the mail and contraband goods." She was sent South, after being held prisoner in her own home for two months, on the evening of May 13, a day after her son William headed to Colorado. After her arrest in March, Margaret McLure's house was stripped of all furniture and goods, which were then sold for the benefit of the Union, and the residence turned into a prison for female supporters of the Confederate cause. Mrs. McLure took the steamboat *Belle Memphis* to Memphis, under the escort of the 1st Nebraska Infantry, and then went southward by rail to La Grange and into Mississippi by ambulance, finally ending her journey in Columbus. Following the fall of Vicksburg, Mrs. McLure went to Demopolis, Alabama, where she remained until the end of the war. Upon her return to St. Louis, Mrs. McLure "was elected president for life" of the first Chapter of the United Daughters of the Confederacy of Missouri, and worked tirelessly in building the Confederate Home in Higginsville, Missouri. She died in St. Louis at the age of 90, following "a serious accident" that left her bed-ridden for two months prior to her passing. "From St. Louis,"

complished, he was by his daring energy and intelligence fitted peculiarly for the military service of his beloved south. He died in the harness, and his heart full of patriotic devotion to Missouri and her people ceased to beat in the din of battle and line of duty. And when the long roll of the day of judgement calls to resurrect his brave heart will with the thousands of others bivouacked in their graves, again throb with patriotic love for Missouri and our common country.

R. H. Musser.

* * * * * * *

Item: Irregular Operations in the Indian Territory, Northwest Arkansas and in Southwest Missouri, 1863-1865, including numerous skirmishes and attacks on Federal trains, by J. W. Cooper.[101]
Published: April 24, 1886.

Roughing It in the Bush

Beaumont, Kas., March 30
Editor *Republican*

In the summer of 1863, I was with two companies of [Charles A.] Carroll's Arkansas Cavalry Regiment on detached service near Bentonville, Ark.[102] Capt.

The Chicago Times, May 15, 1863; Hale, *Branded As Rebels Volume Two*, 216; Nichols, *Guerrilla Warfare, Volume II*, 84–85; Potter & Robbins, 145–150; Mrs. P. G. Robert, "History of Events Preceding and Following the Banishment of Mrs. Margaret A. E. McLure, As Given to Her By Herself," *Reminiscences of the Women of Missouri During the Sixties*, 78, 80–83; Winter, 85–86.

101. James W. Cooper was born in the late 1820s or early 1830s and was living near Memphis, Tennessee, when the Civil War began. He joined what became Company G, 15th Arkansas Infantry and was elected 1st lieutenant of the command in 1861. He lost this position in May 1862, and returned to the Trans-Mississippi, where he joined either Company G or H, of Carroll's Arkansas Cavalry Regiment, rank unknown. Cooper fought at Prairie Grove, after which he remained in northwest Arkansas where he recruited a company in the spring of 1863. Still in Carroll's Regiment, now commanded by L. L. Thompson, Cooper operated as a scout and guerrilla in northwest Arkansas, and later commanded a company serving under Stand Watie. By the end of the war, Cooper was a major at the head of a battalion of guerrillas under Watie's command. He disbanded his battalion on June 1, 1865, and with a few remaining men intended to go to Mexico; however, that task proved too difficult to accomplish, and so he surrender himself and his remaining men at Cassville, Missouri, on July 1, 1865. On July 5, Cooper was paroled and he returned to his home near Memphis, Tennessee. Following the war, Cooper settled in Beaumont, Kansas, where he was living in 1886. Final disposition unknown. *O.R.*, vol. 34, pt. 3:658 *O.R.*, vol. 48, pt. 2:758–759; *O.R.S.*, pt. 2, vol. 2:240, 242, 560; J. W. Cooper, "Battle of Prairie Grove," *Missouri Republican*, February 6, 1886; William Furry, ed., *The Preacher's Tale: The Civil War Journal oaf Rev. Francis Springer, Chaplain, U.S. Army of the Frontier* (Fayetteville, AR, 2001), 115, cited hereafter as Furry.

102. Charles A. Carroll was born in Alabama in about 1830. He moved to Crawford County, Arkansas, in 1854, got married, and relocated to Conway County. There Carroll was a farmer, a close friend of Governor Henry Rector, and a Democratic candidate for the First Arkansas Congressional District in 1859. With the beginning of the Civil War, Carroll was commissioned May 18, 1861, captain of a cavalry company (three months) in the Arkansas Militia, which he had raised in Fayetteville. The 40-man company acted as Ben McCulloch's bodyguard at the Battle of Wilson's

[John A.] Armington [Arrington] was in command, with Capt. [T. P.] Jefferson as junior.[103] I was sent with a dispatch to headquarters, at Fort Smith.[104] On returning, a man near the prairie south of Bentonville warned me of danger.[105] I had a good horse of the best Middle Tennessee breed, and though somewhat fatigued I concluded to go on. Reaching the prairie I could see mounted men in the distance, but

---

Creek and was disbanded at the end of August 1861. After his militia service, Carroll was assigned to duty as a Confederate colonel, commanding the District of Northwest Arkansas on June 3, 1862, where he organized Carroll's Arkansas Cavalry Regiment, and later commanded a cavalry brigade, which he led at the Battle of Cane Hill on November 28, 1862. Carroll was relieved of command on December 3, 1862, following Cane Hill, pending an investigation for cowardice. Carroll returned to Conway County and never reentered to the army, resigning on April 12, 1863. Following the war Carroll moved to little Rock, where he died on February 27, 1877. *O.R.S.*, pt. 2, vol. 2:240; Allardice, *Confederate Colonels*, 91; Kremm, 53; William Garrett Piston and Richard W. Hatcher III, *Wilson's Creek: The Second Battle of the Civil War and the Men Who Fought It*, (Chapel Hill, NC, 2000), 207; Margaret Ross, *Arkansas Gazette: The Early Years 1819–1866* (Little Rock, AR, 1969), 339, 372–373; Special Orders No. 6 (June 3, 1862), No. 20 (October 22, 1862), No. 23 (October 26, 1862) and No. 60 (December 3, 1862), Special Orders Book No. 1, 4, 87–89, 91-92.

103. Captain John A. Arrington commanded Company G, Carroll's Arkansas Regiment, while Captain T. P. Jefferson commanded Company H. Arrington was mustered into the Confederate Service on July 15, 1861, as a captain commanding Company D, 2nd Arkansas Mounted Rifles. At Wilson's Creek, Arrington was praised by Colonel James McIntosh for his performance at the battle, after which his unit was transferred to east of the Mississippi. Upon reorganization of his unit at Corinth, Mississippi, on May 8, 1862, Arrington returned to Arkansas, where he organized Company H, Carroll's Arkansas Cavalry Regiment, which was mustered on August 15, 1862. Arrington was promoted to major, of what was now known as Gordon's or the 4th Arkansas Regiment, on March 25, 1864. During the Camden Expedition, Arrington was again cited for his "gallant conduct" at the Battle of Poison Springs, on April 18, 1864.

Captain T. P. Jefferson organized his Company G on August 10, 1862. He was known to have been in the Battle of Fayetteville, Arkansas, on April 18, 1863, where he was wounded and captured. He was exchanged shortly after the battle, but nothing more is known of Jefferson, save what Cooper has recorded in his piece for the "Confederate Tales." Arrington died on May 10, 1878, while Jefferson's final disposition was not found. *O.R.*, vol. 3:111; *O.R.*, vol. 22, pt. 1:308–309; *O.R.*, vol. 34, pt. 2:792; *O.R.S.*, pt. 2, vol. 2:189, 198, 240, 242; Desmond Wall Allen, *Index to Arkansas Confederate Pension Applications* (Conway, AR, 1991), 32, hereafter cited as Allen, *Index to Arkansas Pensions*; National Archives, Record Group 109, Confederate Muster Rolls, Carroll's Arkansas Cavalry; Sifakis, *Arkansas*, 53, 57–58.

104. Ft. Smith is located on the Arkansas River near the border of Arkansas and the Indian Territory. It was established in 1817, and manned on and off until the Civil War, when it became an important point in the defense of the Arkansas Valley. During the war, Ft. Smith served as a supply depot and assembly point for the Confederates to launch attacks on Missouri or Kansas, while supporting their Indian allies in the Indian Territory. Federal forces under James G. Blunt captured Ft. Smith on September 1, 1863, and retained it for the remainder of the war. Edwin C. Bearss and Arrell M. Gibson, *Fort Smith Little Gibraltar on the Arkansas* (Norman, OK, 1969; reprint ed., Norman, OK, 1979), 8, 244, 268–269.

105. Bentonville, Arkansas, is the county seat of Benton County, the farthest northwest county of the state. The city contained about 1,000 residents prior to 1861. During the course of the Civil War the town was occupied on-and-off by both sides. During the Pea Ridge Campaign, Federal forces under Franz Sigel burned 30 buildings of the town in March 1862, as a response to some rebels who had fired upon his troops. Alternatively, one Federal soldier asserts that the buildings were burned in response to a Union man who had been poisoned at a local hotel. Banasik, *Reluctant Cannoneer*, 74.

could not tell whether friends or foes. Advancing cautiously, I soon saw a soldier in blue off to the right trying to get behind me, while at the same time four or five more advanced in front from cover nearly half a mile away. Turning quickly, I easily got ahead of the single man, and as the others were still quite distant I thought I would have a little fun. I halted, with my gun hanging down but pointing towards my pursuer, who seemed to think I was surrendering. At all events he sheathed his revolver and came forward with an affable smile, evidently not wishing to hurt my feelings. As soon as he had his revolver well stowed away I began deliberately raising my gun. The sudden change that came over his mug as he comprehended the situation and wheeled to "git," was very marked. I fired a shot close enough for the zip of the ball to give him a good send-off, and then, as his comrades were closing in, I put spurs to my horse. He seemed to enjoy a joke, for as we were putting distance between us according to our horses' abilities, I heard his laugh ring across the prairie. The Feds had been on a little raid. Getting into the woods I soon found some of our boys with Geo. Jefferson of Bentonville. We waylaid them on their return and fired on them from a wooded hill on Sugar Creek,

Capturing Some Horses.

That night I crawled up to their camp alone, halted their pickets, got them to fire a volley and firing a single shot in return shouted, "Charge them boys!" There was a great noise, nearly all of which they made themselves, and I was afterwards told they decamped precipitately.

No one comprehended the frightful conditions prevailing in this region by reason of the partisan warfare waged there, unless he had an opportunity to actually see its workings. As it fell to my lot to take an active part in that deplorable struggle I will give you some incidents for the "Tales of the War."

As we were returning from a scout one day we stopped for dinner at Pea Ridge.[106] We were all young fellows, none over 21 years old. We expected to be followed and I selfishly left the rest and rode half a mile ahead to dine with a certain blue-eyed lass, who I knew would welcome me. Dinner was half over when bang! bang! I heard shots in the distance. I jumped up, seized my gun, strapped on

---

106. Pea Ridge was a mountain ridge in northwest Arkansas, where a battle occurred on March 6–8, 1862. There was no town by that name during the Civil War. The nearest was a village known as Leetown, which was about two miles southwest of Elkhorn Tavern. Leetown and Elkhorn Tavern were the two main focal points of the battle. Even while the battle raged General Samuel R. Curtis selected the Union name for the engagement, according to newspaper correspondent William Fayel. Recalling that day, Fayel noted that one man wanted to call it "Ozark Mountains," but Curtis thought that too general. Another suggested Leetown. Fayel suggested Sugar Creek. "The general objected to this on account of the affair two weeks before." Curtis then questioned a local as to the name of the distant ridge. "'Pea Ridge!' said the Butternut. 'That's just it,' said the general." As to surviving buildings in the area by the summer of 1863, Elkhorn Tavern was burned in late 1862, while Leetown still remained, as did some of the surrounding farms. Unknown as to whose farm Cooper was referring in his article. Wm. Fayel, "Curtis Withdrawal From Cross Hollows," *Missouri Republican*, December 19, 1885; Shea & Hess, 327, 329.

revolver and rushed out. As I got in the saddle Little Blue was screaming: "Run, Jim, run!" The boys were already coming along at a full run, there was a stake and rider fence in front, the girl screaming behind and the firing coming closer. I thought my time was come, but managed to get over the fence. Then I wished the girl ten miles away, but as she was right there looking on I tried to look cool.

It should have been easy enough, but it wasn't. The boys made a stand, and as two of the Yanks appeared in an opening, I managed to bring my gun to bear, when it was instantly struck by one of my comrades and Little Blue was speedily joining in their shouts of laughter. The miserable rascals had played me

A Mean Joke.

There were no Yanks. However, I knew we would be followed, and so I took a side road, leaving the boys to follow the main road. When I reached camp that night I found the boys all there, and some without hats. The genuine foe had run them in, and though they were in no humor for joking any more I had the laugh on them.

In the fall of 1863, being detailed with Col. [William W.] Reynolds from near Camden on a scout to northern Arkansas, I was cut off with a squad by the Federals following Gen. Shelby out of Missouri.[107] Our main body of scouts joined Shelby, and my party went towards the Nation line.[108] Falling in with Capt. Wm. Brown, who was pursuing some Federals, we joined him in a sharp engagement at Round Prairies in the western part of Benton County.[109] My squad had the credit

---

107. "Col. Reynolds" was probably Lieutenant Colonel William W. Reynolds, the only Colonel Reynolds found who served in the Trans-Mississippi. Reynolds was elected captain of Company F, 21st Arkansas Infantry Battalion, in December 1861, following the promotion of Captain W. Thompson to major of the regiment. On May 7, 1862, Reynolds was promoted to major, upon reorganization and consolidation of McRae's 21st with Hobbs's and Boone's Regiments. He was promoted to lieutenant colonel on December 16, 1862. The 21st was redesignated the 15th Arkansas Infantry in February 1863, with Reynolds still as the lieutenant colonel. Reynolds was subsequently captured at Vicksburg on July 4, 1863, paroled, and returned to Arkansas, where he was given command of the 1st Consolidated Regiment in January 1864. Reynolds survived the war, married, and died in July 1880. [Note: The *Official Records* misidentifies the Reynolds in volume 22 as Daniel H. Reynolds, who served on the east side of the Mississippi River. The correct Reynolds was William W. Reynolds.] *O.R.*, vol. 22, pt. 1:751, 1006; *O.R.*, vol. 41, pt. 3:968; *O.R.*, vol. 41, pt. 4:1143; *O.R.S.*, pt. 2, vol. 2:557–558, 560; Allardice, *Confederate Colonels*, 65–66, 197; Allen, *Index to Arkansas Pensions*, 246; Sifakis, *Arkansas*, 99, 107; Internet site, www.couchgenweb.com/civilwar.

108. Cooper is mistaken as to when the scouts joined Shelby. Shelby departed the main army on September 22, 1863, and did not return to Washington, Arkansas, until November 3. The incident that Cooper describes next occurred in early September 1863, before Shelby departed on the expedition. *O.R.*, vol. 22, pt. 1:671, 677.

109. William "Buck" Brown was "a good looking fair complected young man, appearing to be about twenty-five or thirty years old," in 1864. Born in the mid-1830s, Brown was the owner of Brown's Mill (the mill was "disabled" on August 30, 1864, to deny its use to local rebels), which was located on Brush Creek, five miles west of Elm Springs, in Benton County, Arkansas. At the beginning of the Civil War, Brown was General Ben McCulloch's personal bodyguard and scout. He fought at Wilson's Creek in 1861, after which he organized a guerrilla company in March 1863,

of turning the enemy's left, which led to their complete rout with a loss of twenty or thirty prisoners.[110]

After this I reported to Gen. Stand Watie on the Canadian River in the Indian Territory and was given a commission with orders, which I carried out, to raise a company in Northwest Arkansas.[111] The general started on a raid about the 15th

---

operating primarily about Fayetteville and in southwest Missouri. Brown's band, including several former slaves, frequently stole "sections of the Union's telegraph lines," successfully stole 240 horses and mules from a Union command that was pursuing him (June 24, 1864), attacked Federal trains passing through northwest Arkansas and "often united with [Stand] Watie for a raid." In April 1863, Brown led his band in the Battle of Fayetteville and later, after the Federals abandoned the city, captured it on August 23, 1863, taking six Federals prisoners. On September 5, at Round Prairie, Brown captured another 23 prisoners. In April 1864, Brown's band attacked a 10-man squad of Federal cavalry "herding stock," killing all but one. Brown was active in 1864, operating from time-to-time in southwestern Missouri, where he was now styled as "Colonel Buck Brown." Michael Hughes labels Brown "the wiliest and most effective Confederate partisan captain in northwest Arkansas." Brown did not survive the war; he was killed on March 13, 1865, near his mill in Benton County. *O.R.*, vol. 22, pt. 2:307, 595, 612, 750–751; *O.R.*, vol. 41, pt. 1:270; *O.R.*, vol. 48, pt. 1:1185; Britton, *Civil War on the Border, 1863–65*, 162; Frank Cunningham, *General Stand Watie's Confederate Indians* (San Antonio, TX, 1959), 114, hereafter cited as Cunningham; Eakin & Hale, 46–47; Furry, 116, 125, 127, 170 (n. 17); Huff, "Guerrillas," 136–137; Michael A. Hughes, "Wartime Gristmill Destruction in Northwest Arkansas and Military Farm Colonies," in *Civil War Arkansas Beyond Battles and Leaders* (Anne J. Bailey and Daniel Sutherland, gen eds.; Fayetteville, AR, 2000), 35, 37, hereafter cited as Hughes, "Wartime Gristmills"; Ingenthron, 292; Bruce Nichols, *Guerrilla Warfare in the Civil War, Volume III, January–August 1864* (Jefferson, NC, 2014), 194, 196, hereafter cited as Nichols, *Guerrilla Warfare, Volume III*; Nichols, *Guerrilla Warfare, Volume IV*, 363; James Anderson Slower, "Autobiography of," Western History Collection, University of Oklahoma, Norman, Oklahoma, 96.

110. The engagement took place on September 5, 1863, beginning a short distance from Flint Creek, ending 12 miles south of Maysville, Arkansas, on Round Prairie. Dubbed the "Skirmish near Maysville" by the compilers of the *Official Records*, the engagement began about mid-morning. The 75-man Federal force from the 1st Arkansas Cavalry (Union), commanded by Captain J. I. Worthington, was escorting Captain John Gardner of the 2nd Kansas Cavalry, who was bearing dispatches to Colonel William Cloud. The Unionists made contact with a 72-man rebel force (not 300 as Federal sources claimed), led by Captain William Brown, after which a running fight of 10 miles took place. Brown's force then broke contact, and the Federals moved on another 8 miles and "stopped to feed" 12 miles south of Maysville; the rebels then charged the feeding Unionists. Fifty men of the 1st Arkansas (Union) ran, while Captain Gardner with the other 25 men held the enemy briefly. "Flanked on the right and left" Gardener fell back, formed again, was again flanked, retreated a half mile and fell back for the last time forming a line on Round Prairie. With no support coming from Captain Worthington's routed troops, Gardner gave the final order to retreat, whereupon he was captured. Federal losses totaled one killed, two wounded, with 23 captured (Dyer has only 22 missing or captured), while Brown lost but one man killed and one man deserted. [Note: The only Federal report on this engagement was written by Captain John Gardner; Captain Worthington made no report.] *O.R.*, vol. 22, pt. 1:612; Britton, *Civil War on the Border, 1863–65*, 162; Dyer, 680; Edwards, *Prairie was on Fire*, 47; Fury, 117.

111. Stand Watie was born on December 12, 1806, in what became modern-day Georgia. He was educated at a mission school, served as a deputy sheriff, clerked in the Cherokee Supreme Court and edited a newspaper. As a member of the "Treaty Party," Watie helped negotiate a treaty which sold the Cherokee lands east of the Mississippi River. Relocated to the Indian Territory (modern-day Oklahoma) in 1837, Watie assumed the leadership of his party in 1839, following the assassination of three of its prominent members. Prior to the Civil War, Watie served on the Cherokee Council and was speaker of the Council from 1855–1861. With the coming of the Civil War, the Five

of December, 1863, to Cain [Cane] Hill.[112] Crossing the Arkansas River, near Fort Gibson he advanced to Illinois Creek, where he was defeated by a force from Fort Gibson, the brigade hardly fighting at all, though commanded by a brave officer.[113]

My company came near to being massacred. Expecting to be supported we charged two howitzers opposite the center of our line. Nearing them, we came upon a body of Indians lying under cover to support the guns. We were so close that we could see the paint on their faces, and not till then did we discover that the rest of line was in retreat. We opened a fire that held in check the Federal Indians, who were not much better soldiers than our own.[114] They let us get away

---

Civilized Tribes joined the Confederacy in October 1861, and Watie became the colonel of the 1st Cherokee Mounted Rifles. Watie fought at Wilson's Creek in Missouri, Pea Ridge in Arkansas, and Honey Springs (July 1863) and Cabin Creek (September 1864) in the Indian Territory, to name but a few of his engagements. He was promoted to general officer on May 10, 1864, and was the last Confederate general to surrender on June 23, 1865. Following the war, Watie returned home, to what is now Delaware County, Oklahoma, where he died on September 9, 1871. Banasik, *Reluctant Cannoneer*, 292–294.

112. Cane Hill, Arkansas, was located about 10 miles southwest of Prairie Grove and 20 miles southwest of Fayetteville. On November 28, General James G. Blunt's 1st Division had a running fight of about 10 miles against a rebel cavalry division commanded by John S. Marmaduke. The Confederates lost 10 killed, 66 wounded, and six missing, while the Federals reported four killed and 36 wounded. *O.R.*, vol. 22, pt. 1:46: Banasik, *Embattled Arkansas*, 287.

113. Fort Gibson was established as a military post in 1830, just prior to the relocation of the Eastern Indians to the Indian Territory. It was located on the east side of the Grand River, about a mile from the river on a bluff, and about three miles from where the Grand met the Arkansas River. The post contained quarters sufficient to hold two companies of troops, along with two stone buildings for quartermaster and commissary stores. Wiley Britton, *The Union Indian Brigade in the Civil War* (Kansas City, MO, 1922), 209–210, cited hereafter as Britton, *Union Indian Brigade*; Wiley Britton, *Memoirs of the Rebellion on the Border 1863* (Chicago, 1882; reprint ed., Florissant, MO, 1986), 207–209.

114. Following the loss of the Arkansas Valley in September 1863, General Douglas Cooper withdrew his forces into the southern part of the Indian Territory, leaving Colonel Stand Watie to harass the Unionists in the northern part of the Territory. Beginning in late October through December 1863, Watie conducted a series of raids north of the Arkansas River, thus "instilling fear into all Union sympathizers," according to Lary and Donald Rampp. On December 16 (not 15th) Watie began his last raid for 1863, leading a band of 650 Cherokee and Creek across the Arkansas River. Watie initially burnt the Creek Agency and then attacked the Ft. Gibson pickets some three miles from the fort, killing two and wounding two. The following day Watie was at Park Hill, where he burned some buildings and looted a local Unionist's home, camping that night on the Illinois River northeast of Park Hill. With Watie again raiding north of the Arkansas, Colonel William A. Philips, commanding at Fort Gibson, dispatched Captain A. C. Spilman with 290 men and one 12-lb howitzer from the Indian Brigade, to reinforce Major John Foreman at Rhea's Mill, Arkansas. Arriving at Park Hill shortly after Watie had left, Spilman learned the direction of Watie's withdrawal and headed toward the Illinois River, following Watie's trail up Barren Fork Creek, where he engaged Watie's Indians. After a two hour fight, Captain Spilman reported that he had "routed" the enemy (Frank Cuningham writes that the Unionists had "edged" Watie in the battle). In either case Spilman reported the loss of one man killed and two wounded, while estimating the rebel loss at "not less than 12 killed and 25 wounded, besides a large number of horses killed and disabled." Of the other primary or secondary sources, only the Rampps believe Spilman's claims of Confederate losses, while Wilfred Knight "congratulates" Spilman "for his creativity" in his report. Watie's troops fought "dismounted," making the loss of horses unlikely and Spilman did not police the battlefield to get an actual count of anything. Despite all the speculation, the adjutant

Without Much Loss.

Leaving the brigade near Cane Hill I went towards Fayetteville, where the enemy had a post.[115] We had just begun picking up deserters and recruits when the weather turned intensely cold, snow falling several inches deep. This compelled us to fall back into the mountains on King's River. About the 1st of February, 1864, with about thirty men I followed a company of raiders, overtaking him two miles from their post at Berryville.[116] They ran at the first gun, and we drove them helter-skelter into town, pickets and all going in together and creating such confusion that the garrison did not follow us, though we rode off deliberately on the main road.[117] The country was full of deserters and independent bands of

---

of the 1st Cherokee Regiment reported the rebel losses as one man killed, one mortally wounded and "several slightly wounded." *O.R.*, vol. 22, pt. 1:781–783; *O.R.*, vol. 22, pt. 2:1047; Britton, *Civil War on the Border, 1863–65*, 234; Britton, *Union Indian Brigade*, 232–233; Cunningham, 112; Dyer, 986; Edwards, *Prairie was on Fire*, 87; Kenny A. Franks, *Stand Watie and the Agony of the Cherokee Nation* (Memphis, TN, 1979), 151–152, hereafter cited as Franks; Wilfred Knight, *Red Fox: Stand Watie's Civil War in Indian Territory* (Glendale, CA, 1988), 184, 190–192, hereafter cited as Knight; Lary C. Rampp & Donald L. Rampp, *The Civil War in the Indian Territory* (Austin, TX, 1975), 53–54, 58; *Union Army*, 5:424.

115. Following the engagement at Barren Fork Creek, Watie continued on towards Rhea's Mill where he intended to attack Major John Foreman's command. On December 20, Watie engaged Foreman's command briefly in the vicinity of Cane Hill. In this skirmish Foreman, reported the loss of three men, after which Watie broke contact and continued northward toward southwest Missouri with half his command, while the remainder headed south to intercept a train from Ft. Smith. Watie passed through Cincinnati, Arkansas, on the evening of December 20, still heading north. By December 23, Watie was in southwestern MacDonald County, Missouri, where he remained briefly until returning south. Passing by Maysville, Watie again divided his command with some of his men continuing on into the Cherokee portion of the Indian Territory, there to gather up their families to escort them south, while the others headed back to the south side of the Arkansas River, thus ending his raid. Meanwhile, the other half of Watie's command successfully intercepted the Union train on December 26, killing one and capturing "6 or 8 prisoners." *O.R.*, vol. 22, pt. 2:746, 751–752; Britton, *Civil War on the Border, 1863–65*, 234–235; Britton, *Union Indian Brigade*, 334; Cunningham, 114; Edwards, *Prairie was on Fire*, 88; Franks, 152–153; Nichols, *Guerrilla Warfare, Volume II*, 293; *Union Army*, 5:218.

116. Berryville, Arkansas, is the county seat of Carroll County. In 1860 the town consisted of 51 buildings, and by the end of the war all had been burned, except "two small residences" and the Hubbert Hotel. The hotel was supposedly saved from the flames because "the Masonic records and regalia were stored in the upper story" of the building. During the war Berryville was the center of guerrilla activity in northern Arkansas and saw frequent Union scouts to the area to break up rebel bands. Ingenthron, 200–201, 221–222, 301, 339, 343, 346, 348.

117. On January 26, 1864, General C. B. Holland, commanding the 4th Missouri Militia District, left Springfield on an expedition into northwest Arkansas. Holland was operating under orders of General John B. Sanborn, commanding the District of Southwestern Missouri, to break up a pending Confederate raid into Missouri, which was forming in Searcy, Carroll, Newton, and Izard Counties, Arkansas. Arriving at Cassville, Holland determined that Berryville was the point of the Confederate concentration. Proceeding forward Holland arrived at Berryville on January 29, where he joined his 200-man force with Captain James Duff, commanding a detachment of the 2nd Arkansas Cavalry (Union), consisting of his own Company I and Company F. Duff had previously arrived at Berryville on January 23. No mention of the incident that Cooper describes was noted in the *Official Records* or *Supplement*, save Holland's remark upon his arrival on January

partisans. Thieves and bushwhackers were robbing friend and foe right and left, all good fighters, but poor soldiers. I could gather a company, but could give no cohesion to the mass. The condition of affairs allowed the evils of a defensive policy.[118] The same condition existed all through, from the Indian Territory to Virginia, as I afterwards learned. The armed men roving in the bush were more than the numbers the same section had in the army. Had our army been pushed upon northern soil these men would have been in. Shortly after the last skirmish I fell in with two independent companies commanded by Capts. Scrugg and Rallie [Raly or Railey][119]. We marched to attack a small detachment that was guarding Blake's Mill in Benton County. As I was ignored in the councils, I followed to await developments. Seeing the advance charging, we hurried forward, and to my astonishment, soon found ourselves going in on horseback against the enemy fortified in a mill. We had no chance to get at them and were quickly defeated. I lost two good men, Williams and Marshall.[120]

29: "Everything was apparently quiet in that locality [Berryville], except some little excitement created by small parties of jayhawkers." Holland remained in Berryville, awaiting his train, which arrived on February 5. Then, leaving a force to protect the town, Holland began operations in Carroll County on February 6, attempting to bring the Confederate forces of Thomas Freeman, Joseph Love, and a Major Gunning to battle. However, Holland failed in that endeavor, though overall the expedition did manage to prevent the raid into Missouri and drive 1,000 "Confederate soldiers and bushwhackers" across the Arkansas River. General Sanborn further reported that the various elements of the expedition, not including Holland, killed 70 and captured 200 rebels. *O.R.*, vol. 34, pt. 1:86–89; *O.R.S.*, pt. 2, vol. 2:69, 74.

118. By February 1864, the two northern tiers of counties in northern Arkansas were awash with various bands of both Union and Confederate guerrillas. "It was a war between friends and neighbors; no quarter asked and none was given," according to Leo E. Huff. Huff states that the war "was characterized by murder, arson, robbery, pillage and ambush...These outlaws called themselves—as best suited their purpose—Confederates and Federals...Some of these bands of freebooters claimed allegiance to either the United States or the Confederacy and confined their" attacks to their opponents' sympathizers or soldiers. In northern Arkansas the most famous bands of Confederate guerrillas were led by James Ingrham, William "Buck" Brown, and James W. Cooper, while the Union bands were captained by William J. "Wild Bill" Heffington of Yell County and William Dark of Searcy County. All these guerrillas were originally in the Confederate Army, but Heffington and Dark both deserted, forming Union guerrilla bands. Another noted Unionist was Martin D. Hart, a Texan, who operated in western and northern Arkansas, until he was caught and hanged in January 1863. Huff, "Guerrillas," 127, 136–138.

119. A review of Edward G. Gerdes's Internet site "couchgenweb" shows only one Raly—Lawson Raly. He enlisted in Company H, 14th Arkansas Infantry (Power's Regiment), at Yellville on July 13, 1861, and was discharged on February 8, 1862. Later he joined the 27th Arkansas Infantry and then John Coffee's Regiment. Captain Raly was found to be active in northwest Arkansas in 1864, attacking Federal trains. A search of the name Scrugg shows two possibilities, apparently brothers, D. H and W. D. Scrugg. Both joined the 4th Arkansas Cavalry Regiment, on August 15, 1862, in Bentonville, Arkansas. They later transferred to guerrilla Captain James Ingrham's Company on May 20, 1863. Final disposition of the Scruggs and Raly not known. *O.R.*, vol. 41 pt. 1:798; Arkansas: Edward G. Gerdes Civil War Home Page. www.couchgenweb.com/civilwar; hereafter cites as Gerdes.

120. Blake's Mill was also known as Black's Mill and was located at Cross Hollows, Arkansas. The engagement took place on February 17, 1864, between the Arkansas guerrillas and a detachment of the 1st Arkansas Cavalry (Union), probably Company H. No further information available

Striking a Train.

Returning to Kings River, crossing the Boston Mountains and scouting along the Arkansas River, thence across the Mulberry Mountain, we struck a train heavily guarded on Mulberry Creek. I posted the company on a bluff at an angle with the road. By some means they discovered us and the escort turned our right up the incline. The company changed front in good order, but as the enemy outnumbered us we fell back fighting until the Federals returned to their train.[121] These affairs were in the latter part of the winter of 1864. Recrossing the Boston Mountains we scouted between King's River and Osage and Buffalo Creek, changing camp every day as the enemy had strong detachments out in every direction. We had a good chance at a force near Huntsville, but a lot of thieves who had joined me for purposes of plunder, refused to fight and caused so much confusion that I could not make an attack.[122]

While we were encamped on Buffalo Creek with Capt. John Cecil [Sissell]

---

other than what Cooper has written in his article. Unknown as to the identity of Williams and Marshall. *O.R.S.*, pt. 2, vol. 2:35; Dyer, 682; Hughes, "Wartime Gristmills," 35, 37; *Union Army*, 5:134.

121. Mulberry Creek or River was located near Ozark, Arkansas. In the latter part of February 1864, the 14th Kansas Cavalry relocated to Ozark, there to scout and escort trains through the area. In all probability a detachment of the 14th Kansas was the escorting unit that encountered Cooper's band in the late winter of 1863–1864 on Mulberry Creek, exact date unknown. However, Company D, 15th Kansas Cavalry, as noted in the *Supplement to the Official Records*, pursued guerrillas on March 7, 1864, killing two of their number. The incident that Cooper describes probably occurred near where the road from Van Buren crosses Mulberry Creek, which was about midway between the two towns—about 15 miles from either Ozark or Van Buren. *O.R.S.*, pt. 2, vol. 21:433, 441; Davis, *Civil War Atlas*, plt. no. 160.

122. Huntsville is the County Seat of Madison County, Arkansas, and is located in the center of the county, a short distance from War Eagle Creek. In January 1863, a soldier in the 19th Iowa Infantry provided this description of Huntsville:

> The place may have contained, in its day of glory, perhaps a hundred and fifty inhabitants. At present, however, it is comparatively deserted—no men in the place, a few women or Negroes left in charge of a few dwellings. Half of the Negroes at present are used by our troops or for government purposes. The town contains one or two fine dwellings, several large extensive store houses which have been arranged with every modern improvement and calculated for large stocks of goods.

In further describing Huntsville, another Federal soldier stated that it contained a courthouse, jail and "an immense old barn of a building, surmounted by a steeple which would have been agony to an architect's apprentice in the North, [which] serves the triple purpose of a church, a school house and a Masonic Hall," the rest of buildings, "about fifty in number, being little more than log hovels." Before the war was over, Huntsville, like most of the county seats in northern Arkansas, was burned by Federal troops. The town was burned in late February 1863, in retaliation for "three men being killed near there," leaving only "three or four residences" and the Masonic Lodge. After the war the Lodge served as the county courthouse until a new one could be built. Desmond Walls Allen, ed., *Turnbo's Tales of the Ozarks: War and Guerrilla Stories. Revised Edition* (Conway, AR, 1989), 17; Charles W. Huff, Civil War Diary, State Historical Society of Iowa (Des Moines, IA), January 8, 1863; Ingenthron, 301–302; Thomas, "Letter From the Twentieth," *Daily Missouri Democrat* (St. Louis), February 12, 1863.

and a lot of rapscallions under a Capt. Patton our pickets were driven in one day about 1 o'clock and followed up pell-mell by the enemy.[123] I had been taking a nap and was aroused by the racket to find the enemy within 150 yards. We had

A Good Position,

however, and my men were quickly in line. There was a creek in our front which had to be crossed by a narrow defile approached by a lane with a bluff on one side and a fence on the other. This we could sweep with a concentrated fire, but just across the creek at Mrs. Casey's house Capt. Cecil lay sick. His horse stood at the gate unsaddled, and at the alarm the captain had gone out bareheaded to mount. Without saddle or bridle he had just got his horse into the road when the enemy were upon him striking him with guns and sabers. He kept his seat, however, and we held our fire until the moment when his horse went down into the creek. Then we gave them a volley which sent them to the right about. Patton's company had fled from us with a few of Cecil's men and we could see them scrambling up the mountainside. The balance of Cecil's men stood with us and sending out a vedette we made haste to saddle up. We soon had some seventy-five men in line,

---

123. There are two possibilities for Captain Cecil. The *Official Records* identifies the man as Captain Sissel. A review of assorted sources names the captain as Jonathan Sissel, who enlisted in what became Company B, 20th Arkansas Infantry, eventually becoming the command's 1st lieutenant, when the unit reorganized in May 1862; after which no further record was found. Sissell's unit was eventually captured at Vicksburg, and Sissel was possibly paroled (or escaped) and returned to the Trans-Mississippi in July–August 1863. Another source identifies the captain as Captain John Cecil, who was born in Tennessee, in about 1822, a farmer by profession and living in Prairie Township, Newton County, Arkansas, at the beginning of the Civil War. Initially Cecil joined a Home Guard unit on June 22, 1861, was later mustered out, and on March 10, 1863, joined Harrell's Arkansas Cavalry Battalion. These men could be one in the same, given the phonetic spelling of the last name. Regardless, Cooper's Captain Cecil or Sissel led a band of Arkansas guerrillas in northwest Arkansas, whom Sidney D. Jackman characterized as "no better fighters on earth." In the fall of 1863, after returning to northern Arkansas, Sissel was elected 1st Lieutenant of a 60-man company. Later, the unit disbanded and Sissel organized his own command, which he operated both independently and with S. D. Jackman's and other guerrilla companies in the region. On April 5, 1864, Sissel's band was engaged at Whiteley's Mill near the headwaters of the Buffalo River, where they, with other rebel bands, including Captain Patton's, beat off a Union attack of the 2nd Arkansas Cavalry (Union). Sissel barely escaped capture by riding through the Union troops as they attempted to unhorse him; his horse was finally killed, but Sissel managed to escape on foot, though quite sick at the time. Nothing else found on Captain Sissel. *O.R.*, vol. 34 pt. 1:872; *O.R.S.*, pt. 2, vol. 2:636; T. Lindsay Baker, ed., *Confederate Guerrilla: The Civil War Memoir of Joseph H. Bailey* (Fayetteville, AR, 2007), 112 n. 19, hereafter cited as Baker; James Troy Massey, *Memoir of Captain J. M. Bailey* (n.c., 1995), 30; Norton & Massey, 43; Sifakis, *Arkansas*, 105.

A search of all the Pattons on Edward Gerdes's Arkansas Internet site has one possibility for Captain Patton; he could be John M. Patton, who was born in Obion County, Tennessee, in about 1831. At the beginning of the Civil War, he enlisted in the 4th Arkansas Infantry Battalion on November 7, 1861, as a sergeant. He was discharged out of the 4th in May 1863, and was conscripted into the Confederate Service in July 1864, serving in the 48th Arkansas Cavalry, where he was a lieutenant. Patton was captured in Lynn County, Kansas, on November 15, 1864, sent to Johnson's Island Prison, where he was released at the end of the war on May 15, 1865.

and learning from our scouts that the enemy in about the same force was waiting for us over on the bluff, expecting he had to charge up the lane, we crossed over through a field to a road which led to their rear. They were wary, however, and began to draw off.[124] A running fight ensued for two miles down the valley, then up Whiting Mountain. They had a cool, brave commander, I think a Captain [William F.] Orr.[125] He disputed all the ground and took skillful advantage of every corner, finally getting off

In Good Order

so that we could get no great advantage. He lost two prisoners and three or four men. Two or three days later we dodged the avenging scout of a battalion under Col. [John E.] Phelps, who followed and defeated Cpt. Cecil in the Limestone Valley.[126] We dropped back on King's River Mountain and were joined by Capt.

---

124. On the morning of April 4, 1864, Captain William F. Orr, commanding a 50-man detachment from Companies C, F and I, 2nd Arkansas Cavalry (Union) departed Clepper's Mill on Crooked Creek in present day Boone County, Arkansas, and headed southwest on a scout to Newton County (during the Civil War Clepper's Mill was in Carroll County). On the afternoon of April 5, Orr's command approached the Confederate position at the headwaters of the Buffalo River by Whiteley's Mill. Alerted to the Federals' approach, the Confederate forces of Captains Sissel, Cooper, and Patton began to form a line to meet the Unionists. Orr launched an immediate assault, which initially caused a panic in the rebel ranks as roughly half the grayclads fled (most of Patton's men with some of Sissel's). The remaining Confederates, numbering about 75 men, stood their ground and traded fire with the Unionists for the next two hours. With his ammunition nearly exhausted, Captain Orr withdrew his command heading first to Carrollton and then back to Clepper's Mill. According to Orr he lost one killed, one wounded with one man missing (presumed killed). Additionally, Orr reported that "the loss of the enemy has not been ascertained, beyond one wounded." Dyer has the Federal loss as four killed, one wounded and one missing, which mirrors closely with what Cooper reported in his article. *O.R.*, vol. 34, pt. 1:871; *O.R.*, vol. 34, pt. 3:121; *O.R.S.* pt. 2, vol. 2:51, 54, 60, 69, 75; Baker, 74 (n. 4); Dyer, 683; Norton & Massey, 54.

125. William F. Orr was born about 1840, and joined the Union Army on April 23, 1861, as a private in the Lyon Guards of Missouri. At the end of his term of service Orr reenlisted on September 21, 1861, in Company I, 10th Illinois Cavalry, as a private. He was appointed 1st lieutenant of what became Company C, 2nd Arkansas Cavalry (Union) on June 30, 1863, at Arcadia, Missouri. In September 1863, he led his company from eastern Missouri to Springfield, where it joined the main body of its regiment and began operations in southwest Missouri and northwest Arkansas. Orr was later promoted to captain, with a date of rank as April 11, 1864, and led his company in anti-guerrilla operations in April 1864, after which his name disappears from the *Official Records* or *Supplement*. Orr survived the war and was mustered out of the 2nd Arkansas on August 20, 1865. *O.R.*, vol. 34, pt. 1:871, 891; *O.R.S.*, pt. 2, vol. 2:62–63; Allen, *Damned Yankees*, "Orr, William F." entry; Albert W. Bishop, *Report of the Adjutant General of Arkansas, For the Period of the Late Rebellion, and to November 1, 1866* (Washington, 1867; reprint ed., Santa Maria, CA, 2012), 62–63, cited hereafter as Bishop, *Report of Adjutant General*.

126. On April 14, Colonel John E. Phelps, commanding the 2nd Arkansas Cavalry (Union) ordered Major James A. Melton's 110-man detachment to take up the pursuit of Captain Sissel's guerrillas, which numbered about 130 men. Meanwhile, Captain John C. Bailey, commanding Company D, of the same regiment was en route for Berryville, when he received orders at Carrollton from Colonel Phelps on April 15 to join Major Melton in encircling Captain Sissel's command. Farther to the south, at Clarksville, Lieutenant William J. Hunter departed Clarksville on April 16 with a detachment of Company M, 1st Arkansas Cavalry on a scout, which happened to be in the direc-

[Richard] Yeager and nine men claiming to belong to Quantrill's band.[127] I would like to hear through your paper whether any of the James or Youngers were with this detachment, or the names of any of them.[128]

The enemy supposed we had been driven out of the country, and they sent a forage train out from Berryville with only sixty men.[129] We went against them

---

tion of Captain Sissel's command, 27 miles northeast of Clarksville. Failing initially to trap Sissel, the three Union parties united, giving Melton about 200 men. Melton pushed on after the elusive rebel who was now reported camped in the Limestone Valley (intelligence probably given by the scout from Clarksville, under Lieutenant Hunter). Breaking camp at 4:00 a.m. on April 17, Major Melton divided his command to assault Sissel, who was but three miles away. The two-pronged attack took Sissel completely by surprise. The rebels briefly formed a line, fired a few volleys, then broke when the flanking party under Captain Orr arrived. The rebels scrambled up an adjacent hill, the Unionists followed, killing in the process 30–31 and capturing eight or nine prisoners. Sissel for his part escaped, while Melton reported no losses. *O.R.*, vol. 34, pt. 1:890–891; *O.R.*, vol. 34, pt. 3:179–180; *O.R.S.*, pt. 2, vol. 2:48, 60, 63, 65, 72, 78; Bishop, *Report of Adjutant General*, 52; *Union Army*, 6:563.

John Elisha Phelps was born on April 6, 1839, in Springfield, Missouri. A wholesale grocer and cattle trader prior to the Civil War, Phelps was the son of John S. Phelps, who became the military governor of Arkansas (July 1862–March 1863) and governor of Missouri (1876–1880) after the war. John E. Phelps was appointed a 2nd Lieutenant in the 3rd U.S. Cavalry on June 11, 1862 (Bishop has the date as June 9), and in August 1863 was appointed a "commissioner" to raise the 2nd Arkansas Cavalry Regiment (Union). For the next several months Phelps labored to organize the 2nd Arkansas and was promoted in the meantime to 1st lieutenant on October 1, 1863. He completed the organization of his regiment and was commissioned colonel of the 2nd on March 18, 1864. Promoted to brevet brigadier general on March 13, 1865, "for gallant and meritorious service during the war," Phelps was mustered out of the service on August 20, 1865. Following the war Phelps returned to Springfield where he became a "commercial traveler, farmer and miner." He died on September 17, 1921, in Pasadena, California. Bishop, *Report of Adjutant General*, 57, 94; Boatner, 650; Faust, 580; Heitman, 2:734; Roger D. Hunt and Jack R. Brown, *Brevet Brigadier Generals In Blue* (Gaithersburg, MD, 1990), 479.

127. See Appendix B for a biography of Richard "Dick" Yeager.

128. Cooper is referring to Alexander Franklin (Frank) (born January 10, 1844) and Jesse James (born September 5, 1847), both of whom rode with Quantrill. There were four Youngers, who were members of the James-Younger gang: Jim (born January 14, 1848), John (born in 1851), Bob (born October 29, 1853), and Thomas Coleman or Cole Younger (born January 15, 1844). Of the four Youngers, all rode with Quantrill at one time or another, with the exception of Bob, who took no part in the Civil War, though he was a member of the James-Younger gang in the post Civil War period. Banasik, *Cavaliers of the Brush*, 147, 171–172; Hansen, 1:282-285.

129. The Union forage train, under the command of Lieutenant Andrew J. Garner, Company B, 2nd Arkansas Cavalry (Union), departed Clepper's Mill on May 1, 1864. Garner commanded a 100-man detachment, composed of elements of Companies B, C, D, F, G, I and K. Assisting Garner was Lieutenant James Hester, also from Company B. The forage expedition reached the Buffalo River near where Richland Creek entered the Buffalo, but was unable to cross at the ford because of high water, causing them to halt on May 2. While the Unionists waited to cross the river they queried the local residents as to possible rebels in the area. According to a Union report, "Every one in the vicinity able or willing to give information was in utter ignorance of the presence of a strong rebel force. Union people living close by had seen none, heard none." The engagement occurred the next day on May 3, 1864, and would be one of the worst defeats suffered by the 2nd Arkansas Cavalry (Union) during the war. And contrary to the *Official Records*, Sidney Jackman was not in command of the rebel forces; instead it was Captain J. W. Cooper. *O.R.*, vol. 34, pt. 1:908–909; *O.R.S.*, pt. 2 vol. 2:51, 54, 64, 66, 70, 72, 76, 78; Allen, *Damned Yankees*, "Hester, James" entry.

with about the same number, striking them about six miles below Kingston, as they were going up a small Valley between timbered hills.[130] On the hill nearest us they posted part of their force in ambush. We discovered them on the right when just abreast of them. We were marching in column and I gave the order, "Twos right, charge!" just as they opened fire. The boys charged right up among them, bearing them back over the hill into a ravine. The train had reached the crest of the opposite hill and there the routed detachment joined the rest of their command. When we attempted to debouch from the defile they gave us such a volley as drove us back. I noticed that the defile bore to the left of the hill they were on, and, following it up with about half the force, I left orders with Yeager to charge with the rest as soon as he should see a commotion among the enemy. I soon gained

Their Right Rear,

and had no sooner moved forward then Yeager was also among them. Between us they were annihilated as an organization, having twenty-four or twenty-five killed and six taken prisoner, the train was burned.[131] The scattered remnants were pursued four or five miles.

The enemy now moved against us from all sides. A battalion from Berryville and encamped at Fairview, another at Kingston, and Col. Phelps, as I understood, moved from Cooked Creek.[132] Several days of heavy rain swelled all the streams,

---

130. Kingston, Arkansas, was located in eastern Madison County, on the east bank of Kings River. It was 25 miles due south of Berryville and about 18 miles southeast of Huntsville. The town was laid out in 1853, and named after the first settler of the town, King Johnson. At the beginning of the Civil War the town had 45 white residents with 14 Negroes. The town was destroyed during the war and rebuilt in 1866. *History of Benton, Washington, Carroll, Madison, Crawford, Franklin and Sebastian Counties, Arkansas, Etc.* (Chicago, 1889), 457–458, hereafter cited as *History of Benton, Washington, etc. Counties, Arkansas.*

131. When Cooper's band attacked, the Union party was divided into three parts; an advance guard, a main body, and a rear guard. It is unclear from the Federal report of the engagement at what point in time the battle took place or the circumstances surrounding it. According to Colonel John Phelps's report, the train was unable to ford the Buffalo River on May 2. It appears that the train left on May 3 and was then attacked while en route back to Clepper's Mill or while searching for another place to ford the river. According to Phelps, the advance guard under Lieutenant Hester was attacked first, surrounded, and summarily destroyed. The main body and rear guard were eventually routed from the field, following a two-hour engagement, according to Federal sources. Initially the 2nd Arkansas reported the loss of 34 killed, including Lieutenant Hester, with eight wounded, but when the official report came out it listed 37 killed with 11 wounded. The Union dead "were buried, it is supposed by females of the neighborhood," according to the adjutant of the 2nd Arkansas. In addition to the reported losses, Company G also reported the loss of three men missing, which were not listed in the official report of the engagement, bringing the known losses to 37 killed, 11 wounded, and three missing; total 51. *O.R.*, vol. 34, pt. 1:909; *O.R.S.*, pt. 2, vol. 2:51, 55, 72; Dyer, 684; *Union Army*, 6:732–733.

132. On May 4, 1864, Colonel Phelps received word, at his Clepper's Mill camp, that his train was taken and the escort mauled. Phelps immediately assembled all available men—110— including several of the survivors of the escort who had made it back to Clepper's Mill, and started in pursuit of Cooper's band, believing he was after Jackman. Riding through the night Phelps made 30 miles by morning and actually found Jackman's camp, not Cooper's, near where his train was taken on

but as soon as the waters receded we decamped in the night, crossing King's River twelve or fifteen miles below Kingston, and moving into Benton County. With a detail of three men I made a long journey, crossing the Arkansas fifty miles above Fort Gibson, and reported to Gen. Stand Watie, near the Texas line. He gave me orders and sent me back with fourteen men and an Indian guide, our ammunition being carried on a pack mule. We swam the Arkansas River at Weber's Falls, crossing the ammunition on a raft, and getting our guns and pistols wet.[133] It was fifty miles to the Arkansas line and I aimed to go through that night as it would not do to stay where we were on the main road between Fort Gibson and Fort Smith. We started for the Sallisaw Creek ten miles away. The guide lost the road and we arrived about daylight with a settlement of hostile Indians close before us.[134] Not a gun was in condition to fire and we believed the guide to be a traitor. In this fix we took a mountain range and followed it to the northeast till noon when we stopped to draw the wet loads from our firearms, leaving pickets out to the rear. In a few minutes they were fired on. We put on a bold face and charged back yelling. This routed them and we pushed forward once more. The same thing was repeated three times. At night, thinking we were beyond the settlements, we went down into the valley, but immediately struck the last village at Flint Courthouse.[135] In-

---

May 3. In the early morning attack, the Federal command dismounted and fought the rebels for an hour and a half. Phelps's troopers finally drove the guerrillas from their "intrenched" camp, which was protected by "earthworks and other defenses." In describing the combat Captain Martin O'Brian, commanding a 30-man detachment of Company G, stated that the rebels were barely visible, fighting from behind "an embankment," and ten feet from his command. "After being repulsed, the enemy fled in confusion," according to O'Brian. When the rebels broke from their first position, they reformed briefly, probably to give time for the wounded to be removed, and then retreated from the battlefield, after Colonel Phelps ordered his command to charge. With the rebels fleeing, Phelps did not pursue, stating "my horses, too weak and famished, could not have stood it." As to losses, Phelps reported that Jackman was wounded and "several more rebels were wounded, but none dead on the field." Federals losses totaled seven wounded, while the editors of the *Union Army* sarcastically recorded, "The Confederate casualties, if any, were not reported." Later Federal reports, citing Confederate sources, put the rebel losses at either six or 16 killed, with 13 wounded, and five taken prisoner. Additionally, Phelps reported capturing 30 mules and $135,000 dollars in Confederate notes. *O.R.*, vol. 34, pt. 1:908–909; *O.R.*, vol. 34, pt. 3:486; *O.R.*, vol. 34, pt. 4:313; *O.R.S.*, pt. 2, vol. 2:51, 55, 72; Allen, *Damned Yankees*, "O'Brian, Martin E.," entry; *Union Army*, 6:732–733.

133. Webber Falls was located on the Arkansas River about 35 miles from Ft. Gibson and an equal distance, by land, from Ft. Smith. Davis, *Civil War Atlas*, plt. 119.

134. Sallisaw Creek was located about 16 miles from Webber Falls and about another 19 from Ft. Smith. At the time of the Civil War the main road from Ft. Smith to Webber Falls crossed the Sallisaw near the Indian village of Kendrow, where the modern-day town of Sallisaw is now located. Ibid.

135. The route that Cooper took was far greater than the 50 miles that he had put forth at the beginning of his piece. If Cooper had taken a direct route to northeast Arkansas to cross where Flint Creek entered the Indian Territory, the route would have been about 50 miles; however, after Cooper crossed at Weber Falls he headed east toward Ft. Smith on the main road and then turned northward, adding another 16 miles to his route. The mountainous area that he referred to was located about twenty miles above the main road, to the north of Kendow. Ibid.

dians were on the alert and headed us off at a bend in the valley. We could not fire a shot, having been unable to get the wet loads out of our guns. The men showed

Signs of Panic

and trying the old game I again ordered a charge. All the men but two or three obeyed; the Indians were again bluffed, but our old pack mule got into the brush and could not be found. Our source of ammunition was gone. In this blight I finally succeeded in rejoining my company.

Having fifty-two men, we attacked a large train of supplies for the enemy at Fort Smith. The train was guarded with 125 men, commanded by a Capt. [James L.] Powell, who had fought bravely on our side at Pea Ridge, and then deserted as did thousands of others, a result of the mistaken defensive policy.[136] We attacked Capt. Powell's rear and had possession of part of the train, when our ammunition failed, and the enemy bringing up reinforcements we retreated. This skirmish was called the Fitzgerald Mountain fight.[137]

Receiving numerous recruits, I organized two companies under Capts. Ed Jennings and George Selvage.[138] Shortly afterwards Capt. John Carroll also reported

---

136. James L. Powell was born about 1838 in Wyth County, Virginia (The *History of Benton, Washington, etc. Counties, Arkansas* says that Powell was born in 1832, in Cannon County, Tennessee). Moving to Arkansas in 1850, Powell settled in Madison County. At the beginning of the Civil War, he enlisted in Company G, 15th Arkansas Infantry (Northwest) and later deserted. On June 1, 1862 (Bishop has the date as June 11), Powell enlisted in Company F, 1st Arkansas Cavalry (Union) and was appointed captain of Company F, 2nd Arkansas Cavalry Regiment (Union) on June 11, to rank from November 23, 1863. Powell survived the war, resigning from the service on May 18, 1865. Allen, *Damned Yankee*, "Powell, James L," two entries; Bishop, *Report of Adjutant General*, 33, 73; *History of Benton, Washington, etc. Counties, Arkansas*, 1111; Hewett, *Confederate Roster*, 12:439; Gerdes.
137. The Federals have the engagement taking place at Gerald Mountain, during an expedition from Cassville to Fayetteville. Captain Powell departed his camp near Cassville on the morning of August 23, 1864, with Company F, 2nd Arkansas Cavalry (Union). The first day's march went fine; however, many of his command were without horses and marched along as infantry. By the second day, August 24, many of the dismounted men complained of sore feet and were allowed to ride in the wagons, while their guns were stored carelessly in the "feed-boxes." Ten miles from Fayetteville, the rear of the train was attacked by Cooper's guerrillas, estimated at between 25–30 men. The rear guard was basically riding in the wagons or on the mules pulling the wagons when the attack began. Panic ensued as the men had no quick access to their weapons. Meanwhile, at the front of the train, Captain Powell gathered his available mounted men and rushed to the rear to drive off Cooper's men. Fortunately for the Union command, Cooper's men were having trouble with their ammunition, causing him to break off the engagement. Powell reported the loss of one man killed and three wounded. *O.R.*, vol. 41, pt. 1:273–274; *O.R.*, vol. 41, pt. 2:923; *O.R.S.*, pt. 2, vol. 2:71, Dyer, 686.
138. Several Edward Jenningses were found when searching the Internet, with the most likely being Edward L. Jennings, who joined the 15th Arkansas Infantry (Northwest) on October 29, 1861. This Jennings later deserted or left the army on November 6, 1862, at Camp McCulloch Arkansas. Nothing was found in any source on Captain George Selvage save what Cooper has written on him. Selvage was from Benton County, remained with Cooper until early 1865, when he was furloughed, but never returned. He was killed sometime after the war. Gerdes.

to me with an excellent company.¹³⁹ These captains were excellent officers. Jennings is now a respected citizen. Selvage was from Benton county, and a regular hotspur. He was killed since the war, while serving as United States Marshal in the Indian Territory. Carroll was a good organizer and brave soldier. Since the war he has served as a mayor of Eureka Springs, and is now Marshal of the Western District of Arkansas. In the latter part of the summer of 1864, while the battalion was in Sugar Creek hills, Carroll's company ran against Capt. [John I.] Worthington with 125 men of the First Arkansas Federal regiment, and was defeated.¹⁴⁰

---

139. John G. Carroll, a Royal Arch Mason, was born on August 30, 1828, in what is now Claiborne County, Tennessee. At the age of eight his family moved to the Indian Territory, settling in the Ft. Gibson area. Carroll "was reared on the frontier, and received his education by his own personal efforts" while living among the Cherokee. His first wife died in 1856, after bearing him two children. Moving to McDonald County, Missouri, in 1857, Carroll again married and had seven more offspring with his second wife. Prior to the Civil War, Carroll relocated to Newton County, Arkansas, where he owned a mill and blacksmith shop on Kings River. Carroll joined the 3rd Arkansas State Troops, at the beginning of the war and was elected captain of Company A. Wounded at Wilson's Creek on August 10, 1861, Carroll later joined the 14th Arkansas Infantry (Power's Regiment), after the 3rd disbanded, being elected captain of Company F on May 24, 1862. In the late winter 1863–1864 or early spring of 1864, he became ill, "received a furlough and went home," and never returned to the regular Confederate Service. While Carroll was absent from the 14th Arkansas, he was dropped from the Confederate rolls on December 3, 1864. Meanwhile, when he arrived home, "the whole country was full of Yankees, and in order to make friends of them and keep from being killed, he made up a company of what he called 'Federal hogskin militia.'" Later, realizing his mistake, he went to Huntsville, seeking protection from the Union garrison under Major E. D. Ham, of the 1st Arkansas Infantry. Ham ignored Carroll's request and immediately branded him a rebel and ordered him out of the town or he would be shot. Carroll then rejoined the Confederate cause, feeling he had no choice. He raised a company in northwest Arkansas, during the summer of 1864 and eventually combined his company with Cooper's battalion, as one of three units in the command. In February 1865 Carroll left Cooper's Battalion with a few of his men and formed an escort for General Stand Watie, remaining with him until the end of the war. After the war Carroll settled first in Huntsville, Arkansas, where he farmed and planned the reconstruction of the courthouse. He was a state representative to the Arkansas House (1866–1868), a member of the State Constitutional Convention (1874), and moved to Eureka Spring in 1879. There he was elected mayor (1880–1884) and became a lawyer in 1884. Relocating to Ft. Smith in 1885, Carroll was appointed a U.S. Marshall of the Western District of Arkansas. While living in Ft. Smith Carroll also founded the *Elevator* newspaper in 1887. Final disposition unknown. Harrell, *Arkansas, Confederate Military History*, 51, 286; *History of Benton, Washington, etc. Counties, Arkansas;*, 375, 377, 436–437, 764, 1049–1050; Gerdes; Norton & Massey, 41, 43, 54, 57–58, 60; Sifakis, *Arkansas*, 75, 95.

140. John I. Worthington was born on June 14, 1826, in Somerset County, Pennsylvania, where he ran away from home at the age of 11. Worthington fought in the Mexican War, returned to Pennsylvania, and married in 1848. Following the death of his wife in 1849, he served in a variety of positions, wandering west and south, finally ending up in Carroll County, Arkansas, where he studied the law and married for a second time. He moved to Granby, Missouri, established a law practice, and rallied the local populace to form a company loyal to the Union. Worthington initially served as a scout for General Nathaniel Lyon and was wounded at Wilson's Creek. Returning home to recover, Worthington later enlisted as a private in Company A, 6th Kansas Cavalry on January 7, but was quickly made a sergeant and then a commissary sergeant on February 1, 1862. Worthington left the 6th Kansas on July 21, 1862, being authorized to raise a company for 1st Arkansas Cavalry Regiment (Union). Worthington was appointed captain of Company H, 1st Arkansas Cavalry on August 7, 1862, and remained with the unit throughout the war. He was

To retrieve this disaster, I went in haste to his aid. His men promptly rallied, and marching against the company of Mountain Federals, or "Hogskins," as we called them, we defeated them.[141] Returning to Sugar Creek hills, we started on a raid into Missouri with Selvage in advance, Carroll was the main column and Jennings in the rear. We passed east of Cassville with its 800 to 1,000 garrison, and at daylight next morning struck Flat Creek, down which we drove rapidly for twenty miles, striking small bodies of militia at nearly every house.[142] The woods were full of them. Thence we moved to King's River where we arrived at 4 p.m., having traveled eighty miles in twenty-six or twenty-seven hours, captured a large

---

promoted to major effective February 28, 1865. Worthington did not survive the war, but was killed on March 12, 1865, 18 miles from Fayetteville near King's River, during an engagement with Cooper's command. The engagement was Worthington's "first scout" after being promoted. To the men of his regiment, the government "sustained a severe loss"...while "the command suffered a loss that could not be repaired." *O.R.*, vol. 48, pt. 1:1168, 1185; Allen, *Damned Yankees*, "Worthington, John I." entry; Bishop, *Report of Adjutant General*, 10, 37; A. W. Bishop, *Loyalty On the Frontier or Sketches of Union Men of the Southwest With Incidents and Adventures In Rebellion On the Border* (St. Louis, 1863), 29–35, 37-38, 41–44, 46–48, 50–51, cited hereafter as Bishop, *Loyalty On the Frontier*; M. La Rue Harrison, "Death of Maj. Worthington," *Fort Smith New Era* (Fort Smith, AR), March 25, 1865; M. La Rue Harrison, "From Fayetteville," *Fort Smith New Era*, March 18, 1865.

The 1st Arkansas Cavalry Regiment (Union) began organizing on July 3, 1862, in Springfield, Missouri. The regiment completed its organization on October 2, 1862, with twelve companies. M. La Rue Harrison, of the 36th Illinois Infantry was appointed the first colonel of the regiment. The regiment operated exclusively in northwest Arkansas and southwest Missouri, participating in two major engagements—Prairie Grove (December 7, 1862) and Fayetteville (April 18, 1863), both in Arkansas. Additionally, the regiment had numerous engagements with guerrilla forces operating in their area. The 1st served until the end of the war, and was mustered out on August 23, 1865. Bishop, *Report of Adjutant General*, 55–56.

141. Little was found on this engagement, other than some scant comments recorded in Federal reports, and even those don't agree with what Cooper has written. On September 12, 1864, Colonel M. La Rue Harrison, commanding at Fayetteville, learned that Cooper's band intended to attack a train that was bound from Ft. Smith to Fayetteville. Harrison dispatched Captain Worthington on a forced march with a 99-man detachment of the 1st Arkansas Cavalry (Union). On the 13th, Worthington attacked a portion of "Buck" Brown's command near Bentonville, scattering them and killing three in the process. The following day Worthington left the train after it passed by Little Sugar Creek, and proceeded on his mission. Per Worthington's orders, he was "to sweep up the White River toward Richland and Huntsville." Later on the 14th, Worthington struck Carroll's 80-man band at Rodger's Crossing, near Jennings' Ferry on the White River. Worthington charged the rebel command, "routed" them, "killing 5 men, and wounding a larger number." Worthington further reported the destruction of a tannery and the capture of 35 guns, with 11 rebel horses killed. As to Cooper's reported pursuit and defeat of Worthington, the *Official Records* makes no mention of it, simply listing Federals losses as "1 man slightly wounded." *O.R.*, vol. 41, pt. 1:797–798; *O.R.S.*, pt. 2, vol. 2.41.

142. Between August 31 and September 30, 1864, the Cassville garrison consisted of Companies A, C, F, I, and L of the 2nd Arkansas Cavalry (Union), commanded by Lieutenant Colonel Hugh Cameron. And this garrison was reduced to Companies A and C on October 16, as the other units moved to Springfield to join their parent regiment, which was concentrating, to take up the pursuit of Sterling Price's invasion force. *O.R.*, vol. 41, pt. 2:976; *O.R.S.*, pt. 2, vol. 2:56, 58, 64, 70–71, 76-77, 79–80.

number of horses and killed several militia men. I heard afterwards that some were killed

After They Had Surrendered.

This was against my orders, but Selvage had a brother murdered a short time before and his guides, who lived on this creek, had been very strongly treated by the militia, and like many of the partisans on both sides, were hard to control.[143]

Returning to the Sugar Creek and White River hills we were shortly afterwards on picket on the Cassville and Fayetteville and Bentonville and Fayetteville road during the days' siege of Fayetteville by the troops of Price on their retreat from Missouri.[144] In the evening, the evening vindettes were run in, and during a

---

143. There is nothing in the *Official Records* on the operation that Cooper describes. However, based on what Cooper has written, the operation took place in the Flat Creek area, which was in Barry County, Missouri, located about 23 miles northeast of Cassville. Two operations are listed in the *Union Army: A History of Military Affairs in the Loyal United States* as occurring in Barry County on October 8 and 29, 1864, but no description of these engagements is given. The October 29 engagement took place at Upshar's farm against guerrillas during Price's Raid, though it did not involve Cooper's band. There was nothing written on the engagement on October 8. However, on October 20, 1864, another incident occurred involving Brown's band, which is mentioned in passing in the *Official Records*. Colonel M. LaRue Harrison was escorting a train from Cassville to Fayetteville when he was attacked by Brown. The two hour skirmish, which took place at Nubbin Ridge, in Benton County, Arkansas, ended when the Confederates broke off the attack. This engagement could have been part of Cooper's retreat from the Barry County area that Cooper previously discussed. *O.R.*, vol. 41, pt. 1:396, 406–407; *O.R.S.*, pt. 2, vol. 2:26, 38; Hinton, 283–284; *Union Army*, 5:82.

144. The Siege of Fayetteville was one of the last actions that occurred during Price's 1864 Missouri Raid. According to Samuel R. Curtis, Fayetteville had been under siege from October 25, 1864 (other sources have the siege beginning on October 18), when General James Fagan arrived late on November 2 and attempted to take to the town. Near midnight on November 3, Curtis received word of the predicament at Fayetteville and immediately began a march, through a snow storm, to relieve the city. Curtis arrived at Fayetteville about 11:00 a.m. the next morning. On the Confederate side, prior to Fagan's arrival, the rebels, under Colonel William H. Brooks had invested the town, supported by William "Buck" Brown's and Cooper's commands. With the notice that Price was in the area Brooks requested assistance from General Price to capture the town. Price agreed, ordering Fagan to make a demonstration at Fayetteville. Fagan then "cobbled together" a 500-man force from Cabell's and Slemons's Brigades, with an 80-man detachment from Elliott's Regiment, and two pieces of artillery. The remainder of Fagan's Division, accompanied by Freeman's Brigade, bypassed the city, heading for northeast Arkansas. Marching through a snowstorm Fagan's command arrived at Fayetteville late on the evening of November 2. The following day at about noon, Fagan made a lackluster attack, using only Cabell's Brigade, while Slemons's Brigade went into camp and did nothing. After taking the local hospital, Fagan stopped the attack, having made the required demonstration, after which he withdrew. Colonel Marcus La Rue Harrison, commanding at Fayetteville, reported his losses as one killed and eight wounded. Rebel losses are not known, though Harrison "claimed...over one hundred casualties in killed, wounded, and captured," while a period newspaper estimated rebel losses at "one lieutenant and several others killed besides several others wounded." Richard J. Hinton put the rebel losses at 75 killed and wounded. Overall Fagan's command committed only 500 men to the demonstration—80 from Shelby's and 420 from Cabell's Brigade; Slemons's Brigade simply camped at Fayetteville and did nothing. (In the *Official Records*, Shelby stated that he sent Elliott with 500 men, while John Edwards says that Elliott had only 80 men, with Collins's artillery. This would further suggest

driving snow the enemy advanced past us. We escaped between their advanced and their main bodies. I sent a courier to Gen. Price and fell back to King's River, whence we went south to Shawnee town, near Red River, I. T., where he remained until about 1st of February, 1865, having about 175 men.[145] Meantime Capt. Carroll was detailed with part of his men as escort for Gen. Stand Watie. Capt. Selvage was given a furlough and I never saw him again. An order was issued to send our horses to the Brazos, where the remainder of the battalion deserted. They believed the order meant that they were to be put in the infantry and kept with the Army. They loved their horses and loved scouting, and though true to the South, they wanted to fight for their own families whose homes are along the border in the hands of the merciless foe. Had an army been north of their homes they would have made the best of soldiers. Next day after the desertions I reported to Gen. (now Senator) Maxey, commanding the Indian department, and suggested as I was without men I was no use there I could go back and, hunt the boys up and continue to harass enemy's communications.[146] He consented and gave us a lot of ammunition. Collecting fourteen or fifteen stragglers I started back.

---

that the overall force committed to the Fayetteville attack numbered only 500 men, with most of the men coming from Cabell's Brigade.) On the other hand, General Curtis reported that Fagan had 8,000 men; Harrison said 5,200; and Wiley Britton has the number as 6,000. *O.R.*, vol. 41, pt. 1:399, 515, 638, 661; *O.R.S.*, pt. 1, vol. 7:411; *O.R.S.*, pt. 2, vol. 14:16, 18; Britton, *Civil War on the Border, 1863–65*, 514; Edwards, *Shelby and His Men*, 461; "From Fayetteville," *Missouri Republican*, November 24, 1864; "From St. Louis," *Chicago Tribune*, November 24, 1864; H. F. Head, "After Price," *National Tribune*, December 19, 1912; Hinton, 287; Sinisi, 329–331; Wright Memoirs, unnumbered pages 101–102.

145. Shawneetown was located in the Chickasaw Nation, on the Canadian River, about 75 miles from the Red River. Davis, *Civil War Atlas*, plt. no. 119.

146. Samuel Bell Maxey was born on March 30, 1825, at Tompkinsville, in Monroe County, Kentucky. Educated locally, Maxey graduated from West Point in 1846 (number 48 of 49). He fought in the Mexican War and was breveted a 1st lieutenant "for gallant and meritorious conduct." Following the war, Maxey was stationed at Jefferson Barracks in St. Louis, became bored, and resigned from the army on September 17, 1849. He returned to Kentucky, settling in Clinton County, where he married in 1853, earned a law degree, then relocated to Paris, Texas, in 1857, where he opened a law office with his father. At the beginning of the Civil War, Maxey organized the Lamar Rifles and was elected captain on May 25, 1861. Later the company was organized with nine other companies on November 26, 1861 to form the 9th Texas Infantry, with Maxey appointed colonel of the regiment. Maxey was promoted to brigadier general on March 4, 1862, and was assigned command of the Indian Territory, a position he held until late in the war. During the Camden Expedition, Maxey led a cavalry division at Poison Springs, after which Kirby Smith promoted him to major general. On February 21, 1865, Maxey was replaced as commander in the Indian Territory by Douglas H. Cooper and was given command of a dismounted cavalry division, a position he held until the end of the war. After the war, Maxey returned to Paris, Texas, resumed his law practice, was elected to the U.S. Senate in 1874, and served two terms (1875–1887). Maxey died at Eureka Springs, Arkansas, following "a period of declining health," and was returned to Paris for burial. See Appendix B for a complete biography. *O.R.S.*, pt. 2, vol. 68:722, 725, 727–729, 731–734; Anne Bailey, "Samuel Bell Maxey," in *Confederate General*, 4:171–172; Boatner, 520–521; Faust, 481–482; Heidler, "Maxey, Samuel Bell," in *Encyclopedia of the Civil War*, 1267–1268; Heitman, 1:698; Roberts, *Texas, Confederate Military History*, 246–248; J. Elden Spencer, "Samuel Bell Maxey," in *Ten More Texans In Gray* (W. C. Nunn, gen ed.; Hillsboro, TX, 1980), 59–61, 64, 67–68, hereafter cited as *Ten More Texans*; Simpson, 86–87; Warner, *Generals in Gray*, 216.

After Passing the Outposts

of our Army, stragglers from the different commands began to join me in squads. Some were deserters, but I had no power to return them to their commands. We crossed the Arkansas River about seventy-five strong some miles below Van Buren, using an old boat for the men and swimming the horses. Night came on when half my men of the force was across and a Federal steamer anchored in midstream, but fortunately it left before daylight and we all crossed. Passing the mountains we found Kingston and many of my men's houses in ashes. Foraging parties of the enemy were plundering the country daily and strange to say these predatory parties were mostly Arkansas absentees with few exceptions of the army, who had joined us to plunder, expecting there would be an invasion of the North, but finding their mistake, went over to the strong side and plundered their friends. They were mostly those Yahoos who have given Arkansas such an unsavory name abroad. Most of those who came across the mountain with me soon left and I began to reorganize the battalion. The remains of Capt. Carroll's company having been collected, Capt. Wiggins was elected to command it.[147] He proved a brave, good officer. Learning that a large forage train was to move on the Kingston road I attacked them with about forty men. The train guard numbered 150, but we found they had a timid commander and harassed them, front, flanks and rear, so we forced them off from the river.[148] Thinking they were gone, we disbanded to hunt forage. While I was eating lunch in a house I heard shots, and going with two or three men up the mountain we could see the flames of burning houses. At the appointed rendezvous that night I found only ten or twelve men. In a cave close by was a prominent family of Kingston, whose house had just been burned and the husband and father murdered, though a noncombatant. We learned that Maj. Worthington had taken command of the federal forces. He was their bravest scout and

---

147. A search of the Internet, for a Captain Wiggins revealed only one possibility from Arkansas—Jannedens or Jannedine or Janaders H. Wiggins. This Wiggins enlisted in the 2nd Arkansas Artillery (Clark County, Arkansas), on July 15, 1861, and was appointed the unit's 1st sergeant. Later, Wiggins was promoted to 1st lieutenant, then to captain in May 1862, after the previous captain had resigned. Captured at Shelbyville, Tennessee (June 23, 1863), Wiggins was sent to Johnson's Island and was later exchanged, date unknown. *O.R.S.*, pt. 2 vol. 2:265; Sifakis, *Arkansas*, 38; Gerdes.

148. Based upon the fact of Cooper's return to northwest Arkansas in mid February 1865, the incident that he describes probably occurred on March 4, 1865. Little was written on this action, save an acknowledgment by the Federals that a forage train was attacked in the King's River area, but the commander of the train is not identified, nor the individuals who attacked the train. However, at the same time, another report placed Cooper in the area with 150 men. As to the attack, it appears that the Federals supposedly killed three of Cooper's men and took two prisoners, while losing none of their own. *O.R.*, vol. 48, pt. 1:1103.

Most Merciless House-Burner.

We could not collect enough men to attack his command. A few days later we attacked and captured a forage train of corn on Buffalo Creek, nine miles east of Kingston. We hauled it into the mountains and were trying to hide it, when Worthington marched into the valley and set the whole neighborhood in flames. People whose houses had already been burned and who were living in rail pens, were robbed of their beds and clothing. An old lady in advanced stage of consumption was dragged out into the snow and her house burned. But Worthington was working his own destruction. My men were so enraged at the outrages that I felt that I could risk a fight with his mounted men, who comprised about half his force. By great exertion I assembled forty-two men to intercept these house burners on their return. We took position at the rocky point which we knew they would pass. Two pickets were replaced on a path half a mile away, with instructions to run for it as the enemy approached. Four of the coolest men were placed at the foot of the hill with instructions to fire and escape when attacked. The main body was formed on a small plateau at the crest of the rocky hill. When the enemy came on, the program was carried out, though one of our pickets was captured. The result was that the mounted force charged up the hill well in advance of their foot troops. Worthington was at their head. As he came on Lieut. Tuck Seltz took deliberate aim at and him and fired. He was seen to stagger, turn and slide.[149] At the same time the company charged, driving the enemy in complete rout. Worthington fell dead near the foot of the hill. This was the last scout of the First Arkansas in this region.[150] I then continued reorganizing the battalion, being reinforced by companies from Bentonville and Berryville under Capts. Jackson and Denny.[151] In one of my expeditions I was taken

---

149. Nothing was found on a "Tuck Seltz" or any variation thereof.
150. Like the previous incident detailed by Cooper, this one is not to be found in the *Official Records*. Indeed, Cooper's description of the fight was the most complete given of any participant. The only mention of Worthington's expedition was made by Colonel M. La Rue Harrison, in a short letter to General John B. Sanborn in which Harrison wrote: "Major J. I. Worthington charged Cooper's command near King's River, and received in the confusion during the charge a mortal wound through the breast and died in fifteen minutes." The incident occurred on Sunday, March 12, 1865. As to the death of Worthington, Sanborn, commander of the area that embraced northwest Arkansas, congratulated Colonel M. La Rue Harrison "upon the rapid destruction of bushwhackers" in his area including Buck Brown, who was killed on March 13. The death of Worthington "was unfortunate," according to Sanborn, "but such casualties must occur in war." *O.R.*, vol. 48, pt. 1:1185, 1193; Bishop, *Arkansas Adjutant General*, 10; M. La Rue Harrison, "From Fayetteville," *Fort Smith New Era*, March 18, 1865.
151. The only possibility of a Jackson found, out of multiple sources checked, is a Captain "Frank" Jackson, who organized a company in northwest Arkansas in the summer of 1864, which later became part of D. C. Hunter's Cavalry Regiment. Captain Jackson participated in Price's 1864 Missouri Raid and is assumed to have left the command after it returned to Arkansas, joining up with Copper's new battalion in the spring of 1865. Captain Denny, was probably John Denny, who originally organized and commanded a Home Guard Company from Berryville at the beginning of the Civil War. Denny's command was assigned to the 4th Arkansas State Troop Regiment, where it was lettered "Company I" and fought at Wilson's Creek in August 1861. Northing more was

With Fever

and rheumatism. Falling in with Dr. [Alvah] Jackson, since famous as the discoverer of Eureka Springs, he told me of a cave in the White and King's River hills, near a spring of medicinal waters, where I could be safe.[152] As it was the route to the rendezvous of one of my companies I went there. The doctor and one of my escorts carried water in their hats and bathed me two or three times a day for ten days, when I recovered and left. The cave or rock house is still to be seen just to the rear of the Southern hotel at the springs and is the confederate hospital mentioned in several histories of the Springs. When the war closed the men were loth to give up and small skirmishes continued until the 1st of June when the main body of the battalion surrendered at Fayetteville. I tried, with a few men, to get mounted to go to Mexico, but as forage was scarce, the horses poor and the citizens grumbling for fear we would bring more depredations upon them, I finally disbanded it and the few who had stuck by me and about the 1st of July went to Cassville to surrender. I was placed under arrest and sent to Springfield by the officer in command, who said I was too late and outlawed.[153] At Marionville my name was discovered by a lot of militia who were loafing around the saloon—just such a gang is often seen in such places in South Missouri and Arkansas.[154] Soon we saw twenty or thirty men armed with

Guns and Pistols

approaching. Their leader demanded that I be given into their hands. My Iowa guard sprang to arms and one of them who had my revolvers motioned to me. I stepped up beside him and laid hold of the weapons and as I did so I looked into the faces of the soldiers who had me in charge. I was greatly relieved to see that they were evidently brave men who didn't intend to have any prisoners taken from them. The militia made the same discovery and wilted like whipped curs. Arriving at Springfield, I was at first put in the stockade, but having made a cartel with a Maj. [James M.] Moon [Moore] a month or two before, I dropped him a

---

found on either Captains Jackson or Denny. Edwards, *Shelby and His Men*, 168, 426; Ingenthron, 91; Norton & Massey, 63–64; Gerdes.

152. Alvah Jackson was born on July 26, 1806, in Georgia and moved to Kentucky, where he married and subsequently fathered five children. Moving to Arkansas in 1838, the Jacksons settled in the northwest part of the state, where they had four more children. In 1856, Jackson discovered Eureka Springs, claiming that a treatment with the waters of the spring cured his eye ailment. During the Civil War, Jackson operated a hospital in a cave in the Eureka Springs area, supporting the Southern cause. After the war Jackson marketed the water of the springs as "Dr. Jackson's Eye" tonic. The town of Eureka Springs was incorporated in 1880, and Dr. Jackson died on May 21 the same year. Today Eureka Springs is a thriving town, noted for its spas. Wikipedia.

153. Major James M. Moore, commanding 3rd Battalion, 15th Missouri Cavalry, headed the Cassville garrison. Moore met with Cooper to settle on the conditions of surrender or a cease fire on May 30, 1865. See note 157 for details of that meeting. *O.R.*, vol. 48, pt. 2:586, 758–759.

154. Marionville was located about 35 northeast of Cassville, in Lawrence County and 25 miles from Springfield.

note reminding him of his promise.[155] He visited me and had me paroled about the 5th of July. I was given transportation to St. Louis with reference to the quartermaster's department. On entering I was sneeringly directed across the street. On entering the building indicated I was shown into a parlor and informed by a lady that she was a member of an association for assisting Confederate soldiers to reach their homes. Not having a dollar, I was constrained to accept their hospitality. I received favors from several prominent men, among whom were Messrs. Kennard & Sons, D. A. January and George Knapp, so long one of the proprietors of the *Republican*.[156] The friendships that formed kept up for many years. The association furnished me transportation to Memphis, near where I lived.

J. W. Cooper.

* * * * * * *

---

155. Major James M. Moore met with Cooper in Berryville, Arkansas, on May 30, 1865, to discuss the surrender of his command. Cooper was reluctant to surrender without direct orders from his superior, which was General Stand Watie. In an ensuing agreement, Cooper agreed to a cease fire and to do the best he could do "in keeping down the stealing etc." The meeting took an hour to complete and Cooper was assured by Major Moore, that regardless of the outcome of their discussion that Cooper was free to go after they had finished. The following day, June 1, Cooper disbanded his command. See Appendix A for the correspondence between Cooper and Moore concerning Cooper's surrender. *O.R.*, vol. 48, pt. 2:758–759.

156. In January 1862 Henry Halleck established a Board of Assessments in St. Louis to fine supporters of the Confederacy. Those who had enlisted or had family members in the Confederate Army were fined the most. John Kennard & Sons were local merchants, who established themselves in St. Louis in 1857, where they owned "the largest carpet house in the United States." Samuel Kennard, one of John's sons, joined the Confederate Army in 1861, and served throughout the war. As such, when the Board of Assessments doled out their fines, Kennard was at the top of Halleck's initial assessment, being fined $800 dollars. To pay the fine the Kennards "had carpets valued at that amount seized." John Kennard was born on August 14, 1809, in Lexington, Kentucky, and moved to St. Louis in 1857. He survived the war, dying on November 18, 1872.

Derrick A. January was also born in Lexington, Kentucky, in August 1814, and moved to St. Louis in the winter of 1836–1837. January was a wholesale grocer, who came from the "elite" of St. Louis, a Conditional Unionist and head of the St. Louis Chamber of Commerce as well as on the board of a local bank. In December 1861, he was branded a "disloyal citizen," but was never exiled from the city, possibly because he either donated a hospital ship to the Union command, or, simply paid to have the ship named after him so that his name "would be firmly tied to the Union cause." January retired from the grocery business in 1875 and died on July 19, 1878.

George Knapp was the "owner and editor the *Missouri Republican*," with his brother John. Both of the Knapps were at one time or another members of the St. Louis Missouri Militia. George was born on September 25, 1814, and moved to St. Louis in 1820. At the age of 12 George was apprenticed to the *Republican*, became a journeyman in 1834, and a part owner of the paper in 1837. The Knapps, with another partner, became co-owners of the *Republican* in 1854, and remained so throughout their lives. During the Civil War George Knapp was elected captain of the "Missouri Republican Guards" in September 1862, a unit made up entirely of employees of his newspaper. George died in 1883 while en route from Germany to the United States, following a visit to the former country. Gerteis, 73, 175, 214–215; Hale, *Branded As Rebels Volume 2*, 176; J. Thomas Scharf, *History of Saint Louis City and County, From the Earliest Periods to the Present Day: Including Biographical Sketches of Representative Men* (2 vols.; Philadelphia, PA, 1883), 1:907, 915–916, 2:1303–1305, 1351; Winter, 42, 81, 140.

Appendix A
Orders, Circulars, and Correspondence

Item: Shelby's Proclamation to Northeast Arkansas in May 1864.[1]

Men of Northeast Arkansas: The land of your birth is struggling in the grasp of a giant, and you are cold to the consequences and indifferent to the results. I have come among you to appeal to your manhood before I appeal to the sword. Every inhabitant of this valley owing military service by law to the Confederate States Government must immediately enroll himself in some company; companies will as rapidly join regiments; and regiments will be assigned to brigades as please the wishes of Lieutenant General E. Kirby Smith. Choice of organization will be allowed until the 10th of June, after which time you shall be considered as conscripts and treated accordingly. I know your past history. I have heard your disgraceful fraternizing with the Federals. I believe you have committed crimes and treason against your country, but I am willing that you shall take up arms and wash out your dishonor in the blood of a common enemy. I call upon all good men to support me, but as plain statements will save future trouble, and as I had rather act than talk, I here announce to you, upon the faith of a soldier and the truth of a gentleman, that all who refuse to rally to their country's flag shall be outlawed, hunted from county to county, and when captured hung as high as Haman. You shall fight for the North or the South. I will enlist you in the Confederate Army; or I shall drive you into Federal ranks. You shall not remain idle spectators of a drama enacted before your eyes. I have ammunition for your muskets, and these shall be taken from the enemy. I come with veterans to fight for your homes, but you must fight, too, or the homes will be desolate and your own blood shall be spilt upon the door-sills. Events gather fast. There is no time to argue now, and I command you to rush at once to arms. Every officer with recruiting papers will report at once to my headquarters, and colonels or generals professing to have regiments or brigades will come immediately to receive orders and instructions for future operations. I do not condemn, but I threaten; I do not bully, but I strike. This beautiful valley shall be quiet and peaceful, or it shall be desolated with fire and sword. If the snake can not be scotched it shall be killed. No more smuggling, no more stealing of cotton, no more dodging conscription and harboring deserters. Come up like men, or go to General Steele like men, but whatever you do, remember the 10th of June.

[JO. O. SHELBY]
[Brigadier-General, Commanding]

* * * * * * *

---

1. Edwards, *Shelby and His Men*, 312–313.

Item: Finding of the Count of Inquiry on the loss of the tinclad *Queen City*.[2]

Mississippi Squadron, Flagship Black Hawk,
Mound City, Ill., September 6, 1864.

    Sir: I enclose herewith a copy of the finding of the Court of Inquiry, convened by your order on the 8th day of August, 1864, to investigate the loss of the U.S.S. *Queen City*. The proceedings are rather voluminous and will follow.

K. R. BREESE
Lieutenant-Commander, U.S. Navy.
Rear-Admiral David D. Porter,
Commanding Mississippi Squadron.

Finding of the Court of Inquiry convened to investigate the loss of the U.S.S. Queen City.

    The court, having maturely considered the evidence adduced, is of opinion that Acting Master Michael Hickey, in himself, did all that could be done in defense of his vessel; that he had taken the usual precautions to guard against surprise and for defense, but that he was not supported by the executive officer, Acting Ensign F. M. Hathaway, and the officers of divisions, Acting Ensign J. S. Roberts and Acting Master's Mate J. W. Pardee.

    Had Acting Master Hickey been properly sustained by his officers, the result of the engagement would have been the same, but the Navy would not have suffered so much in credit.

    From the evidence before it the court deems that Acting Ensigns Hathaway and Roberts did much, by their gross misconduct, to cause a surrender without any damage have been previously inflicted on the enemy.

    The court further finds that General Order No. 84 was not carried out, but that the orders of Lieutenant-Commander S. L. Phelps, commanding district, ordering the *Queen City* to guard the town of Clarendon, were strictly followed, and that at the time of the attack the vessel was lying at the best anchorage for the defense of that place and for self-defense.

K. R. BREESE,
Lieutenant-Commander, U.S. Navy, and President Court.
J. M. Alden
Acting Ensign, Judge-Advocate.

* * * * * * *

---

[2] *O.R.N..*, vol. 26:421.

Item: Letter from Governor Thomas C. Reynolds to Governor Henry Watkins Allen, acknowledging Louisiana's support for the Missouri troops.[3]

Marshall, Texas, 1st Feb., 1865
To His Excellency H. W. Allen, Governor of the State of Louisiana:

Sir—I embraced an early opportunity on my return from Missouri last December, to thank you in person for the generous contributions of the noble people of Louisiana, at your invitation, during the summer and fall, in aid to the gallant Missourians in the Confederate armies.

It is again my pleasant duty to thank you for the language, as eloquent as it is terse, in which you allude to them in your late annual message to the legislature of your State. As the constitutional Executive of the oppressed people of Missouri, I beg leave to assure you, and through you your constituents, that the munificent aid and liberal hospitality of Louisiana to Missouri's soldiers are as gleams of the highest sunshine amid the gloom of their long and weary exile from their cherished homes. From personal intercourse with them I know that they fully appreciate the many kindnesses shown them by Louisianans, and especially by yourself, their warm-hearted and public-spirited Governor.

You generously assure those patriotic soldiers that "the citizens of Louisiana have adopted them." They could have no nobler or better fosterage; of its excellence you yourself, once a Missourian, are an illustrious example. But Missouri does not surrender her interest in you: she claims, with pride, that the qualities which developed in the genial atmosphere of the sunny South, have given you an enviable national reputation for foresight, ability, energy, and patriotism, received their earliest culture in her own clime.

With sentiments of the highest esteem, I have the honor top be, sir,

Very respectfully, your obedient servant,
Thos. C. Reynolds
Governor of the State of Missouri.

* * * * * * *

Item: Confidential letter to General Price directing him to prepare for making "a campaign into Missouri."[4]

[Confidential] Hdqrs. Trans-Mississippi Department
Shreveport, La., June 3, 1864.
Maj. Gen. S. PRICE, *Commanding District of Arkansas:*

General: The commanding general desires that you make such arrangements, through your agents and friends in Missouri, as will enable you to obtain accurate information for him upon the following points:

---

3 Dorsey, 385.
4 *O.R.*, vol. 34, pt. 4:642.

First. The information should all have reference to the prospective condition of affairs during the months of August, September, October, and November next.

Second. It should embrace in detail accurate information as to the supplies to be obtained in the country, giving the localities and amount and nature of the supplies.

Third. All information in regard to movements of the enemy, the number of troops, and names of commanding officers, where they are stationed, and amount of supplies at the various posts.

Fourth. The feeling of the people, prospect of obtaining recruits, and whether they can supply themselves with arms and equipments, and to what extent.

Fifth. Information as to the roads, their condition, whether bridges exist, or are necessary at the crossing of the streams, especially via Crowley's Ridge.

Sixth, Obtain, if possible, copies of U.S. military maps; state between what points telegraphic communications exists.

The general commanding desires this information, as, should our successes continue, the opportunity may offer to make a campaign into Missouri.

I am, general, very respectfully, your obedient servant,

W. R. Boggs,
Brigadier-General and Chief of Staff.

* * * * * * *

Item: Orders, dated August 4, 1864, directing General Price to mount an expedition to Missouri.[5]

Headquarters Trans-Mississippi Department
Shreveport, La., August 4, 1864.
Maj. Gen. S. Price,*Commanding District of Arkansas:*

General: You will make immediate arrangements for a movement into Missouri, with the entire cavalry force of your district. General Shelby should be instructed to have his command in Northeast Arkansas ready to move by the 20th instant. You can instruct him to await your arrival with the column immediately under your command. A brigade of Louisiana troops, under Colonel Harrison, has been ordered to report to you. They should be added to General Marmaduke's command, and with his old brigade constitute his division. General Clark should be transferred to the command of Marmaduke's old brigade. Colonel Greene should be left in Arkansas, together with the other regimental commander whose mutinous conduct has already proved them unfit for command. General Shelby's old brigade, increased by the one raised in East Arkansas, can be organized into a division under his immediate command. General Fagan will command the division composed of Cabell's and Crawford's brigades. These skeleton organizations are best adapted for an expedition in which a large addition to your force is expected.

---

5 *O.R.*, vol. 41, pt. 2:1040–1041.

These weak brigades should be filled by the regiments raised in Missouri, and you should scrupulously avoid the organization of any new brigades. You will carry a supply of ammunition for General Shelby's command in northeast Arkansas, and should yourself be provided with ammunition sufficient for the expedition. You will scrupulously avoid all wanton acts of destruction and devastation, restrain your men, and impress upon them that their aim should be to secure success in a just and holy cause and not to gratify personal feeling and revenge. Rally loyal men of Missouri, and remember that our great want is men, and that your object should be, if you cannot maintain yourself in that country, to bring as large an accession as possible to our force. Your recruits will in all probability be mounted; deal frankly with them, and let them understand that mounted organizations, made through necessity, are liable to be dismounted on their arrival in our lines, where forage, and subsistence will not admit the maintenance of so large a cavalry force. Make Saint Louis the object point of your movement, which, if rapidly made, will put you in possession of that place, its supplies, and military stores, and which will do more toward rallying Missouri to your standard than the possession of any other point. Should you be compelled to withdraw from the State, make your retreat through Kansas and the Indian Territory, sweeping that country of its mules, horses, cattle, and military supplies of all kinds. The division of General Fagan, the senior officer of your command, should be increased as soon as practicable.

By command of General E. Kirby Smith:
W. R. Boggs,
Brigadier-General and Chief of Staff.

* * * * * * *

Item: The cartel ending military operations in the Trans-Mississippi, signed on May 26, 1865.[6]

Terms of a Military Convention entered into this 26th day of May, 1865, at New Orleans, La., between Gen. E. Kirby Smith, C.S. Army, commanding the Department of Trans-Mississippi, and Maj.-Gen. E. R. S. Canby, U.S. Army, commanding the army and division of West Mississippi, for the surrender of the troops and public property under the control of the military and naval authorities of the Trans-Mississippi Department.

I. All acts of war and resistance against the United States on part of the troops under General Smith shall cease from this date.

II. The officers and men to be paroled until duly exchanged, or otherwise released from the obligation of their parole by the authority of the government of the United States. Duplicate rolls of all officers and men paroled to be returned by such officers as may be designated by the parties hereto, officers giving their individual paroles, and commanders of regiments, battalions, companies or detachments signing a like parole for the men of their respective companies.

---

6 Harrell, *Arkansas, Confederate Military History*, 282–283.

III. Artillery, small-arms, ammunition and other property of the Confederate States Government, including gunboats and transports, to be turned over to the officers appointed to receive the same on the part of the Government of the United States; duplicate inventories of the property to be surrendered to be prepared, one copy to be retained by the officer delivering and the other by the officer receiving it, for the information of their respective commanders.

IV. Officers and men paroled under this agreement will be allowed to return to their homes with the assurance that they will not be disturbed by the authorities of the United States as long as they continue to observe the conditions of their paroles and the laws in force where they reside, except that persons resident in northern States and not excepted in the amnesty proclamation of the President, may return to their homes on taking the Oath of Allegiance to the United States.

V. The surrender of the property will not include the side arms or private horses or baggage of officers.

VI. All horses which are in good faith the private property of enlisted men will not be taken from them. The men will be permitted to take such with them to their homes, to be used for private purposes only.

VII. The time, mode and place paroling and surrender of property will be fixed by the respective commanders, and it will be carried out by commissioners appointed by them.

VIII. The terms and conditions of this convention to extend to all officers and men of the army and navy of the Confederate States, or any of them being in or belonging to the Trans-Mississippi Department.

IX. Transportation and subsistence to be furnished at public cost for the officers and men (after being paroled) to the nearest practicable point to their homes.

X. If the United States troops, designated for the garrisons of interior points, should not reach their destinations before the work of paroling is completed, suitable guards will be detailed for the protection of public property. These guards, when relieved, will surrender their arms, and be paroled in accordance with the terms of this convention.[7]

(Signed) S. B. Buckner,
Lieutenant-General and Chief of Staff.
(For Gen. E. Kirby Smith.)
(Signed) P. Jos. Osterhaus.
Major-General of Volunteers and Chief of Staff.
(For Maj.-Gen. E. R. S. Canby, commanding Military Division of West Mississippi.)

* * * * * * *

---

[7] Paragraph X of the cartel was not listed in the *Official Records* but was contained in *Arkansas State Gazette*. "Surrender of the Trans-Mississippi Department," *Arkansas State Gazette* (Little Rock, AR), June 15, 1865.

Item: Additional conditions and terms for ending military operations in the Trans-Mississippi, not covered in the cartel as spelled out in the *Official Records*, but spelled out in the General Orders below. The General Orders was divided into six parts; Part one was listed above as paragraphs 1-9, while paragraph 10 comes from the *Arkansas State Gazette*. The remaining five parts as follows:[8]

Headq'rs Mil. Div. West Mississippi,
New Orleans, May 26, 1865.
General Orders No. 61.

I. See paragraphs 1-9 above.

II. The United States troops sent into the interior of the country will be kept well in hand, in a state of the most exact discipline, and in constant readiness for any service which they may be called upon to perform. When detachments are made for the purpose of protecting the inhabitants against jayhawkers and other lawless characters, and on all marches through the country, the conduct of the officers and men must be such as to inspire the people with confidence and respect, and no depredations, however slight, or interference with the citizens in their lawful pursuits will be permitted.

III. To guard against waste or loss of public property, not under the control of the Confederate military and naval authorities, the civil officers in charge or agents in charge of such property will be relieved by the proper officers and agents of that Government. All sales of such property, or transfers, except to authorized agents of the Government, are forbidden, and any attempt to conceal it or withhold it will work the immediate forfeiture of any private interest that may be involved.

IV. Private property will not be interfered with, unless required for "public use," and where this is necessary, it will be taken in an orderly manner, under the orders of the commanding officers, and the proper receipts will be given. Property so received will be disposed of and accounted for as any other public property.

V. 1. Until the commercial restrictions, and the blockade of the Gulf ports, are removed by the President, no foreign or general commerce with those ports or with the interior of the country west of the Mississippi, (within the limits of this Division) can be permitted, and trade will be limited to the wants of the army and navy, and the necessities of the inhabitants within the limits of military occupation. To the extent of these necessities, military permits and clearances may be given for supplies not prohibited by existing orders, but no permit or clearances will be given to any point that is not occupied by military or naval force.

2. In the neighborhood of military posts the inhabitants may freely bring in their produce, and take out such supplies as may be required for plantation and family use. Live stock, provisions of all kinds, fuel, and other products and materials, required by the army and navy, or for the use of inhabitants, may be freely sold in open market; but no other products of insurrectionary districts can be sold

---

8 Ibid.

or shipped, except by delivery to the Quartermaster's Department for consignment to a purchasing agent of the Treasury Department.

3. No trade store or trade permits for the interior will be permitted or recognized, until the regulations of the Treasury Department can be extended over the country to be occupied and until then no clearances or permits will be granted for any point that is not occupied by the troops of the United States.

VII. Under the authority of the executive order of April 28th, 1865, all well disposed persons, who accept, in good faith, the Presidents's invitation "to return to peaceful pursuits," are assured that they may resume their usual avocations, not only without molestation, but, if necessary, under the protection of the United States troops; conforming to the regulations of the Treasury Department and to the additional condition of not fabricating or dealing in articles contraband of war.

By order of Maj. Gen. E. R. S. Canby

C. T. Christensen,

Lieut. Col. Ass't Adj't General.

* * * * * * *

Item: Eulogy upon the death of ex-Governor Thomas C. Reynolds, by Judge Breckenridge.

Published: April 2, 1887.

Friendship's Tribute

Action of the St. Louis Bar Relative to the Death of Ex-Governor Reynolds Judge Breckenridge Utters A Glowing Eulogy of the Deceased.

There was a meeting of the bar held in the room No. 4 of the circuit court yesterday afternoon to take action with reference to the death of Thomas C. Reynolds. It was largely attended and was called to order by Alex. J. P. Garesche, Judge Breckenridge was called to the chair. James E. Withrow acted as secretary. Judge Breckenridge started the object of the meeting and in so doing paid a high tribute to the life and works of the deceased. He said that death coming in the ordinary course of nature was always shocking, and in this instance it turned in the most lamentable form, making it more than unusually the duty of his former associates to express in emphatic terms their estimate of the great personal worth, the manly character, and the honorable life of the friend whose loss was so deeply deplored. He had sought relief from suffering caused by disease and death, in the words he so recently wrote commending himself "to the mercy of God and the charitable judgment of men," were thus rendered more significant and pathetic. Judge Breckenridge concluded:

> If I am correctly informed, Gov. Reynolds came to the city in the year 1850 and established himself in the practice of the profession. He was possessed of great natural ability, and his mind was both vigorous and acute. He

was of an unusually calm, well-balanced temperate, self-possessed and not easily excited. In character he was positive, resolute, fearless. He had been carefully trained in the best classical and, professional school, both at home and abroad, and some experience important diplomatic service help to complete his thorough preparation for success. Soon secured a high position as a practitioner, and was appointed district attorney of the United States for this district. But a strong political bias in his positive convictions made him a leader of opinion and action, and he was unavoidably involved in the debate, constantly in circumstances increasing in earnestness, which fill the decade immediately preceding the war, and thus for years was drawn away from the profession, was elected lieutenant governor and became a very conspicuous figure in the Southern side of the that great controversy, sharing the fortunes, and at last, the reverses of those whose cause he so warmly espoused. After the storm subsided he lived for a short time in Mexico, and then returned to his own home and resumed the practice of the profession. It was a striking evidence of his real manliness and of that heroic quality in him that though reduced from a high place to humble station and to poverty, he accepted the results of the war with cheerful acquiescence and became again, without despondency or repining, and with all the ardor of youth to construct a new career. Most of you are familiar with the latter portion of his life. He was again successful at the bar, and was again rewarded with important official positions in connection with the practice, and although of recent years he has confined his professional labors chiefly to those departments which brought him less than formally in contact with the body of this professional brethren, he was well known in the courts and recognized by all as a skillful, learned and able lawyer. He was again honored with important public trust, and apparently in the full vigor of his current hours moved among us, commanding the respect and confidence of all men.

How sadly and how suddenly ended!

You will cause to be expressed in permanent form your estimate of his character and your sense of our loss, and I leave to others the sad but pleasant duty of speaking more in detail of his eventful life. I myself have known him during the larger part of his residence here, and have cherished for him a warm personal regards and I grieve with you at this premature and the of a career so full of high purpose, earnest effort and true courage.

Hon. T. G. C. Davis then passed a fitting eulogy of the deceased, and on motion of Mr. R. Cullen it was decided that the bar attend the funeral, which will take place from St. George's church this afternoon at 3 o'clock, in a body.

On motion of the Judge Bakewell the chair appointed Judge R. A. Bakewell, Judge Warwick Hough, H. A. Clover, James O. Broadhead and Alex. J. P. Garesche as a committee to draft a memorial to be submitted to an adjourned meeting of the bar, which will be held in Judge Dillon's Court, Monday afternoon at 3 o'clock.

****

Item: General Shelby's addresses his division at the close of the war, urging them to continue the fight. [9]

Address of General J. O. Shelby
To His Division.

Soldiers of Shelby's Division:

The Crisis of a Nation's fate is upon you. I come to you in this hour of peril and gloom, as I have come when your exultant shouts of victory were proud on the breezes of Missouri, relying upon your patriotism, your devotion, your heroic fortitude and endurance. By the memory of our past efforts, our brilliant reputation, our immortal dead, our wrecked and riven hearthstones, our banished and insulted women, our kindred fate and kindred ruin, our wrongs unrighted and unavenged, I conjure you to stand shoulder to shoulder and bide the tempest out. In union there is strength, honor, manhood, safety, success—in separation, defeat, disgrace, disaster, extermination, death. I promise to remain with you until the end. To share your dangers, your trials, your exile, your destiny, and your lot shall be my lot, and your fate shall be my fate; and, come what may, poverty, misery, exile, degradation, oh! never let your spotless banner be tarnished by dishonor. If there be any amongst you that wish to go from our midst, when the dark hour comes, and the bright visions of peace are paling beyond the sun set-shore, let him bid farewell to the comrades that no danger can appall and no disaster deter, for the curse of the sleepless eye and the festering heart will be his reward, as the women of Missouri, the Paris of a ruined Paradise, shall tell how Missouri's braves fought until the Confederate flag by inches was torn from the mast.

Stand by the ship, boys, as long as there is one plank upon another. All your hopes and fears are there. All that life holds nearest and dearest is there. Your bleeding mother-land, pure and stainless as an angel guarded child, is there. The proud imperial South, the nurse of your boyhood and the priestess of the faith is there, and call upon you, her children, her best and bravest, in the pride of purity of your manhood, and your blood, to rally round her alter-shrine, the blue skies and green fields of nativity, and send your scornful challenge forth: "The Saxon Beasts are equal to the Norman Steel!"

Meet at your company quarters, look the matter fairly and squarely in the face. Think of all you have to lose and all you have to gain. Watch the fires of your devotion, as you would your hopes of heaven. Stand together, act together, keep your discipline and your integrity, and all will be well, as you strike for God and humanity. I am with you until the last, and oh, what glad hozannas will go up

---

9 "Address of General J. O. Shelby to His Division," *Shelby and His Men*, 516–517.

to you, when our land, redeemed, shall rise, beautiful, from its urn of death and chamber of decay, the storms of battle and the anguish of defeat floating away forever!

If Johnston follows Lee, and Beauregard, and Maury, and Forrest, all go' and the Cis-Mississippi Department surrender its arms and quit the contest, let us never surrender. For four long years we have taught each other to forget that word, and it is too late to learn it now. Let us all meet as we have met in many dark hours before, with the hearts of men that have drawn the sword and thrown away the scabbard, and resolve, with the deep, eternal, irrevocable resolution of freemen that we shall never surrender!

If all the regiments of this department go by the board, if coward fear and dastard treachery dictate submission, we will treat every man who leaves his banner now, as a base recreant, and shoot him as we would a Federal. *This Missouri Division surrender*–my God! Soldiers, it is more terrible than death. You, the young and the brave of poor Missouri, that have so often marched away to battle, proudly and gaily, with love in your hearts and light in your eyes for the land that you loved best, you who are worshiped by your friends and dreaded by your enemies; you that have the blood of Cavaliers in your veins—it is too horrible to contemplate.

[Brigadier General]
[J. O. Shelby, Commanding]

* * * * * * * *

Item: Governor Claiborne F. Jackson's Proclamation to Missouri, justifying his call for 50,000 militia to defend the state.[10]

A Proclamation.
To the People of Missouri:

A series of unprovoked and unparalleled outrages have been inflicted upon the peace and indignity of the Commonwealth and upon the rights and liberties of its people by wicked and unprincipled men, professing to act under the authority of the United States Government. The solemn enactments of your Legislature have been nullified, your volunteer soldiers have been taken prisoners, your commerce with your sister States have been suspended, your trade with your fellow-citizens has been and is subjected to the harassing control of armed soldiery, peaceful citizens have been imprisoned without warrant of law, unoffending and defenseless men, women, and children have been ruthlessly shot down and murdered, and other unbearable indignities have been heaped upon your State and yourselves.

To all these outrages and indignities you have been submitted with a patriotic forbearance which has only encouraged the perpetrators of these grievous wrongs to attempt still bolder and more daring usurpations. It has been my earnest

10 *O.R.*, vol. 53:696–698.

endeavor under all these embarrassing circumstances to maintain the peace of the State and to avert, if possible, from our borders the desolating effects of a civil war. With that object in view I authorized Major-General Price several weeks ago to arrange with General Harvey, commanding the Federal forces in this State, the terms of an agreement by which the peace of the State might be preserved. They came, on 21st of May, to an understanding, which was made public. The State authorities have faithfully labored to carry out the terms of that agreement. The Federal Government, on the other hand, not only manifested its strong disapprobation of it by the instant dismissal of the distinguished officer who on its part entered into it, but it at once began and has unintermittingly carried out a system of hostile operations in utter contempt of that agreement and in reckless disregard of its own plighted faith. These acts have lately portended revolution and civil war so unmistakably that I resolved to make one further effort to avert these dangers from you. I therefore solicited an interview with Brigadier-General Lyon, commanding the Federal army in Missouri. It was granted, and on the 10th instant, waiving all questions of personal and official dignity, I went to St. Louis, accompanied by Major-General Price.

We had an interview on the 11th instant with General Lyon and Col. F. P. Blair, jr., at which I submitted to them this proposition: that I would disarm all the companies which had been armed by the State; that I would pledge myself not to attempt to organize the militia under the military bill; that no arms or munitions of war should be brought into the State; that I would protect all citizens equally in all their rights, regardless of their political opinions; that I would repel all attempts to invade it, from whatever quarter and by whomsoever made, and that I would thus maintain a strict neutrality in the present unhappy contest, and preserve the peace of the State. And I further proposed that I would, if necessary, invoke the assistance of the U.S. troops to carry out these pledges. All this I proposed to do upon the condition that the Federal Government would undertake to disarm the home guards which it illegally organized and armed throughout the State, and pledge itself not to occupy with its troops any localities in the State not occupied by them at this time.

Nothing but the most earnest desire to avert the horrors of civil war from our beloved State could have tempted me to propose these humiliating terms. They were rejected by the Federal officers. They demanded not only the disorganization and disarming of the State militia and the nullification of the military bill, but they refused to disarm their own home guards, and insisted that the Federal Government should enjoy an unrestricted right to move and station its troops throughout the State whenever and wherever that might, in the opinion of its officers, be necessary, either for protecting of the "loyal subjects" of the Federal Government or for the repelling of invasion, and they plainly announced that it was the intention of the Administration to take military occupation under these pretexts of the whole State, and to reduce it, as avowed by General Lyon himself, to the "exact condition of Maryland."

The acceptance by me of these degrading terms would not only have sullied the honor of Missouri, but would have aroused the indignation of every brave citizen, and precipitated the very conflict which it has been my aim to prevent. We refused to accede to them, and the conference was broken up. Fellow citizens, all our efforts toward conciliation have failed. We can hope nothing from justice or moderation of the agents of the Federal Government in this State. They are energetically hastening the execution of their bloody and revolutionary schemes for the inauguration of a civil war in your midst; for the military occupation of your State by armed bands of lawless invaders; for the overthrow of your State government, and for the subversion of those liberties which that government has always sought to protect, and they intend to exert their whole power to subjugate you, if possible, to the military despotism which has usurped the powers of the Federal Government.

Now, therefore, I, C. F. Jackson, Governor of the State of Missouri, do, in view of the forgoing facts and by virtue of the power vested in me by the constitution and laws of the Commonwealth, issue this my proclamation, calling the militia of the State, to the number of 50,000, into the active service of the State, for the purpose of repelling said invasion, and for the protection of the lives, liberty and property of the citizens of the State; and I earnestly exhort all good citizens of Missouri to rally under the flag of their State for the protection of their endangered homes and firesides, and for the defense of their most sacred rights and dearest liberties.

In issuing this proclamation, I hold it to be my solemn duty to remind you that Missouri is still one of the United States; that the executive department of the State government does not arrogate to itself the power to disturb that relation; that that power has been wisely vested in a convention, which will at the proper time express your sovereign will, and that meanwhile it is your duty to obey all the constitutional requirements of the Federal Government; but it is equally my duty to advise you that your first allegiance is due to your own State, and that you are under no obligation whatever to obey the unconstitutional edicts of the military despotism which has enthroned itself at Washington, nor to submit to the infamous and degrading sway of the wicked minions of this State. No brave and true-hearted Missourian will obey the one or submit to the other. Rise, then, and drive out ignominiously the invaders who have dared desecrate the soil which your labors have made fruitful and which is consecrated by your homes!

Given under my hand as Governor and under the great seal of the State of Missouri at Jefferson City this 12th day of June, 1861.

Claiborne F. Jackson
By the Governor:
B. F. Massey
Secretary of State

* * * * * * *

Item: Correspondence concerning the resignation of S. D. Jackman, commanding Confederate infantry regiment and orders assigning him to recruitment duty in Missouri.[11]

Camp near White River
Oct. 23d, 1862
[To] Maj. Genl. [Thomas C.] Hindman

Sir: I am commanding a regiment of infantry in the Confederate Service. The regiment is in good condition, the Lt. Col. & Maj. are efficient officers and capable of taking charge of the same. The experience I have had in military affairs has been with mounted men and I desire permission to resign my present command, and if that cannot be given, I want a furlough for a limited period, and authority to proceed to Missouri to raise and organize a Regt. of mounted men for service along the Kansas and Missouri border, to act in conjunction with and under the orders of the officer in command of the army when the same shall proceed into Missouri, performing the scouting and out post duty incident to the advance of the army. If authority is given me for the purpose stated I feel satisfied that I can raise the men in Missouri, brave men who will not leave the state for the ordinary service, but are schooled in the Kansas border wars, and invaluable in the performance of such duties as would devolve on them. Should I be permitted to proceed to Missouri, all the outfit I want would be a reasonable supply of percussion caps. There are some arms and ammunition concealed in the country and the remainder I would expect to capture from the enemy. I expect to recruit the men in the border counties from the Arkansas line to the Missouri River and from my own personal knowledge and the knowledge of the men I would recruit I should always expect to have thorough and complete information of the topography of every portion of the western counties of Missouri and eastern counties of Kansas. I further believe that I can get Capt. [William C.] Quantrill and his men to join me, in the formation of a regiment for the kind of duty indicated.

S. D. Jackman, Col.
1st. Regt. Inf. 2d Brig. A.W.

[Endorsement]

Approved–Make an order as follows:

    1. Accepting Col. [Sidney D.] Jackman's resignation (Which requires him to tender in form.)...

    3. Relieving Lt. Col. [Josiah H.] Caldwell of duty in Col. [William H.] Brooks, and ordering him to report to Br. Gen. Shoup for duty with his regt.

    4. Authorizing Col. Jackman to raise a cavalry regiment in Missouri for the duty before written, to be commanded by him. Other officers to be appointed upon his recommendation from time to time.

---

11 Jackman to Hindman, Letter (October 23, 1862), Miscellaneous Correspondence; Special Orders No. 22 (October 25, 1862), Special Orders Book No. 1.

T. C. H.

* * * * * * *

Hd. Qrs. District of Arkansas
Camp War Eagle, Madison Co. Oct. 25th 1862
Special Orders [Extract]
No. 22

IV. The resignation of Col. S. D. Jackman, of Jackman's regiment of Missouri infantry is accepted and that officer discharged from the service.

V. Brig. Genl. [Francis A.] Shoup, comdg. Shoup's Division will immediately cause the vacancies in Jackman's regt of Missouri infantry, occasioned by the resignation of Col. S. D. Jackman, to be filled according to law.

VI. Col. S. D. Jackman is authorized to raise one regiment of cavalry in the State of Missouri, and to act in that state independently of all other commands, reporting directly to these Hd. Qrs. when this command moves into the state. When the proper number of companies are reported to him organized, Col. Jackman will assign other field officers and the proper staff officers to duty subject to the subsequent confirmation of the War Department...

By Command of
Maj. Genl. Hindman
R. C. Newton
A. A. Genl.

* * * * * * *

Item: Correspondence concerning the surrender of James W, Cooper's Battalion of guerrillas.[12]

Headquarters,
Cassville, June 3, 1865.
Bvt. Maj. Gen. J. B. Sanborn:

Sir: Yesterday I came back from a five days' scout through the northern part of Arkansas. According to your orders I made efforts to accomplish a meeting with the leading Confederate officers in said part of the country. Finding Colonel Coffee was nowhere near, I communicated with Maj. J. W. Cooper, Indian Brigade, in sending him your instructions to me from May 17 last [not found], and requested him (Cooper) to surrender under the terms named therein. His answer you will please find in copy no. 1. I then directed to him what you will see in no. 2 and at about 2 p.m. on the 30th of May last, I, in presence of Capt. Ph. Rohrer and two lieutenants, met Major Cooper, and came after an hour's talk to the following agreement: Cooper would not surrender until caught, or ordered to do so by his superiors, but cease all hostilities against our party, and, furthermore, help

---

12 *O.R.*, vol. 48, pt. 2:758–759.

us all he can in keeping down stealing, etc. I agreed to this, provided it meets your approbation, and with the clear understanding that this quasi armistice would be at an end whenever he did not come up fully with his promise. To explain to you why I wrote Cooper twice, I would say it was pretty troublesome to get him to come. After long private conversations with some of Cooper's friends I was bound, in order to see him, to pledge myself of his safe coming and going whether he would surrender or not.

I am, very respectfully, your obedient servant,
James M. Moore
Major Third Battalion, Fifteenth Missouri Volunteer Cavalry.

[Inclosure No. 1]

Headquarters Cooper's Battalion,
On the Range, May 30, 1865.

Maj. James M. Moore:

I have the honor of receiving your communication of to-day. As for surrendering, I do not think that I am under and compulsion to justify an honorable surrender, and shall not until I am ordered by my commander. Desiring to go to may command, I am willing to meet you in order to prevent depredations on citizens; I am willing to cease hostilities.

Respectfully, your most obedient servant,
James W. Cooper,
Major, Commanding Cooper's Battalion, First Indian Brigade, District of Indian Territory, C.S. Army.

[Inclosure No. 2]

Berryville, Ark., May 30, 1865.
Maj. James W. Cooper:

Yours of the 29th [30th] instant is at hand, and in reply I would say my main object in addressing my last to you was to cause hostilities to cease on peaceable citizens in this country. It is not in the least my intention to seek any ungentlemanly advantage of you. My directions from headquarters are simply such as you saw yesterday. I sincerely wish to see you before to-night, and you can rest assured at the end of our conference that you can go safe to any place you wish, no matter if you surrender or not. The bearer of this, Henry Woods, will specify time and place where our meeting shall take effect.

Very respectfully, your obedient servant,
James M. Moore,
Major, Commanding U.S. Forces.

Appendix B
Selected Biographies

Richard P. Crump

Praised as a "gallant soldier and a genial gentleman," by General Walter P. Lane, Richard Philip Crump was born in January 1824, in Powhatan, Virginia. After briefly attending West Point, Crump moved to Texas in 1842, settling first at Clarksville and then Jefferson. Married twice, Crump was a man of many talents, serving as a local sheriff, saloon keeper, and a river boat owner.

At the beginning of the Civil War, Crump joined the 1st Texas Cavalry Battalion and was elected major on November 4, 1861. He led his battalion at the Battle of Pea Ridge (Elkhorn Tavern) in March 1862, after which his unit was transferred to the east side of the Mississippi River. On May 20, 1862, the 1st Battalion was combined with other Texas units to form what eventually became the 32nd Texas Cavalry (Dismounted). Crump was not reelected in the new regiment He returned to Texas and with Walter P. Lane raised the 1st Texas Partisan Cavalry Regiment, accepting the appointment of lieutenant colonel.

After Colonel Lane took sick, Crump led the regiment at Prairie Grove, where his brigade commander praised him for his "gallantry" and "daring chivalry." During the Red River Campaign, Crump was again cited for his "coolness and bravery," while leading the 1st Texas Partisan. Crump was promoted to full colonel on October 28, 1864, and continued to lead his regiment or commanded a brigade until the end of the war.

Returning to Jefferson, Texas, Crump was arrested for having hanged Martin D. Hart on January 21, 1863. Martin Hart, a brother of a Unionist Texas judge, Hardin Hart, was a Union guerrilla leader and former member of the Texas Senate, who robbed and executed prominent Arkansas citizens, including Colonel DeRosey Carroll, Judge McAllister and a Mr. Samuel Richardson. Crump was imprisoned, escaped, but was never rearrested for killing Hart. Crump became a leading opponent of Reconstruction and joined the "Knights of the Rising Sun" in Jefferson. He was again arrested for killing a former Union officer, tried, and found not guilty. Crump was freed from prison, but fell and never recovered, dying in October 1869.[1]

* * * * * * *

Archibald S. Dobbin

Archibald Stephenson Dobbin (per *O.R.*) or Dobbins (per Allardice, Edwards, and Southern Historical Society) was born near Mount Pleasant, Maury

---

1. *O.R.*, vol. 22, pt. 1:155–156; *O.R.*, vol. 22, pt. 2:774–775; *O.R.*, vol. 34, pt. 1:618; *O.R.*, vol. 41, pt. 3:996, 998–999; *O.R.S.*, pt. 2, vol. 68:34, 264, 268–269, 271–272, 274, 277; Allardice, *Confederate Colonels, 117*; "From North-West Arkansas and Missouri," *Weekly Dallas Herald*, February 4, 1863; Lane, 105; McCaslin, 183; W. J. Weaver, "A Sketch of Mrs. Sophia Kannady, A Heroine of Fort Smith," in *Confederate Women of Arkansas*, 85–86; Wooster, *Lone Star Regiments*, 109, 315.

County, Tennessee, in 1827, and remained in his birth state until 1850, when he married and moved to Arkansas. Settling near Helena, Dobbin became a prosperous planter, specializing in produce and other crops. At the beginning of the Civil War, Dobbin remained in his business and supplied the Confederate Army with assorted foodstuffs; but all that came to an end on July 12, 1862, when a Federal Army, under Samuel R. Curtis took Helena. Dobbin departed for Little Rock, where he offered his services to General Thomas C. Hindman, who appointed Dobbin a volunteer aide-de-camp on August 7, 1862.

Upon organization of the District of Arkansas, Dobbin was reaffirmed as aide-de-camp on September 19. He continued to serve under Hindman until the latter left the Trans-Mississippi Department in March 1863. On October 30, 1862, Dobbin was appointed acting chief of ordnance and 10 days latter was again appointed an aide-de-camp for the 1st Corps Trans-Mississippi Army. While in the 1st Corps, in addition to commanding a squadron of cavalry, Dobbin served in a variety of positions, including ordnance officer, aide-de-camp and provost officer. At the Battle of Prairie Grove, while on Hindman's staff, Dobbin was recognized for his "coolness and disregard of danger."

Archibald Dobbin

Following the Battle of Prairie Grove, Dobbin left Hindman's staff and returned to the Helena area where he raised several companies of cavalry. General T. H. Holmes, commanding the Trans-Mississippi Department, subsequently sent a mustering officer to Dobbin on March 22, to legitimize his command, and then combined it with Francis M. Chrisman's Arkansas Battalion to form Dobbin's Arkansas Cavalry Regiment (sometimes referred too as the 1st Arkansas Cavalry). The regiment was probably organized in late March 1863, when Dobbin was appointed colonel of the regiment. Operating between the White and Mississippi Rivers, Dobbin scouted and harassed the Union garrison at Helena as well as disrupting Mississippi River traffic.

Dobbin's regiment was at the Battle of Helena (July 4, 1863), where it was assigned to Lucius M. Walker's Division and sustained four killed and eight wounded. During the Little Rock Campaign (August 1–September 14, 1863), Dobbin commanded a brigade and then Walker's Division, following Walker's death in a duel with General John S, Marmaduke on September 6. On September

10, 1863, Dobbin's Brigade contested the Federal crossing of the Arkansas River, after which Dobbin, angry with Marmaduke, refused to obey his superior's orders.

This was not the first time that Marmaduke and Dobbin had had a severe disagreement. On April 12, 1863, Marmaduke's command engaged a Federal force at Taylor's Creek in eastern Arkansas. According to Marmaduke, Dobbin was expected to block the enemy's retreat, but he failed to do so. Of the failure, Marmaduke wrote: "Had Dobbin's command fallen upon the rear of the enemy, or even destroyed the bridge, the 350 cavalry & 2 pieces of artillery certainly have been captured & the whole force could have been turned against the other column, which also should have been destroyed or captured; the failure deserves investigation and the punishment of the incompetent party," i.e., Colonel Dobbin.

Relieved of his command for his actions at Bayou Fourche on September 10, Dobbin was later reinstated, pending a court martial. On October 11, 1863, Dobbin's camp was surprised and routed at Tulip, Arkansas, where he lost "all his camp and garrison equipment and transportation" along with "a number of prisoners and horses." Immediately following the incident at Tulip, Dobbin was relieved of command. He then resigned from the service, pending Kirby Smith's approval. On October 27th, Dobbin was ordered to appear before a court martial for disobedience of orders during the engagement at Bayou Fourche; however, the court martial, headed by General T. H. Drayton, was subsequently delayed and dissolved on November 10, 1863. Thirteen days later, on November 23, 1863, Dobbin was "dismissed" from the service, through it was unclear as to whether his resignation had been accepted or he was dismissed for other reasons.

Dobbin was later reinstated and he returned to northeast Arkansas, where he began recruiting in the area between Clarendon on the White River and Helena on the Mississippi River. Prior to recruiting a new command, Dobbin, according to Federal sources, had been in Richmond, where he was commissioned a brigadier general. Various other sources also have Dobbin as a Confederate general, but in most cases, they state that he was never confirmed by the Confederate Congress (*SHSP*, vol. 2:356–357; Heitman, 2:177; Morrow, 245).

With the arrival of J. O. Shelby in northeast Arkansas in May of 1864, Dobbin successfully recruited and organized a new regiment. Shelby in turn ordered Dobbin's new command to blockade the White River and harass the garrison at Helena. Later Dobbin was given command of a brigade of Arkansas Cavalry composed of his own regiment, James H. McGehee's (or McGhee's) Regiment and Allen R. Witt's Regiment, with Blocher's Arkansas Battery. Dobbin then led his brigade during Price's 1864 Missouri Raid, serving in James F. Fagan's Cavalry Division. On the raid Dobbin's Brigade had a mixed record, being the unit that failed to prevent the Federal escape from Pilot Knob in September 1864. Following the raid Dobbin's Brigade returned to northeast Arkansas, where it remained until its surrender in May 1865.

Though General Marmaduke despised him, Colonel Dobbin was well thought of by Shelby's Adjutant, John N. Edwards. To Edwards, Dobbin was an "intrepid" officer, who was a "true and brave" soldier.

Following the war, Dobbin moved to New Orleans, where he entered into a local business. Unable to tolerate Reconstruction, Dobbin moved to Brazil, where he attempted to establish a plantation. Sometime in the latter part of 1869 or 1870, Dobbin is thought to have been murdered by a local resident and his body never found.[2]

* * * * * * *

John N. Edwards

John Newman Edwards was born in Warren County, Virginia, near Port Royal, on January 4, 1838. With but "a common school education," Edwards proved to be an avid reader of classic authors, which in turn encouraged him to write. At the age of 14, he wrote a story which garnered him notoriety in his local area. At the age of 17, Edwards moved to Missouri, settling in Lexington, Lafayette County. Edwards was a printer and became the editor of the *Lexington Expositor*, "a militant and highly influential weekly," that was owned by a rich local businessman; all by the age of 20.

At the beginning of the Civil War, Edwards enlisted as a private on June 14, 1861, in what became Company A, 6th Infantry Regiment, 8th Division, MSG. As a member of the Guard, Edwards was at the Battles of Carthage, Wilson's Creek, Lexington, and Pea Ridge. Following Pea Ridge, Edwards went with the Guard for service on the east side of the Mississippi River, returning to Arkansas in June 1862, as part of J. O. Shelby's Company. Edwards joined the Confederate Service on July 1, 1862, at DeValls Bluff, Arkansas.

From eastern Arkansas, Shelby's Company moved to Van Buren, then up to Waverly, Missouri, where the 5th Missouri Cavalry (CSA) was recruited. Upon organization of the regiment in August 1862, Edwards was appointed adjutant and on September 12, 1862, following the retirement of Captain W. J. McArthur,

---

2. *O.R.*, vol. 22, pt. 1:143, 436, 526; *O.R.*, vol. 22, pt. 2:674, 869, 1043; *O.R.*, vol. 34, pt. 4:598; *O.R.S.*, pt. 2, vol. 2:148; *O.R.S.*, pt. 3, vol. 2:538, 607, 704; Allardice, *Confederate Colonels*, 130; Allardice, *More Generals in Gray*, 79–80; Banasik, *Embattled Arkansas*, 58; Brock, "Confederate Roster," *SHSP*, vol. 2:356–357; Burke, 115; Crute, *Confederate Army*, 60; Edwards, *Shelby and His Men*, 316, 437; General Orders No. 11 (October 30, 1862), Copy Book of General Orders (May 31–December 30, 1862), District of Arkansas, General Hindman's Command, Peter W. Alexander Collection, Columbia University, hereafter cited as Copy Book of General Orders; General Orders No. 24 (November 22, 1862), 1st Corps, Trans-Mississippi Army, Copy Book of General Orders; Harrell, *Arkansas, Confederate Military History*, 272; Letter (February 20, 1863), Hindman to Anderson, Hindman's Command (January 2–March 14, 1863), Peter W. Alexander Collection, Columbia University; Marmaduke, 106–107, 180–182, 281, 287, 304–305, 315; Mobley, 111–112, 173, 184; Jno. P. Morrow, Jr., "Confederate Generals From Arkansas," *Arkansas Historical Quarterly* 21 (Autumn 1962), 245, hereafter cited as Morrow; Sellmeyer, 122, 183–184; Special Orders No. 25 (October 28, 1862), Special Orders Book No. 1; Special Orders Book and No. 38 (November 10, 1862), 1st Corps Trans-Mississippi Army, Special Orders Book No. 1.

John N. Edwards

Edwards was elevated to adjutant of Shelby's Iron Brigade.

Shelby noted Edwards's bravery at the Battle of Prairie Grove (December 7, 1862), in "cheering" the 5th Regiment "on to victory or death." And again during Marmaduke's First Missouri Raid (December 31, 1862–January 25, 1863), Shelby credited Edwards with noble, "well done, good and faithful" service. During Marmaduke's Second Missouri Raid (April 17–May 2, 1863), Edwards was "severely wounded," in the leg, "while gallantly leading and encouraging" his regiment forward at Cape Girardeau on April 26.

Edwards was captured following the engagement at Cape Girardeau and was held in the post hospital (Marble City Hotel) until June 16, when he was sent to Myrtle Street Prison in St. Louis. Forwarded to Sandusky, Ohio, and Johnson's Island Prison, on June 30, 1863, Edwards was later returned to St. Louis where he was exchanged on July 6, 1863, according to the *Official Records*. However, in Jennie Edwards's biography of her husband, she quotes Major J. F. Stonestreet, a comrade of John's, who says Major Edwards was at the Battle of Helena (July 4, 1863), where he "especially distinguished himself for bravery and strategy."

Edwards accompanied Shelby on his October 1863 Missouri Raid, even though no mention is made of him during the expedition. Edwards was no braggart, according to one source who wrote of Shelby's adjutant: "The only thing that exceeded his bravery was his modesty. Not once in the reports or in his lengthy history of Shelby's operations did he mention himself." And a review of the *Official Records* supports this comment, as little is mentioned of Edwards after Marmaduke's Second Missouri Raid, where Edwards was wounded and captured.

Edwards's name does appear again in R. W. Crabb's account, during the attack on the *Queen City* on June 24, 1864. According to Crabb, Edwards "displayed unusual coolness and daring bravery" during the engagement and subsequent attack on three gunboats. And Edwards is also identified as Shelby's inspector general in the summer of 1864, when Shelby's Adjutant was Major W. J. McArthur, who had returned to duty. Promoted to colonel in 1864, when Shelby commanded a division during Price's 1864 Missouri Raid, Edwards remained with Shelby until the end. During the course of the war, "Edwards lost more horses shot from under him in battle than any other member in Shelby's Brigade." He was wounded several times and was in more than 50 battles or skirmishes.

Edwards survived the war, but never surrendered nor was he paroled; instead, he went to Mexico with General Shelby, settling in Mexico City, where he published an English/Spanish newspaper, *The Mexican Times*, with ex-Governor Henry W. Allen of Louisiana. During his Mexico stay Edwards wrote the first of three major books on the war, *Shelby and His Men: or, the War in the West*. Edwards returned to Missouri in 1867, published his book, and wrote a second entitled *Shelby's Expedition to Mexico*. Edwards became a prolific writer and journalist, renowned as one of the best newspapermen west of the Mississippi, if not the best. In 1868, Edwards founded the Kansas City *Times*, with John C. Moore. In time, Edwards would become the owner, editor, or writer for six different Missouri newspapers.

In 1871, Edwards married Miss Mary Virginia "Jennie" Plattenburg, with whom he had three children. His third book *Noted Guerrillas* was written at his father-in-law's house and published it in 1877. However, a dark corner of Edwards's life appeared with his return to Missouri, as he turned to drink. He tried twice to stem the habit, admitting himself to a sanitarium in 1887, and again in 1888. Unable to curb his drinking problem, Edwards died in a Jefferson City hotel on May 4 (or May 9, say Eakin & Hale), 1889, following two days of illness; he was 51. The cause of death was "heart disease," or "inanition of the cardiac nerves."

Upon Edwards's death, the Missouri Legislature went into recess in his honor, following a resolution offered by Senator McGrath of St. Louis. Countless obituaries were written, one declaring that Edwards was "one of the most brilliant writers in the United States," and the "prince of Missouri Newspaper men." Still another recorded that Edwards was "the most brilliant writer Missouri ever nurtured to greatness," and yet another simply wrote that Edwards was the "Napoleon of journalism." Of his writing a Kansas newspaper called Edwards a "brilliant and picturesque...writer...a word-painter, a genius." Of all the comments on Edwards's passing, the one offered by his old commander General Shelby, probably best suited his comrade in arms. General Shelby wrote: "God never created a more noble, magnanimous or truer man than John N. Edwards."[3]

* * * * * * *

General Mariano Escobedo

General Mariano Escobedo was born on January 16, 1826, in San Pablo de los Labradores (modern-day Galena, Mexico). Prior to the Second French Intervention, Escobedo was a "hauling contractor" in northern Mexico, operating out of

---

3. *O.R.*, vol. 22, pt. 1:290–291; *O.R.*, vol. 41, pt. 2:1073; Anonymous, *5th. Missouri Cavalry*, 9; Bartels, *Trans-Mississippi Men*, 142; R. R. Crabb, "Cavalry Fight Against Gunboats," *Missouri Republican*, July 3, 1886; Eakin, *Confederate Records*, 3:6; Eakin & Hale, 128; Eakin, *Missouri Prisoners of War*, "Edwards, J. N." entry; Edwards, *John N. Edwards Biography*, 10–11, 14–18, 24, 27–29, 189, 198, 200, 209, 212–213, 218; Edwards, *Noted Guerrillas*, i–v; Marmaduke, *Order and Letter Book*, 55, 77, 176; National Archives, Record Group M322 (roll no. 38), Confederate Compiled Service Records, 5th. Missouri Cavalry (CSA); Peterson, 239–240; Sellmeyer, 27–28, 98; Schnetzer, *More Forgotten Men*, 72; Sifakis, *Missouri*, 96; Webb, 326–328.

Mariano Escobedo

Monterrey, his home town at the time. After the French arrived, Escobedo joined the Mexican army and was promoted to colonel for bravery at the First Battle of Puebla in May 1862. Later he rose to the rank of general, under Benito Juárez, becoming one of his most trusted and competent officers. Unfortunately, Escobedo was captured when Puebla fell to the French on May 17, 1863. Later, while being transported to the coast and ultimately destined for prison in France, Escobedo escaped with the help of French General Mejia, who took a "liking for the young Escobedo."

Considered the "most talented military man" in the Mexican army, Escobedo commanded Liberal Mexican forces in northeast Mexico, which operated along the Texas-Mexico border, even as our Civil War was winding down. He captured Matamoras on March 23, 1866, and received the surrender of Emperor Ferdinand Maximilian on May 15, 1867, at Queretaro. On June 19, 1867, Escobedo became the "executioner" of the emperor.

Percy Martin labeled Escobedo a "ferocious leader...mainly on account of a complete indifference to the ordinary dictates of humanity." Continuing, Percy noted that Escobedo was a "confirmed liar and trickster," who "was also a great physical coward..., having a horror of flying bullets, and invariably keeping under any available cover which presented itself during an engagement." Another author described Escobedo as "a tall slender man with wire glasses, beard, large ears and steady manner," appearing "more like a professor than a warrior."

After expelling the French from Mexico, Escobedo served for a time as governor of Nuevo Leon, which encompassed his hometown of Monterrey. Later, following the death of Juarez, in July 1872, Mexico descended into a period of unrest. Porfirio Diaz assumed the presidency of Mexico in late 1876, following a short struggle with Sebastian Lerdo; Diaz took control of the Mexican government, setting himself up as a dictator. Escobedo, a loyal Juarista, opposed the new dictator, led a rebellion against Diaz, was captured in 1878, imprisoned, and died on May 22, 1902.[4]

* * * * * * *

---

4. *O.R.*, vol. 41, pt. 2: 1244, 1257, 1259; Martin, 108–109, 219, 307–308; McAllen 88–90, 184; Murray, 164, 232; O'Flaherty, 303; Parkes, 268, 273, 282–284; Internet site, www.wickipedia.org.

Thomas R. Freeman

Thomas Roe Freeman was born on February 22, 1829, in Scott County, Missouri. Prior to the Civil War, Freeman lived in Dent, Crawford, and Phelps Counties, Missouri. A blacksmith, livestock trader, and lawyer, Freeman joined the Dent County Cavalry Company, Missouri State Guard (MSG) in August 1861, and was later elected colonel of the 6th Infantry Regiment, 7th Division, MSG. Freeman was elected to the Confederate Congress on October 31, 1861, at the Cassville Session of the Confederate Missouri State Legislature, but never served. During Price's retreat from Springfield in early 1862, Freeman was captured at Crane Creek, Missouri, on February 14, while serving as the rear guard.

Freeman was sent first to Myrtle Street Prison in St. Louis, then to Alton Prison in Illinois on March 3, 1862. He was paroled on June 18, and exchanged on September 23. Freeman returned to Missouri and raised a Partisan Ranger regiment, which was organized in March 1863. During the remainder of 1863, Freeman conducted operations in southern Missouri. His command was located in eastern Arkansas on January 26, 1864, when it was reorganized and Freeman was elected colonel. Of the regiment, one local resident of northeast Arkansas noted that, "They are very rough looking customers." A strong disciplinarian, Freeman personally shot two of his men for "marauding" during Price's Missouri Expedition.

Freeman was "badly wounded" at Fitzhugh Woods, near Augusta, Arkansas, on April 1, 1864, but recovered and continued operating in eastern Arkansas. With the arrival of General J. O. Shelby in May 1864, Freeman's unit was attached to Shelby's command on May 27. On July 16, 1864, Shelby put Freeman at the head of a small brigade, numbering 700 effective men, composed of his own regiment, E. T. Fristoe's Regiment and B. Ford's Battalion—all Missourians. During Price's 1864 Missouri Raid, General Price declared Freeman "a brave and energetic officer," who provided "brilliant services" while leading a brigade in Marmaduke's Cavalry Division.

At the end of Price's Raid, Freeman returned to eastern Arkansas, where he remained until he was paroled on June 5, 1865, at Jacksonport. Freeman became a lawyer, initially practicing in Arkansas. Later he moved to Shannon County, Missouri, then to Rolla, and finally settled in Waddill, Newton County, where he owned a farm and was the prosecuting attorney for the county. He died at his daughter's house, in Tiff City, McDonald County, Missouri, on February 28, 1893, and was buried in Neosho.[5]

* * * * * * *

---

5. *O.R.*, vol. 8:269; *O.R.*, vol. 34, pt. 4:632; *O.R.*, vol. 41 pt. 1:640; *O.R.S.*, pt. 2, vol. 31:749; *O.R.S.*, pt. 2, vol. 35.301; *O.R.S.*, pt. 3, vol. 1·605; Allardice, *Confederate Colonels*, 153; Bartels, *Trans-Mississippi Men*, 167; Coleman Letters (October 27, 1909 and November 20, 1914); Dyer, 800; Eakin, *Missouri Prisoners of War*, "Freeman, Thos. R." entry; Edwards, *Shelby and His Men*, 317–318; Ingenthron, 96, 318 (n. 9); Mobley, 160, 176, 195; National Archives, Record Group M322 (roll no. 68), Confederate Compiled Service Records, Freeman's Missouri Cavalry Regiment; Peterson, et al., 201, 206; Schnetzer, *More Forgotten Men*, 85; Wright, *General Officers*, 170.

Charles Harrison

Charles, or Charley, Harrison was born in New York (Eakin & Hale say Arkansas), in the later 1820s or early 1830s, and moved west to Utah. Following a reported affair with one of Brigham Young's wives, Harrison fled Utah in 1859 and settled in Denver where he established himself as a "gambler and gunman," who owned the "Criterion gambling hall." Duane Smith describes Harrison as a "suave and dapper gambler...the dime-novel image of the western gambler and gunfighter" that visiting easterners could expect to find in his Criterion establishment. John Edwards recorded that Harrison was "a tall, swarthy, extremely silent, uncommunicative man," who was expert with the revolver.

Harrison sided with the Confederacy at the start of the Civil War, and his gambling hall became the rallying point for sympatric Southerners. Following an incident there, Harrison was placed on trial for "assaulting a Union sentry," convicted, levied a $5,000 dollar fine, and forced to leave Denver under a threat of death. If he did not leave Denver, the 1st Colorado Cavalry threatened to destroy the Criterion by cannon fire. Harrison quickly sold his establishment and departed Denver on September 19, 1861, taking the 7:00 a.m. stage. Heading eastward Harrison joined William Quantrill in March 1862 "at a place called Wellington," which was located seven miles west of Independence, Missouri, on the Missouri River.

Harrison became a captain under Quantrill, was wounded at Pink Hill, Missouri, on June 11, 1862, recovered quickly, and was next noted in Kansas on July 27–28, 1862, when with two companions, he robbed three Mexicans en route for Olathe, Kansas. Later the same day, Harrison also robbed the local sheriff. Pursued by a 30-man party, led by the disgruntled sheriff, Harrison's group was caught, and in the ensuing gunfight, Harrison's two companions were mortally wounded or captured, while Harrison escaped, though wounded in the leg. Following his recovery, Harrison continued his guerrilla activities, and was wounded yet again on October 6, near Sibley, Missouri, in an engagement with the 5th MSM Cavalry.[6]

On November 6, Harrison headed south with Quantrill. He later left the guerrilla chief and joined Emmett MacDonald's Cavalry Regiment, commanding what

---

6. Bartels & Toms have Harrison wounded at Sibley, Missouri, in June 1862, along with Richard Childs, but make no mention of an engagement at Pink Hill. The *Official Records* has no engagement taking place in or near Sibley, in June 1862, save the capture of some suspected guerrillas. John Edwards has Harrison attacking Sibley in the summer of 1862, but gives no specific date. In attacking Sibley, Edwards has Harrison commanding 60 men and being repulsed by Union troops who are in the various buildings of the town. Harrison in turn suffered severe losses of six dead and 37 wounded at Sibley. Further, Edwards has Harrison wounded at Pink Hill, but gives no date; however a reading of the *Official Records* seems to put the date at June 11, 1862. In all likelihood, the Sibley attack that Bartels & Toms and Edwards refer to occurred in October 1862, after which Harrison proceeded south with Quantrill's band. *O.R.*, vol. 22 pt. 1:120–121, 131–132; Carolyn Bartels & Janice Toms, "Charles 'Ki' Harrison," in Duncan E. Hansen *A Reunion in Death: Grave Sites of the Men Who Rode With William Clarke Quantrill* 3 vols.(Independence, MO, 2002), 3:91, hereafter cited as Bartels & Toms; Edwards, *Noted Guerrillas*, 121–122, 125–126, 312–314.

became Company A, 10th Missouri Cavalry. Harrison subsequently fought at Prairie Grove, where he was praised for his performance, after which he resigned on January 15, 1863 to pursue his idea of a Colorado Expedition.

General T. H. Holmes (John Edwards and Lankford say it was T. C. Hindman) commissioned Harrison a colonel with authority to organize a brigade of troops from the Colorado Territory, many of whom had fled Missouri to avoid Union Militia duty. Departing Missouri in mid-May 1862, Harrison led his ill-fated expedition westward toward Colorado. Unfortunately, Harrison was killed on May 15, 1862, near the confluence of the Verdigris and Elk Rivers, during an engagement with the Little and Great Osages. Harrison was then beheaded along with his men, their heads displayed on a pole at the Indian village, minus their scalps, except for Harrison who was bald. Instead, Harrison's black beard "was scalped" from his face as an added Indian trophy.

Warner Lewis, one of the two survivors of the expedition, wrote that Harrison's "entire life had been spent upon the western plains, and he had been a protégé of...Kit Carson. He was tall, athletic, and almost as brown as an Indian, of whose blood he was said to have a mixture. He "knew no fear and he staggered no hardship." Bat Masterson, famous western gunfighter, also knew Harrison, calling him "'the most brilliant pistol handler I ever saw and a far more deadly shot than most of the famous gunfighters.'"[7]

* * * * * * *

Samuel B. Maxey

Samuel Bell Maxey was born on March 30, 1825, at Tompkinsville, in Monroe County, Kentucky. He was admitted to West Point on July 1, 1842, graduated in 1846 (number 48 of 49), and was assigned to duty with the 7th U.S. Infantry. Maxey fought in the Mexican War, where he was breveted a 1st lieutenant in the 8th U.S. Infantry "for gallant and meritorious conduct for the Battles of Contreras and Churubusco," August 19–20, 1847. After the surrender of Mexico City, Maxey was appointed provost marshal of one of five military districts of Mexico City by General Winfield Scott.

Following the Mexican War, Maxey was stationed at Jefferson Barracks, in St. Louis, but became bored with the duty and resigned from the army on September 17, 1849. He returned to Kentucky, settling in Clinton County, where he married in 1853, earned a law degree, and relocated to Paris, Texas, in 1857, opening there a law firm with his father.

Personally and politically, Maxey was a Whig-Democrat and he ran for office

---

7. *O.R.*, vol. 22, pt. 1:59, 131; *O.R.S.*, pt. 2, vol. 38:254; Abel, 237–238; Banasik, *Cavaliers of the Brush*, 144; Bartels & Toms, 3:91–92, 96–97; "Bushwhacking," *The Kansas State Journal*, August 4, 1862; Eakin & Hales, 193; Hale, *Branded As Rebels, Volume 2*, 135; Editor comment, *Leavenworth Daily Conservative*, July 30, 1862; Edwards, *Noted Guerrillas*, 121–123, 126–127; Gregg, 38–39; Josephy, 293; Lankford, 92–93; Lewis, 228–229, 231–232; Nichols, *Guerrilla Warfare in Missouri, 1862*, 44, 93, 207–208; Smith, *Birth of Colorado*, 20–21, 135, 146–147.

Samuel B. Maxey

in the Texas Senate, even as Texas seceded from the Union. Maxey did not take his seat in the Texas Senate (his father replaced him there), preferring to enter the army. Initially, he organized the Lamar Rifles, of which he was elected captain on May 25, 1861. Later, the Lamar Rifles was organized with nine other companies on November 26, 1861, to form the 9th Texas Infantry, with Maxey appointed colonel of the regiment.

Maxey was sent to the east side of the Mississippi River and was promoted to brigadier general on March 4, 1862. He served in the Western Department until August 18, 1863, when he was ordered to report to the Trans-Mississippi, to serve under the command of his old comrade from Mexico, E. Kirby Smith. On December 11, 1863, Maxey was assigned command of the Indian Territory, a position he held 1865.

As commander in the Territory, Maxey "organized the Indians and earned their respect," according to Anne Bailey. He "was particularly careful that no race or color line should be drawn in determining the ranking of others." During the Camden Expedition, Maxey led a cavalry division at Poison Springs, where the Confederates captured a Federal train. Kirby Smith promoted Maxey to major general, effective April 18, 1864, for his performance at Poison Springs, though he was never confirmed in that grade by the Confederate government. On February 21, 1865, Maxey was replaced as commander in the Indian Territory by Douglas H. Cooper. Maxey in turn was given command of a dismounted cavalry division, a position he held until the end of the war.

Following his resignation/parole on May 26, 1865, Maxey returned to Paris, Texas, and resumed his law practice. He was elected to the U.S. Senate in 1874 and served two terms (1875–1887). While in the Senate "he efficiently served on the committees on Territories, on Military Operations, on Education and Labor, and was chairman of the committee on Post Offices." He also authored a bill "asserting" the passage of railroads through the Indian Territory. Noted as an "eloquent" speaker, Maxey proved a strong advocate "on behalf of dealing fairly with the Indians." In 1887, he was defeated for reelection, and returned to Paris and his law practice.

Eight years after leaving the Senate, Maxey died at Eureka Springs, Arkansas, on August 16, 1895, following "a period of declining health." His body was returned to Paris for burial.[8]

* * * * * * *

Thomas H. McCray

Thomas Hamilton McCray was born near Jonesborough, in Washington County, Tennessee, in 1828. He lived there and in Georgia and Arkansas before moving to Texas in 1856, where he was a manufacturer in Tellico, Ellis County. Just prior to the Civil War, McCray moved back to Arkansas, settling in Wittsburg, near the St. Francis River, where he opened a mill. He married twice.

At the beginning of the Civil War, McCray joined Company F, 5th Arkansas Infantry, as 1st lieutenant. He was appointed adjutant of the regiment on July 20, 1861, and remained in that position after the regiment was transferred to Confederate service on July 27, 1861. In December 1861, McCray resigned from the 5th Arkansas shortly after the regiment was transferred to Bowling Green, Kentucky. He was appointed mustering officer for General William J. Hardee and returned to Arkansas to carry out a new recruiting assignment in Pocahontas. In time McCray organized "McCray's Infantry Battalion," of which he was elected major on January 25, 1862, and then lieutenant colonel. McCray's Battalion eventually became the 31st Arkansas Regiment on May 27, 1862, the date of his promotion to colonel.

McCray led a brigade at Richmond, Kentucky, on August 30, 1862, where his division commander praised him "highly" for the "gallantry and coolness" that he displayed on the battlefield. General E. Kirby Smith subsequently recommended McCray for general officer and "it appears," according to Bruce Allardice, that Dandridge McRae received the promotion by mistake. However, Marcus J. Wright recorded in *Arkansas in the War*, that McCray was eventually promoted and ranked a brigadier general from November 3, 1863.

Following the consolidation of the 31st Arkansas in the summer of 1863, McCray returned to Arkansas, but not before a trip

Thomas H. McCray

---

8. *O.R.S.*, pt. 2, vol. 68:722, 725, 727–729, 731–734; Anne Bailey, "Samuel Bell Maxey," in *Confederate General*, 4:171–172; Boatner, 520–521; Cunningham, 133; Faust, 481–482; Heidler, "Maxey, Samuel Bell," in *Encyclopedia of the Civil War*, 1267–1268; Heitman, 1:698; Roberts, *Texas, Confederate Military History*, 246–248; J. Elden Spencer, "Samuel Bell Maxey," in *Ten More Texans In Gray*, 59–61, 64, 67–68; Simpson, 86–87; Warner, *Generals in Gray*, 216.

to the Confederate capital. McCray met with J. A. Seddon, the Secretary of War, and proposed to raise a force in northeast Arkansas to interdict the Mississippi River. Seddon left the decision as to McCray's plan with General Smith, who saw merit in McCray's suggestion.

McCray returned to Arkansas in August 1863, began his recruitment, and within a short period of time had several thousand men answering his call. His new command was noted as being present during Steele's advance on Little Rock in August 1863, but apparently took no part as it was still organizing. By January 1864, McCray's command was actively engaged in northeast Arkansas, where it remained until the arrival of Joe Shelby. When Shelby arrived in the Batesville area, he found the various area commanders cooperative with his efforts to organize northeast Arkansas. Of McCray, Shelby declared the Arkansan to be "a brave, energetic, intelligent officer, one who is willing to work and willing to fight."

With the Iron Brigade protecting northeast Arkansas, McCray successfully trained and organized his command, consisting of Milton Baber's and Lee Crandall's Arkansas Regiments with Timothy Reeve's Missouri Regiment. In time, John Edwards recorded that the brigade "acted admirably...and gave evidence of future firmness and soldierly bearing," though he personally believed that McCray was "unenterprising." McCray led his brigade during Price's 1864 Missouri Raid and then again in northeast Arkansas for the remainder of the war until he surrendered the brigade in Jacksonport on June 5, 1865.

According to the *Arkansas Historical Quarterly*, McCray was promoted to brigadier general on November 7, 1863, though official sources have him as a colonel to the end of the war. Following the war, McCray fled briefly to Mexico and returned to Wittsburg in 1870, where he returned to farming. He later became a traveling salesman and died in Chicago on October 19, 1891. McCray was buried in the Cook County Cemetery at Dunning in an unmarked "potter's field" grave site."[9]

* * * * * * *

William H. Parsons

William Henry Parsons, a man who, according to a member of his regiment never received credit for the acts he performed, was born on April 23, 1826, in New Jersey, near Elizabeth. At an early age, Parsons's family relocated to Montgomery, Alabama, where his father opened a grocery store (or a shoe factory, according to Allardice). While still in his teens, Parsons attended Emory College in Oxford, Georgia, some 40 miles east of Atlanta. At the age of 18, Parsons left

---

9. *O.R.*, vol. 8:685; *O.R.*, vol. 16, pt. 1:934, 941; *O.R.*, vol. 22, pt. 1:964–965, 1081–1082; *O.R.*, vol. 34, pt. 4:670; *O.R.S.*, pt. 2, vol. 2:360, 362, 734; Allardice, *Confederate Colonels*, 261; Allardice, *More Generals In Gray*, 158–159; Brock, "Confederate Roster," *SHSP*, vol. 2:399; Edwards, *Shelby and His Men*, 358; Harrell, *Arkansas, Confederate Military History, Extended*, 529–530; Harrell, *Arkansas, Confederate Military History*, 290; Mobley, 130–131, 150, 204–205; Morrow, 244–245; Sifakis, *Arkansas*, 79, 114–115, 124–125; Marcus J. Wright, *Arkansas In the War 1861–1865* (Batesville, AR, 1963), 68.

school, contrary to his father's wishes, and journeyed to Natchitoches, Louisiana, where he joined the 2nd U.S. Dragoons of Zachary Taylor's army, which was bound for Texas.

After the Mexican War, Parsons settled near Tyler, Texas, where he farmed and edited the *Tyler Telegraph*. He married in 1851 and bought the *Telegraph* in 1852, later selling the newspaper and moving to Johnson County in 1855, to Hill County in 1858, and to Waco in 1859. A lawyer by 1860, Parsons founded the *Southwest* in Waco, a pro-Southern newspaper that advocated reopening the slave trade in the United States.

With the beginning of the Civil War, Governor Edward Clark appointed Parsons a colonel and aide-de-camp on June 10, 1861, and authorized him to raise a

William H. Pasrons

regiment. Laboring through the summer months, Parsons's regiment was officially organized on September 11, 1861, at Rocket Springs, Texas, with Parsons elected colonel. On October 28, 1861, near Hempstead, Texas, the 12th Texas Cavalry (originally known as the 4th Texas Dragoons or 4th Texas Cavalry) was mustered into the Confederate Service.

The 12th Texas languished about Texas through the winter of 1861–1862, anxiously awaiting orders. Finally in March 1862, the regiment headed north, with Little Rock as its ultimate destination. Parsons's command played an important role in holding Little Rock in the spring and summer of 1862, during which time Parsons "highly distinguished" "himself, his regiment and his State all over with glory." As the 1862 Campaign wore on Parsons was appointed a brigade commander, a position he held off-and-on for the remainder of the war.

One of Parsons's men wrote:

> As a horseman I can say he had no superior in the Confederate army; proud, well equipped, he looked a very knight of chivalry; brave and a commanding voice, which could be heard above the din of battle; his white plume could always be seen in the front of battle; with true military genius he was always quick to take advantage of the enemy's mistake; resolute and self-confident and confident of the valor of his men, he often turned what seemed to be defeat into victory.

During the spring of 1863, Parsons operated along the Mississippi River, where his actions were given "no credit," according to one member of the 12th

Texas. During that summer Parsons led a raid on the Mississippi River, breaking up the Federal plantations in western Louisiana and capturing 1,000 slaves. By 1864 Parsons was back in Texas to fend off a potential Union invasion, which never occurred. Called to action in Louisiana, Parsons led a brigade during the Red River Expedition, where he "exhibited courage, energy and perseverance worth the highest praise," according to Richard Taylor. At Yellow Bayou on May 18, Parsons's Brigade fought its last major engagement of the war, suffering its highest losses during the conflict, in 81 killed, wounded and missing. Following the Red River Expedition, Parsons spent the remainder of the war patrolling southwest Arkansas, until shortages of forage forced his command back to Texas, where it remained until the end of the war.

Although he was never officially promoted to general officer, the *Southern Historical Society Papers* listed Parsons as a brigadier general or acting general. As a wartime commander, B. P. Gallaway wrote of Parsons:

> Certainly the commander of the Twelfth Texas Cavalry looked and acted like the western Confederacy's answer to Napoleon Bonaparte. He possessed a contagious confidence and swashbuckling presence that thrilled those around him...[H]e had both the bearing and experience of a born leader. To look at Parsons, decked out in his brass buttons and black hat with white plume, one could see marvelously uniformed soldiers marching into battle amid brilliantly colored flags to the accompaniment of drum rolls and bugle calls....To see Parsons, therefore was to see his regiment.

At the end of the war, Parsons assembled his men one last time, telling them of his intentions of moving to Senora, Mexico. Those that wished to join him should meet him in 60 days for the journey. When Parsons left the States, instead of Mexico he moved to British Honduras. He stayed but a short time and returned to Texas, settling in Houston, where he became a Republican active in railroad promotions, newspapers and politics, and winning election to the Texas Senate (1869–1871). Parsons left Texas in the 1880s and spent the following years living in either Baltimore or New York, where he practiced law or sold real estate. At the time of his death on October 2, 1907, Parsons was living in Chicago.[10]

* * * * * * *

---

10. *O.R.*, vol. 4:95; *O.R.*, vol. 13:38; *O.R.S.*, pt. 1: vol. 6:343, 351; *O.R.S.*, pt. 2, vol. 67:854, 858; Allardice, *Confederate Colonels*, 299; Allardice, *More Generals in Gray*, 177–179; Bailey, 5–7, 15, 47; Brock, "Confederate Roster," *SHSP*, vol. 2:380–381; "The Campaign in Arkansas," *San Antonio Herald* (San Antonio, TX), August 9, 1862; Gallaway, 13–14, 20, 29–30, 33; "Lee's Lieutenants," *SHSP*, vol. 17:426; "Living Generals of the Confederate States Army," *SHSP*, vol. 20:38; Soldat, "Letter from Arkansas," *The Tri-Weekly Telegraph* (Houston, TX), June 3, 1863; Wooster, *Lone Star Generals*, 245; Wooster, *Lone Star Regiments*, 184–185, 188–190, 192, 324.

John F. Rucker

John Flemming Rucker was born near Lynchburg, Virginia, on September 19, 1838, and later moved to Missouri, where he lived in Rocheport, Boone County. He married in June 1853 and was established as a merchant at the beginning of the Civil War. He joined the 3rd Division, MSG, on May 14, 1861, as a member of the Boone County Sturgeon Invincibles, and was elected 2nd lieutenant of his company a week later. Transferring to the Washington Blues, of the 8th Division, MSG, prior to the formation of his regiment, Rucker transferred yet again, prior to the Battle of Wilson's Creek, becoming the 2nd lieutenant of Company D (Bartels says Company A), 1st Infantry Regiment, 3rd Division, MSG on June 14.

Rucker fought at Carthage (July 5, 1861) and Wilson's Creek, where he was wounded. Appointed a captain and Adjutant of the 6th Infantry Regiment, 3rd Division, MSG, on September 21, Rucker fought at Lexington and on November 5, 1861, was elected major of 1st Infantry Regiment, 3rd Division, MSG. At the Battle of Pea Ridge, Rucker commanded his regiment, "was seriously wounded and behaved with great gallantry." Captured at the close of the battle, by the 3rd Iowa Cavalry, Rucker was sent to Springfield, and forwarded to St. Louis on July 7, 1862. Rucker escaped from Gratiot Prison and returned to Boone County, where he began guerrilla style operations and recruited for the Confederacy.

Rucker returned to Ft. Smith, Arkansas and entered the Confederate Service as a major on November 5, 1862. He headed back to Missouri following the Battle of Prairie Grove, but was captured near Linn Creek, Camden County, on January 6, 1863. Sent to Gratiot Prison, Rucker escaped with four other officers (Captains John Stemmons, Harvey Rucker, Robert Maupin, and John Stevenson) on March 13, 1863.

Rucker linked up with S. D. Jackman in Howard County, helped capture General T. Bartholow on April 23, 1863, but later, according to Jackman, betrayed his commander when he unwittingly brought a spy into the guerrillas' camp, resulting in Jackman's wounding on June 18. In later years Jackman believed that Rucker should have been shot for his actions, in failing to identify the spy or assuming command of Jackman's band while Jackman was recovering.

Rucker headed south in September 1863, crossed the Missouri River on September 7, and was cornered by the Federals in Callaway County, a short distance from St. Aubert. Wounded and captured on September 8, Rucker was confined in Jefferson City until he was paroled to Boone County in February 1864. Not fully recovered from his wound, and apparently violating his parole, Rucker had his parole vacated in early June 1864, and was rearrested on June 4.

Rucker spent the remainder of the war in either Gratiot or Alton Prisons. On March 11, 1865, he was again paroled in St. Louis, to serve as an agent for the Confederate government in the distribution of clothing for the inmates of Alton.

Rucker was allowed to return to Boone County in July 1865. He died there on December 28, 1889, in Sturgeon.[11]

* * * * * * *

Richard Waterhouse

Waterhouse was born in Rhea County, Tennessee, on January 12, 1832. He ran away from home to fight in the Mexican War with his father, joining the Tennessee Mounted Volunteers and later the 4th Tennessee Infantry, at the age of 14. Returning home in 1848, Waterhouse moved with his family to Texas the following year, settling in St. Augustine. The young Waterhouse entered the "mercantile business" with his father, married, and had two sons. By the time of the Civil War, the Waterhouse family owned 52 slaves and was worth an estimated $117,300 dollars, ranking as one of the richest families in Texas. On December 31, 1863, the elder Waterhouse was murdered in his store, leaving the family business to his son.

At the beginning of the Civil War, Waterhouse began organizing the 19th Texas Infantry near Jefferson, Texas at Edler's Plantation. The last units were mustered into the Confederate Service on May 10, 1862, and Waterhouse was elected colonel on May 13. The 19th began its march to Little Rock in June 1862, arriving sometime in the latter part of September or early October 1862. Shortly after their arrival they were placed into what became the 3rd Brigade, Walker's Texas Division on October 7, 1862.

Waterhouse's regiment saw its first action at Millikin's Bend, Louisiana, on June 7, 1863. Joseph Blessington, of the 16th Texas, called Waterhouse "gallant and brave" for how he led the 19th Texas. General Henry McCulloch also called Waterhouse gallant, "charging over the levees and entirely through the enemy's camp." McCulloch was so impressed with Waterhouse he added, "from beginning to end of

Richard Waterhouse

---

11. *O.R.*, vol. 8:235, 319; *O.R.*, vol. 53:426; Bartels. *Forgotten Men*, 316; Bartels, *Trans Mississippi Men*, 25, 35; Eakin, *Confederate Records*, 6:197–198; Eakin, *Missouri Prisoners of War*, "Rucker, Jno. F, Major," 3 entries; Griffin Frost, *Camp and Prison Journal* (Quincy, IL; 1867; reprint ed., Iowa City, IA, 1994), 36–37, 230, cited hereafter as Frost; Hale, *Branded As Rebels, Volume 2*, 280; *History of Howard and Cooper Counties*, 273; Mary Jackman, 94; Norton, 151, 170–172, 176–177; Nichols, *Guerrilla Warfare, Volume III*, 414 (n. 1); Peterson, et al., 113, 116, 126, 128, 183; Schnetzer, *More Forgotten Men*, 199; Wood, *Noted Guerrillas*, 195–197, 200, 205–208, 2310, 278 (n.1).

the engagement, the colonel behaved in the most gallant manner, and his officers and men seemed to catch the enthusiasm of their commander, and did their duty nobly and gallantly upon every portion of the field."

The 19th remained inactive for the rest of 1863, but entered the Red River Campaign in March 1864. Waterhouse led his command at Mansfield on April 8 and again at Pleasant Hill, where he was instrumental in preventing "confusion on the right from becoming disastrous." Of his performance the *Houston Daily Telegraph* reported that "Col. Waterhouse by his gallantry, has extorted the praise of all his competitors in the race for freedom or the grave." Among those "competitors" was Colonel Overton Young, who recorded that Waterhouse was "the most dashing of us all."

Pleasant Hill proved to be high point of Waterhouse's military career. General Scurry, commanding the brigade, spoke "highly" of Colonel Waterhouse to General Richard Taylor, who in turn noted Waterhouse's name in his official report. This in turn led to Waterhouse's promotion to brigadier general by E. Kirby Smith, on May 13, 1864, "to date from April 30, 1864, subject to the approval of the President." The Confederate Senate approved the promotion on March 18, 1865, the last day they were in secession.

At Jenkins' Ferry, following the wounding of General Scurry, Waterhouse took command of the brigade. He remained the brigade commander until the final surrender, after which he fled briefly to Mexico. Waterhouse returned home to Texas where he became a land speculator. On March 18, 1876, while visiting Waco, Waterhouse fell down some stairs, which was probably caused by the pneumonia from which he was suffering at the time, and broke his arm. He died two days later and his body was returned to Jefferson, where he was buried.

As a regimental commander, Ralph Wooster recorded that Waterhouse was "one of the better" ones; however, he only rated him as an "average" general officers, but caveated the rating stating— "given greater opportunities he may have shown superior talents."[12]

* * * * * * *

John A. Wharton

John Austin Wharton was born on July 3, 1828 (*The Houston Daily Telegraph* and H. P. Simpson have the date as July 5, 1829), near Nashville, Tennessee. He was originally named Edwin Waller Wharton, after a friend of his father. Edwin's parents had previously settled in Texas on Oyster Creek, Brazoria County, and were visiting Tennessee at the time of John's birth. In 1838, Edwin's uncle

---

12. *O.R.*, vol. 24, pt. 2:467; *O.R.*, vol. 34, pt. 1:568; *O.R.S.*, pt. 1, vol. 4:421; *O.R.S.*, pt. 2, vol. 69:15, 20, 22–23; Bailey, "Richard Waterhouse," in *Confederate General*, 6:108–109; Banasik, *Confederate Tales, 1863*, 179; Blessington, 45–46, 54, 58, 97; Faust, 807; G. A. F., Letter (April 10, 1864) to H. P. (High Private), in *Houston Daily Telegraph*, April 20, 1864; Heitman, 2:71; Letters (June 29, 1862 and September 23, 1862), Copy Letter Book No. 1; Lowe, 56; Roberts, *Texas, Confederate Military History*, 258–259; Warner, *Generals in Gray*, 326–327, 397 (n. 512); Wooster, *Lone Star Generals*, 4–5, 7, 170–172, 237–238.

John A. Wharton

died of a fever that was sweeping Texas, at which time Edwin's name was changed to John Austin Wharton, in honor of his uncle.

Educated locally and by private tutors, John attended South Carolina College (known today as the University of South Carolina), from 1846–1850, where he "graduated with distinction." While attending college he was chosen as commandant of cadets and met his future wife, Penelope Johnson, daughter of the South Carolina governor. Following college Wharton returned to Texas to manage the family plantation, which he had inherited following the death of his father in 1839.

Wharton married in 1854 (Simpson has it as 1848) and was an accomplished lawyer. He was elected district attorney for the 1st Judicial District of Texas in 1859, in addition to being a wealthy planter worth $236,950, including 133 slaves. "As an orator of great power and a debater of knowledgeable ability he occupied a prominent position at the bar." Wharton was interested in politics, prior to the war, but never ran for greater public office, preferring to remain in the background, opposing "efforts by Northerners to place restrictions upon the instruction of slavery." With the coming of the Secession Crisis, Wharton was chosen to represent his county at the Texas Secession Convention.

Following secession, Wharton raised a company and assisted in the capture of the Federal forces that were stationed in Texas at the beginning of the conflict. Following this first mission, he took a ship to New Orleans to purchase weapons for his company, but was captured by a Federal ship on his way back to Texas, returned to New Orleans, and threatened with imprisonment if he failed to take the Oath of Allegiance to the United States. Wharton refused to take the oath saying to his captors "'to Key West forever!'" Detained for two weeks, Wharton was finally released as no weapons had been found on board the schooner, since he had thrown them overboard prior to his capture.

By the time Wharton had returned to Texas, Fort Sumter had been fired upon. He actively recruited what became Company B, 8th Texas Cavalry (Terry's Texas Rangers). The company was mustered on September 7, 1861, and later moved to Bowling Green, Kentucky, where it began active service. In the fall of 1861, Wharton "was seriously impaired by a severe case of the measles, which entirely unfitted him for duty for several weeks."

At its first battle, at Woodville, Kentucky, on December 17, 1861, the regiment's colonel was killed, and on January 9, 1862, the new commander of the regiment died of typhoid fever. Wharton was elected colonel of the 8th Texas, effective January 9 (Simpson has the date as June 13, 1862), and led his regiment, a brigade, or a division for the remainder of his time east of the Mississippi River.

Wharton headed his regiment at the Battle of Shiloh, Tennessee (April 6–7, 1862), where he was wounded in the leg, and cited for his gallantry by General W. J. Hardee. While he recovered from his wound,

> His political friends in Texas were so delighted with his dashing military record, they determined to send him to the Confederate Congress...But his mother...acted on his behalf, and in a card to the public said that she knew the blood that was in her son's veins, that her heart was in full sympathy with his, and that there was no political honor within the gift of the people of Texas, or all the seceding States, that could induce him to lay aside his arms until success was assured.

During the Confederate invasion of Kentucky, Wharton was praised for his actions at Perryville (October 8, 1862) and was subsequently promoted to brigadier general on November 18, 1862. At Stones River, Tennessee (December 31, 1862–January 3, 1863), Wharton "pre-eminently distinguished" himself, commanding a brigade, which General Braxton Bragg labeled "invincible," by capturing over 2,000 prisoners, a battery of artillery, and "destroying a large number of wagons loaded with Government stores." At the Battle of Chickamauga (September 19–20, 1863), Wharton led a division, after which he was promoted to major general, to rank from November 10, 1863, following yet another gallant operation.

In early 1864, following a "long exposure and duty, labor and fatigue...[that had] seriously impaired his constitution and unfitted for longer service in the arduous duties of the cavalry," Wharton requested a transfer to the Trans-Mississippi and went back to Texas in April 1864. With his arrival in the Trans-Mississippi Department, Chaplain R. F. Bunting, of the 8th Texas Cavalry gave an introduction of his old commander to the people of Texas, which read in part:

> In four pitched battles and over two hundred cavalry engagements, he has borne himself as a gallant soldier, a skillful and cool officer, ever leading where bullets flew thickest...In reaching this proud position step by step, he has been guided by a single aim as a soldier; toward this he has directed all the energies of his cultivated mind with a fixedness of purpose that could never brook even partial defeat. That aim was an unflinching determination to distinguish himself in serving his country against a foe whom he despised, and by unwavering devotion to duty and fidelity in its discharge...
>
> He has been a General of Cavalry...Although not known by the press to the extent others who have less merit, but by his true worth, his great genius and unrivaled courage, which have found a development in the long marches, the wary vigils, the weary retreats and the victorious encounters that have marked the progress of the Army of Tennessee, he has elevated himself to his present honorable position, and has created for himself a

name and fame that will ever be cherished by those who have followed him...

His brilliant military record has already become a prominent part in the history of his country. May his career in his native Texas be as successful, honorable and glorious as it has been with the army of Tennessee.

Following the death of Tom Green at Blair's Ferry on April 12, Wharton was assigned to command Green's old corps. Wharton's command pursued and harassed Nathaniel Banks's Union army as it retreated back to New Orleans. On May 18, at Yellow Bayou, Wharton fought his last major engagement in the war, and lost, suffering over 600 casualties. Of Wharton's performance during the Red River Campaign, Richard Taylor wrote:

> Major-General Wharton, commanding the Cavalry Corps, has fully sustained the high reputation which he now [exhibits] in the campaign of the Army of Tennessee, and by his skill, energy and indefatigable industry, [he] has gained fresh laurels. I cannot too highly commend his valuable services.

For the remainder of the war Wharton's command operated in either southeast Arkansas or western Louisiana and finished the war stationed in Texas. On April 6, 1865, following a confrontation with Colonel George W. Baylor at the Fannin hotel in Houston, Texas, Wharton was shot and killed. Wharton was remembered as "a tall, raw-boned, smooth shaven man, wearing a faded uniform without an insignia of rank, constantly engaged where there was fighting to be done." The death of J. A. Wharton was keenly felt with those who knew him, with one veteran writing: "In his death the Confederate army was deprived of an excellent officer, a gallant soldier, and a true gentleman."

George Baylor was charged with murder, but the end of the war complicated the proceedings. Finally tried three years later, the first trial resulted in a hung jury, while a second trial, six months later acquitted Baylor.[13]

* * * * * * *

David A. Williams

David A. Williams was born in Prince Edward County, Virginia, on October 19, 1832, moved to Missouri at an early age, where his family settled first in Livingston, then Mercer County. The son of a large land owner and slave holder, Williams attended Grand River College in Grundy County, Missouri. At the beginning of the

---

13. *O.R.*, vol. 10, pt. 1:569, 670; *O.R.*, vol. 20, pt. 1:665; *O.R.*, vol. 30 pt. 2:19, 522; *O.R.*, vol. 34, pt. 2:943; *O.R.S.*, pt. 1, vol. 6:350; *O.R.S.*, pt. 2 vol. 67:790; Allardice, *Confederate Colonels*, 57, 246; Boatner, 909; R. F. Bunting, "Maj. Gen. Jno. A. Wharton," *Houston Daily Telegraph*, June 13, 1864; Faust, 817–818; E. Polk Johnson, "Some Generals I Have Known," *Southern Bivouac*, 6 vols. (reprint ed., Wilmington, NC, 1993), 4:120; Nunn, 163–164; Roberts, *Texas, Confederate Military History*, 261–263; Simpson, 17, 95, 180; Wooster, *Lone Star Generals*, 65–74.

Civil War, he was a married farmer, merchant, lawyer, and a veteran border ruffian, living in Grundy County.

On July 4, 1861, Williams joined Company A, 3rd Cavalry Regiment, 8th Division, MSG, and was elected 1st lieutenant (Note: Bartels and Peterson have the name as D. H. Williams). He was promoted to captain on September 20, 1861, and appointed regimental adjutant the same day; later, he became the brigade adjutant. Williams resigned on December 15, 1861, but rejoined the 8th Division on February 3, 1862, as adjutant of the 14th Cavalry Regiment.

Williams joined the Confederate Service on June 22, 1862, and was assigned to recruiting services in Missouri, thereafter returning to Arkansas on September 27. Williams was subsequently promoted to captain on January 27, 1863, commanding Company D, 6th Missouri Cavalry Regiment (CSA). During Price's 1864 Missouri Raid, Williams was detached to raise a new cavalry regiment, of which he was elected colonel. John Edwards wrote of Williams, he "was a splendid officer, devoted, intelligent, skilled, experienced and courageous."

Following the war, Williams fled to Mexico, but later returned to Arkansas, where he farmed in Chicot, Jefferson, and Desha Counties. It also appears that Williams returned briefly to Missouri, where he lived in Livingston County, the birthplace of his child Mary. In his final move, Williams relocated to Texas, settling in Dallas in 1876, where he was a lawyer and politician. He died on March 29, 1898, in Terrell, Texas.[14]

****

John I. Worthington

John I. Worthington was born on June 14, 1826, in Somerset County, Pennsylvania, ran away from home at the age of 11, and worked as a "canal boat driver" in western Pennsylvania. He captained his own boat by the age of 16. At 20 he enlisted in Company B, 2nd Pennsylvania Volunteer Regiment and participated in the Mexican War. Wounded in the arm on September 13, 1847, at the storming of Chapultepec, Worthington remained with his command during the entire day. By the end of the war, Worthington had been promoted to 1st lieutenant of his company.

He returned to Pennsylvania and married in 1848; unfortunately his wife died the following year. In the years following he held a variety of jobs, including train conductor, plantation overseer in Mississippi, and school teacher in Louisiana. Returning to Pennsylvania, Worthington remained but a short time and headed to California in 1854. He never made it, but settled instead in Carroll County, Arkansas, where he studied law and was admitted to the bar in 1855.

---

14. Allardice, *Confederate Colonels*, 397; Anonymous, *The Gallant Breed. The 6th Missouri Cavalry: A Roster of the Men Who Rode Under the Flag of Shelby's Iron Brigade* (Independence, MO: Two Trails Publishing, 2009), 69; Arthur, 66; Bartels, *Forgotten Men*, 392; Eakin, *Confederate Records*, 8:65; Edwards, *Shelby and His Men*, 508; National Archives, Record Group M322 (roll no. 44), Confederate Compiled Service Records, 6th. Missouri Cavalry; Peterson, et al., 243, 252–253, 283.

Worthington married a second time and moved to Granby, Missouri, where he established his law practice. With the coming of the secession debate in 1860–1861, Worthington rallied the local populace to form a company loyal to the Union. At the beginning of the war, he offered his services as a scout and guide to General Franz Sigel. Captured before the Battle of Carthage, Worthington was held as a spy, but was able to escape just prior to the Battle of Wilson's Creek on August 10, 1861. He then returned to Sigel's command and was wounded during the battle. Returning home to recover from his wounds, Worthington was viewed as a loyal rebel, having told everyone that he was wounded while fighting on the side of the Confederates; however he was just biding his time. On January 2, 1862, he departed home and headed to Ft. Scott, where he enlisted as a private in Company A, 6th Kansas Cavalry on January 7. The following day he was promoted to sergeant "and detailed to recruit for the regiment." On February 1, 1862, he was promoted to commissary sergeant. While with the 6th, Worthington participated in several scouts, seeking forage for the regiment, and was again wounded on March 2, 1862.

He returned to active service on June 1 and was slightly wounded during a running fight with Tom Livingston's guerrillas a short time later. Worthington left the 6th on July 21, 1862, to raise a company for 1st Arkansas Cavalry Regiment (Union). On August 7, 1862, Worthington was appointed captain of Company H, 1st Arkansas Cavalry Regiment.

While in the 1st Arkansas, Worthington participated in two major battles: Prairie Grove, where he was cited for "coolness and bravery and persistent efforts to rally the men," after his command had been routed from the field; and Fayetteville, on April 18, 1863. Overall, Worthington took part in numerous engagements with guerrillas, in which he was quite successful, including a scout in Carroll County (April 1863), skirmish at Fitzgerald or Gerald Mountain (August 29, 1863), skirmish Near Maysville on Round Prairie (September 5, 1863), scout from Fayetteville with "skirmishing nearly every day" (December 23–25, 1863), Richland Creek (December 25, 1863), Richland Creek (August 16, 1864), and Rogers Crossing (September 14, 1864) to name but a few.

Worthington was promoted to major with a date of rank February 28, 1865, but did not survive the war, being killed on March 11, 1865 (the *Official Records* has the date as March 13, 1865), 18 miles from Fayetteville near King's River, during an engagement with Cooper's command. Worthington's last words were "Go on, boys, and whip them; they have killed me."[15]

* * * * * * *

---

15. *O.R.*, vol. 22, pt. 1:249, 611–612, 779, 913; *O.R.*, vol. 41, pt. 1:261–263; *O.R.*, vol. 48. pt. 1:1168, 1185; *O.R.S.*, pt. 1, vol. 4:32–33; *O.R.S.*, pt. 2, vol. 2:32, 34, 41, 43; Allen, *Damned Yankees*, "Worthington, John I." entry; Bishop, *Report of Adjutant General*, 10, 37; Bishop, *Loyalty On the Frontier*, 29–35, 37–38, 41–44, 46–48, 50–51.

Richard F. "Dick" Yeager

Richard F. Yeager was born March 28, 1839, on a farm near present-day Grand View, Missouri. While in his teens his father "entrusted him with one of his...wagon trains and by 1860 [he] was making regular trips across the plains," freighting goods to various government installations from Fort Leavenworth.

At the beginning of the Civil War Yeager considered himself neutral, though his family had Southern sympathies. That changed in the latter part of 1861, however. Kansas Jayhawkers raided his father's farm and stripped it of over $10,000 dollars of goods and livestock, even though the elder Yeager was a loyal Union man. Following the raid, Dick Yeager initially joined Upton Hays's rebel home guard company and then Quantrill guerrillas, where he was listed as a member on the roster of July 16, 1862. With Quantrill, Yeager would win his reputation as a "young hero famed for dash and courage."

Little is known of Yeager's initial year as a guerrilla, save that he befriended George Todd and operated with him in 1862. On August 10, 1862, he enlisted in what became Company K, 12th Missouri Cavalry, after which he alternated between service as a regular Confederate soldier and a guerrilla. He was at Independence on August 11, 1862, according to one account, where he was wounded and out of action for several months. Leaving Missouri for Arkansas, Yeager rejoined the regular Confederate army, and was promoted to brevet 2nd lieutenant on November 26, 1862. Yeager was probably at Cane Hill on November 28, 1862, and Prairie Grove on December 7, 1862. Absent on sick furlough from December 10, Yeager returned to duty with Company K in February 1863.

Yeager returned to guerrilla operations in the spring of 1863, and was part of a band that raided Council Grove, Kansas, on May 4, 1863. Familiar with Council Grove area from his freighting days on the Santa Fe Road, Yeager stopped for a few hours in the town to have some teeth pulled. Heading back to Missouri, at a "leisurely" pace, Yeager's band robbed serval farms, and the passengers of the Santa Fe stagecoach, who contributed 14 horses and $1,300 dollars to the band. Next Yeager's party robbed the express agent at Gardner, Kansas, and "completely stripped the town." Of the raid the *Wyandotte Commercial Gazette* reported that Yeager's band "committed several murders, stole much property..., and are now back in their homes, in Jackson County, Mo." Yeager

Richard F. Yeager

next took part in the Lawrence Raid in August 1863, serving to guide the command out of Kansas after they had sacked the town.

During the winter of 1863–1864, Yeager returned to the 12th Missouri Cavalry, where he was reported as present on February 28, 1864. Yeager remained in the Camden, Arkansas, area with his command, until some time after March 17, when he headed back to Missouri, leading a squad of nine men (rumors at the time had Yeager already back in Kansas in February 1864). En route to Missouri, Yeager linked up with Captain F. W. Cooper's guerrilla band in northwest Arkansas. On May 3, 1864, Cooper and Yeager's combined forces dealt a devastating blow to the 2nd Arkansas Cavalry (Union) at Richland Creek in Newton County, where they killed 37 Federals, wounded 11 and captured three or more prisoners.

On June 11, near Kingsville, Missouri, Yeager rode with Bill Anderson and ambushed a party of Federals, killing 12 of their number, with only two escaping. Two days later Yeager attacked a detachment of the 2nd Colorado Cavalry commanded by Sergeant Major Martin Hennion, four miles southeast of Westport. Yeager scattered the Federals and captured their wagon, which he burned after taking three of their mules and all the goods. Less than a month later, on July 6, Yeager engaged a 26-man detachment of the 2nd Colorado at the Little Blue or "Gitner's Farm" in a "hand-to hand grapple," driving them from field and killing in the process the commander of the detachment, Captain Seymour Wagoner and seven of his men. Thirteen days later, Yeager was shot in the head and mortally wounded, while raiding Arrow Rock. Local doctors "gave him no hope of recovery; his brains were extruding from the wound's entry and exit in the cranium."

Yeager hid in the woods in northeast Saline County and was cared for by the Ike Flannery family until "a party of soldiers" found and killed him in early September 1864, according to William Goff (Eakin & Hale have the date as "about August 1, 1864"). Hansen says that the party of militia that found Yeager had no idea whom they had killed. John Edwards wrote of Dick Yeager: "It might be said of him that he lived literally with his revolver belt buckled. Pure as a child, simple, tranquil, he did everything possible for his country, nothing against her."[16]

* * * * * * *

---

16. *O.R.*, vol. 34, pt. 2:377, 447–448; *O.R.*, vol. 34, pt. 1:1001–1002; *O.R.*, vol. 41, pt. 1:48–49; *O.R.S.*, pt. 2, vol. 3:399; *O.R.S.*, pt. 2, vol. 38:262; Anonymous, *The Gallant Breed. The 12th Missouri Cavalry: A Roster of the Men Who Rode Under the Flag of Shelby's Iron Brigade* (Independence, MO: Two Trails Publishing, 2009), 99; O.S. Barton, *Three Years With Quantrill: A True Story Told by His Scout John McCorkle* (Armstrong, MO, 1914; reprint ed., Norman, OK, 1992), 127,155; Joanne Chiles Eakin, *Warren Welch Remembers: A Guerrilla Fighter from Jackson County, Missouri* (Independence, MO, 1997), 6; Eakin & Hale, 482–483; Edwards, *Noted Guerrillas*, 234; Goff, vol. 9:80–82; Goff, vol. 11:96, 101, 104–105, 109–112; Gregg, 88; Hansen, 2:191; "The Late Guerrilla Raid," *The Emporia News* (Emporia, KS), May 16, 1863; "The Late Raid," *Wyandotte Commercial Gazette*, May 16, 1863; Nichols, *Guerrilla Warfare, Volume II*, 119, 218; "Quantrill and His Famous Command," *Confederate Veteran* 18 (June, 1910), 279; Williams, *Second Colorados*, 52–53, 59–60.

Index to Previous Biographies

Found in *Missouri Brothers in Gray* (vol. 1), *Serving With Honor* (vol. 2), *Reluctant Cannoneer* (vol. 3), *Missouri in 1861* (vol. 4), *Cavaliers of the Brush* (vol. 5), *Duty, Honor and Country* (vol. 6), *Confederate "Tales of the War," Part One* (vol. 7), *Confederate "Tales of the War," Part Two* (vol. 7), *Confederate "Tales of the War," Part Three* (vol. 7), and *Confederate "Tales of the War," Part Four* (vol. 7).

Allen, Henry W.	vol. 7, pt. 4:144
Anderson, William	vol. 5, 173
Banks, Nathaniel P.	vol. 7, pt. 4:146
Bates, John Francis	vol. 4, 346
Bee, Hamilton P.	vol. 7, pt. 4:148
Black, John Charles	vol. 6, 441
Blair, Francis P.	vol. 7, pt. 1:183
Blunt, James G.	vol. 2, 273
Boudinot, Elias C.	vol. 7, pt. 2:167
Bowen, John S.	vol. 1, 135
Brent, Joseph L.	vol. 7, pt. 4:150
Brown, Egbert Benson	vol. 6, 442
Buchel, August C.	vol. 7, pt. 4:151
Burbridge, John Q.	vol. 3, 378
Canby, Edward Richard Sprigg	vol. 6, 444
Churchill, Thomas J.	vol. 7, pt. 3:161
Clark, Meriwether L.	vol. 7, pt. 2:168
Clark, John B., Jr.	vol. 3, 380
Clark, John B., Sr.	vol. 3, 382
Clarkson, James J.	vol. 7, pt. 1:184
Clayton, Powell	vol. 2, 278
Cloud, William F.	vol. 7, pt. 2:169
Coffee, John T.	vol. 7, pt. 2:170
Coleman, William O.	vol. 3, 383
Curtis, Samuel R.	vol. 2, 279
Dana, Napoleon J. T.	vol. 6, 446
Davidson, John W.	vol. 2, 281
DeBray, Xavier B.	vol. 7, pt. 4:152
Drayton, Thomas Fenwick	vol. 3, 385
Ewing, Thomas	vol. 5, 175
Fagan, James Flemming	vol. 3, 386

Foster, Emory S.	vol. 7, pt. 2:171
Fremont, John C.	vol. 1, 135
Frost, Daniel M.	vol. 1, 138
Green, Martin E.	vol. 4, 347
Green, Thomas	vol. 7, pt. 4:153
Greene, Colton	vol. 7, pt. 2:173
Gregg, William	vol. 5, 176
Grinsted, Hiram L.	vol. 7, pt. 4:158
Halleck, Henry Wager	vol. 4, 348
Harney, William S.	vol. 7, pt. 1:185
Harris, Thomas Alexander	vol. 4, 349
Hays, Upton	vol. 5, 178
Hebert, Louis	vol. 7, pt. 1:187
Herron, Francis J.	vol. 2, 283
Hindman, Thomas C.	vol. 1, 139
Holmes, Theophilus H.	vol. 1, 141
Jackman, Sidney D.	vol. 7, pt. 2:174
Jackson, Claiborne F.	vol. 4, 350
Kirkwood, Samuel J.	vol. 4, 352
Lane, James H.	vol. 2, 286
Lane, Walter P.	vol. 7, pt. 1:188
Lawther, Robert R.	vol. 7, pt. 3:162
Lewis, Levin Major	vol. 7, pt. 3:163
Little, Henry	vol. 7, pt. 2:175
Lyon, Nathaniel	vol. 4, 353
MacDonald, Emmett	vol. 1, 143
Marmaduke, John Sappington	vol. 1, 143
Major, James P.	vol. 7, pt. 4:159
McBride, James H.	vol. 3, 388
McCulloch, Ben	vol. 4, 356
McCulloch, Henry E.	vol. 7, pt. 3:165
McIntosh, James McQueen	vol. 6, 447
McKinstry, Justus	vol. 4, 358
McNeil, John	vol. 7, pt. 2:176
McRae, Dandridge	vol. 7, pt. 3:166
Mitchell, Charles S.	vol. 3, 390
Mouton, Alfred	vol. 7, pt. 4:159
Parsons, Mosby M.	vol. 1, 146

Polignac, Camille de	vol. 7, pt. 4:162
Pope, John	vol. 6, 449
Price, Edwin W.	vol. 7, pt. 2:178
Price, Sterling	vol. 1, 148
Quantrill, William C.	vol. 3, 391
Rains, James S.	vol. 7, pt. 1:190
Randal, Horace	vol. 7, pt. 4:164
Rust, Albert	vol. 7, pt. 2:179
Salomon, Frederick	vol. 2, 288
Schnable, John A.	vol. 3, 392
Schofield, John M.	vol. 4, 360
Scurry, William R.	vol. 7, pt. 4:166
Shaver, Robert G.	vol. 7, pt. 4:169
Shelby, Joseph O.	vol. 1, 150
Sigel, Franz	vol. 4, 362
Smith, Edmund Kirby	vol. 1, 152
Steele, Frederick	vol. 1, 152
Steen, Alexander Early	vol. 1, 155
Sturgis, Samuel D.	vol. 4, 364
Tappan, James C.	vol. 7, pt. 3:168
Taylor, Richard	vol. 1, 157
Todd, George	vol. 5, 179
Totten, James	vol. 2, 289
Vandever, William	vol. 6, 450
Van Dorn, Earl	vol. 1, 157
Walker, John G.	vol. 7, pt. 3: 169
Watie, Stand	vol. 2, 292
Waul, Thomas N.	vol. 7, pt. 4:170
White, Julius	vol. 6, 450
Yates, Richard	vol. 6, 453

Appendix C
Extended Comments on Selected Items
Extended Comments for Chapter 1
Item: Extended Comments on Some of Shelby's Men.

J. C. Boucher

J. C. or "Cam" Boucher was a member of Company D, 6th Missouri Cavalry (CSA). Enlisting on September 12, 1862, as a corporal in Newton County, Missouri, Boucher went Absent Without Leave (AWOL) on November 9, 1862, but returned to his unit by the end of February 1863. He was with Shelby in northeast Arkansas in June 1864, where he served as a member of the brigade's advance guard. Boucher later fled to Mexico as part of Shelby's "Expedition to Mexico" in the summer of 1865. Final disposition not known.[1]

Richard A. Collins

Richard Armstrong Collins was born in Mason County, Kentucky, in December 1841, and later moved to Missouri, date unknown. On April 1, 1861, he joined the 8th Division, MSG, and transferred to Hiram Bledsoe's Battery on May 19, 1861. Collins left the Guard on November 23, 1861, and later joined the Confederate Service at DeValls Bluff, Arkansas, on June 30, 1862. He was assigned to Joseph Bledsoe's Battery on September 20, 1862, as the unit's 1st lieutenant and served in that capacity until December 11, 1863, when Joseph Bledsoe resigned from the service. His first action, while in command, occurred on April 2, 1864, during the Camden Expedition, at Okolona, Arkansas. Collins served out the remainder of the war, participating in the capture of the *Queen City*, and Price's 1864 Missouri Raid. Following the war, Collins went briefly to Mexico with Shelby, taking his cannon with him, which he later sold to the Juaristas. Collins returned to Waverly, Missouri, where he became a lawyer, a member of the Missouri legislature, and "benefactor" to the Confederate Home at Higginsville. Collins married in August 1888, less than a year prior to the death of John N. Edwards, who wrote a glowing piece on Collins's marriage, in the *Kansas City Times*. Collins died at Piedmont, Wayne County, Missouri, on May 20, 1902, at the age of 61, and was buried at his request at Higginsville "among his comrades in the Confederate Home Cemetery."[2]

---

1. Anonymous, *6th Missouri Cavalry*, 56; Edwards, *John N. Edwards Biography*, 258; Edwards, *Shelby and His Men*, 329; National Archives, Record Group M322 (roll no. 41), Confederate Compiled Service Records, 6th Missouri Cavalry.
2. Ankesheiln, *Eight-Hundred Voices*, 2:15–16; Ankesheiln, *Last Guardsmen*, 53; Eakin, *Confederate Records*, 2:84; Eakin, *Trans-Mississippi Men*, 261; Edwards, *John N. Edwards Biography*, 152; Hale, *Branded As Rebels, Volume 2*, 65; Marmaduke, 338; National Archives, Record Group M322 (roll no. 86), Confederate Compiled Service Records, Collins's Light Artillery.

William Moorman

William Moorman or Moreman or Moron, of St. Joseph, Missouri, was born about 1836 or 1840, depending on the source. At the beginning of the Civil War he joined Company C, 1st Cavalry Regiment, 4th Division, MSG, as a private and served from the Battle of Carthage (August 3, 1861) through the siege and capture of Lexington (September 18–20, 1861), after which he left State Service. Joining the Confederate Service on July 26, 1862, he initially served as the junior 2nd lieutenant of Company H, 5th Missouri Cavalry (CSA). Moorman was promoted to 1st lieutenant on February 10, 1863, and to captain in early 1864, after William R. Edwards left the company for recruiting service (the *Supplement to the Official Records* has Edwards deserting). A stalwart in Shelby's Brigade, Moorman was branded a "cool, wary, and intelligent," as well as an "indefatigable" officer by John Edwards. Moorman was captured on October 19, 1864, near Lexington as he was returning from recruiting service and sent to Gratiot Street Prison, then forwarded to Johnson's Island on November 1864. There he remained until the end of the war, taking the Oath of Allegiance on June 16, 1865. Final disposition unknown.[3]

Isaac N. Shelby

Isaac or Ike N. Shelby, a resident of Layfayette County, Missouri, joined Company H, 2nd Infantry Regiment, 8th Division, MSG, on June 17, 1861. He fought in all the battles of his regiment from Carthage to Pea Ridge. Taken prisoner in Bates County, Missouri, Shelby was sent to Johnson's Island, was later exchanged, and joined Company A, 5th Missouri Cavalry (CSA) on August 18, 1862, at Waverly, Missouri. In time he became the "heroic standard bearer" of the 5th Regiment. Shelby survived the war and was paroled in Shreveport in June 1865.[4]

* * * * * * *

Extended Comments for Chapter 2

Item: The 1864 religious revival in the Trans-Mississippi Department.

According to Bell Wiley there were four major factors that "gave rise to large-scale revivalism among Confederates": First—the prevalence of Southern churches that provided a large number of preachers and "well-organized denominational propaganda." Second—the men who made up the army came from a strong Protestant religious background where they had previously experienced

---

3. *O.R.S.*, pt. 2, vol. 38:203; Eakin, *Missouri Prisoners of War*, "Moron, Wm." entry; Edwards, *Shelby and His Men*, 315, 356, 394, 423; Anonymous, *5th Missouri Cavalry*, 111.
4. Anonymous, *5th Missouri Cavalry*, 21; Bartels, *Trans-Mississippi Men*, 153; Eakin, *Confederate Records*, "I. N. Shelly," entry, 7:20; Edwards, *Shelby and His Men*, 327, 585; National Archives, Record Group M322 (roll no. 40), Confederate Compiled Service Records, 5th Missouri Cavalry (CSA); Peterson, et al., 221, 225, 227.

revivals. Third—Southern arms were largely successful from 1861 to April 1863, but defeats or draws at Antietam, Vicksburg, and Gettysburg, caused Southern soldiers to question whose side God was on. "The feeling gained wide currency that God would not permit the South to triumph unless and until her people humbled themselves." Fourth—As the war wore on, soldiers took stock of their lives, realizing that like many before them, their days were numbered.

The first great revival began following the Battles of Antietam and Perryville, in the fall of 1862, and continued on into the spring of 1863. The next revival began following the loss of Vicksburg and the defeat at Gettysburg. In the Trans-Mississippi, interest in revivals was not evident until January 1864, where one was noted as occurring in Louisiana. In the District of Arkansas a revival began in late May 1864, prompting one soldier to call it "the greatest revival he ever saw," and continued until mid-August, when the infantry commands moved forward to support Price's move into Missouri.

Preachers came from the Baptists, Methodists, Presbyterians and even the Catholics, which was odd given the overall population of the United States was highly Protestant at the time of the Civil War. Dozens were baptized on a daily basis, preaching occurred throughout the regiments, while the 10th Missouri Infantry and Pindall's Sharpshooter formed Christian Associations to further their religious beliefs. Of those baptized or immersed, a member of the 10th Missouri estimated that 35 men were being converted every day during the revival. In M. M. Parsons's old brigade, commanded by S. P. Burns, William Hoskins said this of the revival:

> The revival of God's work is going on extensively in our brigade—men are being made to see there [their] awful conditions & are turning to the calling of the gospel—they are turning by 10 & 20 at a time—such interest has not been taken in religious duties since the war began as there is now.

On July 4, "late in the day, drill and all camp duties...[were] dispensed with," according to Captain John Quesenberry, and "all have the privilege of attending preaching." And the longer the revival lasted the larger the crowds grew, even during heavy rains. "Many of the men seem deeply concerned about their eternal salvation," which pleased Captain Quesenberry as well as other religiously-inclined soldiers. Of the revival in Parsons's Division, Captain Eathan A. Pinnell recorded:

> We have one of the greatest revivals of religion going on in the Mo. Div., that I have ever heard of. Preaching or prayer meetings every day in almost all the Reg'ts. Dozens, perhaps scores, are daily baptized and added to the church...Cards and cursing are rapidly giving place to hymn books and sacred music.

Even though the religious fervor waned in the late summer 1864, when the infantry moved from the Camden area, it revived again in October after the units returned from the feint against Little Rock. "The church house was crowded to overflowing every night," according to Silas Turnbo of an Arkansas Regiment, "and nearly all the soldiers attended for the good that was in the preaching and not for mere pastime...[and] the longer it was protracted the more interest was taken in it." Among the many preachers, who used the local Methodist church, was Brigadier General L. M. Lewis, who was a favorite of the troops. Lewis's influence over the men, who attended, was substantial as "great numbers of them quit their wicked ways and turned toward the Great Savior of man."

And so the revival continued on into 1865, according to several sources, encompassing most every command in the region, and existed until the end of the war. "However, subsequent court-martial findings, statements of chaplains, and similar sources make it fairly clear that the consequences of revivals were short-lived." The temptations of camp life were ever present and "many of the converts soon lapsed into previous ways."[5]

* * * * * * *

Item: Extended Comments on the Execution of Captain John Guynes, October 15, 1864.

By the summer of 1864, following Confederate successes throughout the region, the Confederate War Department ordered E. Kirby Smith to transfer Walker's and Polignac's Divisions to the east side of the river. In late July, General Walker, wishing to remain in the Trans-Mississippi gave up his command, while Smith appointed John H. Forney the new commander of the Texas Division. With the impending move to the east, many of the Texas Divisions were reluctant to go, which led to increased desertions and "dangerously low" morale.

Captain John Guynes, for his part, spoke out forcefully against any redeployment, urging his men to desert if ordered to go East. Forney arrested Guynes, court-martialed him, and despite the court's recommendation to grant leniency for past "good character," ordered Guynes executed. General Orders No. 58, District of Arkansas, set the execution date for the following day. A last minute petition appealed to General Magruder to commute the sentence, but was denied. In denying the request, Magruder was supposed to have said: "We cannot execute the private soldier & let the officer be freed when guilty of the same or worse crime."

On October 15, the four divisions (Churchill's, Parsons's, Polignac's and Forney's) at Camden were formed around the condemned and "witnessed the melancholy performance of shooting" the Texas captain. Prior to the execution, Guynes was guarded by a company of the 10th Missouri Infantry as it was feared that

---

5. Banasik, *Serving With Honor*, 174; Barney, 263; Dougherty, 234–235; Goff & Tarbell, 49; Hoskin Diary, June 5, 19, 21, 24, July 24, 28–29, 31, 1864, August 7–8, 15, 1864; Kerby, 395–396; Quesenberry Diary, June 16, 1864, July 3–4, 7, 1864, August 7, 1864; Robertson, 186; Turnbo, 383–384; Wallace Diary, May 31, 1864, June 12, 14, 19–20, 25, 1864, July 3, 10, August 1, 1864; Bell Irwin Wiley, *The Life of Johnny Reb: The Common Soldier of the Confederacy* (Baton Rouge, LA, 1943), 182–184.

those sympathetic to Guynes, who were said to number in the "hundreds," would attempt to free him; however, no attempt was made.

On the day of the execution, Guynes was escorted to the execution site, up-river from Camden, by a drum corps that "beat the dead march." A party of 12 soldiers, six who had loaded guns, were detailed to carry out the execution at 4:00 p.m. Of the execution a member of General Magruder's staff recorded:

> I stood in ten steps of this Captain, and could see him well, and every thing that passed. He spoke a few words, to several friends, and then knelt in prayer. When he was through he got upon his feet and said he was ready, a man then advanced to blind folded [sic] him, but he begged that they would not do it. The space was cleared and we all held our breath waiting the command to fire...The officer in command gave the order—Ready–Aim–Fire–and he was no more, he fell a corpse, with six bullet holes through him. The crowd rushed up to look at him. I had seen enough and turned away from the sad and horrid sight.

Despite the "horrid sight" that Magruder's command had to witness, a member of Pindall's Missouri Sharpshooter noted that, though "very hard,...I think it was right." [6]

* * * * * * *

Extended Comments for Chapter 3

Item: Extended Comments on the Burning of Doniphan, Missouri, September 19, 1864.

On September 16, 1864, General Thomas Ewing, commanding the District of St. Louis, ordered Major James Wilson, commanding at Pilot Knob, to send a scout to the Arkansas line. Lieutenant Erich Pape, from the "Hell-Hounds" of the 3rd MSM Cavalry, was tasked with the mission to scout to the Arkansas border and determine if the rumor of the impending invasion of Price were true. Pape's command was also tasked, according William Nevin of the 3rd MSM Cavalry, to burn Doniphan, Missouri, in retaliation for the treatment that the town had recently given some returning parolees from the 54th Illinois Infantry. Colonel Grenville M. Mitchell, commanding the 54th, "desired redress for the treatment of his men," telling the 3rd MSM "to be sure and burn Doniphan." As to who actually gave the order to burn Doniphan, speculation has Major Wilson issuing the command.

A portion of Pape's force departed Pilot Knob on the morning of September 17 and arrived at Patterson at sundown, where they joined the balance of the scout. On the 18th, Pape departed Patterson, per orders from Captain Robert McElroy,

---

6. *O.R.S.*, pt. 2, vol. 81: 50, 56; Blessington, 279–280; Goff & Tarbell, 54; Harrison, 44, 56; Hoskin Diary, October 15, 1864; Kerby, 324–328; Norris, 81; Thompson, *Tejanos In Gray*, 59–60, 114–115; Turnbo, 378–379; Wallace Diary, October 15, 1864.

commanding the local garrison, and moved toward Doniphan. After making 45 miles during the day, Pape camped briefly at 1:30 a.m. on the 19th, before riding on to Doniphan, which was about 12 miles distant. The Union party entered Doniphan, described as "a crude hamlet, 18 houses around a wooden courthouse," near 5:00 a.m. Brushing aside a few pickets, they engaged M. Rector Johnson's Company, pushing them out of town and chasing them to the Arkansas line.

Pape captured a few pickets during his attack on Doniphan and learned from his prisoners that Price was at Pocahontas with 12,000 men. "Pape did not believe this report," believing rather that only J. O. Shelby was in the area (Mark Lause has the interrogation taking place at 4:00 p.m. on the return trip to Pilot Knob). Still, Pape sent the information back to Pilot Knob, and, upon returning to Patterson, telegraphed Pilot Knob stating that "he placed no confidence in the report" from the rebel wounded, that Price was in Pocahontas.

After chasing the rebels to the Arkansas line, Pape returned to Doniphan at 10:00 a.m., ate lunch, and burned the hapless town. Departing at 1:00 p.m., the Unionists continued on their scout, even as Sam Hildebrand with his guerrilla band entered the still burning town. Hildebrand found the entire town in flames except one house and the Methodist church. Sam burned the lone house, believing it belonged to a Union supporter; however, it belonged to the widow of Colonel Aden Lowe, a loyal Confederate.

Meanwhile, Pape's command moved south toward Martinsburg, which they also burned, and then headed northeast, coming to rest near Ponder's Mill. Camping at the Vandiver farm, Pape sent out scouts, found nothing, and then picketed the area for the night.

Back at Doniphan, Hildebrand did what he could for the town and then took up the pursuit of the Federal raiders. Before dawn the next day, Hildebrand's party had gotten in front of Pape's scout, and waited for the dawn to attack.

Shelby's Division entered Doniphan at 3:30 p.m., and made camp, a little over an hour after Hildebrand had departed the area. Enraged at what had happened there, Shelby promptly ordered a pursuit of the Doniphan raiders. Lieutenant Colonel Benjamin A. Johnson, commanding a 100-man detachment of the 15th Missouri Cavalry from Fagan's Division, was sent in pursuit, being joined by a 30-man party from Jackman's Brigade (probably M. Rector Johnson's Company) and another 120 men from Shank's Brigade. In all Johnson had about 250 men, not including Hildebrand's band, which numbered about 40 men.

Riding though the night, Johnson found the Federal camp, and, with Hildebrand, surrounded it on three sides. Early the next morning Johnson attacked Pape's men, scattering them, while killing and wounding several and capturing others, who were eventually executed. Hildebrand, for his part later reported that he captured 16 prisoners, whom he executed.

According to Jerry Ponder, Pape's command was decimated in the engagement at Ponder's Mill, losing 47 killed (citing Union Post Returns) and 45 wounded, while John Edwards says 40 were killed and 43 captured. However, three rebel sources, one in the *Official Records*, stated that there were only 14 Federal casualties, while Confederate Dr. William McPheeters puts the losses at about 20, and a third report puts the losses at nine killed. Federal sources, including period newspapers, have Pape in one case losing 20 killed, wounded, and missing, and others have him losing between 7–11 killed.

Major James Wilson, commanding at Pilot Knob, reported that Lieutenant Pape returned to Pilot Knob in the latter part of the day on September 20 with 60 men of the scouting party, suggesting that Federal losses totaled no more than 26 of all types. Shelby reported losing six killed and wounded, while other Confederate sources specified rebel losses as two killed and four or five wounded, while S. B. Williams, from Shelby's Division says that the Confederates lost eight killed.

After recuperating from his scout, Pape's 65-man command moved to Pilot Knob, where they joined in the defense of the city, arriving near noon on September 26.[7]

* * * * * * *

Item: Description and Gun Placements at Fort Davidson, Pilot Knob, September 27, 1864, by Orderly Sergeant H. C. Wilkinson.

Fort Davidson was hexagonal and each side 40 yards long, or 240 yards around and 80 yards across. There was a sally port on the south side, just aside from the head of the south rifle pit. So in going into the fort you stepped into the heavy door of the sally port and you were then directly under the south parapet and then to your left was a stair way. On going up the stair way, you emerged through a trap door into the fort. On the east side, facing the old Pilot Knob Ry. [Railroad] Depot, was the gate way with a heavy draw bridge that hinged to heavy timbers at the gate entrance. Then with windlasses inside, attached to high strong posts, this bridge was drawn up by means of ropes extending from the windlasses up over pulleys at the top of the posts, then attached to the outer corners of the bridge. Fort Davidson then mounted four 32-pound siege guns or pivot guns, some 12 or 14 feet long, and if we remember rightly, they weighed 9000 pounds. Then there were three 24-pound howitzers, with limbers so they could be

---

7. *O.R.*, vol. 41, pt. 1:455; Breihan, 131–132; Britton, *Civil War on the Border, 1863–1865*, 391–393; "The Burning of Doniphan," in *Ripley County*, 13–14; Busch, *Missouri Democrat Articles*, 11, 43; Mark J. Crawford, *Confederate Courage on Other Fields: Four Lesser Known Accounts of the War Between the States* (Jefferson, NC, 2000), 101, hereafter cited as Crawford, *Confederate Courage*; Edwards, *Shelby and His Men*, 383; W. T. Fowler, "A Missouri Boy's Experiences," *Confederate Veteran* 40 (December, 1932), 432–433, hereafter cited as "Missouri Boy's Experience;" "From St. Louis," *Chicago Tribune*, September 23, 1864; Gifford, 56–59; Lause, *Price's Lost Campaign*, 32–33, 39; Quoted in Nichols, *Guerrilla Warfare, Volume IV*, 44–46; Ponder, *15th Missouri Cavalry*, 90, 93, 95–97; Ponder, *General Marmaduke*, 166–167; Kirby Ross, "The Burning of Doniphan," *North & South* 6 (November 2003): 79–80; Sinisi, 58–59; Quoted in Suderow, *Arcadia Valley*, 36–40; Thompson, "Great Little Battle of Pilot Knob," 145.

hauled on the field, same as field pieces, as heavy artillery. Also there were two mortars about the same caliber as the 24-pound howitzers.[8]

* * * * * * *

Item: Extended Comments on Shelby's Operations on the St. Louis-Iron Mountain Railroad, September 27, 1864.

While the Battle of Pilot Knob was proceeding on September 27, Shelby divided his command into three parts before advancing on the Iron Mountain Railroad. Ben Elliott was sent to Irondale to destroy the bridge at that point, while B. Frank Gordon, with two regiments, headed north to destroy the three bridges near Mineral Point, which was 26 miles north of Pilot Knob. The remaining men of the division were tasked to destroy the railroad between Mineral Point and Irondale.

After destroying the South Big River Bridge, Gordon moved on to Mineral Point, where he discovered the 3rd Brigade, 3rd Division of A. J. Smith's 16th Corps, commanded by Colonel James Mills, which numbered between 1,500 to 1,650 men, with two pieces of artillery. Not hesitating, Gordon charged Mills's command, which showed little fight, being unsure of what they faced, and withdrew. From Mineral Point, Mills pulled back "to DeSoto for a more commanding position." Gordon then burned yet another bridge and finally the third bridge over Mill Creek by the end of the day. Additionally, Gordon also burned the depot and two rail cars and captured "large quantities of goods."

Meanwhile, Elliott encountered no resistance at Irondale and burned the Irondale Bridge, after which he tore up the track to the city, looted the local stores, and burned the depot.

By noon on the 27th Shelby's main body had destroyed over five miles of track and engaged a Union train of several cars loaded with 250 troops, who were en route to Pilot Knob. However, upon encountering Shelby and seeing the South Big River bridge in flames, the Union troop train backed up to DeSoto, breaking contact with Shelby's command. Shelby then completed the destruction of the railroad and cut the telegraph to Pilot Knob, after which he called in his detachments, ordering them to Potosi.

Jackman's Brigade easily took Potosi, capturing 130 (Edwards says 400, while George Maddox of Jackman's Brigade says it was 365, while Shelby reported 175) of the 50th EMM. They then burned the local depot and seven train cars, while executing several prisoners, who had "rendered themselves obnoxious." Also taken were 175 Enfield rifles, with the "same number of cartridge boxes and belts, and much valuable ammunition." From Potosi, Shelby sent out scouts in several directions, including one toward Hopewell, which was located about five miles southeast from Potosi on the Iron Mountain Railroad.

Lieutenant Shelby Plattenburg, commanding the 30-man Hopewell scout,

---

8. Albert Castel has the fort as a pentagon, with three mortars, not two. Castel, *Sterling Price*, 211; Wilkinson (Letter No. 15).

discovered a Federal wagon train en route from Pilot Knob near the railroad. Plattenburg, according to Federal sources, immediately engaged M. P. Tate's command, causing 38 casualties (23 of whom were Negro teamsters), while destroying 64 wagons, capturing two caissons and "30 fine artillery horses" (Gifford says 70 wagons were taken, while Shelby says that only 25 were captured). Additionally, the Federals also admitted to losing the "traveling forge" and "battery wagons," of Battery H, 2nd Missouri Artillery, while Shelby claimed 130 prisoners, including 100 Negroes.

During the night of the 27th–28th, while encamped at Potosi, Jackman's Brigade "was getting drunk, and men were standing on logs and stumps, making speeches." According to George Maddox, "The Yankees would have had a picnic if they had run on us." Shelby was furious with Jackman's command and ordered them put under arrest; however the balance of the command refused to place the drunkards under confinement.

On the 28th, Shelby "grew uneasy and restless," having received no news from General Price, and moved his division to Caledonia, where he learned of Price's repulse at Pilot Knob. However, according to H. A. Wilkinson, a member of the Fort Davidson garrison, a courier from General Shelby, en route to Price, was captured on the morning of September 28, who revealed that Shelby was aware of Price's plight at Pilot Knob, probably as early as the night before.

All told, Shelby reported suffering only 10 casualties, while inflicting 100 killed and wounded among the Federals during his operations on the St. Louis-Iron Mountain Railroad.[9]

* * * * * * *

Item: A Legend Surrounding the Evacuation of Fort Davidson.

On the evening of September 27, 1864, a carriage arrived near Ironton, carrying two women. The two women, according to Captain T. J. Mackey, lived on a plantation north of Pilot Knob and desired to get a pass from General Price. One of the women was called "Mrs. R." and the other a "Miss H." A staff officer, whom Mackey does not name except by calling him "Captain X," intervened with the ladies, as he had previously met them at the Arcadia Seminary, where they had probably worked in the hospital treating the wounded.

Mrs. R, whose first name was Marian (another article identifies the lady as "Mrs. Marion") and her sister Miss H. were escorted to Price's headquarters where

---

9. *O.R.*, vol. 41, pt. 1:628, 652–653, 673; *O.R.*, vol. 41, pt. 3:977–978; Busch, *Missouri Democrat Articles*, 28, 39–40, 42, 48–49, 55; Cocker, 13; "Damage to the Iron Mountain Railroad," *Missouri Republican*, October 3, 1864; Edwards, *Shelby and His Men*, 385–386; "From the Frontier," *Chicago Tribune*, October 1, 1864; Gifford, 113–114, 119–120, 133–134; Lindsay, *Forge*, October 19, 1865; O'Flaherty, 218; Palmer, 5; Quoted in Nichols, *Guerrilla Warfare, Volume IV*, 51; Norton & Massey, 63; Sellmeyer, 211–213; Sinisi, 65–67; Suderow, *Arcadia Valley*, 94–95; "The War In Missouri," *Chicago Tribune*, September 29, 1864; Wilkinson (Letters No. 17, 18 & 19); Wright Memoirs, unnumbered page 72.

they requested a pass to return to their plantation. Pass obtained, the two ladies were escorted to the north side of Pilot Knob, where they met Colonel Archibald Dobbin. The ladies then invited Colonel Dobbin "and his brigade to partake of a good supper which she had provided for them at her plantation," which was a short distance from Dobbin's camp.

Dobbin was well aware that both ladies supported the Union, but saw no reason to turn down the invitation for a much needed meal. The whole brigade was then marched over to the ladies' plantation, where five steers were being barbequed. With Dobbin's command distracted, Mrs. R. sent her teenaged brother to inform General Ewing that the Potosi Road was cleared of rebel pickets. Ewing then verified that the coast was clear and evacuated Fort Davidson down the lightly or unguarded Potosi Road.

When the Fort Davidson magazine exploded, Dobbin and his command were on their way back to their camp. Dobbin quickly "divined its meaning" and returned to his assigned picket posts shortly thereafter. The next morning Fort Davidson was found evacuated, with none the wiser as to how Ewing escaped undetected.

There are at least two parts of Mackey's story that are somewhat verified, one by Dr. Seymour Carpenter and the other by General Ewing himself. Earlier in the evening a woman identified as a "Mrs. Marion" carried a message from Colonel Alonzo Slayback, according to Carpenter, to General Ewing, urging him to surrender, or, failing to do so, "that in the heat of the assault, not much quarter would be shown." In Mackey's account he has General Price sending a "Union woman," name unknown, to deliver the message to General Ewing.

In the most revealing part of the story, General Ewing in a letter to his son, after the battle, told him "that he knew the road to Potosi was open because a local boy came to the fort and told him the Confederates were not blocking the road."[10]

* * * * * * *

Item: Extended Comments on Confederate Losses at Pilot Knob.

There are basically two schools of thought concerning the Confederate losses at Pilot Knob. Union sources, led by General Ewing, who commanded at Pilot Knob, with Colonel Thomas C. Fletcher, commander of the 47th EMM and Radical candidate for Missouri governor in 1864, put forth the idea that Price lost

---

10. Bartels, *Iowa Boy*, 155; Bartels, *Pilot Knob*, 32; Bartels, "Woman's Work Never Done," in *Civil War Stories of Missouri*, 54–56; Crowley, 138; Britton, *Civil War on the Border, 1863–1865*, 408; "Escape From Fort Davidson," *Civil War Times Illustrated* 13 (April, 1974):30–31; Fletcher, 44; Gifford, 166–168; Lause, *Price's Lost Campaign*, 53–54; "A National Account," in *Rebellion Record*, 11:140–141; Wm. Forse Scott, "The Last Fight For Missouri," *Personal Recollections of the War of the Rebellion Addresses Delivered Before the Commandery of the State of New York, Military Order of the Loyal Legion of the United States* (New York, 1901; reprint ed., Wilmington, NC, 1992), 311, hereafter cited as Scott, "Last Fight;" Thompson, "Great Little Battle of Pilot Knob," 290.

1,500 or more men at Pilot Knob. Then there were the Confederate participants, who put the rebels' losses at about 500.[11]

Confederates who recorded their losses at Pilot Knob immediately following the battle and in the recollections that followed after the war were fairly constant in their record keeping. Unfortunately, reports following the battle were incomplete, though what they did present supports the idea that Price suffered in the neighborhood of 500 casualties.

William Cabell's Brigade, of Fagan's Division, reported the loss of 45 killed with 230 wounded, while J. T. Alexander of his staff put the number at 200 killed and wounded. J. B. Clark's Brigade of Marmaduke's command reported 94 casualties from three of the five participating units. There were no reports for Thomas McCray's or William Slemons's Brigades of Fagan's Division, and Marmaduke's other brigade under Tom Freeman recorded that his losses "were minimal." Further, both Colonel John C. Wright of Cabell's Brigade and Captain T. J. Mackey, Price's chief engineer, reported that Fagan's Division suffered about 350 casualties, implying that Slemons and McCray lost about 75 men between them. Summing up the Confederate losses, Dr. William McPheeters, the medical director of the army recorded—"our men were repulsed, but not badly."[12]

John B. Clark, Jr.

Overall Colonel Wright believed that the Confederates lost about 500 men at Pilot Knob, as did James W. Campbell, a Confederate soldier in Wood's Missouri Battalion, with James Cocker, from Harris's Missouri Artillery, and an unnamed Confederate veteran. The men of Jeffers's 8th Missouri also put the army's losses at 500, so says a Federal report, while C. K. Polk, of the 3rd Missouri Cavalry (CSA), who counted the Confederate dead following the battle, put the rebel losses "at not over four hundred killed, wounded and missing." Even a civilian, Louis Fusz, a resident of St. Louis and one of the owners of the Pilot Knob Iron Works, who had a son in the Confederate Army, also believed the Confederate losses totaled about 500.[13]

---

11. Fletcher writes that Price lost 1,468 men at Pilot Knob, not including "a number of bodies [that] were found on the mountain side...long after the battle." *O.R.*, vol. 41, pt. 3:542; Fletcher, 43.
12. *O.R.*, vol. 41, pt. 1:630, 692, 694, 698, 709; *O.R.S.*. pt. 1, vol. 2:402; J. T. Alexander, Letter (undated, probably October 2, 1864); Freeman Memoir, September 27, 1864; Pitcock & Gurley, 224; Wright Memoirs, unnumbered page 76.
13. *O.R.*, vol. 41, pt. 3:542; Campbell Memoir; Fusz Diary, 3:1; C. K. Polk, Letter, *Iron County Register* (Ironton, MO), October 12, 1905; Cocker, 18.

Fusz recorded in his diary on October 2 that he had met James Harrison, one of the owners of the Ironworks at Pilot Knob and "a gentleman...whose statements deserve the fullest credibility." Harrison related to Fusz that he had met with Price during the battle or shortly thereafter and convinced the general to leave the ironworks untouched. Price also agreed to return all confiscated property, which he subsequently did. Additionally, Harrison met with "numerous" men from St. Louis, including Trusten Polk, former U.S. Senator and aid to General Price; Dr. William McPheeters, Price's Medical Director; and several other officers of Price's staff. Harrison remained in the area, departing on September 29, and headed back to St. Louis where he met with Fusz and granted interviews with the local press.

Harrison arrived in St. Louis, on October 1 (the *Missouri Democrat* says he arrived on October 3), where he met with Louis Fusz, and it appears among the many things he relayed to Fusz, the Confederates lost "some 50 killed and as much as 450 to 500 wounded" at Pilot Knob, or roughly 500–550 casualties all told. Considering that Harrison met freely with the Confederates on Price's staff, it would not be a stretch to believe that some Confederate officer gave Harrison the data on the rebel losses.[14]

Union participants had a different take on the Confederate losses at Pilot Knob. Following the battle, General Ewing began the legend of Confederate losses, claiming in a telegram on September 29 to have inflicted 1,500 casualties on the rebels. Given that Federal forces evacuated Fort Davidson during the night of September 27–28, thus surrendering the position to the rebel forces, it would have been impossible for him to have come up with the figure on September 29 except by pure conjecture.

Dr. Seymour Carpenter, a "boyhood friend" and college roommate of General Ewing, initially put the number at 300 "dead and severely wounded." However, after returning to St. Louis, Dr. Carpenter wrote a letter to Mrs. Ewing, raising the losses to "over 1,000." General Rosecrans, for his part weighed in on the issue on October 6, writing General Henry Halleck, the Chief of Staff of the Army, "that enemy losses will not fall much short of one thousand," thus supporting Carpenter's assertions. And yet another participant, Dr. T. W. Johnson, who stayed behind with the Union wounded following the battle, put the rebel losses at 1,525 weeks after the battle, seemingly to support Ewing's wild estimates. Thus it appears that despite the Confederates' lower estimates of their own casualties, Ewing's initial reports spawned the legend of horrific losses suffered by Price at Pilot Knob. And this was not the last time Ewing would overestimate his enemy's losses, telling a subordinate on October 28 that General Alfred Pleasonton had captured 2,000 prisoners at Mine Creek, where Pleasonton reported taking only 1,000, while actual prisoners were about half that number. From that time on, Federal sources and

---

14. The *Missouri Republican*, per their interview with Harrison, put the losses at "forty men killed and between three and four hundred wounded." Busch, *Missouri Democrat Articles*, 77–78; Fusz Diary, 3:1–2; "Price Certainly in Missouri," *Missouri Republican*, October 3, 1864.

authors, for the most part, have claimed that the Federals inflicted 1,500 or more casualties on the assaulting rebels at Pilot Knob.[15]

Following Ewing's pronouncement as to rebel losses, other participants and supporters fell in line with that number, despite any concrete evidence to support the number. There was one notable exception, General John B. Sanborn, who commanded a division under General Pleasanton during the Expedition. Sanborn put the rebel losses at a mere 300 killed and wounded. Walter Busch, a modern-day historian, chronicled the various Union veterans' associations and reunions that followed the Battle of Pilot Knob, in which the veteran Unionists recorded rebel losses as 400 dead, 175 mortally wounded with another 1,000 wounded, who recovered, total 1,575. And David Murphy, commanding Fort Davidson's artillery put the Confederate loss at a "little less than 1500" men; but he also has Price assaulting with 12,000 armed men, which was a gross overestimation.[16]

Other Federal reports immediately following the Battle of Pilot Knob placed the Confederate casualties at between 800–1,500 men, with 1,500 being the most common number. However, even the *Missouri Democrat* dismissed the larger number, believing that 800–1,000 was closer to the truth. The *Democrat* went on to record that the Battle of Pilot Knob was "one of the fiercest on record, has not been exaggerated, except in the number lost by the rebels...[and] those who suppose that a heavier execution ought to have been done by the small force of a few hundred men under General Ewing, in a few hours, ought to be sent to a lunatic asylum." Dr. Seymour Carpenter, who remained behind after General Ewing evacuated Fort Davidson, estimated the rebel losses at "not less than 150 killed and about 700 wounded," but two days later, when back in St. Louis, he upped the number to "over 1,000," and later to 2,000, before settling on 1,500. Henry Wilkinson, of the 47th EMM, recorded in a paper he wrote years after the battle, that "I understand that the official report of the Confederate officers put their loss at 1,468." However, Wilkinson gives no indication as to who gave him the supposed "official report" of losses.[17]

The controversy continued into the early twentieth century when C. K. Polk, of the 3rd Missouri Cavalry (CSA) wrote the *Iron County Register*, stating that the

---

15. Curiously, the telegraphic message sent by Captain Charles S. Hill, on September 29, stated in the *Chicago Tribune* that the rebels were repulsed with a loss of 150 killed and wounded—a misprint or the truth? Probably the former. *O.R.*, vol. 41, pt. 3:482–483, 656; *O.R.*, vol. 41, pt. 4:298; Bartels, *Iowa Boy*, 141, 147, 154; Bartels, *Pilot Knob*, 30; Busch, *Missouri Democrat Articles*, 457–458; "Pap Price's Raid," *Fort Smith New Era*, November 12, 1864; Cyrus A. Peterson & Joseph Mills Hanson, *Pilot Knob: The Thermopylae of the West* (New York, 194; reprint ed., Cape Girardeau, MO, 1964), 317–318, hereafter cited as Peterson & Hanson; "The War In Missouri," *Chicago Tribune*, September 30, 1864; Williams, *Second Colorados*, 79.

16. Busch, *Fort Davidson*, 66, 74, 93; Hinton, 26–27; Sanborn, "Campaign in Missouri," 144.

17. *O.R.*, vol. 41, pt. 3:553; Bartels, *Pilot Knob*, 30; "The Battle of Pilot Knob," *Missouri Republican*, October 2, 1864; Busch, *Missouri Democrat Articles*, 53, 73, 77–78, 114, 142; Crawford, *Confederate Courage, 118*; Lause, *Price's Lost Campaign*, 53; Lindsay, "Pilot Knob," *Forge*, October 19, 1865; "The War In Missouri," *Chicago Tribune*, October 5, 1864; Wilkinson (Letter No. 18).

Confederates lost no more than 400 killed, wounded, and missing. David Murphy responded, quoting Captain T. J. Mackey, Price's Engineer, who wrote an article in which he stated that Price lost 1,056 (Britton has the number as 1,164 officers and men in 20 minutes) men in 15 minutes; however, immediately following the Expedition, at Price's Court of Inquiry, Mackey stated that the rebel losses at Pilot Knob totaled 430. Murphy also referred to Dr. Thomas W. Johnson, a Union surgeon at Pilot Knob, who wrote a letter to General Ewing on October 14, 1864, in which he stated that he saw a list from an unnamed Confederate non-commissioned officer with the names of 335 dead. Johnson then extrapolated the Confederate wounded to be 1,200 or 1,600 casualties overall. Even David Murphy in recounting his friendly sources admits, in one case, that the rebels losses were about 800 killed and wounded, and then boosts the total to "anywhere from 1600 to 2400, citing a combination of unnamed sources and pure guessing." All of which should raise serious questions as to Union reporting on Confederate losses, given that the North did not regain the area of Pilot Knob until mid-October 1864.[18]

Major H. H. Williams, an aide-de-camp of General Ewing, was sent to Pilot Knob to re-occupy the city in mid-October 1864, and among his many tasks, he was to determine the composition and strength of Price's Army. Williams was also tasked to determine the rebel losses at the Battle of Pilot Knob. On October 16, two days after Dr. Johnson wrote his correspondence to General Ewing on rebel losses, Major Williams wrote: "The [Confederate] surgeon in charge of the hospital will not admit to loss of more than 300 killed and wounded, but that only includes those that were badly wounded." Clearly Major Williams was trying to have the rebel surgeon support what General Ewing, Colonel Fletcher, and Dr. Johnson were saying in the local press and in their inflated reports about the Confederate losses at Pilot Knob.[19]

And when that didn't work, they simply ignored Confederate reports on the losses, like David Murphy did in 1905. In responding to C. K. Polk's letter to the *Iron County Register*, on Confederate losses at Pilot Knob, Murphy wrote that Williams "found no estimate of the Confederate losses in killed and wounded, from any source, below 1500." This was clearly an incorrect statement as shown above. Williams simply ignored any report that didn't fit the narrative that General Ewing had established on September 29.

Among modern-day authors, Michael J. Forsyth puts the loss at between 1,000 and 1,500, basing his number on statements provided by Dr. Johnson. Forsyth writes that since Price "did not record a count of the casualties...Therefore, we must give credence to Union estimates which are based upon Ewing's surgeon, Thomas J. [W.] Johnson." Ultimately, authors Forsyth and William Crowley believe that

---

18. *O.R.*, vol. 41, pt. 1:709; Britton, *Civil War on the Border, 1863–1865*, 412–413; Peterson & Hanson, 317–318; C. K. Polk, Letters, *Iron County Register* (October 12, November 23, 1905 & January 11, 1906); David Murphy, Letter (October 19, 1905), *Iron County Register*, November 23, 1905).

19. *O.R.*, vol. 41, pt. 3:685; *O.R.*, vol. 41, pt. 4:8.

Price lost not "less than 1,000 men," while Robert Kerby puts the rebel loss at "more than 750 dead and wounded." However, author Douglas Gifford writes that there is "no way of knowing exactly how many wounded Confederates were sent south, how many slightly wounded men remained with their units, and exactly how many were buried on the battlefield." In other words, Crowley, Gifford, and Forsyth are trusting in the unsubstantiated Union accounts, ignoring Confederate reports of actual losses, and not bothering to analyze what Price probably lost.[20]

Walter Busch, in his 2004 biography of Thomas Ewing, writes that, "Most present-day historians prefer a count of 1,030 Confederate dead and wounded for the assaults on the fort without including casualties over the entire" battle. This would suggest losses greater than the 1,030 that Busch listed above. However, in 2010 Busch penned another book on Pilot Knob, where he diplomatically hedged his comments on Confederate losses, writing: "How many died and were wounded is a good question, but claims of 300 to 400 Rebel dead and 900 to 1,200 wounded are not impossible." This seems to suggest that losses between 1,200 to 1,600 were within the realm of possibility.[21]

One of the first modern authors to realistically tackle the rebel losses at Pilot Knob was Lumir Buresh. In his 1977 book, *The Battle of Mine Creek*, Buresh put the Confederates' Pilot Knob casualties at 600, becoming the first author to correctly identify the overall rebel losses at the battle. Nine years later, Bryce Suderow, who helped research Buresh's book, wrote his ground-breaking book on the battle, *Thunder In Arcadia Valley*, in which he presented the most detailed analysis of the Confederate losses at Pilot Knob. Suderow placed the Confederate losses at about 510 killed and wounded—160 for Marmaduke's Division and 350 for Fagan's command. Kyle Sinisi, who also wrote an account of the battle in his book *The Last Hurrah*, supports Suderow's estimates. Douglas Gifford in *Where Valor and Devotion Met*, acknowledges Suderow's work, but believes the 500-man loss to be "undoubtedly too low." Mark A. Lause acknowledges that Suderow is the "most knowledgeable" historian on the Battle of Pilot Knob, but incorrectly cites Suderow's estimate of rebel loss as "some 800 casualties."[22]

So what was the likely number of men lost by Price at Pilot Knob? Was it the 500- plus that many of the Confederates claimed or the 1,000 to 1,600 that many Union participants and most modern-day authors believe? See Appendix E for my breakdown of estimated Confederate losses at Pilot Knob, which I put at 544.

Analysis of Confederate Losses

In analyzing the Confederate losses at Pilot Knob, it might be useful to look at another Confederate attack on a fortified position. On July 4, 1863, Confederate

---

20. Crowley, 138; Forsyth, *Great Missouri Raid*, 137–138; Gifford, 195–196; Kerby, 343; Lause, *Price's Lost Campaign*, 53; Williams, *Second Colorados*, 79.
21. Busch, *Fort Davidson*, 39; Busch, *General*, 115.
22. Buresh, 39; Gifford, 195–196; Lause, *Price's Lost Campaign*, 53; Sinisi, 85–86; Suderow, *Arcadia Valley*, 121, 138–139.

forces under General T. H. Holmes assaulted the town of Helena, Arkansas. At the time, Helena was defended by four emplaced land batteries, Fort Cutis, the gunboat *Tyler*, and 13 field guns from three other units, a total of 35 pieces of artillery. Fort Curtis contained six heavy siege guns, while the *Tyler* provided eight more. The other batteries provided an assortment of lighter field guns of varied calibers and styles.

The rebel forces assaulting Helena numbered 8,146 men, while the Federal defenders numbered 4,129. Holmes began his attack an hour before sunrise and six hours later withdrew from the area. During the six hour battle Holmes's troops were subjected to musket and artillery fire at point-blank rage, similar to what was experienced at Pilot Knob. Rebel losses, excluding captured, numbered 173 killed and 651 wounded for a total of 824. Overall the command lost 10.1 percent (824 / 8,146 = .101) of the men engaged, excluding those who were captured.[23]

At Pilot Knob the main attack lasted about one and a half hours, according to General Ewing, followed by half "an hour of ineffective musketry and artillery fire." During the battle, the fort had no more than 13 guns in play. Of the 13 guns, one 32-pounder fell off the parapet during Slemons's and McCray's assault, reducing the fort's main battery by 25 percent, before the other commands even assaulted the fort. Also, at least four other guns, at one time or another, rolled or fell off the parapet and had to be man-handled back on, thus reducing the fort's firepower each time it happened. Additionally, two 3" rifled guns of Montgomery's Battery were essentially useless during the assault, being abandoned on the outside of the fort after their horses were killed.

If one accepts the rebel loss of 1,500 men at Pilot Knob one would also have to believe that 10 artillery pieces did more damage in about two hours at Pilot Knob than the entire garrison of Helena, with 35 guns and four times the manpower, did in six hours. Further, at Fort Davidson there were only four guns on the east or southeast side of the fort, where the main assault took place, with four more on the southwest or west side. The remaining guns were on the north or northwest corner of the fort, with the one 32-pound gun on the northeast corner that was made useless when it rolled off the parapet early in the main assault. This would suggest that only four of Ewing's guns could immediately bear on Fagan's Division, without firing over his own troops stationed on the parapets. Colonel Thomas Fletcher, commanding the 47th EMM, recorded that two of Montgomery's 3" rifles were elevated to fire over the parapet, but failed to say where they were placed. Assuming that these guns were probably on the west or southwest walls, they probably used ball ammunition, instead of canister, to better control their shots so as to not hit their own men. They essentially lobbed their shells over their own men, which was not a very accurate way of directing fire on a charging enemy.[24]

---

23. Banasik, *Confederate Tales, 1863*, 67–69 (note nos. 18 & 20), 187; Edwin C. Bearss, "The Battle of Helena, July 4, 1863," *Arkansas Historical Quarterly* 20, (Autumn 1961), 294–295; "The Opposing Forces in Arkansas," in *BLCW*, 3:460.
24. Fletcher, 35.

Marmaduke's Division, Price's other division in the assault, was actually subject to as many as seven guns that could fire directly on it. This might explain why the left wing of Marmaduke's Division never really made any serious attack on Fort Davidson given the number of guns that could bear on its assault. And when Marmaduke's attack faltered, the guns on the southwest, west, and north could have fired on Fagan's Division, but would have had to fire over their own troops on the parapet, and probably used different ammunition other than grape or canister, assuming they even fired at Fagan's Division.

Following the battle General Ewing reported that he had seven guns firing canister at Cabell; however, this was misleading. According to period accounts, even when the rebels were charging the fort, the fort concentrated its fire on the rebel artillery and didn't use anti-personnel canister and grape rounds until the rebels were withdrawing from the fort. According to the *Missouri Republican*:

> The rebels who had been able to advance to the trenches were unable to hold their ground, and commenced falling slowly back, keeping up their fire till the battery on the mountain was silenced, when the guns of the fort together with the infantry, directed their fire to such effect that the rebel lines were broke,...the grape canister and minie balls mowing them down by scores.[25]

Given the placement of Fort Davidson's guns (see diagram of Fort Davidson) this would have meant that of the three guns in the southwest part of the fort, two would have been raking the fort's south parapet with canister. Other accounts imply that only five guns could bear on Cabell during his charge, which seems more likely. And during Cabell's charge, the northeast 32-pound gun was already off the parapet and unavailable as well as the two 3" rifles from Montgomery's Battery that were outside the fort. This would have left the four guns in the southeast corner, one gun from the southwest corner and the two elevated guns, to conduct the fire on Cabell's command—two of which were probably lobbing ball ammunition at the attackers.[26]

Given the placement of the Federal guns bearing on Fagan's Division, the length of the attack, and the thick "dense cloud" of smoke that covered the area, which one participant described as "like the wings of countless ravens," it doesn't seem possible that the Confederates suffered the horrific losses described by Union accounts of the battle. And when General Cabell read a St. Louis newspaper of September 30, that reported the rebel loss of 1,500 men and his death at Pilot Knob, he simply remarked that, "It was a whole issue of falsehoods."[27]

Further, Federal authorities had ulterior motives for over-reporting rebel losses. From the beginning of the campaign, Federal leaders had woefully underestimated the rebel invasion of Missouri and were totally unprepared for the

---

25. "The Battle of Pilot Knob," *Missouri Republican*, October 2, 1864.
26. Ibid.; "Arrival of Captain Hills," *Missouri Republican*, September 30, 1864.
27. J. T. Alexander, Letter (undated, probably October 2, 1864).

scope of the invasion. By reporting huge rebel losses, it was clear that the Federal leaders were attempting to downplay Price's invasion, build up morale for the upcoming campaign, and dispel any rumor of being unprepared, while furthering their future political or military ambitions. And what better way of assuring the population of Missouri that the rebels could be easily defeated than by hyping their losses at the Battle of Pilot Knob.

That said, there is little doubt that the Confederates took terrible losses at Pilot Knob on September 26–27, but they did not have 1,500 or even 1,000 casualties that many believe they suffered. At Helena the Confederates lost 10.1 percent of those engaged, over a six hour period—four hours more than the battle at Pilot Knob lasted. At Pilot Knob the Federals had 13 pieces of artillery verses 35 at Helena. And at Helena the attacking rebel force was about the same as that at Pilot Knob, while the defenders at Helena outnumbered the defenders at Pilot Knob by over four to one. Finally, at Pilot Knob a similar loss of 10.1 percent would have equated to 680 (6,737 x .101 = 680) casualties—far less than the 1,500 that was generally accepted. And this assumes the Battle of Pilot Knob lasted three times longer than it actually did.[28]

Overall the Confederate losses at Pilot Knob are correctly estimated at 544 (See Appendix E for details) out of 6,737 engaged or 8.1 percent (544 / 6,737 = .0807) of the assaulting force.

****

Item: Extended Comments on the Effect of the Battle of Pilot Knob on the Confederate Army and the Overall Impact on the Remainder of the Campaign.

In analyzing the Battle of Pilot Knob, modern-day historians agree on a few points. Common to all was the saving of St. Louis, which came about because Price did not bypass Pilot Knob and move immediately on the city, and the loss of Confederate morale. Additionally, Bryce Suderow believes Price's defeat cost him Jefferson City and "permanently weaked [weakened] its faith in its leaders." Douglas Gifford agrees with Suderow, noting further that the defeat inflicted a "psychological scar on the Army of Missouri," from which the Confederate army never recovered. According to Gifford, the rebel army "performed poorly for the remainder of the campaign." Joseph Thompson espouses all the above effects of the Battle of Pilot Knob and further writes that "Pilot Knob was of decisive importance to the success or failure of Price's invasion"—and in this case it would seem that Pilot Knob ultimately cost Price a successful Expedition.

In his analysis, Michael Forsyth states simply that Marmaduke's and Fagan's Divisions had their "fighting spirit...sapped" from them, causing a loss of morale. Not only was the rebel morale affected, according to Howard Monnett, but both Marmaduke's and Fagan's men (except Cabell's Brigade), "showed a decided

---

28. *O.R.*, vol. 41, pt. 1:448; *O.R.S.*, pt. 1, vol. 7:402; Busch, *Missouri Democrat Articles*, 58, 84; Busch, *Pilot Knob*, 47; Cole, 417.

aversion to fighting." To Albert Castel "the fighting edge of Fagan's division was badly blunted for the remainder of the campaign, Marmaduke's division was exposed as unreliable in battle," and army desertions began to increase. And to William Crowley, the Confederate defeat at Pilot Knob so disheartened Price's army that "the whole expedition became nothing but a long drawn-out retreat."

Of all the modern writers on the subject, Kyle Sinisi provides probably the best overall assessment of the effect of Pilot Knob on the Expedition. Sinisi writes: "If Price could take comfort in anything...it was in the fact that his army remained a potent threat. Pilot Knob was a setback, but it was not debilitating given his relatively slight losses."

But what of the Confederate soldiers themselves? Surprisingly, there were few comments from Confederate soldiers following the battle expressing more than relief that the Federals were gone. There were no comments about poor morale, increased loss of men, or any indications that the fighting ability of the army had been affected. Don Palmer, a conscript from Connecticut, who was unwillingly placed in Shelby's Division, and who had every reason to complain, wrote: "I seldom heard a murmur of discontent." If anything, the few comments that existed had to do with the shortcomings of generalship in the rebel command, and the superior generalship of the Federals.

General William Cabell in his later years wrote: "It made me feel sad to think that so many brave men had sacrificed their lives through bad generalship and a mistake in the strength of the enemy's position. We should have never attempted to take this fort by direct assault." John C. Darr of Cabell's Brigade wrote that the charge "was one of the most unreasonable blunders ever made...It was a useless sacrifice of a large number of brave and true officers and men."

That said, during the Court of Inquiry following the Expedition, Colonel James R. Shaler, Price's inspector general, noted that there was no "distrust or want of confidence in the leadership of Major-General Price on the part of the troops of the campaign."

Union veterans, typified by David Murphy, commander of Fort Davison's artillery, wrote that "the Battle of Pilot Knob deserves to be ranked among the most important and decisive battles ever fought on the American Continent." Murphy believed that not only did the battle save St. Louis, it prevented a Southern movement into Illinois and Indiana.[29]

And remember, Pilot Knob was just the beginning of the Expedition. There would be other engagements and there would be successes, like Glasgow, Sedalia, Lexington, the Little Blue and Big Blue. The morale of the army would remain relatively intact until the Battle of Mine Creek, when it was finally shattered. Until

---

29. *O.R.*, vol. 41, pt. 1:724; *O.R.S.*, pt. 1, vol. 7:394; Busch, *Fort Davidson*, 97; Campbell Memoir; Castel, *Sterling Price*, 218–219; Crowley, 138; Darr, 360; Forsyth, *Great Missouri Raid*, 138; Gifford, 176, 219–220; Monnett,, 24–25; Moore, *Missouri, Confederate Military History*, 182; Palmer, 24; Sinisi, 91; Suderow, *Arcadia Valley*, 121–122, 135; Thompson, "Great Little Battle of Pilot Knob," 140, 294.

then the Army of Missouri remained a viable threat to Missouri and with a more competent general could have been successful.

****

Item: Extended Comments on the Execution of Major James S. Wilson and His Men on October 3, 1864.

"Probably no action in Missouri during the Civil War has been so enshrouded in propaganda," according to Jerry Ponder, "as the execution of [James S.] Wilson, first by the U.S. Army at the time of the execution and since by the U.S. Government and by members of Union veterans descendent organizations." Ponder does little to clarify or support his comments with actual references in his account of the execution, which he detailed in his book on the 15th Missouri Cavalry. By piecing together the various accounts of Wilson's fate, including Ponder's account, I have produced the following story of Major James S. Wilson's capture and execution.[30]

Wounded and captured at the Battle of Pilot Knob on September 27, Union Major James S. Wilson had been second in command of the garrison. Following the battle, Dr. Seymour Carpenter dressed Wilson's wound and received assurance from an old friend, Lieutenant Colonel Thomas M. Gunter, that Wilson would be treated as a prisoner of war. Wilson for his part was not so sure, believing that he was marked for death, when his old enemies of southeast Missouri discovered that he had been captured. In time, Wilson was recognized by Colonel Timothy Reeves, commanding the 15th Missouri Cavalry (CSA). Reeves would subsequently request that Wilson be tried by court-martial, after which he was to be executed. As Price's Army moved northward, the prisoners, including Wilson, were carried along with the main body and would remain with them until October 3. With the number of prisoners swelling to well over 400, Price paroled 200 on October 3, with "more than that number" the next day.[31]

Prior to paroling the prisoners, "the field officer of the day [FOD] of the rebel army," who was identified as Colonel James R. Shaler, Price's inspector general, asked the men whether they were "citizens, soldiers or militia;" if a solider or a militiaman, they were further asked what was their assigned unit. If they answered the 3rd MSM Cavalry, they were separated from the rest, while those who identified themselves as civilians or citizens were conscripted into the rebel army. During this process, three members of the 3rd suspecting that they might be marked for execution, gave a false unit, while another believing that this was the first group to be paroled gave his unit as the 3rd, even though he was not a member.[32]

---

30. Ponder, *15th Missouri Cavalry*, 98, 100–106.
31. Bartels, *Battle of Pilot Knob*, 35–36; Mobley, 193.
32. Mark Lause says the FOD was probably John T. Coffee, while Ponder says it was Joe Shelby, neither of which is incorrect. The FOD was identified by several sources as Price's IG, who was

Those separated from the parolees were then handed over to Colonel Timothy Reeves, commander of the 15th Missouri Cavalry (CSA). Reeves, who was "branded a 'murderous fiend, a blood-stained outlaw'" by a resident of southeast Missouri, was also an arch enemy of Major Wilson and the 3rd MSM, and wanted revenge for Wilson's past acts. The execution subsequently took place at about 9:30 a.m., October 3, according to both James M. Kitchen, one of those who found the bodies of Wilson and his men, and Captain Franz Dinger, who was captured with Major Wilson. Kitchen had heard the shots fired at 9:30 on October 3, from the direction where the bodies were eventually found on October 23, while Dinger, was told the time from some of the other paroled men, who heard the shots.[33]

Of the actual execution of Major Wilson and party, Colonel J. J. Oliphant, a lieutenant at that time in the 47th Arkansas Mounted Infantry, and witness to the actual execution wrote:

> Col. Reeves addressed Maj. Wilson and told him that he had been ordered by Gen. Price to take them out and shoot them, when Maj. Wilson looking straight into the eye of Col. Reeves, said, "You do not mean to say that you are going to shoot us without a trial?" To which Col. Reeves replied, "You have been tried, and such are my orders," and ordered "forward."... Before the order to fire was given, Maj. Wilson and the men were asked if they had anything to say, and none but the boy said anything...Maj. Wilson took his hat off and laid it on the ground in front of him, and he and the five others stood facing the detail, apparently without a tremor, but the boy continued to cry. When the fire was ordered, Maj. Wilson was shot dead with many bullets...The men were stripped of their clothing, such as could be used as trophies, and especially Maj. Wilson, and they were left where they fell.[34]

As to why Major Wilson and party were killed there are two distinct opinions. Union commentary, whether officially or unofficially, was that Wilson's execution was murder and unjustified. Initially the *Missouri Democrat* reported that Wilson was killed "in retaliation for the alleged killing of some of Reeve's men," but later

---

Colonel James R. Shaler. It should also be noted that Colonel Shaler, as Price's IG, was responsible for paroling all the prisoners captured on the raid. On October 6, General Shelby sent a report of his operations to General Price, from Westphalia. As a P.S. to the letter Shelby wrote: "I leave about 100 prisoners here for Colonel Shaler to parole." This leaves little doubt, that Shaler was the officer tasked with identifying and selecting the men from the 3rd MSM Cavalry for execution. *O.R.*, vol. 41, pt. 1:719; *O.R.*, vol. 41, pt. 3:985; Busch, *Missouri Democrat Articles*, 240, 247–248; Crawford, *Confederate Courage*, 110; Crute, *Confederate Staff Officers*, 159; "How Price Treats his Prisoners," *Freedom's Champion*, November 3, 1864; Lause, *Price's Lost Campaign*, 141; Palmer, 14; Ponder, *General Marmaduke*, 188–189.

33. Busch, *Missouri Democrat Articles*, 288–289; Crawford, *Confederate Courage*, 91.
34. Charles Edward Nash, *Biographical Sketches of Gen. Pat Cleburne and Gen. T. C. Hindman Together With Humorous Anecdotes and Reminiscences of the Late Civil War* (Little Rock, AR, 1895; reprint ed., Dayton, OH, 1977), 170–173.

subscribed to the view that Wilson was murdered. To Southerners, Major Wilson and party were killed, according to John Edwards, as "an act of eminent justice for he was a common murderer, and entirely destitute of manly and soldierly feelings." General M. Jeff Thompson saw the execution as "entirely justifiable, only it should have been done by such order and form that retaliation would have been avoided." Thompson blamed Wilson's fate on the "blackened ruins and lonely graves in Ripley County," that were caused by Wilson's 3rd MSM Cavalry.[35]

Jerry Ponder, a modern-day author, who is decidedly biased toward the Confederacy, says that Wilson was executed for the 1863 Christmas Day Massacre at the Pullman farm, in southwest Ripley County, where "62 civilians, including some babies" were killed. According to Ponder, who says there was "ample proof" of Wilson's "brutal actions," the party they attacked was "having Christmas religious services and a community dinner." Wilson's men then "killed and wounded soldiers, civilians, men, women, children and babies, without discrimination." Later, after Wilson was caught, General Price had a hearing on the matter, without Wilson being present, where witnesses were called and the verdict of guilty and death were given.[36]

Michael Forsyth totally ignores the Christmas Day Massacre, believing that Wilson's only "'crime' deserving of execution was his effectiveness in combating guerrillas." Douglas Gifford, another author, puts little store in Wilson's execution because of the Christmas Day Massacre, believing instead Wilson's Official Report on the Christmas day attack. Within Wilson's report of the Christmas day battle, he reported killing or mortally wounding 32 rebels while wounding only three. This disproportionate loss between killed and wounded would suggest that Wilson didn't believe in taking any wounded prisoners, though he did report capturing 112 prisoners. Since Wilson failed to mention any loss of civilians of any type, Gifford believes that, "The 'Wilson Massacre' seems to be mostly modern spin placed on local tradition of dubious reliability by one flawed historian"—in this case he probably means Jerry Ponder. Ponder for his part considers many, if not most, Federal reports or for that matter, modern accounts of the war, to be mere "Union war propaganda." And to be fair to historians, both current and past, in many of Ponder's books, he fails to site sources, though he does occasionally list a bibliography. This in turn allows one to question the reliability of his writings, particularly concerning the Wilson affair.[37]

Gifford also seems to imply, that since the warfare in southeast Missouri was a "no quarter given" policy, that had Wilson been executed upon immediate capture at Pilot Knob, the execution would have been appropriate. The problem with

---

35. Britton, *Civil War on the Border, 1863–1865*, 413; Busch, *Missouri Democrat Articles*, 101, 115; Edwards, *Shelby and His Men*, 389; Fletcher, 41; Nichols, *Guerrilla Warfare, Volume IV*, 56; Stanton, et al., 294.
36. Ponder, *15th Missouri Cavalry*, 77, 101; Ponder, *General Marmaduke*, 169.
37. *O.R.*, vol. 22, pt. 1:184; Forsyth, *Great Missouri Raid*, 231; Gifford, 220–221; Ponder, *General Marmaduke*, 183.

that assessment is that Wilson was not captured by Reeves's men at Pilot Knob. However, once it was known that Wilson was captured, it seems reasonable to expect that Reeves would have requested Wilson's execution. And said execution took place on October 3, 1864, by the men of the 15th Missouri Cavalry (CSA).

To Jerry Ponder, "The death of Major James Wilson was not murder, but a legally ordered death by firing squad carried out, not by guerrillas as reported by the North, but by soldiers of the Confederate Army acting under general orders. The capture and execution of James Wilson was probably the greatest achievement of General Price's Invasion."[38]

Nor do the tales of Wilson's execution end here. When paroled prisoners reached St. Louis they told local officials that Major Wilson and six of his men had been turned over to Timothy Reeves for execution. General Rosecrans immediately retaliated, per a longstanding order issued by President Lincoln, on July 30, 1863, which stated "that for every soldier of the United States killed in violation of the laws of war, a rebel soldier shall be executed." Rosecrans issued General Orders No. 277, which specified that a rebel major and six men be held in "solitary confinement" at the Alton, Illinois Prison. These prisoners would then receive the same treatment as the Wilson party—if Wilson's party was found dead, then the rebel prisoners' fate was sealed.[39]

William S. Rosecrans

On October 23 partially buried and decomposed bodies were found near the banks of St. Johns Creek, on the Jefferson farm, about 10 miles west of Union in Franklin County. Two young boys out gathering persimmons came upon the bodies and immediately reported the scene to Federal authorities. Upon examination of the remains, papers found on Wilson's body identified the victim as the major.[40]

Events moved very quickly after Wilson's body was found. On October 26, General Ewing issued General Orders No. 51, telling the public that Major Wilson's body had been found and that he and his men had been murdered. He urged his

---

38. Ponder, *General Marmaduke*, 190.
39. *O.R.*, vol. 41, pt. 3:657–658; Bartels, *Battle of Pilot Knob*, 36; Britton, *Civil War on the Border, 1863–1865*, 413; Busch, *Missouri Democrat Articles*, 99, 101, 240, 287–289; Fletcher, 41; Lause, *Price's Lost Campaign*, 141; "The War In Missouri," *Chicago Tribune*, October 8, 1864; Quoted in Ross, "Burning of Doniphan," 83.
40. Busch, *Missouri Democrat Articles*, 236, 240, 264; Nichols, *Guerrilla Warfare, Volume IV*, 53.

comrades to "justly avenge his fiendish murder." The following day Wilson's body arrived in St. Louis, where he received a hero's funeral and later burial at Troy, Missouri, his hometown. On October 28, various statements were taken from members of the 3rd MSM, who identified the remains as well as potential rebels, who were to be executed. And before the 28th had ended, Joseph Darr, the acting provost marshal, Department of Missouri, ordered that the provisions of Special Orders No. 277 be carried out the following day.[41]

Even though it was shown that none of the condemned Confederates at Alton were involved in the execution of Major Wilson, they were sentenced to die. The *Missouri Democrat* justified their execution, stating: "In the instances of the victims on whom retribution is now especially to fall, it has been thoroughly proven that they have repeatedly, and in aggravated forms, committed the crime by which by law their lives are forfeited—the crime of treason to the National Government." A crime that technically all who supported the Confederacy could be charged with.[42]

On October 29, 1864, lots were drawn to determine who was to be executed. If the unlucky soldier drew a black marble from a bag he was slated as one of the six enlisted men to be shot. Those selected were Privates John W. Gates (3rd Missouri Cavalry), John A. Ferguson and Charles W. Minnekin (46th Arkansas Mounted Infantry Regiment), Harvey H. Blackburn (Coleman's Missouri Regiment), John Nicholds (12th Missouri Cavalry) and Asa V. Ladd (4th Missouri Cavalry). Prior to the execution Ferguson was removed from the list because "he never bore arms and was only employed as a teamster," and George F. Bunch (3rd Missouri Cavalry) was substituted in his stead. The men to be executed were not notified of their fate until the morning of the 29th, leaving virtually no time to prepare for their deaths. A Catholic priest and an Episcopalian minister baptized five of the condemned, while Asa Ladd, a Methodist, had previously been baptized. At 2:00 p.m. on the 29th, the condemned were taken in a wagon to Fort No. 4, which was just south of Lafayette Park, in St. Louis, where they were executed for crimes which they did not commit, save being in the Confederate Army.[43]

Of the six men only Minnekin gave a final statement, prior to being shot, which was as follows:

> Soldiers, and all of you who hear me, take warning from me. I have been a Confederate soldier four years, and have served my country faithfully. I am now to be shot for what other men have done, that I had no hand in, and know nothing about...I am sorry to be shot for what I had nothing to do with, and what I am not guilty of. When I took a prisoner I always treated

---

41. Busch, *Missouri Democrat Articles*, 259–260, 265–273.
42. Ibid., 259.
43. Anonymous, *Gallant Breed, 12th Missouri* 71; Busch, *Missouri Democrat Articles*, 273, 289–291; Crawford, *Confederate Courage*, 102, 106.

him kindly, and never harmed a man after he surrendered. I hope God will take me into his bosom when I am dead. O'Lord, be with me![44]

At 3:00 p.m., on October 29, the six rebel solders were executed by a detachment from the 10th Kansas and 41st Missouri Infantries. However, there still remained the issue of a Confederate major to be executed. Following the Battle of Mine Creek on October 25, two majors were among the captives. They were sent to St. Louis, and lots were drawn to determine who would be shot to avenge the death of Major Wilson. Major Enoch O. Wolf, of Ford's Missouri Battalion, was selected and marked for death on November 11. However, on November 10th President Lincoln stayed Wolf's execution, pending review of the case. Nine days later Lincoln addressed a letter to General Rosecrans to ensure that Rosecrans was not executing Wolf "merely for revenge," thus suspending Wolf's execution until further ordered. In the end Major Wolf was not executed. He was transferred to Johnson's Island Prison on Lake Erie, where he was released in the spring of 1865, thus ending the saga of Major James S. Wilson's execution at the hands of Colonel Timothy Reeves.[45]

* * * * * * *

Item: Extended Comments on General M. Jeff Thompson's Sedalia Expedition, October 14–17, 1864.

On October 14, the Army of Missouri made camp at 10:00 a.m. near Jonesborough in Saline County, at which time General Price ordered General Clark to conduct his Expedition to Glasgow, while General M. Jeff Thompson was tasked to take Sedalia. Thompson was also directed to drive a herd of cattle and mules, estimated at 2,000 head, back to the army. For the Expedition, which departed at 3:00 p.m. on the 14th, Thompson fielded 1,200 men, with two pieces of Richard Collins's Artillery, under Lieutenant John L. Harris. Guiding the Expedition was Major James C. Wood, who was a resident of Pettis County.[46]

According to orders, Thompson headed south on the road to Longwood, where he linked up with Alonzo Slayback's 500-man battalion sometime after dark. From Slayback, Thompson learned the location of the Federal forces in the area—General Sanborn was reported to the west, having passed through Georgetown heading toward Cook's Store, while A. J. Smith's infantry was reported at California, to the east, en route for the La Mine Bridge. The next morning, realizing that he was between the two Federal forces, yet far enough away so that they couldn't affect him, Thompson decided to press on to Sedalia. By continuing his advance on Sedalia, Thompson hoped to draw Sanborn back to that town, thus

---

44. Busch, *Missouri Democrat Articles*, 291; Quoted in Crawford, *Confederate Courage*, 108–109; Mobley, 194.

45. Busch, *Missouri Democrat Articles*, 341; Crawford, *Confederate Courage*, 111, 113, 123.

46. *O.R.*, vol. 41, pt. 1:664; *O.R.*, vol. 41, pt. 3:1012; *O.R.*, vol. 41, pt. 4:41–42, 44; *History of Pettis County*, 443, 449; Pitcock & Gurley, 231.

allowing Price with the main army to proceed westward without interference.⁴⁷

Thompson moved at daybreak on the 15th, proceeding southward toward Sedalia. Reaching the Georgetown area at 9:30, Thompson halted at the intersection of the Otterville/Cook's Store Roads, to give time for Sanborn's and Smith's forces to further distance themselves from his command. However, unknown to Thompson, instead of heading north after Price, Smith's command was moving slowly westward on the Georgetown Road toward Thompson's command. By noon, Thompson felt secure and proceeded on to Sedalia, where he arrived about 2:30 p.m.⁴⁸

M. Jeff Thompson

Meanwhile in Sedalia, Union Colonel John D. Crawford had been tasked by General Rosecrans to raise a force with which to defend the town. By October 15, Crawford had assembled between 500 and 800 militia, depending on the source, to defend Sedalia. Even as Crawford assembled his command, he was urged by General E. B. Brown, the district commander, to "take his horses and arms and leave Sedalia to its own fate." After consulting his fellow officers, "the word went out, 'We will stay until driven out.'"⁴⁹

Early on the morning of October 15, Crawford was warned by an A. M. Forbes that a large rebel force was near. But Crawford ignored the warning, believing that it was one of many false alarms that reached the city on a daily basis. Meanwhile, a Union scout hastily returned to Sedalia about noon, reporting, that indeed, rebels were in the woods a short distance from Sedalia and advancing on the city. Crawford ordered his command into the trenches and two forts that protected the town.⁵⁰

To the north of Sedalia at about 2:30 p.m., Thompson ordered his advance unit, Elliott's Battalion, which was clad in blue overcoats, to approach Sedalia "at

---

47. See Appendix D for the strength of Slayback's command. *O.R.*, vol. 41, pt. 1:388, 665; *O.R.*, vol. 41, pt. 4:1000; *History of Pettis County*, 434, 436; Lothrop, 197; Sanborn, "Campaign in Missouri," 169–170; Sinisi, 135–136; Stanton, et al., 242–243.
48. *O.R.*, vol. 41, pt. 1:665; Busch, *Missouri Democrat Articles*, 163, 313; Sellmeyer, 224; Sinisi, 136.
49. *O.R.*, vol. 41, pt. 1:364; *History of Pettis County*, 434–436; Britton, *Civil War on the Border, 1863–1865*, 441; Busch, *Missouri Democrat Articles*, 313; Lause, *Collapse of Price's Raid*, 35–36; Occasional, "From Sedalia," *Missouri Republican*, October 24, 1864; Sellmeyer, 224; *Union Army*, 6:781.
50. A. M. Forbes noted assorted times during the Sedalia engagement, which were one hour later than reported by other sources. A.M. Forbes, "The Capture of Sedalia," *Missouri Republican*, November 4, 1864, hereafter cited as Forbes; Occasional, "From Sedalia," *Missouri Republican*, October 24, 1864.

a steady walk," hoping to take the city by surprise. When they were within forty yards of the Federal picket, a Negro boy, who was working in an adjacent field started to run, alerting the defenders of the rebel ruse. The picket fired a ragged volley at the oncoming rebels, then beat a hasty retreat. Elliott charged after the pickets straight into Sedalia, routing the bluecoats, and taking the outer rifle pits with numerous prisoners. The remainder of the Thompson's command followed at a gallop deploying in an open field a short distance from Sedalia, while Harris's artillery was placed in the cemetery and commenced firing.[51]

In Sedalia, Crawford's command recovered quickly from Elliott's charge and drove him out of the city, even as Federal reinforcements arrived. A 33-man detachment from the 7th MSM Cavalry was en route to Georgetown at the time to secure some ammunition for Sanborn's command, which was located 16 miles away. Discovering that rebels were headed to Sedalia, Captain Oscar B. Queen, commander of Company M, 7th MSM Cavalry, rushed to the city and offered his services to Crawford, who dismounted 23 men of the 7th and placed them in the city entrenchments.[52]

By 2:45 p.m., rebel artillery began to throw shells at the Union forts, which were quickly abandoned by the skittish militia. With his artillery firing, Thompson sent detachments of his command to encircle the city, which they did in short order. Assaulted from all directions, the Union defense quickly collapsed, except for a small fort occupied by a steadfast 16-man company of German Home Guards commanded by Lieutenant Frank McCabe, and another occupied by Queen's MSM Cavalry. "It was quite a fierce struggle" while it lasted, recalled one rebel trooper, but in the end the garrison surrendered. The time was 3:00 p.m.[53]

As Sedalia was secured General John Sanborn's Federal Division arrived at Cook's Store, well to the northwest of the town, ensuring that no Union force would be able to interfere with Thompson's operations at Sedalia from the west. To Sanborn's east, Colonel David Moore's 1st Brigade, 3rd Division of A. J. Smith's 16th Army Corps, was slowly making its way to Sedalia down the railroad, but would not arrive in time. Thompson had successfully threaded the needle between the Union commands and captured Sedalia, with little or no trouble.[54]

With the resistance ending in Sedalia, rebel troopers swarmed into the local businesses to procure whatever they could. A short time later General Thompson arrived and immediately ordered his men to form up, so as to halt the pillaging. In the case of one trooper who failed to heed Thompson's orders, Thompson shot the man's mule, killing it, and wounded the soldier in his leg. With order restored

---

51. *O.R.*, vol. 41, pt. 1:665; Forbes; *History of Pettis County*, 436; Sellmeyer, 224; Stanton, et al., 243–244.
52. *O.R.*, vol. 41, pt. 1:364; *Union Army*, 6:781.
53. *O.R.*, vol. 1, pt. 1:364; Busch, *Missouri Democrat Articles*, 313; Forbes; *History of Pettis County*, 437–438, 441; "Missouri Boy's Experience," 432; Sinisi, 136–137.
54. *O.R.*, vol. 41, pt. 4:40–41, 314; *History of Pettis County*, 447; Sanborn, "Campaign in Missouri," 170.

Thompson directed his quartermaster, commissary "and ordnance officers to make their selections of what was needed or desired" of the available supplies.

Between 8:00–9:00 p.m. Thompson left town "and headed on a road that... [he] did not intend to follow," but when out of sight crossed over to the Lexington Road. The rear guard of Thompson's command departed Sedalia near midnight, even as 2,500 Union troops under Colonel David Moore arrived, the horse's feet of their advanced element covered with rags to muffle their approach. Not finding Thompson, the Federals camped for the night, while the rebels were well on their way back to the main army.

In addition to over 300 prisoners,[55] several wagon loads of "clothing, boots, etc." that were "suitable for soldiers," were taken, with most of the goods being procured from Cloney, Crawford & Company. Overall the goods were valued at $13,000. The Confederates also burned the railroad's water tower, a Negro shanty town, and attempted to burn the train depot, but some "young ladies" prevented it, arguing effectively with General Thompson that if the depot was fired much of the town would burn. Not wanting to destroy private property Thompson left without burning the depot. Other spoils included 300 hundred Austrian rifles, 400 pistols, 15,000 rounds of ammunition, and a herd of 2,000 cattle, sheep, horses, and mules, all at the cost of five killed and 13 wounded (the *Missouri Republican* said the rebels lost 10 killed and 12 wounded), while the Federals, according to the *Missouri Republican*, lost seven killed or wounded. Additionally, prior to leaving Sedalia, nine or ten Negroes who had assisted in building the defenses for Sedalia were all executed, shot in the head at close range (the *Republican* said seven were killed). As to the Federal prisoners, all were verbally paroled. However, General Rosecrans later vacated the paroles saying they were not valid and ordered the men back to duty.[56]

After departing Sedalia, Thompson's command successfully evaded Federal troops and finally rejoined the main army at Grand Pass, about seven miles east of Waverly on October 17.[57]

* * * * * * *

Item: Extended Comments on the Concentration of the Federal Command in October 1864.

As shown in Chapter 2, the Union command was slow to react or understand the scope of Price's invasion of Missouri in 1864. And it wasn't until the Battle

---

55. Edwards says 700 were captured, which is clearly wrong according to period accounts which put the total Union force at less than 500 officers and men. Thompson says he unconditionally paroled "several hundred," including 125 EMM and U.S. volunteers. Edwards, *Shelby and His Men*, 417.
56. *O.R.*, vol. 41, pt. 1:665, 670–671; *O.R.*, vol. 41, pt. 4:41–42; *O.R.S.*, pt. 2, vol. 35:482–483; Busch, *Missouri Democrat Articles*, 163, 225, 313–314; *History of Pettis County*, 442, 446, 448–449; Monnett, 31; Occasional, "From Sedalia," *Missouri Republican*, October 24, 1864; Sellmeyer, 225; Sinisi, 137; Stanton, et al., 244–246.
57. *O.R.*, vol. 41, pt. 1:666, 704; Cruzen, 28; Sellmeyer, 229; Stanton, et al., 246.

of Pilot Knob at the end of September 1864, that General William Rosecrans, the commander of the Department of Missouri, realized that a significant rebel incursion was taking place. Unfortunately, by that time, the Federal command was hopelessly scattered throughout Missouri and numbered but 17,966 men, including almost 4,000 EMM, as compared to Price's invasion force of over 17,000 officers and men.[58]

On September 24, as the invasion was developing, General Rosecrans contacted acting Missouri Governor Willard Hall, alerting him to the possible need of calling out the Missouri Militia. Governor Hall complied the following day, and General Rosecrans followed up by issuing General Orders No. 176, which officially alerted the people of Missouri of Price's invasion. In his orders Rosecrans wrote that Price brought with him "men from other States to plunder, murder, and destroy you," all in an effort to arouse Missourians to action.[59]

To the south of Price's invaders, in Arkansas, Union General Joseph Mower tried vainly to catch the rebel army as it headed north into Missouri, but had to give up his cross country quest, and moved to Cape Girardeau for river transport to St. Louis. After arriving in St. Louis, Mower linked up with the 3rd Division, 16th Army Corps. The reunited Right Wing, 16th Corps, under A. J. Smith then took up the pursuit of the Confederates, who had bypassed St. Louis and headed west. The infantry of Smith's command would never catch up to Price's army, while his cavalry, under Colonel Edward Winslow, would join in the pursuit under Alfred Pleasonton.

Pleasonton had arrived in St. Louis on September 30, moved to Jefferson City on October 8, and assumed command of the local area. On October 19, Pleasonton moved forward to Dunksburg, where he took command of a provisional division originally headed by John Sanborn. Pleasonton then reorganized his force into four cavalry brigades commanded by Generals E. B. Brown, John McNeill, John Sanborn, and Colonel Edward Winslow. The following day Pleasonton's command, constituting the eastern portion of the Union pursuit force, headed northwest toward Lexington. In all, Pleasonton's complement numbered about 6,500 cavalry, with 10 pieces of artillery, while A.J. Smith's infantry, which followed within supporting distance of the cavalry, numbered about 9,500 infantrymen.[60]

To the west, Kansas Governor Thomas Carney and General Samuel R. Curtis, Commander of the Department of Kansas, were kept informed of Price's progress as the latter moved into Missouri. General Curtis initially interpreted rebel moves across the Arkansas River as a pending invasion of Kansas via Fort Scott and requested that the governor call out the Kansas State Militia. Upon closer review,

---

58. For Confederate strength see Appendix D. *O.R.*, vol. 41, pt. 2:967.
59. *O.R.*, vol. 41, pt. 3:342, 365–366, 379–380.
60. The 1st Division numbered about 5,000 men, while the 3rd Division numbered 4,500 men with a total aggregate present on September 30, 1864, of 10,006. *O.R.*, vol. 39, pt. 2:554; *O.R.*, vol. 41, pt. 1:240; *O.R.*, vol. 41, pt. 3:508, 612, 660; Hinton, 152; Shalhope, 269; Titterington, 68; Williams, "Westport," 3.

Governor Carney rejected the call, believing that there was no immediate threat to Kansas. Meanwhile, as a precaution, Curtis began preparing Kansas for a possible invasion by erecting fortifications and concentrating his scattered volunteer force.

Price at the time was located in eastern Missouri, heading toward St. Louis, and posing no immediate threat to Kansas. On October 2, General Rosecrans telegraphed Curtis that Price had bypassed St. Louis and was headed west. Still the Kansas governor refused to react. And much of this refusal was a result of the current election cycle that pitted Governor Carney's supported candidates against Jim Lane's men, who were also supported by Curtis. Simply put Carney did not trust Curtis's motives in asking for the militia. On October 5, Curtis wrote Governor Carney, imploring him to call out the militia, while at the same time detailing the rebel army's path of destruction. Still, even with Price at Jefferson City, Carney hesitated to call out the militia, "disliking to take citizens of a whole state from their peaceful operations." Finally, on October 9, following repeated pleas for the KSM, Governor Carney ordered the militia to assemble, setting rally points for the various counties (Britton says it was October 8). George Deitzler was placed in command of the KSM, subject to the orders of General Curtis.[61]

Alfred Pleasonton

Within days the KSM began to assemble and "nearly all the male inhabitants had gone to the front as soldiers," according to a member of the 2nd KSM. The roads were clogged with men heading to the assembly points. "No where, at no time," wrote the Kansas Adjutant General, "and under no circumstances, had such an uprising been witnessed. It was wide spread and complete."[62]

As the various commands came together, General James G. Blunt, who had been on the plains fighting a mixed force of Cheyenne, Arapaho, and Kiowa Indians, was given leadership of the Provisional Cavalry Division or 1st Division, Army of the Border, and ordered to assemble at Olathe, Kansas. The division would eventually contain four brigades commanded by Colonels Charles Jennison, Thomas Moonlight, Charles W. Blair, and James H. Ford, with a total

---

61. Britton, *Civil War on the Border, 1863–1865*, 436; Collins, 186, 188–189; Hinton, 28, 30, 32–35; "How the Federals Fought," in Shelby Scrapbook; Sinisi, 150–153, 156.

62. G. G. Gage, *The Battle of the Blue of the Second Regiment KSM October 22, 1864. The Fight. The Captivity. The Escape* (Chicago, n.d.; reprint, ed., Shawnee Mission, KS, n.d.), 11, 15, hereafter cited as Gage.

complement of about 5,000 men. The KSM, under Deitzler, was designated the 2nd Division, Army of the Border, with its headquarters at Olathe. The KSM then assembled at Olathe, Atchison, Paola, Mound City, Fort Scott, and Wyandotte, though without a stated brigade structure. However, each militia assembly point did have an assigned general officer, each of whom historian Samuel J. Crawford implies commanded a brigade, even though there were no official brigades established within the Army of the Border for most of the KSM. Initially, Major General George Deitzler's command concentrated at Paola, about 14 miles from the Missouri line, before moving up in Shawnee or Shawneetown, which was about 25 miles north of Paola and eight miles from the Missouri border. In all, 16,000 men answered the call for the KSM, with some 10,000 eventually entering Missouri.[63]

On October 14, General Blunt's command moved forward to Hickman Mills, just south of Kansas City, where he massed his command, while the rest of the KSM continued to assemble. By late afternoon on October 16, General Curtis ordered Blunt to proceed to Warrenburg, Missouri, but not before Blunt's KSM staged a mutiny. Led by Brigadier General William H. M. Fishback, the Kansans started back to Kansas, believing that the southeast part of their state and their home counties were the targets of Price's invasion. Taking his headquarters staff and a section of Napoleon guns, Blunt raced ahead of the militia, cut them off at a creek and threatened to fire on them if they refused to return to camp. The militia complied and Blunt promptly ordered the arrest of several key officers, including General Fishback. With the situation resolved, Blunt headed east at 7:00 p.m., with his 1st and 2nd Brigades, which numbered 2,000 cavalry, and eight mountain howitzers. By October 18, Blunt was in place at Lexington to confront Price's advance, having added en route a 300-man Missouri Militia unit from Warrenburg.

James G. Blunt

Meanwhile, the remainder of the Army of the Border under Curtis headed to Independence, Missouri, the lead elements arriving on October 17, and fortified their position at the Big Blue River. Curtis wanted to go deeper into Missouri, but the KSM refused, citing the Kansas law that limited their operations to Kansas. In the end,

---

63. Of the KSM, Fishback's Brigade was numbered the 5th Brigade. Collins, 184, 191; Connelley, 181; Crawford, *Kansas In the Sixties*, 143; Forsyth, *Great Missouri Raid*, 249–250; Hinton, 37–38, 46–48, 58, 64.

Curtis gave in and waited for Price to arrive. It was October 19, and Price was now faced with the prospects of fighting off two armies: General Curtis's Army of the Border from the west and the Department of Missouri troops under Alfred Pleasonton and A. J. Smith from the east.[64]

* * * * * * *

Item: Extended Comments on the "Action" at Lexington, October 19, 1864.

Price's command began its march at "daybreak" on the morning of October 19, led by Thompson's Brigade, which moved to the front of the column on the Waverly-Lexington Road, which was also known as the Dover Road. They were followed by Jackman's Brigade, Fagan's Division, the army trains, with Marmaduke's Division bringing up the rear. About eight miles outside of Lexington, Shelby's Division made a "flank march" to the southwest at Tabo Creek, intent on approaching Lexington via the Salt Pond Road. The plan called for encircling the town and trapping the Federal troops who were reported there under Jim Lane, Charles Jennison, and James Blunt—all hated by Missourians for their past actions in the state.

On the Salt Pond or Camden Road, Thompson's advance hit Blunt's pickets, who were posted about five miles from Lexington near 11:00 a.m. Holding the position as long as they could, the advanced troops dispatched couriers to inform General Blunt of the rebel presence. About noon, Blunt was alerted by his pickets from both the east and southeast that the rebels were approaching Lexington. Federal pickets near Taboo Creek, on the Dover Road, had apparently detected Shelby's move to the southwest and reported their findings at about the same time. General Blunt quickly deployed his command for combat, placing Charles "Doc" Jennison's 1st Brigade to the east of the fairgrounds and about a mile from the city. Jennison's "Lilliputian brigade" connected with Thomas Moonlight's 2nd Brigade, which held the left at the Masonic College. Three miles to the front of Moonlight, on the Dover Road, Captain H. E. Palmer held a strong position with about 250 men, including the Warrenburg Militia under Captain George Grover, who were armed with "Martin-Henry breech loading rifles...that could fire sixteen times before reloading."

Meanwhile, after Shelby moved off the Dover Road, Fagan's command, led by Cabell's Brigade, continued down the main road to Lexington. Seemingly moving at a slower pace, Fagan's command didn't make contact with Federal pickets west of Tabo Creek until near 1:00 p.m., when they began active skirmishing. Back at Salt Pond Road, Thompson deployed his brigade to the east of Jennison's line with the "strong regiments" of B. Frank Gordon, Moses Smith, and William H. Erwin occupying his right, while the smaller commands of Ben Elliott, Alonzo

---

64. *O.R.*, vol. 41, pt. 4:59; Busch, *Missouri Democrat Articles*, 164; Collins, 192; Connelley, 182; Gage, 24; Hinton, 60, 62–63, 65, 80; Sinisi, 166, 169, 181.

Slayback, and John T. Coffee (now commanded by John T. Crisp), with the newly organized battalion of M. Rector Johnson holding the left.

By 2:00 p.m. Thompson launched his attack, skirmishing with the enemy. On the Dover Road, Cabell's Brigade continued to push the Federals back and by 2:00 p.m. were within three miles of Lexington where they came to a halt, being confronted by Captain Palmer's Federals. At 3:00 p.m., the scope of the engagement changed when Collins's Parrot guns arrived and began shelling the Union position from the Salt Pond Road. In the meantime, while Thomson and Cabell were engaged, Shelby led Jackman's Brigade to the Warrenburg Road in an attempt to trap Blunt's command. However, shortly after Collins began shelling the Union position, Blunt saw it was time to withdraw. Outflanked and now outranged by the rebel artillery, Blunt ordered a retreat. Seeing the Yankees pulling out, Slayback's Battalion struck, chasing Jennison, who moved to the west and northwest in a rapid, though controlled retreat. Slayback was followed by the rest of Thompson's Brigade.

Back on the Dover Road, Cabell's Brigade made several unsuccessful probes or charges against the Yanks stationed at that point. To the rebels' surprise, the Federals under Captain Palmer counter-charged, capturing 15 men, whom they later verbally paroled. Cabell never did break through and occupied the Union position only after the northerners had abandoned the area.

From the very beginning of the engagement, Blunt realized that he had no real chance of defeating the rebel advance, since requested reinforcements were never provided. His stand at Lexington became an exercise in delay and determining the exact composition of the rebel force that he faced. As such, Blunt conducted a controlled retreat for the next several hours through Lexington and down the road to Independence, using the 500-man 11th Kansas Cavalry to cover his rear. The 11th accomplished its mission in fine fashion by forming successive lines, firing, and then retreating, thus successfully covering Blunt's withdrawal.

Dogging the Federal retreat, Slayback's Battalion eventually gave way to Gordon's Regiment with the approaching darkness. Gordon's boys carried on the rebel pursuit for several miles and into the dark of the night. The 5th Missouri was encouraged by bugler George Cruzen, who would signal a charge, at which time the Unionists invariably fled, leaving the 5th behind time and time again. Hampered by steep hills and thick tree cover, Gordon's Regiment could do little damage to the 11th Kansas, and they too gave up the chase at Sni-a-bar Creek, about three miles east of Wellington. It was midnight when Gordon's command was recalled. Returning to Lexington, Gordon's boys watered their horses in the Missouri River and bedded down for the night, ending the "Action" at Lexington for October 19. Camped about the town was the Army of Missouri, while Thompson's Brigade rested in the streets of the city.

Overall the engagement at Lexington had begun in earnest at 2:00 p.m. and was over by mid-night, having ranged over 14 miles, according to one source, from start to finish. There was little damage done to either side. Federal losses were variously reported at 40–50 casualties, with General Curtis reporting the loss of 50 men, while General Blunt recorded "losing but few men." R. Fuller, a member of the 11th Kansas remarked, "Our loss in killed will not exceed 12 individuals...we had none wounded," while a piece of captured correspondence from the Army of the Border noted the losses as 40. Of those Federal units reporting losses, Captain George Grover's Warrenburg Militia reported at least two killed; Company D, 11th Kansas, R. Fuller's unit, shows one killed and one missing; and Company H, 11th Kansas lost one wounded. Michael Forsyth writes in *The Great Missouri Raid* that Moonlight's 11th Kansas lost 100 men at Lexington, which seems out of line, given the known losses that were published in the *Supplement to the Official Records*.

Confederate losses were recorded as "very slight" according to one account, while George Cruzen noted that three men from Gordon's command were wounded toward the end of the contest. All other Union and Confederate accounts are silent on the matter of casualties, suggesting that they were indeed very light, notwithstanding Forsyth's estimation.[65]

* * * * * * *

Item: Extended Comments on Cabell's Rear Guard Action, October 22, 1864, at Independence.

Shortly after the Federal Army crossed the Little Blue River on October 22, confusion entered into the picture as to which command or commands General McNeil was facing. In his Official Report, McNeil stated that "he attacked the enemy's rear guard, composed of two brigades." However, this is not entirely correct. In his commentary on the October 22nd engagement, General William Cabell states that his brigade was the only one sent back from Fagan's Division to protect the rear of the army, while Colonel John C. Wright, of W. F. Slemons's Brigade, clearly states in his memoirs, that his regiment was the only command of Slemons's Brigade on picket at the Little Blue to engage the Federal advance. So McNeil's statement is only partially correct, in that he was fighting one brigade and a portion of a second. Unfortunately, in retelling the story of the Confederate retreat from the Little Blue to Independence, historians, for the most part, have latched onto McNeil's report and have Pleasonton fighting two rebel brigades—Cabell's

---

65. *O.R.*, vol. 41, pt. 1:573–574, 582–583, 646, 657, 666; *O.R.*, vol. 41, pt. 4:140–141; O.R.S., pt. 1, vol. 7:397; O.R.S., pt. 2, vol. 21:409, 423; Britton, *Civil War on the Border, 1863–1865*, 442–444; Busch, *Missouri Democrat Articles*, 213–214; Captured Union Correspondence, in Confederate Correspondence (MSS 03-26, box no. 1, file no. 3), R. Fuller to Daughter (October 20, 1864) and Letter, Army of the Border (October 20, 1864); Connelley, 194–185; Cruzen, 28; Darr, 360; Davis, *Civil War Atlas*, plt. no. 161; Dyer, 813; Forsyth, *Great Missouri Raid*, 176; Grover, 171, 174; Harrell, *Arkansas, Confederate Military History*, 442; Hinton, 84–88; Lause, *Collapse of Price's Raid*, 65–67, 69; Monnett, 50–51; Palmer, 27; Moore, *Missouri, Confederate Military History*, 185; Occasional, "From Lexington," *Missouri Republican*, November 2, 1864; Pitcock & Gurley, 233; Sellmeyer, 330–332; Sinisi, 174–178; Stanton, et al., 247–248; Wright Memoirs, unnumbered pages 88–89.

William L. Cabell

and Slemons's—before reaching Independence. Further compounding the confusion, Wiley Britton also implies, as do other others, that Fagan's entire division was assaulted at Independence, a fact that author Paul Jenkins disputes. Jenkins, in his book on the Battle of Westport, states that Fagan's Division, including Slemons's Brigade, was following behind the army's trains, occupying the center of Price's column as it headed for the Big Blue. Further, two wounded men (unknown as to rebel or yank), who departed Independence at noon on the 22nd, reported that the rebel train was moving west, with "Fagan's division in the rear." This last statement can be taken to mean that Fagan was following the train or that his command was the rear guard. However, according to prisoners captured at Independence, Cabell's comments on the rear guard action, and Wright's memoirs, it's more likely that Fagan's Division, less Cabell's Brigade, was heading west with the trains. Simply put, with the exception of Cabell's Brigade, "Fagan was guarding the train."[66]

As to Cabell's rear guard action, it really began after Wright's Arkansas Regiment passed through Cabell's command, en route for the rear and a much need rest. When McNeil's Federals approached Independence at 2:00 p.m. they dismounted and deployed for action. A short time later General John Sanborn arrived with Pleasonton's 3rd Brigade, deploying on McNeil's right, which eventually overlapped Cabell's left flank. Cabell initially repulsed Sanborn's advances, but sensing trouble on his left flank, Cabell ordered an immediate retreat through Independence "before another attack could be made." Even as Cabell was pulling back, General Pleasonton arrived at about 3:00 p.m., with the remainder of E. B. Brown's 1st Brigade, which he held in reserve. Quickly assessing the situation, Pleasanton ordered an immediate advance by Sanborn's and McNeil's commands.

---

66. Of all the prisoners captured on October 22, four were from Thomas McCray's Brigade, three of whom were either sick in the hospital or a nurse when captured. The fourth was Colonel Milton Baber, commander of the 45th Arkansas, who "was captured while taking a ride." The rest of the POWs were from William Cabell's or J. B. Clark's Brigades. *O.R.*, vol. 41, pt. 1:371; *O.R.*, vol. 41, pt. 4:183; *O.R.S.*, pt. 1, vol. 7:398, 409; "The Battle of Westport," Shelby Scrapbook; Britton, *Civil War on the Border, 1863–1865*, 463–465; Buresh, 49–50; Hinton, 115; Jenkins, 67, 74; Monnett, 77, 86; Report of Prisoners, Bryce Suderow Collection, Western Historical Manuscript Collection, State Historical Society of Missouri (Columbia), List of Prisoners at Leavenworth (December 12, 1864), hereafter cited as Suderow, Report of POWs; Sinisi, 210; Wright Memoirs, unnumbered page 91.

Sanborn rapidly "moved forward through gardens, yards and streets," while McNeil's command was directed to mount and charge the enemy.

Caught by surprise, Cabell did not made it out of Independence before his command was struck on the flanks. Colonel E. C. Catherwood, leading the 13th Missouri Cavalry, "made a gallant saber charge," hitting Cabell's command as it exited Independence to the west. A fierce battle raged over William M. Hughey's Arkansas Battery. It was "a furious hand to hand fight," according to one Union participant, "in which the rebels were stricken down like so many worthless weeds." The battery was "magnificently defended and no less bravely attacked," according to another witness. But in the end the two guns were taken, and according to Federal sources, 17 rebels lay dead among the captured artillery. In the attack on Hughey's Battery, the 13th Missouri lost seven wounded (Sinisi has the 13th losing 10 wounded, which was not correct; the 13th lost seven wounded in capturing the guns, with another four killed and wounded from the Little Blue to Independence.).

His flank smashed and his brigade in disorder, Cabell headed out of town as best he could, barely escaping capture by jumping his horse over an artillery piece and losing his sword in the process. Exiting the melee, Cabell eventually reestablished order in his command, thanks to the timely arrival of a battalion of the 10th Missouri Cavalry under Lieutenant Colonel Merrit Young. For Cabell's Brigade, the battle was over as it headed to the rear, but it was just beginning for Marmaduke's Division, which was positioned west of Independence to hold off the Union advance while the army with its train headed southwest toward Byram's Ford on the Big Blue.[67]

In driving Cabell from Independence various sources, including General Pleasonton, report that 100 or more prisoners were taken; however, later, when Pleasonton wrote his Official Report on the Expedition, he records only that "a number of prisoners were taken" and does not mention any specific amount. And the *Missouri Democrat* later noted that 41 men were captured with Colonel Milton Baber, "on the Big Blue near Independence," while a member of John Sanborn's Brigade simply noted in his diary that "some prisoners" were taken. Further, a member of the 1st MSM, from Brown's Brigade, recorded that just 25 prisoners were taken, which corresponds fairly closely with Cabell's losses in Independence.

In recalling the disaster at Independence, General Cabell wrote that he had 200 to 300 men "cut off." General Price made a similar statement in his Official

---

67. T. J. Hughes of the 5th MSM recalled that only 16 members of Hughey's Battery were killed. *O.R.*, vol. 41, pt. 1:340, 371, 389; *O.R.*, vol. 41, pt.4:185, 204; *O.R.S.*, pt. 1, vol. 7:398; *O.R.S.*, pt. 2, vol. 35:748; Britton, *Civil War on the Border, 1863–1865*, 464; Brown Court-Martial, J. H. Little Testimony, 163; Brown Court-Martial, Pleasonton Testimony, 19; Busch, *Missouri Democrat Articles*, 336, 379; T. J. Hughes, "A Missouri Man's Experience on the Price Raid," *National Tribune*, July 17, 1890, hereafter cited as Hughes, "A Missouri Man's Experience"; Jenkins, 69, 72; Quoted in Kirkman, 100; Sanborn, "Campaign in Missouri," 177; Sinisi, 211–212; Wright Memoirs, unnumbered page 91.

Report of the Expedition which appears to be the basis for authors like Kyle Sinisi, Mark Lause, and others, putting the number of captured Confederates at between 300 and 400. And even Henry Luttrell mentions that 300 prisoners were reported taken. However, the plight of the supposed prisoners is clarified in the *Official Records*, where it is noted that General Marmaduke, who was in Independence during Cabell's rout, "led Cabell's men and cut his way to the command." John Edwards also states that Marmaduke "safely led" the cut off men "though to the army." In reviewing the prisoner of war records for the Expedition, a total of 89 names were listed, including doctors, nurses, and the wounded in the rebel hospital when the city was taken. However, of those names, 48 were repeated, some more than once, leaving only 41 prisoners captured at or near Independence on October 22. Of those 41 names, 23 were from Cabell's Brigade, 14 were from Clark's Brigade, and four were from McCray's Brigade, the last being identified as the colonel of the 45th Arkansas, who supposedly commanded the rear guard, with the others being either nurses or the sick in the hospital.[68]

* * * * * * *

Item: Extended Comments On Shelby's Operations on the Big Blue for October 22, 1864.

Following the Battles of Little Blue and Independence, on October 21, the Federal command pulled back to the west side of the Big Blue River, to positions previously prepared by General Samuel R. Curtis. General James G. Blunt, for his part, disagreed with General Curtis "relative to the probable movements of Price," following the battles of October 21. Curtis insisted that Price would attack down the main road to Kansas City, and deployed his troops accordingly. Blunt disagreed with Curtis, believing that Price would feign an attack down the main road while he maneuvered farther south to cross the Big Blue. Despite his misgivings, Blunt followed Curtis's orders and deployed his command.[69]

Curtis's defensive line was approximately 15 miles long, stretching from the mouth of the Big Blue at the Missouri River on the left, to the Hickman Road Crossing or the Russell's Ford on the far right. The main Federal line extended six miles from the left and was primarily defended by elements of the KSM, from General George Deitzler's command. Next came Blunt's 3rd Brigade of KSM, commanded by Charles Blair. To the right of Blair, James H. Ford's 4th Brigade, including the 10th and 12th KSM, took their post, and then Moonlight's 2nd Brigade, which anchored Curtis's main line at Simmon's Ford. The remainder of the army was farther

---

68. *O.R.*, vol. 41, pt. 1:646; Bray Diary, October 22, 1864, 11; Edwards, *Shelby and His Men*, 427; Kirkman, 98; Lause, *Collapse of Price's Raid*, 96–97; H. J. McBrayer, "Hurried Price Right Briskly," *National Tribune*, August 25, 1904, hereafter cited as McBrayer; Monnett, 87; Sellmeyer, 242; Sinisi, 212; Suderow, Report of POWs, Gratiot Prisoner List no. 74 and 79 (November 10, 1864), Gratiot Prisoner List no. 81 (December 31, 1864), Gratiot Prisoner List no.84 (January 10, 1865), Leavenworth List (December 12, 1864).

69. Blunt, "Civil War Experiences," 257.

south, with Blunt's 1st Brigade under Charles "Doc" Jennison placed at Byram's Ford and supported by the 4th KSM. Russell's Ford was occupied by the 1,200-man 1st Brigade, KSM, commanded by General Melvin S. Grant. All the fords crossing the Big Blue were covered from the mouth of the river to Russell's Ford, except for two: Hinkle's or Cattleman's Ford, between Byram's and Simmon's Fords and another Cattle Ford to the south of Byram's Ford, both of which were left unguarded. In all, Curtis deployed about 15,000 men (10,000 KSM, nominally assigned to Deitzler, and 5,000 KSM and volunteers under Blunt), with 34 pieces of artillery to confront Price at the Big Blue on the 22nd.[70]

The battle of the Big Blue River opened early on the morning of October 22nd, with picket fire on the Kansas City Road just before 8:00 a.m. Back in Independence, S. D. Jackman's Brigade led out Shelby's advance at 9:00 a.m., heading toward the picket firing on the Kansas City Road. Jackman was instructed by General Shelby to drive back the enemy pickets "and guard the right flank of the army until the train passed," at which time Fagan's Division would take over. To accomplish his mission, which was nothing more than a feint to hold Curtis's line in place while the army crossed the Blue at Byram's Ford, Jackman used DeWitt C. Hunter's and W. O. Coleman's Regiments to hold the flank. After pushing back the Union pickets, Jackman awaited the arrival of Fagan's command, after which he hurried off to Shelby, with John Schnable's and C. H. Nichol's commands to join the main push across the Big Blue.[71]

M. Jeff Thompson's Brigade followed Jackman, taking the Westport Road, but "was slow in getting started," according to Thompson, "as so many of our men had friends to see, and all were so tired." About 11:00 a.m. Thompson's Brigade approached Byram's Ford, accompanied by Joe Shelby and the engineers from Marmaduke's Division. The road leading to the ford and the ford itself were found to be obstructed with fallen trees and abatis, making the ford "almost impregnable," necessitating their removal before the army's train and artillery could cross. However, the road was so badly blocked, that Shelby ordered a new road cut to the ford. With the engineers working on the road, Thompson dismounted part of his brigade to secure the crossing and protect the engineers, which proved to be quite difficult. Time and time again Thompson's men were repulsed as Doc Jennison successfully held the ford. Still, it took only 90 minutes for the engineers to clear the area to the east of the ford; the rest would be completed after the ford was secured.[72]

In the early afternoon, Byram's Ford still held firm, necessitating a change in strategy by General Shelby if he had any hope of crossing the Blue. Turning to B. F. Gordon, commanding the 5th Missouri, Shelby ordered him to proceed

---

70. Ibid., 258; Mark Lause writes that Curtis's line numbered only 5,000 men with 12 pieces of artillery; clearly wrong. *O.R.*, vol. 41, pt.1:479; Hinton, 122–126, 129; Lause, *Collapse of Price's Raid*, 85–87; Monnett, 69, 71–72, 142–143; Sellmeyer, 237; Sinisi, 195–196.
71. *O.R.*, vol. 41, pt. 1:658, 675; Lause, *Collapse of Price's Raid*, 90; Monnett, 77–78; Sellmeyer, 237; Sinisi, 199.
72. *O.R.*, vol. 41, pt. 1:584, 710; Cruzen, 29; Hinton, 128; Jenkins, 74; Monnett, 79; Sellmeyer, 239; Sinisi, 198–199; Stanton, et al., 249.

upstream, to a reported Cattle Ford, cross, and proceed to the Wornall Road, turn toward Westport and then hold. To Alonzo Slayback he gave a similar order, but Slayback was directed downstream to the Hinkle or Cattlemen's Ford, flanking Doc Jennison's position. In both cases the men found unprotected fords allowing them to cross with ease.[73]

Back at General Curtis's headquarters, the nervous Union commander had received early reports of only limited attacks on his main line. Curtis had been "out generaled" by Sterling Price, wrote Thomas Moonlight. Price had marched off to the southwest from Independence, bypassing Curtis's main line. Curtis, according to Moonlight, seemed to be "wandering in his mind" on the 22nd. "There was a lack of decision of character," Moonlight continued, with "a lack of action, a lack of everything that bespoke determination to fight it out to the bitter end." And Moonlight was not the only senior officer to question Curtis's "lack of action." Colonel Samuel Crawford, who severed on Governor Carney's staff, wrote: "The old gentleman lost his nerve." Even though Curtis failed to act decisively on the 22nd, he did attempt to keep his subordinates advised of the situation. At 9:00 a.m., he sent an aide to General Grant at Russell's Ford, directing him to watch for a possible rebel move on his position. Curtis also moved his headquarters farther west, to better control the situation, and sent riders to Blunt to apprise him of the situation; but Blunt never received any orders or intelligence, leaving him in the dark as to his commander's intentions.[74]

Receiving Curtis's warning at about 10:00 a.m., Grant dispatched the 2nd KSM, which he accompanied, to scout the east side of the Blue. After proceeding down the Hickman Mills Road and a mile beyond the Blue, the 2nd stopped to feed and rest their horses, having met the 21st KSM from Grant's command and a battalion of the 15th Kansas, from Jennison's Brigade, both of which were scouting east of the Blue. After a short rest, Grant heard gunfire to the north, at about 1:00 p.m. from Byram's Ford, and ordered the other units to continue their scout, while he returned to Russell's Ford, with George Veale's 2nd KSM. Meeting another rider at Russell's Ford, Grant was informed that Byram's Ford, had been flanked, and further the supports Grant had left at Russell's Ford had been ordered back to Westport. Back went Grant and the 2nd KSM, at a gallop, heading toward the gunfire "on the prairie" at Mockbee Farm, via the Wornall Road.[75]

---

73. Monnett and Sinisi have the time as 2:00 p.m. while George Cruzen writes that it was "after noon." Cruzen, 29; Forsyth, *Great Missouri Raid*, 186; Hinton, 129–130; Kirkman, 95–96; Monnett, 79–80; Sinisi, 199; Shalhope, 271.

74. *O.R.*, vol. 41., pt. 1:479–480; Blunt, "Civil War Experiences," 258; Crawford, *Kansas in the Sixties*, 147; Gage, 83–84; Monnett, 78; *Moonlight Reminiscences*, 35.

75. Sinisi says the prairie firing was from Gordon's engagement with elements of the 3rd and 13th KSM, which Cruzen does not acknowledge, recording instead: "We got out of the timber still going S.W., and not seeing any enemy, kept on going." The first enemy the 5th Missouri encountered was the 2nd KSM Artillery. *O.R.*, vol. 41., pt. 1:479; *O.R.S.*, pt. 1, vol. 7:385–386; P. I. Bonebrake, "Recollections of the Second Day's Fight In the Battle of Westport," in Fred L. Lee, ed. *The Battle of Westport* (Kansas City, MO, 1976), 33, hereafter cited as Bonebrake; Cruzen, 30; Gage, 40, 70–71, 83–84; *Moonlight Reminiscences*, 35; Sinisi, 202–204.

By 2:00 p.m., as the army's trains were approaching Byram's Ford, Slayback struck Jennison's left flank, causing the Union force to retreat rapidly to the west. And while Slayback struck, Thompson finally secured Byram's Ford, pouring his men across after Jennison's retreating Federals, pressing them back toward Westport and the Kansas line. General Blunt, who had heard artillery firing at 1:00 p.m. from Jennison's position, reacted quickly, and without orders from General Curtis. A courier was sent to Moonlight, ordering him to Jennison's assistance; but it was too late. Jennison had been flanked, causing Curtis's position at the Blue to be untenable. Moonlight then headed for the Kansas state line to link up with Jennison, which he did, while Blunt directed Deitzler's command to fall back to Kansas City. Meanwhile, per orders, Thompson halted his drive short of the Kansas line, picketed the area with the W. H. Erwin's 12th Missouri Cavalry and returned to the division's assembly point for the night.[76]

Back at Byram's Ford, Shelby secured the area and began clearing the debris, which took about an hour, after which the train could pass. At about the same time Jackman came up with Nichol's and Schnable's commands, while three miles away at the Mockbee Farm the 2nd KSM Artillery wheeled into position, having been fired upon by some hidden rebels (probably the advance from Gordon's 5th Missouri). At this point in time, the 2nd KSM Artillery was unsupported, being in the rear of the column that had retreated from Russell's Ford. The 3rd, 13th, and 23rd KSM, which were in front of 2nd KSM Artillery, had fled when they encountered Gordon's advance, failing to offer any resistance; besides they had orders to get to Westport.

Deserted by his supports, Captain Ross Burns, commanding the 22-man battery, immediately deployed his single gun—a 24-pound, brass howitzer. Within minutes, the main body of Gordon's 5th Missouri arrived at the Wornall Road and were fired on by the battery at 200 yards, which missed, according to George Cruzen of the 5th. Fortunately for Burns, Colonel G. W. Veale galloped up with the remainder of the 2nd KSM, deploying to the right of the battery. After deploying the 2nd KSM, "General Grant and his staff fell back from the field," according to Veale, and escaped the area, leaving the 2nd KSM to its fate. Meanwhile, Gordon also deployed, dividing his regiment into two battalions; Lieutenant Colonel Yandell H. Blackwell led five companies commanding the left of the line, while Colonel Gordon led the other four companies on the right.[77]

While Gordon surveyed the situation and his command skirmished with the Yankees, he sent George Cruzen, his bugler, to a vantage point where he could view the battle area. Further, Gordon wanted Cruzen to inspect a draw or gully

---

76. *O.R.*, vol. 41. pt. 1:575, 666–667; Blunt, "Civil War Experiences," 257–258; Busch, *Missouri Democrat Articles*, 219, 235; Kirkman, 85; Sinisi, 199–201.

77. Of the first firing of the artillery, G. G. Gage, of the battery, recorded that the gun fired at 100 yards and that "the lane in front of us was strewed thick with dead of wounded men and horses." P. I. Bonebrake, of Company G, 2nd KSM, stated that the first three shots missed, which seems to agree with Cruzen's account and not Gage's. *O.R.*, vol. 41, pt. 1:658; *O.R.S.*, pt. 1, vol. 7:386; Bonebrake, 33, 35; Cruzen, 30; Gage, 20, 26, 40–41, 72–73, 84–85; Sinisi, 199–200, 204.

that he had spotted. When Cruzen returned, he described the Union force as 400 if infantry and 225 if cavalry. Cruzen also described the draw, or "a swell in the prairie" as coming out in the rear of the Federal position. Blackwell's Battalion was then moved down the draw where it waited for the signal to charge. Meanwhile, back at Byram's Ford, Jackman's two-unit command rushed to the front to support Gordon. The engagement had been ongoing for about 30 minutes, when Jackman neared the Mockbee Farm and fronted his command with that of Gordon's. It was at that time that Cruzen, per Gordon's orders, blew the charge, and away the 5th went, "with the usual rebel yell." With Jackman's men to their right, "the whole command swept forward, in a gallant style, driving the Federals, utterly routed and demoralized, from their shelter, pursuing them across the prairie, killing and capturing them in considerable number." Colonel Jackman with 100 men and Blackwell's Battalion continued their pursuit of the fleeing foe until dark, pushing them back toward Indian Creek and the Big Blue, where the 21st KSM, with the 15th Kansas sat idly by, watching the 2nd KSM be destroyed. Unwilling to re-cross the Blue, Blackwell and Jackman returned to their respective brigades for the night. The remnants of the 2nd KSM, along with the other units of Grant's Brigade on the east side of the Blue, retreated to Olathe and were not a factor in the battle of October 23.[78]

The engagement at the Mockbee Farm had cost the 2nd KSM 24 killed, 24 wounded, and a loss of 68 prisoners, out of the 300-man unit. The 4th, 19th and 23rd KSM also lost heavily in Gordon's and Jackman's charge, suffering 12 killed, 19 wounded, with 37 more captured, for a grand total of 179. The 2nd KSM also lost nine wagons and their artillery, while other KSM units also lost part of their train. Jackman reported his losses as "slight," but "quite a number of horses were killed or wounded." Neither Thompson nor Shelby made any mention of losses at the Big Blue. However, Dr. William McPheeters of Price's staff recorded that the hospital he had established after the fighting at Mockbee Farm contained 27 men, not including the dead. Further, during the Court of Inquiry following the Expedition, it was also recorded that the losses on October 22 were "very light." And G. G. Gage, in his book on the 2nd KSM, recorded that some of their men, who were prisoners counted 43 rebels either killed or wounded upon the field, following the battle. Other Federal losses from Blunt's command were minimal, with Jennison recording the loss of but 15, while Moonlight and Ford reported none. Overall "losses on both sides were slight," at the Blue, according to one Union source, without considering the Mockbee Farm.[79]

---

78. In his account of Gordon's operations Sinisi has the 5th engaging the two regiments of Grant's KSM as they retreated from Russell's Ford. However, Cruzen makes no mention of it, writing instead that their first contact was with the 2nd KSM Artillery. O.R., vol. 41, pt. 1:675; Cruzen, 30–31; Bonebrake, 34–35; Quoted in Lause, *Collapse of Price's Raid*, 93; Sinisi, 203, 207.
79. John Edwards put the Kansans' losses at Mockbee Farm at 217 dead with 207 prisoners; clearly out of line, given that Colonel Veale gave a by-name account of losses in his command, totaling 116, while other KSM commands lost 63 more. And even Dr. McPheeters of Price's staff recorded on the 22nd that Shelby captured "some 60 prisoners," clearly more in line with the Federal offi-

Appendix C / 331

By the end of the pursuit, following the engagement at the Mockbee Farm, the sun was setting, ending the day for Shelby's Division. Shelby had a victory and secured a crossing of the Blue, allowing the Confederate army's trains to cross which they safely did, followed by the rest of the army.

* * * * * *

Item: Extended Comments on Union Losses at the Big Blue on October 23, 1864.

Overall Kyle Sinisi places the Union losses at Byram's Ford at less than 100, which as shown below is clearly not correct, being too low. Howard Monnett and Paul Kirkman put the Union losses at 200 (probably based upon Hinton's comments), which is too high, but closer to the truth. That said, the losses of the Union command at the Big Blue on October 23 are generally known, though there are some minor differences, depending on the source, with period newspapers putting the loss at just 120 killed and wounded—again too low.[80]

Note: John McNeil's 2nd Brigade is not including below as it was engaged with the rebel train near Russell Ford. The artillery is also not listed below, having suffered no losses on October 23.

Philip's Brigade. Colonel John Philip's Brigade lost 15 killed, 74 wounded, with the slightly wounded not counted in the 1st or 7th MSM. Grand Total 89. Additionally in a post-war interview Colonel Philips stated that his command suffered 124 casualties. The difference with the number shown below probably reflects the slightly wounded who were not previously listed or could be simply Philips not remembering what he lost on October 23.[81]

Philips 1st Brigade:

    1st MSM Cav.   3 K, 11 W, 0 M[82]

    4th MSM Cav   8 K, 48 W, 0 M[83]

---

cial report. *O.R.*, vol. 41, pt. 1:676, 710; *O.R.S.*, pt. 1, vol. 7:387; Bonebrake, 33; Edwards, *Shelby and His Men*, 425; Gage, 45, 86, 93; Hinton, 140, 143; Pitcock & Gurley, 235; Sellmeyer, 241; *Union Army*, 5:122.

80. Hinton, 173; Kirkman, 114; Monnett, 115; Occasional, "Pursuit of Price," *Missouri Republican*, November 4, 1864; Sinisi, 241.

81. Interview with Judge John F. Philips, "General Jo O. Shelby," in Shelby Scrapbook; Occasional, "Pursuit of Price," *Missouri Republican*, November 4, 1864; Bryce Suderow, "The Battlefield of Westport as Seen by a Federal Infantryman," *The Westport Historical Quarterly* 10 (June 1974), 14, hereafter cited as Suderow, "Battlefield of Westport."

82. The *Missouri Democrat* provided a partial list of casualties, in the 1st MSM, but does not list the losses for Companies D and G. However, the *Supplement to the Official Records* does list the by-name losses in the 1st MSM, including the missing units as three killed and 11 wounded. And neither of these sources agrees with the official report that lists three killed and nine wounded. *O.R.*, vol. 41, pt. 1:360–361; *O.R.S.*, pt. 2, vol. 34:498–499; Busch, *Missouri Democrat Articles*, 396; Suderow, "Battlefield of Westport," 14.

83. The *Supplement* reports losses as four killed, 32 wounded, with four missing; excluding Company F. Additionally, Company K was escorting the ration wagons and was not present, while

7th MSM Cav	4 K, 15 W, 0 M[84]
Total Philips	15 K, 74 W, 0 M

Sanborn's Brigade. With the exception of the 2nd Arkansas Cavalry (Union), Sanborn's units have known losses for October 23. During the Expedition the 2nd Arkansas reported the loss of one killed with 11 wounded; one man was killed at Boonville, with another known to have been wounded on October 25. This leaves nine wounded unaccounted for; however, based upon John Phelps description of the action on October 23, where the rebels "planted the [artillery] shells in the column with an unerring accuracy," I would suspect that the regiment lost the remaining nine wounded at Westport.[85]

Sanborn's 3rd Brigade:

2nd Ark.	0 K, 9 W, 0 M[86] [E]
6th MSM	1 K, 10 W, 0 M
6th EMM	2 K, 17 W, 0 M
7th EMM	0 K, 0 W, 0 M [Not Engaged]
8th MSM	0 K, 11 W, 1 M
Total Sanborn	3 K, 47 W, 1 M

Winslow's Brigade. Colonel Winslow recorded that his losses "did not exceed 25 killed and wounded." However, the 3rd and 4th Iowa recorded four killed and 17 wounded; the 4th and 10th Missouri lost three killed and 17 wounded; and the rest of the brigade had no reports. Total 41 known casualties for Winslow.

Winslow's 4th Brigade:

3rd Iowa Cav.	1 K, 12 W, 0 M[87]
4th Iowa Cav.	3 K, 5 W, 0 M[88]
4th Mo. Cav/7th Ind.	2 K, 4 W, 0 M
10th Mo. Cav.	1 K, 13 W, 0 M
Total Winslow	7 K, 34 W, 0 M[89]

---

neither Companies L or M appear to have been with the command. Suderow has the command losing nine killed, with 47 wounded. *O.R.*, vol. 41, pt. 1:363; *O.R.S.*, pt. 2, vol. 35:34, 43, 51, 58, 66, 82, 90, 93, 101, 104; Suderow, "Battlefield of Westport," 14.

84. Busch, *Missouri Democrat Articles*, 432; Suderow, "Battlefield of Westport," 14.

85. *O.R.*, vol. 41, pt. 1:403; Bishop, *Report of the Adjutant General of Arkansas, 75*; Suderow, "The Battlefield of Westport," 15.

86. *O.R.*, vol. 41, pt. 1:403; Bishop, *Report of the Adjutant General of Arkansas, 75*; Suderow, "The Battlefield of Westport," 15.

87. S. H. M. Byers gives the overall loss in the brigade, while Nathaniel Baker gives the by-name loss in the 4th Iowa Cavalry. Suderow has the loss as 13 wounded. Nathaniel B. Baker, *Report of the Adjutant General and Acting Quartermaster General of Iowa. January 11, 1864, to January 1, 1865* (Des Moines, IA, 1865), 962; S. H. M. Byers, *Iowa in War Times* (Des Moines, 1888), 583; Suderow, "The Battlefield of Westport," 15.

88. Scott, *Fourth Iowa*, 568.

89. Suderow, "The Battlefield of Westport," 15.

Total Federal Losses At Byram's Ford

Total Philips	15 K, 74 W, 0 M
Total Sanborn	3 K, 47 W, 1 M
Total Winslow	7 K, 34 W, 0 M
Grand Total Pleasonton	25 K 155 W, 1 M

Confederate losses at the Big Blue were spotty. Freeman had no report and only three of Clark's regiments (3rd, 7th & 10th Missouri) reported losing nine killed with 16 wounded. The other units also had an estimated loss of nine killed and 16 wounded (See Appendix G, Losses at the Byram's Ford Front for details). But Byram's ford was just one part of the Battle of Westport. See Appendix G for the Confederate Order of Battle at Westport, including estimated strengths and losses.[90]

* * * * * * *

Item: Extended Comments on the Confederate Train.

"The saga [of the trains] starts with the realization," according to Kyle Sinisi, "that historians have not only exaggerated the size of the trains, but they have never properly noted the route and the attendant combat actions." In his book on Price's Raid, Sinisi provides interesting evidence of the train's size, quoting from a "Union informer," who counted the wagons as they passed through Independence. The informer noted, "The whole army was moving in a compact body, the trains in the center, wagons moving two abreast, about 250 in number." This was somewhat supported by a Confederate observer, who said that the train was "stretched out for 2 miles" on October 23. At 40 feet per wagon, with 4 mules or horses, this would equate to about 269 wagons (10,760 ft. / 40 ft. = 269). And James W. Campbell of Wood's Battalion recalled in his memoirs, that on October 23, the Confederate trains contained 300 wagons. But did this train also include the civil conveyances that accompanied the Expedition?[91]

Following the Battle of Mine Creek, Price ordered the destruction of a portion of his train, including civilian conveyances. In all about one third of the train was destroyed on the night of October 25, after which, according to General Shelby, about 300 wagons still remained. This would suggest the train numbered about 450 wagons for both the military and civilians who accompanied the Expedition. This would be further supported by a Union spy who noted on October 29 at Newtonia that the train numbered "about 300 wagons, mostly loaded with plunder." For his part Sinisi writes that the rebel train was down to but 50 wagons, which appears to be wrong, unless the other 250 wagons were all civilian-owned,

---

90. Ibid.
91. Campbell Memoir; Edwards, *Shelby and His Men*, 247; "How the Federals Fought," in Shelby Scrapbook; Sinisi, 174–175, 249.

which is highly unlikely. Additionally, a member from the 3rd Wisconsin Cavalry recorded in his diary of the 25th, that Price "destroyed over one hundred wagons heavily loaded with ammunition and captured goods," while local newspapers placed the number at "about 200." This, with the number that Shelby gives would suggest a train that numbered between 400–500 wagons, which is echoed by Governor Reynolds in his article to the *Marshal Republican*, on December 23, 1864.[92]

Most authors, period newspaper accounts, and Union scouts have the trains gradually increasing from 250, at the beginning of the Expedition, up to as many as 600. And in the opinions of virtually all, the trains were loaded with booty taken from the citizens of Missouri. However, according to Sinisi, Price needed the wagons, not to carry booty or plunder, though there were probably some illicit goods carried in a few of the wagons, but to convey supplies for the army, such as forage, food, ammunition, forges, assorted quartermaster goods, along with the sick and wounded—all to support an army estimated to number in excess of 25,000, including unarmed recruits and camp followers. Further, according to Freeman Mobley, Price need to load up his train with assorted foodstuffs before hitting the open prairies of western Missouri and eastern Kansas, where supplies were short or non-existent, a tactic that Mobely labels a "grassland strategy."

The vast majority of the illicit "plunder" taken by the Confederates was done by individual soldiers, who were mostly stragglers, deserters, "sneaks and deadheads," and who carried their loot on their persons or on their horses, according to Missouri Governor Reynolds. However, according to at least one Federal and one Confederate source, that was not entirely true. A Union supporter from Boonville recorded that the "men and horses are loaded down with plunder, but their wagons are empty. They are saving them, doubtless to fill them up with valuable commodities on the eve of their retreat to the South." Captain James T. Alexander, of Fagan's staff says the following, which supports what the Federal witnessed:

> We have come through a magnificent country all through Mo. Every little town is full of goods of every description. There is nothing you can imagine that you cannot find in these stores & our army sacks every town they come to. You cannot conceive of the amount of goods that our soldiers carry along with them & finally have to abandon for want of transportation. Well I have for you & Mrs. Eakin some calico, domestic hoops, shoes, etc.

Price had issued "strict orders" against looting, going so far as to have men shot who resisted arrest for pillaging. Price also arrested Lieutenant Colonel C. H. Nichols of Jackman's Brigade for looting on October 3 at Potosi, but upon

---

92. *O.R.*, vol. 41, pt. 1:705; Busch, *Missouri Democrat Articles*, 298; Confederate Correspondence (MS 03-026, box no. 1, file no. 4), Board of Survey at Clarksville, TX (November 29, 1864), General J. O. Shelby Testimony; "Latest From the Field," *Missouri Republican*, October 12, 1864; Monnett, 133; Pitcock & Gurley, 237; Porter, *In the Devil's Dominion*, 172; Schultz, 145; Sellmeyer, 257; Shalhope, 273; Sinisi, 304–305; Volunteer, "Interesting Particulars of the Late Campaign Against Price," *Daily Conservative*, November 5, 1864; "The War In Missouri," *Chicago Tribune*, November 9, 1864.

review released him. In one case, Colonel Thomas Freeman personally executed two men for looting, and in another General M. Jeff Thompson shot a man in Sedalia for failing to halt his thieving. To further curb pillaging, Price appointed John P. Bull as the army's provost marshal, who organized nine companies from the various brigades to serve as provost guards. "Each day the guards were deployed along the line of march to prevent straggling, depredating, etc. This proved difficult, as at times the column was stretched out five or six miles." This helped curb indiscriminate looting, but never eliminated it. Overall, any large volume of goods taken by the Confederates was done by the various quartermasters, who paid for them in either Confederate money or some type of voucher, which for Union supporters was the same as stealing or plundering. In the final analysis the vast majority of "plundered goods" were generally dedicated to the support of the army and not for the benefit of the private individual.[93]

John P. Bull

As to the route taken by the train, Sinisi, as well as period participants, are in general agreement. In the early morning hours of October 23, the livestock herd crossed at Russell Ford on the Big Blue River, having followed the Harrisonville-Hickman Mills Road southward from Byram's Ford. The herd was followed by the wagons which could only cross the ford one at a time. The route taken by the trains then moved about three miles southeast before turning southwest toward Little Santa Fe and then south to safety.

When it comes to describing the defense of the train, Sinisi falters in a few points. According to William Cabell, Charles Tyler's Brigade led the way at the front of the train, not Thomas McCray's Brigade, as Sinisi writes. (Colonel John C. Wright in his memoirs also says that McCray led the train, as do other authors who have misinterpreted Price's Official Report.) A close reading of Price's comments on the issue implies that McCray was leading the train; however, Price

---

93. *O.R.*, vol. 41, pt. 1:648, 720, 722, 725; *O.R.*, vol. 41, pt. 3:980; J. T. Alexander, Letter (undated, probably October 2, 1864); Busch, *Missouri Democrat Articles*, 113, 136–137, 143, 211; Castel, *Sterling Price*, 222–223; Edwards, *Shelby and His Men*, 435; Forsyth, *Great Missouri Raid*,195; Mobley, 198; "The Occupation of Franklin," *Missouri Republican*, October 3, 1864; "Price Certainly in Missouri," *Missouri Republican*, October 3, 1864; Schultz, 143; Sinisi, 240; Stanton, et al., 244–245.

ordered a portion of McCray's Brigade "forward" to engage the Union left that was confronting the train, near Hickman Mills. If McCray were leading the train how could he be ordered "forward"? Price also noted in his report that he deployed his escort and the unarmed men at the front of the train, where he awaited the arrival of a portion of McCray's Brigade, again clearly indicating that McCray was not leading the train; where, if he had been, McCray would have already been there and deployed. In this case Price simply wrote a clumsy statement as to the placement of McCray's Brigade, meaning merely that McCray's Brigade came from the rear of the train.[94]

The actual assaults that took place against the train are well covered by Sinisi, though a few points are missing. John McNeil's Brigade approached Hickman Mills about 10:00 a.m., following an all night march that began at midnight from Independence. Arriving near Hickman Mills, McNeil discovered the rebel train passing about three miles to his front. Considering the size of the train and the escort that guarded it, McNeil approached cautiously, taking a position to the north of Hart Grove Creek. It was about noon when McNeil sent skirmishers forward, across the creek, only to retreat when confronted by Confederate artillery (probably Harris's Battery, which had arrived from Byram's Ford; not Hughey's Battery, as claimed by several authors, since this battery had been captured at Independence the previous day).

Back at Byram's Ford, Tom Freeman's Brigade had withdrawn from combat about 10:00 a.m. and per orders rode to Russell Ford to help protect the train. Arriving at the train, General William Cabell, who was responsible for the train, deployed Freeman's command, as well as a portion of McCray's Brigade which had arrived at Russell Ford. And so from about noon to 2:00 p.m., long rage skirmishing and artillery fire took place between the forces of Generals Cabell and McNeil. By 3:00 p.m., with the rear of the train turning to the southwest, McNeil finally, and briefly, crossed over Hart Grove Creek, but then retreated out of rebel artillery range. And to ensure that McNeil remained a safe distance away from the train, Cabell ordered the tall prairie grass fired, causing the flames to push McNeil's Federals back even further until they were no longer in contact with the train.[95]

The Confederate train had been saved, but this would only be short lived as the events of October 25 would show. For his lackluster performance at Hart Grove Creek, General McNeil would later be court-martialed, charged with "Disobeying the lawful command of a superior officer," as well as two other nonrelated charges. In the end General McNeil would be found guilty and suspended for

---

94. *O.R.*, vol. 41, pt. 1:636; *O.R.S.*, pt. 1, vol. 7:398; Forsyth, *Great Missouri Raid*, 195; Monnett, 118–119; Wright Memoirs, unnumbered page 95.

95. *O.R.*, vol. 41, pt. 1:341, 372, 379, 383; *O.R.S.*, pt. 1, vol. 7:398–399; Darr, 361; McNeil Court-Martial, Charge no. 3, 10; McNeil Court-Martial, John F. Beveridge Testimony, 29, 39–40; McNeil Court-Martial, Nelson Cole Testimony, 46; Monnett, 119–120; Sinisi, 252–254; Freeman Memoir, October 23, 1864.

three months without pay or rank; however, upon appeal, the charges were dismissed and McNeil was restored to his rank.[96]

****

Extended Comments for Chapter 4
Irregular Operations

Item: Extended Comments on the Composition of Harrison's Expedition to Colorado.

Various sources place the composition of Harrison's Expedition at from 16–46 men, all officers. Warner Lewis, the only member to survive both the expedition and the Civil War, puts their number at 19, as do most sources. Of the 19 men in the expedition, 14 are known and are listed below. Clark Hockensmith was listed as a survivor by John Edwards—one of only two. Given Warner Lewis's account of the expedition, the inclusion of Hockensmith is suspect and probably not correct, though he is included below as part of the fourteen.

From the papers recovered, including officer commissions, by a detachment from the 15th Kansas Cavalry, it was determined that the expedition had three colonels, one lieutenant colonel, one major and four captains. It is assumed that the rest were lieutenants of some type, numbering 10. The list below contains two colonels, two lieutenant colonels, two captains, and the remainder either lieutenants or men of unknown ranks.[97]

Captain Bowen.

In Lewis's account of the expedition, Captain Bowen was from Howard County. This Bowen could be William H or N. Bowen, who enlisted in Saline County, Missouri, in December 1861, and was subsequently captured at Milford on December 19, along with William P. McLure. Sent to Alton Prison, Bowen was paroled in August 1862.[98]

Colonel Charles Harrison.

Colonel Charles or Charley Harrison commanded the expedition to Colorado. He was shot in the face, according to Warner Lewis, and was the fourth to be taken by the Indians. And like the other captives, he was tortured and killed. John Edwards, in *Noted Guerrillas*, has Harrison bravely fighting to the bitter end, being the last man killed by the Indians. Of Harrison's death Edwards wrote:

> Lewis left Harrison dying as the Indian always dies—killing to the last. Behind his dead horse, both legs broken, jaw shattered, and four fingers of

---

96. Forsyth, *Great Missouri Raid*, 268 (n. 64); Jenkins, 102; McNeil Court-Martial, Charge no. 1, 9.
97. *O.R.*, vol. 22, pt. 2:286; Abel, 237–238; Britton, *Civil War on the Border, 1863–1865*, 228; Cottrell, 67; Edwards, *Noted Guerrillas*, 127; "Fort Scott Correspondence," *Chicago Tribune*," May 25, 1863; "From St. Louis," *Chicago Tribune*, May 27, 1863; Lankford, 93; Nichols, *Guerrilla Warfare, Volume II*, 101.
98. Eakin, *Battle of Blackwater*, "Bowen, W. N." roster entry; Eakin, *Confederate Records*, 1:121.

his left hand gone, he shot while a load was left in a single pistol. There came then finally a rush and a volley—then great stillness. Harrison had been the last to go, and it had taken him three-quarters of an hour to die.

As shown under Harrison's biography (see Appendix B), he was shot, captured, and killed early in the engagement with the Osages. Following Harrison's death, he was scalped, in a non-traditional way, as he was "shiny bald," with no hair to remove. Instead, the Osages "cut off 'his magnificent fan-shaped beard,'" in addition to beheading him.[99]

Lieutenant Colonel John Henderson.

Little is known of John Henderson, though this could be Captain John Henderson, of the 7th Division, MSG. This Henderson was appointed a captain and drill master on November 11, 1861, and was later assigned to Little's Missouri Brigade. However, the most likely John Henderson that Musser was referring to was probably a lieutenant colonel, in the 8th Division, MSG, serving on the staff of General Rains in September 1862. This second Henderson was noted for his service under Colonel Douglas Cooper at the Battle of Newtonia, September 30, 1862. Of Henderson, Cooper wrote: He rendered "valuable service...in carrying orders, in leading troops and placing them into position."[100]

Clark L. Hockensmith.

Clark L. Hockensmith (rank unknown) was born on February 21, 1843, in Missouri, probably Jackson County. He was a "top scout and spy," serving under Quantrill. According to John Edwards, Hockensmith accompanied Harrison's Expedition, but managed to survive, along with Warner Lewis. According to Warner Lewis, only himself and Raferty survived the expedition, however. Lewis makes no mention of Hockensmith. It was possible that Hockensmith started with the expedition, but left before it had gone far from its starting point. That said, in the latter part of the war Hockensmith accompanied Quantrill to Kentucky, where he was killed on May 10, 1865.[101]

Lieutenant Douglas Huffman or Hoffman.

Douglas Huffman or Hoffman was the first man killed when Harrison led a charge on the Indians. Warner Lewis, who had lost his horse in this charge took Hoffman's mule, but later exchanged his mule for Colonel Woodson's horse, as the latter preferred mules to horses. This would later cost Woodson his life as the horse proved faster than the mule, allowing Woodson to be caught and killed.[102]

J. B. Kimbaugh.

---

99. Edwards, *Noted Guerrillas*, 127; Josephy, 293; Lewis, 230.
100. *O.R.*, vol. 13:300; Eakin & Hale, 200; Lankford, 93; Peterson, et al., 211; Schnetzer, *More Forgotten Men*, 110.
101. Edwards, *Noted Guerrillas*, 127; Lankford, 93, 104; Lewis, 231.
102. Lankford, 93; Lewis, 229.

Little is known of J. B. Kimbaugh (probably a lieutenant) save that he rode with Harrison and was killed on May 23, 1863, south of Coffeyville, Kansas.[103]

Colonel Warner Lewis.

Colonel Warner Lewis was one of only two survivors of the expedition. Wounded in shoulder early in battle, he managed to hide from the Indians and escaped with Lieutenant John Raferty after the pair abandoned their horses and hid under the embankment of a creek or river bed. A full biography has been previously presented; see Chapter 2 note no. 85 for details.[104]

Captain William P. (or Parkinson or Park) McLure (or McClure).

Captain William P. McLure, a prominent attorney from St. Louis, went to Denver, Colorado, in 1859, where he met Harrison and established a "lucrative position" in the local area. Wounded in a duel in Denver, McLure recovered and returned to St. Louis at the beginning of the Civil War. He tendered his service to Missouri, joining the MSG in the latter part of 1861. He was captured at Backwater River (Milford) on December 19, 1861, sent to Alton Prison, and exchanged in September 1862 (or released on having been forced "to take the Oath of Allegiance"), after which he joined Harrison's Expedition to Colorado. McLure fell off his horse and was the third man captured or killed by the Indians, according to Warner Lewis. In McLure's case he was captured alive and then brutally tortured and killed.[105]

Reuben or Rube Pickwell (or Pickerel or Pickral).

No other information has been found on Reuben or Rube Pickwell (or Pickerel or Pickral), save that he rode with Harrison on his Colorado Expedition. Pickerel broke his arm as the command rushed out of an Indian encirclement, and was eventually killed when the men made a final stand two miles farther on at the Verdigris River.[106]

Lieutenant John B. Raferty (or Raftery).

In reviewing the *Official Records*, the *Supplement*, and other sources, the name Raferty, as a Confederate, is rare. Lieutenant John B. Raferty could be the Captain Raferty mentioned as commanding the Emmett Guards, a 50-man company, of the 4th Military District, Missouri Militia, operating under Colonel M. Jeff Thompson. This Raferty was a resident of St. Joseph at the beginning of the war, but is not mentioned in any official documents or records. According to Warner

---

103. Lankford, 93, 131; Lewis, 231–232.
104. Lewis, 229–230.
105. Carolyn M. Bartels, *True Tales: Civil War in Missouri* (Independence, MO, 2002), 140; Eakin, *Battle of Blackwater*, "McClure, W. P." roster entry; Eakin, *Missouri Prisoners of War*, "McClure, W. P." entry; Eakin & Hale, 290; Frost, 40, 178; Lankford, 93; Letter, Ruxton to Brown (May 10, 1863), in Eakin, *Battle of Blackwater*; Lewis, 23; Peterson, et al., 299; Potter & Robbins, 145–148; Winter, 86.
106. Lankford, 93; Lewis, 230.

Lewis, Raferty was the only other man who escaped the Osage Indians, only to be killed a month later at Cowskin Prairie, after having returned to Missouri.[107]

Frank Roberts.

The only Frank Roberts or Franklin Roberts (rank unknown, though probably a low ranking officer) or variation thereof that could be found was F. M. Roberts, who was wounded at Corinth, Mississippi, in October 1862, and a "citizen" of the same name, who was sent to Alton Prison and later paroled in January 1863. No other candidates were found in the *Official Records*, the *Supplement*, or other sources listed in the bibliography. Both Rose Lankford and Warner Lewis include Roberts as part of the Harrison Expedition, but nothing else is known, except that Lewis says that Roberts was the second man killed, shot in head, after which Lewis took Roberts's horse, giving up his mule, as Lewis trusted the horse more so than the mule— particularity in the running fight that ensued.[108]

Captain Edward West.

Edward West was probably the assistant quartermaster captain of the 1st Cavalry Regiment, 8th Division, MSG. This West was born in Kentucky in about 1824, and lived near Independence, Missouri, at the beginning of the Civil War. He enlisted in Company A, 2nd Cavalry Regiment, 8th Division, MSG, on June 2, 1861, served out his term, and was discharged on December 3. Three days later West was appointed quartermaster of the 1st Cavalry Regiment. After leaving the Guard on February 28, 1862, West joined what became the 10th Missouri Cavalry, where he was an assistant quartermaster. It appears that West departed the 10th with Colonel Harrison, who had commanded Company A of the same regiment. West was killed at the unit's final stand at the Verdigris River on May 23, 1863.[109]

Lieutenant Colonel Branham H. Woodson.

Branham H. Woodson of Springfield, Missouri, joined the 8th Division, MSG, as lieutenant colonel and aide-de-camp on August 16, 1861. Prior to officially joining the Guard, Woodson had served under General James Rains at Carthage, on July 5, 1861, where he was cited for his performance of duty. During Harrison's Expedition, Woodson was the fifth man caught or killed, as Harrison's party broke for Verdigris River.[110]

Lieutenant John Y. Yeater.

No additional information was found on John Y. Yeater. He is only listed in the sources cited as a member of the Harrison Expedition, killed by the Indians.[111]

---

107. Lankford, 93; Lewis, 230–231; G. S. Parsons's Report (January 18, 1861), Missouri Militia Papers, Missouri Historical Society; Peterson, et al., 170; Stanton, et al., 51.
108. Bartels, *Trans-Mississippi Men*, 68; Eakin, *Missouri Prisoners of War*, "Roberts, F. M" and "Roberts, Francis M." entries; Lankford, 93; Lewis, 229–230.
109. *O.R.S.*, pt. 2 vol. 38:253, 298; Bartels, *Forgotten Men*, 385; Bartels, *Trans-Mississippi Men*, 239, 278; Eakin & Hale, 461; Lankford, 93; Peterson, et al., 245.
110. *O.R.*, vol. 3:22; *O.R.*, Index, 1104; Bartels, *Forgotten Men*, 401; Lewis, 230; Peterson, et al., 211.
111. Eakin & Hale, 483; Lankford, 93.

Appendix D
Army of Missouri Order of Battle and Additions to the Army
Army of Missouri Order of Battle
September 19, 1864

Abbreviations (Used throughout the various Orders of Battle):

Ark. = Arkansas	Inf. = Infantry
Bn. = Battalion	K = Killed
Brig. = Brigadier	Lt. = Lieutenant
Capt. = Captain	Ltc. = Lieutenant Colonel
Cav. = Cavalry	M = Missing
Cdr. = Commander	Maj. = Major
Col. = Colonel	Mo. = Missouri
Co. = Company	Mtd. = Mounted
Cos. = Companies	MW = Mortally Wounded
Div. = Division	SB = Smoothbore
(E) = Estimate	Sec. = section
EFF = Effectives	Ukn. = Unknown
Gen. = General	WIA = Wound In Action

Organizational Notes:

1. If not otherwise specified, units are considered regiments with ten companies. Additionally it appears that cavalry companies that formed in 1864, with few exceptions, contained 60 enlisted men, with four officers. As such if not stated or unknown, regiments raised during the Expedition (e.g., Tyler's Brigade) will be rated as containing 640 officers and men with a staff of six officers for a total of 646 or 64 officers and men per company. Effective strength, per Thomas Livermore, if fully armed would be 549 (646 x .85 = 549.1). Additionally, the mounted infantry units (e.g., 45–47th Arkansas Mounted Infantry or Cavalry) appeared to have contained 80 enlisted men per company (See Freeman's Brigade for details), with four officers per company. As such, where not known or stated, all units identified as mounted infantry units will be rated as 84 officers and men per company, with a staff of six officers giving the command 719 (846 x .85 = 719.1) effective officers and men per regiment; battalions will be similarly calculated based upon the number of companies in the unit.[1]

---

1. *O.R.*, vol. 41, pt. 1:699; Thomas L. Livermore, *Numbers & Losses in the Civil War in America: 1861–1865* (Bloomington, IN, 1957), 68–69, hereafter cited as Livermore; Muster Roll, Company

2. It is also clear from previous strength reports in the Trans-Mississippi, that Price's report of "men" was meant to embrace only the enlisted personnel of the army or men with "muskets," not the officers, staff, engineers, or the men who manned the artillery pieces. Since the Expedition was organized just before it left Arkansas, it's assumed, unless otherwise indicated, that the various units were at full strength for officers. The officer strength of each regiment, where not known, will have 10 captains (excluding staff), 10 1st lieutenants and 20 2nd or 3rd lieutenants; total 40. The command staff of each regiment will include a colonel, a lieutenant colonel, a major with an adjutant, a commissary & quartermaster and an ordnance officer; total six, which gives each regiment 46 officers. Battalions will be assigned a command staff of a lieutenant colonel, a major, an adjutant, a commissary & quartermaster and an ordnance officer for a total of five. The number of companies varies, depending on the battalion and will be addressed on a case by case basis. Allowing for an 85 percent effective strength for cavalry units (per Thomas Livermore) will give a typical regiment 39 (46 x .85 = 39.1) effective officers, while battalions vary depending on the number of assigned companies.[2]
3. As the Expedition began General Price issued General Orders No. 12, dated September 21, 1864, which specified that brigade staffs would consist of an acting assistant adjutant general, an acting assistant inspector general, an acting assistant quartermaster, an acting assistant commissary of subsistence, an acting ordnance officer and a brigade surgeon—"No other staff officers will be allowed." With the exception of the brigade surgeon, all members of the staff will be considered effective, giving the brigade staff, including the commander, a total of six officers. Staffs also included various amounts of aides-de-camp, even though they were not included in Price's order; this was shown by the various commands that had aides-de-camp listed (e.g., Cabell's Brigade) and are included in the brigade staff numbers, where appropriate.[3]

* * * * * * *

General References:
1. *O.R.*, vol. 41. pt. 1:641-642; *O.R.S.*, pt. 1, vol. 7:391.
2. Buresh, 204–207; 216–221.
3. Forsyth, *The Great Missouri Raid*, 242–244.

C. Wood's Battalion (June 30, 1864), Missouri Historical Society, hereafter cited as Muster Roll, Company C, Wood's Battalion; Muster Roll, Company G, William's Missouri Regiment, Samuel M. Bartley Papers, Missouri Historical Society; Muster Roll, Stallard's Escort Company, Company D, 5th Missouri Cavalry (CSA), Missouri Historical Society, hereafter cited as Muster Roll, Stallard's Company.
2. *O.R.*, vol. 41, pt. 1:699; *O.R.*, vol. 22, pt. 2:1127; *O.R.*, vol. 34, pt. 3:803; *O.R.*, vol. 41, pt. 4:1002, 1137–1139; Banasik, *Confederate Tales, 1864*, 176–178; Livermore, 68–69.
3. *O.R.*, vol. 41, pt. 3:943–944, 947; Crute, *Confederate Staff Officers*, 30, 58, 131–132, 173–174; General Orders No. 12 (September 21, 1864), Army of Missouri Papers, Missouri Historical Society.

4. Harrell, *Arkansas, Confederate Military History*, 273–274.
5. Lause, *Price's Lost Campaign*, 208–209.
6. Monnett, 139–141.

* * * * * * *

Introduction to the Army of Missouri.

Armed verses Unarmed Men. When General Price began the Expedition, he reported his strength as "12,000 men," 4,000 of whom were unarmed. However, prior to departing Pocahontas, Arkansas, Price issued General Orders No. 8, which specified that "All property captured from the enemy to be issued under directions of the division commander." The original unarmed men were all subsequently armed shortly after the Expedition left Boonville in early October 1864, making the idea of unarmed men a moot consideration in preparing this Order of Battle. This was further supported by John C. Wright, who commanded an Arkansas cavalry regiment during the Expedition. Of the initial lack of arms, Wright wrote: "We soon captured a sufficient number of guns for the whole command, but as we marched through the state, unarmed recruits continued to join us, so that when we reached Kansas City we had a mob of not less than ten thousand men without guns, or organization."[4]

And despite Wright's comments on newly arriving unarmed recruits, author Mark Lause interprets the unarmed condition differently, writing: "In a region where adult white men carried arms in peacetime, this probably did not mean that these men had no weapons, but that the military authorities had not issued the arms" that they carried.[5]

Even though "4,000 unarmed men" were present when the Expedition began, many of the original unarmed men served as horse holders, stretcher bearers, or protected the trains as the army advanced into Missouri, until such time as they were armed. They essentially served as a pool of ready replacements for those lost in combat, according to General William L. Cabell. The same could be said for the dismounted men, who accompanied the Expedition, e.g., following the Battle of Pilot Knob, several hundred horses were immediately available for men who lacked mounts. "In any case" writes Lumir Buresh "sufficient guns were on hand to arm 12,000 troops or most of the army."[6]

Early Recruiting for the Expedition. Even before General Price arrived in northeast Arkansas, General Shelby had been actively recruiting for the Expedition, incorporating a combination of volunteers, deserters, and previously paroled prisoners into his command. And by the time Price had arrived in northeast Ar-

---

4. Wright Memoirs, unnumbered pages 70–71.
5. Lause, *Price's Lost Campaign*, 16.
6. See Appendix I, Small Arms and Artillery for details on the number of weapons captured during the Expedition. Buresh, 216–217.

kansas, Shelby reported having recruited 8,000 men for the Missouri Expedition, which did not include those men he brought with him, which numbered between 1,500–2,000 (some Federal accounts put Shelby's strength at from 2,500–3,000 men when he crossed the Arkansas River in May 1864). Those new men were eventually organized into brigades commanded by Colonels S. D. Jackman, T. H. McCray and A. Dobbin, "with several unattached regiments and battalions." Additionally, when Price organized the expedition at Pocahontas he attached various unassigned regiments to assorted brigades or divisions and formed Thomas Freeman's Brigade. There were also several units, not included in the original organization, which joined as the Expedition progressed, with some joining as the army entered Missouri and were never listed in Price's Order of Battle, e.g., Doc Rayburn's Body Guard, M. Rector Johnson's Battalion, W. O. Coleman's Regiment, and A. Slayback's Battalion, all of which were in southeast Missouri recruiting at the time or had been sent forward as a kind of advanced party. Their numbers would also boost the overall Confederate strength (See Additions to the Expedition, following this Order of Battle for details.).[7]

Strength of the Army of Missouri. All the modern-day writers who have dealt with the subject accept Price's assessment of 12,000 men; that is, 4,000–5,000 men for Fagan's Division, 3,000–4,000 men for Marmaduke's Division, and 3,000 men for Shelby's command. Other authors simply accept the 12,000 figure without assigning the value to any of the commands. However, even a cursory review of official published documents and unofficial letters should give one pause before blindly accepting Price's numbers without further analysis. And all this despite Governor Thomas Reynolds's statement, following the Expedition, that Price had "not known the strength of his own forces, for returns were neither made nor insisted on."[8]

At the beginning of the Expedition, within Fagan's Division, reports of the various brigade commanders contradict the assessment that the division contained 4,000–5,000 men, without even considering the impact of officers or artillerymen. General Cabell recorded that his command numbered 2,500 armed men when he left Princeton. Reports from the field at the end of July 1864 put Dobbin's command at 865 well-armed men, while Thomas McCray's Brigade numbered 1,700. Colonel W. F. Slemons wrote his wife in late August 1864 that he would "be able to take 1,000 men" on the Expedition. The total of Fagan's command would then number at least 6,065 men; however, this figure does not include Witt's Arkansas Regiment, which was left out of Dobbin's 865 figure, nor three additional

---

7. *O.R.*, vol. 34, pt. 3:670, 687, 803, 832; *O.R.*, vol. 41, pt. 1:651; Britton, *Civil War on the Border, 1863–1865*, 387; Coleman Letters (November 20, 1914).

8. *O.R.*, vol. 41, pt. 1:627; Britton, *Civil War on the Border, 1863–1865*, 390; Crowley, 136; "Dardanelle Taken," *Fort Smith New Era*, May 21, 1864; Edwards, *Shelby and His Men*, 383; Forsyth, *Great Missouri Raid*, 110; Kerby, 340; Lause, *Price's Lost Campaign*, 1; Moore, *Missouri, Confederate Military History*, 179–180; O'Flaherty, 218; Ponder, *General Marmaduke*, 161; Schultz, 140; Sellmeyer, 208–209; Shalhope, 263.

companies that were added to Harrell's Arkansas Battalion, after the command reached Pocahontas, nor the "200–300 unarmed men who joined the different regiments [of Cabell's Brigade] a few days before leaving for Missouri." Also missed were the two half-sized engineer companies attached to Fagan's Division, which adds another 79 effective officers and men to his total. These four additional acquisitions add about 1,030 more effectives, boosting the division's total to about 7,095 men, without including Fagan's 168-man escort, Anderson's Arkansas Battalion, which was assigned after the command reached Pocahontas. This would mean that the other two divisions numbered but 4,737 (12,000 - 7,095 - 168 = 4,737) men between them; clearly not correct as shown below.[9]

Similarly, within Marmaduke's Division, most writers have missed the fact that the 8th Missouri Cavalry (CSA) was detached from Clark's Brigade on September 16–17 and sent into Missouri ahead of the main army. And Wood's Battalion was assigned to Marmaduke's Division at the beginning of the Expedition, but was not attached to Clark's Brigade until after it left Pocahontas, thus boosting his strength by almost another 400 men. And nowhere do you find the mention of Marmaduke's Pioneer Company, which further increases the divisional strength.[10]

Within Shelby's Division, authors have accepted Shelby's report of September 17, which has Jackman's Brigade at 1,596 men. However, Jackman in his official report of the Expedition, puts his strength at 1,500 armed and 500 unarmed men, which is 404 more men than Shelby reported. In the case of Jackman's Brigade, it appears that he was reporting officers and men, as well as including late arriving recruits, where Shelby excluded officers.[11]

Overall the figures presented below will show that the Army of Missouri numbered over 17,000 effective officers and men, including all staff, escorts, officers, artillerymen, engineers, pioneers and unattached units, when the invasion began. The 9,000–12,000 man figure put forth by General Price and Colonel James R. Shaler should not be accepted as correct, because they simply did not know the true number and probably gave lower figures to support the idea that the Expedition had no real chance to succeed. This was further supported by Missouri Governor Thomas Reynolds, who noted that Price did "not know the strength of his own forces."

This 17,000-man figure is further supported by assorted Union and Confederate accounts as well as my research as detailed below, which put the initial invasion force between 15,000–20,000 effective men. Even Jerry Ponder, who is not known for overestimating Confederate troop strength, places the force at between

---

9. *O.R.*, vol. 41, pt. 1:738; *O.R.*, vol. 41, pt. 2:1036; *O.R.*, vol. 41, pt. 3:69. 79; Cruzen, 21–22; Edwards, *Shelby and His Men*, 383; Forsyth, *Great Missouri Raid*, 110; Lause, *Price's Lost Campaign*, 16; Sinisi, 30–31, 45; W. F. Slemons Letters (August 24, 1864), Museum of the Confederacy, Richmond, VA, hereafter cited as Slemons Letters.

10. *O.R.*, vol. 41, pt. 1:627, 642, 719; *O.R.*, vol. 41, pt. 3:929; *O.R.S.*, pt. 2 vol. 38:272; Buresh, 218; Campbell Memoirs; Crute, *Confederate Army*, 204; Gifford, 55; Sifakis, *Missouri*, 102–103; Suderow, *Arcadia Valley*, 139.

11. *O.R.*, vol. 41, pt. 1:678; *O.R.*, vol. 41 pt. 3:940.

16,000–18,000, including those who preceded Price to Missouri by a few days. C. K. Polk, of the 3rd Missouri Cavalry (CSA) put the invasion force at no more than 15,000, not including acquisitions as they proceeded into Missouri. Lieutenant Colonel D. J. Haynes, of the 17th Illinois Cavalry, who was captured at Glasgow during the raid, and conversed with his captors, recorded that Price "entered the state with 18,000." Finally, General William S. Rosecrans, commander of the Department of Missouri, upon "development" of Price's movements estimated the number at about "15,000 effective fighting men" in addition to Price's "merciless conscription of every arms-bearing inhabitant who is not in the State or National service."[12]

Within the pages of the *Missouri Democrat* and the *Missouri Republican* are several pieces that deal with the strength of the invasion, of which there are two of note from the *Democrat*. The first written on October 3, 1864, states:

> That we do not over-estimate the magnitude of the invading movement is shown by several circumstances. The best information puts Price's invading force at not less than 15,000 well armed and well organized men. This is formidable, but it is not all. The invaders will be joined by a large number of recruits, many of them old soldiers of Price, who have been scattered through the more disloyal districts of the State on recruiting service, awaiting the coming of their old leader to join him with such accessions as they have been able to collect. In this way will the invading army be likely to grow rapidly in strength. These views are sustained by predictions which the disloyal residents of Missouri have long been indulging. Nothing is more certain than that they have been preparing for months with a view to co-operating in the present movement. Large number of lodges of the treasonable Order of the American Knights have been established throughout the States, and arms and munitions of war, through their agency have been distributed in much greater abundance than the loyal public had any idea...The only safe conclusion is that Missouri is in imminent peril.[13]

Further, historian Walter E. Busch, Natural Resource Manger at the Fort Davidson State Historic Site at Pilot Knob, also believes that Price carried more than 12,000 men into Missouri. Busch has made a study of the invasion, compiling a by-name list of Confederates who participated in the Expedition, and he places the initial invasion total at between 15,000 and 18,000; considerably higher that what General Price reported.[14]

---

12. *O.R.*, vol. 41, pt. 3:633; Busch, *Missouri Democrat Articles*, 203; Monaghan, 311; C.K. Polk, Letter, *Iron County Register*, October 12, 1905; Ponder, *General Marmaduke*, 161; Schultz, 140; Scott, "Last Fight," 302.
13. Busch, *Missouri Democrat Articles*, 60; "Magnitude of the Invasion," *Missouri Democrat*, October 3, 1864.
14. Busch, *Missouri Democrat Articles*, 21, 26, 69, 99–100 203; Gifford, 55 (n. 119); Wilkinson (Letters No. 15 & 18).

Appendix D / 347

Confederate Artillery. There are differing opinions in the various accounts on Price's Raid as to the number of artillery pieces that the Confederate Army had in hand for the Expedition. Depending on the source, the number varies from a low of 10 guns up to 18. Price for his part recorded that he began the Expedition with 14 pieces of artillery, but specified no caliber or type. Most secondary writers accept Price's number of 14 guns, which will be shown below as the correct amount; however, the caliber and assignment of cannon to the various batteries is where the assessment becomes confused. And in virtually all cases, the writers simply ignore the caliber and type of guns, or incorrectly place them due to incomplete or faulty research. Also, during the Expedition Price captured several pieces of artillery, some of which were added to his command, while others were spiked or destroyed.[15]

John C. Moore, who wrote the Missouri volume of Clement Evans's *Confederate Military History*, places the number of guns at 12. Paul Jenkins, author of *Battle of Westport*, writes that Price's artillery "consisted chiefly of twelve-pounder mountain howitzers and small artillery pieces, with one or two remarkable products of rustic blacksmith shops." Price had, according to Jenkins, "at least eight large Parrot rifled guns (twenty-pounders)." W. L. Webb supports Jenkins's assessment and further believes that Price started the Expedition with "about thirty guns in all," including "a wicked little one-inch gun used very effectively in picking off artillery men at long range." This last gun was actually a 2-pound Woodruff gun, which was manufactured in Quincy, Illinois, while the ammunition appears to have been made in the St. Louis Arsenal. It was a steel, smoothbore cannon that weighed 256 pounds, was 36" long, but was rarely used in combat during the war. The Woodruff had a bore of 2.125 inches and could be deployed either by infantry or cavalry. During the course of the Expedition the Confederates captured two Woodruff guns at Pilot Knob and assigned them to Colonel Archibald Dobbin's Brigade.[16]

Modern-day author Joseph Thompson gives Price 14 pieces of artillery, consisting of "12-pounder mountain howitzers and 20-pounder Parrot guns, all captured from the Union army," which is not correct—the number of guns is the same as Price reported, but the calibers are completely wrong, save for the presence of two 12-pound mountain howitzers. Douglas Gifford, also a modern-day writer, has Price initially with 16 guns, which comprised "12-pounder field guns and outdated 6-pounder field guns," with one "14-pounder James Rifle" and "two 20-pounder Parrot Rifles"; however, the two 20-pounder Parrots were sent back to Princeton/Camden on August 31, due to the lack of "suitable horses," leaving Price with 14 guns. In listing the loss of the two large Parrots, Gifford believes

---

15. *O.R.* vol. 41, pt. 1:627, 641; Britton, *Civil War on the Border, 1863–1865*, 390; Castel, *Sterling Price*, 205; Scott, "Last Fight," 303; "The War In Missouri," *Chicago Tribune*, September 27, 1864.
16. *O.R.*, vol. 41, pt. 1:719; *O.R.*, vol. 41, pt. 3:961; Jenkins, 31; John R. Margrieter, "The Woodruff Gun," *Civil War Times Illustrated* 12 (May, 1973), 33, 37, hereafter cited as Margrieter; Moore, *Missouri, Confederate Military History*, 180; Ripley, 174, 177, 188; Webb, 209–210.

the *Official Records* report of the two "iron guns" being sent back, must have referred to the 20-pound Parrots; however, we know from previous accounts, that Hughes's Battery contained four 6-pound iron guns and no 20-pound Parrots. Additionally, there were no 14-pound James Rifles on the Expedition, as will be shown below.[17]

In General Price's Court of Inquiry following the Expedition, Colonel James R. Shaler shed some light on the composition of the initial 14 guns in Price's artillery. Shaler has Fagan's Division with four guns; two each in Cabell's and Slemons's Brigades; Marmaduke had a battalion of artillery with two batteries of three guns each; and Shelby's command had four guns, divided into two sections. Shaler further noted that Shelby had two Parrots.[18]

Of all the accounts that deal with the artillery in Price's Army, there are two that generally have the right number of guns with which Price began the Expedition, including the caliber, with the exception of one light rifled piece. The *Missouri Democrat* states that Price had 16 guns: "two Parrots, two James rifles, two brass mountain howitzers, two iron howitzers, six smooth-bore guns and one 1 1/6-inch rifled" piece. The *Missouri Republican* has a similar statement, but further acknowledges the presence of two 1½ inch Woodruff guns. In making its report the *Democrat* only listed 15 guns, not 16; however it should have counted two 2-pound Woodruff guns, as were reported by the *Republican*, which Price captured at Pilot Knob. This would have made 16 guns in all, as reported by the *Democrat*. Additionally, there was also one discrepancy in the caliber of one of the guns, which will be covered below. As to which batteries or sections had which guns, the following paragraphs should prove ample to answer that question.[19]

Shelby's Divisional Artillery. Following the Camden Expedition (March 23–May 3, 1864), Richard Collins's Battery was refurbished. Its 12-pound James Rifles were removed and replaced by two 10-pound Parrot Rifles. The James Rifles were then apparently sent to Pratt's Battery for use on the Mississippi River Operations, along with the remaining 12-pound howitzer from Collins's command. Collins in turn received an additional two 12-pound iron howitzers, which it took on the Missouri Expedition. For the Expedition, Collins's Missouri Artillery was divided into two sections, one for Shanks's Brigade and one for Jackman's command.

Captain Richard Collins commanded the section in Shanks's Brigade which deployed the two 10-pound Parrot Rifles. First Lieutenant Jacob D. Conner led the second section, in Jackman's Brigade, consisting of two 12-pound iron howitzers.[20]

---

17. Banasik, *Confederate Tales, 1864*, 219; Busch, *Missouri Democrat Articles*, 52; Darr, 359; Farmer Memoir, 11; Gifford, 54; Thompson, "Great Little Battle of Pilot Knob," 145.
18. *O.R.*, vol. 41, pt. 1:719.
19. Busch, *Missouri Democrat Articles*, 335; Margreiter, 36–37; "Price's Forces," *Missouri Republican*, November 7, 1864.
20. Banasik, *Confederate Tales, 1864*, 228; Bartels, *Trans-Mississippi Men*, 23; Smith, "Queen

Fagan's Divisional Artillery. Fagan's command comprised two batteries of two guns each: Hughey's Battery was commanded by Lieutenant William M. Hughey, while a two-gun section of Blocher's Battery was commanded by Lieutenant J. V. Zimmerman. The caliber of the guns in Fagan's Division was identified from Federal sources as "five 6-pounders and one 12-pounder howitzer." Given that Hughey's Battery originally had four guns, before it left Princeton and that Blocher's Battery contained two guns, one of which was a 12-pound howitzer; this must mean that the remaining two guns in Hughey's Battery were 6-pound smoothbore guns. This is further supported by Union accounts of the Battle of Pilot Knob, which reported two 6-pound guns on Shepherd Mountain.

At the Battle of Independence (October 22), the Federals would report capturing two pieces of artillery, described as brass and rifled; however, the pieces, having been in "constant use [had] almost worn out the thread or rifle." The two pieces were actually 6-pound, brass smoothbores and not rifled guns, which fits the profile of calibers and types previously reported in the *Missouri Republican* of the Confederate artillery available for the Expedition.

Thus, Hughey's Battery contained two 6-pound, brass smoothbores, while Zimmerman's Section contained one 6-pound brass smoothbore and one 12-pound brass howitzer.[21]

Marmaduke's Divisional Artillery. Of the three divisions, in Price's army, Marmaduke's was the least documented as to its artillery content. The division contained two batteries, of three guns each.

S. S. Harris's Battery, commanded by Lieutenant T. J. Williams, had its roots in Griswald's Missouri Battery. Samuel S. Harris was appointed commander of the unit in February 1864, when the battery contained four 12-pound mountain howitzers. For the Missouri Expedition, the battery was reduced to three guns, which J. A. Cocker, a member of the battery identified as one 6-pound smoothbore, one 12-pound James Rifle, and a "twelve pound smooth bore," which was a 12-pound mountain howitzer.[22]

Pratt's Texas Battery also contained three guns and was commanded by Captain Henry C. Hynson. J. A. Corker has this battery as containing one 6-pound smoothbore, with two 12-pound mountain howitzers. In this case, I believe Cocker was mistaken. Instead of the two mountain howitzers, the battery contained one 12-pound James Rifle, with one 12-pound mountain howitzer. This would correspond with what was reported in the *Missouri Democrat* and *Republican*, which identified the Confederate artillery as containing two mountain howitzers (one each for Harris and Hynson); and two 12-pound James Rifles (one

---

City," 120; Sellmeyer, 347 (n. 4).

21. Later in the Expedition, Dobbin's Brigade added two 2-pound Woodruff guns. *O.R.*, vol. 41, pt. 1:642; *O.R.*, vol. 41, pt. 4:79, 183–185; Banasik, *Confederate Tales, 1864*, 219; Busch, *Missouri Democrat Articles*, 52, 305, 364–365; Farmer Memoir, 11.
22. Banasik, *Confederate Tales, 1863*, 190 (n. 65); Cocker, 13.

each for Harris and Hynson), while the remaining gun was, according to Cocker, a 6-pound smoothbore.[23]

The only discrepancy noted with what the *Missouri Democrat* reported, as to caliber, was six smoothbore guns. As shown above the various batteries numbered five 6-pound smoothbores, with the addition of a 12-pound howitzer.

Losses during the Expedition. Listed below within [ ] are the known losses that specific units suffered during the Expedition. And as will be shown, only a handful of commands are represented. Total estimated losses, embracing the entire Expedition are shown in Appendix I.

* * * * * * *

Item: Army of Missouri at the beginning of Price's Raid.

Army of Missouri (Maj. Gen. Sterling Price): Staff = 14[24]
    Bodyguard: Rayburn's Indept. Ark. Co. (Capt. Howel A. "Doc" Rayburn).
        EFF = 55[25]
        Escort:[26]
            Company K, 2nd Mo. Cav. (Windsor Guards; Capt. Robert
                Collins).[27] EFF = 55
            Officers and men of unknown assignments, including band.[28] EFF
                = 188
        Total Army HQ = 312

---

23. Busch, *Missouri Democrat Articles*, 335; Cocker, 13.
24. Not included in the staff are the corps surgeon and the "medical field purveyor," but does include the corps commander. *O.R.*, vol. 41, pt. 2:1090.
25. On September 4, 1864, "Doc" Rayburn's command was reported as between 50–60 men; say 55 for this Order of Battle. In Federal reports, they spell his name as Rayborne, which is not correct. The company served throughout the Expedition. *O.R.*, vol. 41, pt. 3:55. Edwards, *Shelby and His Men*, 285; *White County Heritage Civil War Collection Volume 1–25* (Searcy, AR, n.d.), 2:3, 19:14.
26. As the march to northeast Arkansas began, Dr. William McPheeters, surgeon general of the army, who traveled with Price's headquarters, reported that Price's entourage consisted of 300 officers and men. Deducting Price and staff leaves 286 (300-14 = 286) of whom 243 (286 x .85 = 243.1) would be considered effective. Additionally, Price's Escort did not number 243 officers and men; more likely about 55. It was unknown as to what function the remaining 188 officers and men performed. Pitcock & Gurley, 216.
27. R. B. Coleman stated that the captain was Benjamin L. Quarles, while R. O. Nelson recorded that the captain was Robert Collins. In making his claims for Quarles, Coleman was part of some recruits making their way to the army, under Captain Quarles. Quarles was listed in the *Supplement to the Official Records* as a lieutenant in the company while Collins was listed as the captain. Quarles probably became the captain sometime after the army returned from the Expedition. *O.R.S.*, pt. 2, vol. 50:145; R. B. Coleman, "Various Small fights In Missouri," *Confederate Veteran* 14 (March, 1906), 120, hereafter cited as Coleman, "Small Fights"; Confederate Correspondence, Nelson to Maclean (December 15, 1864); Eakin & Hale, 361.
28. According to Jerry Ponder and the *Missouri Republican*, Price had a band with the Expedition that played while the army marched. Additionally, these 188 men also included "a long list of civilians and politicians," and with the band made a "grand parade" that was talked about fifty

* * * * * * *

Fagan's Division

Fagan's Division General Information. Fagan's escort was generally unknown, but was subsequently identified as Anderson's Arkansas Battalion. Originally commanded by Captain William L. Anderson, it appears that Anderson gave up the command of his battalion, on September 18, 1864, and accepted a position on General Fagan's Staff. Captain N. Terry Roberts, who commanded Company A, Anderson's Battalion then assumed command of the battalion, according to Colonel John C. Wright. The battalion consisted of three companies, according to Wright, who also has Roberts as a major, which was probably a brevet rank. The battalion had an estimated effective strength of 168 (3 x 64 = 192 x .85 = 163 + 5 staff = 168) officers and men (See Organizational Note no. 1 for strength of companies).[29]

Fagan's Division was considered the largest of Price's three divisions, containing by most accounts over 5,000 men, while John Edwards has it numbering but 4,000. However, the number was actually much higher, when officers, staff, engineers, and artillerymen who seemed to have been left out are added. Kyle Sinisi presents the largest assessment of Fagan's Command, putting it well above 6,000 men, i.e., Cabell at 2,700; Slemons at 1,000; Dobbin at 800 and McCray at 1,700; plus three battalion sized units of unspecified strength. However, Sinisi also misses the addition of Witt's Arkansas Regiment, which was not part of Dobbin's Brigade when the 800 figure was listed (Witt's command was escorting an ammunition train to Shelby's Division at the time). Witt's Cavalry would have added a significant increase to the size of Dobbin's Brigade.[30]

Fagan's Division (Maj. Gen. James F. Fagan):
  Staff = 10 EFF[31]
  Escort: Anderson's Ark. Cav. Bn. (Capt. N. Terry Roberts). EFF = 168
  HQ & Escort Total = 178

Cabell's Brigade General Information. Cabell reported his strength as 2,500 armed men, with between 200–300 unarmed men (use 250 as average), when the brigade departed Princeton, Arkansas, or roughly 2750 men, officers excluded.

---

years after the war had ended. "Latest From the Rebel Invasion," *Missouri Republican*, September 27, 1864; Ponder, *General Marmaduke*, 156; Thompson, "Great Little Battle of Pilot Knob," 142.

29. Roberts was originally the Captain of Company F, 1st Arkansas Mounted rifles and later transferred to Anderson's Battalion, date unknown, where he commanded Company A. *O.R.*, vol. 41, pt. 1:719; *O.R.*, vol. 48, pt. 2:439; *O.R.S.*. Index, vol. 4:4429; *O.R.S.*, pt. 2, vol. 2:160; Crute, *Confederate Staff Officers*, 58; Schultz, 193; Wright Memoirs, unnumbered pages 81, 94.
30. *O.R.*, vol. 41, pt. 1:738; *O.R.*, vol. 41, pt. 2:1036; *O.R.*, vol. 41, pt. 3:69. 79; Cruzen, 21–22; Edwards, *Shelby and His Men*, 383; Forsyth, *Great Missouri Raid*, 110; Lause, *Price's Lost Campaign*, 16; Sinisi, 30–31, 45.
31. The divisional surgeon W.B. Welch was excluded from the staff as non-effective. *O.R.*, vol. 41, pt. 3:944.

The command added three more companies to Harrell's Battalion after it reached northeast Arkansas. The three companies, added another 153 (3 x 60 = 180 x .85 = 153) effective men to the brigade total (see Organizational Note No. 1), giving the command 2,903 effective men, excluding officers, staff, and the battery (both officers and men) from the brigade (see Harrell's Battalion/ Regiment below for details). The 153 added men would be considered unarmed, giving the brigade 403 unarmed men.

The number of officers is calculated per Organizational Note No. 1 as follows: officers strength of Cabell's Brigade would be 247 (5 regt. x 46 = 230 x .85 = 195.5; plus two bns. of six companies each x 29 = 58 x .85 = 49.3; plus Proctor's Company 4 x .85 = 2.55 for a total of 247.35). This would give Cabell's Brigade 3,150 effective officers and men, not including brigade staff or the battery officers and men. The staff would normally add another 13 officers; however, of the 13, including General Cabell, the brigade surgeon and chaplain were not considered effective, leaving 11. The battery would add another 31 (42 - 10 men - 1 officer = 31) officers and men to the total, after deducting the loss of two guns early in the Expedition. With the brigade staff and battery manpower added in, the brigade entered Missouri with about 3,192 effective officers and men; however see final calculation below under the various units in the brigade.[32]

Hughey's Arkansas Battery. The battery started the Expedition with four guns; however, on August 31, two of the guns were returned to Princeton, "not having suitable horses." On October 31, the Artillery Corps for the District of Texas numbered 26 guns with 273 officers and men present for duty and assumed to be effective, or 10.5 officers and men per gun. There is no reason to suspect that Price's Artillery would have numbered any more or less. As such 10.5 officers and men are assigned to each gun that was taken with the command to Missouri, with the exception of Hugheys's Battery. Since two of the guns were sent back to Princeton, 11 officers and men are deducted from the battery total of 42, to escort the guns back to Princeton, leaving 31 effectives for the 2-gun battery.[33]

Harrell's Arkansas Battalion/ Regiment. When this unit departed Princeton, it contained only seven companies; however, upon arrival in northeast Arkansas three companies were added, bringing the unit up to regimental strength. Harrell's Battalion was reported by Federal scouts as containing 400 men while en route to northeast Arkansas and prior to receiving its three additional companies. Those companies would have added 163 (64 x 3 = 192 x .85 = 163.2) effective officers and men, giving the command 563 effective officers and men, assuming all were armed. Additionally, a Federal report has Harrell's Battalion with only 200 men at Pilot Knob, which would suggest that the other 363 men were part of the unarmed

---

32. *O.R.*, vol. 41, pt. 3:947; *O.R.S.*, pt. 1., vol. 7:391; Crute, *Confederate Staff Officers*, 30; Livermore, 68–69.
33. *O.R.*, vol. 41, pt. 1:642; *O.R.*, vol. 41, pt. 4:79, 1023.

or unorganized portion of the brigade. The fact that 163 officers and men (the men probably unarmed) were added at Pocahontas, pairs well with Cabell's report that when he left Princeton he had between 200–300 unarmed men, i.e., 250 unarmed were from Harrell as they marched to northeast Arkansas, with another 153 men (officers considered armed) were added after they reached northeast Arkansas, giving the command 403 unarmed men.[34]

Monroe's, Gordon's, Morgan's and Hill's Arkansas Cavalry Regiments. After the Federals re-occupied Pilot Knob, and, upon questioning the various wounded prisoners, Federal sources reported that each of these commands numbered 500 men. Earlier reports of Hill's and Gordon's Regiments placed their strengths at 500 and 400 men respectively. As such, 500 will be used for each of these regiments. Each regiment would then add in 39 officers (46 x .85 = 39.1), giving each regiment 539 officers and men. Given that Cabell originally reported that his command consisted of 2,500 armed and 250 unarmed men, these numbers don't appear to be unreasonable. Additionally, Company C, Gordon's Regiment, was Cabell's Escort, which would deduct 54 (539 / 10 = 53.9) from Gordon's command giving him 485 (539 - 54 = 485) officers and men. All four of these regiments, including Cabell's escort, would be considered armed, or roughly 2,000 men.[35]

Gunter's Regiment/ Witherspoon's and Woosley's Battalion with Proctor's Company. Of all the sources available, only William Cabell's and John C. Darr's accounts of the Expedition list Gunter's command as a regiment composed of Witherspoon's and Woosley's Battalions and Proctor's Company. Further more, upon closer investigation, it was found that Woosley's Battalion was actually Gunter's Battalion, commanded by Woosley.

As to the strength of Gunter's Regiment, the same Federal report that listed the strengths of Monroe's, Gordon's Morgan's and Hill's strength, has Gunter's and Witherspoon's Battalions at 200 men each. Officers would add 25 (29 x .85 = 24,65) to each battalion giving them 225 effective officers and men. Additionally, Proctor's Company appears to have been part of Witherspoon's Battalion, though for some reason Cabell listed it as a separate unit, within Gunter's Regiment. Given that Gunter's command numbered 13 companies would equate to 31 (400 / 13 = 30.7) men per company. This would make Procter's command 34 (31 + 3 officers = 34) effective officers and men, while Witherspoon and Woosley's Battalions would now contain 210 (450 - 31 = 419 / 2 = 209.5) effective officers and men. Four hundred of Gunter's command would have been considered armed for Pilot Knob.[36]

---

34. *O.R.*, vol. 41 pt. 3:254; *O.R.*, vol. 41, pt. 4:79; *O.R.S.*, pt. 1, vol. 7:391.
35. *O.R.*, vol. 41, pt. 1: 743, 758–759; *O.R.*, vol. 41, pt. 3:254; *O.R.*, vol. 41, pt. 4:79.
36. *O.R.*, vol. 41, pt. 4:79; *O.R.S.*, pt. 1, vol. 7:391; *O.R.S.*, pt. 2, vol. 2:851; Internet site, www.history–sites.com., "The Arkansas in the Civil War Message Board," Key word "Witherspoon;" Darr, 359; Sifakis, *Arkansas*, 64.

Cabell's Brigade Summary Comments. Overall the brigade totaled 3,215, which is 23 more men than was calculated under Cabell's Brigade General Information, above. This is less than half of a percent difference between the two numbers. Also, as shown above, 2,500 men of the brigade would have been considered armed at the beginning of the Expedition, with more weapons added as the Expedition progressed, until the entire command was armed.

Cabell's Arkansas Bde. (Brig. Gen. William L. Cabell, captured Oct. 25, 1864; Ltc.. Thomas M. Gunter). EFF = 11[37]
    Escort: Company C, Gordon's Arkansas Cav. Regt. (1st Lt. Robert J. Wilson).[38] EFF = 54
    HQs. & Escort Total = 65 EFF
        Monroe's Ark. Regt. (Col. James C. Monroe, WIA Sept. 27; Ltc. A. V. Reiff).[39] EFF = 539
        Gordon's Ark. Regt. (Col. Anderson Gordon, WIA, date ukn; Ltc. William H. Fayth).[40] EFF = 485 [106 K, W, M][41]
        Morgan's Ark. Regt. (Col. Thomas J. Morgan).[42] EFF = 539
        Hill's Cav. Regt. (Col. John F. Hill, WIA Sept. 27; Maj. James L. Adams).[43] EFF = 539
        Gunter's Ark. Regt. (Ltc. Thomas M. Gunter)
        James Woosley's Bn. (Maj. James Woosley).[44] EFF = 210

---

37. As the senior surviving officer, Lieutenant Colonel Thomas M. Gunter commanded the brigade after Cabell was captured, not Lieutenant Colonel A. V. Reiff as several sources, including the *Official Records,* reported. *O.R.*, vol. 41, pt. 1:641; *O.R.*, vol. 41, pt 3:947; *O.R.S.*, pt. 1, vol. 7:391, 403, 410; Buresh, 204; Crute, *Confederate Staff Officers*, 30; Darr, 361; Forsyth, *Great Missouri Raid*, 242.
38. Sadler was placed on recruiting service on September 18, 1864, leaving command of the company to 1st Lt. Robert J. Wilson. A typical cavalry company in 1864 contained 64 officers and men; or 55 (64 x .85 = 55) effective officers and men. See Organizational Note No. 1 for details. *O.R.S.*, pt. 1, vol. 7:395; *O.R.S.* pt. 2 vol 2:241, 243; Internet site, www.couchgenwed.com, 4th Arkansas Cavalry, Company C.
39. Also known as the 1st or 6th Arkansas Cavalry with the moniker the "Rawhide" Regiment. *O.R.S.*, pt. 2, vol. 2:150; Allardice, *Confederate Colonels*, 276; Buresh, 204; Crute, *Confederate Army*, 41; John L. Ferguson, *Arkansas and the Civil War* (Little Rock, AR, 1965), 312, hereafter cited as Ferguson; William G. Hazen Letter (December 21, 1864); Moore, *Missouri, Confederate Military History*, 182; Sinisi, 320.
40. Gordon's Regiment was also known by several different names including the 1st, 2nd, 4th, 9th, or the 11th Arkansas Cavalry Regiment. *O.R.S.*, pt. 2, vol. 2:240; Allardice, *Confederate Colonels*, 158; Darr, 363; Ferguson, 313.
41. Crute, *Confederate Army*, 61.
42. Originally organized as the 5th Arkansas Cavalry Regiment, it was later reorganized as Morgan's or the 8th Arkansas Cavalry Regiment. Ferguson, 313.
43. Also known as the 7th Arkansas Cavalry Regiment. At Pilot Knob, Colonel Hill was seriously wounded, while Lieutenant Colonel Oliver Basham was killed, leaving the command to Major James L. Adams, who was promoted to his position on March 31, 1864. Ferguson, 313; *O.R.S.*, pt. 2, vol. 2:232; Darr, 360.
44. As noted above this was actually Gunter's Battalion, commanded by Woosley.

Witherspoon's Ark. Bn. (Maj. J. L. Witherspoon).[45] EFF = 210
Proctor's Co. (Cdr. ukn.). EFF = 34
Harrell's Ark. Regt. (Lt. Col. John M. Harrell).[46] EFF = 563
Hughey's Ark. Battery (Capt. William W. Hughey).[47] 2 guns, 6-pound iron SB EFF = 31 (E)
Brigade Total = 3,215 EFF

* * * * * * *

Dobbin's Brigade General Information. Dobbin's Brigade was a newly organized command, composed largely of recruits. At Pilot Knob, on September 27, several sources reported the command having between 1,500–1,600 men. However, Shelby reported that Dobbin's strength was 835 effective, well-armed men on July 27, which probably did not include officers. This was also a number used by many authors to specify the strength of Dobbin's Brigade for the Missouri Expedition; however, the brigade was far from complete and still had almost two more months for recruiting. And by the time the Expedition was launched, Dobbin's units would have been at the "maximum number allowed by the law," according to J. O. Shelby's Adjutant General, W. J. McArthur.[48]

At the time that Dobbin's strength was reported at 835 effectives, it included Dobbin's Regiment, McGhee's Battalion and probably Gordon's Missouri Regiment, which was attached to Dobbin at the time. And during the months leading up to the Expedition these units suffered a combined loss of "eight killed, forty wounded, with five men captured," according to of Deryl Sellmeyer, with one of the wounded coming from Gordon's Missouri Regiment. On yet another occasion Dobbin was reported to have lost an additional 17 men, exclusive of Gordon's command. Total loss for Dobbin's and McGhee's commands was 69 (8 + 40 + 5 + 17 = 70 - 1 = 69) prior to completing their organizations.[49]

McGhee's or McGehee's Regiment was also known as the 44th Arkansas Mounted Infantry, suggesting that it consisted of ten companies with 84 officers and men per company. Per the Organizational Note No. 1 above, this would equate to a strength of 714 (84 x .85 = 71.4 x 10 companies) effective officers and men;

---

45. Also known as the 13th or 16th Arkansas Cavalry Battalion. Witherspoon was captured on November 11, 1863, and was later known to be a prisoner at Ft. Smith, Arkansas, in April 1865. During Price's Raid his battalion was probably commanded by the senior captain or the adjutant of the battalion, names unknown. *O.R.*, vol. 41, pt. 1:1018; *O.R.S.*, pt. 2, vol. 2:252; Internet site, www.couchgenweb.com, Key Word "Witherspoon;" Sifakis, *Arkansas*, 81.
46. Also known as the 17th Arkansas Cavalry Battalion. *O.R.S.*, pt. 2, vol. 2:253.
47. Also known as the 8th Arkansas Field Battery. *O.R.*, vol. 41, pt. 1:642; *O.R.*, vol. 41, pt. 4:79, 1023; Banasik, *Confederate Tales, 1864*, 219; Busch, *Missouri Democrat Articles*, 52; Crute, *Confederate Army*, 62; Farmer Memoir.
48. *O.R.*, vol. 41, pt. 2: 1036; Britton, *Civil War on the Border, 1863–1865*, 403; Schultz, 180; Sinisi, 45; Wright Memoirs, unnumbered page 77.
49. *O.R.*, vol. 41, pt. 1:241; Cruzen, 21; Sellmeyer, 199.

and with the regimental staff of six it would number a maximum of 720, before any reduction for the summertime losses.[50]

Both Dobbin's and Witt's Regiments were cavalry regiments. As shown in Organizational Note No. 1, above, once recruited to full strength each of these units should have numbered about 549 effective officers and men per unit. Further, Witt's Regiment did not join Dobbin's Brigade until just prior to the beginning of the Expedition, having escorted an ammunition train across the Arkansas River at Dardanelle about a week before the main army crossed the river. As such Witt's Regiment was not part of Dobbin's Brigade that Shelby reported on July 27, 1864, being added to said command sometime after it arrived in northeast Arkansas. And like McGhee's command, their summertime losses must be taken into account.[51]

Dobbin's and McGhee's Regiments. Considering the comments above, Dobbin's Regiment, also known as the 1st Arkansas Cavalry Regiment, started out with a maximum of 549 effective officers and men. Assuming that 66 percent of the losses sustained before the Expedition began were lost by Dobbin's Regiment (69 x .66 = 46) this would leave the regiment with 503 (549 - 46 = 503) effective officers and men for the regiment when the Expedition began.[52]

In a like manner McGhee's Regiment started out with a maximum of 720 effective officers and men. Assuming that 33 percent of the losses sustained before the Expedition began were lost by McGhee's command (69 x .33 = 22.7), this would leave the regiment with 697 (720 - 23 = 697) effective officers and men for the regiment, when they entered Missouri.

Witt's Arkansas Cavalry Regiment. Organized in the summer of 1864, following the Camden Expedition, Witt's command was also known as the 10th Arkansas Cavalry Regiment. Prior to the Missouri Expedition, Witt lost seven killed and five captured on September 2, while escorting an ammunition train to General Shelby in northeast Arkansas. This would suggest that its pre-invasion strength was 537 (549 - 12 = 537) effective officers and men.[53]

Summary of Dobbin's Brigade. Considering the comments above, on Dobbin's, Witt's and McGehee's commands, Dobbin's Brigade numbered about 1,845 effective officers and men, including the battery and the brigade staff, but without deducting any losses sustained in August and September 1864. Dobbin lost 52 killed wounded and missing on July 31 and another 17 men in mid-August 1864; total 69, while Witt lost another 12 on September 2. This would suggest that the

---

50. Allardice, *Confederate Colonels*, 264–265.
51. *O.R.*, vol. 41, pt. 1:738; *O.R.*, vol. 41, pt. 3:69.
52. At the time that Dobbin sustained his losses McGhee was half the strength of Dobbin's command; as such Dobbin's regiment suffered two-thirds of the losses. *O.R.S.* pt. 2, vol. 2:148; Ferguson, 312.
53. *O.R.S.*, pt. 2, vol. 2:237; Ferguson, 313; Sifakis, *Arkansas*, 60.

brigade entered Missouri with 1,764 effective offices and men. The addition of the artillery strength of 21 and brigade staff of six, including Colonel Dobbin, would boost the command to 1,791. If the 124 effective officers (4 x 30 Cos. = 120 + 24 staff and 2 artillery officers = 146 x .85 = 124.1) and 19 artillery men are removed from the brigade it would leave 1,560 (1,791 - 124 - 19 = 1,648) men at Pilot Knob; this compares favorably to the 1,500–1,600 men who were reported as in Dobbin's Brigade and blocking the Federal retreat from Pilot Knob on September 27.[54]

Based on the above comments, Dobbin's Brigade entered Missouri as follows:

Dobbin's Ark. Bde. (Col. Archibald S. Dobbin)
    Staff = 6
    Dobbin's Cav. (Ltc. Unknown).[55] EFF = 503
    McGhee's Cav. (Col. James McGhee or McGehee; wounded October 23 & 25, 1864; Ltc. Jesse S. Grider, Oct. 25, 1864).[56] EFF = 697
    Witt's Cav. (Col. Allen R. Witt). EFF = 537
    Blocher's Battery (one sec.) (Lt. J. V. Zimmerman)[57] 2 guns; 1 6-pound SB and 1 12-pound How. EFF = 21
        Dobbin's Brigade Total = 1,764 EFF

McCray's Brigade General Information. Kyle Sinisi has McCray's Brigade at 1,700 men at the beginning of the Expedition, this figure probably not including officers. The brigade contained thirty companies at four officers per, or 120 officers, with six command staff officers per regiment and another six officers for the brigade command staff giving the brigade 144 (4 x 30 = 120 + 18 + 6 = 144) officers. Effective officers would number 122 (144 x .85 = 122.44). Adding in the enlisted men would give the brigade an effective strength of 1,822 officers and men. A Federal report places the strength of McCray's Brigade at 2,000 men on September 13, as the Expedition was concentrating in northeast Arkansas, which would support the 1,822 figure, i.e., 1,700 men / .85 = 2,000 men present.[58]

The 45th and 47th Arkansas were mounted infantry, suggesting that they should each consist of ten companies with 84 officers and men per company. Per

---

54. *O.R.*, vol. 41, pt. 1:241; Cruzen, 21; Sellmeyer, 199.
55. The *Missouri Democrat* noted that Dobbin's Regiment was commanded by an unknown lieutenant colonel. Busch, *Missouri Democrat Articles*, 305.
56. Allardice has McGhee being wounded at both Westport (October 23) and at Mine Creek (October 25); however, since McGhee was wounded in the chest at Westport, it seems unlikely that he could have even participated in the Battle of Mine Creek. It is assumed that the next in command of McGehee's Regiment, Lieutenant Colonel Jesse S. Grider, would have taken command of the regiment following the Battle of Westport. Grider, according to John Edwards, was also wounded at Westport, but managed to escape capture. Edwards also has Grider as a major. Allardice, *Confederate Colonels*, 264; Edwards, *Shelby and His Men*, 437; Kirkman, 142; Monnett, 139; Sifakis, *Arkansas*, 65; Sinisi, 229–230.
57. Per Hughey's Arkansas Battery above, the battery effective strength was estimated at 21 officers and men (10.5 officers and men per gun x 2 = 21). *O.R.*, vol. 41, pt. 4:79, 1023.
58. *O.R.*, vol. 41, pt. 2:1046; Busch, *Missouri Democrat Articles*, 11; Sinisi, 45.

the Organizational Note No. 1 above, this would equate to a strength of 714 (84 x .85 = 71.4 x 10 companies) effective officers and men for each regiment; and with the regimental staff of six it would number 720.[59]

The 15th Missouri Cavalry (CSA) was organized in the summer of 1864, and according to Stewart Sifakis, it "apparently never completed its organization." The unit had been actively engaged in operations in southeast Missouri for several months and probably at less than organizational strength. Given the calculated brigade strength above, this would give the 15th Missouri 364 (1,822 - 720 - 720 - 6 = 376) effective officers and men.[60]

McCray's Bde. (Col. Thomas H. McCray)
    Staff = 6 EFF
    45th Ark. Inf. (Mtd.) (Col. Milton D. Baber, captured, Oct. 22; Ltc. J. W. Clark).[61] EFF = 720
    47th Ark. Inf (Mtd) (Col. Lee Crandall, captured, Oct. 25, 1864; Ltc. R. M. Davis (?).[62] EFF = 720
    15th Mo. Cav. (Col. Timothy Reeves). EFF = 376
        McCray's Brigade Total = 1,822 EFF

Slemons's Brigade General Information. W. F. Slemons in a letter home to his wife on August 24, 1864, stated that "I shall be able to take 1,000 men" on the Missouri Expedition. However, this should be taken as the minimum, as new acquisitions were probably added after the command reached Pocahontas, plus the number of sick in Slemons's Brigade had been improving "rapidly," and there was still another six days before the command headed north. And, like the other units in Price's command, Slemons probably did not include officers.

Overall officers would add 156 (46 per regt. x 4 = 184 x .85 = 156.4) effective officers to the command, not including brigade staff who add another six to the command. These additions would then suggest that Slemons's Brigade totaled about 1,162 (156 + 6 + 1,000 = 1,162) effective officers and men.[63]

John C. Wright's Arkansas Cavalry Regiment. Colonel Wright put the strength of his command at "about three hundred men" at the beginning of the Expedition, officers not included. Officers would have added 46 more (See Organizational note No. 1 above), giving the command about 345 officers and men. Effectives

---

59. Allardice, *Confederate Colonels*, 264–265.
60. Sifakis, *Missouri*, 103.
61. After the capture of Baber the next in the command chain would have been Lieutenant Colonel J. W. Clark. Eakin, *Missouri Prisoners of War*, "Baber, Milton P." entry; Ferguson, 313; Suderow, Report of POWs, List no. 74 (November 10,1864); Sifakis, *Arkansas*, 120.
62. A review of the Internet site couchgenweb shows that in addition to Crandall, the major, and, it appears also, the lieutenant colonel of the unit were also captured at Mine Creek; however there is no record of R. M. Davis's or W. S. Nanna's capture. The next in command would have been either the senior captain of the regiment or the Adjutant, Captain E. Hewitt. *O.R.*, vol. 41, pt. 1:624; internet site couchgenweb.com.
63. Sinisi, 30–31; W. F. Slemons Letters (August 24, 1864).

would have been 294 (346 x .85 = 294.1) officers and men. This was rounded up to 295 to fit the brigade profile of 1,162 effective officers and men calculated above.[64]

Carlton's, Crawford's, and 2nd Arkansas Cavalry Regiments. These three regiments have an estimated strength, based upon and average of all three, after deducting the strength of Wright's Regiment. This would give each of these commands 287 (1,162 - 295 - 6 for staff = 862 / 3 = 287.33) effective officers and men per regiment.

Slemons's Arkansas Bde. (Col. William F. Slemons, captured Oct. 25, 1864; Col. William A. Crawford)
    Staff = 6 EFF
    2nd Cav. (Ltc. Thomas M. Cochran).[65] EFF = 287
    Crawford's (Col. William A. Crawford).[66] EFF = 287
    Carlton's Cav. (Col. Charles H. Carlton, WIA, Oct. 22,1864; Ltc. R. H. Thompson).[67] EFF = 287
    Wright's Cav. (Col. John C. Wright).[68] EFF = 295
        Slemons's Brigade Total = 1,162

General Information Unattached Units. Little is known of Lyles's or Rogan's Regiments, except that they were organized in late September 1864, or, were organized as the Expedition progressed. As such they will be treated the same as other 1864 cavalry regiments. Each regiment will have an effectives strength of 549 (10 x 64 = 640 + 6 Regt. staff = 646 x .85 = 549.1) effective officers and men, assuming they were armed. See Organizational Note No. 1 for details.[69]

Unattached.
    Lyles's Ark. Cav. (Col. Oliver P. Lyles). EFF = 549
    Rogan's Ark. Cav. Bn. (Col. James W. Rogan).[70] EFF = 549
    Pioneer Co. (Cdr ukn.).[71] EFF = 79

---

64. Wright Memoirs, unnumbered page 59.
65. With Slemons commanding the brigade, the command of the regiment fell upon Thomas M. Cochran. For the Expedition, according to Stewart Sifakis, the 2nd Arkansas was "reduced to a battalion and designated as the 18th Cavalry Battalion." The 2nd was also known as the 4th Arkansas Cavalry Regiment. *O.R.S.*, pt. 2, vol. 2:182; Sifakis, *Arkansas*, 52; Wright Memoirs, unnumbered page 71.
66. Also known as the 1st or the 10th Arkansas Cavalry Regiment. *O.R.S.*, pt. 2, vol. 2:143; Ferguson, 312.
67. Kirkman, 142.
68. Also known as the 12th Arkansas Cavalry Regiment. *O.R.S.*, pt. 2, vol. 2:247; Ferguson, 313.
69. *O.R.*, vol. 41, pt. 3:929; Allardice, *Confederate Colonels*, 326.
70. Most writers have Rogan's unit as a regiment; however, William C. Wright, commanding a regiment in Slemons's Brigade, says it was a battalion. Wright Memoirs, unnumbered page 70.
71. Captain Thomas J. Mackey, Corps of Engineers, on Price's staff, stated that the Expedition was accompanied by portions of two engineer companies, assigned to the army, with a pioneer company attached to Fagan's Division. The two engineer companies numbered 75 men as a combined

Unattached Total = 1,173

Summary of Fagan's Division.

HQ. and Escort	178
Cabell's Brigade	3,215
Dobbin's Brigade	1,764
McCray's Brigade	1,822
Slemons's Brigade	1,162
Unattached	1,177
Division Total	9,318[72]

* * * * * * *

Marmaduke's Division

Pontoon Train/Engineers. Captain Thomas J. Mackey, Corps of Engineers, on Price's staff, stated that the Expedition was accompanied by portions of two engineer companies, assigned to the army, with a Pioneer Company attached to Fagan's Division. The two engineer companies numbered 75 men as a combined strength and were originally listed as part of Marmaduke's Division, Clark's Brigade, but should have been listed under division control; four officers added into the total gives them 79 officers and men. This company would have been in addition to all the other units in Marmaduke's Division. As the Expedition progressed General Price ordered the Engineer units to be at the front of the march, to quickly overcome obstacles. The Pontoon Train consisted of 25 wagons, according to General Cabell, 18 of which carried pontoons. Captain Mackey recorded that 14 of the pontoon wagons were destroyed after crossing the Arkansas River as they were no longer needed. The remaining four pontoon wagons were retained for use by the engineers, reducing the overall engineer train to 11 wagons.[73]

Marmaduke's Division (Maj. Gen. John S. Marmaduke, captured Oct. 25, 1864; Brig. Gen. John B. Clark, Jr.).
 Staff = 17[74]
 Escort: Co. D, 5th Mo. Cav. (Capt. David R. Stallard). EFF = 55[75]

---

strength; 4 officers added into the total, giving them 79 officers and men. There was no reason to believe that the pioneer company would have any fewer men than the other two engineer companies, who were of only partial strength. Crute, *Confederate Staff Officers*, 158; Schultz, 186.

72. A deserter from Price's Army places the strength of Fagan's command at 8,000 cavalry at the beginning of the Expedition, but does not indicate whether this included officers or not. "The War in Missouri," *Chicago Tribune*, September 27, 1864.
73. Crute, *Confederate Staff Officers*, 158; Schultz, 186, 194; Sinisi, 39.
74. Crute, *Confederate Staff Officers*, 131–132.
75. Stallard's Company shows an organizational strength of 64 officers and men for the beginning of the campaign. This would give the command 55 (64 x .85 = 55) effective officers and men, per Livermore. Buresh, 217; Livermore, 67–68; Muster Roll, Stallard's Company.

Engineer Co./ Pontoon or Engineer Train (Capt. James T. Hogane).
EFF = 79
HQ Total = 151 EFF

Marmaduke's Brigade General Information. When the brigade began the Expedition, General John B. Clark, commanding the brigade, reported his effective strength as 1,200 men, which probably did not include officers. Clark listed several units as part of his command, implying that they were part of the 1,200 number; however, that was not true. A review of Clark's command shows that Davies's Battalion, which was attached to Kitchen's 7th Missouri Cavalry, joined the brigade at Bollinger's Mill, Missouri, after it left Pocahontas on the evening of September 24. Likewise, Robert Wood's 14th Missouri Cavalry Battalion (CSA) traveled with the army as it marched from the Princeton, Arkansas, area on August 30, 1864, but was not part of Clark's Brigade. Instead it was attached to Marmaduke's Division Headquarters and was subsequently assigned to Clark's Brigade sometime after it left Pocahontas. Further, in January 1864, Colonel Salomon Kitchen, with 15 officers from the command, were detached for recruiting service in northeast Arkansas and southeast Missouri. Kitchen would subsequently recruit Davies's Battalion in addition to roughly 343 recruits for the brigade.[76]

Eliminating Davies's and Wood's Battalions from Clark's reported command leaves the 3rd, 4th, 7th, 8th, and 10th Missouri Cavalries (CSA) to represent the 1,200 effective men in the brigade when it began the Expedition from Princeton. Also excluded from this 1,200 figure would be the battery men and the brigade staff. The five regiments would have numbered 50 companies, yielding 200 officers (4 x 50 = 200); regimental staff would add 30 (5 x 6) more officers, giving the brigade 196 (230 x .85 = 195.5) effective officers, not including the brigade staff. However that figure was further reduced by the loss of Colonel Kitchen and 15 officers, leaving 180 (196 - 16 = 180) effective officers in the brigade. The 3rd, 4th, 7th, 8th, and 10th Missouri Cavalries would number 1,380 effective officers and men.

The 3rd and 8th Missouri Cavalries are calculated below to contain 724 effective officers and men, leaving the 4th, 7th and 10th Missouri Cavalries Regiments 656 (1,380 - 724 = 656) effective officers and men at the beginning of the Expedition. This would equate to about 219 (656 / 3 = 218.6) effective officers and men per regiment for the 4th, 7th, and 10th Missouri Cavalries, when the Expedition began.

3rd Missouri Cavalry (CSA). On September 27, 1864, Colton Greene reported his effective strength as 145, which was "about one-half of the effective total of"

---

76. Bryce Suderow has Kitchen's entire regiment in northeast Arkansas prior to the raid; however, a review of the W. C. Ballard Diary, a lieutenant in Company D, shows that the 7th Missouri Cavalry was with the brigade when it departed Princeton on August 30, 1864. *O.R.*, vol. 41 pt. 1:627, 642, 719; *O.R.*, vol. 41, pt. 2:1090; *O.R.*, vol. 41, pt. 3:953; *O.R.S.*, pt. 2, vol. 50:223; Ballard Diary, August 30, 1864; Marmaduke, 358; Suderow, *Arcadia Valley*, 139.

the 3rd Missouri Cavalry (CSA). This would suggest that his total force numbered 290 men. Additionally, a few days prior to the Battle of Pilot Knob, Green detached two of his companies to recruit, leaving him only eight companies for the assault. The other two companies would have added 72 men (290 / 8 = 36.25 men per company) to the command, giving the regiment 362 effective men (290 + 36 + 36 = 362). Officers would add another 39 (46 x .85 = 39.1) effectives, giving the 3rd Missouri 401 effective officers and men for the Battle of Pilot Knob. However, at the beginning of the Expedition, 61 of those men would have been recruits and returning officers added by Colonel Kitchen's efforts in northeast Arkansas and southeast Missouri, after the Expedition had begun (See Additions to the Army, listed below, for recruits for Clark's Brigade). Thus the 3rd's effective strength at the beginning of the Expedition numbered 340 (401 - 61 = 340) officers and men.[77]

7th Missouri Cavalry (CSA). Authors Bryce Suderow and Kyle Sinisi have Solomon Kitchen's command operating in northeastern Arkansas and southeastern Missouri when Clark's Brigade started on the Expedition. At the time Colonel Kitchen was indeed in northern Arkansas with 15 officers from his brigade on recruiting service; however, the 7th Missouri Cavalry was still with the main army. Operating under Lieutenant Colonel Jesse Ellison, the 7th participated in operations on the Mississippi River during the time that Kitchen was in northern Arkansas. When the Expedition began, Ellison led the regiment northward with the brigade on August 30, linking up with Colonel Kitchen on September 24 at Bolliger Mill, Missouri. This is further supported in the *Official Records*, where Davies reports that the 7th Missouri left Princeton with the other units of Clark's Brigade on August 30.[78]

8th Missouri Cavalry Regiment (CSA). Commanded by William L. Jeffers, the regiment was detached from the brigade at Powhatan about September 16 (Sinisi says Jeffers was detached at Pocahontas, while Suderow has the date as "about September 13," both of which are wrong) and entered Missouri as part of the army advance. When the 8th Missouri subsequently attacked Bloomfield on September 22, Federal reports put Jeffers's strength at "at least 200," but later adjusted the figure to between 400–500; say 450 officers and men. The 450 figure is further supported by J. A. Cocker, who briefly transferred to Jeffers's regiment when it entered Missouri, before reverting back to Harris' Missouri Battery. Overall Jeffers's strength was higher than what it had been during the Camden Expedition, which was estimated to number about 300 effective officers and men. It is assumed that the command recruited itself following the Camden Expedition and

---

77. The two detached companies rejoined the regiment before October 9. *O.R.*, vol. 41, pt. 1:687–688.
78. *O.R.*, vol. 34, pt. 1:831, 934; *O.R.*, vol. 34, pt. 2:453–454, 506, 523, 1097–1098; *O.R.*, vol. 34, pt. 4:165, 296, 684; *O.R.*, vol. 41, pt. 1:695; *O.R.*, vol. 41, pt. 2:8, 24, 36; *O.R.*, vol. 41, pt. 3:929, 953; Ballard Diary, May 1–August 30, 1864; Marmaduke, 358; Sinisi, 45; Suderow, *Arcadia Valley*, 139.

summer river operations. The 450 figure suggests an effective strength of 383 (450 x .85 = 382.5) officers and men; 36 of whom were officers (three were with Kitchen on recruiting service.[79]

14th Missouri Cavalry Battalion. Though eventually assigned to Clark's Brigade sometime after it left Pocahontas, in September 1864, the battalion served initially as an unattached unit in Marmaduke's Division, having been assigned to the division on August 30. As such, Wood's Battalion was not part of the reported 1,200 effectives that Clark listed when it started from Princeton. The 14th entered Missouri with "400 men," according to James H. Campbell of the battalion. Officers calculated based upon six companies (4 x 6 = 24 + 5 staff = 29) gives the battalion 429 officers and men when it left Arkansas. Effective strength would then be 365 (429 x .85 = 364.65) officers and men.[80]

Marmaduke's Mo. Bde (Brig. Gen. John B. Clark; Col. Colton Greene, October 25, 1864).
    Staff = 8[81]
    3rd Cav. (Col. Colton Greene, WIA Oct. 22; Capt. Benjamin S. Johnson).[82] = 340
    4th Cav. (Col. John Q. Burbridge, WIA Oct. 21; Ltc. William J. Preston).[83] EFF = 219
    7th Cav. (Col. Solomon G. Kitchen, WIA Oct. 23; Ltc. John F. Davies).[84] EFF = 219
    8th Cav. (Col. William L. Jeffers). EFF = 383
    10th Cav. (Col. Robert R. Lawther). EFF = 219 [16 K, 56 W, 73 M][85]
    Pratt's Art. Bn. (Maj. Joseph Pratt, WIA Oct. 26, 1864)[86]
        Hynson's Tx. Battery or 10th Tx. Lt. Art. (Capt. Henry C. Hynson) 3 guns; 6-pound. brass SB, 12-pound James Rifle, 12-pound Mt. How.[87] EFF = 32 (E)

---

79. Banasik, *Confederate Tales, 1864*, 238–239; *O.R.*, vol. 41, pt.3: 303, 361; Cocker, 9; Sinisi, 59; Suderow, *Arcadia Valley*, 40.
80. *O.R.*, vol. 41, pt. 1:627, 642, 719; *O.R.*, vol. 41, pt. 2:1090; Buresh, 218; Campbell Memoirs; Crute, *Confederate Army*, 204; Sifakis, *Missouri*, 102–103; Suderow, *Arcadia Valley*, 139.
81. *O.R.*, vol. 41, pt. 2:1095.
82. Greene was wounded on October 21 at the Little Blue, but didn't turn over command to Johnson until the 22nd. On the 24th Greene briefly resumed command of the regiment, until after the Battle of Mine Creek, when he assumed command of the brigade, after J. B. Clark assumed command of Marmaduke's Division. *O.R.*, vol. 41, pt. 1:634, 690–691, 693.
83. *O.R.*, vol. 41, pt. 1:682, 684; Kirkman, 143.
84. The combined unit of the 7th Missouri and Davies's Battalion was also known as the "Missouri and Arkansas Legion." Bartels, *Trans-Mississippi Men*, 17.
85. *O.R.*, vol. 41, pt. 1:698–699.
86. *O.R.*, vol. 41, pt. 1:679; Bailey, *Between the Enemy and Texas*, 311 (n. 7); Wooster, *Lone Star Regiments*, 306.
87. Per Hughey's Arkansas Battery above, the battery effective strength was estimated at 32 officers and men (10.5 officers and men per gun x 3 = 31.5). *O.R.*, vol. 41, pt. 1:719; *O.R.*, vol. 41, pt. 4:1023; Cocker, 13.

Harris' Mo. Battery (Capt. S. S. Harris) 3 guns; 6-pound. brass SB, 12-pound James Rifle, 12-pound Mt. How.[88] EFF = 32 (E)
Brigade Total = 1,452 EFF

Freeman's Brigade General Information. Freeman reported his "Present For Duty Strength" on September 20, 1864, as follows, ( ) = officer strength:

Unit	Present For Duty	.85 Percent	EFF
Freeman's Regt	550 (46)	468 (39)	507
Fristoe's Regt	530 (46)	451 (39)	490
Ford's Bn.	276 (29)	235 (25)	260

In reporting his "Present for Duty" it appears that Freeman did not include officers. This would add 39 (45 x .85 = 39.1) effective officers to each regiment; Ford's Battalion, based upon six companies, would add 25 effective officers (6 x 4 = 24 + 5 staff = 29 officers x .85 = 25); while the brigade staff would add another six men, giving the brigade (507 + 490 + 260 + 6 = 1,263) effective officers and men.[89]

On October 6, 1864, upon arrival at Linn, Freeman's Brigade was detached from the division "and marched under Major-General Price's orders with the main column," to guard the army's trains. By the Battle of Independence, on October 21, the brigade was again part of Marmaduke's Division.[90]

Freeman's Bde. (Col. Thomas R. Freeman)
  Staff = 6
  Freeman's Mo. Cav. (Ltc. Joseph B. Love, POW Oct. 23; Maj. M. V. Shaver).[91] EFF = 507 [13 K, 20 W, 148 M][92]
  Fristoe's Mo. Cav. (Col. Edward T. Fristoe). EFF = 490 [11 K, 40 W, 65 M][93]
  Ford's Ark. Bn. (Lt. Col. Barney Ford). EFF = 260 [3 K, 5 W, 11 M][94]
    Brigade Total = 1,263 [27 K, 65 W, 224 M]

Unattached.
  14th Cav. Bn. (Lt. Col. Robert C. Wood). EFF = 365
Summary of Marmaduke's Division.

---

88. Per Hughey's Arkansas Battery above, the battery effective strength was estimated at 32 officers and men (10.5 officers and men per gun x 3 = 31.5). *O.R.*, vol. 34, pt. 3:830; *O.R.*, vol. 41, pt. 1:719; *O.R.*, vol. 41, pt. 4:1023; Cocker, 13.
89. *O.R.*, vol. 41, pt. 1:344, 364, 699; Livermore, 68–69.
90. *O.R.*, vol. 41, pt. 1:681, 685.
91. Paul Kirkman says that Major William Cook took over the command after Love was captured. Buresh, 206; Kirkman, 143; Suderow, Report of POWs, List no. 74 (November 10, 1864).
92. *O.R.*, vol. 41, pt. 1:671; Crute, *Confederate Army*, 206–207.
93. *O.R.*, vol. 41, pt. 1:699; Crute, *Confederate Army*, 207.
94. *O.R.*, vol. 41, pt. 1:671; Crute, *Confederate Army*, 60.

Division Staff and Escorts	151	EFF
Clark's Brigade	1,453	EFF
Freeman's Brigade	1,263	EFF
Unattached	365	EFF
Division Total	3,232	EFF

* * * * * * *

Shelby's Division

Shelby's Division General Information. On September 17, 1864, just prior to the launch Expedition Shelby's Division numbered 3,051 mounted and dismounted men, of whom 1,433 were unarmed. However, given the arms captured during the Expedition, the command would have been completely armed and mounted by the time it left Boonville in mid-October 1864. It was also clear from S. D. Jackman's report that he had significantly more men in his command than was indicated by Shelby on September 17. Jackman numbered his command at 2,000 men, which probably included officers and enlisted men, while Shelby's report probably did not include officers.[95]

Shelby's Division (Brig Gen. Joseph O. Shelby)
  Staff = 12 EFF[96]
  Escort: Co. E, 12th Mo. Cav. (Capt. Maurice M. Langhorne).[97] EFF = 55
  Advance Party: Johnson's Co. (Capt. Matthew Rector Johnson).[98] EFF = 43
    HQ Total = 110 EFF

Shelby's Brigade General Information. On September 17 General Shelby reported the strength of Shanks's Brigade as 1,455, with 278 unarmed and 48 of that number dismounted. However, the unarmed and dismounted portion of the brigade would evaporate within days of the Expedition beginning, as sufficient arms and horses were procured the deeper the brigade moved into Missouri. At the time of the report, General Shelby also noted that a portion of the men from the brigade were attached to Wood's Battalion, but he gives no number.

At the beginning of the Expedition the brigade consisted of three cavalry regiments, one battalion of cavalry and a two-gun battery. The three regiments added 114 (29 companies x 4 = 116 officers + 18 for three staffs = 134 x .85 = 113.9)

---

95. *O.R.*, vol. 41, pt. 1:678; *O.R.*, vol. 41, pt. 3:940.
96. The divisional surgeon, Junius Terry, was excluded from the staff as non-effective. *O.R.*, vol. 41, pt. 3:943–944; Crute, *Confederate Staff Officers*, 173–174.
97. Strength based upon the typical cavalry company in 1864, i.e., 64 officers and men of whom 55 (64 x .85 = 55) would be considered effective, per Livermore. *O.R.*, vol. 41, pt. 1:662; Edwards, *Shelby and His Men*, 501; Livermore, 67–68; Muster Roll, Stallard's Company; Whitsett Letter.
98. For details on Johnson's command see Additions to the Expedition, Johnson's Battalion at the end of this Appendix. E-mail (May 11, 2008), Lars Gjertveit, Internet site, on "The Missouri Civil War Message Board," hereafter cited as Gjertveit letter.

effective officers; while Elliott's Battalion of four companies added 18 (4 x 4 = 16 + 5 staff = 21 x .85 = 17.85) effective officers to the brigade. Total additions to the brigade for all officers, including eight brigade staff and two from Collins's Battery gives the brigade 142 (114 + 18 + 10 = 142) effective officers. This indicates that the brigade began the Expedition with 1,597 (1,455 + 142 = 1,597) effective officers and men, excluding only the 19 men from the artillery company. With the artillery men added in, the brigade totaled 1,616 effective officers and men.

Note: One company was deducted from the 12th Missouri, to reflect the loss of the company as the Escort for the commanding general.

Elliott's Cavalry Battalion. Elliott's command appears to have started out as a four-company battalion. Later, as the Expedition progressed, Elliott increased his command to regiment size at Boonville between October 9–12, 1864, by adding another six companies. However, R. P. Mitchell, who was "Elliott's Orderly from the time the Brigade was organized until...[it was] rounded up at Shreveport," recorded that the unit was always just a battalion. Further, that Elliott was never officially promoted to lieutenant colonel, much less full colonel. Mitchell's assertions are supported by the *Official Records*, which has Elliott still listed as a major on December 31, 1864. However, the *Official Records* has a report by Elliott dated May 8, 1864, where he signs as "Lieutenant-Colonel, Commanding Battalion." Additionally, Elliott, in recounting his wartime experiences says he was promoted to full colonel, in command of a regiment at Boonville during Price's Raid. Given the *Official Records* remarks that Elliott was only a major in December 1864, I suspect that he was never officially promoted to either lieutenant-colonel or colonel. And Elliott's Regiment, the 9th Missouri Cavalry Regiment, was not officially organized until after the Expedition returned to Arkansas. See Ben Elliott's and Robert Wood's Battalions under Additions to the Expedition below for additions to their battalions.[99]

Gordon's 5th Missouri Cavalry Regiment (CSA). The strength of this unit was reported in mid-July 1864 as 500, by George Cruzen. On September 24 Cruzen has Companies H and I at 75 men at Farmington, Missouri; with six officers, would give the commands 81 effective officers and men. This would suggest that the regiment had 410 (5 x 81 = 405 + 5 staff = 410) effective officers and men. The average between the July date and September date would yield 455 (500 + 410 = 910 / 2 = 455) effective officers and men for the beginning of the Expedition.[100]

---

99. *O.R.*, vol. 34, pt. 1:840–841; *O.R.*, vol. 41, pt 1:631, 645; *O.R.*, vol. 41, pt. 4:1144; Allardice, *Confederate Colonels*, 139; Bartels, *Elliott's Scouts*, 61; Edwards, *Shelby and His Men*, 403; Marshall Letter; Moore, *Missouri, Confederate Military History, Extended*, 286; Sellmeyer, 221, 223.

100. *O.R.*, vol. 41, pt. 1:670; Crute, *Confederate Army*, 199; Cruzen, 22–23; Moore, *Missouri, Confederate Military History*, 177.

The 11th and 12th Missouri Cavalries (CSA), With Elliott's Missouri Cavalry Battalion. These units comprised a total of 23 companies and constituted the remaining officers and men of the brigade not enumerated above. The estimated strength of the brigade at the beginning of the Expedition was 1,616. From this number we deduct the brigade staff of 8, the artillery company of 21 and Gordon's Regiment of 455 leaving 1,132 (1,616 - 8 - 21 -455 = 1,132) for the other three units of the brigade. The unknown commands totaled 23 companies or 49 (1,129 / 23 = 49.2) effective officers and men per company. This suggests that the 11th Missouri contained 492 (10 x 49.2 = 492) effective officers and men, including staff; the 12th Missouri contained 443 (9 x 49.2 = 442.8) effective officers and men, including staff; and Elliott's command contained 197 (4 x 49 = 196.8) effective officers and men, including staff at the beginning of the Expedition.

Note: Rounding reduces the brigade strength by two to 1,611.

Shelby's Mo. Cav. Bde. (Col. David Shanks, severely wounded, captured Oct. 6, 1864; Brig. Gen. M. Jeff Thompson, Oct. 7, 1864)[101]
    Staff = 8 EFF
        5th Cav. (Col. B. Frank Gordon). EFF = 455 [15 K, 50 W, 41 M][102]
        11th Cav. (Col. Moses W. Smith, MW, captured Oct. 28, 1864; Ltc J. C. Hooper).[103] EFF = 492 [10 K, 40 W, 20 M][104]
        12th Cav. (Lt. Col. William H. Erwin). EFF = 443 [3 K, 22 W, 10 M][105]
        Elliott's Cav. Bn. (Lt. Col. Ben Elliott). EFF = 197 [7 K, 18 W, 0 M][106]
        Collins Battery (one sec.) (Capt. Richard A. Collins) 2 guns, 10-pound Parrots.[107] EFF = 21 [1 K, 0 W, 2 M][108]
        Brigade Total = 1,616

Jackman's Brigade General Information. On September 17, 1864, General Shelby reported that Jackman's command numbered 441 armed men and 1,155 unarmed men; total 1,596, of whom 1,463 were mounted. However, in his offi-

---

101. Shanks was later reported as dying in Federal custody on December 2, 1864, with a gunshot to the breast; however, he survived the war, dying in Denver, Colorado, in 1870. Following the wounding of Colonel Shanks, on October 6, Colonel Moses W. Smith took immediate command of the brigade, being relieved by General Thompson the following day. *O.R.*, vol. 41, pt. 1:654–655, 663; Anonymous, *12th Missouri Cavalry*, 10; Sellmeyer, 309–310.
102. *O.R.*, vol. 41, pt. 1:670.
103. James C. Hooper was the lieutenant colonel of the 11th and known to have been on the Expedition. He would have replaced Smith upon his wounding at Newtonia. Allardice, *Confederate Colonels*, 210; Confederate Correspondence (MSS 03-26, box no. 1, file no. 3), Hooper to Thompson (October 12, 1864); Edwards, *Shelby and His Men*, 418, 501.
104. *O.R.*, vol. 41, pt. 1:670; Crute, *Confederate Army*, 203–204.
105. Ibid.
106. *O.R.*, vol. 41, pt. 1.670.
107. Collins's section contained the two Parrots, one of which he lost on October 23, when it burst at the Battle of Westport. Per "Hughey's Arkansas Battery" above, the battery effective strength was estimated at 21 officers and men (10.5 officers and men per gun x 2 = 21). *O.R.*, vol. 34, pt. 3:687; *O.R.*, vol. 41, pt. 1:656, 658; *O.R.*, vol. 41, pt. 4:1023.
108. *O.R.*, vol. 41, pt. 1:670.

cial report of the Expedition, Jackman recorded that he "moved into the State with about 500 armed men and 1,500 unarmed"; total 2,000. The difference could have been additional acquisitions after Jackman's September 17 report along with officers and artillerymen, which were not figured within the original 1,596 men. Officers would have added 142 (4 x 20 = 80 + 12 staff = 92 for Hunter's and Jackman's Regiments; Schnable and Coffee had four companies each, adding 32 + 10 staff = 42 officers; brigade staff of six and two more officers from the artillery gives the brigade a total of 142 officers). Total effective officers would be 121 (142 x .85 = 120.7).

This would give the brigade 1,736 (121 + 1,596 + 19 artillerymen = 1,736) effective officers and men as compared to Jackman's command strength on July 26, which was 1,710. Additionally on August 10, four companies were added to John A. Schnable's command, so "that his regiment may be filled up and organized according to law." These four companies would have added 218 (64 x 4 = 256 x .85 = 217.6) effective officers and men to the brigade, giving the brigade 1,954 (1736 + 218 = 1,954) effective officers and men. Additionally, at the same time that Schnable's command was increased by four companies, D. C. Hunter's Regiment also received "the remainder of the recruits" that were available at that time. These two final additions would have rounded out the brigade at about 2,000 effective officers and men, as recorded by S. D. Jackman when he entered Missouri.

As to why there are 404 men missing from Shelby's September 17 report, I would suspect that in addition to not including officers, the report failed to include the additional manpower that was added to the brigade because they were not organized. The figures presented below for the various regiments and battalions were pro-rated based upon the number of companies in the command. The brigade contained 32 companies; 10 each for Hunter and Jackman's Regiments, four for Coffee, and eight for Schnable. The pro-rated value would be 61.6 (2,000 - 21 for artillery - 6 for brigade staff = 1,973/ 32 = 61.65) effective officers and men per company.

As to the unarmed men, upon the capture of Glasgow, Jackman's Brigade would have been fully armed, given the substantial number of arms that were captured from the enemy. Further, according to Jackman, "after the deduction of all losses... [he] came out [of Missouri] with about the same number almost entirely armed." Prior to the start of the Expedition, Jackman reported only 500 of his men were armed, while 1,500 were not.[109]

John T. Coffee's Battalion. Coffee was supposed to recruit a regiment of troops for Price's Expedition, but failed to do so, raising instead a battalion of four companies, which he organized in the spring of 1864. The battalion, probably under Lieutenant Colonel John T. Crisp, Coffee's second in command, was detached from Jackman's Brigade and ordered to report to General Price on October 3. Coffee was then left behind in eastern Missouri, to recruit additional men for his

---

109. *O.R.*, vol. 41, pt. 1:678; *O.R.*, vol. 41, pt. 2:1036, 1053–1054; *O.R.*, vol. 41, pt. 3:940.

regiment. Meanwhile, Coffee's Battalion, under Crisp, was probably armed and then assigned back to Shelby's command, date unknown.

As shown in the *Official Records*, D. A. Williams's Regiment was not assigned to Jackman's Brigade until October 30, and there is no reason to believe that Coffee's unit was immediately assigned to Tyler's Brigade. Further, as also shown within the *Official Records*, Crisp's unit was not listed in the Army of Missouri Order of Battle, while Coffee's command was listed under Tyler's Brigade. In all probability, Coffee's command was placed in Tyler's Brigade sometime before the end of the Expedition, similar to what happened to Williams's Regiment.

Another name associated with Coffee's Battalion was Major Thomas J. Shaw. He first appeared in the *Official Records* at the Battle of Newtonia on October 28, 1864, as commanding a unit in Jackman's Brigade. It is supposed that Crisp had been incapacitated following the engagement at Mine Creek or was otherwise assigned to other duties. Previous to that date Shaw is noted as commanding Company C, in Coffee's Battalion, being promoted to major in October 1864. This would further indicate that Coffee's command was not assigned to Tyler's Brigade until after October 28 (See also comments on John T. Crisp's Battalion below).[110]

John A. Schnable's Battalion. Schnable's Battalion was organized in the summer of 1864 with four companies (Sifakis says six companies) of "raw recruits" and added two (Crute says he added four more) more before it departed for the Missouri Expedition. Overall, Crute has the command with eight companies while Sifakis has the unit with six companies; eight seems to be the correct number.[111]

John T. Crisp's Battalion. One of the units identified by several sources as being part of Shanks's Brigade, Shelby's Division, was John T. Crisp's Battalion. However, a review of the *Supplement to the Official Records* shows Crisp as a member of Coffee's Regiment, in the role of lieutenant colonel. This would further suggest that Coffee's Regiment (actually a battalion) was commanded by Lieutenant Colonel John T. Crisp. As such, I believe that when various writers were referring to Crisp's unit they are actually referring to Coffee's Battalion, as commanded by Crisp.

Originally Crisp organized an "independent" company in Texas from Missourians living there in the summer of 1862. Leading a two-company command, Crisp proceeded to southwest Missouri where his unit was ordered into the Confederate Service in August 1862. In September 1862 Crisp was elected captain of Company I, 6th Missouri Cavalry (CSA)—Coffee's Regiment. In early January 1864 Crisp returned to Texas on furlough, having been granted a 50 day leave, but never returned to his command; instead, he probably linked up with John T.

---

110. *O.R.*, vol. 41, pt. 1:673, 677; Allardice, *Confederate Colonels*, 104–105; Busch, *Missouri Democrat Articles*, 106, 289; Edwards, *Shelby and His Men*, 303, 385; Hulston & Goodrich, 292–293; Danny Odom Letter (June 10, 2013), Internet site "The Arkansas Civil War Message Board," key word "John T. Coffee;" "The War In Missouri," *Chicago Tribune*, October 8, 1864; Winns, 538.

111. *O.R.*, vol. 41, pt. 2:1053–1054; Crute, *Confederate Army*, 210; Sifakis, 108.

Coffee, who was in southwest Missouri and northwest Arkansas in September 1864, to form a new command for the upcoming invasion of Missouri.

Additionally, Lieutenant Colonel John T. Crisp's name appears in M. Jeff Thompson's memoirs as commanding the rear guard of the army at Ironton, on September 29, while Coffee was located at Fredericktown on a recruiting mission on October 5. Hulston and Goodrich in their biography of Coffee noted that Coffee traveled with the Expedition "to Fredericktown, Missouri [where] he hoped to fill his quota of men, but by October 3, he had not done so. Shelby relieved Coffee from Jackman's brigade and ordered him to report to Price."

It's also clear from assorted Confederate reports on Price's Expedition, that Coffee's name was missing from all the recorded reports of the Expedition after Pilot Knob, suggesting that he was no longer with the army.

As to Coffee's Battalion, now commanded by Crisp, Price eventually assigned it back to Shelby, probably after it was better armed, to use as he saw fit. Crisp's unit was then attached to Shanks'/Thompson's Brigade, where it operated for most of the Expedition. And by the time the Expedition had ended, Coffee's Battalion was assigned to Tyler's Brigade. It should also be noted that most writers had Crisp as a major at the time, although that is not correct. In correspondence, concerning the Expedition, Crisp signed his name as a lieutenant colonel.[112]

Jackman's Mo. Cav. Bde (Col. Sidney Jackman):
  Staff= 6 EFF
  Coffee's Cav. Bn. (Col. John T. Coffee, relieved to recruit, Oct. 3; Ltc. John T. Crisp; Maj. Thomas J. "Commodore" Shaw, sometime after October 25; Bn. Detached Oct. 3, 1864 to Army, though still operated with Shelby's Div.). EFF = 246 (E)
  Jackman's Cav. (Lt. Col. C. H. Nichols). EFF = 617 (E)
  Hunter's Cav. (Col. DeWitt C. Hunter). EFF = 617 (E)
  Schnable's Cav. Bn. (Lt. Col. John A. Schnable). EFF = 493 (E)
  Collins's Battery (one sec.; Lt. Jacob D. Conner) 2 guns; two 12-pound iron how.[113] EFF = 21 (E)
    Brigade Total = 2,000 EFF

The 46th Arkansas Mounted Infantry Regiment. Upon release from arrest on January 1, 1864, William O. Coleman returned to Missouri to recruit a new com-

---

112. *O.R.S.*, pt. 2, vol. 38:269; Allardice, *Confederate Colonels*, 104–105; Anonymous, *Gallant Breed the 6th Missouri Cavalry*, 122; Bunch, *Missouri Democrat Articles*, 106, 289; Confederate Correspondence (MSS 03-26, Box no. 1, file no. 3), Crisp to McLean (October 16, 1864); Edwards, *Shelby and His Men*, 419; Forsyth, *Great Missouri Raid*, 243; Hulston & Goodrich, 292–293; Lause, *Price's Lost Campaign*, 141; Monnett, 141; Henry Ellison Skaggs Papers (1831–1899), Deposition A (November 4, 1895), Western Historical Manuscript Collection, State Historical Society of Missouri (Rolla, MO); Stanton, etc., 238, 301; Sellmeyer, 231; Winns, 538.

113. Per "Hughey's Arkansas Battery" above, the battery effective strength was estimated at 21 officers and men (10.5 officers and men per gun x 2 = 21). *O.R.*, vol. 41, pt. 4:1023; Bartels, *Trans-Mississippi Men*, 23; Sellmeyer, 347 (n. 4).

mand. He eventually raised three companies of Missouri cavalry in south-central Missouri and then moved to eastern Arkansas, under the direction of General Shelby. Coleman then raised an additional seven companies and, with his previous three, formed the 46th Arkansas Mounted Infantry, of which he was elected colonel. John W. Crabtree was elected lieutenant colonel with a man named Stone being made the major, according to Coleman.

In August 1864 Coleman was allowed by General Shelby to detach the three Missouri companies from the 46th and return to Missouri to complete an all Missouri command, prior to the invasion. However, Coleman didn't have sufficient time to complete the task. Later, when Shelby entered Missouri with his division, he assigned "Coleman's Regiment" to Jackman's Brigade; the date was probably right after the division crossed into Missouri on September 19 (see Additions to the Expedition, for more on Coleman's Command).[114]

The remaining seven companies of the 46th were attached to Shelby's Division at the beginning of the Expedition. There is no indication that the 46th was ever assigned to a specific brigade within the division. With Coleman gone, the command of the 46th fell to Lieutenant Colonel John W. Crabtree. Since the 46th was identified as a mounted infantry unit, it will be rated at 84 officers and men per company, with a staff of five officers giving the command 504 (84 x 7 companies = 588 + 5 staff = 593 x .85 = 504) effective officers and men (See Organizational Note No. 1 above for details).

Unattached:
    46th Ark. Inf (Mtd) (Ltc. John W. Crabtree). EFF = 504 EFF

Summary of Shelby's Division:

Division Staff and Escort	110 EFF
Shanks' Brigade	1,616 EFF
Jackman's Brigade	2,000 EFF
Unattached	504 EFF
Division Total	4,230 EFF[115]

Army of Missouri Starting Strength.

Army HQ	312 EFF
Fagan's Division	9,318 EFF
Marmaduke's Division	3,232 EFF
Shelby's Division	4,230 EFF
Army Total	17,092 EFF[116]

---

114. Coleman Letters (October 27, 1909 and November 20, 1914); Ferguson, 313; Gifford, 224; Sellmeyer, 209.
115. The *Official Records* and the *Chicago Tribune* reported that Shelby's strength was 4,000–5,000 men when he occupied Fredericktown on September 23, 1864. *O.R.*, vol. 41, pt. 3:342; "The War in Missouri," *Chicago Tribune*, September 27, 1864.
116. This number is further supported by Lieutenant Colonel D. J. Hynes, of the 17th Illinois Cav-

Final Analysis and Summary of the Army of Missouri.

The 17,092 effective strength of Price's Army of Missouri when it left Arkansas is considerably different than what Price recorded in his reports on the Expedition. The figure above includes officers, staff, engineers and artillerymen, all of whom it appears that Price left out of his army total. Price also appears to have not counted units that were attached to the various divisions as will be seen in the following paragraphs.

Removing all the officers, staffs, escorts, and engineer units leaves the command with about 14,840 (17,092 - 312 HQ - 1,049 Fagan - 473 Marmaduke - 414 Shelby = 14,844) men. This still leaves 2,884 men unaccounted for.

From the 14,844 we also remove the 400-man difference between General Shelby's September 17 report and Colonel Jackman's report of the Expedition. In a like vein, General Cabell recorded receiving between 200–300 (say 250) more men just before he went into Missouri. These two reductions bring the army strength to 14,194 (14,844 - 650 = 14,194) men, as defined by Price.

Additionally, the 8th Missouri Cavalry (CSA) was detached from the army several days prior to the army entering Missouri. It is estimated that the 8th Missouri had a strength of 347 (383 - 36 officers, including recruiters = 347) men. Deducting the 8th Missouri leaves the army with 13,847 (14,194 - 347 = 13,847) men.

After all the above adjustments are made we are still left with 1,843 men, whom Price did not consider part of the army when they entered Missouri. Major J. R. Shaler, inspector general of the Army of Missouri, sheds some light on these units, based upon testimony he gave at Price's Count of Inquiry following the Expedition. When questioned as to the organization of the army, Shaler gave a breakdown as to the number of divisions, brigades and artillery assigned to the various commands and even mentions partisan companies, which he did not consider part of the army's organization. Also noticeably missing from Shaler's comments were any remarks on the unattached regiments or battalions that were part of the army. These included Rogan's, Lyles's and the 46th Arkansas Regiment, with Anderson's Cavalry Battalion. Though noted as a detached unit, Anderson's Battalion served as Fagan's Escort and was deducted under that previous deduction for escorts. Deducting the other three commands leaves the army with 12,347 (13,847 - 510 men for Rogan - 510 men for Lyles and - 480 men for the 46th Arkansas = 12,347) men.

Removing the officers and men from the artillery units would reduce the overall strength of Price's army to 12,185 (12,347 - 52 Fagan's Art. - 64 Marmaduke's Art. - 42 Shelby's Art. = 12,189) effective men, excluding all officers, escorts, engineers, artillerymen and attached units.

There was also one other unit, Wood's Battalion, not commonly accepted as

---

alry, who was captured at Glasgow and later paroled. Hynes says Price entered Missouri with 18,000 men. Busch, *Missouri Democrat Articles*, 203.

an unattached unit at the beginning of the Expedition. Wood's Missouri Battalion, which served in Marmaduke's Division, was normally considered attached to Clark's Brigade; however, Wood's Battalion was not attached to Clark's Brigade until after it had departed Pocahontas. Deducting Wood's strength from the total leaves the army with 11,824 (12,189 - 365 = 11,824) men in the Army of Missouri when it crossed into Missouri. This figure or the previous 12,185 figure pairs well with General Price's report that he entered Missouri, "with nearly 12,000 men."[117]

The previous paragraphs are understood to be educated speculation on my part, as there is limited empirical evidence to support my suppositions, one way or the other. That said, we do know that based upon Cabell's, Clark's, Slemons's, and Dr. McPheeters' comments on the army's strength when it left Princeton, that the command totaled roughly 5,000 (2,500 for Cabell, 1,200 for Clark, 1000 for Slemons and 300 for the headquarters = 5,000) effectives. Further, B. Frank Gordon, a regimental commander in Shelby's Division, wrote a letter home on September 7, where he has Price heading for northeast Arkansas with 5,000–6,000 cavalry. A Union report dated September 16 puts Price's command at 6,000 as it marched to northeast Arkansas. At the same time General Shelby reported that he had recruited 8,000 men in northeast Arkansas, with a month of recruiting still to go; and, with his own command of about 1,500 this would have given Price 14,500 men (5,000 + 8,000 + 1,500 = 14,500), well above the 12,000 figure that he commonly used. Finally, a captured Federal officer, who conversed with his captors at Glasgow put the invasion force at 18,000.

In the final analysis, Mark Lause, author of several pieces on Price's Expedition, writes that the Army of Missouri's "commanders likely had only a vague idea how large" the army was "at any given point." And this was easily seen by the testimony of Colonel James R. Shaler, in Price's Court of Inquiry, when he placed the army's beginning strength at 7,000 armed and 2,000 unarmed men, total 9,000. This was far below Price's own original total of 12,000. So the idea that the Army of Missouri numbered over 17,000 effective officers and men seems reasonable given all the evidence presented above.[118]

* * * * * * *

Additions to the Army of Missouri
September 20-December 2, 1964

Timothy Reeve's 15th Missouri Cavalry. As the Expedition entered Missouri, General Shelby reported that Lieutenant Colonel Benjamin A. Johnson of the 15th

---

117. *O.R.*, vol. 41 pt. 1:627, 642, 678–679, 719; *O.R.*, vol. 41, pt. 3:940; *O.R.S.*, pt. 1, vol. 7:391.
118. *O.R.*, vol. 34, pt. 3:670, 687, 803; *O.R.*, vol. 41, pt. 1:627, 651, 722; *O.R.*, vol. 41, pt. 3:212; *O.R.S.*, pt.1 vol. 7:391; Britton, *Civil War on the Border, 1863–1865*, 387; Busch, *Missouri Democrat Articles*, 13–14, 203; Mark A. Lause, "Army of Missouri," in *Encyclopedia of the Civil War*, 85; Pitcock & Gurley, 216; Slemons Letters (August 24, 1864).

Missouri Cavalry (CSA) recruited 100 men, which were to be added to his regiment, the 15th Missouri.[119]

15th Missouri Cav. Regt. (Col. Timothy Reeves) EFF = 100 Recruits added

William O. Coleman's Missouri Regiment. This unit never reached regimental strength, having a reported complement of "200 men" when it joined Shelby's Division on September 25 at Fredericktown. Coleman had proceeded to Missouri in August 1864 with three companies of Missourians that he had originally recruited for the 46th Arkansas Mounted Infantry. It was estimated that Coleman's command was assigned to Jackman's Brigade shortly after his arrival on September 25. Coleman's command was not part of the strength report issued on September 17, as the command was not with its brigade or even in the vicinity.

As a mounted infantry unit Coleman's Command would have number about 219 (3 x 84 = 252 + 5 staff = 257 x .85 = 219) effective officers and men, similar as to what was reported.[120]

Sept. 19, 1864 Coleman's Mo. Regt. (Col. William O. Coleman). EFF = 219

Alonzo Slayback's Battalion or Regiment. Slayback's unit joined the Expedition on September 23 (Sinisi says the 24th) and was added to Shanks's Brigade, Shelby's Division when the command entered Union, Missouri, on October 2. The *Official Records* has the unit as a battalion; John Edwards says the unit had 10 companies, which makes it a regiment; however, it appears from Edwards writings, the command initially contained four companies, adding six more over time. As such, on September 23, Slayback's four-company command consisted of 223 effective officers and men, at 64 officers and men per company or 222 (64 x 4 = 256 + 5 staff = 261 x .85 = 221.85) effective officers and men for the battalion.

The additional six companies are assumed to have been added at Boonville between October 10–12. They would have added 326 (6 X 64 = 384 x .85 = 326.4) effective officers and men to the battalion.[121]

Sept. 23, 1864 Slayback's Cav. Bn. (Ltc. Alonzo W. Slayback). EFF = 222
Oct. 10-12, 1864 Slayback's Bn. to Regt. EFF = 326

Recruits for Shanks's or Thompson's Iron Brigade. On October 14, 1864, Shelby reported that the Iron Brigade, commanded by M. Jeff Thompson, was sent on an expedition with 1,200 men while another 600 were on furlough, suggesting that the brigade had contained at least 1,800 men. On this same date Shelby also remarked that he had sent D. A. Williams with 150 men to the north side of the Missouri River to recruit. These additional troops suggest a brigade strength on October 14 of about 1,950, as compared to the 1,455 men that started with the Expedition. This would further suggest that the Iron Brigade received at

---

119. *O.R.*, vol. 41, pt. 1:945.
120. *O.R.*, vol. 41, pt. 3:956–957; Busch, *Missouri Democrat Articles*, 11; Coleman Letters, (October 27, 1909 and November 20, 1914).
121. *O.R.*, vol. 41, pt. 1:645; Edwards, *Shelby and His Men*, 391–392; Sellmeyer, 215; Sinisi, 64.

least 495 (1,950 - 1,455 = 495) recruits after the Expedition began, not including Alonzo Slayback's Battalion, which was detached at the time that Shelby made his report on October 14. This number probably included 101 (107 - 6 officers = 101) additional men for M. Rector John's Battalion, with another 312 (330 - 18 = 312) men for Elliott's newly formed regiment. This would leave 82 (495 - 101 - 312 = 82) recruits for the brigade, plus any losses suffered prior to October 14, estimated at 41 for Farmington (September 24), Operation on Iron Mountain RR (September 27–28), Leasburg (September 29), Jefferson City (October 6) and Boonville (October 10). This indicates that the brigade received 123 (82 + 41) recruits for the 5th, 11th and 12th Missouri Cavalries (CSA) by October 14 or 41 men per regiment.[122]

Additionally, on October 17, 1864, Captain George S. Rathbun returned to the Iron Brigade, now commanded by M. Jeff Thompson, having recruited or conscripted a force of 500 men, of whom 100 came from Lexington. Of the Lexington men, according to Federal sources, "most" later deserted before reaching the army, and returned home. Those men recruited by Rathbun "were probably the best armed" of the recruits received by the Iron Brigade, being armed with shotguns. The loss of most of the Lexington men would leave the brigade with about 420 recruits.[123]

Sept. 19–Oct. 14, 1864 Recruits for Shanks' Bde. EFF = 123
Oct. 17, 1864 Recruits for Thompson's Bde. EFF = 420

John T. Coffee's Battalion. John T. Crisp, who commanded the battalion after Coffee departed on October 3, continued to recruit for his unit as well as organizing companies for other units. On October 16, Crisp reported that he had raised "about 115" men for his command. At 85 percent effective this would give the battalion 92 (115 x .85 = 92) additional men.[124]

Oct. 16, 1864 Recruits for Crisp's/Coffee's Bn. EFF = 92

J. F. Davies's Battalion. After it was organized, Davies's Battalion was attached to Kitchen's 7th Missouri Cavalry during the Expedition. It had 307 men, with 250 arms. The 307 men suggests five companies (about 60 men each), which seems to be the standard size for a Trans-Mississippi cavalry company organized in 1864. The company officers would have added 20 (4 x 5 = 20) more, with five staff officers, giving the battalion 332 (307 + 20 + 5 = 332) officers and men. J. H. Knox, a member of Davies's Battalion, places the command's strength at 500 men by the time of the Battle of Mine Creek on October 25, suggesting eight companies, which indicates that the command probably added three more companies

---

122. For details on Slayback see Slayback's Battalion / Regiment see below. *O.R.*, vol. 41, pt. 3:1012.
123. *O.R.*, vol. 41, pt. 1:614; Captured Union Correspondence, in Confederate Correspondence (MSS 03–26, box no. 1, file no. 3), Major Later to Editor of the Leavenworth Times (October 18, 1864); Edwards, *Shelby and His Men*, 419; Sinisi, 122.
124. Confederate Correspondence (MSS 03-26, Box no. 1, file no. 3), Crisp to McLean (October 16, 1864).

during the Expedition. Per Livermore, a cavalry command would have been 85 percent effective, allowing for men without horses, medical, quartermaster department, etc. This would suggest a battalion effective strength on September 24, when they joined the Expedition, of 282 (332 x .85 = 282.2) officers and men. The battalion added three cavalry companies sometime after the Expedition began (probably in October), or 163 (3 x 64 = 192 x .85 = 163.2) effective officers and men. By the time the campaign was winding down on November 3, the command had just 34 officers and men remaining, the rest "having gone home or deserted," most of which occurred after the Battle of Mine Creek.[125]

Sept. 24, 1864 Davies's Bn. (Maj. J. F. Davies). EFF = 282
Oct. 1864 Davies' Bn. Addition (3 Cos.). EFF = 153

Recruits for Marmaduke's Brigade, General John B. Clark commanding. Colonel Salomon Kitchen was detached from the brigade in January 1864, along with 15 officers, to recruit for his command in northeast Arkansas and southeast Missouri. Kitchen subsequently recruited and organized J. F. Davies's Battalion in the spring and summer of 1864. In addition to Davies's Battalion, which numbered 307 men, Kitchen was said to have raised between 600–700 men on September 14, 1864—say 650 for an average. Deducting Davies's 307 would leave Kitchen with 343 men for the other regiments of the brigade. This gives an additional strength of 58 (343 x .85 = 291.55 / 5 = 58.3) effective recruits for the 3rd, 4th, 7th, 8th, and 10th Missouri Cavalries (Wood's Battalion was excluded from the recruits as it was not part of the brigade when Kitchen went to northeast Arkansas and would not have had any recruiting officers with Kitchen.). The returning 15 recruiting officers would add three additional members to each command, giving them 61 effective officers and men.[126]

Sept. 24 3rd Missouri Cav. (recruits) EFF = 61
4th Missouri Cav. (recruits) EFF = 61
7th Missouri Cav. (recruits) EFF = 61
8th Missouri Cav. (recruits) EFF = 61
10th Missouri Cav. (recruits) EFF = 61
Total Recruits 305 EFF

Captured Artillery at Pilot Knob. On September 28, 1864, upon the capture of Pilot Knob, two Woodruff guns were added to Dobbin's Brigade, while Hughey's Battery acquired one 24-pound Coehorn mortar. The Woodruff was a 2-pound smoothbore gun that was used by both infantry and cavalry, requiring two horses to pull its caisson. In both cases the new acquisitions were provided "with a com-

---

125. *O.R.S.*, pt. 2, vol. 38:272; Evault Boswell, *Texas Boys in Gray* (Plano, TX, 2000), 111, hereafter cited as Boswell; Lause, *Price's Lost Campaign* 19; Livermore, 68–69.
126. *O.R.*, vol. 34, pt. 4:667; *O.R.*, vol. 41, pt.:695; *O.R.*, vol. 41, pt. 2:458; *O.R.*, vol. 41, pt. 3:929; *O.R.S.*, pt. 2 vol. 38:272; Livermore, 68–69.

pliment of ammunition." It's assumed that men were provided to work the new pieces of artillery, probably from the unarmed men of the brigade.[127]

Dobbin's Artillery (Cdr. ukn.) two 2-pound SB. EFF = 22

Mortar Sec.; Hughey's Battery (Cdr. ukn.) one 24-pound Mortar. EFF = 11

Provost Guard Companies. A Provost Guard was organized for each brigade of the army, shortly after September 28–29, 1864. Each provost company contained 50 men with four officers. Additionally, one major was added to the staff of each division to serve as provost marshal general for the Division. Unknown as to armament, if any, for the various provost guards. There were initially eight brigades and three divisions, which gives 435 more effectives for the command; this assumes that whether armed or not the provost had some type of weaponry to enforce their duties. Additionally, the Provost Guard was probably pulled from the existing men of the various brigades and did not affect the overall strength of the Expedition or the brigades to which they were assigned. Also, upon formation of C. H. Tyler's Brigade it is assumed that a ninth provost company would have been organized, adding another 46 officers and men to the overall Provost Command, for a total 501.[128] Lieutenant Colonel John P. Bull of Morgan's 2nd Arkansas Cavalry Regiment was wounded at Pilot Knob and appointed Provost Marshall General, Army of Missouri following the battle.

Artillery Captured At Herman. An "old six pounder gun" was captured at Herman on October 3. Since the army could always use more artillery, regardless of how old it was, I would suspect that it was added to either Hynson's or Harris's Battery of Clark's Brigade, which had captured the piece; in this case a pure guess would be Harris. It appears that the gun was abandoned by November 7, when the army crossed the Arkansas River. The gun was subsequently recaptured by the Federal Army on November 8, when General Curtis arrived at the Arkansas River.

There are a few legends surrounding the Herman artillery piece and what happened to it. In one account "the cannon was manned by a few old men who had received training in the German Army." After firing about four rounds, the cannoneers spiked the gun and fled Herman. The Confederates, in turn threw the cannon into the river.

In a second account, local militia manned the gun and upon the approach of the Confederate Army, they fired a few rounds, spiked the gun, then threw it in the Missouri River. After the rebels abandoned Herman, the local militia retrieved the artillery piece from the river and sent it to Jefferson City. Governor Hamilton Gamble then had the piece restored and returned it to Herman. However, Gamble died on January 1, 1864, and thus could not have restored the gun. The governor

---

127. *O.R.*, vol. 41, pt. 1:719; *O.R.*, vol. 41, pt. 3:961; Margreiter, 36–37; Ripley, 177, 188.
128. *O.R.*, vol. 41, pt. 1:648; Schultz, 202.

of Missouri at the time was Lieutenant Governor William Hall, who was serving out the remainder of Gamble's term.[129]

Oct. 3, 1864 Harris's Mo. Battery (added) one 6-pound Iron SB. EFF = 11

Charles Tyler's Brigade. Tyler's Brigade was added to the army at Boonville between October 9–12. Coffee's Regiment was not assigned to the brigade until after October 28, as previously stated. There is no indication that the units of the brigade were organized as infantry commands; as such, their initial organization will be assigned as cavalry regiments, per Sifakis. Perkins's and Searcy's Regiments were newly organized with an estimated strength of 645 for each unit, including staff. Captain James Kennedy further supports the strength of Searcy's Regiment, recalling in his later years that he "was on the Westport battlefield as a captain with six hundred men." Effective strength, per Livermore, if fully armed would be 549 (645 x .85 = 549) officers and men (see Organizational Note No. 1 above for details).

According to General Price, when organized the two regiments had about 200 arms between them, or enough for 100 men per regiment. However, J. W. Halliburton, a member of Company F, Searcy's Regiment, disagrees with the notion that his command was unarmed or nearly so. Halliburton wrote: "Probably one-third had not any kind of arms, and two-thirds carried muzzle-loading shotguns, muskets, squirrel rifles, and revolvers of various kinds and

makes, from a navy to a six-inch Smith and Wesson, my gun being one of the latter."

This would add 426 (645 x .66 = 425.7) arms to the brigade, giving Tyler's Brigade 400 to 626 armed men. Searcy's Regiment would have had 426 arms, while Perkins was probably similarly armed. Additionally, regardless of how the men were armed the officers would be considered armed and not part of the armed men that Price noted in his *Official Report* or Halliburton cited above. This suggests that Perkins's and Searcy's Regiments each added 39 armed officers (46 x .85 = 39.1). However, officers were probably embraced in the 426 figure that was calculated above.[130]

Oct. 9-12, 1864:

Tyler's Mo. Cav. Bde. (Col. Charles H. Tyler):[131]

Staff = 6 (6 armed)

Coffee's Cav. (Col. John T. Coffee); From Jackman's Brigade

---

129. *O.R.*, vol. 41, pt. 1:680, 688; *O.R.*, vol. 41, pt. 3:544; Boatner, 322; Brugioni, 113; James G. Downhour, "Gamble, Hamilton Brown," in *Encyclopedia of the Civil War*, 805–806; "The Fag–End of Price's Army," *Missouri Republican*, November 26, 1864; Hinton, 292; Scott, "Last Fight," 323.

130. *O.R.*, vol. 41, pt. 1:636, 699; Eakin, *Confederate Records*, 3:171; Halliburton, 264; "Capt. James Kennedy," *Confederate Veteran* 36 (January 1928), 25; Livermore, 68–69; Schultz, 201; Sifakis, *Missouri*, 108.

131. The brigade was formed when the Expedition arrived at Boonville between October 9–12, 1864. *O.R.*, vol. 41, pt. 1:645, 719.

Perkins Cav. (Col. Caleb Perkins). EFF = 549 (426 armed)
Searcy's Cav. (Col. James J. Searcy). EFF = 549 (426 armed)
Brigade Total = 1,104 (858 armed)

Ben Elliott's and Robert Wood's Battalions. Both of these battalions were increased to regiments while at Boonville between October 10–12. Wood's Battalion added four companies, while it was estimated that Elliott added six companies at 64 officers and men per company, or 55 (64 x .85 = 55) effective officers and men per company. This would give 220 (4 x 55 = 220) more officers and men for Wood's and 330 (6 x 55 = 330) for Elliott.[132]

Oct. 10-12, 1864:
    Elliott's Bn to Regt. EFF = 330
    Wood's Bn. to Regt. EFF = 220

Guerrilla Units

Sam Hildebrand's Guerrilla Company. This unit joined the Expedition after it crossed into Missouri on September 19, operating with Shelby's Division, where it served as the "advance guard" of Price's Army. A few days after the attack on Farmington (September 24), Hildebrand recruited his command up to a full company by adding 23 officers and men, for a total of 64 effective officers and men by September 28. Hildebrand remained with the army until it reached the vicinity of his home at Big River, at which time he departed with his men, probably by September 28, following the destruction of the Mineral Point Depot and one of the bridges over the Big River. A few days after leaving the army and while on recruiting service, Hildebrand was camped with Major Dick Berryman at Tyler's Mill on Big River with about 300 men, where they were attacked and scattered by a Union force.[133]

Advance Guard (Capt. Sam Hildebrand)
    Sept. 19, 1864. EFF = 41
    Sept. 28, 1864. EFF = 23 (men added to complete the co.)

Captain William "Bloody Bill" Anderson's Guerrilla Company. This group arrived in Price's camp at Boonville on October 11, with 100 men (Edwards puts the number at 300). He was assigned the mission of destroying the North Missouri Railroad and never actively campaigned with the main army. When he arrived in Boonville, Anderson, according to one source was made a colonel in the Confederate Army by Sterling Price, while Governor Thomas Reynolds commissioned Anderson in the MSG. William C. Quantrill arrived with his guerrilla band at the same time as Anderson. Quantrill was assigned the mission of destroying the Han-

---

132. Campbell Memoirs; Moore, *Missouri, Confederate Military History, Extended*, 286; Muster Roll, Company C, Wood's Battalion; Muster Roll, Stallard's Company.
133. *O.R.*, vol. 41 pt. 1:456, 673; Breihan, 129, 131–132; Cruzen, 23; Nichols, *Guerrilla Warfare, Volume IV*, 49.

nibal & St. Joseph Railroad, in particular the "large railroad bridge that was in the end of St. Charles County." In both cases, Anderson and Quantrill did some damage to their targets, but in the "main object" failed to accomplish their missions.

Oct. 11, 1864 Anderson's Guerrillas. EFF = 100

Captain William C. Quantrill. Quantrill arrived at Boonville at the same time that Anderson did. His strength was unknown, though 100 would be a fair guess.

Oct. 11, 1864 Quantrill's Guerrillas. EFF = 100 (E)

George Todd's Guerrilla Company. Todd joined Price's Expedition on October 18, with about 140 officers and men. Later, upon the insistence of General Price, Todd's command, now led by Dave Poole (Todd had been killed), departed the army about October 23, after it was learned that the Federals were executing Shelby's men, believing they were part of Quantrill's guerrillas.[134]

Oct. 18, 1864 Todd's Guerrillas. EFF = 140

Oct. 23, 1864 Departed the army.

****

Captain David R. Stallard's Escort Battalion. On October 16, while waiting at the Keiser Bridge on the Salt Fork River, Stallard was directed by General Marmaduke to organize a battalion to serve as the division's advance. Stallard added Captain Page's Company to his battalion and an incomplete company of 40 men under Orderly Sergeant W. L. Armstrong, giving his battalion 89 effective officers and men as follows:[135]

Page's Co. = 64 x .85 = 55

Armstrong's Co. = 40 x .85 = 34

Oct. 16, 1864 Stallard's Bn. (new units added). EFF = 89

David A. Williams's Missouri Battalion. Williams's Battalion was recruited during the campaign on the north side of the Missouri River. Returning to Shelby's Division on the evening of October 21, it was officially assigned to Jackman's Brigade on October 30. The unit was noted by Shelby as being completely armed. To the 600 men are added the officers. The 600 total would suggest a regiment of 10 companies, which would give the command 45 (10 x 4 = 40 + 5 staff = 45) officers of whom 39 would be considered effective (40 x .85 = 39). Overall the battalion would have had 510 (600 x .85 = 510) effective enlisted men with 39 officers for a total of 549 effective officers and men.[136]

Oct. 21, 1864 Williams Cav. Bn. (Ltc. D. A. Williams). EFF = 549

---

134. *O.R.*, vol. 41, pt. 1:632; Barton, 170, 173; Busch, *Missouri Democrat Articles*, 249–250; Edwards, *Shelby and His Men*, 398, 423; Gibson, 158; Nichols, *Guerrilla Warfare, Volume IV*, 178, 180; "The War In Missouri," *Chicago Tribune*, September 29, 1864.

135. Brown Journal, October 16, 1864; Livermore, 67–68; Muster Roll, Stallard's Company.

136. *O.R.*, vol. 41, pt. 1:634, 657–658; Allardice, *Confederate Colonels*, 397; Livermore, 68–69.

Artillery Captured at the Big Blue on October 22. After crossing the Big Blue River on October 22, Shelby's Division engaged the 2nd KSM, capturing their 24-pound brass howitzer. The gun was then added to Collins's Battery and used at the Battle of Newtonia on October 28. The gun was later abandoned before Collins crossed the Arkansas River on November 7.[137]

Oct. 22, 1864 Collins's Battery–adds one piece of artillery, 24-pound Brass How. EFF = No additional men needed.

Matthew Rector Johnson's Cavalry Battalion. Johnson, of Neosho, Missouri, was a member of Elliott's Battalion of Shelby's Iron Brigade during the early part of the war. He was noted as being in Marmaduke's Second Missouri Raid, where he was "severely wounded" on April 20, 1863, at Patterson. After recovering, Johnson was next heard of during Shelby's Missouri Raid in October 1863, and again during the Camden Expedition, after which it appears that he was sent into southwest Missouri as a recruiting officer.

Prior to Price's Expedition, Johnson organized a partial company, which was part of Piercey's Battalion (formerly Livingston's or Pickler's), that operated in southwest Missouri. At the time, Johnson commanded Company D of the battalion, which was also known as the 1st Missouri Cavalry Battalion, Indian Brigade. As the Expedition developed it appears that a portion of Picker's Battalion (now commanded by Piercey) was incorporated into S. D. Jackman's Regiment, while the majority of the battalion remained in southwest Missouri, where it operated as an independent unit.

Johnson's Company subsequently moved east and was still recruiting, according to one source, in the Doniphan area when the Expedition began. Serving as the advance of Shelby's Division, Johnson's 40-man unit was pushed out of Doniphan on September 19.

A review of the *Official Records* leads one to believe that Lieutenant Colonel Rector Johnson led a party of men to destroy the Federal force that attacked and burned Doniphan. However, M. R. Johnson was not in command of the pursuit force, though he was in command of the force that was driven out of Doniphan. Further, Johnson was a captain at the time not a lieutenant colonel, which Shelby acknowledged a few days after Doniphan, when Captains M. R. Johnson and Thomas J. Shaw took Farmington.

General Shelby, in his record of the Doniphan incident, noted that Lieutenant Colonel Johnson was from Fagan's Division and would rejoin Fagan after dispatching the Union raiders. This suggests that there were two Johnsons involved in the Doniphan incident: M. Rector, who made the initial contact in Doniphan and Benjamin A., who led the pursuit.

In his book on the 15th Missouri Cavalry (CSA) Jerry Ponder has M. Rector

---

137. The battery had previously lost a gun at Westport on October 23; as such, the men previously detailed to man that gun would have been placed on the howitzer. *O.R.*, vol. 41, pt. 1:675; Cruzen, 34.

Johnson taking up the pursuit with about 250 men, along with another 500 or more men from the 15th Missouri Cavalry. The men of the 15th were commanded by Lieutenant Colonel Benjamin A. Johnson, not M. Rector Johnson. Ponder also says the men who were initially driven from Doniphan were members of Company A, 15th Missouri Cavalry, which is clearly not correct according to J. O. Shelby. Further, it appears from a book on Sam Hildebrand, that his command was the one that got ahead of the Federal raiders, trapping them between himself and Ben Johnson's 15th Missouri, not M. Rector Johnson.

A few days after Doniphan, Captain Thomas J. Shaw, commanding Company C, Coffee's Battalion, was ordered by Shelby to proceed to Farmington with his company and 20 men of Captain M. Rector Johnson's Company to take the city. This is supported by a member of Shaw's command who accompanied the Farmington attack. Clearly M. Rector Johnson was not familiar enough with the area and lacked seniority to lead a small expedition against Farmington, much less a 250-man pursuit force to engage the Doniphan raiders.

That said, sometime after Farmington, Johnson's command was increased to battalion strength, and he was probably made brevet major of the unit, not a lieutenant colonel. In all likelihood M. Rector Johnson's Battalion was a "small" battalion of three or four companies, as implied by M. Jeff Thompson later in the campaign. Further, Johnson's Battalion, like other irregular or guerrilla commands, was probably attached to a division and used to support whichever brigade needed help at a particular time. A fair estimate of his strength would have been about 150 officers and men.

M. Rector Johnson's Cavalry Battalion was formed sometime after the Expedition began. Initially the command operated as an independent company under General Shelby with 40 men and an estimated three officers, which would give the command 43 effective officers and men, who were however not part of Shelby's reported strength on September 17, 1864. An additional 107 effective officers and men were added sometime after the Expedition began, giving the battalion an estimated 150 effective officers and men.[138]

Johnson's Bn. (Maj. M. Rector Johnson). EFF = 107 (added during the campaign); 150 by October 22, 1864.

---

138. The *Official Records* identifies a Lieutenant Colonel Johnson as Rector Johnson, in reference to the pursuit of the Doniphan burners, citing pages 945–946. However, this is not true; only the citation on page 956 was Rector Johnson, as verified by a member of Captain Shaw's Company, who accompanied Johnson on the attack on Farmington, while the other references list "Johnson" without a first name. The compilers of the *Official Records* assume that the Johnson on page 956 must have been the same Johnson. *O.R.*, vol. 22, pt. 1:289; *O.R.*, vol. 41, pt. 1:194, 652, 668,1077; *O.R.*, vol. 41, pt. 2:1054, 1193; *O.R.*, vol. 41, pt. 3:60, 368, 945–946, 956–957, 1074; Breihan, 131–132; Buresh, 206; Confederate Correspondence, Tyler to McClean (October 27, 1864); Eakin & Hale, 240; Edwards, *Shelby and His Men*, 152, 222, 267, 385; Forsyth, *Great Missouri Raid*, 243; Fowler, "A Missouri Boy's Experience," 432; Gifford, 56; Gjertveit letter; Lause, *Price's Lost Campaign*, 33; Nichols, *Guerrilla Warfare, Volume IV*, 21, 45–46; Odom Letter (June 10, 2013); Ponder, *15th Missouri Cavalry*, 81, 86, 88, 90; Ross, "Burning of Doniphan," 81; Sellmeyer, 95; Sinisi, 58–59; Stanton, etc., 247, 250; Winns, 538–539.

General James S. Rains MSG Battalion. General Rains accompanied the Expedition with Governor Thomas C. Reynolds, intent on recruiting for the MSG. There is no indication, that during the Expedition Rains did anything of importance save recruit his command. On October 12, he was reported in Licking, Texas County, with 400 men. Sometime thereafter Rains returned to Arkansas, camping near Richmond with 200 men. These men were subsequently ordered into the Confederate Army and were combined with Slayback's command to form a new regiment.[139]

Sept. 19–Oct. 31, 1964 Rains's Bn. MSG. EFF = 200

****

Summary of Known Additions to the Army, Excluding General Recruits for Unknown Commands and Guerrilla Commands

Sept. 19 15th Missouri Cav. Regt. (Col. Timothy Reeves). EFF = 100 recruits added

Sept. 19 Coleman's Missouri Regt. (Col. William O. Coleman). EFF = 222 (E)

Sept. 19–Oct. 14 Recruits for Shanks'/ Thompson's Bde. EFF = 123 (E)

Sept. 19–Oct. 31 Rains's MSG Bn. (James S. Rains). EFF = 200

Sept. 23 Slayback's Cav. Bn. (Ltc. Alonzo W. Slayback). EFF = 223

Sept. 24 Davies's Cav. Bn. (Maj. J.F. Davies) EFF = 282

Sept. 24 Recruits for 3rd, 4th, 7th, 8th, and 10th Mo. Cav. EFF = 305

Sept. 28 Dobbin's Artillery (Cdr. ukn.) two 2-pound SB. EFF = 22

Hughes's Battery Mortar Sec. one 24-pound Mortar. EFF = 11

Sept 28–29 Provost Guards for the Army; 54 officers and men per brigade, with one Provost Marshal, at the rank of major added to each division. Men pulled from existing men within the individual brigades.

Oct. 3 Harris' Mo. Battery (added) one 6-pound Iron SB. EFF = 11

Oct. 9–12 Tyler's Mo. Bde. (Col. Charles H. Tyler)
    Staff = 6 (6 armed)
        Coffee's Cav. (Col. John T. Coffee); From Jackman's Brigade
        Perkins Cav. (Col. Caleb Perkins). EFF = 549 (426 armed)
        Searcy's Cav. (Col. James J. Searcy). EFF = 549 (426 armed)
            Brigade Total = 1,104 (858 armed)

Oct. 10–12 Elliott's Bn to Regt. EFF = 330

Slayback's Bn. to Regt. EFF = 326

Wood's Bn. to Regt. EFF = 220

Oct. 13–20 Davies's Bn. (3 cos. added). EFF = 153

Oct. 16 Recruits for Crisp/Coffee. EFF = 92

Oct. 16 Stallard's Bn. (1 ½ Cos. Added). EFF = 89

Oct. 17 Recruits for Thompson's Bde. EFF = 420

---

139. *O.R.*, vol. 41, pt. 3, 817; *O.R.*, vol. 41, pt. 4:1093, 1107.

Oct. 21 Williams Cav. Regt. (Ltc. D. A. Williams). EFF = 549
By Oct. 22 Johnson's Bn. (Maj. Matthew Rector Johnson). EFF = 107
(recruits added to Bn.)
   Grand Total of Known Additions: EFF = 4,861 officers and men.

Unassigned Recruits or Assigned Recruits Units Not Known

Sept. 24[140] At Fredericktown: 400 recruits, including 40 mounted from Potosi.
Oct. 5[141] From Howard & Callaway Counties; 800 recruits.
Oct. 1–12 From Franklin County: 300 recruits.[142]
Sept. 19– Oct. 19[143] Chariton County; 1,500 recruits.
Howard County; above 1,100 recruits.[144]
Boone County; 2,000 recruits.
Randolph County; 1,000 Recruits.
Callaway County; 400 recruits.[145]
Monroe County; 800 recruits.
Oct. 1–31 Saline County; 207 conscripts
Pettis County; 49 conscripts[146]
   Total Unassigned Recruits/ Conscripts = 8,556

Note: Some of these recruits may have been incorporated into some of the units listed above. As such this listing should be used by the reader to get an idea where the various Southern supporters resided. That said, Colonel John C. Wright, of Slemons's Brigade noted that by the Battle of Westport the army had 10,000 unarmed recruits, which would have been in addition to all the "Known Additions to the Army" listed above.[147]

Additions to the Army: Guerrilla Units

Sept. 19 Sam Hildebrand's Guerrilla Company
 Advance Guard (Capt. Sam Hilderband) EFF = 41 (Sept. 19) EFF = 23
 (added Sept. 28, 1864)
Note: Hildebrand departed the army about Sept. 30, 1864.
Oct. 11 Captain William "Bloody Bill" Anderson's Guerrillas. EFF = 100
Note: Upon receiving his assignment to raid the railroads north of the
 Missouri River, Anderson departed the army, never to return.
Oct. 11 Capt. William Quantrill Guerrillas. EFF = 100

---

140. Sinisi, 64; "The War in Missouri" *Chicago Tribune*, September 27, 1864.
141. Busch, *Missouri Democrat Articles*, 159.
142. Ibid., 146.
143. Ibid., 191.
144. Amount reduced from 1,500 to 1,100 to account for previous report of October 5.
145. Amount reduced from 800 to 400 to account for previous report of October 5.
146. *The Advertiser* (Sedalia, MO), January 21, 1865.
147. Wright Memoirs, unnumbered pages 70–71.

Note: Upon receiving his assignment to raid the railroads north of the Missouri River, Quantrill departed the army, never to return.

Oct. 18 George Todd's Guerrilla Company. EFF = 140

Note: Departed the army on Oct. 23, to prevent further executions of Confederate soldiers in Shelby's Division.

Grand Total of Guerrilla Units: EFF = 445 officers and men

Note: There were other guerrilla units operating at the time of Price's Expedition; however, the ones listed above are known to have reported to Price for orders, while the others have no record of ever contacting Price.

Summary of Additions to the Army of Missouri
(September 19–December 2, 1864)

Recruits for Known Units and New Units	4,861
Unassigned Recruits	8,556
Total	13,417

Note: Known guerrilla commands that cooperated with the army totaled 445 officers and men; however, in all cases they departed after serving but a brief time with the army.

Appendix E
Confederate Order of Battle
Pilot Knob (September 27, 1864)

General Information. There was no reason to believe that the Confederate Order of Battle changed remarkably from what it was when Price's command entered Missouri, except for a few units and known recruits that joined the Expedition between September 19 and 27, 1864. Additionally, any losses suffered by the army prior to the battle, either by desertion, sickness, or casualty would have been made up by new acquisitions, who joined the army when it marched into Missouri, excluding any new, organized units that were added.

Of the 4,000 unarmed men that Price reported at the beginning of the Expedition, 1,433 belonged to Shelby's Division, leaving 2,563 for Fagan's and Marmaduke's commands. Cabell's Brigade, as shown in Appendix D, had 403 unarmed men, leaving 2,160 (2,563 - 403 = 2,160) unaccounted for. Little was known of Lyles's and Rogan's Regiments, of Fagan's Division. These two regiments were probably not organized when the Expedition began or were organized at the last moment. As such, Lyles's and Rogan's Regiments were probably unarmed, which deducts another 1,098 men (see Appendix D for details on Lyles's and Rogan's Regiments) from the unarmed total, leaving 1062 (2,160 - 1,098 = 1,062) unarmed men not accounted for.[1]

For the Battle of Pilot Knob, Colonel Freeman's Brigade was combined with Slayback's Missouri Battalion giving the combined unit 1,485 (1,263 + 222 = 1,485) effective officers and men, without considering their armed condition (see Appendix D for specifics on the effective strength of these units). Freeman was tasked to provide "*every* available [armed] man" for the upcoming assault. Given that about 1,062 unarmed men are unaccounted for, the combined effective strength of Freeman's Brigade and Slayback's Battalion probably numbered about 423 (1,485 - 1,062 = 423) armed officers and men. Freeman, in his memoir, noted that the combined armed strength was "approximately 500 armed men," while General Marmaduke recorded that his command numbered between "4 or 500 men." In this case 500 is adopted for the combined strength of Freeman's and Slayback's commands. This would also suggest that the estimate of 4,000 unarmed men at the beginning of the Expedition was not unreasonable.[2]

Note: The numbers presented below, under the various units, in ( ) represents the armed and effective officers and men, who were engaged in the battle, while

---

1. *O.R.*, vol. 41, pt. 3:929.
2. Suderow, in his book on Pilot Knob, puts Freeman's and Slayback's combined strength at 500. Letter (September 27, 1864), Marmaduke to MacLean, Confederate Correspondence (MSS 03-26 Box 1 File 2); Suderow, *Arcadia Valley*, 101, 139; Freeman's Memoir, September 27, 1864; Letter (September 26, 1864), Marmaduke to Freeman, Army of Missouri File, Missouri Historical Society; Suderow, *Arcadia Valley*, 139.

the unbracketed numbers represent all men present, including those who were unarmed, horse holders, or part of the Infirmary Corps, but does not include the sick or men on detail. Also, all the strengths listed below, with but few exceptions, are estimates (E). Losses are as stated, but in some cases they are estimated, which are designated by (E).

* * * * * * *

Army of Missouri (Maj. Gen. Sterling Price)

Staff = 14 (14)[3]
Bodyguard
    Rayburn's Indept. Ark. Co. (Capt. Howel A. "Doc" Rayburn).[4] EFF = 55 (55)
Escort[5]
    Company K, 2nd Mo. Cav. (Windsor Guards; Capt. Robert Collins).[6] EFF = 55 (55)
    Officers and men of unknown assignments. EFF = 188 (0)
        Total Army HQ = 124[7]

* * * * * * *

Fagan's Cavalry Division

General Information for Fagan's Division. Of Fagan's four brigades only three participated in the Battle of Pilot Knob: Cabell's, McCray's and Slemons's. Dobbin's Brigade served as the reserve and guarded the Federal escape route up the Potosi Road. Also, there was no evidence that Lyles's or Rogan's commands par-

---

3. Not included in the staff are the corps surgeon and the "medical field purveyor," but does include the corps commander. *O.R.*, vol. 41, pt. 2:1090.
4. On September 4, 1864, "Doc" Rayburn's command was reported as between 50–60 men; say 55 for this Order of Battle. In Federal reports, they spell his name as Rayborne, which is not correct. *O.R.*, vol. 41, pt. 3:55. Edwards, *Shelby and His Men*, 285; *White County Heritage Civil War Collection Volume 1–25* (Searcy, AR, n.d.), 2:3, 19:14.
5. As the march to northeast Arkansas began, Surgeon General Dr. William McPheeters, who traveled with Price's headquarters, reported that Price's entourage consisted of 300 officers and men. Deducting Price and staff leaves 286 (300 -14 = 286) of whom 243 (286 x .85 = 243.1) would be considered present. Additionally, Price's Escort did not number 243 officers and men; more likely about 55. It is not known what function the remaining 188 officers and men had. Pitcock & Gurley, 216.
6. *O.R.S.*, pt. 2, vol. 50:145; Confederate Correspondence, Nelson to Maclean (December 15, 1864); Eakin & Hale, 361.
7. This may be an overreach in believing that the various elements of Price's headquarters were all effective, armed and engaged. There was no direct evidence that either Price's escort or Rayburn's company were involved in the assault, though they could have been used as couriers. Staff officers were routinely used to carry messages and orders to the assorted commanders. As such, staff, at all levels, will always be considered effective.

ticipated in the assault, probably because they were either not armed or not fully organized (see comments above on the unarmed condition of the army).

    Fagan's Division (Maj. Gen. James F. Fagan):
        Staff = 10 EFF (10) [0 K, 1 W, 0 M][8]
        Escort: Anderson's Ark. Cav. Bn. (Capt. N. Terry Roberts). EFF = 168 (131)[9]
        HQ & Escort Total = 178 (141) [0 K, 1 W, 0 M]

General Information for Cabell's Brigade. Cabell's Brigade began the Expedition with 3,215 effective officers and men of whom only 2,500 were armed. Horse holders and the Infirmary Corps would have been drawn from the unarmed portion of the brigade, which numbered 403 (see General Information under Cabell's Brigade in Appendix D). Subtracting the 403 unarmed men from the brigade gives the command 2,812 (3,215 - 403 = 2,812) effective armed officers and men prior to the Battle of Pilot Knob. Allowing one horse holder for every 4.5 horses (some authors have horse holders as one for every four while others have one for every five) would mean that the command needed 625 (2,812 / 4.5 = 624.8) men holding horses. Additionally the Infirmary Corps, while in the field, would per regulations consist of one nurse per company. Cabell's Brigade contained 64 companies, thus requiring 64 nurses. This suggests that Cabell's Brigade carried 2,123 (2,812 - 625 - 64 = 2,123) armed officers and men into the battle.

However, the 403 unarmed men noted above would have been used as horse holders or as part of the Infirmary Corps as follows: 100 of the men would have held the horses of all the unarmed men, while the other 303 would have relived men with arms to hold their horses while they joined the effective armed officers and men that were available for the battle. This would give the brigade an effective strength of 2,426 (2,123 + 303 = 2426) armed officers and men for the battle.

The 2,426 was further reduced by the headquarters staff, escort, and artillerymen leaving 2,330 (2,426 - 65 - 31 = 2,330) armed officers and men for the various regiments and battalions. The strength was further prorated based upon their status upon entry into Missouri on September 19, 1864, as shown below. The battery would be unaffected as all the men would be considered effective.

Since General Cabell participated in the assault, at Pilot Knob, it's reasonable to believe that his escort was also involved in the assault. The escort company was calculated at 43 (55 / 4.5 = 12) after the horse holders were removed (55- 12 = 43). This would adjust the headquarters and escort to 54, giving the brigade and overall strength of 2,415 (2,330 + 54 + 31 = 2,415)[10]

---

    8. The Divisional Surgeon W.B. Welch was excluded from the staff as non-effective. *O.R.*, vol. 41, pt. 3:944.
    9. Horse holders are calculated at 4.5 horses for one man, giving the battalion 37 (168 / 4.5 = 37.3) or an effective and armed strength of 131 (168 - 37 = 131).
    10. Busch, *Missouri Democrat Articles*, 56; Confederate States War Department, *Regulations for the Army of the Confederate States, 1863. Corrected and Enlarged With A Revised Index* (Richmond,

Appendix E / 389

Unit	Strength on Sept. 19	(Pro-rated) Strength on Sept. 27
HQ/ Escort	65	54
Monroe's Regt.	539	403
Gordon's Regt.	485	362
Morgan's Regt.	539	403
Hill's Regt.	539	403
Woosley's Bn.	210	157
Witherspoon's Bn.	210	157
Proctor's Co.	34	25
Harrell's Regt.	563	421
Hughey's Battery	31	31
	3,215	2,415

Note: Pro-rated value was 74.7 percent (2,330/ 3,215 - 65 - 31 = .747)

Harrell Adjustment. As shown in Appendix D and supported by a Federal report following the Battle of Pilot Knob, Harrell's command fielded about 200 for the battle on September 27. The remaining men were considered unarmed and served as the horse holders for the brigade. Thus the 221 excess men in Harrell's command (from above) would have increased the numbers available to the other units in the brigade giving them the following totals:[11]

Unit	Harrell Adjustment Strength on Sept. 19	(Pro-rated) Strength on Sept. 27
HQ	65	54
Monroe's Regt.	539	450
Gordon's Regt.	485	404
Morgan's Regt.	539	449
Hill's Regt.	539	449
Woosley's Bn.	210	175
Witherspoon's Bn.	210	175
Proctor's Co.	34	28
Harrell's Regt.	563	200
Hughey's Battery	31	31
	3,215	2,415

Note: The new pro-rated value was 83.3 percent (2,330 - 200/3,215 - 65 - 31 - 563 = .833)

VA, 1863; reprint ed., Harrisburg, PA, 1980), 238 (para. 1189), hereafter cited as Confederate States War Department, Regulations; "Price's Invasion," *Chicago Tribune*, November 3, 1864; Sinisi, 79; Suderow, *Arcadia Valley*, 138.

11. *O.R.*, vol. 41, pt. 4:79.

Cabell's Ark. Cav. Bde. (Brig. Gen. William L. Cabell). EFF = 11[12]
Escort
    Company C, Gordon's Ark. Cav. Regt. (1st Lt. Robert J. Wilson).[13] EFF = 54 (43)[14]
    HQs. & Escort Total = 54 (43)
Monroe's Regt. (Col. James C. Monroe, WIA).[15] EFF = 539 (450) [27 K, 69 W, 0 M][16]
Gordon's Regt. (Col. Anderson Gordon).[17] EFF = 485 (404)
Morgan's Regt. (Col. Thomas J. Morgan).[18] EFF = 539 (449) [42 K, W, M][19]
Hill's Regt. (Col. John F. Hill).[20] EFF = 539 (449)
Gunter's Regt. (Ltc. Thomas M. Gunter)
    James Woosley's Bn. (Maj. James Woosley).[21] EFF = 210 (175)
    Witherspoon's Cav. Bn. (Maj. J. L. Witherspoon).[22] EFF = 210 (175)
    Proctor's Co. (Cdr. ukn.). EFF = 34 (28)
Harrell's Cav. Regt. (Ltc. John M. Harrell).[23] EFF = 563 (200)
Hughey's Battery (Capt. William W. Hughey).[24] 2 guns, 6-lb brass. EFF = 31 (31)
    Cabell Bde. Total = 3,215 EFF Present,

---

12. *O.R.*, vol. 41, pt. 3:947; *O.R.S.*, pt. 1, vol. 7:391, 403; Crute, *Confederate Staff Officers*, 30.
13. Captain James O. Sadler was placed on recruiting service on September 18, 1864, leaving command of the company to 1st Lt. Robert J. Wilson. *O.R.S.*, pt. 1, vol. 7:395; *O.R.S.*, pt. 2, vol. 2:241, 243; Internet site, www.couchgenwed.com, 4th Arkansas Cavalry, Company C.
14. A typical cavalry company in 1864 contained 64 officers and men; or 55 (64 x .85 = 55) effective officers and men. For Pilot Knob, 12 (55 / 4.5 = 12.2) horse holders were required, leaving the company with 43 (55 - 12 = 43) effective, armed officers and men. See Appendix D, Organizational Note No. 1 for details.
15. Also known as the 1st or 6th Arkansas Cavalry. *O.R.S.*, pt. 2, vol. 2:150; Edwards, *Shelby and His Men*, 388; Ferguson, 312; Moore, *Missouri, Confederate Military History*, 182.
16. Hazen Letter; Suderow, *Arcadia Valley*, 121.
17. Gordon's Regiment was also known by several different names including, the 1st, 2nd, 4th, 9th, or the 11th Arkansas Cavalry Regiment. *O.R.S.*, pt. 2, vol. 2:240; Ferguson, 313.
18. Originally organized as the 5th Arkansas Cavalry Regiment, this unit was reorganized as Morgan's or the 8th Arkansas Cavalry Regiment. John Edwards says that John C. Bull led the regiment at Pilot Knob, where he was wounded. Edwards, *Shelby and His Men*, 388; Ferguson, 313.
19. Crawford, *Confederate Courage*, 108; Sifakis, *Arkansas*, 55.
20. Also known as the 7th Arkansas Cavalry Regiment. *O.R.S.*, pt. 2, vol. 2:232; Ferguson, 313.
21. This was actually Gunter's Battalion, commanded by Woosley. See Appendix D for details.
22. Also known as the 13th or 16th Arkansas Cavalry Battalion. Witherspoon was captured on November 11, 1863, and was later recorded as a prisoner at Fort Smith in April 1865. During Price's Raid, his battalion was probably commanded by the senior captain or the adjutant of the battalion, names unknown. *O.R.*, vol. 41, pt. 1:1018; *O.R.S.*, pt. 2, vol. 2:252; Internet site, www.couchgenweb.com, Key Word "Witherspoon;" Sifakis, *Arkansas*, 81.
23. Also known as the 17th Arkansas Cavalry Battalion, the unit was increased to a regiment when the battalion arrived at Pocahontas in September, 1864. *O.R.S.*, pt. 2, vol. 2:253.
24. Also known as the 8th Arkansas Field Battery. Busch, *Missouri Democrat Articles*, 52; Crute, *Confederate Army*, 62; Farmer Memoir, 11.

Appendix E / 391

$$= 2,415 \text{ EFF (Engaged \& Armed)}^{25}$$
Total Losses = [45 K, 230 W, 0 M]²⁶

General Information for Dobbin's Brigade. Present at the battle but not engaged.²⁷

    Dobbin's Ark. Brigade (Col. Archibold Dobbin)
        Brigade Total = 1,764 EFF (Present, not engaged)

General Information for McCray's Brigade. Like Cabell's Brigade, McCray's would have used horse holders and established an Infirmary Corps for the battle. When the Expedition began McCray's Brigade had about 1,822 effective officers and men, all or most of whom were armed. As shown with Cabell's Brigade, McCray's command would have required 405 (1,822 / 4.5 = 404.8) horse holders, with an Infirmary Corps of 30 or one nurse per assigned company. This would reduce the effective strength of the brigade to 1,387 (1,822 - 405 - 30 = 1,387) armed officers and men, including staff. This strength is then pro-rated based upon the strength of the brigade when it began the Expedition or 76 percent (1,387 / 1,822 = .761).²⁸

Unit	Strength on Sept. 19	(Pro-rated) Strength on Sept. 27
HQ	6	6
45th Ark. Regt.	720	547
47th Ark. Regt.	720	547
15th Mo. Regt.	376	287
	1,822	1,387

    McCray's Bde. (Col. Thomas H. McCray)
        Staff = 6 EFF
        45th Ark. Inf. (Mtd.) (Col. Milton D. Baber). EFF = 720 (547)
            [10 K, W, M]²⁹
        47th Ark. Inf (Mtd) (Col. Lee Crandall). EFF = 720 (547)
        15th Mo. Cav. (Col. Timothy Reeves). EFF = 376 (287)
        McCray's Brigade Total = 1,822 EFF Present,
                            = 1,387 EFF (Engaged & Armed)
        Losses = [8 K, 43 W, 0 M] (E)³⁰

---

25. Mark J. Crawford places Cabell's strength at 1,800. Crawford, *Confederate Courage*, 104.
26. *O.R.S.*, pt. 1, vol. 7:402.
27. *O.R.*, vol. 41, pt. 1:709; Sinisi, 78.
28. *O.R.*, vol. 41, pt. 2:1046.
29. Mamie Yeary, *Reminiscences of the Boys in Gray 1861–1865* (Dallas, TX, 1912; Reprint ed., Dayton, OH, 1986), 200, hereafter cited as Yeary.
30. See calculation and reasoning below under Losses in Fagan's Division. A member of McCray's Brigade noted that overall his command lost only "a few in killed and wounded," while a member of the 45th Arkansas recorded that his command suffered 10 casualties. Wilson Memoirs, 13; Yeary, 200.

General Information for Slemons's Brigade. Like the other brigades in Fagan's Division, Slemons's command would have used horse holders and established an Infirmary Corps for the battle. When the Expedition began Slemons's Brigade had about 1,162 effective officers and men, all or most who were armed. As shown in the other brigades, Slemons's command would have required 258 (1,162 / 4.5 = 258.2) horse holders with an Infirmary Corps of 40, or one nurse per assigned company. This would reduce the effective strength of the brigade to 864 (1,162 - 258 - 40 = 864) armed officers and men, including staff. This strength is then pro-rated based upon the strength of the brigade when it began the Expedition or 74 percent (864 / 1,162 = .743).

Unit	Strength on Sept. 19	(Pro-rated) Strength on Sept. 27
HQ	6	6
2nd Ark. Regt.	287	213
Crawford's Regt.	287	213
Carlton's Regt.	287	213
Wright's Regt.	295	219
	1,162	864

Slemons's Arkansas Bde. (Col. William A. Crawford)[31]
   Staff = 6 EFF
   2nd Cav. (Ltc. Thomas M. Cochran).[32] EFF = 287 (213)
   Crawford's (Col. William A. Crawford).[33] EFF = 287 (213)
   Carlton's Cav. (Col. Charles H. Carlton). EFF = 287 (213)
   Wright's Cav. (Col. John C. Wright).[34] EFF = 295 (219)
     [4 K, 21 W] (E)[35]
     Slemons's Bde. Total = 1,162 EFF (Present),
                   = 864 EFF (Engaged & Armed)
   Losses = [8 K, 41 W, 0 M] (E)[36]

Fagan's Division Summary.

HQ	141 EFF	(Engaged & Armed)
Unattached		(Not Engaged)

---

31. Gifford, 136; Wright Memoirs, unnumbered page 74.
32. With Crawford commanding the brigade, the command of the regiment fell upon Lieutenant Colonel Thomas M. Cochran. For the Expedition, according to Stewart Sifakis, the 2nd Arkansas was "reduced to a battalion and designated as the 18th Cavalry Battalion." The 2nd was also known as the 4th Arkansas Cavalry Regiment. *O.R.S.*, pt. 2, vol. 2:182; Sifakis, *Arkansas*, 52; Wright Memoirs, unnumbered page 71.
33. Also known as the 1st or the 10th Arkansas Cavalry Regiment. *O.R.S.*, pt. 2, vol. 2:143; Ferguson, 312.
34. Also known as the 12th Arkansas Cavalry Regiment. *O.R.S.*, pt. 2, vol. 2:247; Ferguson, 313.
35. See calculation and reasoning below under Losses in Fagan's Division.
36. Ibid.

Cabell's Bde.	2,415 EFF	(Engaged & Armed)
Dobbin's Bde.		(Not Engaged)
McCray's Bde.	1,387 EFF	(Engaged & Armed)
Slemons's Bde.	<u>864 EFF</u>	(Engaged & Armed)
Fagan's Div. Total	4,807 EFF	(Engaged & Armed)

Losses in Fagan's Division. Of the three brigades engaged at Pilot Knob, only Cabell's has a recorded loss of 45 killed with 230 wounded; total 275. The rest of Fagan's command lost 75 more men, according to Colonel John C. Wright of Slemons's Brigade. Wright put the combined losses of McCray's and Slemons's Brigades at only 3.69 percent (75 / 2,251 - 219 for Wright's Regiment = .369). It appears that all the Federal fire at Fagan's command was concentrated on Cabell's Brigade, after the other two brigades got but a hundred yards out on the Fort Davidson plain, thus minimizing their loss. At that time the bulk of Slemons's and McCray's Brigades buckled and took shelter in a ditch, while Cabell's command, with Wright's Arkansas Cavalry, continued on to the fort. Captain T. J. Mackey also stated that Fagan lost about 350 officers and men, supporting Wright's comments.

Based on a proportional loss, equivalent to those engaged, this would suggest that McCray suffered 68.2 percent (1,387 / 2032 = .682) of the 75 casualties or 51 killed and wounded (1,387 / 2032 = 51.1), while Slemons's Brigade (less Wright's Regiment) lost the other 24. Since Wright's Regiment, made it all the way to the fort's ditch, its losses would have been similar, in proportion to that of Cabell's Brigade or 11.3 percent (275 / 2,415 = .113) of those engaged or 25 casualties (219 x .113 = 24.7). This would then suggest that Fagan's Division lost 375 (275 + 75 + 25 = 375) officers and men.[37]

Further, the breakdown of losses in McCray's and Slemons's Brigades, with Wright's Regiment would be based upon the same proportion as the losses in Cabell's Brigade which were 16.3 percent (45 / 275 = .163) killed with 83.7 percent wounded (100 - 16.3 = 83.7). This would suggest that losses would be as follows:

Unit	Total Casualties	Killed (16.3%)	Wounded (83.7%)
HQ	1	0	1
McCray's Bde.	51	8	43
Slemons's Bde.	24	4	20
Wright's Regt.	25	4	21

Summary of Losses in Fagan's Division:

    Cabell's Bde. = [45 K, 230 W, 0 M]
    McCray's Bde. = [8 K, 43 W, 0 W] (E)
    Slemons's Bde. = [8 K, 41 W, 0 M] (E)
    Total Losses Fagan's Div. = [61 K, 315 W, 0 M] (E)

---

37. *O.R.*, vol. 41, pt. 1:709; Wilson Memoirs, 13; Wright Memoirs, unnumbered page 76.

394 / CONFEDERATE TALES OF THE WAR IN THE TRANS-MISSISSIPPI

* * * * * * *

Marmaduke's Cavalry Division

General Information Marmaduke's Division. Of Marmaduke's two brigades only Clark's fully participated in the assault on Pilot Knob, with the exception of Kitchen's 7th Missouri Cavalry, with Davies's Battalion. Kitchen's command was detached to guard the trains at the St. Francis River. Additionally, Freeman's Brigade was combined with Slayback's Battalion to protect the western approaches to Pilot Knob and supplement the northern defenses of the army to prevent the escape of the Federal troops. As such, Freeman's command was only lightly engaged, basically from long ranged fire, suffering but "minimal" casualties according to Freeman.[38]

Marmaduke's Division (Maj. Gen. John S. Marmaduke).
Staff = 17 (17)[39]
Escort: Co. D, 5th Mo. Cav. (Capt. D. P. Stallard). EFF = 55 (43)[40]
Engineer Co./ Pontoon or Engineer Train (Capt. James T. Hogane).
EFF = 79 (0)[41]
HQ Total = 151 (60) EFF

General Information Marmaduke's Brigade. Like the other brigades in the assault, Clark's command would have used horse holders and established an Infirmary Corps for the battle. Prior to the Battle of Pilot Knob, Clark's Brigade received 305 effective recruits and officers for the 3rd, 4th, 7th, 8th, and 10th Missouri Cavalries. The brigade also added Wood's and Davies's Missouri Battalions to the command equaling another 365 and 282 effective officers and men, respectively. Overall Marmaduke's Brigade had 2,404 (1,452 + 365 Wood + 282 Davies + 305 recruits = 2,404) effective officers men of all types available for the Battle of Pilot Knob.

The 7th Missouri Cavalry, with Davies's Battalion, was guarding the trains during the battle, which reduced the brigade effective strength to 1,842 (2,404 - 219 7th Mo. - 61 recruits 7th Mo. - 282 Davies = 1,842).

For the battle on September 27, the 3rd Missouri Cavalry fielded only 145 officers and men; the remaining men of the regiment were either on recruiting service or unavailable for some other reason. The 4th, 8th, 10th Missouri Cavalries and Wood's Battalion would then have 1,369 (1,842 - 8 Bde. staff - 145 3rd Missouri engaged - 61 recruits 3rd Missouri - 195 3rd Missouri not engaged - 64 artillery

---

38. *O.R.*, vol. 41, pt. 1:679, 695; Freeman Memoir, September 27, 1864.
39. Crute, *Confederate Staff Officers*, 131–132.
40. Horse holders are calculated at 4.5 horses for one man, giving the company 12 (55 / 4.5 = 12.2) or an effective and armed strength of 43 (55 - 12 = 43) officers and men.
41. The Engineer Company would be considered unarmed.

= 1,369) effective officers and men for the 4th, 8th, 10th Missouri Cavalries and Wood's Battalion.

Allowing 4.5 men as horses holders (1,369 / 4.5 = 304) or 304 horse holders would leave the remaining units with 1,065 (1,369 - 304 = 1,065) effective officers and men. The Infirmary Corps would deduct another 36 (one per assigned company), giving these units a total of 1,029 (1,065 - 36 = 1,029) effective officers and men. The pro-rated strength for the Battle of Pilot Know would be 75 percent (1,029 / 1,369 = .751).

Unit	Strength on Sept. 27	Pro-Rated Strength on Sept. 27
4th Mo. Cav.	280	211
8th Mo. Cav.	444	333
10th Mo. Cav.	280	211
Wood's Mo. Bn.	365	274
Total	1,369	1,029

Pratt's Artillery Battalion. The battalion contained 64 effective officers and men, to man and service the guns (see Appendix D for details). This would not have changed for the Battle of Pilot Knob. According to Federal sources, Pratt's Battery (i.e., both Harris's and Hynson's Batteries) "did most of the fighting."[42]

Marmaduke's Mo. Bde. (Brig. Gen. John B. Clark).
  Staff = 8 (8)[43]
  3rd Cav. (Col. Colton Greene). EFF = 401 (145) [3 K, 26 W, 0 M][44]
  4th Cav. (Col. John Q. Burbridge). EFF = 280 (211)
    [4 K, 31 W, 0 M] (E)[45]
  7th Cav. (Col. Solomon G. Kitchen).[46] EFF = 280 (0) [Not engaged]
  Davie's Cav. Bn. (Lt. Col. J. F. Davies). EFF = 282 (0) [Not engaged]
  8th Cav. (Col. William L. Jeffers). EFF = 444 (333)
    [13 K, 11 W, 0 M (E)][47]
  10th Cav. (Col. Robert R. Lawther). EFF = 280 (211)
    [4 K, 26 W, 0 M][48]
  14th Cav. Bn. (Lt. Col. Robert C. Wood). EFF = 365 (274) [
    5 K, 40 W, 0 M (E)][49]
  Pratt's Art. Bn. (Maj. Joseph Pratt)[50]

---

42. *O.R.*, vol. 41, pt. 4:79.
43. *O.R.*, vol. 41, pt. 2:1095.
44. *O.R.*, vol. 41, pt. 1:688, 692.
45. Burbridge reported his actual losses as 35 killed, wounded, and missing. For details on the further breakdown, see Losses in Marmaduke's Division below. *O.R.*, vol. 41, pt. 1:694.
46. Guarding the trains during the battle.
47. For calculation and explanation see Losses in Marmaduke's Division, below.
48. *O.R.*, vol. 41, pt. 1:698.
49. For calculation and explanation see Losses in Marmaduke's Division, below.
50. The battalion was in reserve during the battle; however, Henry C. Luttrell, in his account implies

Hynson's Tx. Battery (Capt. Henry C. Hynson).[51] 3 guns; 6-lb. brass SB, 12-lb James Rifle, 12-lb Mt. How.[52] EFF = 32 (E) [ukn.]

Harris' Mo. Battery (Lt. T. J. Williams).[53] 3 guns; 6-lb. brass SB, 12-lb James Rifle. EFF = 32 (32) [0 K, 0 W, 0 M][54] 12-lb Mt. How.[55] EFF = 32 (32) [0 K, 0 W, 0 M][56]

Marmaduke's Brigade Total = 2,404 EFF Present,
= 1,246 EFF (Armed & Engaged)
Losses = [29 K, 134 W, 0 M] (E)

General Information Freeman's Brigade. For the Battle of Pilot Knob, Colonel Freeman was tasked to provide "*every* available [armed] man" from his brigade, with Alonzo Slayback's Battalion to support the battle. As shown at the beginning of this Appendix, after deducting the unarmed men, Freeman was left with 423, effective armed officers and men. However, since Freeman reported having about 500 armed men, 500 will be accepted as his strength. No deductions are made for horse holders or Infirmary Corps, as the unarmed men within Freeman's Brigade more than covered any requirements that were needed. Additionally, it appears that Freeman's command never dismounted during the attack, thus requiring no horse holders.[57]

Freeman's Brigade (Thomas R. Freeman).[58] EFF = 1,263 (377)
Slayback's Bn. (Ltc. A. Slayback). EFF = 222 (123)
Freeman's Bde. Total = 1,485 EFF (Present)
= 500 EFF (Armed & Engaged)
Losses = [1 K, 4 W, 0 M] (E) [59]

---

that Pratt's Battalion took some type of action during the engagement. *O.R.*, vol. 41, pt. 1:679; H. C. Luttrell, "Battle of Pilot Knob," *Missouri Republican*, October 24, 1885.
51. Also known as the 10th Texas Light Artillery. Wooster, *Lone Star Regiments*, 306.
52. Per Hughey's Arkansas Battery above, the battery effective strength was estimated at 32 officers and men (10.5 officers and men per gun x 3 = 31.5). *O.R.*, vol. 41, pt. 1:719; *O.R.*, vol. 41, pt. 4:1023; Cocker, 13.
53. *O.R.S.*, pt. 2, vol. 38:348; Cocker, 17.
54. Cocker, 17.
55. Per Hughey's Arkansas Battery above, the battery effective strength was estimated at 32 officers and men (10.5 officers and men per gun x 3 = 31.5). Ibid., 13; *O.R.*, vol. 34, pt. 3:830; *O.R.*, vol. 41, pt. 1:719; *O.R.*, vol. 41, pt. 4:1023.
56. Cocker, 17.
57. Freeman Memoir, September 27, 1864; Marmaduke to Freeman, Letter (September 26, 1864), Army of Missouri File, Missouri Historical Society.
58. The assigned values are a pure guess, though the overall value of 500 comes from Thomas R. Freeman. Freeman Memoir, September 27, 1864.
59. Ibid.; *O.R.*, vol. 41, pt. 1:630 Suderow, *Arcadia Valley*, 139.

Marmaduke's Division Summary.

HQ	60	
Marmaduke's Bde.	1,246	(Engaged & Armed) [29 K, 134 W, 0 M]
Freeman's Bde.	500	(Engaged & Armed) [1 K, 4 W, 0 M]
Div. Total	1,806	(Engaged & Armed)
Div. Losses		[30 K, 138 W, 0 M] (E)

Losses in Marmaduke's Division. Bryce Suderow puts Marmaduke's losses at 170 killed and wounded, citing three unofficial sources which add to Price's stated losses of 94. Twenty of the losses come from Freeman's and Slayback's command, while thirty each are assigned to both Wood's Battalion and the 8th Missouri Cavalry, which suffered "heavy losses" according to Joseph Thompson, while J. A. Cocker, a former member of Jeffers's regiment recalled that the 8th Missouri, with Greene's 4th Missouri, "suffered most" of Clark's Brigade losses.

Freeman described his losses as "minimal," which Bryce Suderow interprets as 20 killed, wounded and missing. I believe that five would be a better number, since Freeman did not feel the need to list any specific losses. In reporting the losses of Marmaduke's Division, Price noted that the command suffered 94 casualties. This number actually reflects the losses in the 3rd, 4th, and 10th Missouri Cavalries, suggesting that Freeman lost only a few, all probably slightly wounded, which Price decided not to record.

Based on the 567 officers and men that the 3rd, 4th, and 10th Missouri Cavalries, carried into the battle, the losses can be estimated for the remaining units of the brigade. The 567 men, who participated in the assault suffered 94 casualties or 16.5 percent (94 / 567 = 16.5) of the men engaged. This suggests that Wood's Battalion lost 45 (.165 x 274 = 45.2) officers and men, which can be further broken down into killed and wounded as shown below.

Losses for Jeffers's regiment can be calculated based upon its overall losses during the Expedition, which were 22 killed and 35 wounded. Of those casualties, eight (two killed and six wounded) were suffered at Boonville (October 11), Glasgow (October 15) and Little Osage River (October 25). The unit didn't appear to have been engaged at the Little Blue on October 21, but at Independence on the 22nd their losses were described as "heavy." However, given that the other units of Clark's Brigade lost a total of only five wounded at Independence, this would suggest the loss of two killed and three wounded for Jeffers would have been considered heavy. On October 23, at Byran's Ford, the 8th lost an estimated seven (three killed and four wounded; see Appendix G for details). This would suggest that the 8th lost 17 (22 - 7 = 15) killed, with 25 (35 - 13 = 22) wounded at Pilot Knob and Mine Creek.[60]

---

60. See Appendix G for details of the 8th Missouri's losses at Byram's Ford. *O.R.*, vol. 41, pt. 1:683,

At the Battle of Mine Creek the 8th was in reserve supporting Pratt's Artillery Battalion and would have suffered similar proportional losses as the 3rd Missouri which was also in reserve. At Mine Creek the 3rd Missouri lost one killed and 10 wounded. The 8th Missouri was only slightly larger than the 3rd Missouri with 294 effective dismounted men versus 254 or 1.16 (294 / 254 = 1.16) more officers and men (see Appendix G for details). This suggests that the 8th lost 13 (1.16 x 11 = 12.76) killed and wounded at Mine Creek or two killed and 11 wounded. This would then suggest that Jeffers lost 13 (15 - 2 = 13) killed and 11 (22 - 11 = 11) wounded at Pilot Knob.[61]

The various units that have an estimated loss or only list a total of killed, wounded, and missing, can be further broken down using the same percentages that known units of Marmaduke's Division experienced at the battle: which was 11.8 percent (7 / 59 = .118) of the total losses would be killed, while the remaining 88.2 percent would represent wounded men. This would suggest the following breakdown for the 4th and Wood's Missouri units, along with Freeman's command:

Units with Estimated Losses

Unit	Total Losses	Killed (16.3%)	Wounded (83.7%)
4th Mo. Regt.	35	4	31
Wood's Bn.	45	5	40
Freeman's Bde.	5	1	4

Units with Known Losses with the 8th Mo.

Unit	Total Losses	Killed	Wounded
3rd Mo. Regt.	29	3	26
8th Mo. Regt	24	13	11
10th Mo. Regt.	30	4	26
Grand Total	168	30	138

The losses of Freeman, Slayback, the 8th Missouri, and Wood's Battalion added to Price's report of 94 casualties would suggest that Marmaduke's Division lost (94 + 24 + 45 + 5 = 168) officers and men.[62]

Losses in Marmaduke's Div. = [30 K, 138 W, 0 M] (E)

* * * * * * *

---

61. *O.R.*, vol. 41, pt. 1:691; McGhee, *Campaigning With Marmaduke*, 26.
62. *O.R.*, vol. 41, pt. 1:630; *O.R.S.*, pt. 1, vol. 7:402; Cocker, 18; Freeman Memoir, September 27, 1864; Suderow, *Arcadia Valley*, 139–140; Thompson, "Great Little Battle of Pilot Knob," 284.

Battle of Pilot Knob

Army of Missouri Total Engaged & Armed

HQ & Staff	124
Fagan's Division	4,807
Marmaduke's Division	1,806
	6,737[63]

Summary of Losses at Pilot Knob
(September 27, 1864)

HQ & Staff	0 K	0 W	0 M
Fagan's Division	61 K	315 W	0 M (E)
Marmaduke's Division	30 K	138 W	0 M (E)
Total Army of Missouri	91 K	453 W	0 M (E)

Total Casualties = 544

---

63. Various authors give different numbers of Confederates who made the assault at Pilot Knob. Wiley Britton says there were 5,600 men. Captain T. J. Mackey says that Price had between 7,000–7,500 men as does Joseph Thompson; 4,000 for Fagan, with Marmaduke having between 3,000–3,500 men. Thomas Fletcher, a Union participant, puts the number of rebels at 10,000. Author Bryce Suderow puts the number at 4,682. And Mark Lause has the number at 4,800; 1,100 for Clark, 2,000 for Cabell and 1,700 for Slemons and McCray. *O.R.*, vol. 41, pt. 1:709; Britton, *Civil War on the Border, 1863–1865*, 405; Crawford, *Confederate Courage*, 107; Fletcher, 37; Lause, *Price's Lost Campaign*, 49-50; Suderow, *Arcadia Valley*, 139; Thompson, "Great Little Battle of Pilot Knob," 139, 283, 294.

Appendix F

Confederate and Union Orders Of Battle

Glasgow, Missouri (October 15, 1864)

Confederate Command

General Information. For the Battle of Glasgow, the Confederate forces comprised two basic parts. General John B. Clark commanded a Provisional Division, containing his brigade and that of Colonel Sidney D. Jackman. The second part of the Glasgow attack force was assigned only as Clark's Division was crossing the Missouri River at Arrow Rock, en route for Glasgow. Having been informed that Glasgow was guarded by a rumored tinclad gunboat, Clark requested that the Glasgow attack be supported by a section of artillery from the western side of the river. General Price agreed, sending General Shelby with a detachment to support the Glasgow force.[1]

Clark's Provisional Division

General Information Clark's Provisional Division. At the time of the Battle of Glasgow, newspaper accounts placed the Confederate strength at between 1,500–2,000 men on the north side of the Missouri River, with one battery of artillery. One newspaper account garnered from eyewitnesses stated that Clark had "about 1,600 men" with him after taking Glasgow, while acknowledging that Jackman was also present, but giving no total for his command. General Clark, for his part gives no details on the size of his force.

Shelby's command on the west bank of the Missouri River contributed another 125 men (Edwards says it was 200 men, while other sources place the number at 300, and period newspapers say Shelby had 2,000–3,000), with a two gun section of Collins's Battery. In this case, Shelby's account is used in the Order of Battle below.[2]

Note: The numbers presented below under the various units in ( ) represent the armed and effective officers and men who were engaged in the battle, while the unbracketed numbers represent all men present, including horse holders and the Infirmary Corps. Also, all the strengths listed below are estimates (E).

Provisional Division. (Brig. Gen. John B. Clark, Jr.)
   Staff = 6 (6)[3]

---

1. *O.R.*, vol. 41, pt 3:1010–1011; Denny, 2–3; *History of Howard and Cooper Counties*, 288; Sellmeyer, 223.
2. *O.R.*, vol. 41, pt. 3:1012; Britton, *Civil War on the Border, 1863–1865*, 431; Busch, *Missouri Democrat Articles*, 141; Denny, 3; Edwards, *Shelby and His Men*, 404; "From St. Louis," *Chicago Tribune*, October 15, 1864; "General Clark in North Missouri," *Missouri Republican*, October 13, 1864; *History of Howard and Cooper Counties*, 288; "The War in Missouri," *Chicago Tribune*, October 13, 1864.
3. Since Clark's Brigade suffered no loss of staff at the Battle of Pilot Knob, it's assumed that all eight members, including the commanding general were present and available for Glasgow. Greene

General Information Colton Greene's Brigade. For the upcoming battle, Wood's Battalion was absent in Saline County, recruiting four new companies to make the unit a regiment. At the same time, Major James C. Wood was scouting Sedalia with a 60-man force for a possible attack. When Wood returned to the main army he reported the condition of things at Sedalia which resulted in an expedition sent out on October 14 to capture the city, with James C. Wood as the guide.

According to Colton Greene, only Harris's Battery of Pratt's Battalion was present on the north side of the river. Hynson's Battery probably remained with the main army protecting the train.[4]

Brigade and unit strengths for Glasgow are calculated based upon the starting values as enumerated in Appendix D and adjusted for known losses at Pilot Knob (September 27), Leasburg (September 29–30), Russellville (October 9), California (October 9), and Boonville (October 11). Since one of the primary reason for sending Clark's Brigade north of the Missouri River was to allow it to recruit for its various regiments in their home counties, no additions were added to the regiments following Pilot Knob.[5]

Unit	Starting Strength	Losses	Max Strength
3rd Mo. Cav.	401	40	361
4th Mo. Cav.	280	35	245
7th Mo. Cav.	280	9	271
Davies's Bn.	282	0	282
8th Mo. Cav.	444	27	417
10th Mo. Cav.	280	37	243
	1,967	148	1,819

The original officer strength of these six units totaled 203 effectives (see Appendix D, Clark's Brigade and Davies's Battalion). This would suggest that these units carried 1,616 men (1,819 - 203 = 1,616) into the fight at Glasgow, excluding all officers, staff, and artillerymen. This number pairs fairly well with the reported strength of Clark's Brigade at Glasgow of about 1,600 men. Since all the units at one time or another operated as dismounted during the battle, one man was needed to hold 4.5 horses, as previously shown at Pilot Knob, while the Infirmary Corps would have totaled 10 men per regiment and five for Davies's Battalion, giving the following effective strengths for the Battle of Glasgow.[6]

---

received two members of Clark's staff plus two couriers, giving him a total of five members, including himself for his staff. This left Clark with a staff of six, including himself. *O.R.*, vol. 41, pt. 1:689; *O.R.*, vol. 41, pt. 2:1095.

4. *O.R.*, vol. 41, pt. 1:689; Campbell Memoirs; *History of Pettis County*, 443, 449.
5. See Appendix E for losses at Pilot Knob. *O.R.*, vol. 41, pt. 1:692, 697-698.
6. Originally the brigade numbered 206 effective officers, three of whom were wounded at Pilot Knob, which reduced the officers' corps to 203. *O.R.*, vol. 41, pt. 1:692; Busch, *Missouri Democrat Articles*, 202; Confederate States War Department, Regulations, 238.

Unit	Max Strength	Horse Holders	Infirmary Corps	EFF Strength
3rd Mo. Cav.	361	80	10	271
4th Mo. Cav.	245	54	10	181
7th Mo. Cav.	271	61	10	200
Davies's Bn.	282	63	5	214
8th Mo. Cav.	417	88	10	319
10th Mo. Cav.	243	54	10	179
	1,819	400	55	1,364

Marmaduke's Brigade (Col. Colton Greene)
   Staff = 5 (5) EFF
   3rd Cav. (Capt. B. S. Johnson).[7] EFF = 361 (271) [4 K, 26 W, 0 M]
   4th Cav. (Col. John Q. Burbridge). EFF = 245 (181) [2 K, 9 W, 0 M][8]
   7th Cav. (Col. Solomon G. Kitchen). EFF = 271 (200) [0 K, 2 W. 0 M]
     Davies's Cav. Bn. (Lt. Col. J. F. Davies). EFF = 282 (214)
   [embraced in 7th Cav.]
   8th Cav. (Col. William L. Jeffers). EFF = 417 (319) [0 K, 4 W, 0 M]
   10th Cav. (Col. Robert R. Lawther). EFF = 243 (179) [1 K, 4 W, 0 M][9]
   Harris's Mo. Battery (Lt. T. J. Williams).[10] 3 guns; 6-lb. brass SB, 12-lb
     James Rifle, 12-lb Mt. How.[11] EFF = 32 (32) [0 K, 0 W, 0 M]
   Greene's Brigade Total = 1,824 EFF Present
                    = 1,369 EFF Dismounted
   Losses = [7 K, 45 W, 0 M]

Jackman's Brigade General Information. Though directed to take 500 men of his command to support the Glasgow attack, according to General Shelby Jackman actually took 800 men with him when he crossed the Missouri River.[12]

At the Battle of Glasgow, Jackman's Brigade consisted of four commands: D. C. Hunter's and Jackman's Regiments, with William O. Coleman's and J. A. Schnable's Battalions. As will be shown below, Schnable's unit, or a two-company detachment thereof, was part of General Shelby's supporting force that attacked from the western bank of the Missouri River. That left Jackman's Brigade with no more than 29 companies available. It's assumed that the arms within the brigade would have been evenly distributed to the various companies, to take advantage

---

7. *O.R.*, vol. 41, pt. 1:689.
8. Burbridge put his losses at one killed and eight wounded. In this case I used the higher value reported by the brigade. *O.R.*, vol. 41, pt. 1:694.
9. Lawther reported losing one killed, with four wounded, while the brigade reported that he lost one killed and two wounded. I suspect that the additional two wounded were only slightly wounded, which the brigade report excluded. *O.R.*, vol. 41, pt. 1:692, 697.
10. *O.R.S.*, pt. 2, vol. 38:348; Cocker, 17.
11. Per Hughey's Arkansas Battery as shown in Appendix D, the battery effective strength was estimated at 32 officers and men (10.5 officers and men per gun x 3 = 31.5). *O.R.*, vol. 34, pt. 3:830; *O.R.*, vol. 41, pt. 1:719; *O.R.*, vol. 41, pt. 4:1023; Cocker, 13.
12. *O.R.*, vol. 41, pt 3:1012; Edwards, *Shelby and his Men*, 405.

of the entire command structure within the brigade. For Glasgow, since Jackman had only 800 men, the remaining unarmed portion of his command would have remained behind with the main body of the army. This suggests that each company numbered 28 (800 / 29 = 27.58) officers and men per company. The brigade staff would add an additional six men to the total.

The various units are then reduced to account for horse holders at one for every four horses, since the command was newly recruited; and, for the Infirmary Corps, 10 men per regiment, and six for Schnable's Battalion and three for Coleman's command, giving the brigade's effective strength at Glasgow as follows:[13]

Unit	Max Strength	Horse Holders	Infirmary Corps	EFF Strength
Jackman's Regt.	276	69	10	197
Hunter's Regt.	275	69	10	196
Coleman's Bn.	84	21	3	60
Schnable's Bn.	165	41	6	118
	800	200	26	571

Note: Jackman's Regiment would have a maximum effective strength of 27.58 x 10 = 276; horse holders would be 276/ 4 = 69, while the Infirmary Corps numbered 10. This would then give Jackman's Regiment 197 (276 - 69 - 10 = 197) effective officers and men for the Battle of Glasgow. The other units are similarly calculated.

    Jackman's Brigade (Col. S. D. Jackman)
        Staff = 6 (6) EFF
        Jackman's Regt. (Ltc. C. H. Nichols). EFF = 276 (197)
        Hunter's Regt. (Col. D. C. Hunter). EFF = 275 (196)
        Coleman's Bn. (Col. William O. Coleman). EFF = 84 (60)
        Schnable's Bn. (Ltc. J. A. Schnable). EFF = 165 (118)
            Brigade Total = 806 EFF Present
                        =577 EFF Dismounted
        Losses (E) = [3 k, 19 W]

Estimated Losses in Jackman's Brigade. There is no reason to believe that Jackman's command lost more or less heavily than Greene's Brigade. Greene's command lost seven killed and 45 wounded out of 1,369 engaged or 3.8 percent (52 / 1,369 = .0379) of those engaged. That suggests that Jackman lost 22 (.038 x 577 = 21.93) officers and men. Of the losses suffered by Greene's command

---

13. The 800 figure is assumed to be officers and men, as Jackman seems to have reported his command as such from the beginning of the Expedition. Further, for the Battle of Glasgow, Jackman appears to have been the one that reported to General Shelby that he was taking 800 men. See Appendix D, Shelby's Division, Jackman's Brigade for details. *O.R.*, vol. 41, pt. 1:431; *O.R.*, vol. 41, pt. 3:1012; Coleman Letters (October 27, 1909); Confederate States War Department, Regulations, 238; "Valiant Coleman, Veteran of Two Wars," *Confederate Veteran* 17 (September, 1909), 212.

13.4% (7 / 52 = 13.4 percent) were killed, while 86.6% were wounded, which equates to three killed (.134 x 22 = 2.94), with 19 wounded.

Shelby's Detachment

General Information on Shelby's Detachment. In his report on the Glasgow engagement Shelby noted that he took only 125 men. John Edwards clarifies what commands these men came from, noting that they were Captain Maurice M. Langhorne's Company from the 12th Missouri Cavalry (CSA), along with men from Schnable's command. In his report on the Glasgow attack, General Clark stated that Shelby took a regiment to support the attack, suggesting that it was more than the 125 men that General Shelby says that he had. However, without better evidence, the 125 figure will be used.

Langhorne's Company was part of the 12th Missouri Cavalry, serving as Shelby's Escort Company, with an initial strength of about 55 (see Appendix D, Shelby's Division for details) officers and men. However, allowing for the liberal furlough policy that Shelby implemented when at Boonville, where a full one-third of the Iron Brigade received leave to spend time with their families, this would suggest that Langhorne's Company numbered probably about 37 (55 x . 66 = 37), with two officers and 35 men.

Elements from John Schnable's Battalion made up the rest of Shelby's Detachment, excluding Collins's Artillery. Based on Shelby's comment that he took only 125 men, this would suggest that Schnable's command was just a detachment of about 90 men (125 - 35 for Langhorne = 90) or two companies, officers not counted. Estimating three effective officers per company would give Schnable's Detachment 96 (90 + 6 = 96) effective officers and men.

Captain Richard Collins commanded a section of his battery at Glasgow, consisting of two 10-lb Parrot Rifles. Since they had suffered no appreciable losses prior to Glasgow, its full compliment of 22 officers and men would have been present and effective.[14]

With the exception of Shelby's staff, which probably remained mounted, the other cavalry units would have required one horse holder for every four horses in Shelby's Detachment and one for every six in the escort company. The Infirmary Corps would have been minimal and was not considered for Shelby's Detachment. The number noted below in ( ) reflects the number of effectives after removing the horse holders.

General Shelby's Detachment (Brig. Gen. J. O. Shelby)
    Staff = 12 (12) EFF[15]
    Detachment Schnable's Mo. Bn. (Cdr. ukn.).[16] EFF = 96 (72)

---

14. Edwards, *Shelby and His Men*, 405; Whitsett Letter.
15. The Divisional Surgeon Junius Terry was excluded from the staff as non-effective. *O.R.*, vol. 41, pt. 3:943–944; Crute, *Confederate Staff Officers*, 173–174.
16. The commander was probably a senior captain or major of the battalion, both of whom are un-

Co. E, 12th Mo. Cav. (Capt. M. M. Langhorne).[17] EFF = 37 (31)
Section Collins Mo. Battery (Capt. Richard A. Collins). 2 guns, 10-lb Parrot Rifle. EFF = 22 (22)
Total Shelby's Detachment = 167 EFF Present
= 137 EFF Dismounted
Losses (E) = [1 K, 4 W, 0 M]

Estimated Losses in Shelby's Detachment. There was no reason to believe that Shelby's Detachment lost more or less heavily than Greene's Brigade. Greene lost seven killed and 45 wounded out of 1,369 engaged or 3.8 percent of those engaged. That would suggest that Shelby lost five (.038 x 138 = 5.24) officers and men. Of the losses suffered by Greene's command 13.4 % (7 / 52 = 13.4 percent) were killed, while 86.6 % were wounded, which equates to one killed (.134 x 5 = .67), with four wounded in Shelby's Detachment.

Confederate Summary of the Battle of Glasgow

Engaged

Clark's Provisional Division:

Greene's Brigade	1,369
Jackman's Brigade	571
Shelby's Detachment	137
Grand Total CSA Forces	2,077[18]

Losses

	Killed	Wounded	Missing
Greene's Bde	7	45	0
Jackman's Bde.	3	20	0
Shelby's Detch.	1	4	0[19]
Total Losses	11	69	0[20]

* * * * * * *

known.

17. Anonymous, *12th Missouri Cavalry*, 47; Edwards, *Shelby and His Men*, 405.
18. Mark Lause has the total Confederate force "engaged" at from "1,800 to 2,000." Lause, *Collapse of Price's Raid*, 50.
19. Lieutenant Colonel D. J. Hynes of the 17th Illinois reported that Federal snipers shot seven or eight men. "The War in Missouri," *Chicago Tribune*, October 29, 1864.
20. A newspaper account from the *Chicago Tribune* stated that "the rebel loss, by actual count, was eighty-five killed, and from 180 to 200 wounded." This seems highly unlikely given the known loss in Greene's Brigade. "The War in Missouri," *Chicago Tribune*, October 29, 1864.

Union Order of Battle
Glasgow, Missouri (October 15, 1864)

General Information Colonel Chester Harding's Command. In his official report on the Battle of Glasgow, Colonel Chester Harding reported that his command "consisted of 481 officers and men of the Forty-third Missouri, the Ninth Missouri State Militia and the Thirteenth Missouri Cavalry, and the Seventeenth Illinois Cavalry, for duty and about 150 militia and citizens," suggesting a total force of 631 officers and men. However, a review of assorted sources finds that is not true. Local newspapers reported that his command numbered as high as 1,100 men, while Captain Oscar Kirkhan, commanding company G, 43rd Missouri, stated that Harding's command did not exceed 750. General J. B. Clark, who captured Glasgow, put the number of his prisoners, including four companies of militia, at between 800–900 officers and men. And Richard J. Hinton says that Harding had 300 armed citizens when he arrived at Glasgow, in addition to his own command. Captain Mayo's men add another 300, suggesting that the Glasgow garrison totaled about 1,086 officers and men, i.e., Mayo had 300; militia and citizens 300; and Harding 486 (see following paragraph on the 43rd Missouri.).[21]

43rd Missouri Infantry (Companies A, C, D, E, G, & H). The *Supplement to the Official Records* shows that of the six companies in the 43rd Missouri that were at Glasgow, Companies C, D, and G listed their paroled, killed, and missing total as 243 (C = 79; D = 87; G = 77) officers and men or an average of 81 officers and men per company (243 / 3 = 81). Companies A, E, and H have no comments in the *Supplement* on the number paroled, killed, or missing; however, based upon the other three units in the regiment these three commands would have added another 243 officers and men. Also, prior to leaving for Glasgow, Harding ordered the concentration of his regiment at Macon, where he requested transportation for "870 men and four car loads of baggage." This suggests that the ten companies averaged 87 men each, including the staff. The average of 81 men per Companies A, E, and H seems reasonable, even when the regimental staff of five is added in. Overall I would estimate that the 43rd had 491 (243 + 243 + 5 = 491) effective officers and men at Glasgow.[22]

Citizens and Militia. There were militia units from three localities at Glasgow, according to local newspapers—units from Saline and Chariton Counties, plus the Glasgow City Guards. These three commands provided 310 officers and men to the garrison, according to local accounts.

The Saline County command appears to have consisted of two companies, one commanded by a Captain Turner and the other by Captain George Bingham.

---

21. *O.R.*, vol. 41, pt. 1:436–437, 682; Britton, *Civil War on the Border, 1863–1865*, 456–457; Hinton, 71; "The War in Missouri," *Chicago Tribune*," October 20, 1864.

22. *O.R.*, vol. 41, pt. 3:568; *O.R.S.*, pt. 2, vol. 38:21, 23–24, 26–27.

Colonel Harding noted that Bingham's command numbered 86 officers and men, which is further supported by the *History of Saline County*. Added investigation shows that Bingham's command was actually Company H, 71st EMM. There are also indications that the other company was composed of men from Company F, 71st EMM, as noted in the *History of Saline County*. This second company, according to the *Missouri Democrat*, was commanded by Captain Turner and numbered 60 men from the EMM.

The Chariton County Militia was from the 46th EMM and numbered 70 officers and men, commanded by Lieutenant John Vance (the *Missouri Democrat* and *Republican* called Vance a captain, but the commanding general of Vance's Military District says that Vance was a lieutenant).

Sources do not give a number for the Glasgow City Guards, but we can estimate that the local defenders numbered 94 (310 - 86 - 70 - 60 = 94) officers and men for the Battle of Glasgow.

Mark A. Lause, in the *Collapse of Price's Raid*, identified another militia unit that was at Glasgow, from Ray County. Commanded by Captain Clayton Tiffin, the unit numbered but 21 men, including the commanding officer. This raises the known militia command strength to 341 officers and men.[23]

Volunteer Cavalry (9th MSM, 13th Missouri and 17th Illinois). There were three unit detachments from the volunteer cavalry at Glasgow: the 13th Missouri, the 9th MSM, and the 17th Illinois. The detachment from the 13th Missouri Cavalry numbered 26 officers and men, according to the *Supplement to the Official Records*. And a member of the 9th MSM Cavalry wrote a piece for the *Missouri Democrat* where he listed the two companies that participated in the Battle of Glasgow and their strengths, giving the detachment 99 officers and men. Further, Captain George Holloway, of Colonel Harding's staff, says that the 9th MSM numbered only 85 men. In Holloway's case it's clear that he did not count the officers and non-commissioned officers that led the two companies that were in the battle.

Lieutenant Israel Eldridge of the 17th Illinois reported there were "several men" from the 17th at the Battle of Glasgow. Lieutenant Colonel D. J. Hynes, of the 17th, who had been scouting the area prior to the battle, was notified of the imminent threat to the city. Hynes, decided to stay in Glasgow to help defend the city and dismissed his escort of "about fifty men and joined the party."

This gives a total of about 149 officers and men for the 9th MSM and the detachment of the 17th Illinois. However, Colonel Robert Lawther, commanding the 10th Missouri Cavalry (CSA), reported capturing 157 cavalry on his portion of the field, which was defended by the 9th MSM and the 17th Illinois Cavalry.

23. O.R., vol. 41, pt. 1:433, 436, 1029; "Attack Upon Glasgow," *Missouri Republican*, October 21, 1864; Busch, *Missouri Democrat Articles*, 187, 200, 223; Hinton, 71; *History of Saline County, Missouri, Carefully Written and Compiled From the Most Authentic Official and Private Sources, Including A History of the Townships, Cities, Towns and Villages, etc.* (St. Louis, 1881), 345, 352; Lause, *Collapse of Price's Raid*, 46.

This would seem to suggest that the 17th numbered 58 (157 - 99 = 58) officers and men.[24]

Maximum Number Surrendered of the Glasgow Garrison. Overall the garrison of Glasgow numbered 981 officers and men at the beginning of the battle. However, as the battle progressed 41 men from Captain George Bingham's Company of the Saline County Militia fled, retreating to Macon City, which boosts the missing from the Union command from 40 to 81, thus reducing the garrison to no more than 889 men (981 - 11 killed - 81 Missing = 889) to be surrendered. Of those missing, 69 were from the militia, while 12 were from the 43rd Infantry and the 13th Cavalry.

Additionally, when the surrendered garrison returned to Federal lines, on parole, the *Chicago Tribune* noted that the total was "between 500 to 600, and 200 or 300 citizens" or 700–900 prisoners in all.[25]

   Glasgow Garrison (Col. Chester Harding)
      Staff = 8 EFF[26] [1 K, 0 W, 0 M]
      43rd Mo. Inf. (Cos. A, B, D, E, G, and H; Maj. B. K. Davis). EFF = 486 [8 K, 26 W, 9 M][27]
      13th Mo. Cav. (Detch., 1st Bn.; Capt. John H. Mayo). EFF = 26 [0 K, 2 W, 3 M][28]
      9th MSM Cav. (Detch., Cos. B and M; Capt. S. A. Hunter). EFF = 99 [0 K, 0 W, 0 M]
      17th Il. Cav. (Detch., Lt. Israel H. Eldridge). EFF = 58 [0 K, 0 W, 0 M]
      Garrison Total = 651 [9 K, 28 W, 12 M]
   Militia and Home Guard (Maj. James W. Lewis)[29]
      Saline County Militia (Capt. Turner)[30]
         Co. F, 71st EMM (Capt. Turner). EFF = 60 [0 K, 1 W, Ukn. M]

---

24. *O.R.*, vol. 41, pt. 1:430, 436–437, 699; *O.R.S.*, pt. 2, vol. 35:749; Busch, *Missouri Democrat Articles*, 187, 200, 307–308; "The War in Missouri," *Chicago Tribune*, October 29, 1864.
25. *O.R.*, vol. 41, pt. 1:436, 439; "The War in Missouri," *Chicago Tribune*, October 20, 1864.
26. Colonel Harding was assisted by Lieutenant Colonel D. J. Hynes (17th Illinois Cavalry); Major J. B. Moore (post commissary); Captain G. A. Holloway, adjutant (General Fisk's staff); Captain J. A. Cotton, commissary; Joseph Thompson (43rd Mo., adjutant); Redman (43rd Mo., quartermaster) and Lieutenant George Simmonds (62nd U.S. Infantry, colored troops). *O.R.*, vol. 41, pt. 1:437; Busch, *Missouri Democrat Articles*, 226, 229–230.
27. Busch, Missouri *Democrat Articles*, 328–329.
28. Ibid.
29. Ibid., 200.
30. This was probably John H. Turner, who was previously a major on the staff of General Thomas Bartholow, commander of the 8th Missouri Militia District. Turner had resigned on August 31, 1863, and no further record was found on him. I suspect that he volunteered his services and was elected captain of the company. Gray, *Missouri Adjutant General Report*, 391.

Co. H, 71st EMM (Capt. George Bingham).[31] EFF = 86
[0 K, 0 W, Ukn. M]
Chariton County Militia (1st Lt. John Vance).[32] EFF = 70 (E)
[0 K, 1 W, Ukn. M]
Ray County Militia (Capt. Clayton Tiffin). EFF = 21 [0 K, 1 W, 0 M]
Glasgow City Guards (Capt. Samuel Steinmetz). EFF = 94 (E)
[2 K, 1 W, Ukn. M]
Militia and Home Guard Total = 331 [2 K, 4 W, 18 M]
Total Union Strength at Glasgow = 981.
Initial Losses at Glasgow = [11 K, 33 W, 81 M][33]
Reevaluated Losses = [11 Killed, 32 Wounded, 30 Missing][34]
Total Surrendered = 889.

---

31. Lause says that Bingham's unit contained only 61 officers and men, while Colonel Harding has Bingham's Company at 86 officers and men. Further, no mention was made of Turner's Company, which was noted in the *Missouri Democrat* as commanding the Saline County Militia, implying that there was more than one company from Saline County. *O.R.*, vol, 41, pt. 1:436; Busch, *Missouri Democrat Articles*, 187, 200; Lause, *Collapse of Price's Raid*, 46.

32. *O.R.*, vol. 41, pt. 1:433; Busch, *Missouri Democrat Articles*, 200; Lause, *Collapse of Price's Raid*, 46.

33. Forty-one of the missing had fled Glasgow as the battle developed, retreating to Macon City, thus avoiding capture. The missing of the 9th MSM and the 13th Missouri Cavalry eventually returned to their commands, having avoided capture. The fate of the other missing militia remains unknown. *O.R.*, vol. 41, pt. 1:436; *O.R.S.*, pt. 2, vol. 38:23–24; Busch, *Missouri Democrat Articles*, 229, 308.

34. Busch, *Missouri Democrat Articles*, 328–329.

Appendix G
Confederate Order of Battle
Westport (October 23, 1864)

General References:

1. *O.R.*, vol. 41. pt. 1:641–642; *O.R.S.*, pt. 1, vol. 7:391.
2. Buresh, 204–207; 216–221.
3. Forsyth, *Great Missouri Raid*, 242–244.
4. Harrell, *Arkansas, Confederate Military History*, 273–274.
5. Lause, *Price's Lost Campaign*, 208–209.
6. Monnett, 139–141.
7. Suderow, "Battlefield of Westport," 16–17.

Assumptions:

1. The engagements on October 23, 1864, at Byram's Ford, Hickman Mills Road, and south of Westport are all considered part of the Battle of Westport.
2. All the strengths presented below are estimates and considered armed, except where otherwise noted.
3. Arkansas commands received no additional manpower during the Expedition, whereas the Missouri units received recruits throughout, which are reflected in Appendix D and incorporated below.
4. There were no deductions taken for the assorted staffs, unless a specific officer was killed, wounded or captured; and those are noted in the appropriate place in the Order of Battle below. Staff lost within a brigade would have been replaced, as brigades had limited staff members to begin with, while those of the army and division commanders were probably not replaced, as they were numerous.
5. All commanding officers of regiments, battalions, companies, or batteries remain as indicated in Appendix D, except for those known to have been previously killed, wounded or captured.

Westport Order of Battle Introduction. "The Battle of Westport was the largest battle in point of numbers engaged that was fought west of the Mississippi River," according to Paul Jenkins, as well as other authors. According to Jenkins, 20,000 Federal and 9,000 Confederate troops were engaged at Westport, totals agreed on by several sources; however, all the current literature fails to identify the numbers engaged or even present at the battle. And even General Price who put his strength at "8,000 armed men" gave no indication what this number included. Below the reader will find a detailed look at the Army of Missouri at the Battle of Westport, with its roughly 18,000 effective rebels available or 14,000 effective dismounted rebels available on October 23. As to how sources have accounted for the Confederate command on October 23, more will be presented in the analysis at the end of the Order of Battle. And like all of my Orders of Battle, this one will likely change over time as additional information becomes available, especially regarding Fagan's Division, which is almost totally void of sources.[1]

General Information on the Battle of Westport. The Army of Missouri had been actively engaged in Price's Raid since September 18, 1864, and as such several troop acquisitions were made, as shown in Appendix D. These in turn have been incorporated into the Order of Battle below. Adjustments have been made to the various units to reflect the battlefield losses experienced from the beginning to the Expedition. Adjustments have also been made to reflect the losses from sickness and desertion, while numbers of horse holders varied, depending on the brigade.

A review of the various sources cited in the bibliography have horse holders ranging from one for every four, as recorded by M. Jeff Thompson, to as many as one for every eight, as noted by Don Mc. N. Palmer of the Iron Brigade, during the actual Expedition. From other sources it has been noted that one man held the horses for five men. As such, when dealing with the horse holders in the Iron Brigade or Thompson's command, one man for every six will be used (this is the average of four and eight). In veteran units, like Cabell's and Slemons's Brigades, one for every four and a half will be used. And in new brigades like McCray's, Dobbin's, and Freeman's or in new unattached regiments, such as Lyles's and Rogan's, one for every four will be used.[2]

To account for losses due to desertion, sickness, etc., Thomas Freeman's Brigade provides us with a basis to use for non-veteran commands, while veteran commands will be treated on a case by case basis. At the beginning of the Expedition, Freeman's effective force numbered 1,159 (excluding officers). And by the Battle of Independence on October 22, it was down to 900 effectives. This would suggest a loss of all types, including battlefield losses, desertion, and sickness, of 20.6 percent (1,159 - 900 = 239 or 239/ 1,159 = 20.6 %). At Pilot Knob, the brigade's only other engagement prior to the Battle of Independence on October 22, it was estimated that the brigade suffered only five casualties (see Appendix E). As such no subtractions were made to the brigade to account for battlefield losses, so in this case the loss was strictly from sickness and desertion.[3]

For all other commands or recently raised units, including McCray's, Dobbin's, as well as Freeman's and several unattached units, 20.6 percent will be deducted from the various brigades' starting strengths. Jackman's Brigade is a

---

1. Lause says that the Confederates had between 10,000–14,000 men while the Unionists numbered 25,000. Forsyth has the rebel total at 12,000 engaged, while the Federals numbered 22,000 to 23,000. *O.R.*, vol. 41, pt. 1:636; D. Brown, 41; Boatner, 906; Forsyth, *Great Missouri Raid*, 198; Jenkins, 154, 173–174; Lause, *Collapse of Price's Raid*, 129; Mark A. Lause, "Battle of Westport," in *Encyclopedia of the Civil War*, 2093; Monaghan, 336; Howard N. Monnett, "Decisive Conflict: The Battle of Westport," in *Battle of Westport*, 3, 6, 12.
2. Palmer, 22; Stanton, etc., 248; Suderow, *Arcadia Valley*, 138.
3. Freeman Memoir, October 22, 1864.

special case and will be addressed under the General Information for Jackman's Command. This would suggest that these units contained the following effective strength, excluding officers, which increase the brigade's size, and battlefield losses, which will decrease the brigade's size. Additionally, officers would have had a higher effective rate than the enlisted men, say 90 percent of what the brigade showed at the beginning of the Expedition, less any known losses, while any artillery or escort companies would have remained basically unchanged. All battlefield losses, horse holders, and Infirmary Corps will be adjusted below under the specific brigade.[4]

Brigade	At Start EFF Men	Less 20.6 % EFF Men	At Westport EFF Officers/Men
Freeman's	1,154 (109)	700 (98)	798[5]
McCray's	1,700 (122)	1,350 (110)	1,460
Dobbin's	1,648 (124)	1,309 (112)	1,421

Note: Number of EFF Officers in ( ).

And finally, for the Order of Battle below two numbers are provided: the unbracketed number represents the maximum effective strength of a particular unit, if the entire command was mounted. The bracketed number represents the effective strength of the unit after removing horse holders and the Infirmary Corps. As was seen under the narrative for the Battle of Westport, units operated both mounted and dismounted, and it is impossible to tell exactly what a unit's strength was at any particular time in the battle.

Losses in the Army of Missouri. Under normal circumstances losses and the explanation for them would be included under the appropriate command. However, due to the lack of empirical information regarding losses, the issue will be addressed following the Order of Battle after all the effective strengths have been calculated. In calculating losses, the effective dismounted strength of a command and its location on the battlefield became determining factors; as such, the need to cover losses after the Order of Battle was complete. The losses will, however, be listed under the specific brigade below.[6]

Army of Missouri (Maj. Gen. Sterling Price)
    Staff = 14 (14)
    Bodyguard

---

4. See Appendix D for starting strength for the various brigades. Additional changes will be made under the individual brigades below.
5. Freeman Memoir, October 22, 1864.
6. Of all the Confederate commands at Westport, only Jackman's and Cabell's Brigades, three units of Clark's Brigade, and McGhee's Regiment have known losses on October 23. *O.R.*, vol. 41, pt. 1:686, 692, 697, 699; Bryce Suderow, "Battle of Westport Opening Phase," Internet site, "The Missouri Civil War Message Board," hereafter cited as Suderow, "Battle of Westport Opening Phase."

Rayburn's Indept. Ark. Co. (Capt. Howel A. "Doc" Rayburn).
EFF = 55 (55)
Escort: Company K, 2nd Mo. Cav. (Windsor Guards; Capt. Robert Collins). EFF = 55 (55)
Officers and men of unknown assignments, including band. EFF = 188 (0)
Total Army HQ = 312 (124) [0 K, 1 W, 0 M]

Fagan's Cavalry Division

General Information for Fagan's Division. Of Fagan's four brigades Slemons's and Dobbin's participated in the Battle of Westport; Cabell's and McCray's Brigades guarded the army's trains; and, it also appears that a portion of McCray's Brigade, which was guarding the rear of the train, was also engaged against Pleasonton's Division in the latter part of the Battle at Byram's Ford. There is no substantial evidence that Lyles's or Rogan's commands participated in any of the actions surrounding the battles of October 23, save guarding the train in some capacity.

The strength of the various brigades and unattached units are adjusted for the Battles of Pilot Knob (September 27, 1864), Boonville (October 11-12, 1864) and Independence (October 22, 1864). Additional adjustments are also made for losses based upon sickness and desertion as enumerated above. Total available strength is represented by the unbracketed numbers below, while the dismounted effective strength in ( ) reflects the loss of horse holders and Infirmary Corps.

Fagan's Staff and Escort Battalion. For the Battle of Westport, Fagan's Staff had only eight officers, having lost two staff officers since the beginning of the Expedition: Lieutenant Colonel Wyatt C. Thomas was wounded and captured at Pilot Knob, while Captain Lewis D. Holsemlake was captured on October 20. Anderson's Arkansas Battalion suffered few if any casualties prior to Westport; however, as noted above its original strength is reduced by 20.4 percent for enlisted men, which allows for sickness, desertion, and any unknown casualties giving the command a strength of 122 (180 x .85 = 153 x .794 = 121.4) enlisted men. Officers are calculated based upon 17 original officers, reduced by 10 percent, giving the battalion 15 effective officers, for a maximum effective strength of 137. Horse holders calculated at one man for every four horses, as the command was newly recruited, giving the battalion 34 (137 / 4 = 34.25) horse holders. This leaves the battalion with an effective dismounted strength of 103 (137 - 34 = 103) officers and men.[7]

Fagan's Division (Maj. Gen. James F. Fagan):
Staff = 8 (8)

---

7. *O.R.*, vol. 41, pt. 3:944; Suderow, Report of POWs, no. 74 (November 15, 1864) & no. 84 (January 12, 1865).

Escort: Anderson's Ark. Cav. Bn. (Capt. N. Terry Roberts). EFF = 137(103)
HQ & Escort Total = 145 (111) [0 K, 0 W, 0 M]

General Information for William Cabell's Brigade. Cabell's Brigade began the Expedition with 3,215 effective officers and men. At Pilot Knob Cabell's Brigade lost 275 killed and wounded. Of those 96 were in Monroe's Regiment and 41 were in Morgan's command. This would have left 137 (275 - 138 = 137) casualties for the other units in the brigade. This would suggest the following losses based upon a proportional distribution as follows:

Unit	Strength on Sept. 27 (percent of total)	Losses on Sept. 27
Gordon's Regt.	403 (25.5%)	34.9
Hill's Regt.	403 (25.5%)	34.9
Gunter's Regt.		
Woosley's Bn.	157 (09.9%)	13.5
Witherspoon's Bn.	191 (12.1%)	16.5
Harrell's Regt.	421 (26.7%)	36.5
Total	1,575 (99.7%)	136.4

Note: Strength on September 27, reflects the number after horse holders and the Infirmary Corps are removed.

At Boonville (October 11, 1864) Cabell lost 21 killed and wounded, while the specific units affected were not known. The same was true at Independence on October 22. There various Federal reports have Cabell losing either 40 or 17 killed or as an average 29 killed (40 + 17 = 57 / 2 28.5; see Appendix C, Cabell's Rearguard Action for details), with 23 prisoners. Wounded are calculated at only twice the number of killed given the circumstances of how the men were killed, for a total of 58 wounded. This would suggest that at Independence, including the 23 prisoners, Cabell suffered 110 (29 killed, 58 wounded and 23 prisoners; total = 110) additional losses, which need to be deducted from Cabell's starting strength. The combined losses between Boonville and Independence total 108, excluding POWs from Independence.

From the unit's starting strength as shown in Appendix D, the losses of September 27 are deducted as well as the losses the brigade suffered at Boonville and Independence. Losses are then pro-rated based upon available strength on October 22, with the exception of prisoners which were: Monroe, five; Gordon, one; Morgan, twelve; Hill, four; Staff one.

Additionally, under normal circumstances Cabell's veteran command would have lost about 10 percent of its strength due to sickness and desertion. However, by October 18 Fagan's Division, including Cabell's Brigade, had been short on rations for some time and sickness had increased significantly, largely because of the changing weather. This in turn no doubt resulted in abnormal loss of manpower in all the brigades of the division including Cabell's. As such, Cabell's Brigade will also suffer the loss of an additional 20.6 percent of its strength to reflect the disaffection in his brigade.[8]

Unit	Strength on Sept. 19	Available on Oct. 22
HQ/ Escort	65 (1)	64 [00/01 = 1]
Monroe's Regt.	539 (96)	352 [17/05 = 22]
Gordon's Regt.	485 (35)	357 [17/01 = 18]
Morgan's Regt.	539 (42)	395 [18/12 = 30]
Hill's Regt.	539 (35)	400 [19/04 = 23]
Gunter's Regt.		
Woosley's Bn.	210 (14)	156 [08/00 = 08]
Witherspoon's Bn./ Proctor's Co.	244 (16)	180 [09/00 = 09]
Harrell's Regt.	563 (37)	418 [20/00 = 20]
Total	3,184 (275)	2,322 [108/23 = 131]

Notes:
1. ( ) losses on September 27.
2. Available on October 22 was calculated after removing losses from Pilot Knob and multiplying the remainder by 79.4% to reflect losses by sickness, desertion, etc., from Sept. 18–October 22; e.g., for Monroe's Regiment it would be 539 - 96 = 443 x .794 = 352. The other commands are similarly calculated.
3. [Losses/ POWs]–Losses at Boonville and Independence calculated on the prorated strength of the various units, excluding the escort, times 108. Prisoners were added in after the prorated losses were calculated; e.g., for Monroe's Regiment it would be 352 / 2,258 = .155 x 108 = 16.8 + 5 prisoners = 21.8 or 22. The other units were similarly calculated. Some rounding is used to obtain 108 in total losses. This suggests that Monroe's Regiment had 330 (352 - 22 = 330) effective officers and men available for October 23, before deducting horse holders and the Infirmary Corps.

Unit	Available on Oct. 23	Horse Holders (Infirmary Corps)	EFF For Oct. 23
Staff	9	00 (00)	9
Escort	54	12 (00)	42
Monroe's Regt.	330	74 (10)	246
Gordon's Regt.	339	76 (09)	254
Morgan's Regt.	365	81 (10)	274
Hill's Regt.	377	84 (10)	283

8. *O.R.*, vol. 41, pt. 4:1003–1004; Busch, *Missouri Democrat Articles*, 335, 439; Mobley, 196.

Gunter's Regt.
  Woosley's Bn.   148   33 (06)   109
  Witherspoon's   171   38 (07)   126
   Bn./Proctor's Co.
Harrell's Regt.   <u>398</u>   <u>88 (10)</u>   <u>300</u>
Total   2,191   486 (62)   1,643

Note: Since Cabell's Brigade was a veteran command, horse holders were calculated at one man for four and a half horses, including the escort. Infirmary Corps was one man per assigned company, escort not included in this case.

    Cabell's Arkansas Cav. Bde. (Brig. Gen. William L. Cabell). EFF = 9 (9)[9]
        Escort: Company C, Gordon's Arkansas Cav. Regt. (1st Lt. Robert J. Wilson). EFF = 54 (42)
        HQs. & Escort Total = 63 (51)
        Monroe's Regt. (Ltc. A. V. Reiff).[10] EFF = 330 (246)
        Gordon's Regt. (Col. Anderson Gordon). EFF = 339 (254)
        Morgan's Regt. (Col. Thomas J. Morgan). EFF = 365 (274)
        Hill's Regt. (Col. John F. Hill). EFF = 377 (283)
        Gunter's Regt. (Ltc. Thomas M. Gunter)
            James Woosley's Bn. (Maj. James Woosley).[11] EFF = 148 (109)
            Witherspoon's Cav. Bn. (Maj. J. L. Witherspoon).[12] EFF = 171 (126)
        Harrell's Cav. Regt. (Ltc. John M. Harrell). EFF = 398 (300)
            Cabell's Bde. Total = 2,191 EFF Available
                      = (1,643) EFF Dismounted
        Total Losses = [3 K, 9 W, 0 M][13]

General Information for Dobbin's Brigade. Prior to the battle on October 23, Dobbin's Brigade had little contact with the enemy, save picket duty and scouting.

---

9. Captain David W. Corder was captured at Pilot Knob. Major Herman Carlton, Cabell's Inspector General, was captured on October 22. Suderow, Report of POWs (received at Gratiot Prison, November 10, 1864) also List no. 74 (November 15, 1864).
10. James Monroe was wounded and "disabled" at Pilot Knob, leaving command of the regiment to Lieutenant Colonel A. V. Reiff. *O.R.*, vol. 41, pt. 1:641, 647; Allardice, *Confederate Colonels*, 276; Sifakis, *Arkansas*, 51.
11. This was actually Gunter's Battalion, commanded by Woosely. See Appendix D for details. *O.R.S.*, pt. 2, vol. 2:851.
12. I've incorporated Proctor's Company into Witherspoon's Battalion, where Appendix D listed it as a separate unit when the Expedition began.
13. Cabell put his losses at just three killed with "several" wounded; wounded are estimated at nine, or three for every man killed. General McNeil recorded that his command found "about 40" dead rebels on the field after their fight with Cabell. However, McNeil's report was probably just an effort on his part to show how fierce his engagement was with Cabell. A few weeks after he wrote his report, McNeil was court-martialed for his performance against the rebel train and no doubt wanted to show that he had carried out his orders as best he could. *O.R.*, vol. 41, pt. 1:372; *O.R.S.*, pt. 1, vol. 7:399.

As such the 1,421 effectives, as shown above will be used as the brigade's effective strength at Westport, less horse holders and Infirmary Corps. The various unit strengths are prorated based upon the overall strength of the brigade at the beginning of the Expedition. The brigade staff and artillery section are considered to be as strong as when they began the Expedition, with any losses replaced from the brigade's regiments. As such, 27 is deducted from the 1,421 leaving 1,394 (1,421 - 27 = 1,394) to be distributed to the three regiments of the commands as follows:

Unit	Strength on Sept. 19	Prorated Strength on Oct. 23	EFF on Oct. 23
Dobbin's Regt.	503 (29%)	404	293 [101/10]
McGhee's Regt.	697 (40%)	558	408 [140/10]
Witt's Regt.	527 (31%)	432	314 [108/10]
Total	1,727 (100%)	1,394	1,015 [349/30]

Notes:
1. ( ) percent of total times 1,394 gives the maximum effective strength, on October 23, less horse holders and Infirmary Corps.
2. [Horse Holders/ Infirmary Corps] Horse holders calculated at 1 for every 4; Infirmary Corps, 1 per assigned company.
3. Dobbin's Regiment calculated as follows: .29 x 503 = 404 / 4 = 101 horse holders; Infirmary Corps = 10; 404 - 101 -10 = 293. The other regiments are similarly calculated.

    Dobbin's Ark. Bde. (Col. Archibald S. Dobbin)
        Staff = 6 (6) EFF
        Dobbin's Cav. (Ltc. Unknown).[14] EFF = 404 (293)
        McGhee's Cav. (Col. James McGhee, WIA; Ltc. Jesse S. Grider, Oct. 25, 1864).[15] EFF = 558 (408)
        Witt's Cav. (Col. Allen R. Witt). EFF = 432 (314)
        Blocher's Battery (one sec.) (Lt. J. V. Zimmerman), 2 guns; 1 6-lb SB and 1 12-lb How. EFF = 21 (21)
            Dobbin's Brigade Total = 1,421 EFF Available
                              = (1,042) EFF Dismounted
            Losses = [27 K, 64 W, 35 M][16]

---

14. According to the *Missouri Democrat* an unknown lieutenant colonel commanded Dobbin's Regiment, while Dobbin commanded the brigade. Busch, *Missouri Democrat Articles*, 305.
15. Allardice has McGhee being wounded at both Westport (October 23) and at Mine Creek (October 25); however, McGhee was wounded in the chest at Westport, which makes it unlikely that he could have even participated in the Battle of Mine Creek. It is assumed that the next in command of McGhee's Regiment, Lieutenant Colonel Jesse S. Grider, would have taken command of the regiment following Westport. Grider, according to John Edwards was wounded at that battle, but managed to escape capture. Edwards also has Grider as a major. Allardice, *Confederate Colonels*, 264; Edwards, *Shelby and His Men*, 437; Monnett, 139; Sifakis, *Arkansas*, 65; Sinisi, 229–230.
16. For details on losses, see Losses on the Westport Front below.

General Information for McCray's Brigade. Prior to the battle on October 23, McCray's Brigade participated in but one engagement of note, the Battle of Pilot Knob, where it was estimated that they suffered 43 casualties (see Appendix D, Losses in Fagan's Division for details). The remainder of the time McCray's Brigade was apparently used on picket duty, scouting, or train guard. As such the 1,417 (1,460 - 43 = 1,417), effectives as shown above will be used as the brigade's effective strength at Westport, less horse holders and Infirmary Corps. The various unit strengths are prorated based upon the overall strength of the brigade at the beginning of the Expedition. The brigade staff and artillery section are considered to be as strong as when they began the Expedition, with any losses replaced from the brigade's regiments. As such, six is deducted from the 1,417 leaving 1,411 (1,417 - 6 = 1,411) to be distributed to the three regiments of the commands as follows:

Unit	Strength on Sept. 19	Prorated Strength on Oct. 23	EFF on Oct. 23
45th Ark. Regt.	720 (40%)	564	413 [141/10]
47th Ark. Regt.	720 (40%)	564	413 [141/10]
15th Mo. Regt.	376 (20%)	281	201 [070/10]
Total	1,816 (100%)	1,411	1,027 [352/30]

Notes:
1. ( ) percent of total times 1,411 gives the maximum effective strength, on October 23, less horse holders and Infirmary Corps; e.g., the 45th Arkansas would be 564 (.4 x 1,411 = 564).
2. [Horse Holders/ Infirmary Corps] Horse holders calculated at one for every four; Infirmary Corps, one per assigned company.
3. The 45th Arkansas Regiment calculated as follows: 564 / 4 = 141 horse holders; Infirmary Corps = 10; 564 - 141 -10 = 413. The other regiments are similarly calculated.

   McCray's Bde. (Col. Thomas H. McCray)
   Staff = 6 (6) EFF
   45th Ark. Inf. (Mtd.) (Ltc. J. W. Clark).[17] EFF = 564 (413)
   47th Ark. Inf (Mtd) (Col. Lee Crandall). EFF = 564 (413)
   15th Mo. Cav. (Col. Timothy Reeves). EFF = 281 (201)
   McCray's Brigade Total = 1,417 EFF Available
                          = (1,033) EFF Dismounted
   Losses = [2 K, 5 W, 0 M][18]

---

17. After the capture of Baber the next in the command chain would have been Lieutenant Colonel J. W. Clark. Eakin, *Missouri Prisoners of War*, "Baber, Milton P." entry; Ferguson, 313; Suderow, Report of POWs, List no. 74 (November 15, 1864); Sifakis, *Arkansas*, 120.
18. For details on losses, see Losses from the Train Guards below.

General Information for Slemons's Brigade. Prior to the battle on October 23, Slemons's Brigade participated in but one engagement of note, the Battle of Pilot Knob, on September 27, where it is estimated that they suffered 20 casualties (see Appendix D, Losses in Fagan's Division for details), with the exception of Wright's Arkansas Regiment which lost an estimated 25 officers and men. The remainder of the time Slemons's Brigade was apparently used on picket duty, scouting, or train guard. As such, the 2nd Arkansas, Crawford's, and Carlton's Regiments had a strength of 841 (861 -20 = 841), while Wright's command had 270 (295 -25 = 270) effective officers and men; total 1,111, following the Battle of Pilot Knob (i.e., about 280 (841 / 3 = 280.3 effective officers and men per regiment for the 2nd Arkansas, Crawford and Carlton). This strength was further reduced by sickness, desertion, etc., by 20.6 percent, for the same reason that Cabell's command was similarly reduced, giving the brigade 882 (841 + 270= 1,111 x .794 = 882) effective officers and men for Westport on October 23. Additionally, as a veteran unit, one man can hold four and a half horses as noted above. The brigade staff lost one man at Pilot Knob, but he would have been replaced prior to the Battle of Westport. As such the various units' strengths are calculated as follows:

Unit	Strength on Sept. 28	Prorated Strength on Oct. 23	EFF on Oct. 23
2nd Ark. Regt.	280 (222)	222 [50/10]	162
Crawford's Regt.	280 (223)	223 [50/10]	163
Carlton's Regt.	281 (223)	223 [49/10]	164
Wright's Regt.	270 (214)	214 [48/10]	156
Total	1,111 (882)	882 [197/40]	645

Notes:
1. ( ) = September 28 value times .794 gives the maximum effective strength of various regiments in Slemons's Brigade on October 23, less horse holders and Infirmary corps; e.g., for the 2nd Arkansas it would be 222 (280 x .794 = 222.3). Other units similarly calculated.
2. [Horse Holders/ Infirmary Corps] Horse holders calculated at one for every four and a half; Infirmary Corps, one per assigned company.
3. The 2nd Arkansas Regiment calculated as follows: 222 / 4.5 = 49.5 horse holders; Infirmary Corps = 10; 222 - 50 - 10 = 162. The other regiments are similarly calculated.

Slemons's Arkansas Bde. (Col. William F. Slemons)
    Staff = 6 (6) EFF
    2nd Cav. (Ltc. Thomas M. Cochran). EFF = 222 (162)
    Crawford's (Col. William A. Crawford). EFF = 223 (163)
    Carlton's Cav. (Col. Charles H. Carlton). EFF = 223 (164)
    Wright's Cav. (Col. John C. Wright). EFF = 214 (156)

Slemons's Bde. Total = 888 EFF Available
= (651) EFF Dismounted
Losses = [9 K, 27 W, 7 M][19]

General Information Unattached Units. In reviewing the assorted sources as listed in the bibliography, nothing was found on Lyles's or Rogan's Regiments. It doesn't appear that either command was engaged at Westport or for that matter in any of the major engagements during the Expedition. It is assumed that they were relegated to defending the train throughout the Expedition or possibly served as provost guards. As such, their effectives, as shown in Appendix D, at the beginning of the Expedition would have been reduced by 20.6 percent for sickness, desertion, service as teamsters, replacements for the Pioneer Company or in the Provost Guard, giving each of the regiments 436 (549 x .794 = 435.9) effective officers and men. The Pioneer Company would have remained unchanged as any losses would have been made up from either unarmed recruits or from details from other units, such as Lyles's or Rogan's commands. The adjustments in the unattached units gives the following results:

Unit	Strength on Sept. 19	Strength on Oct. 23	EFF on Oct. 23
Lyles' Regt.	549	436	317 [109/10]
Rogan's Regt.	549	436	317 [109/10]
Pioneer Co.	79	79	0
Total	1,177	951	634 [218/20][20]

Notes:
1. Strength on October 23 obtained by multiplying strength on September 19 times .794, i.e., Lyles's and Rogan's Regiments would each be 436 (549 x .794 = 435.9).
2. [Horse Holders/ Infirmary Corps] Horse holders calculated at one for every four; Infirmary Corps, one per assigned company. No horse holders or Infirmary Corps for the Pioneer Company.
3. Effective strength on October 23 calculated as follows for Lyles's Regiment: 317 (436 / 4 = 109 horse holders; Infirmary Corps = 10; 436 - 109 - 10 = 317) effective officers and men. Rogan's Regiment would be identical to Lyles's command.

Unattached.
  Lyles's Ark. Cav. (Col. Oliver P. Lyles). EFF = 436 (317)
  Rogan's Ark. Cav. Bn. (Col. James W. Rogan). EFF = 436 (317)

---

19. For details see Losses on Westport Front listed below.
20. It's assumed that the Pioneer Company would have been unarmed or lightly armed as it main mission was to build bridges and clear the road for the army's movement, while other armed commands provided security.

Pioneer Co. (Cdr ukn.). EFF = 79 (0)
Unattached Total = 951 EFF Available
= (634) EFF Dismounted
Losses = [0 K, 0 W, 0 M]

Fagan's Division Summary

Unit	EFF Available (EFF Dismounted)	
HQ	145 (111)	[0 K/ 0 W/ 0 M]
Cabell's Bde.	2,191 (1,643)	[3 K/ 9 W/ 0 M]
Dobbin's Bde.	1,421 (1,042)	[27 K/ 64 W/ 35 M]
McCray's Bde.	1,417 (1,033)	[2 K/ 5 W/ 0 M]
Slemons's Bde.	888 (651)	[9 K/ 25 W/ 7 M]
Unattached	951 (634)	[0 K/ 0 W/ 0 M]

Fagan's Div. Total = 7,013 EFF Available
= (5,114) EFF Dismounted
Losses = [41 K, 103 W, 42 M][21]

* * * * * * *

Marmaduke's Division

General Information Marmaduke's Division. Shortly after the start of the Expedition, Marmaduke's Division began adding recruits and increasing units from battalions to regiments, thus building its overall strength. It also fought in several engagements where men were lost, including Pilot Knob, Russellville (October 9), Boonville (October 11), Glasgow (October 15), Little Blue (October 21), and Independence (October 22) before fighting the Battle of Westport on October 23. All of these engagements cost the command some casualties, with nearly all of them falling in Clark's Brigade. All additions and losses are reflected in the paragraphs below. Additionally, it appears that John B. Clark's Brigade did not suffer the losses from desertion or sickness that was experienced in Fagan's command. In fact, according to Henry Luttrell, by the Battle of Westport his regiment, the 10th Missouri Cavalry, was twice the size it was when it began the Expedition. As such, any losses from desertion or sickness would be a non-factor in determining the strength of the various units in Clark's Brigade. Freeman's Brigade has a stated value for the Battle of Westport and will not be affected by any losses or gains for the battle on October 23.[22]

---

21. Suderow puts Fagan's losses at 75 killed and wounded, with 100 captured; Cabell lost 15 killed and wounded, Dobbin lost 50 killed and wounded, with 100 captured; Slemons lost 10 killed and wounded with none captured; and McCray, with the two unattached commands suffered no losses. Suderow, "Battlefield of Westport," 17.

22. *O.R.*, vol. 41, pt. 1:688, 692; Luttrell, "Price's Great Raid," *Missouri Republican*, March 6, 1886.

Stallard's Escort Battalion. On October 16, 1864, while camped at the Keiser Bridge, David Stallard's Escort Company was increased to a battalion by adding one company and part of another, totaling 89 effectives. This gave the Escort Battalion 144 (55 + 89 = 144) effective officers and men. The command then lost five men at the Little Blue on October 21, reducing its total to 139, before deducting horse holders and Infirmary Corps. Horse holders would be one man for every four and a half horses, or 31 (139 / 4.5 = 30.8), with two men for the Infirmary Corps. This would give the command 106 (139 - 31 -2 = 106) effective dismounted officers and men. See Appendix D, Additions to the Army of Missouri, Captain David R. Stallard's Escort Battalion for details.

Losses from September 19–October 22. The losses listed below are mostly complete, with missing values estimated. That said, in the case of Independence on October 22, it appears that Thomas Freeman's Brigade suffered the majority of the Confederate killed and wounded, which Kyle Sinisi estimates at less than 50 for Marmaduke's Division. The men captured in Clark's Brigade, on October 22, are included in the losses below. As such no losses for killed and wounded are deducted for October 22, as Freeman recorded his strength for October 23, taking into account the losses he had previously suffered.[23]

Unit	Losses on Sept. 27	Losses on Oct. 9–15	Losses on Oct. 21	Total
3rd Mo. Cav.	29	41 (3)	31	104
4th Mo. Cav.	35	11	0	46
7th Mo Cav./ Davies' Bn.	0	14 (9)	15	38
8th Mo. Cav.	24	7	0	31
10th Mo. Cav.	30	13 (5)	20	68
Wood's Bn.	45	0 (3)	22	70
Total	163	52 (20)	88	357

Note: Known prisoners = ( )

Marmaduke's Division (Maj. Gen. John S. Marmaduke).
Staff = 17 (17) EFF

---

23. See Appendix E and F for details on losses for September 27 and October 15, 1864. The losses for Wood's command on October 21 were estimated at 22, being the average of the other three units of Clark's Brigade engaged at the Little Blue. The remainder of Clark's losses on October 21 per the *Official Records*. Losses for Boonville on October 11 per the *Official Records*. The losses in the Escort command have been previously addressed. The artillery losses were not considered, as men would have been detailed to make up any losses as the Expedition progressed. Also note, that in Clark's report of casualties for the Expedition, he excluded those who were captured, while my figures include prisoners. *O.R.*, vol. 41, pt. 1:692, 694, 697–699; Freeman Memoirs, October 23, 1864; Sinisi, 214; Suderow, Report of POWs, Gratiot Prisoner Lists nos. 74 (November 15, 1864) and 79 (November 10, 1864), no. 81 (December 31, 1864), no.84 (January 10, 1865) and Leavenworth List (December 12, 1864).

Escort: Stallard's Battalion (Capt. David R. Stallard).[24]
    EFF = 139 (106)
Engineer Co./ Pontoon or Engineer Train (Capt. James T. Hogane).
    EFF = 79 (0)
        HQ Total = 235 (123) EFF [0 K, 0 W, 0 M]

Note: Parenthesis ( ) around a number reflects the unit's effective strength if the command operated dismounted, while the non-parenthesis number represents available effectives, if the unit operated mounted. The Engineers were carried in wagons and were generally unarmed; however, they played an integral part in clearing roads and building make-shift bridges, making them, in my estimation, effective soldiers.

Marmaduke's Brigade General Information. Shortly after the Expedition began, Marmaduke's Missouri Brigade, commanded by General John B. Clark, began adding units and recruits. Excluded from the table immediately below is the 10th Missouri Cavalry, which will be addressed separately.

The 7th Missouri and Davies's Cavalry Battalion. On September 24, Colonel Solomon Kitchen joined Clark's Brigade in eastern Missouri, bringing with him J. F. Davies's Battalion of 282 effective officers and men. In the first part of October 1864, Davies received three new companies for his command, which added 153 effectives. Kitchen also brought with him, on September 24, 305 additional recruits for Clark's Brigade, or 61 officers and men per assigned unit (see Appendix D, Additions to the Army, J. F. Davies's Battalion and Recruits for Marmaduke's Brigade for details).

Harris's Artillery Battery. With the capture of Herman on October 4, the 3rd Missouri Cavalry, of Clark's Brigade, acquired one 6-lb iron smoothbore, which apparently was added to Harris's Battery. Men appear to have been detailed from the 3rd Missouri to man the captured gun, adding both the gun and 11 effective men to the battery.[25]

Wood's 14th Missouri Cavalry Battalion/ Regiment. Robert Wood's Battalion was not part of Clark's Brigade when it left Princeton on August 29, 1864, but was assigned to the brigade sometime after it left Pocahontas. This would have added 365 effective officers and men to the brigade. On October 11, following the occupation of Boonville, Major Robert C. Wood, commanding the battalion, organized four additional companies, thus making his unit a regiment. Wood was subsequently promoted to lieutenant colonel, then colonel of his regiment. Rais-

---

24. Escort composed of Company D, 5th Missouri Cavalry; Captain Page's Company and part of a company commanded by Orderly Sergeant W. L. Armstrong. Anonymous, *5th Missouri Cavalry*, 49; Brown Journal, October 16 & 21, 1864.
25. Ankesheiln, *Eight–Hundred Voices*, 1:155–156.

ing Wood's unit to a regiment added 220 effectives (see Appendix D, Additions to the Army, Ben Elliott and Robert Wood's Battalions for details).[26]

Unit	Strength on Sept. 19	Additions before Oct. 23 (losses)	EFF at Westport on Oct. 23
3rd Mo. Cav.	340	61 (104)	297 [66/10]
4th Mo. Cav.	219	61 (46)	234 [52/10]
7th Mo. Cav.	219	61 (19)	261 [58/10
Davies's Bn.[27]	0	282 (19)	263 [66/08]
8th Mo. Cav.	383	61 (31)	413 [92/10]
10th Mo. Cav.	See Below	See Below	See Below
Wood's Bn.	0	585 (70)	515 [115/10]
Total	1,161	1,111 (289)	1,983 [449/58]

Notes:
1. Losses are those that occurred September 19–October 22, 1864. Excluding October 22, as noted above.
2. [Horse holders / Infirmary corps] Effectives at Westport reflect the available mounted officers and men of the command. Horse holders are calculated at one for every four and a half in all commands except for Davies's Battalion which was one for every four. The 8th Missouri is calculated as follows: 383 + 61 - 31 = 413; 413 / 4.5 = 92; 413 - 92 - 10 = 311 EFF, dismounted on October 23. Other units similarly calculated.
3. The overall losses in the 7th Missouri and Davies's Battalion were evenly divided among the two commands.

3rd and 4th Missouri Cavalries. In his memoirs Colonel Thomas Freeman stated that for the defense of Byram's Ford on October 23, he was also given command of the 3rd and 4th Missouri Cavalries, totaling about 600 men. Officers would have added (39 + 39 = 78 x .9 = 70.2) 70 effectives, giving the two commands 670 effective officers and men (see appendix D for details). The numbers shown above have the two commands with 531 effective officers and men. This would suggest that these two commands, in addition to the recruits as previously noted, received 141 (670 - 531 = 139) additional recruits not previously recorded.[28] This would boost each unit by 70 or 69 men, giving these new values for October 23:

3rd Missouri Cav. 295 + 70 = 365 [81/10]; 365 - 91 = 274
4th Missouri Cav. 234 + 69 = 303 [67/10]; 303 - 77 = 226

---

26. *O.R.*, vol. 41 pt. 1:627, 642, 719; *O.R.*, vol. 41 pt. 2:1090; Allardice, *Confederate Colonels*, 405; Buresh, 218; Campbell Memoirs; Crute, *Confederate Army*, 204; Sifakis, *Missouri*, 102–103; Suderow, *Arcadia Valley*, 139.
27. Losses embraced in the 7th Missouri Cavalry.
28. Freeman Memoir, October 23, 1864.

Lawther's 10th Missouri Cavalry. The 10th Missouri began the Expedition with 219 effective offices and men (see Appendix D). In his account, Henry Luttrell recorded that at the Battle of Westport, "The old Tenth is twice as large as now as it was when we left Arkansas." This would suggest an effective strength of 438 officers and men; horse holders would be 97 (438 / 4.5 = 97), with an Infirmary Corps of 10. This gives the command 331 (438 - 97 - 10 = 331) effective officers and men for October 23.[29]

    Marmaduke's Mo. Bde. (Brig. Gen. John B. Clark).
        Staff = 8 (8)
        3rd Cav. (Capt. Benjamin S. Johnson). EFF = 365 (274)[3 K, 6 W, 2 M]
        4th Cav. (Ltc. William J. Preston).[30] EFF = 303 (226)
          [2 K, 4 W, 0 M] (E)
        7th Cav. (Col. Solomon G. Kitchen, wounded Oct. 23).[31]
          EFF = 261 (193) [5 K, 8 W, 0 M]
        Davies's Bn. (Ltc. John F. Davies). EFF = 263 (189)
        8th Cav. (Col. William L. Jeffers). EFF = 413 (311) [3 K, 4 W. 0 M] (E)
        10th Cav. (Col. Robert R. Lawther). EFF = 438 (331) [0 K/ 2 W/ 0 M]
        Wood's Regt.(Ltc. Robert C. Wood).
          EFF = 515 (390) [4 K, 5 W, 0 M] (E)
    Pratt's Art. Bn. (Maj. Joseph Pratt).
        Hynson's Tx. Battery or 10th Tx. Lt. Art. (Capt. Henry C. Hynson),
          3 guns; 6-lb. brass SB, 12-lb James Rifle, 12-lb Mt. How.
          EFF = 32 (E)
        Harris's Mo. Battery (Capt. S. S. Harris), 4 guns; 6-lb. brass SB,
          6-lb iron SB, 12-lb James Rifle, 12-lb Mt. How.
          EFF = 43 [0 K, 2 W, 0 M] (E)
        Brigade Total = 2,641 EFF Available
                    = (1,997) EFF Dismounted
        Losses = [18 K, 32 W, 2 M]

Freeman's Brigade General Information. Thomas Freeman reported that his "effective strength...was less than 700 men" on October 23. His officer strength at the beginning of the Expedition was estimated at 103. Allowing for a 10 percent loss for assorted causes would leave the brigade 93 effective officers, brigade staff not included. This suggests a brigade strength of 793 (700 + 93 = 793) effective officers and men. This would then be proportionally distributed among the brigade's three commands as follows:

---

29. Henry Luttrell, "Price's Great Raid," *Missouri Republican*, March 6, 1886.
30. Freeman Memoir, October 23, 1864.
31. The combined unit of the 7th Missouri and Davies's Battalion was also known as the "Missouri and Arkansas Legion." Davies assumed command of both the 7th Missouri Cavalry and Davies's Battalion after Kitchen was wounded. Losses are assumed to include Davies's Battalion. *O.R.*, vól. 41, pt. 1:696; Bartels, *Trans-Mississippi Men*, 17.

Unit	Starting Strength Sept. 19 (% Total)	Available EFF on Oct. 23	Dismounted EFF on Oct. 23 [HH / IC]
Freeman's Regt	507 (40.3)	320	230 [80/ 10]
Fristoe's Regt.	490 (38.9)	309	222 [77/ 10]
Ford's Bn.	260 (20.6)	164	117 [41/ 06]
Total	1,257	793	569 [198/26]

Notes:
1. Available EFF on October 23 for Freeman's Regiment would be 320, calculated as follows: 320 (793 x .403 = 319.5) effective officers and men. The other commands are similarly calculated.
2. The Dismounted EFF on October 23 would have the horse holders [HH] removed at one man for every four horses; Infirmary Corps [IC] would deduct another man for every assigned company; i.e., this would give Freeman's Regiment 80 (320 / 4 = 80) horse holders, an Infirmary Corps of 10, with an EFF dismounted strength on October 23 of 230 (320 - 80 - 10 = 230). The other commands are similarly calculated.

 Freeman's Bde. (Col. Thomas R. Freeman)
  Staff EFF = 6 (6)
  Freeman's Mo. Cav. (Ltc. Joseph B. Love). EFF = 320 (230)
  Fristoe's Mo. Cav. (Col. Edward T. Fristoe). EFF = 309 (222)
  Ford's Ark. Bn. (Lt. Col. Barney Ford). EFF = 164 (117)
   Brigade Total = 799 EFF Available
     = (575) EFF Dismounted
   Losses = [5 K, 9 W, 5 M][32]

General Information Charles H. Tyler's Brigade. Organized at Boonville between October 9–12, 1864, the brigade consisted of two regiments, commanded by Colonels Caleb Perkins and James J. Searcy. John T. Coffee's Battalion was later added to the brigade following the Battle of Newtonia on October 28. Prior to that, Coffee's command, led by Lieutenant Colonel John T. Crisp, had followed in the rear of the army, serving as the recruiting command for Price. At the Battle of Westport, Coffee's Battalion was assigned to M. Jeff Thompson's Brigade. The brigade was eventually attached to Shelby's Division, according to the *Official Records* Order of Battle; however, during the bulk of the Expedition it operated as a detached command, as indicated in the assorted correspondence from the Expedition. Further complicating the assignment of Tyler's Brigade is the fact that following the Expedition Colonel Tyler filed a report on his operations, sending it to General Marmaduke. Additionally, in Price's Court of Inquiry, Colonel James R. Shaler stated that Tyler's Brigade was placed in Marmaduke's Division, but

---

32. For losses see details below under Losses at Byram's Ford.

did not specify when. For the Battle of Westport, it appears to have been assigned to Marmaduke's Division, but was detached as an independent command, serving directly under General Price.[33]

Since Perkins's and Searcy's Regiments were organized less than two weeks before the Battle of Westport, no deductions are taken from the commands, save the reduction of 15 percent, to coincide with the standard loss of present for duty strength versus effective strength, as shown in Livermore. As shown in Appendix D, under Additions to the Army of Missouri, Tyler's Brigade, each of these regiments arrived with 645 officers and men, which equates to (645 x .85 = 549) effective officers and men if armed. However, as shown in Appendix D, only 426 officers and men were armed, leaving each regiment with 123 (549 - 426 = 123) unarmed men. For the Battle of Westport, each unit would need 137 (549 / 4 = 137 horse holders) with an Infirmary Corps of 10. The unarmed, effective men could serve as horse holders, with another 24 men deducted from each of the regiments to give their effective dismounted strength on October 23; i.e., 549 - 123 - 24 = 402 EFF Dismounted officers and men. The mounted EFF Strength for each regiment would be 426.

Tyler's Mo. Cav. Bde. (Col. Charles H. Tyler). [Detached]
    Staff = 6 (6) EFF
    Perkins Cav. (Col. Caleb Perkins). EFF = 426 (402)
    Searcy's Cav. (Col. James J. Searcy). EFF = 426 (402)
        Brigade Total = 858 EFF Available
                = (810) EFF Dismounted
      Losses = [0 K, 0 W, 0 M]

Marmaduke's Division Summary

Unit	EFF Available (EFF Dismounted)	
HQ/ Escort	235 (123)	[0 K, 0 W, 0 M]
Clark's Brigade	2,641 (1,997)	[18 K, 32 W, 2 M]
Freeman's Brigade	799 (575)	[5 K, 9 W, 5 M]
Tyler's Brigade	858 (810)	[0 K, 0 W, 0 M]

    Marmaduke Div. Total = 4,533 EFF Available
                      = (3,505) EFF Dismounted
    Losses = [23 K/ 41 W/ 7 M][34]

* * * * * *

---

33. *O.R.*, vol. 41, pt. 1:719; *O.R.*, vol. 41, pt. 4:1013, 1067.
34. Suderow puts Marmaduke's losses at 50 killed and wounded, with five prisoners; Clark lost 40 killed and wounded, with five prisoners, while Freeman lost 10 killed and wounded, with none captured. Suderow, "Battlefield of Westport," 17.

Shelby's Division

Shelby's Division General Information. Of the three divisions in the Army of Missouri, Shelby's received more new units than any other, including Slayback's and Williams's Regiments, with Johnson's Battalions. They also received numerous recruits that flocked to the army, adding 543 recruits for Thompson's Brigade, with another 239 in Jackman's command, in addition to increasing Elliott's Battalion to a regiment. The division also fought in several engagements prior to Westport, where some men were lost and some captured; however, despite their losses, according to Sidney Jackman, who commanded one of Shelby's brigades, he completed the Expedition, "after the deduction of all losses...with about the same number almost entirely armed." As such, limited adjustments are made for losses from various causes, including sickness, desertion, furloughs, and battlefield casualties. These adjustments will be made on a case by case basis as stated under the various commands. The starting values of all units upon entering Missouri will remain the same for Westport, with adjustments made for horse holders and the Infirmary Corps. For horse holders, as previously indicated, the rate will generally be one man for every six horses in Thompson's Brigade, except as noted below. Under previous calculations, newly raised commands, like Jackman's Brigade, would need one man for every four horses; however, by Westport, Jackman's Brigade demonstrated that it was of veteran quality. As such, one man will be deducted for every four and a half horses in Jackman's Brigade.

Collins's Artillery Battery. On October 22, Jackman's Brigade captured a 24-pound howitzer at the Mockbee Farm, complete with caisson and ammunition. There are no indications that the gun was used at Westport, though it was later used at Newtonia. So, for Westport, the gun will not be available or listed under Collins's command.

> Shelby's Division (Brig Gen. Joseph O. Shelby)
> Staff = 12 (12) EFF[35]
> Escort: Co. E, 12th Mo. Cav. (Capt. Maurice M. Langhorne).
> EFF = 55 (55)[36]
> HQ Total = 67 (67) EFF [0 K, 0 W, 0 M]

Thompson's Brigade General Information. By the Battle of Westport, Thompson's Brigade had increased its strength significantly. It had added Alonzo Slayback's Battalion, which had grown to a regiment by the time of Westport, as well as had Elliott's Battalion. Thompson also added M. Rector Johnson's Battalion,

---

35. The Divisional Surgeon Junius Terry was excluded from the staff as non–effective. *O.R.*, vol. 41, pt. 3:943–944; Crute, *Confederate Staff Officers*, 173–174.
36. Strength based upon the typical cavalry company in 1864, i.e., 64 officers and men of whom 55 (64 x .85 = 55) would be considered effective, per Livermore. *O.R.*, vol. 41, pt. 1:662; Edwards, *Shelby and His Men*, 501; Livermore, 67–68; Muster Roll, Stallard's Company; Whitsett Letter.

in addition to John T. Crisp's command. Crisp's unit was actually John T. Coffee's command, which most authors associate with C. H. Tyler's Brigade, but which was not attached to Tyler's Brigade at the Battle of Westport (see Appendix D, Jackman's Brigade, John T. Coffee's Battalion, and John T. Crisp's Battalion for details). Additionally, D. A. Williams's Regiment of recruits was also added to the brigade for Westport, while several sources, including the *Official Records*, place it in Jackman's Brigade. However, Williams's command was not assigned to Jackman until October 30, when Jackman's Brigade reentered Arkansas and was broken up with portions sent on furlough to northern Arkansas. The brigade also received numerous recruits for the original veteran units, all of which will be detailed below.[37]

The brigade had previously participated in several engagements prior to Westport, but any losses would have been replaced by new recruits that flocked to the brigade as it marched across Missouri. As such, no adjustments were made for the losses previous to Westport on October 23, or for men still on furlough or sick.

Benjamin Elliott's Regiment. At Boonville, between October 10–12, 1864, Elliott's Battalion added six companies, making it a regiment. At the same time the battalion would have replaced any losses that it had taken in previous engagements. Sickness, desertions, and loss from non-returning furloughs would have been minimal; say, no more than five percent of the total command, including new recruits. The battalion began the Expedition with 197 effective officers and men, adding 330 effective recruits at Boonville, giving the command 527 effective officers and men before any reductions. The loss from assorted causes would leave the command 501 (527 x .95 = 501) effective officers and men for Westport. Horse holders would be one for every four and a half, as the command contained numerous recruits and untrained horses, requiring 111 (501 / 4.5 = 111) horse holders. The Infirmary Corps would require 10 men. The dismounted effective strength would be 380 (501 - 111 - 10 = 380) officers and men (see Appendix D, Additions to the Army of Missouri, Ben Elliott's and Robert Wood's Battalions).

Alonzo W. Slayback's Regiment. Slayback's command joined the Expedition on September 23 and consisted of about 222 effective officers and men. At Boonville, between October 10–12, the command was recruited up to regimental strength, adding 326 effective officers and men, for a total strength of 548, before reduction for horse holders or the effects of the march. As most of the command joined just two weeks before the Battle of Westport, 10 percent was deducted from the command's strength, instead of 20.4 percent for new units. This would give the regiment 493 (548 x .9 = 493) effective officers and men. Horse holders would be at the rate of one for every four horses, as the command was made up of recruits, or 123 (493 / 4 = 123) horse holders, with an additional 10 removed for the Infirmary

---

37. *O.R.*, vol. 41, pt. 1:642, 667, 677; Forsyth, *Great Missouri Raid*, 244; Jenkins, 164; Kirkman, 144; Lee, 22; Monnett, 141; Stanton, etc., 250.

Corps. Thus the regiment totalled 360 (493 - 123 - 10 = 360) effective officers and men for October 23 (see Appendix D, Additions to the Army of Missouri, Alonzo Slayback's Battalion or Regiment for details).

D. A. Williams's Regiment. D. A. Williams arrived in Independence on the evening of October 21 with "about 600 men." Officers would have added 45 (4 x 10 companies = 40 + 5 staff = 45). Effective officers and men would then number 549 (645 x .85 = 549) for the Battle of Westport. Since the unit was not deployed until Westport and had but two days to lose any men, no adjustments are needed for sickness, desertion, etc., save the need for horse holders, at one for every four, and the Infirmary Corps of 10 men. This would give the regiment 137 (549 / 4 = 137) horse holders. Williams's Regiment would then have 402 (549 - 137 - 10 = 402) effective dismounted officers and men for October 23.

John T. Coffee's Battalion (John T. Crisp's command). Within the *Official Records* no mention is made of Crisp's command in the Army of Missouri Order of Battle, but John T. Coffee's command is noted. As shown in Appendix D, Shelby's Division, Jackman's Brigade, John T. Coffee's Battalion and John T. Crisp's Battalion, Coffee's Battalion was not assigned to Tyler's Brigade until after October 28. And prior to that, Lieutenant Colonel Crisp generally commanded the battalion from October 3 until the end of the Expedition. The command was not seriously engaged in any combat prior to the Battle of Westport. Prior to Westport, the battalion served as the recruiting command for the army, with Crisp tasked to organize companies and forward them to the other commands. During this period of time Crisp reported recruiting "about 115 men" for his battalion, which equates to 92 (115 x .85 = 92) additional effective men. When added to Coffee's starting strength this would give the command 338 (246 + 92 = 338) effective officers and men. However, as noted in the beginning of this Appendix, as a new unit, many of whose recruits were conscripted, the effective strength will be reduced by 20.6 percent, giving the command 268 (338 x .794 = 268) effectives before considering horse holders or the Infirmary Corps. Horse holders would be one for every four horses or 67 (268 / 4 = 67), with an Infirmary Corps of six (it's assumed that the additional men would have produced two additional cavalry companies). This suggests that Coffee's or Crisp's command carried 195 (268 - 67 - 6 = 195) effective dismounted officers and men into the battle on October 23.[38]

It should also be noted that Crisp probably recruited additional men for his command prior to October 23; however, since no other deductions are taken for other causes, the figures presented above are considered reasonable for the battalion at the Battle of Westport.

M. Rector Johnson's Battalion. Johnson's Battalion began the Expedition as a

---

38. *O.R.*, vol. 41, pt. 1:641–642; Crisp to McLean (October 16, 1864), Confederate Correspondence (MSS 03–26, Box no. 1, file no. 3).

40-man company and was expanded to a small battalion by the Battle of Westport, giving the command an estimated 150 effective officers and men. As a mixed unit of recruits and veterans Johnson's Battalion needed one horse holder for every four and a half horses or 33 (150 / 4.5 = 33) men, with an Infirmary Corps of three. This gives the battalion 114 (150 - 33 - 3 = 114) effective dismounted officers and men. The unit was first engaged at Lexington where it suffered few if any losses, and any subsequent losses would not have affected its overall strength (see Appendix D, Additions to the Army of Missouri, Matthew Rector Johnson's Battalion for details).[39]

Recruits for Thompson's Brigade: the 5th, 11th and 12th Missouri Cavalries. Between September 19 and October 17, the brigade received 543 recruits. These recruits would have been for the 5th, the 11th, and 12th Missouri Cavalries, as the other units in the brigade have been previously covered. Each of these regiments would have received an additional 174 effective men, which would give the various commands the following strength for the Battle of Westport on October 23. Considering these three units were the premier regiments of the brigade, a minor adjustment of five percent was made to each of the commands' original strength to reflect the loss from sickness, absentees from furlough, or other assorted causes.

Unit	Strength on Sept. 19 {5 % loss}	(Recruits) EFF on Oct. 23	Strength on Oct. 23
5th Mo. Cav.	455 {23}	606 (174)	495 [101/10]
11th Mo. Cav.	492 {25}	642 (175)	525 [107/10]
12th Mo. Cav.	443 {22}	595 (174)	487 [99/9]
Total	1,390 {70}	1,843 (523)	1,507 [307/29]

Notes:
1. The EFF on October 23 reflect the total effective officers and men available. The number in { } reflects the number of recruits each units received prior to Westport.
2. [Horse holders/ Infirmary Corps] Strength on October 23 reflects the effective officers and men dismounted strength.
3. The 5th Missouri calculated as follows: EFF on October 23 was 606 (455 +174 - 23 = 606). Dismounted strength would be 495 (606 / 6 = 101 horse holders; 606 -101 - 10 = 495) effective dismounted officers and men. Other units similarly calculated.

Shelby's Mo. Cav. Bde. (Brig. Gen. M. Jeff Thompson)
    Staff = 8 (8) EFF
        5th Cav. (Col. B. Frank Gordon). EFF = 606 (495)
        11th Cav. (Col. Moses W. Smith). EFF = 642 (525)
        12th Cav. (Lt. Col. William H. Erwin). EFF = 595 (487)

---

39. *O.R.*, vol. 41, pt. 1:666.

Elliott's Regt. (Col. Ben Elliott). EFF = 501 (380)
Slayback's Regt. (Ltc. Alonzo W. Slayback). EFF = 493 (360)
Williams' Regt. (Capt. D. A. Williams). EFF = 549 (402)
Coffee's Bn. (Ltc. John T. Crisp). EFF = 268 (195)
Johnson's Bn. (Maj. M. Rector Johnson). EFF = 150 (114)
Collins's Battery (one sec.) (Capt. Richard A. Collins) 2 guns, 10-lb Parrots. EFF = 22 (22)
Brigade Total = 3,834 EFF Available
= (2,988) EFF Dismounted
Losses = [40 K, 127 W, 6 M]

Jackman's Brigade General Information. Shortly after the Expedition began William O. Coleman's Battalion joined Shelby's Division, and was assigned to Jackman's Brigade. The brigade lost John T. Coffee's command on October 3, but later received it back for the Battle of Newtonia on October 28. Two days after Newtonia, Coffee's Battalion was assigned to C. H. Tyler's Brigade, where it remained until the Army returned to its winter camps in Texas.

At the beginning of the Expedition most of the brigade had been newly recruited, having seen limited action during Shelby's operations against Little Rock in August 1864. By the Battle of Westport, the command was a veteran unit, requiring only one man to hold every four and a half horses. Additionally, since the command came largely from southern and southeast Missouri or northeast Arkansas, it received limited recruits as the Expedition progressed. And by the end of the Expedition the brigade contained "about the same number" of men as when it began the campaign. This would suggest that as a minimum the brigade received as many recruits as men lost in combat. According to Jackman, he lost 187 killed and wounded during the Expedition, while his prisoners numbered about 52. This would suggest a minimum of 239 recruits received into the brigade during the course of the Expedition. However the bulk of Jackman's losses occurred after October 22, with just 54 occurring between September 19–October 22. This would then reduce the available recruits to 185 (239 - 54 = 185) for the Battle of Westport.[40]

These recruits can then be apportioned based upon the various units' starting strengths, including Coleman's Battalion as shown below, with the estimated strength on October 23. Horse holders based upon one for every four and a half, as previously indicated, with one man from every company for the Infirmary Corps.

---

40. See Appendix F for losses at Glasgow on October 15. The other losses are given by Jackman for Union (October 1), Jefferson City (October 8), Boonville (October 12), Byram's Ford and Westport (October 22–23), Mine Creek (October 25) and Newtonia (October 28). For October 21 at the Little Blue, Jackman was not engaged save for Nichol's Regiment, and it appears that he lost few if any men. *O.R.*, vol. 41, pt. 1:673–677; Suderow, Report of POWs, nos. 74 (November 15, 1864), 75 (November 15–20, 1864), 76 (November 25, 1864), 78 (December 5, 1864), 81 (December 31, 1864), 84 (January 25, 1865), 85 (January 31, 1865), 86 (February 5, 1865), 89 (February 20, 1865), 90 (February 25, 1865) and 91 (March 5, 1865).

Unit	Strength on Sept. 19	Recruits Assigned	Strength on Oct.23	EFF on Oct. 23
Nichol's	617 (31.7%)	59	676	516 [150/10]
Hunter's	617 (31.7%)	59	676	516 [150/10]
Schnable's	493 (25.3%)	47	540	412 [120/ 8]
Coleman's	219 (11.3%)	20	239	183 [53/ 3]
Total	1,946 (100 %)	185	2,131	1,627 [473/31]

Jackman's Mo. Cav. Bde. (Col. Sidney Jackman):
    Staff= 6 (6) EFF [0 K, 1 W, 1 M].[41]
    Jackman's Cav. (Lt. Col. C. H. Nichols). EFF = 676 (516)
    Hunter's Cav. (Col. DeWitt C. Hunter). EFF = 676 (526)
    Coleman's Cav. Bn. (Col. William O. Coleman). EFF = 239 (183)
    Schnable's Cav. Bn. (Lt. Col. John A. Schnable). EFF = 540 (412)
    Collins Battery (one sec.; Lt. Jacob D. Conner), 2 guns; 2, 12-lb iron how.[42] EFF = 21 (21)
        Brigade Total = 2,158 EFF Available
                    = (1,654) EFF Dismounted
        Losses = [22 K, 72 W, 4 M]

General information for 46th Arkansas (Mounted) Infantry. As a newly recruited unit the 46th Arkansas probably suffered the loss of men from sickness, desertion, etc., as noted at the beginning of this Appendix. As such, the command is reduced by 20.6 percent for assorted causes, including any men lost in combat. This would give the command (504 x .794 = 400) effective officers and men for October 23, without considering horse holders or the Infirmary Corps. The unit would have required one man to hold every four horses or 100 (400 / 4 = 100) horse holders, with an Infirmary Corps of seven for the unit's seven companies. For the Battle of Westport, the 46th would then number 293 (400 - 100 - 7 = 293) effective dismounted officers and men.

    Unattached:
        46th Ark. Inf (Mtd) (Lt. Col. John W. Crabtree). EFF = 400 (293)

Shelby's Division Summary:

HQ/ Escort	67 (67)	[0 K, 0 W, 0 M]
Thompson's Bde.	3,834 (2,988)	[40 K, 127 W, 6 M]
Jackman's Bde	2,158 (1,654)	[22 K, 72 W, 4 M]
Unattached	400 (293)	[0 K, 0 W, 0 M]

---

41. Captain William J. Thompson was captured, while a Major Brown, Jackman's Assistant Adjutant General was wounded. *O.R.*, vol. 41, pt.1:676.

42. Per "Hughey's Arkansas Battery" above, the battery's effective strength was estimated at 21 officers and men (10.5 officers and men per gun x 2 = 21). *O.R.*, vol. 41, pt. 4:1023; Bartels, *Trans-Mississippi Men*, 23; Sellmeyer, 347 (n. 4).

Division Total = 6,459 EFF Available
        = (5,002) EFF Dismounted
Losses = [62 K, 199 W, 10 M][43]

* * * * * * *

Army of Missouri at Westport Summary

Army HQ & Staff	312 (124)	[0 K, 1 W, 0 M]
Fagan's Division	7,013 (5,114)	[41 K, 103 W, 42 M]
Marmaduke's Division	4,533 (3,505)	[23 K, 41 W, 7 M]
Shelby's Division	6,459 (5,002)	[62 K, 199 W, 10 M]

Army Total = 18,317 EFF Available
      = 13,748 EFF Dismounted
Losses = [126 K, 344 W. 59 M]

Comments on the Strength of the Army of Missouri. As shown above, the composite strength of the Army of Missouri was considerably larger than has been commonly accepted throughout the years. However, a lot depends on just how one approaches the reported Confederate strength at the battle on October 23. According to most writing on the subject, only Marmaduke's and Shelby's Divisions were engaged in the battle, with the support of Slemons's and Dobbin's Brigades from Fagan's command. Those commands guarding the trains seemed to have had no place in the Confederate strength at the Battle of Westport, as will be shown below.

If one ignores the units guarding the trains, including Tyler's, Cabell's, and McCray's Brigades, with the assorted division escorts and unattached commands, the Order of Battle would show an Effective Dismounted Strength as follows:

Unit	Available EFF	Dismounted EFF
Thompson's Bde.	3,834	2,988
Jackman's Bde.	2,158	1,654
Clark's Bde.	2,641	1,997
Freeman's Bde.	799	575
Dobbin's Bde.	1,421	1,042
Slemons's Bde.	888	651
Total	11,741	8,907

The above figures for the Dismounted Effectives seem to correspond with what has been generally accepted as the Confederate strength at Westport. They would also suggest that Price was so intent on saving his train that roughly 36.5

---

43. Suderow puts Shelby's losses at 155 killed and wounded, with 125 prisoners; Thompson's Brigade lost 80 killed and wounded, with 100 prisoners, while Jackman lost 75 killed and wounded, with 25 prisoners. Suderow, "Battle Field of Westport," 16.

percent of his army was devoted to guarding it. And one wonders what would have been the outcome of the battle if Price had committed Cabell's Brigade to the defense of Byram's Ford, instead of wasting it guarding the trains?

General Information on Confederate Losses at Westport. The generally accepted losses for the Army of Missouri normally run from 1,000 to 1,500 men, including prisoners, with some estimates running as high as 2,800. Unfortunately most of these figures are pure guesswork and seem to have little or no foundation. Howard Monnett places the Confederate losses at "a conservative" figure of 1,500, citing incomplete Confederate reports of the Expedition. Mark Lause writes that "the Confederates were in denial when they wrote their reports," believing that they had lost "at least 700 to 1,000 with thousands having gone 'missing' for at least the duration of the battle." And Fred Lee, in his small book on Westport, puts the Confederate losses at 200 killed and wounded, with 61 captured; total 261. Lee further lists the three-day total, from October 21–23, as 492 killed, wounded, and captured. However, within all the literature on the battle, there is a little known article and study, written by Bryce Suderow in 1974, for The Westport Historical Quarterly, which makes a worthy attempt to define the losses for the rebels at Westport. In his analysis, Suderow uses the available casualty reports, with estimates for the missing units, and places the Confederate losses at 280 killed and wounded, with 230 captured, for a total of 510. Kyle Sinisi is the only author to acknowledge and support Suderow's groundbreaking research, calling it "the best estimate of casualties" available.[44]

Since making his initial analysis, Suderow did additional research at the National Archives on the rebel prisoners captured on October 23 at Westport. Those figures put the number of prisoners at 59, which would have reduced Suderow's overall loss estimate to 339 (280 + 59 = 339) killed, wounded, and missing. Using a different method for calculating the Confederate losses at Westport, my estimate fills in the blanks for the killed and wounded that Suderow did not cover and will show a loss of 529 killed, wounded, and missing. Admittedly, the information below would be better served if more Confederate accounts, as to losses, were available for the Battle of Westport. And hopefully, over the years, new information will better clarify the rebel losses on October 23, 1864. Additionally, under the individual division totals I note the losses that Suderow first proposed in 1974, for comparison purposes with the numbers I have put forth.[45]

The analysis and figures below are my attempt to update and expand upon Suderow's work in 1974, by looking at what was officially reported by Confederates sources, adding in known prisoners caught on October 23, as listed in the

---

44. D. Brown, 41; Castel, *Sterling Price*, 236; Forsyth, *Great Missouri Raid*, 198; Jenkins, 157; Lause, *Collapse of Price's Raid*, 134–135; Fred L. Lee, "Casualties of Opposing Armies Action Before Westport, October 21–23, 1864," in Lee, *Battle of Westport*, 23; Monnett, 124; Sinisi, 258; Stalnaker, 54; Suderow, "Battlefield of Westport," 17.
45. Letter (August 14, 1976), Suderow to Lumir Buresh, Suderow Collection, State Historical Society of Missouri (Columbia), Western Historical Manuscript Collection.

National Archives POW Lists, and filling in the blanks by estimating losses based upon units with known losses. In estimating the losses, I've divided the battlefield into three distinctive areas; the Westport front, Byram's Ford and the trains. I am assuming that units engaged on the various fronts would have suffered similar losses as a command, on the same front, that had known losses and known or estimated strength.

Losses at the Westport Front. Within Shelby's Division, on the Westport front, Sidney Jackman recorded that his brigade lost 25 killed and 80 wounded from October 22–23. Jackman portrayed his losses on October 22 as "slight," which I interpret as no more than 10 percent of the 105, or 11 officers and men. This would mean that Jackman lost 94 officers and men on October 23, not including prisoners, which numbered four officers and men. Total losses for Jackman number 98.[46]

Using Jackman's losses of killed and wounded for October 23 as a guide will further serve to estimate the losses on the Westport front for Thompson, Dobbin's, and Slemons's Brigades. Overall Jackman lost 5.6 (94 / 1,654 = .056) percent of the men engaged as killed and wounded. Of the men Jackman lost on October 22–23, 23.8 (25 / 105 = .238) percent were killed, while 76.2 percent were wounded. On October 23 this would equate to 22 (94 x .238 = 22) killed and 72 wounded for Jackman's Brigade. The other brigades on the Westport front would have the following estimated losses:

Brigade	Estimated Dismounted EFF on Oct. 23	Estimated Losses on Oct. 23 [Killed/ Wounded/ Missing]
Jackman	1,654	[22 K, 72 W, 4 M]
Thompson	2,988	[40 K, 127 W, 6 M]
Dobbin	1,042	[27 K, 64 W, 35 M]
Slemons	651	[9 K, 27 W, 6 M]
Total	6,355	98 K, 290 W, 51 M

Notes:
1. Thompson's Brigade calculated as follows: 2,988 x .056 = 167 killed and wounded or 40 (167 x .238 = 39.7) killed, with 127 wounded. Prisoners number six.[47]
2. Dobbin's Brigade (less McGhee's Regiment) calculated as follows: 628 x .056 = 35 killed and wounded or 8 (35 x .238 = 8) killed with 27 wounded. McGhee lost 19 killed, with 37 wounded. Prisoners for the brigade number 35, all from McGhee.[48]

---
46. *O.R.*, vol. 41, pt. 1:676; Suderow, Report of POWs, nos. 74 (November 15, 1864), 84 December 31, 1865) and 85 (January 31, 1865).
47. Suderow, Report of POWs, nos. 84 (January 25, 1865), 85 (January 31, 1865), 88 (February 25, 1865) and 91 (March 5, 1865).
48. Suderow, "Battle of Westport Opening Phase;" Suderow, Report of POWs, nos. 85 (January

3. Slemons's Brigade calculated as follows: 651 x .056 = 36.4 or 36 killed and wounded or 9 (36 x .238 = 8.54) killed with 27 wounded. Prisoners number six[49]

Losses at the Byram's Ford Front. On the Byram's Ford front three of J. B. Clark's six units have known losses of 25 killed and wounded, with an estimated Effective Dismounted Strength of 980. This would give three units a loss rate of just 2.5 percent (25 / 980 = .025) of the troops engaged. Of the 25 men lost, nine were killed or 36 (9 / 25 = .36) percent of the men lost, with 64 percent wounded. This would suggest that the 4th and 8th Missouri, with Wood's Battalion and the artillery, also lost 25 (.025 x 984 Effective Dismounted Strength = 24.6) officers and men. This equates to nine killed and 16 wounded; the same as the other units in the brigade as follows:

Unit	Dismounted Strength (Percent of Total)	Losses
4th Mo. Regt.	218 (22%)	2 K/ 4 W
8th Mo. Regt	301 (30%)	3 K/ 4 W
Wood's Regt.	390 (49%)	4 K/ 6 W
Pratt's Bn.	75 (8%)	0 K/ 2 W
Total	984 (100%)	9 K/ 16 W

Freeman's Brigade was also deployed with Clark's Brigade at Byram's Ford and would have lost men in the same proportion as Clark's Brigade. This suggests that Freeman suffered 14 (575 x.025 = 14) casualties; the killed would have numbered five (14 x .36 = 5), while the wounded would have been nine. Freeman reported the loss of 200 men, who "simply melted away in the woods during the confusion of the battle," implying they were lost on October 22, as his command withdrew from Independence. For Westport Freeman's Brigade lost five prisoners.[50]

For the Battle of Westport Marmaduke's Division lost the following officers and men:

Brigade	Estimated Dismounted EFF on Oct. 23	Estimated Losses on Oct. 23 [Killed/ Wounded/ Missing]
Clark	1,972	[18 K, 32 W, 2 M]
Freeman	575	[5 K, 9 W, 5 M]
Total	2,547	[23 K, 41 W, 7 M]

31, 1865), 88 (February 25, 1865), 91 (March 5, 1865) and Ft. Leavenworth List (December 12, 1864).

49. Suderow, Report of POWs, nos. 84 (December 31, 1865) and 91 (March 5, 1865).

50. Freeman Memoir, October 23, 1864; Suderow, Report of POWs, nos. 74 (November 15, 1864), 76 (November 25, 1864), 85 (January 31, 1865) and 91 (March 5, 1865).

Losses from the Train Guards. Three units were involved in guarding the train; Cabell's Brigade, which reported the loss of three killed with an estimated loss of nine wounded (three per man killed); Tyler's Brigade which reported no loss while defending the train on October 23; and McCray's Brigade with Price's escort. Cabell lost .7 (12 / 1,643 = .007) percent of his command, of which .25 percent were killed. This would suggest that McCray suffered 7 (1,033 x.7 = 7) casualties, including two killed and five wounded. Price's escort lost an estimated one (110 x.007 = .77) man wounded.[51]

* * * * * * *

Summary of Confederate Losses For October 23

Unit	Dismounted EFF	Losses (E) [K , W, M]
Army Escort	110	[0 K, 1 W, 0 M]
Army HQ	14	[0 K, 0 W, 0 M]
Fagan's Division		[0 K, 0 W, 0 M]
HQ/ Escort	111	[3 K, 9 W, 0 M]
Cabell's Brigade	1,643	[27 K, 64 W, 35 M]
Dobbin's Brigade	1,042	[9 K, 27 W, 7 M
Slemons's Brigade	651	[2 K, 5 W, 0 M]
McCray's Brigade	1,033	[0 K, 0 W, 0 M]
Unattached	634	
Marmaduke's Division		
HQ/ Escort	123	[0 K, 0 W, 0 M]
Clark's Brigade	1,997	[18 K, 32 W, 2 M]
Freeman's Brigade	575	[5 K, 9 W, 5 M]
Tyler's Brigade (Detached)	810	[0 K, 0 W, 0 M]
Shelby's Division		
HQ/ Escort	67	[0 K, 0 W, 0 M]
Thompson's Brigade	2,988	[40 K, 127 W, 6 M]
Jackman's Brigade	1,654	[22 K, 72 W, 4 M]
Unattached	293	[0 K, 0 W, 0 M]
Army Total	13,826	[126 K/ 346 W/ 59 M]

Notes:
1. Dismounted EFF does not include divisional staff or escort commands, with the exception of Price's escort.
2. There is no indication that the unattached units from Shelby's or Fagan's Division participated in the battle and have not been figured into the numbers above, when calculating losses.

---

51. Buresh, 136.

Appendix H
Confederate Losses At Mine Creek
(October 25, 1864)

General Information. The losses suffered by the Confederate forces at Mine Creek vary depending on the source reviewed. Modern day authors, such as Michael Forsyth, put the losses as 300–400 killed and wounded with another 500 or 600 prisoners. Kyle Sinisi estimates the losses at "no less than three hundred Confederate killed and 250 wounded," with 730 captured. Mark Lause gives no estimate of losses at Mine Creek, instead relies on period reporting which produced wildly varied numbers, while Robert Shalhope deals only with the number captured, which he places at 500. William Crowley and Albert Castel both write that Price lost 300 killed and wounded with 900 captured. And Jerry Stalnaker puts the Confederate losses at between 200–400 killed, with 200 wounded and 500 prisoners, or between 900–1,000 casualties.[1]

The Union authorities who participated in the Battle of Mine Creek, never really dealt with the Confederate killed and wounded, but instead focused on the number of prisoners taken. However, there are a few exceptions. William Scott, of the 4th Iowa Cavalry, recorded the rebel losses as 300 killed and wounded, with 900 captured, while Wilson George of the same command recalled that they "killed about 300 rebels." Richard Hinton, of General Blunt's staff, put the number at 200 killed, who were buried by local civilians, with over 200 wounded, while the prisoners numbered over 800.[2]

Of those who focused on the prisoners taken, General Sanborn noted that 800 Confederates were captured. William Rosecrans and Alfred Pleasonton recorded that the rebels lost 1,000 prisoners at Mine Creek, which number was echoed in the Union Army Series. Though unsupported by actual numbers Pleasonton's prisoner figure is a common thread in many of the post Civil War accounts, this despite General Curtis's report that they took only 500 prisoners. Pleasonton's figures also represent one of the highest totals noted by Union participants. However, even that number continued to grow to 2,000 or more rebel prisoners, long before the first prisoners arrived in St. Louis.

Despite the inflated number recorded by Rosecrans and Pleasonton, Clifford Thompson, one of Pleasonton's assistant adjutants, put the prisoners at "over 600." Additionally, Lieutenant Colonel J. J. Sear, Provost Marshal, Army of the Border, recorded that following the battle he had collected just 495 prisoners. Further, Colonel Samuel J. Crawford, a candidate for Kansas

---

1. Boatner, 508; Crowley, 143; Castel, *Sterling Price*, 341; Forsyth, *Great Missouri Raid*, 210; Lause, *Collapse of Price's Raid*, 151–162; Shalhope, 273; Sinisi, 288; Stalnaker, 95–95.
2. Wilson B. George, "Drive After Price," *National Tribune*, March 13, 1924; Hinton, 212–213; Scott, *Fourth Iowa Cavalry*, 336.

governor, gave a definitive number, when he wrote to the Fort Smith New Era, putting the rebel captured at 447 men, 50 lesser officers, with six senior officers, for a total of 503. And the *Missouri Democrat* reported that a total of 620 prisoners captured at Mine Creek arrived in St. Louis. However that number is suspect as at least seven of the officers (Colonel Baber, Lieutenant Colonel Love, Major Carleton, Captain Davidson, Lieutenant Curtis, Surgeon Lamkin and Lieutenant Collier) were actually captured at Westport or before and not at Mine Creek, as the newspaper reported. Further, following their arrival at St. Louis the captured officers were sent on to Johnson's Island, but "nearly all the rebel officers" escaped at Cincinnati. Captain Henry J. Biscoff, Company C, 41st Missouri Infantry was cited for incompetence for allowing the officers to escape.

Clearly Pleasonton was padding the numbers to make his accomplishments seem greater than they actually were, while the vast majority of the participants consistently reported 500–600 prisoners taken. However, there is one period newspaper, the Weston Border Times, that went so far as to declare that an astonishing 5,000 rebels were taken. This in turn encouraged one Union veteran to also put the number of captured rebels at 5,000—both of which were clearly wrong.

Of all the sources that dealt with the Confederate losses at Mine Creek, only Lumir Buresh makes a credible attempt to define the numbers, using actual Prisoner of War Lists, from the National Archives, as well as casualty reports, when available. The number of killed and wounded in battle can be realistically estimated as will be shown below; however, the number of those executed during and following the battle is nothing more than an educated guess.[3]

Executed Prisoners. Within a typical battle the ratio of killed to wounded normally runs between one to three or higher. At Pilot Knob the Confederates lost one killed for about every five wounded; at Glasgow they suffered one killed for every six; and at Westport the ratio was one killed for every

---

3 . *O.R.*, vol. 41, pt. 1:313, 341, 520; *O.R.*, vol. 41, pt. 4:288: Bray Diary, October 25, 1864; Busch, *Missouri Democrat Articles*, 256, 258, 296, 325, 329, 334, 340, 342, 401; Edwards, *Shelby and His Men*, 442; Forsyth, *Great Missouri Raid*, 214; "From Harrisonville, MO," *Missouri Republican*, November 3, 1864; "From St. Louis," *Chicago Tribune*, November 3, 1864; Hughes, "A Missouri Man's Experience;" "From the Front," *Daily Conservative*, October 28, 1864; "From St. Louis," *Chicago Tribune*, November 22, 1864; Gray, *Missouri Adjutant General Report*, 138; John W. Lanley, "After Price In Missouri," *National Tribune*, May 4, 1911; "The Late Battles With Price," *Missouri Republican*, November 4, 1864; "The Latest From Old Pap," *Fort Smith New Era*, November 5, 1864; McLarty, 56; "Price's Invasion," *Chicago Tribune*, November 3, 1864; A. B. Scholes, "Army of the Frontier How They Drove Old Price out of Missouri," *National Tribune*, March 13, 1890; Sanborn, "Campaign In Missouri," 195; H. A. Seiffert, Letter (November 19, 1864), Leighton Family Papers, Special Collection, University of Arkansas Libraries (Fayetteville); *Union Army*, 6:584; William H. Ward, "Flight of Price's Army," *National Tribune*, May 31, 1917.

three wounded. But in the case of Mine Creek the ratio, as shown by Richard Hinton and others, was a startling one killed for every one man wounded. As to the disproportionate number of killed versus wounded, Kyle Sinisi writes: "The only real explanation for the high number of Confederate killed at Mine Creek is that the vast majority were killed while trying to surrender. There is no possible way to know the exact numbers who were killed, but it is safe to say that Mine Creek ended more as a massacre and less as a battle. It was a massacre and orgy of blood."[4]

There was no official count taken of the number of rebels executed at Mine Creek, though there is plenty of evidence, from both Union and Confederate participants, that the executions took place. Even John Philips, who commanded a brigade at Mine Creek, had no difficulty admitting to the executions, recording simply that "a number" were killed. Philips justified his unit's actions stating that he was authorized to execute any rebels caught in Union uniforms. As shown in Chapter 3, General William Cabell complained to Colonel William Cloud that wounded Confederates were being killed. And Peter Brooks, of Sanborn's command, noted that even soldiers partially clad in blue were subject to execution. On October 25, Brooks recorded in his diary: "When we came over the rise we were in the rear of the brigade. I saw rebs being rounded up, men in blue coats and parts of uniforms. I know what will happen to them." And Confederate Colonel John C. Wright found himself cut off and was going to surrender. But seeing other surrendering soldiers shot down while holding their hands up, prompted Wright to make a run for it and escape.[5]

Lumir Buresh, in his book on Mine Creek, misquotes Philips, stating that "the number of prisoners executed 400;" however the correct quote is "the number of prisoners exceeded 400." Given Richard Hinton's and William Scott's comments on the number of killed, those executed numbered no more than 80; however, part of this number probably represents wounded rebels who remained on the battlefield too long and simply died from lack of care, or were consumed by prairie fires that were set by the fleeing grayclads.[6]

Confederate Prisoners Taken At Mine Creek. The number of Confederate prisoners captured is fairly clear cut as enumerated by Lumir Buresh. The following is a breakdown of rebel prisoners captured at Mine Creek, excluding those prisoners who were executed for being dressed in Union uniforms.[7]

---

4 . Sinisi, 289.
5 . *O.R.*, vol. 41, pt. 1:352; *O.R.S.*, pt. 1, vol. 7:402; Brooks Diary, October 25, 1864; Wright Memoirs, unnumbered page 98.
6 . Two days after Philips noted that he captured 400 prisoners, Philips sent a dispatch to a friend in Sedalia, telling Captain F. I. Parker that he had taken only 200 prisoners. Buresh, 228; Busch, *Missouri Democrat Articles*, 303; Hinton, 225–226.
7 . Buresh, 228–232.

Unit	POWs Mine Creek	Wounded POWs in Hospitals	Total
Fagan's Div.			
HQ/ Unattached	2	3	5
Cabell's Bde.	120	8	128
Slemons' Bde.	31	13	44
Dobbin's Bde	7	6	13
McCray's Bde	18	4	22
Total Fagan's Div.	178	34	212
Marmaduke's Div			
HQ/ Escort	2	1	3
Clark's Bde	229	34	263
Freeman's Bde.	48	5	53
Total Marmaduke's Div.	279	40	319

Total Army of Missouri (POWs) = 457 (Mine Creek column)
= 531 (including wounded)

Note: Wounded POWs in hospitals were not included in POWs Mine Creek column, but reflect those soldiers captured on October 25, who were not transported to St. Louis, but were instead sent to Ft. Scott and Mound City hospitals. Of the 81 POWs in this category, 24 eventually died, 35 were forwarded to St. Louis, while the final 22 escaped. Any other wounded POWs captured on October 25 are embraced in units not associated with the Battle of Mine Creek, but come from the other engagements later in the day.[8]

Overall the Army of Missouri lost 457 prisoners at Mine Creek, who were identified as soldiers. The army also lost 71 men who were identified as either teamsters or civilians traveling with the army. Additionally, the army lost another 25 prisoners captured from other units not engaged at Mine Creek, but were taken at either The Mounds, Little Osage or at Charlot Farm, and came from Shelby's Division (12 men), Tyler's Brigade (five men) or unattached commands (10). Adding in the civilians and POWs taken elsewhere, in the vicinity of Mine Creek gives a total of 553 (457 + 25 + 71 = 553) prisoners taken on October 25, excluding wounded prisoners which numbered 81; the grand total of POWs was 634 (553 + 81 = 634) prisoners of all types taken on October 25.[9]

For the number of killed and wounded, Lumir Buresh, uses a combination of actual reports, and estimates to come up with an estimated total of "300 or more killed, including those dying on the field and those executed." The wounded are

---

8. Ibid., 228–229.
9. In his book on Mine Creek, Buresh double counts the POW's from Marmaduke's Division headquarters, which gives him a total of 281 POW's for the division, instead of the 279 that I have listed above. Ibid., 228–232.

estimated at 228. In reviewing the data presented by Buresh in his book on Mine Creek a few adjustments could be made in the losses that he presents.[10]

* * * * * * *

Losses in Marmaduke's Division. Buresh puts the losses of Stallard's Escort at eight wounded for the Expedition, with five of these occurring at Mine Creek. This is not correct. According to a member of the escort, the command sustained five wounded at the Little Blue (October 21), which would give the command a loss of three wounded at Mine Creek.[11]

Marmaduke's Division.
Div. HQ/ Escort 0 K, 3 W, 2 M[12]

Losses in Clark's Brigade. In Clark's Brigade, Buresh has overestimated the losses in Jeffers's 8th Missouri. In his analysis, Buresh uses the overall loss of the 8th during the Expedition to obtain its loss at Mine Creek, which he estimates at nine killed and 21 wounded out of 57 total killed and wounded or 53 percent of the total losses for the entire Expedition. However, in making his estimate Buresh ignores the losses reported in the *Official Records* at Boonville (October 11), Glasgow (October 15), the Little Blue (October 21), and fails to estimate any losses for Independence (October 22) and Byram's Ford (October 23), which added together totals seven killed and 13 wounded, while Pilot Knob cost the command its greatest losses of an estimated 13 killed and 11 wounded(See Appendix E, Losses in Marmaduke's Division, for details).

At the Battle of Mine Creek the 8th was in reserve supporting Pratt's Artillery Battalion and would have suffered similar proportional losses as the 3rd Missouri which was also in reserve. At Mine Creek the 3rd Missouri lost one killed and 10 wounded. The 8th Missouri was only slightly larger than the 3rd Missouri with roughly 294 effective dismounted verses 254 or 1.16 (294 / 254 = 1.16) more officers and men (see Appendix G for details). This would suggest that the 8th lost 13 (1.16 x 11 = 12.76) killed and wounded at Mine Creek or two killed and 11 wounded. And when all the above casualties are compiled, it indicates that the 8th Missouri lost 22 killed and 35 wounded on the Expedition. This would then reduce Buresh's estimated casualties by seven killed and 10 wounded at Mine Creek.[13]

The 4th Missouri Cavalry (CSA) has a similar problem as shown under the 8th Missouri—an overestimation of losses. Buresh uses Burbridge's report on

---

10. Ibid., 233.
11. Ibid., 227.
12. The wounded includes one man who was sent to the hospital at Ft. Scott. National Archives, Record Group 94, Hospital Records (Register no. 15), Ft. Scott, Kansas.
13. *O.R.*, vol. 41, pt. 1:686, 691–692; Buresh, 225; McGhee, *Campaigning With Marmaduke*, 26.

the Expedition, where Burbridge stated that his loss at Mine Creek, "as best as I have been able to ascertain, was about 40 killed and wounded." And from this estimation Buresh assigned the losses as 13 killed with 27 wounded, based upon a ratio of two wounded for every man killed. However a closer look suggests that the losses were probably much lower.

Burbridge submitted his Expedition report, with a December 9, 1864 date, which was then used by John B. Clark to write the divisional report, which was dated December 19. In his report of losses in the 4th Missouri, Clark stated that there were 13 killed and 51 wounded for the Expedition. A review of the *Official Records* shows that the 4th lost six killed and 40 wounded at Pilot Knob and Glasgow, with an estimated loss of two killed and four wounded at Byram's Ford on October 23. This would mean that the 4th lost five (13 - 8 = 5) killed and seven (51 - 44 = 7) wounded at Mine Creek. This in turn would suggest that the 4th lost eight less killed and 20 less wounded than Buresh puts forth in his book on Mine Creek.[14]

The loss that Buresh shows for Wood's Regiment is five killed and 17 wounded; however it appears that Buresh made a error in his calculated totals. Buresh says that Wood's loss was estimated based upon "one-half of the 4th, 7th and 8th Regiments." Under Buresh's calculation the killed would be five (13 + 6 + 9 = 28 / 3 = 9.3 / 2 = 4.6); the wounded wound be 10 (27 + 12 + 21 = 60 / 3 = 20 / 2 = 10), not 17. In this case, it appears that Buresh simply missed the last division by two. Using Buresh's logic, with my new figures above, Wood's Regiment lost two (11 / 3 = 3.6 / 2 = 1.8) killed; and four (20 / 3 = 6.6 / 2 = 3.3) wounded.[15]

However, I believe there is a better way to estimate Wood's losses, based upon the losses of known units in Clark's Brigade that were in the front line and their estimated strength remaining following the Battle of Westport. The 4th, 7th and 10th Missouri Cavalries were in the front line, with Wood's command. Following the Battle of Westport these units had 1,247 (298 + 513 + 436 = 1,247) effective officers and men remaining. On October 25, they lost 22 killed and 40 wounded or 4.9 (62 / 1,247 = .049) percent of their force present. This would suggest that Woods lost 25 (506 x .049 = 24.7) killed and wounded. At a two wounded for one killed ratio this would mean a loss of eight killed and 17 wounded.[16]

Finally, I see no reason to change the values that Buresh puts forth for Pratt's Artillery Battalion. Overall this suggests that Clark's Brigade lost the following:

---

14. See also Appendix E, Losses in Marmaduke's Division and Appendix G, Losses at the Byram's Ford Front for details. O.R., vol. 41, pt. 1:692, 694.

15. Buresh, 235.

16. See also Appendix G, Marmaduke's Division, Marmaduke's Brigade. For the 4th Missouri see above calculation. *O.R.*, vol. 41, pt. 1:692, 697, 699.

Appendix H / 445

Unit	Losses (POWs)	Wounded POWs in Hospitals [Total POWs]	Total Losses
HQ/ Escort	(1)	1 [2]	2
3rd Mo. Regt.	1 K, 10 W (29)	1 [30]	41
4th Mo. Regt.	5 K, 7 W (30)	6 [36]	48
7th Mo. Regt./	6 K, 14 W (24)[17]	5 [29]	49
Davies' Bn.	(14)	1 [15]	15
8th Mo. Regt.	2 K, 11 W (16)	4 [20]	33
10th Mo. Regt.	9 K, 21 W (46)	6 [52]	82
Wood's Regt.	8 K, 17 W (46)	3 [49]	74
Pratt's Art. Bn.			
Hynson's Tx.	3 K, 6 W (1)	0 [1]	10
Harris's Mo.	2 K, 2 W (22)	7 [29]	33
Total	36 K, 88 W (229)	34 [263]	387

Freeman's Brigade. During the Expedition Freeman's command lost 27 killed and 65 wounded. Its previous engagements included Pilot Knob (September 17), Independence (October 22), and Byram's Ford (October 23). At Pilot Knob the brigade lost one killed with four wounded (see Appendix E) and at Byram's Ford it was estimated that the brigade lost five killed, with nine wounded (see Appendix G, Losses at Byram's Ford Front). Following the Battle of Independence, Freeman noted that he lost a "number of men, who were attempting to mount,"—say one third of his total losses or nine killed and 21 wounded. This would have left him 12 (27 - 15 = 12) killed and 30 (65 - 35 = 30) wounded for October 25. Buresh has a similar number stating that Freeman lost one half of his total Expedition losses at Mine Creek, which would have been 14 and 32. Note, that in his book on Mine Creek, Buresh has the wrong totals for Freeman's loss during the Expedition, recording that Freeman lost 27 killed and 61 wounded.[18]

This could be further broken down, assigning losses based upon proportional strength as follows:

Unit	EFF Strength Oct. 25	Loss On Oct. 25 (POWs) [POWs in hospital]	Total
HQ		(1)	1
Freeman's Regt.	312 (40 %)	5 K, 13 W (27)[2]	49
Fristoe's Regt.	301 (40%)	5 K, 13 W (16)[2]	37
Ford's Bn.	161 (20%)	2 K, 4 W (4)[1]	10
Total	774	12 K, 30 W (48)[5]	97

---

17. Includes the losses suffered at the Little Osage River on October 25. *O.R.*, vol. 41, pt. 1:692.
18. Buresh, 226–227; Freeman Memoir, October 23, 1864.

Notes:
1. Losses for Westport proportioned based upon unit strengths, i.e., 40 percent for Freeman and Fristoe and 20 percent for Ford.
2. Loses for Freeman calculated as five (12 x .4 = 4.8) killed and 13 (30 x .4 = 12) wounded; the same for Fristoe.
3. Losses for Ford calculated as two (12 x .2 = 2.4) killed and six (30 x .2 = 6) wounded; however, the command only lost three killed and five wounded for the entire Expedition. One additional wounded added to both Freeman and Fristoe, which leaves four wounded for Ford's Battalion, instead of the six.[19]

Summary of Losses in Marmaduke's Division.

HQ/ Escort	0 K 3 W 2 M
Clark's Brigade	36 K, 88 W, 263 M
Freeman's Brigade	12 K, 30 W, 53 M
Total	48 K, 118 W, 316 M[20]

* * * * * * *

Losses in Fagan's Division. With the exception of William Cabell's Brigade, little is known of losses suffered by Fagan's Division at Mine Creek. As such Cabell's command will serve as a blueprint for the other three brigades in Fagan's Division, by using the estimated strength of the brigade following the Battle of Westport and its reported losses at Mine Creek.

At the Battle of Westport, Cabell's Brigade suffered the loss of only three killed and nine wounded (see Appendix G, Losses from the Train Guards for details). The present effective strength of Cabell's Brigade at Mine Creek is estimated to be 2,179 (2,191 -12 = 2,179), including escort and staff. Cabell reported his loss as 40 killed and 50 wounded, which equates to 4.1 (90 / 2,179 = .041) percent of effectives present. The killed represented 44 percent of the casualties, while the wounded represented 56 percent of the losses.

Within Fagan's Division, Cabell's Brigade, by all accounts, suffered the greatest losses of the division on October 25. Slemons's Brigade, which was to the left of Cabell, would have lost half as much as Cabell or 2.05 percent, while Dobbin's Brigade, would have lost even less, probably only one percent. In the case of Dobbin, his brigade was the only one of Fagan's Division that was able to somewhat reform following the rout at Mine Creek, thus indicating that they were the least affected by the collapse of the Fagan's command. And McCray's Brigade, which was on the south

---

19 . Freeman Memoir, October 23, 1864.

20 . This does not include those prisoners who were executed. Additionally, Buresh double counts the prisoner loss in the division headquarters, which was two captured not four, which changes the number of POW's to 279 instead of 281. Buresh, 227, 230–232.

side of Mine Creek, during the battle, would have suffered only minor losses, say .5 percent of their effectives present at the battle.

Considering the above statements, the losses in Fagan's Division would be as follows:

Brigade (Strength)	Losses on Oct. 25	Prisoners on Oct. 25	Total
HQ/ Escort(145)[21]	0 K, 0 W	2 M [3]	5
Cabell's (2,179)	40 K, 50 W	120 M [8]	218
Slemons' (845)	7 K, 10 W	31 M [13]	61
Dobbin's (1,295)	6 K, 7 W	7 M [8]	28
McCray's (1,410)	3 K, 4 W	18 M [4]	29
Total	56 K, 71 W	178 M [36]	341

[ ] = Wounded In hospital at either Ft. Scott or Mound City following the battle and not embraced in the other Prisoners.

Notes:
1. Prisoners are from the National Archives records as stated in Buresh, 229–230.
2. Slemons's losses calculated as follows: EFF after Westport = 845 (888 - 43 = 845); Total Losses = 17 (845 x .0205 = 17.3) or 7 (17 x .44 = 7.48) killed and 10 wounded.
3. Dobbin's losses calculated as follows: EFF after Westport = 1,295 (1,421 - 126 = 1,295); Total Losses = 13 (1,295 x .01 = 12.95) or 6 (13 x .44 = 5.72) killed and seven wounded.
4. McCray's losses calculated as follows: EFF after Westport = 1,410 (1,417 - 7 = 1,410); Total Losses = seven (1,410 x .005 = 7.05) or three (7 x .44 = 3.1) killed and four wounded.

Buresh, for his part, combines Slemons's and Dobbin's loss as one figure, assigning their loss as 16 killed and 20 wounded, while my figures show a combined loss of 13 killed and 17 wounded. For McCray's Brigade, Buresh has the loss as four killed and eight wounded, while my estimate totals three killed and four wounded.[22]

Shelby's Division with Tyler's Brigade. Shelby's Division, with Tyler's Brigade did not fight at the Battle of Mine Creek, but was instrumental in saving the Army of Missouri from complete destruction on October 25. As shown in Chapter 3, Shelby's command conducted a rear guard action by forming a battle line, firing a volley, feigning a charge, and then withdrawing before the command became seriously engaged. "This game lasted for two or three hours," according to M. Jeff Thompson, and "after

---

21. There is no indication that Anderson's Escort Battalion was engaged at the battle, though they did lose some prisoners. Buresh, 230.
22. Ibid., 227–228.

a dozen more charges and a dozen more formations," Shelby formed his final line two miles from the Marmiton.²³

In the actions that followed, Jackman's Brigade executed a charge on the Federal line at the end of the day, losing four killed and 10 wounded. Charles Tyler's Brigade also charged the Federal line during the final combat of the day, losing 11 killed and 24 wounded. Thompson, for his part reported that his "loss was small" for the day, probably on a level with Jackman's command, say four killed and 10 wounded. Additionally, Shelby's division lost 12 prisoners, while Tyler's Brigade five.²⁴

* * * * * * *

Summary of Losses at Mine Creek and Supporting Actions

Losses at Mine Creek

Marmaduke's Division	
HQ/ Escort	0 K, 3 W, 2 M
Clark's Brigade	36 K, 88 W, 263 M
Freeman's Brigade	12 K, 30 W, 53 M
Total	48 K, 121 W, 318 M
Fagan's Division	
HQ/Escort	0 K, 0 W, 5 M
Cabell's Brigade	40 K, 50 W, 128 M
Slemons's Brigade	8 K, 10 W, 44 M
Dobbin's Brigade	6 K, 8 W, 15 M
McCray's Brigade	3 K, 4 W, 22 M
Total	<u>57 K, 72 W, 219 M</u>
Total Losses at Mine Creek	105 K, 193 W, 537 M

Supporting Actions

Shelby's Division¹	
HQ/ Escort	0 K, 0 W, 0 M
Thompson's Brigade	4 K, 10 W, 10 M
Jackman's Brigade	4 K, 10 W, 2 M
Total	8 K, 20 W, 12 M
Tyler's Brigade	11 K, 24 W, 5 M
Total Losses Supporting Actions	<u>19 K, 44 W, 17 M</u>
Total Losses on October 25	124 K, 237 W, 554 (625) M

---

23 . Hinton, 228–230, 233; Sellmeyer, 255; Stanton, et al., 256–257.
24 . *O.R.*, vol. 41, pt. 1:668, 677, 700; Buresh, 231.
1 . The losses in Thompson's Brigade is a pure guess. The brigade never charged the enemy like Jackman's command, and was only subject to long range fire for the battle. And again, according to Thompson, his "loss was small." Prisoners per Buresh. Buresh, 231.

(Missing includes 71 Teamsters and Civilians POWs).

In his account of the Battle of Mine Creek Lumir Buresh places the "Preliminary minimum figures" at 121 killed, 228 wounded, with 459 soldiers captured. He later included the wounded Confederates who were taken from the battlefield and sent to the hospitals at Ft. Scott and Mound City, Kansas, which increases the number to "about 559." The number of killed Buresh puts at "300 or more," which includes "those dying on the field and those executed." In contrast to Buresh's account, Samuel J. Crawford put the number of captives, exclusive of wounded prisoners at 503 officers and men; with the wounded it would be 584 (503 + 81 = 584); and with the teamsters the total would be 655 (584 + 71 = 655).[2]

---

2 . Ibid., 228, 233; "Latest From Old Pap," *Fort Smith New Era*, November 5, 1864.

Appendix I
Summary of Price's 1964 Missouri Expedition
Introduction

As to Price's actual physical accomplishments during his Missouri Raid, Federal sources disagreed with his findings as shown in note 175, Chapter 3, even before Price made his official report on the Expedition. The *Chicago Tribune* and the *Missouri Republican* provided similar takes on the Expedition well before the general made his conclusions known. On November 5, 1864, the *Tribune* wrote: "What Price accomplished during his raid may be summed up thus: He received 2,000 recruits, the same number of conscripts, captured about 1,500 stand of arms, paroled 2,000 prisoners, and destroyed some $5,000,000 worth of property." The *Tribune* went on to list what the Expedition had cost Price, recording that he had

> lost at least 3,000 men in battle, besides many hundreds of deserters, about fifteen pieces of artillery, 250 wagons with their spoils, and several thousand horses and small arms. He carried very little out of the state, except many horses and stolen clothing on the backs of his thieving followers. The raid has been marked more for damages to the people than benefit to the rebels.[1]

And of the devastation wrought by Price's army, the *Republican* recorded:

> The enemy have invaded the State, and remained in our borders for over thirty days. They have plundered our towns, ravaged our country, robbed, killed and carried off as prisoners our citizens; they have crippled commerce, interrupted trade, drawn to this department troops from other places where they were more needed—all this has been done and the enemy, loaded with spoils, and their ranks filled with recruits and conscripts, allowed to escape.[2]

What is the truth of the claims made by both sides as to the successes, losses, and material costs enjoyed, suffered, and inflicted by Price during his Missouri Expedition? A brief review may suffice to answer those questions.

* * * * * * *

Federal Prisoners Captured During the Expedition

During the Expedition Price claimed to have paroled 3,000 prisoners, while Federal sources put the number at 2,000. Below is an accounting of prisoners known to have been captured and paroled by the Confederate army. The list does

---

1. Occasional, "Pursuit of Price," *Missouri Republican*, November 4, 1864; "War In Missouri," *Chicago Tribune*, November 5, 1864.
2. Occasional, "Pursuit of Price," *Missouri Republican*, November 4, 1864.

include other captives of lesser numbers, that were not recorded in the *Official Records* or any other of the sources I reviewed.

- Patterson (75—September 22), Jackson (18—September 24), Farmington (14—September 25), and Pilot Knob (129—September 27), all in Missouri.[3]
- Shelby's Operations on the Iron Mountain Railroad, including Potosi (130—September 27) and Hopewell (130—September 27).[4]
- Linn (100—October 4).[5]
- Operations in Franklin County, Union (70—October 1).[6]
- Osage River Bridge (75—October 5).[7]
- Boonville (300—October 9).[8]
- Glasgow (889—October 15).[9]
- Sedalia (425—October 15).[10]
- Carrolton (300—October 17).[11]
- Big Blue (105—October 22).[12]

Total Known Prisoners Captured = 2,660

The numbers given above would seem to support General Price's assertion that he captured and paroled about 3,000 officers and men. However, of the prisoners noted above, General Rosecrans appealed to the Office Commissary-General of Prisoners, questioning the legality of the paroles issued by General Price at Pilot Knob and J. B. Clark at Glasgow. On October 23, the Commissary-General responded, vacating the paroles of those captured at Pilot Knob, and four days later he did the same for those prisoners captured by General Clark. In responding to the queries, W. Hoffman wrote: "The paroles within referred to and all others of the same character are in violation of the cartel and are null and void, and all troops so paroled should be ordered immediately to join their respective commands for duty." In a similar vein, General Rosecrans also ordered the paroles given by M. Jeff Thompson at Sedalia to be voided and ordered the men back to duty.[13]

The voiding of these various paroles would have reduced the number of captured prisoners to no more than 1,217 (2,660 - 129 -425 - 889 = 1,217) officers and

---

3. The Pilot Knob number includes all those captured at Pilot Knob or on the following retreat, including wounded. See notes 18, 20, 21, and 54, Chapter 3; Suderow, *Arcadia Valley*, 141.
4. See Appendix C, Shelby's Operations on the Iron Mountain Railroad.
5. See note 69, Chapter 3.
6. See note 57, Chapter 3.
7. "Rebels on the Pacific Railroad," *Missouri Republican*, October 7, 1864. See also note 69, Chapter 3.
8. See also note 79, Chapter 3. Sinisi, 115.
9. See Appendix F.
10. *O.R.*, vol. 41, pt. 1:670–671; Occasional, "From Sedalia," *Missouri Republican*, October 24, 1864.
11. *O.R.*, vol. 41, pt.1:634.
12. See Appendix C, note 92 for details.
13. *O.R.*, Series 2, vol. 7:1023–1024, 1051.

men. In taking this action the Commissary-General cited General Orders No. 207, dated July 3, 1863, which specified in paragraph two that only the commanders of opposing armies may give the paroles. And in the case of virtually all the captives taken by the Army of Missouri, the paroles were given by subordinate officers conducting independent operations and not General Price. This effectively voided all the paroles issued by the Army of Missouri, reducing the number of captured prisoners to zero. That said, of the 2,660 men known to have been captured by the Army of Missouri, none returned in time to participate in any other actions during the Expedition, and their weapons remained with the rebel army.[14]

* * * * * * *

Small Arms and Artillery Captured and Lost

Small Arms. During the Expedition the Army of Missouri supplied itself with numerous captured weapons as detailed below to equip its unarmed recruits. Additional weapons doubtless came from men no longer capable of bearing arms, like those killed or wounded at Pilot Knob, where the weapons would have been recovered and redistributed; however these weapons were not counted among the ones that had been captured.

- At Bloomfield, September 22, 75 small arms.
- At Potosi, September 27, Shelby captured 150 arms.
- At Pilot Knob, September 27–28, Price reported capturing "a large number of small arms," which I estimate was no more than 100.[15]
- At Union, October 1, about 100 arms.
- At Miller's Station, October 3, 400 Sharps Rifles with 800 other arms.
- At Linn, October 4, 100 arms.
- At the Osage River Bridge, October 6, 75 arms.
- At Boonville, October 9, 300 arms.
- At Glasgow, October 15, one source says 1,200 small arms were captured while another says 2,000 arms. Say 1,600 as an average.
- At Sedalia, October 15, 300 rifles and 400 pistols.
- At Carrollton, October 17, 300 arms.

Total Small Arms Captured = 4,700

While the rebel army captured a minimum of 4,700 arms, they also lost several small arms following the Battles of Westport and Mine Creek. At Westport 150 arms were reported captured from the rebels and at Mine Creek another 1,000 were taken. Additionally as the army moved southward various Federal reports talked about the "large number of small arms" that were taken from or thrown

---

14. *O.R.*, Series 2, vol. 6:78–79; *O.R.S.*, pt. 2, vol. 35: 482–482.
15. In addition to the captured weapons, 500 additional small arms were redistributed from the wounded and killed men, which aided in arming the unarmed men in the rebel army.

away by the retreating rebel army, but no numbers were given. Barring other concrete information this would suggest that Price netted about 3,550 (4,700 - 150 -1,000 = 3,550) small arms.[16]

Federal reports noted that Price crossed the Arkansas with at least 6,000 armed men on November 7 (General Magruder believed Price had only 2,000–3000 arms remaining), but failed to give an accounting of arms remaining in Dobbin's, McCray's, Freeman's and Jackman's Brigades, which were detached from the army prior to crossing the Arkansas. Assuming that these commands retained at least 2/3 of their weapons after Mine Creek, they carried a minimum of about 3,570 (5,409 x .66 = 3,570) weapons, as enumerated below. Also remember that when Jackman's Brigade left with the Expedition it only had 500 armed men, but returned with 2,000 men, "entirely armed."[17]

Unit	Strength at Westport	Losses on Oct. 23, 25	Remaining Strength
Freeman's Bde.	799	114	685
Jackman's Bde.	2,191	114	2,077
Dobbin's Bde.	1,421	155	1,266
McCray's Bde.	1,417	36	1,381
Total	5,828	419	5,409

When Price entered Missouri he came with roughly 8,000 armed men, and when he returned to Arkansas his armed men, including those who remained behind in northeast Arkansas, numbered about 9,570 (6,000 + 3,570 = 9,570) men. This would suggest that Price netted about 1,570 weapons, which was half of what he reported and nearly identical to Federal estimates.

General Magruder paints a different picture in a preliminary accounting of weapons in Price's command, stating that Price returned with 5,000–6,000 fewer small arms them when he began the Expedition. Thus Price would have returned with between 5,570 (2,000 + 3,570= 5,570) and 6,570 (3,000 + 3,570 = 6,570) arms, including those carried by the men in northeast Arkansas. This would further suggest that overall Price lost 1,430 to 2,430 small arms during the Expedition. However, not only did Magruder not consider the men who went to northeast Arkansas, he failed to consider the large number of men who were on furlough from Thompson's, Cabell's and Slemons's Brigades, and who carried their weapons home with them. Later, Magruder would acknowledge that Price had at least

---

16. See also notes 20, 21, 66, 69, 95, Chapter 3, for details and Appendix C for weapons captured at Sedalia. *O.R.*, vol. 41, pt. 1:319, 623, 627, 630–634, 652–654, 670, 680, 682, 696; Buresh, 216–217; Busch, *Missouri Democrat Articles*, 187; "From the Front," *Daily Conservative*, October 28, 1864; "From Kansas City," *Chicago Tribune*, October 24, 1864; Harrell, *Arkansas, Confederate Military History, Extended*, 442; Suderow, *Arcadia Valley*, 135; Wright Memoirs, unnumbered pages 70–71.

17. See Appendix G for the strengths and losses at Westport; also Appendix H for losses at Mine Creek. *O.R.*, vol. 41, pt. 1: 678; Busch, *Missouri Democrat Articles*, 439.

3,500 effectives (not including officers) "on hand," excluding Tyler's Brigade, which was partially armed. Allowing at least 500 small arms for Tyler's command, with an additional 500 for his officers, would suggest that Price probably netted no small arms (3,500 + 3,570 + 500 + 500 = 8,070); though that number would be much higher if all the armed, furloughed men returned with their weapons.

Overall, I suspect that when the Army of Missouri was officially reorganized and the troops incorporated into Trans-Mississippi Army in early January 1865, Price's Expedition would have shown a net gain of about 1,500 small arms. And his loss of weapons, as first perceived, would have turned into a small gain of some type. That said, clearly Price did not return with "3,000 stands of small arms," as he recorded in his official report.[18]

Artillery. During the Expedition the Army of Missouri captured Pilot Knob, securing seven heavy guns, six Woodruff light guns and two Coehorn mortars, for a total of 13 pieces of artillery and two mortars. At Herman the army captured one piece of artillery and at the Big Blue they captured one more gun; total guns captured were 15 pieces of artillery and two mortars. Of the captured guns and mortars, five were added into the Confederate Army while the rest were abandoned or destroyed. In his report of the Expedition Price reported capturing 18 pieces of artillery, of which he included mortars in the total. However, as shown above, he captured only 17 pieces of artillery including mortars, and he further failed to mention that he returned to Arkansas with only three pieces of artillery, having lost all the rest. Also, following the reoccupation of Pilot Knob, the Federal command remounted and repaired six of the heavy guns, which only needed new carriages. Thus, even though Price's comments about the captured artillery may have been basically correct, it was hardly credible, given the fact that he lost everything he had captured, plus 11 guns that he had had at the beginning of the Expedition.[19]

* * * * * * *

Confederate Prisoners Lost (Not Including Recruits or Conscripts)
Casualties Suffered, and Recruits Acquired

Prisoners Lost and Casualties Suffered. During the course of the Expedition, the Confederate army lost the bulk of its prisoners and suffered most of its killed and wounded at Independence (October 22), Westport (October 23), and Mine Creek (October 35). They also lost prisoners when they abandoned their sick and wounded following the before mentioned engagements, in addition to the wounded men left behind at the Marmiton River (October 26) and Cane Hill (November 4). Other wounded who were captured at Marias des Cygnes River and at Mine Creek, are embraced within the totals of the Battle of Mine Creek. Below is a summary of losses as listed in Appendices E (Pilot Knob), F (Glasgow), G (Westport) and H

---

18. *O.R.*, vol. 41, pt. 1:640; *O.R.*, vol. 41, pt. 4:1098, 1107–1108, 1111–1112, 1140.
19. *O.R.*, vol. 41, pt. 4:37, 138.

Appendix I / 455

(Mine Creek), in addition to Sedalia (October 15, see Appendix C) and Newtonia (October 28, see note 165, Chapter 3).

Battle	Killed	Wounded	Missing
Pilot Knob (Sept. 27)	93	456	0
Glasgow (Oct. 15)	11	69	0
Sedalia (Oct. 15)	5	13[20]	0
Westport (Oct. 23)	126	344	59
Mine Creek (Oct. 25)	124	237	554[21]
Newtonia (Oct. 28)	20	50	0
Total	379	1169	613

In addition to the numbers listed above, wounded prisoners were also captured at Pilot Knob (215—October 12), Marmiton (125—October 26) and at Cane Hill (100—November 4). These prisoners numbered about 440 and were incorporated into the number of wounded listed above. This would suggest that Price lost 379 killed, 729 wounded, 440 wounded prisoners and 613 unwounded prisoners; total prisoners would be 1,053.

Additionally losses were also suffered at several other places as enumerated in Chapter 3, including Jefferson City (October 7), Boonville (October 11–12), Lexington (October 19), Little Blue (October 21), Independence (October 22) and Big Blue (October 22), which are not embraced in the totals above.

The known losses suffered at Jefferson City totaled four killed with 14 wounded (see note 78, Chapter 3), while Boonville saw the loss of about 13 killed and 35 wounded (see notes 81 and 88, Chapter 3). Lexington losses were noted as "very slight" for the Confederates, as such it doesn't affect the overall numbers already presented. These lesser engagements cost the Confederates an estimated 17 additional killed and 49 wounded, with none missing.[22]

Other engagements are not as clear cut as these, requiring some estimation to arrive at reasonable figures. At the Little Blue (October 21), the Confederates were estimated to have suffered 100 casualties. Of the commands engaged, at the Little Blue, Marmaduke's Division had a known loss of seven killed, 58 wounded, with six missing or captured; total 71. This would suggest that Shelby's division suffered about 29 casualties. Using Marmaduke's division as a guide, 89 percent (58 / 65 = .892–missing excluded from calculation) of Shelby's casualties were wounded and 11 percent were killed. This translates into three killed (.11 x 29 = 3.19) and 26 wounded for Shelby, while the army lost an estimated 10 killed, 84 wounded, and six missing at the Little Blue.[23]

---
20. The *Missouri Republican* reported the number as 10 killed and 12 wounded. The numbers I use come from the *History of Pettis County*, 442; Occasional, "From Sedalia," October 24, 1864.
21. Not included in this figure were 71 teamsters.
22. See note 169, Chapter 3. *O.R.*, vol. 41, pt. 4:811; Sinisi, 86, 305.
23. See note 110, Chapter 3, for details.

At Independence Confederate casualties were estimated at between 100–200. Cabell's command lost 29 killed (40 + 17 = 57 / 2 = 28.5; average between conflicting Union reports; see Appendix C, Cabell's Rearguard Action, for details) and 23 prisoners; wounded are calculated at only twice the number of killed given the circumstances of how the men were killed, for a total of 58 wounded. The estimated losses in Freeman's Brigade, Marmaduke's Division, were nine killed and 21 wounded (see Appendix H, Freeman's Brigade, for details). Marmaduke's other brigade, Clark's, lost five wounded with 15 prisoners, with only Jeffers's 8th Missouri not recording his losses. Given how light the losses were in the rest of Clark's Brigade, it is estimated that Jeffers lost two killed with three wounded at Independence, as Clark reported that the losses in the 8th Missouri were "heavy" (see Appendix E, Losses In Marmaduke's Division, for details on the losses in Jeffers's Regiment). Other prisoners captured at Independence totaled three from Fagan's other brigades. Overall this would give the Confederates an estimated loss at Independence of 31 killed, 61 wounded, and 41 prisoners. These lesser reported engagements then resulted in the following estimated losses:[24]

Engagement	Losses (E)
Jefferson City (Oct. 6)	4 K, 14 W, 0 M
Boonville (Oct. 11-12)	13 K, 35 W, 0 M
Little Blue (Oct. 21)	10 K, 84 W, 6 M
Independence (Oct. 22)	31 K, 61 W, 41 M[25]
Total	58 K, 194 W, 47 M

The above numbers, excluding any unknown small skirmishes, but including all the major engagements, give a total of 437 killed, 923 wounded, 440 wounded prisoners, with 660 additional prisoners, excluding all deserters, for a total loss of 2,460 casualties. In his report on the Expedition, Price listed the loss of 1,000 prisoners, including wounded; the above numbers suggest that Price lost 1,100 prisoners, excluding deserters or conscripts, who were later captured or who tuned themselves in to Federal authorities, but including wounded, who were captured. Also keep in mind that some of the wounded were probably counted more than once, as this figure includes those slightly wounded who were again wounded at a latter date, as was noted by John Edwards, who wrote that several of the officers in Shelby's Division, were wounded more than once.[26]

For actual losses suffered by specific units during the Expedition see Appendix D. These losses fall primarily in Clark's, Freeman's, and Thompson's (or Shank's) Brigades; the rest being silent on the matter.

Recruits Gained. The number of Confederate recruits and conscripts enlisted

---

24. *O.R.*, vol. 41, pt. 4:184; Hughes, "A Missouri Man's Experience."
25. The missing include those men wounded at Lexington on October 19 and left behind in Independence, where they were captured on October 22.
26. Edwards, *Shelby and His Men*, 501–502.

in the Confederate Army of Missouri is impossible to state accurately, as no record was kept of the number, save the number that Price recorded or that can be gleaned from assorted accounts as mentioned in Appendix D, under Additions to the Army. This listing includes recruits added to the various units that began the Expedition, as well as new units that were formed from recruits and those who had no assigned unit.

New units formed from recruits include Coleman's, Davies's, Perkin's, Searcy's, Slayback's and Williams's commands. Units that obtained substantial recruits include Clark's and Thompson's Brigades, along with Elliott's and Wood's Battalions, which were increased to regiment size, as well as several lesser commands. These additions netted about 4,769 officers and men, not including unassigned recruits, who were not organized or placed into any specific units until after the Expedition. This last category numbered about 8,556 men, suggesting that the army recruited a minimum of 13,325 men. Of those, it was unknown how many actually returned to the Confederate camps in Arkansas, including those in northeast Arkansas.

However, according to Richard Hinton, who served on General Blunt's staff, the rebel army had suffered 10,056 killed, wounded, prisoners, and deserters since leaving Lexington, until they had left Cane Hill; losses prior to those dates, as shown above, are estimated at 713 killed and wounded, giving a grand total of 10,769. That said, in citing the rebel losses, Hinton claims that a Major Parrott of Price's staff gave him the information; however, there was no Major Parrott on Price's staff, though there was a Major James Parrott, who was in Wood's Missouri Battalion. Another Federal report estimated that Price's total losses of the entire Expedition numbered 13,000. This suggests that Price, at a minimum, returned to Arkansas with between 325 to 2,556 recruits, not including recruits who continued to arrive, which would have added several thousand.[27]

Of those who commented on the recruits returning to Arkansas, Governor Thomas C. Reynolds wrote that the Expedition "enabled thousands of our citizens to join our ranks," without specifying numbers. Modern authors generally ignore the issue, save for Albert Castel, who believes that Price returned with "at least 5,000" recruits, while another 2,000 joined the army during the coming months. To others, it seems not worthy of discussion. They focus instead on what Price failed to accomplish verses anything that he succeeded in, which admittedly was little.[28]

Adding the recruits who arrived after Price returned to Arkansas, I believe that a fair estimate, including newly formed units and men assigned to existing units, would be that Price netted at least the 5,000 men that he reported in his summary of the Expedition. However, the vast majority of these recruits did not make up

---

27. *O.R.*, vol. 41, pt. 1, 680; Crute, *Confederate Staff Officers*, 157–159; Hinton, 289–290; Lause, *Collapse of Price's Raid*, 188; "Letter From Ft. Gibson," *Freedom's Champion*, November 21, 1864; Sinisi, 341–343.
28. *O.R.*, vol. 41, pt. 4:1098, 1105; Castel, *Sterling Price*, 251; Schultz, 150.

for the veterans that he lost during the Expedition, though in time they could have been trained as worthwhile replacements. Overall, after taking into account the loss of roughly 1,500 killed and captured, as shown above, and not including deserters, Price gained about 3,500 men over the number with which he began the Expedition. This assumes that most of the wounded, as noted above, would have eventually returned to their commands.

****

Property Destroyed, Captured, or Stolen during Price's Missouri Expedition
(September 19–December 2, 1864)

Introduction. The amount and type of property taken by the Confederates during Price's 1864 Missouri Raid included a variety of goods, in addition to horses, cattle, and foodstuffs that the command needed for basic survival. Among the reported goods taken or stolen one finds clothing of all types, including items suited for women and children, along with household goods, such as bedding and linens. Also common was the taking of money, watches, jewelry, and "ladies' finery," such as feathers and boas. Goods that could not be taken were oftentimes destroyed or burned, such as furniture.

In many cases of the supposed pillaging and robbery, Confederate commissaries or quartermasters offered Confederate money to compensate the owners, as directed by General Price; however, in virtually all cases, the various merchants refused Confederate money, so their goods were simply confiscated.[29]

Known Losses in the Arcadia Valley

- Arcadia lost $10,000 worth of goods on September 27; Dr. McPheeters appropriated five horses and a carriage.
- Ironton had seven stores looted, losing $31,000 worth of goods on the evening of September 27. Upon reevaluation, an additional $4,000 added to goods merchants lost, "besides plundering private houses of everything valuable." Later private home losses were added that totaled $17,000. Total lost at Ironton was $42,000.
- In Pilot Knob the losses of businesses and citizens totaled $29,500 on September 27.
- Peck, Trow & Company later changed their reported losses in Pilot Knob, from $5,000 to $16,124.03, adding $11,124.03 to their total loss when the rebels took the Arcadia Valley.[30]

---

29. Busch, *Missouri Democrat Articles*, 143, 169; Crisp to McLean (October 16, 1864), Confederate Correspondence (MSS 03–26, Box 1, File 3).
30. Of those who lost property in the Arcadia Valley, four are known to have taken up arms and fought inside Fort Davidson: William Delano, C. R. [or F. T.] Peck, W. T. Leeper, and Richard

- The Pilot Knob Iron company initially reported losses of "up to $25,000," however this proved to be a misprint. The real loss was $250,000.[31]
- The Pilot Knob Iron Company also reported the loss of 100 head of horses and mules, estimated to be worth $200.00 each, or $20,000 dollars total.
- Other losses from the iron companies in the Pilot Knob area totaled $28,000 dollars, not including the money lost to the cost of rebuilding.
- "A pile of charcoal...as large as the Lindell hotel," estimated to contain 700,000–800,000 bushels, was burned, valued at $75,000.[32]
- Additional losses in Pilot Knob and Arcadia taken from private residents not included in the above, $50,000.

Total Known Losses Arcadia Valley = $525,624.03[33]

Known Losses in Franklin County, Excluding Railroads

- Richmond (Virginia Mines): 1000 pig bars of lead, noted as being "an invaluable acquisition," value unknown.
- Twelve merchants of Washington lost $38,970, while Mr. Everts, a saddler, lost everything, and two leading men "lost eleven head of horses, of choice and blooded stock." Horses valued at $200.00 each, adding $2,200 to the total, giving a result of $41,170.00.
- The Washington Brewery lost $10,795 worth of goods, including 600 barrels of beer, valued at $6,000.
- Losses re-evaluated from Washington, including four other merchants not previously known, $20,000 in additional losses.
- Merchandise lost from Franklin County was increased by $11,030 with 3,000 horses; horses valued at $200 each or $600,000 total. Overall loss of property destroyed in Franklin County was valued at $500,000, not including property or goods freely given by southern supporters.
- At Herman, on October 3: "3,000–4,000 gallons of wine and also several hundred 'greenbacks,'" value unknown.

Total Known Losses in Franklin County = $1,173,068.00[34]

Trow. "The Battle of Pilot Knob by One Who Was There;" Busch, *Missouri Democrat Articles*, 143; Fletcher, 35; Suits Against Rebels," *Forge*, January 25, 1866.

31. The losses sustained at the ironworks on Pilot Knob Mountain should not be confused with those owned by the firm Chouteau, Harrison & Valle on Iron Mountain; the latter works sustained no damage, per orders of General Price. In fact, the works continued to operate, according James Harrison, one of the owners, even while the battle progressed. Busch, *Missouri Democrat Articles*, 77–78, 319; Fusz Diary, October 2, 1864; "Late From Pilot Knob," *Missouri Republican*, October 2, 1864; Lause, *Price's Lost Campaign*, 67.
32. The *Democrat* said it was worth $80,000 while the *Republican* put the loss at $70,000, for an average of $75,000. Fletcher, 44; "Late From Pilot Knob," *Missouri Republican*, October 2, 1864.
33. Busch, *Missouri Democrat Articles*, 319–320; "From St. Louis," *Chicago Tribune*, October 15, 1864; "Late From Pilot Knob," *Missouri Republican*, October 2, 1864; "Price Certainly in Missouri," October 3, 1864.
34. It was initially reported that Franklin County had lost 2,000 horses and mules, which was later revised upward to 3,000. Additionally, by the time the Confederates had left Franklin County,

Losses to the Railroads

Note: *Chicago Tribune* values are in [ ]

Losses on the St. Louis-Iron Mountain RR:

- Loss of the Mooney Bridge, just above Victoria, value unknown.
- Loss of the DeSoto Bridge, value unknown.
Total Known Loss St. Louis-Iron Mountain RR = $300,000 (estimated).[35]

Losses on the main branch of the Pacific Railroad:

- Bailey Creek Bridge: 110 feet destroyed, $6,600.
- Boeuf Creek Bridge: 230 feet totally destroyed; it cost $13,800 in 1855.
- Big Berger Bridge: 190 feet destroyed, "Loss, $11,400."
- Cole [or Cold] Creek Bridge: 160 feet, "Total loss about $10,000" [$16,000].
- Gasconade Bridge: 759 feet, all spans destroyed, valued "at a cost of more than $45,000" [$55,000].
- Herman Creek Bridge, value unknown.
- Little Berger Bridge, 90 feet, valued at $6,000.
- Moreau Bridge, value unknown.
- Osage Bridge: 1,122 feet, five of six spans destroyed, valued at "not less than $67,000" [$70,000].
- Depots burned: Franklin ($14,000), Gray's Summit ($1,200), South Point ($1,500), Washington ($2,400), Miller's Landing ($2,000), and Herman ($2,400).
- Miscellaneous buildings, water tanks, etc., $23,500.
- Loss of RR stock "estimated at some $217,000," including 33 cars, valued at $40,000.
- Loss of an additional 12 cars, estimated value $14,500.

Note: In all, about 3,402 feet of bridges was burnt on the main line.[36]

Total Known Loss Main Branch Pacific RR = $262,300–279,300.

---

they left behind "about 1,200 broken down horses and mules, some of them marked 'C.S.,' but most of the mules were branded 'U.S.'" Further, the city of Washington originally reported the loss of $38,970 worth of goods, while a follow up report put the loss of "at least $50,000." The difference was $11,030. Busch, *Missouri Democrat Articles*, 145, 169, 178–179, 196; Gregory, 12–13, 19; *History of Franklin County*, 25; Mallinckrodt, 121; "The War In Missouri," *Chicago Tribune*, October 1, 1864.

35. *O.R.*, vol. 41, pt. 3:541, 614; "Destruction of Railroad Property," *Missouri Republican*, October 16, 1864; "From St. Louis," *Chicago Tribune*, October 20, 1864.

36. As noted above, the Moreau River Bridge was also burned, but by the 7th Missouri Cavalry (Union), to prevent its use by the rebels. Busch, *Missouri Democrat Articles*, 109–110; "Destruction of Railroad Property," *Missouri Republican*, October 16, 1864; "Rebel Destruction of Property," *Chicago Tribune*, October 12, 1864; "The War in Missouri," *Chicago Tribune*, October 6, 8 & 19, 1864.

Losses on the S.W. Branch of Pacific RR:

- Brush Creek Bridge: 110 feet, "Loss about $7,000."
- Maramec Bridge No. 1; 525 feet, two of five spans burned, "Loss $13,600."
- Maramec Bridge No. 2 (or Moselle Bridge): 865 feet, of which 380 feet were burned, "Loss some $22,800."
- Depots, "water stations," and "stationary engines": $17,500. Depots included Bourbon, Cuba, Moselle, St. Clair, and Stanton, value unknown.
- Loss of RR stock estimated "at some $55,000."
- Also lost were 15,000 cords of wood for which no value was assigned.

Note: In all about 1,020 feet of bridges burnt on the S.W. Branch.[37]

Reevaluation of bridge losses, including the loss of the Scott Bridge, the water stations, and the depots at California and Lookout recorded above added $28,600 to the value of the destroyed bridges.[38]

Total Known Losses S.W. Branch Pacific RR = $144,500

Summary of Railroad Losses:

St. Louis-Iron Mountain RR	$300,000	
S.W. Branch Pacific RR	$144,500	
Main Branch Pacific RR	$262,300	[$279,300]
Losses to business due to RR destruction	$300,000[39]	
Labor cost to repair RR	$250,000[40]	
Grand Total of Known RR Losses	$1,256,800	[$1,273,800]

Losses from Jefferson City to Boonville Areas, Including Marshall and Otterville

Destruction in Jefferson City Area, not listed above.

- Depot at Osage River Bridge, estimated value $2,000.
- Mr. McKerman's warehouse and mill, value unknown.
- Three "small bridges" over Graves or Gray's Creek on October 7, 6 miles west of city, value unknown.

Total Known Losses Jefferson City = $2,000+[41]

---

37. Busch, *Missouri Democrat Articles*, 109–110; "Rebel Destruction of Property," *Chicago Tribune*, October 12, 1864; "The War In Missouri," *Chicago Tribune*, October 19, 1864.
38. Busch, *Missouri Democrat Articles*, 131; "Destruction of Railroad Property," *Missouri Republican*, October 16, 1864.
39. "Destruction of Railroad Property," *Missouri Republican*, October 16, 1864; "War In Missouri," *Chicago Tribune*, October 19, 1864.
40. Ibid.
41. *O.R.*, vol. 41, pt. 3:645–646, 990; Busch, *Missouri Democrat Articles*, 176.

At Boonville from October 10–12, 1864:

- Roasu & Co., Millers lost 10,000 sacks of flour.
- Stephen, Bruce & Co "Livery stable was stripped of all it contained," valued at $6,000.
- M. J. Wertheimer Clothing striped of its men's clothing, valued at $5,000.
- William Harley's Co. "lost 1,000 gallons of Catwaba wine and much beer," valued at $2,000.
- John B. Miller's stock of wine…"was deliberately spilled until it stood 'shoe top' deep in the cellar."
- William Johnson Clothier lost $1,500 worth of goods. Later reevaluated to $4,300.
- Twenty-three other merchants also lost everything from food, shoes, dry goods, and clothes, valued at $41,200.
- Caleb's farm lost an assortment of products totaling about $3,000.
- "Produce in market," valued at $2,000.
- Losses from the "robbing of private houses and the taking of horses," valued at $41,300.

Known Losses at Boonville = $101,800.[42]

At Otterville on October 8–10: The Lamine Bridge, water tank, and depot; value unknown.[43]

At Marshall: Post Office and area ransacked; $136,000 worth of goods and money taken.[44]

Summary of Known Losses from Jefferson City to Boonville, Including Marshall and Otterville.

Jefferson City	$2,000+
Boonville	$101,800+
Marshall/ Otterville	$136,000+
Total	$239,800+

Known Losses at Sedalia

At Sedalia on October 15, 1864:

- Water tanks destroyed, value not stated.
- "Clothing, boots, etc." taken from Cloney, Crawford &Co., valued at $13,000.
- Five additional merchants lost $4,500.
- Government property lost valued at $8,000.
- 300 horses at $200 each for a total of $60,000.

---

42. Busch, *Missouri Democrat Articles*, 337–338; DaVal to Fagan (October 12, 1864), Confederate Correspondence (MSS 03–26, Box 1, File 3); Thoma, 141.
43. Busch, *Missouri Democrat Articles*, 189; Sellmeyer, 222.
44. Sinisi, 144.

- 20 wagons and a herd of livestock estimated at 2,000 head of cattle and sheep, value unknown.

Total Known Loss at Sedalia = $85,500[45]

Known Losses at Glasgow

Losses suffered at Glasgow on October 15, 1864, as a result of a fire and goods taken (as reported by the *Missouri Republican):*

- Seven assorted business and private houses burned, including contents, valued at $36,600.
- Boone, Borstrick & Co. wholesale mercantile business, with contents, valued at $50,000 [$40,000].
- The City Hall burned, valued at $20,000.
- 50,000 rations burned in City Hall, $30,000.
- Four other buildings burned, value unknown.
- Tobacco Factory of Lewis & Brothers, lost goods valued at $40,000 or $50,000.
- Tobacco factory of William Spear & Co., lost goods valued at $25,000.
- Government property such as uniforms, blankets, with commissary and quartermaster stores lost, valued at $30,000.00.
- Five hundred rebel women, from the local area descended upon Glasgow, following its capture to loot the local stores. "They helped themselves freely to hoop skirts, bonnets, shawls, ribbons, laces etc.... They laid in their winter supplies, and dry goods...The rebel soldiers held the town while these squaws were engaged in their work of plunder and made no effort to prevent it." Value lost unknown.

Total Known Losses at Glasgow = $231,000 [$241,000.][46]

Summary of Known Losses in Missouri during Price's 1864 Missouri Raid in Property Destroyed, Captured, or Stolen

Arcadia Valley	$525,624.03
Franklin County	$1,173,068.00
Railroads	$1,273,800.00
Jefferson City, etc.	$239,800.00
Sedalia	$85,500.00
Glasgow	$231,000.00
Total	$3,528,792.03

---

45. Busch, *Missouri Democrat Articles*, 163; "From St. Louis," *Chicago Tribune*, October 22, 1864; Occasional, "From Sedalia," *Missouri Republican*, October 24, 1864.

46. The loss at the tobacco factory was estimated as $40,000, by the *Missouri Democrat*, while James Denny says it was $50,000. "Attack Upon Glasgow," *Missouri Republican*, October 21, 1864; Busch, *Missouri Democrat Articles*, 201–202, 309; Denny, 23.

The overall loss suffered by Missourians and Kansans was obviously much higher than has been presented above. There were also several other bridges destroyed of unknown value, as well as huge numbers of horses, livestock, and quantities of foodstuffs that were taken to sustain the army, other than that enumerated above, for which there is no associated value. Also, according to most Union newspaper accounts and many Confederates accounts, "every little town" that the Army of Missouri entered was subsequently sacked. This would include cities like Lexington, Dover, Waverly, Potosi, Richwoods, Patterson, Fredericktown, and Union, as well as many others, which would have added significantly to the above totals. Also not included, as noted by the *Missouri Republican*, was the economic impact on the state, including lost business and man hours worked. As such, $5,000,000 must be accepted as the minimum loss experienced by Missouri (not including Kansas) during Price's invasion, with $10,000,000, as recorded by Price, being very possible when all factors are fully known.

* * * * * * *

Closing Comments on Price's Raid

When General Price began his Expedition, lofty goals were set by both himself and his Department commander, E. Kirby Smith. General Smith tasked Price to capture St. Louis, which Price failed to do. Next, General Smith was looking for an infusion of new recruits and supplies to build up the Army of the Trans-Mississippi, for which Price reported that he had recruited 5,000 men when he returned to Arkansas; and in this goal Price had some measure of success, as seen above. In addition to Smith's objectives, Price added his own goals to be accomplished, including the capture of Jefferson City and the reinstatement of Thomas Reynolds as governor of Missouri, in which Price failed. Additionally, though not intended, the *Missouri Republican* credited Price's invasion for "carrying the State for Lincoln and Fletcher," the Radical candidate for Missouri governor in the November elections. Price also intended, by most accounts, to winter in Missouri, thus reestablishing a permanent presence in the state; and again he failed.[47]

Overall the grand goals that were set for the Expedition were a failure. However there was one positive, unintended item that Price accomplished: he drew A. J. Smith's 16th Corps to the Trans-Mississippi, thus delaying operations against Mobile, Alabama. However this has been seen as a minor accomplishment by most authorities on the subject of the Expedition.

Of Price's material accomplishments, he did secure numerous recruits, while wreaking havoc on the Missouri economy; however, the cost to his army was far greater than he surely intended. He began the Expedition with 250 wagons but returned with less than 50; he left with 14 pieces of artillery and returned with but three; he left with 8,000 armed men and returned with about the same, but instead

---

47. "Price's Late invasion," *Missouri Republican*, November 15, 1864.

of a cohesive, veteran army, they were a disorganized, scattered mob, having lost many seasoned troops and half their horses.

In summing up the Expedition, there were numerous comments written by the participants. James T. Alexander of General Fagan's staff, who had high hopes for the Expedition when it began, also saw the danger in having General Price, an infantry commander, leading the army. And the disaster that Alexander feared came to pass, for even as the Expedition was drawing to a close he recorded: "suffice it to say that it is one of the most disastrous of the whole war."[48]

Governor Thomas Reynolds, who was no supporter of Price and demanded that Jefferson Davis dismiss Price from the service following the Expedition, made this assessment:

> Though the expedition has failed to accomplish the grander objects aimed at, yet the good results inevitable under even the worse management, have been obtained. It produced some diversion in favor of Forrest, and enabled thousands of our citizens to join our ranks; some came out with the army and others are gradually finding their way to our lines. Thus the army of the department is really stronger than ever.[49]

And Colonel Samuel J. Crawford, who was elected governor of Kansas following the Expedition, called the raid "ill-advised" and went on to record that: "The Price Raid was a stupendous blunder from the beginning. It tarnished the record of General Price, both as a man and a soldier, and wiped his army out of existence."[50]

Thus ended the "Great Missouri Raid" that, in the end, "For the Federals," according to Michael Forsyth, "amounted to little more than an irritant to their cause."[51]

---

48. J. T. Alexander, Letter (November 12, 1864).
49. On December 14, Governor Reynolds address a letter to General Price stating that he was sending a "memoir" to Jefferson Davison, requesting that Price "cease to be an officer in the Confederate States." Reynolds to Price (December 14, 863), Confederate Correspondence (MSS 03–26, Box 1, File 4); Schultz, 150.
50. Crawford, *Kansas in the Sixties*, 179, 181.
51. Forsyth, *Great Missouri Raid*, 135.

Bibliography

Books/Pamphlets/Articles

Abel, Annie Heloise. *The American Indian in the Civil War, 1862-1865*. Cleveland, OH: A. H. Clark Co., 1919. Reprint. Lincoln, NE: University of Nebraska Press, 1992.

Adamson, Hans Christian. *Rebellion in Missouri: 1861 Nathaniel Lyon and His Army of the West*. Rahway, NJ: Quinn & Boden Company, 1961.

Alberts, Don E., ed. *Rebels of the Rio Grande: The Civil War Journal of A. B. Peticolas*. Albuquerque, NM: University of New Mexico Press, 1984.

Album, Portraits of Companions of the Commandery of the State of Illinois, Military Order of the Loyal Legion of the United States. Chicago, 1892. Reprint. Wilmington, NC: Broadfoot Publishing Co., 1993.

Allardice, Bruce S. *Confederate Colonels: A Biographical Register*. Columbia, MO: University of Missouri Press, 2008.

———. *More Generals in Gray*. Baton Rouge, LA: Louisiana State University Press, 1995.

Allen, Desmond Wall. *Arkansas' Dammed Yankees: An Index to Union Soldiers in Arkansas Regiments*. Conway, AR: n.p., 1987.

———. *Index to Arkansas Confederate Pension Applications*. Conway, AR: Arkansas Research, 1991.

———. *Turnbo's Tales of the Ozarks: War and Guerrilla Stories. Revised Edition*. Conway, AR: n.p., 1989.

Anderson, Ephraim McD. *Memoirs: Historical and Personal; Including the Campaigns of the First Missouri Confederate Brigade*. St. Louis: Times Printing Co., 1868. Reprint. Dayton, OH: Morningside Bookshop, 2005.

Ankesheiln, Wade. *Eight-Hundred Voices: Each with a Story to Tell. A Guide to the Confederate Memorial Cemetery Missouri Historical Site Higginsville, Missouri*. 2 vols. Independence, MO: Two Trails Publishing, 2009.

———. *The Last Guardsmen*. Independence, MO: Two Trails Publishing, 2008.

Anonymous. Bartels, Carolyn M. and James E. McGhee, eds. *The Gallant Breed the 5th Missouri Cavalry: A Roster of the Men Who Rode Under the Flag of Shelby's Iron Brigade*. Independence, MO: Two Trails Publishing, 2009.

———. *The Gallant Breed. The 6th Missouri Cavalry: A Roster of the Men Who Rode Under the Flag of Shelby's Iron Brigade*. Independence, MO: Two Trails Publishing, 2009.

———. *The Gallant Breed. The 12th Missouri Cavalry: A Roster of the Men Who Rode Under the Flag of Shelby's Iron Brigade*. Independence, MO: Two Trails Publishing, 2009.

Arthur, Anthony. *General Jo Shelby's March*. New York: Random House, 2010.

Bailey, Anne J. and Daniel Sutherland, gen. eds. *Civil War Arkansas: Beyond Battles and Leaders*. Fayetteville, AR: The University of Arkansas Press, 2000.

Bailey, Anne J. *Between the Enemy and Texas: Parsons's Texas Cavalry in the Civil War*. Fort Worth, TX: Texas Christian University Press, 1989.

Baker, T. Lindsay, ed. *Confederate Guerrilla: The Civil War Memoir of Joseph Bailey*. Fayetteville, AR: The University of Arkansas Press, 2007.

Banasik, Michael E. *Cavaliers of the Brush: Quantrill and His Men*. Unwritten Chapters of the Civil War West of the River, Volume V. Iowa City, IA: Camp Pope Publishing, 2003.

———. *Confederate "Tales of the War" In the Trans-Mississippi Part One: 1861*. Unwritten Chapters of the Civil War West of the River, Volume VII. Iowa City, IA: Camp Pope Publishing, 2010.

———. *Confederate "Tales of the War" In the Trans-Mississippi Part Two: 1862*. Unwritten Chapters of the Civil War West of the River, Volume VII. Iowa City, IA: Camp Pope Publishing, 2011.

———. *Confederate "Tales of the War" In the Trans-Mississippi Part Three: 1863*. Unwritten Chapters of the Civil War West of the River, Volume VII. Iowa City, IA: Camp Pope Publishing, 2012.

———. *Confederate "Tales of the War" In the Trans-Mississippi Part Four: 1864*. Unwritten Chapters of the Civil War West of the River, Volume VII. Iowa City, IA: Camp Pope Publishing, 2015.

———. *Duty, Honor and Country: The Civil War Experiences of Captain William P. Black, Thirty-seventh Illinois Infantry*. Unwritten Chapters of the Civil War West of the River, Volume VI. Iowa City, IA: Camp Pope Publishing, 2006.

———. *Embattled Arkansas: The Prairie Grove Campaign of 1862*. Wilmington, NC: Broadfoot Publishing Company, 1996.

———. *Missouri Brothers in Gray: The Reminiscences and Letters of William J. Bull and John P. Bull.* Unwritten Chapters of the Civil War West of the River, Volume I. Iowa City, IA: Camp Pope Publishing, 1998.

———. *Missouri in 1861: The Civil War Letters of Franc B. Wilkie, Newspaper Correspondent.* Unwritten Chapters of the Civil War West of the River, Volume IV. Iowa City, IA: Camp Pope Publishing, 2001.

———. *Reluctant Cannoneer: The Diary of Robert T. McMahan of the Twenty-fifth Independent Ohio Light Artillery.* Unwritten Chapters of the Civil War West of the River, Volume II. Iowa City, IA: Camp Pope Publishing, 2000.

———. *Serving With Honor: The Diary of Captain Eathan Allen Pinnell of the Eighth Missouri Infantry (Confederate).* Unwritten Chapters of the Civil War West of the River, Volume III. Iowa City, IA: Camp Pope Publishing, 1999.

Barkley, Roy R. and Mark F. Odintz. *Portable Handbook of Texas.* Austin: The Texas State Historical Association, 2000.

Barney, William L. *The Oxford Encyclopedia of the Civil War.* New York: Oxford University Press, Inc., 2001.

Bartels, Carolyn M. *Battle of Pilot Knob as told by Dr. Seymour Carpenter: An Eyewitness Account by a Participant.* Independence, MO: Two Trails Publishing, 1995.

———. *Civil War Stories of Missouri.* Shawnee Mission, KS: Two Trails Publishing, 1995.

———. *Elliot's Scouts 9th Missouri Cavalry Battalion.* Independence, MO: Two Trails Publishing, 2005

———. *The Forgotten Men: The Missouri State Guard.* Shawnee Mission, KS: Two Trails Publishing, 1995.

———. *Iowa Boy Makes Good: Dr. Seymour D. Carpenter, Lieutenant-Colonel in the War for the Union, Medical Director of the Department of Missouri.* Shawnee Mission, KS: Two Trails Genealogy Bookshop & Publishing, 1996.

———. *Missouri Confederate Surrender: New Orleans & Shreveport May–June 1865.* Independence, MO: Two Trails Publishing, 1991.

———. *Trans-Mississippi Men at War, Volume I: Missouri C.S.A.* Independence, MO: Two Trails Publishing, 1998.

———. *True Tales: Civil War in Missouri.* Independence, MO: Two Trails Publishing, 2002.

Barton, O. S. *Three Years with Quantrill: A True Story Told by His Scout John McCorkle.* Armstrong, MO: Armstrong Herald Print, 1914. Reprint. Norman, OK: University of Oklahoma Press, 1992.

Bearss, Edwin C. and Arrell M. Gibson. *Fort Smith: Little Gibraltar on the Arkansas.* Norman, OK: University of Oklahoma Press, 1969. Reprint. Norman, OK: University of Oklahoma Press, 1979.

———. "The Battle of Helena, July 4, 1863." *Arkansas Historical Quarterly* 20 (Autumn 1961): 256–295.

———. *Steele's Retreat from Camden and the Battle of Jenkins' Ferry.* Little Rock, AR: Pioneer Press, 1966.

Bevier, R. S. *History of the First and Second Missouri Confederate Brigades 1861–1865. And From Wakarusa to Appomattox, A Military Anagraph.* St. Louis: Bryan, Brand & Company, 1879.

Bishop, Albert W. *Loyalty on the Frontier or Sketches of Union Men of the Southwest, With Incidents and Adventures in Rebellion on the Border.* St. Louis: E. P. Studley and Co., 1863.

Blessington, Joseph Palmer. *The Campaigns of Walker's Texas Division.* New York: Lange, Little & Co., Printers, 1875.

Block, William Neil. *Shades of Gray: Confederate Soldiers and Veterans of Randolph County, Missouri.* Shawnee Mission, KS: Two Trails Genealogy Shop, 1996.

Blunt, James G. "General Blunt's Account of His Civil War Experiences." *The Kansas Historical Quarterly* 1 (May 1932): 211–265.

Boatner III, Mark Mayo. *The Civil War Dictionary.* New York: David McKay Company, Inc., 1959.

Boggs, Karen Carmichael and Louise Muir Coutts. *Howard County Cemetery Records.* N.p.: n.d.

Borland, Wm. P. "General Jo. O. Shelby." *Missouri Historical Review* 7 (October 1912): 10–19.

Boswell, Evault. *Texas Boys in Gray.* Plano, TX: Republic of Texas Press, 2000.

Box, Sam. "End of the War—Exiles in Mexico." *Confederate Veteran* 11 (March 1903): 121–123.

Bradley, W. H. "Shelby's Expedition into Mexico." *Confederate Veteran* 22 (December 1914): 551–552.

———. "Through Mexico in 1865." *Confederate Veteran* 23 (July 1918): 311–315.

Breihan, Carl W. *Sam Hildebrand, Guerrilla*. Wauwatosa, WI: Leather Stocking Books, 1984.

Britton, Wiley. *The Civil War on the Border: A Narrative of Military Operations in Missouri, Kansas, Arkansas, and the Indian Territory, During the Years 1861–62, Based Upon Official Reports of the Federal Commanders, etc., Volume 1*. New York: G. P. Putnam's Sons, 1899.

———. *The Civil War on the Border: A Narrative of Military Operations in Missouri, Kansas, Arkansas, and the Indian Territory, During the Years 1863–65, Based Upon Official Reports and Observations of the Author, Volume 2*. New York: G. P. Putnam's Sons, 1899.

———. *Memoirs of the Rebellion on the Border, 1863*. Chicago, IL: Cushing, Thomas & Co., Publishers, 1882. Reprint. Florissant, MO: Inland Printer Limited, 1986.

———. *The Union Indian Brigade in the Civil War*. Kansas City, MO: Franklin Hudson Publishing Co., 1922.

Brock, R. A., ed. *Southern Historical Society Papers*. 52 vols. Richmond, VA: Southern Historical Society, 1876–1959. Reprint. Wilmington, NC: Broadfoot Publishing Company, 1990–1992.

Brooksher, William Riley. *Bloody Hill: The Civil War Battle of Wilson's Creek*. Washington, DC: Brassey's, 1995.

Brown, D. Alexander. "The Battle of Westport." *Civil War Times Illustrated* 5 (July 1966): 4–11, 40–45.

Brugioni, Dino A. *The Civil War in Missouri As Seen From the Capital City*. Jefferson City, MO: Summers Publishing, 1987.

Buresh, Lumir. *October 25th and the Battle of Mine Creek*. Kansas City, MO: The Lowell Press, 1977.

Burke, W. S. *Official Military History of Kansas Regiments during the War for* the *Suppression of the Great Rebellion*. Leavenworth, KS: W. S. Burke, 1870. Reprint. Ottawa, KS: Kansas Heritage Press, n.d.

Busch, Walter E. *Fort Davidson and the Battle of Pilot Knob: Missouri's Alamo*. Charleston, SC: History Press, 2010.

———. *General Sterling Price's Great Missouri Raid: The Missouri Democrat Articles*. Jefferson City, MO: Missouri Department of Natural Resources, 2010.

———. *General, You Have Made the Mistake of Your Life*. Independence, MO: Two Trails, 2004.

Byers, S. H. M. *Iowa in War Times*. Des Moines: W. D. Conduit & Co., 1888.

Callahan, Edward W. *List of Officers of the Navy of the United States and of the Marine Corps, From 1775 to 1900, etc.* New York: L. R. Hamersly & Co., 1901.

"Capt. James Kennedy." *Confederate Veteran* 36 (January 1828): 25.

Castel, Albert. *A Frontier State at War: Kansas, 1861–1865*. Ithaca, NY: Cornell University Press, 1958. Reprint. Westport, CT: Greenwood Press, 1979.

———. *General Sterling Price and the Civil War in the West*. Baton Rouge, LA: Louisiana State University Press, 1968.

Castro, David E. *Arkansas Late in the Civil War: The 8th Missouri Volunteer Cavalry, April 1864–July 1865*. Charleston, SC: The History Press, 2013.

Cater, Douglas John. *As It Was: Reminiscences of a Soldier of the Third Texas Cavalry and the Nineteenth Louisiana Infantry*. Austin, TX: State House Press, 1990.

Clarke, Norman E., Sr., *Warfare along the Mississippi: The Letters of Lieutenant Colonel George E. Currie*. Ann Arbor, MI: Central Michigan University, 1961.

The Civil War in Ripley County, Missouri. Doniphan, MO: The Prospect News, 1992.

Coggins, Jack. *Arms and Equipment of the Civil War*. Wilmington, NC: Broadfoot Publishing Company, 1987.

Cole, Birdie Haile. "The Battle of Pilot Knob." *Confederate Veteran* 22 (September 1914): 417.

Coleman, R. B. "Various Small fights in Missouri." *Confederate Veteran* 14 (March 1906): 120–121.

Collins, Robert. *General James G. Blunt: Tarnished Glory*. Gretna, LA: Pelican Publishing Company, 2005

Donnelley, William. *Life of Preston B. Plumb*. Chicago: Browne, & Howell, Company, 1913.

Cottrell, Steve. *Civil War in the Indian Territory*. Gretna, LA: Pelican Publishing Company, 1995.

Crandall, Warren Daniel and Denison Newell. *History of the Ram Fleet and the Mississippi Marine Brigade in the War for the Union on the Mississippi and Its Tributaries*. St. Louis, MO: Buchart Brothers, 1907.

Crawford, Mark J. *Confederate Courage on Other Fields: Four Lesser Known Accounts of the War Between the States*. Jefferson, NC: McFarland & Company, Publishers, 2000.

Crawford, Samuel J. *Kansas in the Sixties*. Chicago: A. C. McClurg & Company, 1911.

Creel, George. *Rebel at Large: Recollections of Fifty Crowded Years*. New York: G. P. Putnam's Sons, 1947.

Crowley, William. *Tennessee Cavalier in the Missouri Cavalry: Major Henry Ewing, C.S.A., of the St. Louis Times. A Biographical Sketch*. Columbia, MO: Kelly Press, Inc., 1978.

Crute, Joseph H. *Confederate Staff Officers 1861–1865*. Powhatan, VA: Dewent Books, 1982.

———. *Units of the Confederate States Army*. Midlothian, VA: Derwent Books, 1987.

Cunningham, Frank. *General Stand Watie's Confederate Indians*. San Antonio, TX: The Naylor Company, 1959.

Cutrer, Thomas W., ed. "'An Experience in Soldier's Life': The Civil War Letters of Volney Ellis, Adjutant Twelfth Texas Infantry Walker's Texas Division, C.S.A.." *Military History of the Southwest* 22 (Fall 1992): 109–172.

Darr, John C. "Price's Raid in Missouri." *Confederate Veteran* 11 (August 1903): 359–362.

Davis, Edwin Adam. *Fallen Guidon: The Saga of Confederate General Jo Shelby's March to Mexico*. College Station, TX: Texas A & M University Press, 1995.

———. *Heroic Years: Louisiana in the War for Southern Independence*. Baton Rouge, LA: Vail-Ballou Press, Inc., 1964.

Davis, William C., ed. *The Confederate General*. 6 vols. Harrisburg, PA: National Historical Society, 1991.

Dawson III, Joseph G., ed. *The Louisiana Governors: From Iberville to Edwards*. Baton Rouge, LA: Louisiana State University Press, 1990.

Denny, James M. *The Battle of Glasgow, Missouri*. Independence, MO: Blue & Grey Bookshope, 2001.

Dorsey, Sarah A. *Recollection of Henry Watkins Allen, Brigadier General Confederate States Army, Ex-Governor of Louisiana*. New York: M. Dallied, 1866.

Dougherty, Kevin J. *Encyclopedia of the Confederacy*. San Diego, CA: Thunder Bay Press, 2010.

Draper, John Ballard. *William Custis Ballard: His Ancestors and Descendants*. TX: By author, 1979.

Dyer, F. H. *A Compendium of the War of the Rebellion*. Des Moines, IA, 1908. Reprint. Dayton, OH: Morningside Bookshop, 1978.

Eakin, Joanne C. and Donald R. Hale. *Branded as Rebels: A List of Bushwhackers, Guerrillas, Partisan Rangers, Confederates and Southern Sympathizers from Missouri During the War Years*. Independence, MO: Wee Print, 1993.

Eakin, Joanne C. *Battle of Blackwater River Milford, Johnson County, Missouri, on December 19, 1861, Including a List of 736 Captured*. Independence, MO: 1995.

———. *Battle of Independence, August 11, 1862*. Independence, MO: Two Trails Publishing, 2000.

———. *Battle of Lone Jack, August 16, 1862*. Independence, MO: Two Trails Publishing, 2001.

———. *Confederate Records from the United Daughters of the Confederacy Files*. 8 vols. Independence, MO: Two Trails Publishing, 1995–2001.

———. *The Little Gods: Union Provost Marshals in Missouri, 1861–1865*. Shawnee Mission, KS: Two Trails Genealogy Shoppe, 1996.

———. *Missouri Prisoners of War From Gratiot Prison & Myrtle Street Prison, St. Louis, Mo. and Alton Prison, Alton Illinois Including Citizens, Confederates, Bushwhackers and Guerrillas*. Independence, MO: Two Trails Publishing, 1995.

———. *Warren Welch Remembers: A Guerrilla Fighter from Jackson County, Missouri*. Independence, MO: Two Trails Publishing, 1997.

Edwards, Jennie. *John N. Edwards Biography, Memoirs, Reminiscences and Recollections and Also A Reprint of Shelby's Expedition to Mexico An Unwritten Leaf of the War*. Kansas City, MO: Jennie Edwards, 1889.

Edwards, John Newman. *Noted Guerrillas, or the Warfare of the Border*. St. Louis: Bryan, Brand & Company, 1877. Reprint. Dayton, OH: Morningside Bookshop, 1976.

———. *Shelby and His Men, or the War in the West*. Cincinnati, OH, 1867: Reprint. Waverly, MO: General Joseph Shelby Memorial Fund, 1993.

Edwards, Witt. *The Prairie Was on Fire: Eyewitness Accounts of the Civil War in the Indian Territory*. Oklahoma City, OK: Oklahoma Historical Society, 2001.

"Escape From Fort Davidson." *Civil War Times illustrated* 13 (April, 1974): 30–31.

Etcheson, Nicole. *Bleeding Kansas: Contested Liberty in the Civil War Era*. Lawrence, KS: University of Kansas Press, 2004.

Evans, Clement A., ed. *Confederate Military History*. 13 Vols. Atlanta, 1899. Reprint. Secaucus, NJ: Blue & Gray Press, 1974.

Evans, Clement A. and Robert S. Bridgers, eds. *Confederate Military History Extended Edition*. 19 Vols. Atlanta, 1899. Reprint. Wilmington, NC: Broadfoot Publishing Company, 1987.

Ewing, Thomas. "Battle of Pilot Knob and Leesburg, Missouri." *Rebellion Record*, 11:135–139. See under Moore, Frank.

Faust, Patricia L., ed. *Historical Times Illustrated Encyclopedia of the Civil War*. New York: Harper Perennial, 1986.

Fellman, Michael. *Inside War: The Guerrilla Conflict in Missouri During the American Civil War*. New York: Oxford University Press, 1989.

Ferguson, John L. *Arkansas and the Civil War*. Little Rock, AR: Pioneer Press, 1965.

Ferguson, John L. and J. H. Arkinson. *Historic Arkansas*. Little Rock, AR: Arkansas History Commission, 1966.

Fletcher, Thomas C. "The Battle of Pilot Knob, and the Retreat to Leasburg." in *War Papers and Personal Reminiscences. 1861–1865. Read Before the Commandery of the State of Missouri, Military Order of the Loyal Legion of the United States*. St. Louis: Becktold & Co., 1892. Reprint. Wilmington, NC: Broadfoot Publishing Company, 1992. Vol. 14: 29–53.

Forsyth, Michael J. *The Camden Expedition of 1864 and the Opportunity Lost by the Confederacy to Change the Civil War*. Jefferson, NC: McFarland & Company, Inc., 2003.

———. *The Great Missouri Raid: Sterling Price and the Last Major Confederate Campaign in Northern Territory*. Jefferson, NC: McFarland & Company, Inc., 2015.

Fowler, W. T. "A Missouri Boy's Experience." *Confederate Veteran* 40 (December 1922): 432–435.

Franks, Kenny A. *Stand Watie and the Agony of the Cherokee Nation*. Memphis, TN: Memphis State University Press, 1979.

Frazier, Margaret Mendenhall. *Missouri Ordeal 1862–1864: Diaries of Willard Hall Mendenhall*. New Hall, CA: Carl Boyer, 1985.

Fremantle, Arthur J. L. *Three Months in the Southern States, April–June 1863*. New York: John Bradburn, 1864. Reprint. Lincoln, NB: University of Nebraska Press, 1991.

Frost, Griffin. *Camp and Prison Journal*. Quincy, IL: Quincy Herald Book and Job Shop, 1867. Reprint. Iowa City, IA: Press of the Camp Pope Bookshop, 1994.

Fry, Alice L. *Following the Fifth Kansas Cavalry: The Letters*. Independence, MO: Two Trails Publishing, 1998.

Furry, William, ed. *The Preacher's Tale: The Civil War Journal of Rev. Francis Springer, Chaplain, U.S. Army of the Frontier*. Fayetteville, AR: University of Arkansas Press, 2001.

Gage, G. G. *The Battle of the Blue of the Second Regiment K.S.M. October 22,*

1864. The Fight. The Captivity. The Escape. Chicago: W.T.P.A., n.d.. Reprint. Shawnee Mission, KS: Two Trails Publishing, n.d.

Gallaway, B. P. *The Ragged Rebel: A Common Soldier in W. H. Parsons' Texas Cavalry, 1861–1865.* Austin, TX: University of Texas Press, 1988.

Gaughan, T. J., ed. *Letters of a Confederate Surgeon.* Camden, AR: The Hurley Co., Inc., 1960.

Geer, Gene, ed. "'Up and In Line at Day Break; Considerable Skirmish.' The Taylor Bray Diary, September 27, 1864–July 5, 1865." *White River Historical Quarterly* 1 (Summer 1964): 2–15.

Gerteis, Louis S. *Civil War St. Louis.* Lawrence, KS: University Press of Kansas, 2001.

Gibbons, Tony. *Warships and Naval Battles of the Civil War.* New York: W. H. Smith Publishers, Inc., 1989.

Gibson, J. W. (Watt). *Recollections of a Pioneer.* St. Joseph, MO: The Press of Nelson-Hanna, 1912. Reprint. Independence, MO: Two Trails Publishing, 1999.

Gifford, Douglas L. *Where Valor and Devotion Met: The Battle of Pilot Knob.* Winfield, MO: Historynutt Books, 2014.

Gilmore, Donald L. *Civil War on the Missouri-Kansas Border.* Gretna, LA: Pelican Publishing Company, 2006.

Goff, April and John Tarbell, eds. *Traveled Through a Fine Country: The Journal of Captain Henry Brockman Company K, 10th Missouri Volunteer Infantry, C.S.A.* Little Rock, AR: Arkansas History Commission, 2011.

Goff, William A. "Captain Dick Yeager, Guerrilla." *The Westport Historical Quarterly* 9 (December 1973): 80–86

———. "Captain Dick Yeager, Guerrilla." *The Westport Historical Quarterly* 11 (March 1974): 96–116.

Goodrich, Thomas. *Black Flag: Guerrilla Warfare on the Western Border, 1861–1865.* Bloomington, IN: Indiana University Press, 1995.

Gregory, Ralph. *Price's Raid in Franklin County, Missouri.* Washington, MO: Washington Missourian, 1990.

Grover, Geo. S. "The Price Campaign of 1864." *Missouri Historical Review* 6 (July 1912): 167–181.

Hale, Donald R. *Branded as Rebels, Volume 2*. Independence, MO: Blue & Grey Book Shoppe, 2003.

———. *Jackson County and the Civil War*. Independence, MO: Blue & Grey Book Shoppe, n.d.

Hale, Douglas. *The Third Texas Cavalry in the Civil War*. Norman, OK: University of Oklahoma Press, 1993

Halliburton, J. W. "That Charge." *Confederate Veteran* 28 (July 1920): 264.

Hanna, H. L., ed. *The Press Covers the Invasion of Arkansas, 1862-Vol. 2 July–December*. Widener, AR: Southern Heritage Press, 2012.

Hansen, Duncan E. *A Reunion in Death: Grave Sites of the Men Who Rode With William Clarke Quantrill*. 3 Vols. Volume 1, Independence, MO: Two Trails Publishing, 2002. Volumes 2 and 3. Harrisonville, MO: Burnt District Press LLC & Carolyn M. Bartels, 2013.

Harrison, Jon, ed. "The Confederate Letters of John Simmons." *The Chronicles of Smith County, Texas* 14 (Summer 1975): 25–57.

Hearn, Chester G. *Ellet's Brigade: The Strangest Outfit of All*. Baton Rouge, LA: Louisiana State University Press, 2000.

Heidler, David S. and Jeanne T. Heidler, eds. *Encyclopedia of the American Civil War: A Political, Social, and Military History*. New York: W. W. Norton & Company, 2000.

Heitman, Francis B. *Historical Register and Dictionary of the United States Army from Its Organization, September 29, 1789, to March 2, 1903*. 2 vols. Washington: Government Printing Office, 1903. Reprint. Gaitherburg, MD: Olde Soldiers Books Inc., 1988.

Hewett, Janet, ed. *The Roster of Confederate Soldiers 1861–1865*. 16 vols. Wilmington, NC: Broadfoot Publishing Company, 1995–1996.

———, ed. *Supplement to the Official Records of the Union and Confederate Armies*. 100 vols. Wilmington, NC: Broadfoot Publishing Company, 1994–2001.

Hickman, W. Z. *History of Jackson County Missouri*. Topeka, KS: Historical Publishing Company, 1920.

Hinton, Richard J. *Rebel Invasion of Missouri and Kansas*. Chicago: Church & Goodman, 1865. Reprint. San Bernardino, CA: Old South Books, 2015.

Hinze, David C. and Karen Farnham. *The Battle of Carthage: Border War in Southwest Missouri, July 5, 1861*. Campbell, CA: Savas Publishing Company, 1997.

History of Audrain County, Missouri, Written and Compiled from the Most Authentic Official and Private Sources, Including a History of Its Townships, Towns and Villages. St. Louis: National Historical Company, 1884.

History of Benton, Washington, Carroll, Madison, Crawford, Franklin and Sebastian Counties, Arkansas, Etc. Chicago: The Goodspeed Publishing Co., 1889.

History of Franklin, Jefferson, Washington, Crawford & Gasconade Counties of Missouri. Chicago: Goodspeed Publishing Company, 1888.

History of Howard and Chariton Counties, Missouri, Written and Compiled from the Most Authentic Official and Private Sources Including a History of Its Townships, Towns and Villages. St. Louis: National Historical Company, 1883.

History of Howard and Cooper Counties, Missouri, Written and Complied From the Most Authentic Official and Private Sources, Etc. St. Louis: National Historical Company, 1883.

History of Pettis County, Missouri, Including an Authentic History of Sedalia, Other Towns and Townships, etc. Reprint. Clinton, MO: The Printery, n.d.

History of Saline County, Missouri, Carefully Written and Compiled From the Most Authentic Official and Private Sources, Including A History of the Townships, Cities, Towns and Villages, etc. St. Louis: Missouri Historical Company. 1881.

Holister, Ovando J. *Colorado Volunteers in New Mexico 1862*. Denver, CO: Thos. Gibson & Co., 1863. Reprint. Chicago: R. R. Donnelley & Company, 1962.

Hope, F. M. Statement. *Confederate Veteran* 33 (February 1925): 73.

Huff, Leo E. "Guerrillas, Jayhawkers and Bushwhackers in Northern Arkansas during the Civil War." *Arkansas Historical Quarterly* 24 (Summer 1965): 127–148.

Hughes, Nathaniel Cheairs, Jr. *The Battle of Belmont: Grant Strikes South*. Chapel Hill, NC: The University of North Carolina Press, 1991.

Hultston, John K. and James W. Goodrich. "John Trousdale Coffee: Lawyer, Politician, Confederate." *Missouri Historical Review* 85 (October 1990): 272–295.

Hunt, Roger D. and Jack R. Brown. *Brevet Brigadier Generals in Blue*. Gaithersburg, MD: Olde Soldier Books, Inc., 1990.

Ingenthron, Elmo. *Borderland Rebellion: A History of the Civil War on the Missouri-Arkansas Border*. Branson, MO: The Ozark Mountaineer, 1980.

Jenkins, Paul B. *The Battle of Westport*. Kansas City, MO: Franklin Hudson Publishing Company, 1906. Reprint. Digital Copy. BCR Self 2 Life: n.d.

Johnson, E. Polk. "Some Generals I Have Known." In *Southern Bivouac*, 4:120–122. Reprint ed. Wilmington, NC: Broadfoot Publishing Company, 1993.

Joiner, Gary D. *Through the Howling Wilderness: The Red River Campaign and the Union Failure in the West*. Knoxville, TN: The University of Tennessee Press, 2006.

Jones, Michael Dan. *General Mouton's Regiment: The 18th Louisiana Infantry*. N.p.: n.p., 2012.

Josephy, Alvin. M. *The Civil War in the American West*. New York: Alfred A. Knopf, Inc., 1991.

"Capt. James Kennedy." *Confederate Veteran* 36 (January 1928): 25.

Kerby, Robert L. *Kirby Smith's Confederacy: The Trans-Mississippi South, 1863–1865*. New York: Columbia University Press, 1972.

Kiel, Herman Gottlieb. *The Centennial Biographical Dictionary of Franklin County, Missouri*. Washington, DC: by author, 1925.

Kirkman, Paul. *The Battle of Westport: Missouri's Great Confederate Raid*. Charleston SC: History Press, 2011.

Kirkpatrick, Arthur Roy. "Missouri's Secessionist Government, 1861–1865." *Missouri Historical Review* 45 (January 1951): 124–137.

Knight, Wilfred. *Red Fox: Stand Watie and the Confederate Indian Nations during the Civil War Years in Indian Territory*. Glendale, CA: The Arthur H. Clark Company, 1988.

Kremm, Thomas W. *The Lion of the South: General Thomas C. Hindman*. Macon, GA: Mercer University Press, 1993.

Krister, John S. "Captured Guns at Lone Jack, Mo." *Confederate Veteran* 24 (April 1916): 184.

Lane, Walter P. *Adventures and Recollections of General Walter P. Lane, A San Jacinto Veteran, Containing Sketches of the Texan, Mexican and Late Wars with Several Indian Fights Thrown In.* Marshall, TX: News Messenger Pub. Co., 1928.

Lankford, Rose Mary. *The Encyclopedia of Quantrill's Guerrillas.* Evening Shade, AR: n.p., 1999.

Lause, Mark A. *The Collapse of Price's Raid: The Beginning of the End in Civil War Missouri.* Columbia, MO: University of Missouri Press, 2016.

———. *Price's Lost Campaign: The 1864 Invasion of Missouri.* Columbia, MO: University of Missouri Press, 2011.

Lee, Fred L., ed. *The Battle of Westport.* Kansas City, MO: Westport Historical Society, 1976.

Lewis, Warner. "Civil War Reminiscences." *Missouri Historical Review* 2 (April 1908): 221–232.

Lindberg, Kip. "Chaos Itself: The Battle of Mine Creek." *North & South* 1 (1998): 74–85.

Litter, Loren K. *"Bleeding Kansas" The Border War in Douglas and Adjacent Counties.* Baldwin City, KS: Champion Publishing, 1987.

Livermore, Thomas L. *Numbers & Losses in the Civil War in America: 1861–1865.* Bloomington, IN: Indiana University Press, 1957.

Lord, Francis A. *Civil War Collectors Encyclopedia, Volumes I & II.* Dayton, OH: Morningside Bookshop, 1995.

Lothrop, Charles H. *A History of the First Regiment Iowa Cavalry Veteran Volunteers, From Its Organization in 1861 to the Muster Out of the United State Service in 1866. Also, A Complete Roster of the Regiment.* Lyons, Iowa: Beers & Eaton, Printers, Mirror Office, 1899.

Lowe, Richard. *Walker's Texas Division C.S.A. Greyhounds of the Trans-Mississippi.* Baton Rouge, LA: Louisiana State University Press, 2004.

Mallinckrodt, Anita M. *A History of Augusta, Mo. and Its Area (I) 1850s–1860s As Reported in St. Charles Democrat.* Washington, MO: John Miller Publishing, 1998.

Margrieter, John R. "The Woodruff Gun." *Civil War Times Illustrated* 12 (May 1973): 33–39.

Marmaduke, John S. *Confederate States Trans-Mississippi Order and Letter Book*. Independence, MO: Two Trails Publishing, 2000.

Marshall, Albert O. *Army Life; From A Soldier's Journal*. Juliet, IL: Chicago Legal News Company, 1883.

Martin, Percy F. *Maximilian in Mexico: The Story of the French Intervention (1863–1867)*. London: Constable and Company Ltd., 1914.

Massey, James Troy. *Memoir of Captain J. M. Bailey*. N.p: n.p., 1995.

McAllen, M. M. *Maximilian and Carlota: Europe's Last Empire in Mexico*. San Antonio, TX: Trinity University Press, 2014.

McCaslin, Richard B. *Tainted Breeze: The Great Hanging at Gainsville, Texas, 1862*. Baton Rouge, LA: Louisiana State University Press, 1994.

McElroy, John. *The Struggle for Missouri*. Washington, DC: National Tribune Co., 1909.

McGhee, James E. *Campaigning With Marmaduke: Narratives and Roster of the 8th Missouri Cavalry Regiment, C.S.A.* Independence, MO: Two Trails Publishing, 2002.

———. *Letter and Order Book Missouri State Guard 1861–1862*. Independence, MO: Two Trails Publishing, 2001.

McLarty, Vivian Kirpatrick. "The Civil War Letters of Colonel Bazel F. Lazear." *Missouri Historical Review* 45 (October 1950): 47–63.

McMurray, Mrs. J. W. "Sketch of Mrs. D. H. Reynolds, of Lake Village." In *Confederate Women of Arkansas in the Civil War, Memorial Reminiscences*, 132–134. Little Rock, 1907; reprint ed., with Intr. by Michael B. Dougan, Fayetteville, AR: M & M Press, 1993.

Miles, Kathleen White. *Bitter Ground: The Civil War in Missouri's Golden Valley Benton, Henry, and St. Clair Counties*. Warsaw, MO: The Printery, 1971.

Miller, Robert E. "General Mosby M. Parsons: Missouri Secessionist." *Missouri Historical Review* 80 (October 1985): 33–57.

Mobley, Freeman K. *Making Sense of the Civil War in Batesville-Jacksonport and Northeast Arkansas, 1861–1874*. Batesville, AR: P. D. Printing, 2005.

Monaghan, Jay. *Civil War on the Western Border 1865–1865*. New York: Bonanza Books, 1955.

Moneyhon, Carl H. *The Impact of the Civil War and Reconstruction on Arkansas: Persistence in the Midst of Ruin*. Baton Rouge, LA: Louisiana State University Press, 1994.

Monnett, Howard N. *Action before Westport, 1864. Revised Edition* Niwot, CO: University Press of Colorado, 1995.

Moore, Frank, ed. *The Rebellion Record: A Diary of American Events*. 12 vols. Vols. 1–6, New York: Putnam, 1861–1863. Vols. 7–12, New York: Van Nostrand, 1864–1868. Reprint ed. New York: Arno Press, 1977.

Morrow, Jno. P., Jr. "Confederate Generals from Arkansas." *Arkansas Historical Quarterly* 21 (Autumn 1962): 231–246.

Mullins, Mrs. Mary Jackman. "Sketch of Col. Sidney D. Jackman." In *Reminiscences of the Women of Missouri during the Sixties,* 93–96. Jefferson City, MO: Missouri Division, United Daughters of the Confederacy, 1911.

Murray, Robert Hammond, ed. *Maximilian, Emperor of Mexico: Memoirs of his Private Secretary Jose Luis Blasio*. New Haven, CT: Yale University Press, 1934.

Musicant, Ivan. *Divided Waters: The Naval History of the Civil War*. New York: Harper Collins Publisher, 1995.

Nash, Charles Edward. *Biographical Sketches of Gen. Pat Cleburne and Gen. T. C. Hindman Together With Humorous Anecdotes and Reminiscences of the Late Civil War*. Little Rock, AR: Tunnah & Pittard, Printers, 1895. Reprint. Dayton, OH: Morningside Bookshop, 1977.

"A National Account." *Rebellion Record,* 11:139–142. See under Moore, Frank.

Nichols, Bruce. *Guerrilla Warfare in Civil War Missouri, 1862*. Jefferson, NC: McFarland & Company, Inc., 2004.

———. *Guerrilla Warfare in Civil War Missouri, Volume II, 1863*. Jefferson, NC: McFarland & Company, Inc., 2004.

———. *Guerrilla Warfare in the Civil War Missouri, Volume III, January– August 1864*. Jefferson, NC: McFarland & Company, Inc., 2014.

———. *Guerrilla Warfare in Civil War Missouri, Volume IV, September 1864– June 1865*. Jefferson, NC: McFarland & Company, Inc., 2014.

———. *Johnson County Missouri in the Civil War*. Independence, MO: Two Trails Publishing, 1974.

Norton, Richard L. *Behind Enemy Lines: The Memoirs and Writings of Brigadier General Sidney Drake Jackman*. Springfield, MO: Oak Hills Publishing, 1997.

Norton, Richard L. and Troy Massey, eds. *Hard Trials and Tribulations of an Old Confederate Soldier*. Van Buren, AR: Argus Office, 1897. Reprint. Springfield, MO: Oak Hills Publishing, 1997.

Norris, L. Davis, ed. *With the 18th Texas Infantry: The Autobiography of Wilburn Hill King*. Hillsboro, TX: Hill College Press, 1996.

Nunn, W. C., ed. *Ten More Texans in Gray*. Hillsboro, TX: Hill Jr. College Press, 1980.

O'Flaherty, Daniel. *General Jo Shelby: Undefeated Rebel*. Chapel Hill, NC: University of North Carolina Press, 1954. Reprint. Wilmington, NC, 1987.

"The Opposing Forces in Arkansas." In *Battles and Leaders of the Civil War*. 4 vols., 3:459–461. New York: The Century Company, 1887–1888.

"The Opposing Forces at Roanoke Island and New Bern, N.C." In *Battles and Leaders of the Civil War*. 4 vols., 1:670. New York: The Century Company, 1887–1888.

Palmer, Don Mc. N. *Four Weeks in the Rebel Army*. New London, CT: D. S. Ruddock, 1865.

Parkes, Henry Bamford. *A History of Mexico*. Boston: Houghton Mifflin Company, 1960.

Parks, Joseph H. *General Edmund Kirby Smith, C.S.A.* Baton Rouge, LA: Louisiana State University Press, 1954.

Peterson, Cyrus A. and Joseph Mills Hanson. *Pilot Knob: The Thermopylae of the West*. New York: Neale Publishing Company, 1914. Reprint. Cape Girardeau, MO: Ramfire Press, 1964.

Peterson, Richard C., et al. *Sterling Price's Lieutenants: A Guide to the Officers and Organization of the Missouri State Guard*. Jefferson City, MO: Two Trails Publishing, 1995.

Phillips, Christopher. *Damned Yankee: The Life of General Nathaniel Lyon*. Columbia, MO: University of Missouri Press, 1990.

Phisterer, Frederick. *Statistical Record of the Armies of the United States.* New York: Charles Scribner's Sons, 1907.

Piston, William Garrett and Richard W. Hatcher, III. *Wilson's Creek: The Second Battle of the Civil War and the Men Who Fought It.* Chapel Hill, NC: University of North Carolina Press, 2000.

Pitcock, Cythia Dehaven and Bill J. Gurley. *I Acted Out of Principle: The Civil War Diary of Dr. William M. McPheeters, Confederate Surgeon in the Trans–Mississippi.* Fayetteville, AR: The University of Arkansas Press, 2002.

Pleasanton, A. "General Pleasonton's Narrative." *Rebellion Record*, 11:388–395. See under Moore, Frank.

Pollock, Joseph. "Shelby's Old Iron Brigade." *Confederate Veteran* 32 (January 1924): 50.

Ponder, Jerry. *A History of the 15th Missouri Cavalry Regiment, C.S.A.* Doniphan, MO: Ponder Books, 1994.

———. *Major General John S. Marmaduke, C.S.A.* Mason, TX: Ponder Books, 1999.

Porter, Charles W. *In the Devil's Dominion: A Union Soldier's Adventures in "Bushwhacker Country."* Nevada, MO: Bushwhacker Museum, 1998

Porter, David D. *Naval History of the Civil War.* New York: n.p., 1886. Reprint. Secaucus, NJ: Castle, 1984.

"Quantrill and His Famous Command." *Confederate Veteran* 18 (June 1910): 278–279.

Rampp, Lary C. and Donald L. Rampp. *The Civil War in the Indian Territory.* Austin, TX: Presidial Press, 1975.

Reid, Thomas. *Spartan Band: Burnett's 13th Texas Cavalry in the Civil War.* Denton, TX: University of North Texas Press, 2005.

Reynolds, Thomas C. *General Sterling Price and the Confederacy.* Edited by Robert G. Schultz. St. Louis, MO: Missouri History Museum Press, 2009.

Ripley, Warren. *Artillery and Ammunition of the Civil War.* New York: Litton Educational Printing, Inc., 1970.

Robert, Mrs. P. G. "History of Events Preceding and Following the Banishment of Mrs. Margaret A. E. McLure, As Given to Her By Herself." In *Reminiscences of the Women of Missouri during the Sixties,* 78–84. Jefferson City, MO: Missouri Division, United Daughters of the Confederacy, 1911. Reprint. Dayton, OH: Morningside House, Inc., 1988.

Robertson, James I., Jr. *Soldiers Blue and Gray.* Columbia, SC: University of South Carolina, 1988.

Robley, T. F. *History of Bourbon County, Kansas, to the Close of 1865.* Fort Scott, KS, 1894; reprint ed., 2nd printing, Fort Scott, KS, 1976.

Rolle, Andrew F. *The Lost Cause: The Confederate Exodus to Mexico.* Norman, OK: University of Oklahoma Press, 1965.

Ross, Kirby. "The Burning of Doniphan." *North & South* 6 (November 2003): 76–84.

Ross, Margaret. *Arkansas Gazette: The Early Years 1819–1866.* Little Rock, AR: Arkansas Gazette Foundation, 1969.

Roth, Don. *General J. O. Shelby at Clarendon, Arkansas: The Capture and Destruction of the U.S.S. Queen City.* Iowa City, IA: Camp Pope Publishing, 2017.

Rowan, Steven, ed. *Memoirs of a Nobody: The Missouri Years of an Austrian Radical, 1849–1866.* St. Louis: Missouri Historical Society Press, 1997.

Ryle, Walter Harrington. *Missouri: Union or Secession.* Nashville, TN: George Peabody College for Teachers, 1931.

Sanborn, John B. "The Campaign in Missouri in September and October, 1864." In *Glimpses of the Nation's Struggle. Third Series. Papers Read Before the Minnesota Commandery of the Military Order of the Loyal Legion of the United States.* 70 vols., 28:135–204. St. Paul, MN: D. D. Merrill, Company, 1893. Reprint. Wilmington NC: Broadfoot Publishing Company, 1992.

Scharf, J. Thomas. *History of Saint Louis City and County, From the Earliest Periods to the Present Day: Including Biographical Sketches of Representative Men.* 2 vols. Philadelphia, PA: Louis H. Everts & Co., 1883.

Scherneckau, August. *Marching With the First Nebraska: A Civil War Diary.* Edited by James E. Potter and Edith Robbins. Norman, OK: University of Oklahoma Press, 2007.

Schnetzer, Wayne H. *Men of the Tenth: A Roster of the Tenth Missouri Infantry Confederate States of America.* Independence, MO: Two Trails Publishing, n.d.

———. *More Forgotten Men: The Missouri State Guard*. Independence, MO: Two Trails Publishing, 2003.

Schrantz, Ward L. *Jasper County, Missouri in the Civil War*. Carthage, MO: The Carthage, Missouri Kiwanis Club, 1923.

Scott, William Forse. "The Last Fight for Missouri." In *Personal Recollections of the War of the Rebellion Addresses Delivered Before the Commandery of the State of New York, Military Order of the Loyal Legion of the United States. Third Series*, 3:292–328. New York: G. P. Putnam's Sons, 1907. Reprint. Wilmington, NC: Broadfoot Publishing Company, 1992.

———. *The Story of a Cavalry Regiment: The Career of the Fourth Iowa Veteran Volunteers From Kansas to Georgia 1861–1865*. New York: C. F. Putnam's Sons, 1893. Reprint. Iowa City, IA: Press of Camp Pope Bookshop, 1992.

Sellmeyer, Deryl P. *Jo Shelby's Iron Brigade*. Gretna, LA: Pelican Publishing Company, 2007.

Shalhope, Robert E. *Sterling Price: Portrait of a Southerner*. Columbia, MO: University of Missouri Press, 1971.

Sharp, Arthur G. "Battle at Lake Chicot." *Civil War Times Illustrated* 21 (October 1982): 18–23.

Shea, William L. & Earl J. Hess. *Pea Ridge: Civil War Campaign in the West*. Chapel Hill, NC: University of North Carolina Press, 1992.

Shelby, Bettie. "War Experiences." In *Reminiscences of the Women of Missouri during the Sixties*, 103–105. Jefferson City, MO: Missouri Division, United Daughters of the Confederacy, 1911. Reprint. Dayton, OH: Morningside Bookshop, 1988.

Sifakis, Stewart. *Compendium of the Confederate Armies: Florida and Arkansas*. New York: Facts on File, 1992.

———. *Compendium of the Confederate Armies: Kentucky, Maryland, Missouri, The Confederate Units and the Indian Units*. New York: Facts on File, 1995.

———. *Who Was Who in the Confederacy: A Comprehensive, Illustrated Biographical Reference to More Than 1,000 of the Principal Confederacy Participants in the Civil War*. New York: Facts on File, 1988.

———. *Who Was Who in the Union: A Comprehensive, Illustrated Biographical Reference to More Than 1,500 of the Principal Union Participants in the Civil War*. New York: Facts on File, 1988.

Simons, Don R. *In Their Words: A Chronology of the Civil War in Chicot County, Arkansas and Adjacent Waters of the Mississippi River*. Sulphur, LA: Wise Publications, 1999.

———. *Texas in the War 1861–1865*. Hillsboro, TX: The Hill Junior College Press, 1965.

Singletary, Otis A. *The Mexican War*. Chicago: The University of Chicago Press, 1960.

Sinisi, Kyle S. *The Last Hurrah: Sterling Price's Missouri Expedition of 1864*. New York: Rowman & Littlefield, 2015.

Smith, Coleman. "Capture of the Gunboat Queen City." *Confederate Veteran* 22 (March 1914): 120–121.

Smith, Duane A. *The Birth of Colorado: A Civil War Perspective*. Norman, OK: University of Oklahoma Press, 1989.

Smith, E. Kirby. "The Defense of the Red River." In *Battles and Leaders of the Civil War*. 4 vols., 4:369–374. New York: The Century Company, 1887–1888.

Snead, Thomas L. *The Fight for Missouri from the Election of Lincoln to the Death of Lyon*. New York: Charles Scribner's Sons, 1866.

Sperry, A. F. *History of the 33rd Iowa Infantry Volunteer Regiment 1863–1866*. Des Moines, IA: Mills & Company, 1866.

Stalnaker, Jerry D. *The Battle of Mine Creek: The Crushing End of the Missouri Campaign*. Charleston SC: History Press, 2011.

Stanton, Donal J., Goodwin F. Berquist, and Paul C. Bowers, eds. *The Civil War Reminiscences of General M. Jeff Thompson*. Dayton, OH: Morningside Bookshop, 1988.

Starr, Stephen Z. *Jennison's Jayhawkers: A Civil War Cavalry Regiment and Its Commander*. Baton Rouge, LA: Louisiana State University, 1973.

Stephenson, Wendell Holmes. *Publications of the Kansas State Historical Society Embracing the Political Career of General James H. Lane*. Topeka, KS: Kansas State Historical Society, 1930.

Stuart, A. A. *Iowa Colonels and Regiments, Being a History of Iowa Regiments in the War of the Rebellion; And Containing a Description of the Battles in Which They Have Fought*. Des Moines, IA: Mills & Co., 1865.

Suderow, Bryce A. "The Battlefield of Westport as Seen by a Federal Infantryman." *The Westport Historical Quarterly* 10 (June 1974): 10–18.

———. *Thunder In Arcadia Valley: Price's Defeat, September 27, 1864*. Cape Girardeau, MO: The Center for Regional History and Cultural Heritage, Southeast Missouri State University, 1986.

Switzler, William F. *History of Boone County, Missouri, Written and Compiled From the Most Authentic Official and Private Sources; Including a History of Its Townships, Towns and Villages. etc.* St. Louis, MO: Western Historical Company, 1882.

Thoma, James F. *This Cruel Unnatural War: The American Civil War in Cooper County, Missouri, Second Edition*. Kingsport, TN: James F. Thoma, 2006.

Thompson, Jerry, ed. *Tejanos in Gray: The Civil War Letters of Captains Joseph Rafael de la Garza & Manuel Yturri*. College Station, TX: Texas A & M University Press, 2011.

Thompson, Joseph Conan. "The Great Little Battle of Pilot Knob." *Missouri Historical Review* 83 (January 1989): 139–160, (April, 1989): 271–294.

Titterington, Dick. *A Day Late and a Dollar Short: The Fate of A. J. Smith's 16th Army Corps during Price's 1864 Missouri Raid*. Oakland Park, KS: Trans-Mississippi Musing Press, 2014.

Tunnard, W. H. *A Southern History. The History of the Third Regiment Louisiana Infantry*. Baton Rouge, LA: W. H. Tunnard, 1866.

The Union Army: A History of Military Affairs in the Loyal United States 1861–18675—Records of the Regiments in the Union Army—Cyclopedia of Battles—Memoirs of Commanders and Soldiers. 8 vols. New York: Federal Publishing Company, 1908. Reprint. Wilmington, NC: Broadfoot Pub. Co., 1998.

The United Confederate Veterans of Arkansas. *Confederate Women of Arkansas in the Civil War Memorial Reminiscences*. Little Rock, 1907. Reprint. Intr. by Michael B. Dougan, Fayetteville, AR: M & M Press, 1993.

"Valiant Coleman, Veteran of Two Wars." *Confederate Veteran* 17 (September 1909): 212–213.

Vandiver, W. D. "Reminiscences of General John B. Clark." *Missouri Historical Review* 20 (January 1926): 223–235.

Viles, Jonas. "Documents Illustrating the Troubles on the Border, 1860. The Southwest Expedition." *Missouri Historical Review* 2 (October 1907): 61–77.

Warner, Ezra J. *Generals in Blue: Lives of the Union Commanders*. Baton Rouge, LA: Louisiana State University Press, 1964.

———. *Generals in Gray: Lives of the Confederate Commanders*. Baton Rouge, LA: Louisiana State University Press, 1959.

Weaver, W. J. "A Sketch of Mrs. Sophia Kannady, A Heroine of Fort Smith." In *Confederate Women of Arkansas in the Civil War Memorial Reminiscences*, 79–87. Little Rock, 1907; reprint ed., with Intr. by Michael B. Dougan Fayetteville, AR: M & M Press, 1993.

Webb, W. L. *Battles and Biographies of Missourians or the Civil War Period of Our State*. Kansas City, MO: Hudson-Kimberly Pub. Co., 1900. Reprint. Springfield, MO: Oak Hills Publishing, 1999.

Werner, Michael S. *Encyclopedia of Mexico: History, Society, and Culture*. 2 vols. Chicago: Routledge, 1997.

West, Emmet C. *History and Reminiscences of the Second Wisconsin Cavalry Regiment*. Portage, WI: State Register Print, 1904. Reprint. Rochester, MI: Grand Army Press, 1982.

White County Heritage Civil War Collection, Volume 1–25. Searcy, AR: White County Historical Society, n.d.

White, James A. and Carolyn M. Bartels. *The Men Who Rode with Capt. Wm. C. Quantrill & Capt. Wm. T. Anderson: Their lives, Their Loves, Their Stories*. Independence, MO: n. p., 2015.

Wiley, Bell Irwin. *The Life of Johnny Reb: The Common Soldier of the Confederacy*. Baton Rouge, LA: Louisiana State University Press, 1943.

Williams, Ellen. *Three Years and a Half in the Army; or History of the Second Colorados*. New York: Fowler & Wells Company, 1885. Reprint. Albany, MO: Century Reprints, 1999.

Winns, R. M. "Scouting in Arkansas and Missouri." *Confederate Veteran* 21 (November 1913): 538–539.

Winter, William C. *The Civil War in St. Louis: A Guided Tour*. St. Louis: Missouri Historical Society Press, 1994.

Wood, Larry. *Other Noted Guerrillas on the Civil War in Missouri*. Joplin, MO: History Press, 2007.

———. *The Two Civil War Battles of Newtonia*. Charleston, SC: History Press, 2010.

Wooster, Ralph A. *Lone Star Generals in Gray*. Austin, TX: Eakin Press, 2000.

———. *Lone Star Regiments in Gray*. Austin, TX: Eakin Press, 2002.

Worley, Ted R. "A Letter Written by General Thomas C. Hindman in Mexico." *Arkansas Historical Quarterly* 15 (Winter 1956): 265–268.

Wright, Marcus J. *Arkansas in the War 1861–1865*. Batesville, AR: The Independence County Historical Society, 1963.

———. *General Officers of the Confederate Army*. New York: The Neale Publishing Company, 1911.

Yeary, Mamie. *Reminiscences of the Boys in Gray 1861–1865*. Dallas, TX: Press of Wilkinson Printing Company, 1912. Reprint. Dayton, OH: Morningside Bookshop, 1986.

Government Sources

Baker, Nathaniel B. *Report of the Adjutant General and Acting Quartermaster General of Iowa*. January 11, 1864, to January 1, 1865. Des Moines, IA: State Printing Office, 1865.

Bishop, Albert W. *Report of the Adjutant General of Arkansas, For the Period of the Late Rebellion, and to November 1, 1866*. Washington: Government Printing Office, 1867. Reprint. Santa Maria, CA: Janaway Publishing, Inc., 2012.

Confederate States War Department. *Regulations for the Army of the Confederate States, 1863. Corrected and Enlarged with a Revised Index*. J. W. Randolph: Richmond, VA, 1863. Reprint. Harrisburg, PA: The National Historical Society, 1980.

Davis, George B., Leslie J. Perry and Joseph W. Kirkley. *Atlas to Accompany the Official Records of the Union and Confederate Armies*. Washington, DC: Government Printing Office, 1891–1895.

Gorgas, J. *The Ordnance Manual for the Use of the Officers of the Confederate States Army*. Charleston, SC: Evans & Cogswell, 1863. Reprint. Dayton, OH: Morningside Bookshop, 1976.

Gray, John B. *Annual Report of the Adjutant General of Missouri for 1864*. Jefferson City, MO: W. A. Curry, State Printer, 1864.

Library of Congress. *Newspapers in Microform, United States, 1848–1983, Vol I A–O*. Washington, DC: Government Printing Office, 1984.

National Archives. Confederate Muster Rolls. Assorted units. Washington, DC.

———. Record Group 94. Hospital Records (Register no. 15), Ft. Scott, Kansas.

———. Record Group 109. Confederate Correspondence. Assorted Boxes and Files.

———. Record Group 153, Union General Court Martial. Assorted Individuals.

———. Record Group M322. Confederate Compiled Service Records: Missouri. Assorted rolls and units. Washington, DC.

———. Record Group M861. Records of Confederate Movements and Activities. Assorted rolls and units. Washington, DC.

Naval History Division. Navy Department. *Civil War Naval Chronology*. Washington, DC: Government Printing Office, 1971.

United States War Department. *The War of the Rebellion: A Compilation of the Official Records of the Union and Confederate Armies*. 70 volumes comprising 128 books. Washington, DC, 1880–1901. Reprint. Harrisburg, PA: National Historical Society, 1985.

———. *The War of the Rebellion: Official Record of the Union and Confederate Navies*. 31 volumes. Washington, DC: Edwards Brothers, 1894–1922.

Internet Sites

Arkansas: Edward G. Gerdes Civil War Home Page: www.couchgenweb.com/civilwar.

Assorted names and units:

    The Arkansas in the Civil War Message Board: http://history-sites.com/cgi-bin/bbs62x/arcwmb/webbbs_config.pl.
    Key word "Witherspoon."
    Key Word "John T. Coffee." Danny Odom Letter (June 10, 2013).
    Key Word "Thomas Freeman Memoir." Bryce Suderow Letter (November 2, 2014).

"Charles Harrison (And the Confederate Cause in the Colorado Territory)," by Patrick Gerity: http://nebula.wsimg.com/80bce074b2a0a280b403e086b-4cf422f?AccessKeyId=F7559C48D68C23EC2E5B&disposition=0&allow-origin=1.

The Daily Ranchero: chroniclingamerica.loc.gov/lccn/SN83025706.

"The Memoirs of Dr. Robert J. Christie": http://flanaganfamily.net/genealo/memoirs.htm.

The Missouri in the Civil War Message Board: http://www.history-sites.com/cgi-bin/bbs62x/mocwmb/webbbs_config.pl.

>Campbell, James W. Memoir.
>E–Mail (May 11, 2008). Lars Gjertveit.
>Suderow, Bryce. "Battle of Westport Opening Phase."

"The Osage: A Historical Sketch," by George E. Tinker: https://ualrexhibits.org/tribalwriters/artifacts/Tinker_Osage-Historical-Sketch.html.

Surname: McKinney: www.tribalpages.com/tribe/familytree?uid=styxmark&surname=McKinney.

Whitsett, William E. Letter (July 13, 1900): http://history-sites.com/cgi-bin/bbs62x/arcwmb/webbbs_config.pl?md=read;id=24208

www.wikipedia.org.

Manuscripts/Special Collections

Chapel Hill, NC. University of North Carolina.
>Southern Historical Collection.
>>Alexander, James Trooper. Correspondence.
>>Polk, Trusten. Diary
>>Wallace, James T. Diary (1862–1865).

Columbia, MO. State Historical Society of Missouri.
>Western Historical Manuscript Collection:
>>"Address of General J. O. Shelby to His Division."
>>Baker, J. H. P. Collection. J. H. P. Baker Diary (October 1, 1864–May 31, 1865).
>>"The Battle of Pilot Knob by One Who Was There."
>>Bolton, James E. Memoir.
>>Gregg, William H. "A Little Dab of History Without Embellishment."
>>Hazen, William G. Letter (December 14, 1864).
>>Hoskin, William N. Civil War Diary.
>>Logan, Charles W. "Roster and Battles of Company A, 10th Missouri Confederate States Infantry."
>>Quesenberry, John P. Manuscript Diary.
>>Shelby Scrapbook (C3558):
>>>"The Battle of Westport."

"Deeds of Gallantry."
"How the Federals Fought."
Interview With Judge John F. Philips. "General Jo O. Shelby."
Watts, Hemp B. "Shelby At Newtonia."
Suderow, Bryce. Collection:
   Letter (August 14, 1976). Suderow to Buresh.
   Report of Prisoners of War.
Westlake, Thomas W. Memoirs (C186)
Wilson Family Papers (C348): Wilson, John. Memoirs.

Des Moines, IA. State Historical Society of Iowa.
   Huff, Charles W. Diary.

Fayetteville, AR. University of Arkansas.
   Special Collections:
      Leighton Family Papers.

Independence, MO. Jackson County Historical Society.
   Williams, Valerie. "Battle of Westport." Collection no. 720.

Little Rock. AR. Arkansas History Commission.
   Lotspeich, C. B. Typescript Diary (January 17–September 26, 1863).
   Lotspeich, C. B. Unpublished manuscript. "Personal Experiences of C. B. Lotspeich."
   Skaggs, W. L. Collection:
      Coleman, William O. Letters.
      Farmer, Benjamin. Memoir.
      Marshall, R. P. Letter.
   Wright, John Crowell. Papers.
      Typescript copy. "Memoirs of Colonel John C. Wright C.S.A."

Little Rock, AR. University of Arkansas.
   Turnbo, S. C. "History of the Twenty-seventh Arkansas Confederate Infantry With Many Interesting Accounts of the Countries Through Which it Passed During the Civil War and Accurate Accounts of the Battles in which it Engaged."

New York. Columbia University:
   Peter W. Alexander Collection:
      Burbridge, John Q. Letters.
      Copy Book of General Orders, May 31–December 30, 1862. Hindman's Command.
      Copy Letter Book, June 1–Dec. 18, 1862. Hindman's Command.
      Copy Letter Book, January 2–March 14, 1863. Hindman's Command.

Marmaduke, John S. Letters.
Parsons, Mosby M. Letters.
Miscellaneous Correspondence.
Special Orders Book, June 1–Dec. 18, 1862. Hindman's Command.
Telegrams Collection. Assorted Files. Hindman's Command.

Norman, OK. Western History Collection.
Slower, James Anderson, Sr. "Autobiography of."

Richmond, VA. Museum of the Confederacy.
Slemons, W. F. Letters.

Rolla, MO. State Historical Society of Missouri.
Western Historical Manuscript Collection:
Jacob Bess Journal (R1330)
Skaggs, Henry E. Deposition A (November 4, 1895).
Henry Ellison Skaggs Papers (1831–1899)—(R237).

Springfield, IL. Abraham Lincoln Presidential Library.
Black Family Collection.
Black, John C. Letters.

St. Louis, MO. Missouri Historical Society.
Bartley, Samuel M. Papers: Muster Roll. Company G, William's Missouri Regiment.
Brown, R. L. Journal.
Civil War Collection. "Army of Missouri" file:
Diary of the Raid (September 19–October 15, 1864).
General Orders No.12 (September 21, 1864).
Letter. Ewing to Freeman (September 26, 1864).
Order of March (October 5–15, 1864).
Cruzen, George R. "Story of My Life."
Ford, S.H. Reminiscences.
Fusz, Louis. Diary.
Kennerly Papers.
Letter. J. Marmaduke.
Missouri Militia Papers:
Parsons, G. S. Report (January 18, 1861)
Muster Roll. Company C. Wood's Battalion (June 30, 1864).
Muster Roll. Stallard's Escort Company. Company D, 5th Missouri Cavalry (CSA).
Parsons, M. M. Papers:
Bell, Mrs. R. J. Diary (January–August, 1864).
L. A. Pindall Letter (February 3, 1869).

Letter. Parsons to Parents (June 5, 1865).
Peterson Pilot Knob Collection:
  Henry Wilkinson Letters.

Topeka, KS. Kansas State Historical Society.
  Thomas Moonlight Collection.
    Lindberg, Kip (Transcriber), "Wartime Reminiscences of Colonel Thomas Moonlight."

Washington, DC. The Library of Congress.
  Ewing, Thomas. Papers:
    Cocker, J. A. Recollections of.

Private Collections

Terry Justice Collection. Brooks, Peter. Diary (September 26–November 11, 1864).

Newspapers

Alabama:
  Mobile Daily Advertiser and Register (Mobile).

Arkansas:
  Arkansas State Gazette (Little Rock).
  Fort Smith New Era (Fort Smith).
  Washington Telegraph (Washington).

District of Columbia:
  National Tribune (Washington).

Illinois:
  Chicago Daily Tribune (Chicago).
  The Chicago Times (Chicago).

Indiana:
  The Indianapolis Daily Journal (Indianapolis).

Louisiana:
  The Shreveport Weekly News (Shreveport).

Iowa:
  Muscatine Daily Journal (Muscatine).

Kansas:
  The Emporia News (Emporia).

Freedom's Champion (Atchison).
The Kansas State Journal (Lawrence).
Leavenworth Daily Conservative (Leavenworth).
Wyandotte Commercial Gazette (Wyandotte).

Mexico:
Mexican Times (Mexico City).

Missouri:
The Advertiser (Sedalia).
Daily Journal of Commerce (Kansas city).
The Daily Missouri Democrat (St. Louis)
    See also, Busch, *Price's Missouri Raid.*
The Daily Missouri Republican (St. Louis).
The Forge (Ironton).
Iron County Register (Ironton).

Texas:
Galveston Tri–Weekly News (Galveston).
The Houston Daily Telegraph (Houston).
Marshall Republican (Marshall)
San Antonio Herald (San Antonio)
Tri–Weekly Telegraph (Houston).
The Weekly Dallas Herald (Dallas).
The Weekly State Gazette (Austin).Credits

Credits

Photographs and Illustrations

Album, Portraits of Companions of the Commandery of the State of Illinois, Military Order of the Loyal Legion of the United States, 54: John Sanborn.

Carlisle, PA. U.S. Army Military History Institute: Sidney D. Jackman.

Columbia, MO. State Historical Society of Missouri: Richard Yeager.

Confederate Veteran, 5:417: John A. Wharton.

findagrave.com: William Henry Parsons.

fr/wikipedia.org: Pierre Jeanningros.

Republic, MO. Wilson's Creek National Battlefield Park: M. Jeff Thompson, WICR 31454.

Springfield, MO. Private Collection of Garin Ferguson: John P. Bull.

St. Louis, MO. Missouri Historical Society. Peterson Pilot Knob Collection. Wilkinson Collection: Figure No. 1, Gun Emplacements of Fort Davidson.

Topeka, KS. Kansas State Historical Society: James G. Blunt.

Washington, DC. Library of Congress. Simon B. Buckner, LC-DIG-ppms-ca-41840; William L. Cabell, LC-DIG-cwphh-00472; John B. Clark, Jr., LC-cwphh-03655; Alfred W. Ellet, LC-DIG-cwpb-05613; Thomas Ewing, LC-DIG-cwpb-06174; John B. Magruder, LC-USZ62-62496; Samuel B. Maxey, LC-DIG-cwpbh-04972; Joseph A. Mower, LC-DIG-cwpb-06128; Alfred Pleasonton, LC-DIG-cwpb-06452; William S. Rosecrans, LC-DIG-cwpb-06052; Andrew J. Smith, LC-USZ62-90950; Sir Edward Thornton, LC-DIG-cwpbh-00543.

Washington, DC. Naval History and Heritage Command: *U.S.S. Tyler*, NH95020.

Wikimedia Commons: Egbert B. Brown; Servando Canales; Juan N. Cortina; Archibald Dobbin; John Newman Edwards; William M. Gwin; Thomas H. McCray; Joseph O. Shelby; Richard Waterhouse.

Wikimexico: Mariano Escobedo.

Maps

Michael E. Banasik: Battle of Ditch Bayou June 6, 1864.

Battles and Leaders of the Civil War, 1:263: Price in Missouri, 1864. Modified and enhanced by Michael E. Banasik.

Battles and Leaders of the Civil War, 4:348: Price's Raid: From Princeton to Pocahontas. Modified and enhanced by Michael E. Banasik.

Crandell & Newell, *History of the Ram Fleet and the Mississippi Marine Brigade*, 330: Operations on the Mississippi River. Enhanced by Michael E. Banasik.

Davis, *Civil War Atlas,* plt. no. 47, 1: Price's Raid: From Maysville, Arkansas to Laynesport, Texas. Modified by Michael E. Banasik.

Hinton, *Rebel Invasion of Missouri and Kansas*, 258: Battleground of Newtonia, October 28, 1864; 148: Battleground of Westport, October 23, 1864; 120: Westport and Big Blue, October 22 & 23, 1864.

O.R., vol. 41, pt. 1:708: Pilot Knob, MO and Its Approaches.

Scott, *The Story of a Cavalry Regiment*, facing 332: Battle of Marais Des Cygnes (or "Osage;" or "Mine Creek,"), Oct. 25, 1864.

Index

Alexander, Capt. James T., 22, 48–49, 90,300, 334
Allen, Gov. Henry W., 43, 60–61; Bio., 43
Anderson, Capt. William "Bill," 125, 131, 178, 194, 216, 379; Bio., 216
Arkansas Cities/ Towns
  Augusta, 27–28
  Batesville, 26–29, 89–90, 209–210; Description of, 210
  Benton, 50,88
  Bentonville, 223–225,230,233–235,243–244; Description of, 224
  Berryville, 229–230, 233–235 243–244
  Brownsville, 54, 160,190
  Cane Hill, 51, 169, 171, 193,224, 228–229
  Clarendon, 27–30, 33–38, 55
  Clinton, 89–90, 118
  Columbia, 5–6, 8–11, 13–14, 20
  Dardanelle, 26, 88–89
  DeValls Bluff, 3,28–29, 32–33, 37, 54, 290
  Dover, 89, 202
  Eunice, 10,22
  Fayetteville, 15, 41, 160, 171, 223–224, 227–229, 232, 237, 239–241, 243–244
  Gaines' Landing, 9
  Helena, 26, 28, 30, 32, 35–36, 40, 46, 57, 158–159, 192, 209, 305,307
  Hookrum, 90
  Huntsville, 197, 206, 211, 216, 231, 235, 238–239; Description of, 231
  Jacksonport, 26–29, 72, 202; Description of, 27
  Kingston, 235–236, 242–243
  Lake Village, 9, 11, 14,–15, 21; Description of, 15; Sack of, 19
  Little Rock, 1–4, 15, 26, 29, 32, 41, 49–52, 54, 63–64, 88, 104, 111, 160, 183, 209, 214, 224, 293, 310
  Luna Landing, 5–6, 20
  Maysville, 169, 227, 229
  Monticello, 4, 49–51, 53, 55–56, 112
  Mt. Elba, 25, 50–51, 53, 85–87
  Pine Bluff, 1, 4, 50, 53, 104, 111, 159–160
  Powhatan, 46, 52, 90–91
  Princeton, 2, 41, 50–51, 55, 86, 88, 203
  Sunnyside Landing, 13–14
  St. Charles, 54, 113
  Tulip, 3, 41, 46, 88
  Tyro, 85–87, 123, 174
  Warren, 2, 50–51, 87
  Washington, 49–50, 56, 172, 174, 226
  White River Station, 9, 11, 22, 25
Arkansas Troops
  Confederate
    1st Cav. (Dobbin), 356
    2nd Cav. (Cochran), 359
    4th Cav. (A. Gordon), 90, 224, 230, 353
    10th Cav. (Witt), 356
    1st Inf. Cons., 51, 146, 226
    14th Inf., 51, 230, 238, 328
    15th Inf., 223, 226, 237
    17th Inf., 51
    21st Inf., 51, 226
    27th Inf., 56–57, 230
    44th Mtd.Inf. (McGhee), 146, 355–356

45th Mtd. Inf., 324, 326, 357
46th Mtd. Inf., 313, 370–371, 374, 433
47th Mtd. Inf., 310, 357
48th Cav., 232
Cabell's Bde., 13, 77, 86, 89, 90, 95, 100, 102–103, 110, 113, 118–120, 122–123, 125, 130, 136, 138–139, 141, 143, 147, 153, 156, 167–168, 171–172, 174, 240, 300, 306–308, 351–355; at Pilot Knob, 388–391; at Westport, 414–416
Carlton's Cav. Regt., 359
Churchill's Div., 41–43, 45, 50, 56
Crawford's Cav. Regt., 359
Dobbin's Bde., 130, 144, 146, 151, 153, 161, 171, 355–357; at Pilot Knob, 391; at Westport, 416–417
Dobbin's Cav. Regt. (See 1st Ark. Cav.)
Dockery's Bde., 50, 56
Fagan's Division, 50, 86, 88–92, 95, 99–103, 107, 113, 118–121, 240, 295, 300, 304–308, 351–360; Art. Added, 376–377; at Pilot Knob, 387–393; at Westport, 413–421; Losses at Pilot Knob, 393
Gordon's Cav. Regt. (See 4th Ark. Cav.)
Gunter's Bde. (See Cabell's Bde)
Gunter's Cav. Regt., 353
Harrell's Cav. Regt., 352–353, 389
Hawthorn's Bde., 50, 56
Hill's Cav. Regt., 353
Hughey's Art., 13, 17–18, 88, 90, 100–101, 103, 119, 139, 325, 336, 349, 352; Capture of 325; Composition of, 349
Lyle's Cav. Regt., 359
McCray's Bde., 27, 143, 146–147, 153, 162, 171, 324, 326, 335–336, 357–358; at Pilot Knob, 391; at Westport, 418
McGhee's Cav. Regt. (See 44th Ark.)
Monroe's Cav. Regt., 90, 100, 353
Morgan's Cav. Regt., 353
Rogan's Cav. Regt., 359
Slemon's Bde., 86, 89, 95, 103, 118, 125, 144, 146, 151, 153, 156, 168, 172, 174, 240, 300, 323–324, 358–359; at Pilot Knob, 392; at Westport, 419
Witt's Cav. Regt. (See 10th Ark. Cav.)
Wright's Cav. Regt., 125, 130, 138–139, 168, 324, 358–359
Zimmerman's Art., 156, 340; Composition of, 340
Union
1st Inf., 238
1st Cav. (Harrison), 227, 230, 233, 237–239
2nd Cav. (Phelps), 120, 132, 147, 151, 229, 232–234, 237, 239, 332
3rd Cav., 89–90

Baber, Col. Milton, 324–325
Bache, Capt. George, 29, 33, 35
Banks, Gen. Nathaniel, 41, 43–44
Battles, Affairs, Skirmishes, etc.
 Barren Fork Creek, IT (Dec. 7, 1863), 228–229
 Camden Expedition, AR (Mar–April, 1864), 1–3, 28, 63, 104, 111–112, 159–160, 224, 241, 290
 Camp Jackson, MO (May 10, 1861), 85, 97, 183–184, 189, 209
 Cane Hill, AR (Nov. 28, 1862), 238
 Carthage, MO (July 5, 1861), 185
 Colorado Expedition (May 12–19, 1863), Members of, 217, 220,

Index / 501

222, 337–340; Purpose of 215, 217–218
Ditch Bayou, AR (June, 6, 1864), 7, 11, 14–15, 17–18; Losses, 19, 23
Dug Springs, MO (Aug, 2, 1861), 185
Elkhorn Tavern, AR (See Pea Ridge)
Helena, AR (July 4, 1863), 26, 28, 30, 35, 40, 46, 57,159, 192, 209, 305, 307; Losses compared to Pilot Knob, 304–305, 307
Independence, MO (Aug. 11, 1862), 188–189, 323–326
Jenkins' Ferry, AR (April 30, 1864), 1–2, 40, 43, 46, 54–55, 85; Losses, 1–2
Lexington, Mo (Sept. 13–20, 1861), 63–64, 85, 115, 187–189, 197, 202, 209, 291
Lone Jack, MO (Aug. 15, 1862), 1, 72, 77, 124, 138, 177, 189–191, 205, 207
Mansfield, LA (April 8, 1864), 42–43, 53
Oak Hills, MO (See Wilson's Creek)
Pea Ridge, AR (Mar. 6–8, 1862), 40, 42, 52–53, 63, 83, 85, 96, 111, 179, 183, 185, 187–189, 194, 197, 202, 209, 214, 216, 224–225, 228, 237, 291
Pleasant Hill, LA (April 9,1864), 21, 42–43, 85, 138
Prairie De'Ane, AR (April 10, 1864) 112–113
Prairie Grove, AR (Dec. 7, 1862), 5, 26, 42, 45–46, 52, 77, 85, 104, 158, 179, 183, 190, 193, 209, 215, 223, 228, 239
Red River Campaign, LA (Mar.–May, 1864), 21–22, 45, 52, 54, 63
Southwest Expedition, MO (Fall, 1860), 182–183

White River Station, AR (June 22, 1864), 9, 11, 22–25; Losses, 23–24
Wilson's Creek, MO (Aug. 10,1861), 42, 45, 51, 53, 63–64, 66, 85, 115, 177, 179, 185–186, 189–191, 209, 216, 222–224, 226, 228, 238, 243

Battles, Affairs, Skirmishes, etc., Guerrilla Operations in Northwest Arkansas
Blake or Black Mills (Feb.17,1864), 230–231
Gerald Mountain (Aug. 24, 1864), 237
Kings River (Mar. 4, 1865), 242
Kings River (Mar. 12, 1865), 243
Kingston (May 3, 1864), 234–235
Kingston (May 5, 1864), 235–236
Limestone Valley (April 17, 1864), 233–234
Maysville (Sept. 5, 1863), 226–227
Mulberry Creek (Feb. 1864), 231
Whitely's Mill (April 5, 1864), 232

Battles, Affairs, Skirmishes, etc., Price's 1864 Raid
Big Blue River, MO (Oct. 22), 138, 141, 308, 326–331; Byram's Ford, 141, 325, 327–330; Losses, 330; Mockbee Farm, 143, 146, 328–331
Boonville, MO (Oct. 8, 11); 121, 125
California, MO (Oct. 9), 121–123
Castor River, MO (Sept. 22), 92–93
Charlot Farm (See Marmiton River)
Doniphan, MO (Sept. 19), 92, 295
Dover, MO (Oct. 20), 132
Farmington, MO (Sept. 25), 93, 95
Fayetteville, AR (Oct. 18–Nov. 3), 171, 240–241
Franklin, MO (Oct. 1), 110, 113
Glasgow, MO (Oct. 15), 126–129,

400–409; Losses, 128, 402–405,408–409; Orders of Battle, 402–405, 408–409
Glass Village, AR (Sept. 8), 90
Herman, MO (Oct. 3), 114–115
Independence, MO (Oct. 22), 138–141, 323–326; Losses, 138, 325–326; POWs 324–326
Linn, MO (Oct. 4), 116
Little Blue, MO (Oct. 21), 133–137, 308, 326; Losses, 136
Little Blue, MO (Oct. 22), 138, 323, 325
Leasburg, MO (Sept. 29), 106, 109–110
Lexington, MO (Oct. 19), 131, 133, 136, 308, 321–323; Losses, 323
Marmiton River, KS (Oct. 25), 161–162
Mine Creek, KS (Oct. 25), 88, 131, 149–151,153–160, 163, 301, 304, 308, 314, 333; Losses, 163, 439–449; Strengths at, 154
Moreau River Bridge (Oct. 7), 118–119
Mounds, KS (Oct. 25), 150–151, 187
Newtonia, MO (Oct. 28), 165, 167–168; Losses, 168
Norristown, AR (Sept 6), 89
Old Jackson, MO (Sept. 23), 93, 95
Osage River Crossing (Oct. 6), 116–117
Osage River Bridge (Oct. 5), 116–117
Pilot Knob, MO (Sept. 27), 96–97, 99–107, 109, 296–309; CSA Assault, 101–104; Order of Battle, See Appendix E; Effect on CSA Army, 307–309; Evacuation of, 105,108; Losses, 106, 109, 299–307, 399
Ponder's Mill MO (Sept. 20), 92, 295–296
Price's 1864 Missouri Expedition; Accomplishments, 175,450–453; Additions to Army, 373–385; Army of Missouri Organized, 91; Captured or Destroyed Goods, Property & Supplies, 114–115,128, 317, 458–459, 462–463; CSA Artillery, 347–350; CSA Trains, 333–337; Initial Strength, 344–346, 350–373; Objectives, 86, 113; Orders Initiating, 248–250; Parole of POWs, 114, 451–452; Preparing for, 25, 48–49, 84–85,91; Retreat Through Indian Terr., 171–174; Return to Texas, 174
Union, MO (Oct. 1), 110–113
Russelleville, MO (Oct.8), 120, 122
Sedalia, MO (Oct. 15), 126,314–317; Losses, 317
Shelby's Opn. Iron Mountain. RR (Sept. 27), 297–298;Webster, MO (Sept. 29), 109
Westport, MO (Oct. 23), 143–148, 331–333; Big Blue/Byram's Ford, 143–144, 146–149, 331–333, 335–336; CSA Trains, 335–337; Losses, 331–333, 435–438
Wilkin's Bridge, MO (Oct. 12), 125–126
Bell, Dr. Joseph Bell, 46–47; Bio., 46
Bennet, Maj. George W. C., 104; Bio., 104
Benteen, Col. Frederick, 147, 153–154, 160, 162, 165
Blackwell, Lt. Col. Yardell H., 329
Blair, Col. Charles W., 76, 319, 326
Bleeding Kansas, 181–183
Blunt, Gen. James G., 131, 133–136, 143–144, 146, 149, 165, 167–168, 192–193, 216, 224, 319–323, **320**,

326–329; Bio., 192–193
Boats
  Adams, 7–8, 11, 13–14, 25
  Arthur, 13
  Autocrat, 7, 13
  Baltic, 6–9, 11
  Bright Star, 113
  Clara Eames, 11
  Cricket, 28
  Delta, 6
  Diana, 7–11, 14, 20
  Diane, 6–7
  Empress, 25
  Fairchild, 25
  Lebanon, 10
  Leviathan, 10
  Marmora, 10
  Monarch, 13
  Nicolas Longworth, 5–6,8–9
  Ohio Belle, 176
  Old Kentucky, 175–176
  Rocket, 11,13
  West Wind, 127–128
  Wide Awake, 113, 190
  Ironclads
    Lexington (IC), 23–24, 28
    Louisville (IC), 19, 13
    Tyler (IC), 5,10, 28–30, 33–37,305; Description of, 35
  Tinclads, 1, 7, 29
    Curlew (TC No. 12), 5, 34
    Exchange (TC), 13
    Fawn (TC No. 30), 29,33–38; Description, 36
    Naumkeag (TC No. 37), 29, 33–38; Description of, 36
    Prairie Bird (TC No. 11), 8–10
    Queen City (TC No. 26), 25, 28–34, 37–38, 290; Description of, 31
    Romeo (TC No. 3), 5–6, 9–10
Bowie, Maj. James W., 119
Brent, Gen. Joseph I., 47, 58

Broadhead, Col. James O., 76, 201; Bio., 76
Broadwell, Col. William, 60
Brown, Gen. E. B., 118, 139–**140**, 144, 315, 318
Brown, Capt. William "Buck," 178, 226–227, 230, 239–40, 243; Description of, 226–227
Buckner, Gen. Simon B., **46**, 47–48, 58; Bio., 47
Buell, Lt. Col. James T., 188–189
Bull, Lt. Col. John P., 217, **335**
Burbridge, Col. John Q., 14, 110, 127, 160; Bio., 160
Burns, Capt. Ross 329
Burns, Col. S. P., 40, 46, 56, 206, 208, 292; Bio., 208

Cabell, Gen. William, 86, 89, 90, 103, 107, 110, 119–120, 122, 136, 139, 147, 151, 153, 156, 306, 308,322–325, **324**, 335–336; Capture of, 156
Camp Life
  Doghouses (See Shelter Tent)
  Food/Rations, 19, 45, 55, 90–91, 108, 117, 123–124, 126, 128–129, 133, 138, 143, 164–165, 167, 169, 171–173, 211, 221, 334
  Furloughs, 46, 57, 131, 150, 169, 172, 237–238, 241
  Leisure, 13, 45
  Pay, 68, 71, 78, 201, 206, 245, 337
  Religious Revivals, 55, 216, 291–293
  Shelter Tent, 45
  Sickness/ Disease, 85–87, 132–133, 238
Canales, Gen. Servando, **67**–68, 70, 80
Canby, Gen. Edward R. S., 14, 22, 50
Carney. Gov. Thomas, 318–319
Carpenter, Dr. Seymour, 88, 100, 103, 105, 107, 207, 299, 301–302, 309

Carr, Gen. Eugene A., 38
Carroll, Col. Charles; Bio., 223–224
Carroll, Capt. John G., 237–239, 241–242; Bio., 238
Chisum, Col. Isham, 53; Bio., 53
Churchill, Gen. Thomas J., 44, 56, 293
Clark, Gen. John B., Jr., 25, 40, 49, 70, 72, 77, 82, 85–87, 99–102, 109, 111, 114–115, 121,–122, 126–128, 134–135, 139, 141, 144, 151, 163, 172, 194, 203, 211, 218, 242, **300**, 314, 337, 338; Bio., 85
Clark, Gen. John B., Sr., 60; Bio., 66
Clayton, Gen, Powell, 50–51
Cloud, Col. William, 156, 227
Cockrell, Col. Jeremiah V., 124, 138, 155, 176, 188, 191, 214; Bio., 188
Coffee, Col. John T., 93, 190, 214, 309, 322; Bio., 190
Cole, Col. Nelson, 99, 140
Colorado Troops
  1st Colorado Art., 146
  2nd Colorado Cavalry, 137, 150–151
Coleman, Col. William O., 64, 169, 313, 327
Collins, Capt. Richard, 28, 35–37, 134, 148–149, 290, 319–322, 348; Bio., 290
Conrow, Aaron H., 63–64, 68, 70–71, 74; Bio., 64
Cooper, Gen. Douglas, 173, 192, 228, 241, 338
Cooper, Maj. James W., 178, 223–226, 229–240.242–245; Bio., 223; Surrender of, 245, 260–261
Cortina, Gen. Juan N., 68–**69**, 71–72
Cravens, Col. Jordan E., 51; Bio., 51
Crawford, Col. John D., 315–316
Crawford, Col. Samuel, 320,328
Crisp, Lt. Col. John T, 322
Crittenden, Co. Thomas, 140
Crump, Col. R. P., 52–53; Bio., 52, 262

Currie, Lt. Col. George E., 6–8, 11, 14, 15, 17–20
Curtis, Gen. Samuel R., 2, 96, 101, 130–131, 133–135, 137, 141, 143–144, 147, 149, 163, 165, 169, 171–172, 188, 200, 210, 225, 240, 305, 318–321, 323, 326–329

Davies, Maj. J. F., 110, 122, 127
Deitzler, Gen. George, 319–320, 327
Dennis, Gen. E. S., 54
Dobbin, Col. Archibold, 27, 153, 171, **263**, 299; Bio. 262–265
Dockery, Col. Thomas, 50, 56
Douglas, Stephen A., 180
Dwight, Col. Charles C., 57

Edwards, Maj. John N., 27–28, 32, 34–38,59–62, 64–65, 68–69, 71, 75, 78, 81, 85, 92, 104, 116, 118, 120, 131, 134, 137, 174, 215, 217, 240, 265–267, **266**, 290–291, 295, 297, 311, 317, 326, 330, 337–338; Bio., 265–267
Ellet, Gen. Alfred W., 6, 7, 14
Ellet, Charles 7
Elliott, Col. Benjamin, 75, 117, 240, 297, 316, 321
Ellison, Lt. Col. Jessie, 17
Eppstein, Col. Joseph, 125–126
Erskine, Col Albert, 51,53
Erwin, Col. William H., 321
Escobedo, Gen. Mariano, 68–69, 74; Bio., 74, 267–**268**
Ewing, Gen. Thomas, 13, 49, **95**, 99, 101, 104–105, 107, 109–110, 117, 137, 294, 299, 301–306, 312

Fagan, Gen. James F., 48, 88–91, 93, 95, 101, 103, 110, 113, 118, 130, 138, 146–147, 150, 153, 167, 171–172, 174, 240, 324
Fisk, Gen. Clinton, 118

Fishback, Gen. William H. M., 320
Figueros, Louis, 68–69, 71
Ford, Col. James, 135–137, 144,167–168, 319, 330
Forney, Gen. John H., 56, 293
Forts
  Fort Curtis, MO, 96, 305; Armament, 96, 296–297; Price's Hqs, 101
  Fort Davidson, MO, 96–97, 104–105, 296, 298–299, 301–302, 304, 306, 308; Armament, 97–98; Description of, 96–97, 99; Evacuation of, 104–105, 298–299
  Fort Gibson, IT, 228, 236, 238; Description of, 228
  Fort Jackson, LA, 60, 66, 79
  Fort Scott, KS, 150, 161, 165, 218–222, 320, 337
  Fort Smith, AR, 51, 158, 171, 192–193, 224, 229, 236–239, 243, 302; Description of, 224
Foster, Maj. Emory, 138, 189–190; Bio., 189–190
Freeman, Col. Thomas R., 27, 99, 101–102, 136, 138–141, 143–144, 148, 153, 169, 171, 230, 300, 333–336; Bio., 269
Frost, Gen. Daniel M, 77, 182–183, 201; Bio., 183

Gamble, Gov. Hamilton, 205–206; Bio., 206
Gordon, Col. B. Frank, 117, 297, 321–322, 327–330
Gordon, Maj. George P., 59
Grant, Gen. Melvin S., 327–330
Grant, Gen. U. S., 20, 47, 57, 171, 203; Bio., 20
Gravely, Col. Joseph J., 118, 120, 125
Greene, Col. Colton, 2, 4–6, 8–11, 13–14, 17–20, 22, 25, 83, 85, 102, 115, 122, 127, 135, 153, 156, 159, 162, 174; Bio., 85; Cmd. Of Marmaduke's Bde., 2–4, 6, 8–11, 13, 17, 19, 21–22, 25, 83,174; at Glasgow, 127–129, 131
Greenville, MS, 5–8, 11, 13, 14, 21; Burned, 20–21
Gunter, Col. Thomas, 167, 171, 309
Guynes, Capt. John, 56, 293–294
Gwin, William M., 78–**79**, 82; Bio., 79

Harding, Col. Chester, 127–128
Harney, Gen, William S.; Bio., 184
Harris, Gov. Isham, 60
Harris, Capt. Samuel S., 14,100,150, 332, 349
Harrison, Col. Charles, 77, 178, 213–220, 222, 337–340; Bio. 215, 270–271; Description of, 215
Harrison, Col. I. F., 88
Harrison, Col. Marcus La Rue, 239–240, 243
Hawthorn, Gen. Alexander T., 50, 56
Hays, Col. Upton, 181, 188–191, 204; Bio. 189
Herron, Gen. Francis J., 62–63, 65, 176, 193; Bio., 63
Hickey, Acting-Master Michael, 31, 33–34; Bio., 33–34;Court of Inquiry, 247
Hickox, Col. Franklin, 118
Hildebrand, Capt. Sam, 92, 295
Hindman, Gen. Thomas C., 96, 106, 158, 177, 188, 191–193, 205, 217; Bio., 158
Holland, Gen. C. B., 229–230
Holmes, Gen. T. H., 182, 192–193, 214, 217, 305; Bio.,192
Hoyt, Lt. Col. George, 167
Hubbard, Col. L.F., 15, 17
Hughes, Col. John T., 188–189, 214; Bio., 189
Hughey, Capt. William M., 13, 17, 18,

88, 90, 100, 101, 103, 119, 139, 325, 336, 349, 352, 355, 357, 363, 364, 367, 370, 376, 377, 389, 390, 396, 402, 433
Hunter, Col. DeWitt C., 169, 190–191, 202, 205, 207–208, 214, 243, 327; Bio., 190
Hynson, Capt. Henry C., 4, 100, 349–350

Illinois Troops
  10th Cav., 233
  13th Cav., 53
  17th Cav., 128–129
  33rd Inf., 96
  36th Inf., 239
  47th Inf., 15, 17
Iowa Troops
  3rd Cav., 141, 156, 332
  4th Cav., 15, 144, 154–155, 332
  1st Inf., 63
  8th Inf., 2
  12th Inf., 22–24
  14th Inf., 109
  35th Inf., 17

Jackman, Col. Sidney D., 60, 65, 72–73, 82, 123, 125–127, 136, 144, 146, 162–163, 178–188, **180**, 191–201, 200–208, 214, 232, 234–236, 327, 329–330; Bio., 72, 179–204; Capture of Gen. Bartholow, 196–201; Guerrilla Opn. 195–202; Recruiting in Missouri, 205–207, 259–260
Jackson, Gov. Claiborne F., 64, 85, 183–186; Call for Troops, 256–258
Jackson, Col. Congreve, 196–107; Bio., 196–197
Jeanningros, Gen. Pierre, 65, **74**, 75, 77, 78
Jeffers, Col. William L., 4, 93, 95, 156
Jennison, Col. Charles "Doc," 131, 135–136, 186–187, 319, 321, 327, 329–330
Johnson, Lt. Col. Benjamin A., 92, 295
Johnson, Lt. Col. H. P., 187
Johnson, Maj. M. Rector, 92–93, 295, 322, 381–383
Johnson, Dr. Thomas W., 301, 303

Kansas Cities, Towns, etc.
  Lawrence, 186–187, 216
  Paola, 164, 173, 320
  Trading Post, 150
  West Point, 149–150
Kansas Troops
  2nd Cav., 156, 227
  5th Cav., 53
  6th Cav., 328
  7th Cav., 187
  9th Cav., 220
  11th Cav., 134–135, 322–323
  14th Cav. 231
  15th Cav., 220, 231, 328, 330, 337
  16th Cav., 168
  1st Inf., 13
  3rd Inf. 182, 192
  10th Inf., 314
Kansas State Militia (KSM), 135, 137, 143, 146, 149, 318–320, 326–330
  2nd KSM, 143, 319, 328–330
  3rd KSM, 328–329
  3rd Bde. KSM, 330
  4th KSM, 327, 330
  9th KSM, 330
  10th KSM, 326
  12th KSM, 326
  13th KSM, 328–330
  19th KSM, 330
  21st KSM, 328, 330
Army of the Border, 130–131, 137, 141, 149, 163, 319–321, 323
  Blunt's 1st Div., 131, 133–137, 141, 147, 149–150, 163, 165, 167–168, 171, 320–322, 326, 330
  1st Bde. (Jennison), 135, 144, 147,

167–168, 321–322, 327–329
2nd Bde. (Moonlight), 134–135, 137, 144, 321, 323, 326
3rd Bde. (Blair), 144, 326
4th Bde. (Ford), 135, 137, 140, 144, 167–168, 314, 326
Kansas–Nebraska Act, 181
Kitchen, Col. Solomon, 141, 310

Lane, Sen. James, 187, 319, 321; Bio., 186–187
Lane, Gen. Walter P., 52–53 ; Bio., 52–53
Lawther, Col. Robert, 2, 5–6, 13, 23, 106, 111–113, 116, 122, 128,134–135; Bio., 111
Lewis, Gen. Levin M., 293
Lewis, Col. Warner, 77, 182, 213,215, 217, 219–222, 336–340; Bio., 77
Lincoln, Pres. Abraham, 57, 79, 216, 312, 314
Louisana Cities, Town etc.
  Alexandria, 22, 41–44, 194
  Haynesville, 44
  Minden, 44
  Shreveport, 1, 9, 23, 40, 42–43, 48–49, 53, 55–59, 61–65, 81, 124, 131, 155, 164, 175–177, 201, 291
Lyon, Gen. Nathaniel, 42, 183–184, 186, 238

MacDonald, Col. Emmett, 2, 104, 215, 217
Mackey, Capt. T. J., 89, 97, 99, 101, 298, 300, 303
Magruder, Gen. John B., **47**–48, 56–57, 60, 174, 293
Marmaduke, Gen. John S., 10, 13, 15, 17, 18, 20–21, 25, 28–29, 33, 83, 85, 89–91, 93, 95, 99, 101, 104, 107–111, 113, 115–119, 122–123, 125–128, 130, 134–136, 138–139,

141, 143, 150–151, 153, 156, 161, 163, 165, 167, 169, 171–172, 174, 184, 202, 228, 290, 296, 310–312, 326; Bio., 83–84; Captured, 156, 161
Maxey, Gen. Samuel B., 241; Bio., 241, 271–273, **272**
Maximilian, Archduke Ferdinand, 48, 59, 62, 66, 68, 71,74–75,77, 79; Bio., 68
McArthur, Gen. John, 13, 33
McCray, Col. Thomas H., 27, 103, 171, 300, 335–336;Bio., **273**–274
McCulloch, Gen. Ben, 42, 185–186, 237; Bio., 185
McFerran, Col. James, 139–140, 144
McGhee, Col. James, 146
McKinney, Col. Harvey G., 202–203; Bio., 202–203
McNeil, Gen. John, 118, 138, 143, 147–149, 151, 162–163, 165, 171, 323, 336–337
McPheeters, Dr. William, 41, 50, 89–90, 113, 117, 119–120, 123,132, 171, 296, 300–301, 330
Mexico Cities, Towns, etc.
  Camargo, 65–67, 69
  Carlota, 59,69
  China, 45, 64, 67, 69, 73, 79
  Cordova, 75, 83
  Las Flores, 69, 71
  Matamoras, 62, 65, 66, 68, 72–74, 77–79, 81;
  Description of, 78
  Mexico City, 43, 59, 60, 62, 68, 74, 75
  Monterrey, 60–62, 65–69, 73–75, 77–79, 82, 203
  Piedras Negras, 65, 75
  Vera Cruz, 68–69, 75, 83
Missouri Cities, Towns, etc.
  Arrow Rock, 126
  Bloomfield, 91, 93

Boonville, 85, 121–123, 125–126, 128, 184, 207, 332, 334
California, 120–123, 125–126, 314
Carthage, 149, 163–165, 167, 184–185, 206, 208, 291, 340
Cassville, 171, 185, 223, 229, 237, 239, 240, 244
Cuba, 110
Doniphan, 91–92, 189, 294–296, 312; Burning of 294–295
Dover, 132, 321–322
Farmington, 93, 95, 97
Franklin, 110, 113
Fredericktown, 51, 91–93, 95, 97, 99, 116
Glasgow, 126–132, 178, 194, 196–197, 199–201, 203, 308, 314
Herman, 113–116, 210
Hickman Mills, 143, 146, 210, 320, 328, 335–336
Independence, 1, 9, 13, 24, 28–29, 31–32, 37, 46, 52, 55, 64, 77, 87–88, 104, 112, 115, 126, 133–135, 137–141, 143, 179, 182, 186, 189, 197, 214, 219, 320, 322–328, 339–340
Irondale, 96, 297
Ironton, 91, 93, 95–97, 99–101, 298, 300
Jefferson City, 20, 26, 37, 42, 50, 61, 63, 72, 86, 93, 111, 113, 115–120, 183–184, 190, 196, 307, 318–319; Defense of, 118; Price Abandons attack, 119–120
Kansas City, 137–138, 140–141, 143–144, 168, 290, 320, 326, 329
Lexington, 126, 130–133, 184, 187–188, 191, 291, 317–318, 320; Description of, 178
Linn, 116, 118
Little Santa Fe, 143, 147–149, 335
Mineral Point, 96, 105, 107, 297

Newtonia, 167–169, 189, 192, 333, 338
Osceola, 37, 186–187
Pacific City (See Franklin)
Pilot Knob, 91, 93, 95, 107, 109, 113, 117, 119, 294–298; Arcadia Valley, 95–97, 99; Area Surrounding, 98–99; Cedar Mountain, 95, 97, 103; Ironton Gap, 95, 100–101; Pilot Knob Mountain, 97, 101,103; Shepherd's Mountain, 95, 97, 99–103, 195
Potosi, 95, 97, 99, 101, 105, 107, 110, 297–299, 334; Shelby at, 105, 107
Richmond, 64, 208
Rolla, 63, 106, 110, 117, 208, 212
Russellville, 89, 118–120, 122
Sedalia, 123, 126, 130, 308, 314–317, 335
St. Clair, 110–111, 113, 124, 205, 208, 212
St. Louis, 8, 21, 40, 50, 54, 63, 76–77, 83, 85–87, 93, 103, 111, 113–114, 117,132, 157–158, 175, 177, 179, 183–184, 187–188, 190, 194–195, 198–199, 213, 215, 217, 220, 222, 241, 245, 300–302, 306–308, 312–314, 318–319, 339
Steelville, 106, 211
Sullivan, 110
Tipton, 125
Washington, 111, 113–114
Waverly, 26–27, 130, 290–291, 317, 321
Webster, 107–109, 124
Westphalia, 116, 310
Westport, 72, 86–88, 134, 138–140, 143–144, 146–149, 189, 324, 327–329, 331–333
Missouri Troops
 Confederate

1st Cav. 111, 157
3rd Cav. (Greene), 4–5, 11, 13, 17, 83, 85, 101–102, 110, 115, 121–122, 127, 135–136, 139, 141, 143–144, 151, 153, 156–157, 159, 197, 300, 302, 313, 333, 361–362, 424
4th Cav. (Burbridge/Preston), 4, 9, 11, 13–14, 17, 85, 87, 101–102, 108, 110, 127, 129, 131, 134, 136, 141, 143–144, 151, 155–156, 160, 313, 361, 424
5th Cav. (Gordon), 60, 117, 132, 136, 143, 210, 291, 321–323, 327–330, 366
6th Cav., 76, 290
7th Cav. (Kitchen), 4, 17–18, 85, 110, 121–122, 127, 135–136, 141, 151, 155, 313, 361–362, 423
8th Cav. (Jeffers), 4, 11, 13–14, 17–18, 48, 85, 91, 93, 99, 101–102, 111, 115, 118, 126–127, 136, 141, 143–144, 151, 156, 160, 300, 361–363
10th Cav.(Lawther), 1–3, 5–6, 8–9, 11, 13–14, 17–18, 22, 20–25, 40, 52, 54, 83, 85, 87, 89, 96, 101–102, 104, 106–109, 111, 113, 115–116, 121–122, 124–125, 127, 129, 131, 134–135, 139–141, 144, 148–149, 151, 153, 155–158, 160, 163–165, 167–169, 173–177, 215–216, 292–293, 325, 332–333, 340, 361, 425; Hist. of, 2
11th Cav. (M. Smith), 102, 104, 121, 321, 367
11th Cav. Bn. (See 10th Mo. Cav.)
12th Cav. (Erwin), 60, 169, 210, 313, 321, 329, 367
14th Cav. Bn. (Wood), 85, 102, 123, 135–136, 141, 143–144, 151, 155–156, 333, 361, 363,

423; From Bn. to Regt., 370
15th Cav. (Reeves), 92, 295, 309–310, 312, 358, 373–374
8th Inf. (Mitchell), 40, 64–64
9th Inf. (Musser), 40, 63, 85, 179, 213
9th SS Bn. (Pindall), 40, 292, 294
11th Inf., 40
12th Inf., 40
10th Inf., 46, 54–55, 57–58, 176, 208–209, 212, 292–293
16th Inf., 14, 24, 40, 43, 51, 91, 128–131, 173
Anderson's Guerrillas, 379–380
Burns's Bde. (Parsons's), 46, 56, 58, 175, 208–209, 292
Clark's (Marmaduke) Bde., 1, 11, 49, 67, 83, 85, 88–89, 93, 95, 100–103, 107–109, 111, 113–115, 118, 121, 126–127, 129–130, 132, 134–136, 139, 141, 143–144, 151, 153–157, 300, 324, 326, 333, 361–364, 376; at Pilot Knob, 394–396; at Westport, 423–425; Recruits for, 376
Clark's Prov. Div., 400–405
Coleman's Regt., 169, 313, 327, 374
Coffee's Bn., 368–370, 375
Coleman's Cav. Regt., 374
Collins's Art., 127, 136, 146, 160, 167, 171, 240, 314, 322, 430; Composition of, 348
Crisp's Bn. (see Coffee's Bn.)
Davies's Bn., 127, 135–136, 155, 361, 375–376, 423
Elliott's Bn./ Regt., 31, 92, 117, 132, 210, 240, 315, 321, 366, 429; From Bn. to Regt., 379
Freeman's Bde., 26–27, 105, 126, 130, 136, 139–141, 143–144, 148, 151, 153, 155–156, 169,

171, 240, 336, 364; at Pilot
  Knob, 396; at Westport, 425–426
Greene's Bde. (See Clark's Bde.)
Harris's (Williams's) Art., 14, 85,
  100, 128, 135, 144, 148, 151,
  300, 316, 336; Composition of,
  340, 423
Hildebrand's Guerrillas, 379
Hunter's Cav., 202, 208, 243, 327
Iron Brigade (See Shelby's Bde.)
Jackman's Bde., 122, 125–130,
  136, 138, 143–144, 146,
  162,167, 172, 321–322, 327,
  330, 334, 367–370; at Westport,
  432–433
Jackman's Regt., 136, 169, 327,
  329
M. Rector Johnson's Co. or Bn.,
  92–93, 295, 322, 381–382,
  430–431
Lesueur's Art., 40, 51
Marmaduke's (Clark's) Div., 2–4,
  88, 91, 93, 99–101, 108, 110,
  113, 116, 118, 120–123, 125,
  132, 134, 146–150, 162–164,
  167, 172–174, 177, 300,
  304, 306, 308, 321, 325, 327
  360–365, 394–398; at Westport,
  421–427; Losses at Pilot Knob,
  307–308
Parsons's Div., 40–46, 49–52,
  56–57, 60, 62, 64, 208, 292–293
Schnable's Cav. Bn., 126, 169,
  327, 329, 369
Shelby's Bde. (Shank or Thompson), 3–4, 26–35, 37–38, 60, 77,
  91, 95–96, 112, 117, 121–123,
  130, 132, 136–138, 144, 146–
  150, 160–162, 164–165, 167–
  169, 171, 173–174, 222, 314–
  317, 321–322, 327, 365–367; at
  Westport,428–432; Recruits for,
  374–375

Shelby's Div. 57, 59, 91–92, 95,
  99, 101–102, 105, 107–110, 113,
  116, 118, 120–123, 125–126,
  131–132, 134, 136, 138, 141,
  143–144, 148–150, 163–165,
  167–169, 171, 173–174, 202,
  295–296, 297, 308, 321, 331
  365–371; at Westport, 428–434
Slayback's Bn., 60, 99,101, 144,
  169, 322, 374, 429
Stallard's Co./Bn., 134–136, 380
Todd's Guerrillas, 380
Tyler's Bde., 134, 138, 143, 147,
  162, 173–174, 335, 378–379; at
  Westport, 426–427
Williams's Art. (See Harris's Art.)
Williams's Regt., 76, 380,430
Windsor's Guards, 149
Wood's Cav. (See 14th Mo. Cav.
  Bn.)
Missouri State Guard (MSG)
  1st Div., 36
  2nd Div., 46
  3rd Div. (Clark), 63, 66, 85, 160,
    194, 196–197, 202
  4th Div., 64, 189, 291
  5th Div. 104, 209
  6th Div. (Parsons), 37, 40, 42, 45
  7th Div., 338
  8th Div. (Rains), 37, 72, 76–77,
    81, 115, 177, 184–186, 188–191,
    208, 290–291, 338, 340
  Rains's MSG Bn., 383
Union
  7th Cav.,188
  10th Cav., 154,332–333
  13th Cav., 128, 325
  15th Cav., 244
  33rd Inf., 17
  41st Inf., 314
  Bat. H, 2nd Art., 97, 100, 109,
    305–306
  Enrolled Missouri Militia (EMM)

9th EMM, 195
34th EMM, 116
45th EMM, 119, 195
47th EMM, 299, 302, 305
48th EMM, 119
61st EMM, 207
Missouri State Militia Cavalry (MSM)
  1st MSM, 139–140, 154, 156, 163, 325, 331
  3rd MSM, 76, 92, 104, 114, 294, 309–311, 313
  4th MSM, 140, 331
  5th MSM, 125, 132, 208, 211, 325
  6th MSM, 118–119, 150, 332
  7th MSM, 117, 140, 144, 189, 316, 331–332
  8th MSM, 118–119, 150–151, 332
  9th MSM, 127–128, 195
  13th MSM, 127
Thurber's Art., 121–122
Pleasonton's Div., 138–141, 146–150, 154, 169, 171, 318, 324
  1st Bde. (Brown/Philips), 139–149, 143, 147, 153–154, 324–325, 331–333
  2nd Bde. (McNeil), 138–139, 143, 146, 149, 160–163, 323–325, 331, 336 160
  3rd Bde. (Sanborn), 139, 144, 147, 151–152, 160, 324–325, 332
  4th Bde. (Winslow/Benteen), 140–141, 144, 147, 151, 153–156, 160, 162–163, 165, 171, 332
Sanborn's Prov. Div., 120–121, 125–126, 315–316
  1st Bde.(Philips), 120–121, 125
  2nd Bde. (Beveridge), 121, 125
  3rd Bde. (Gravely), 120, 121, 125
Montgomery, Col. James, 182–183, 186–187; Bio., 182

Montgomery, Capt. William C. F., 97, 100, 109, 305–306
Moonlight, Col. Thomas, 134–136, 144, 319, 321, 328–330
Moore, Col. David, 14, 316–317
Moore, Maj. James M., 244–245
Moore, Maj. John B., 128
Moore, Gov. Thomas O., 60
Morehead, Gov. Charles S., 60
Mower, Gen. Joseph, **17**–19, 54, 318
Murrah, Gov. Pendellton, 60
Musser, Col. Richard H., 63, 69, 72, 179–180, 187, 191, 193, 195–197, 202, 204, 213, 215, 217, 223, 338; Bio., 54
Murray, Capt. Thomas, 24, 74, 108, 131, 137, 154, 176

Nichol, Lt. Col. C. H., 136, 169, 327, 329

Ore, Capt. William F.; Bio., 233
Osage Indians, 178, 213, 218–220, 340
Osterhaus, Gen. Peter J., 58
Owen, E. K. Lt. Cdr., 10–11, 21

Parsons, Gen. Mosby M., 40–42, 44–54, 56–58, 61–75, 78, 80, 208, 212, 293; Bio., 42
Parsons, Gen. William H., 4, 5–54; Bio., 53–54, 274–276, **275**
Perkins, Col. Caleb, 194, 201; Bio., 194
Phelps, Col. John S., 120, 151, 168, 233–236, 332; Bio., 234
Phelps, Lt. Cdr. L. S., 33, 37–38
Philips, Col. John F., 120, 121, 140, 144, 147, 153, 331–333
Phillips, Col. William A., 228
Pindall, Col. L. A., 69–70
Pleasonton, Gen. Alfred, 120, 130, 137–141, 143–144, 151, 153, 156,

163, 301, 318, **319**, 321, 323–325, 333
Poindexter, Col. John A., 214
Polignac's Div., 56
Pope, Gen. John, 57
Porter, Admiral David D., 10–11, 22, 31, 34, 36–37
Porter, Col. Joseph, 214
Pratt, Maj. Joseph, 4–5, 9, 17, 99–100, 122, 154
Preston, Lt. Col. William, 134, 143
Price, Gen. Sterling, 1, 3–4, 21, 25–27, 29, 38, 42, 46–52, 54–55, 58–60, 63, 76, 81, 83, 85–93, 95–97, 99, 101, 103–105, 107–108, 110–111, 113–116, 118–121, 123, 125–126, 131, 137, 139–140, 143–144, 147–148, 150, 154, 160–165, 169, 172, 174–175, 178–179, 184–188, 190, 193–194, 203, 209, 216, 239–241, 243, 292, 295, 298–304, 306–312, 314–315, 318–319, 321, 325–328, 333–336; Bio., 83
Price–Harney Agreement, 184
Prichett, Cdr. James, 5, 22

Quantrill, Capt. William C., 31, 178–179, 187, 189, 214–216, 234, 380; Bio., 216

Railroads
  Destruction of, 460–462
  Iron Mt. RR, 93, 95–97, 297, 298; Losses, 460–461
  Pacific RR, 106, 109–110, 118, 120; Losses, 460–461
Rains, Gen. James S., 184–186, 340, 383; Bio., 184
Reeves, Col. Timothy, 195, 206, 309–310, 312, 314
Reynolds, Gen. D. M., 14
Reynolds, Gov. Thomas C., 43, 48, 50, 60, 86, 107, 113, 120, 334

Reynolds, Col. William W., 226; Bio., 226
Rivers/ Lakes
  Arkansas River, 22–23, 26, 29, 33, 36, 49–50, 53, 55, 88–89, 171–172, 202, 209, 224, 228–231, 236, 242, 318
  Bayou Deview, 28, 38
  Bayou Mason, 4, 10, 14–15, 19
  Big Blue River, 134, 137, 141, 143–144, 146–147, 158, 308, 320, 324–327, 330–331, 333, 335
  Black River, 51, 91, 93
  Blackwater River, 115, 126, 130
  Cache River, 28, 34, 37
  Canadian River, 172, 227, 241
  Castor River, 92–93
  Ditch Bayou, 7, 10–11, 13–15, 17–19, 21–22
  Gasconade River, 116
  Kansas River, 143
  Kings River, 231, 235, 238
  Lake Chicot (See Ditch Bayou)
  Lake River (See Ditch Bayou)
  Marmiton River, 161, 163
  Mississippi River, 1, 3–4, 7, 10–11, 13, 15, 21–22, 25, 40, 47, 51–52, 54, 56, 63, 76, 176, 191, 197, 226–227, 241
  Missouri River, 113, 116, 119, 123, 126, 129–130, 132, 184, 187, 194–195, 202, 205, 210, 222, 322, 326
  Old River Lake (See Ditch Bayou)
  Osage River, 116–118, 149–150, 153, 184
  Ouachita River, 2, 41
  Petit Jean River, 88
  Rio Grande River, 61, 65, 69, 72
  Saline River, 1, 50–51, 87–88, 125
  St. John River, 82
  Strawberry River, 90
  White River, 9, 11, 22, 25–31,

33–34, 36, 38–39, 54–55, 90, 149, 210–211, 239–240
Rosecrans, Gen. William, 99, 169, 301, **312**, 314–315, 317–319
Rucker, Maj. John, 193–194, 196–198; Bio., 193, 277–278
Ruthven, Maj. John B., 46; Bio., 46

Sanborn, Gen. John B., **86**–87, 118, 120–122, 125–126, 139–140, 143,147, 150–151, 153, 160, 162, 164–165, 168–169, 171, 229–230, 243, 302, 314–316, 318, 324–325, 332–333
Sanchez, Col. Rafael Plato, 67–71
Schofield, Gen. John M., 76; Bio., 76
Schnable, Col. John, 120
Scudder, Lt. Col. T. W., 53
Shaler, Col. James R., 107, 114, 308–310
Shanks, Col. David, 38, 116–117, 189
Shelby, Gen. J. O., **26**–39, 50, 54, 57–62, 65, 74–75, 77, 85, 90–93, 95–96, 101, 105, 107–109, 111, 113, 116–117, 119–121, 125–127, 132, 134, 136, 138, 141, 143–144, 146–147, 160–164, 167–168, 171–172, 174, 192, 210, 214, 217, 226, 240, 244, 290–291, 295–298, 309–310, 321–322, 327, 329–331, 333–334; Bio., 26
Sissel, Capt. John or Jonathan, 232–234
Slayback, Col. Alonozo, 61, 76, 299, 314, 322, 328, 329
Slemons, Col. William F., 86, 95, 103, 118, 156, 300, 305, 323, 358; Captured, 156
Smith, Gen. Andrew J., 14, 17–19, **21**–22, 54, 107, 130, 314, 316, 318, 321; Bio., 21
Smith, Gen. E. Kirby, 2–3, 41, 44, 46–48, 50, 57–58, 60,75, 174, 203, 241, 294; Bio., 44
Smith, Col. Moses, 121, 321
Snead, Col. Thomas L., 60
Sprague, Col. John T., 57
Standish, Austin M., 40, 45, 63–64, 68–71, 73–74; Bio., 45
Steele, Gen. Frederick, 1–2, 29, 33, 37, 50–51, 54–55, 57, 88, 112–113; Bio., 1–2
Steele, Gen. William, 52
Steen, Col. Alexander E., 209; Bio., 209
Surrender of Trans-Mississippi Department, 250–253

Tappan, Gen. J. C., 50
Texas Cities, Towns, etc.
  Austin, 64, 72, 229
  Brownsville, 54, 62. 72–73, 81; Description of, 72
  Corsicana, 59
  Eagle Pass, 61–62, 65, 75
  Laredo, 61–62
  Roma, 62,72
  San Antonio, 60–62, 75, 79, 185, 203
  Tyler, 54, 81
Texas Troops
  2nd Part. Cav., 53
  3rd Cav., 53
  8th Cav., 52
  12th Cav., 54
  9th Inf. 241
  18th Inf., 56
  22nd Inf., 56
  10th Art. (Pratt or Hynson), 3–5, 8–11, 13–15, 17–18, 85, 99–100, 111, 121–122, 136, 139, 144, 154–157, 161; Composition of, 4, 100, 349–350
  Hynson's Art. (See 10th Texas Art.)
  Pratt's Art. (See 10th Texas Art.)
  Walker's Div., 41, 43, 44, 56, 77,

293
Thompson, Col. Gideon W., 188, 214
Thompson. Gen. M. Jeff, 110, 121, 126, 130, 134, 136, 144, 146–147, 150, 160–162, 311, 314–317, **315**, 321–322, 327, 329–330, 335, 339; Assumes Cmd. of Iron Bde., 121
Thornton, Sir Edward 67, **71**
Todd, Capt. George, 124, 136–137, 178
Tracy, Col. John C., 1, 190–191, 214; Bio., 191
Tyler, Col. Charles, 162

Union Troops Miscellaneous
  5th Minn. Inf., 17, 20
  16th Corps, 3, 14, 19–22, 54, 107, 297, 314–316,318; Hist. Of, 22
    1st Div., 14, 17–18, 318
    3rd Div., 14, 18, 297, 316, 318
  17th Corps, 3, 14
  Marine Bde., 6–8, 11, 14–15, 17–20

Walker, Gen. John G., 41–42, 44, 47–48, 132, 293
Watie, Gen. Stand, 178, 223, 227–229, 236, 238, 241; Bio., 227–228; 1st Cherokee Cav., 228, 229
Warren, Gen. Fitz, 138
Washburn, Gen. C. C., 22, 54
Waterhouse, Gen. Richard, 77–78; Bio., 77–78, **278**–279
Weapons, 114–115
  Enfield Rifle, 22, 111, 139, 148, 159, 297
  Sharps Carbine, 115
  Sharps Rifle, 112, 115
Wharton, Gen. John A.,52; Bio., 52, 279–282, **280**
Williams, Col. David A., 76–77, 117; Bio., 76, 282–283
Williams, Maj. H. H., 302–303
Williams, Lt. T. J., 127–128, 135, 349

Wilson, Maj, James, 103, 114,294, 296, 309–314; Execution of, 309–314
Winslow, Col. E. F., 54, 140–141, 144, 318, 332–333
Wisconsin Troops
  2nd Cav., 15, 18
  8th Inf., 17
Wolfe, Col. Edward H., 110
Wood, Lt. Col. Robert C., 116, 155; Bio., 155
Wood, Maj. James C., 123, 314
Woodson, Col. B. H., 217, 220, 338, 340
Worthington, Maj. John I., 227–239, 242–243; Bio., 238–239, 283–284; Death of 245
Wright, Col. William C., 95,103, 118–119, 138–159, 153, 160, 167–168, 300, 323, 335

Yeager, Capt. Richard F. "Dick," 234–235; Bio., **285**–286
Young, Lt. Col. Merit, 140, 325

Zimmerman, Lt. J. V., 349

www.ingramcontent.com/pod-product-compliance
Lightning Source LLC
Chambersburg PA
CBHW032012230426
43671CB00005B/59